"This revolutionary text makes social theory more teachable. It has helped achieve one of my key goals: allowing students to see the relevance of theory to their own lives and the world around them. Particularly useful is the website. Student activities such as 'Writing Out Loud' and 'Interactive Readings' are extremely helpful. Teachers can comment on students' work individually within the website. The site allows instructors to devote more course time to the additional goals of the course."

—**Margo Ramlal-Nankoe**, *Fairfield University*

"I found many things outstandingly unique to this text….I love the introductory summaries, and so do my students."

—**Selina Gallo-Cruz**, *College of the Holy Cross*

"This companion website is especially useful to make connections between abstract theoretical texts and real world events, research, and contexts that make the in-class material concrete and real for the students."

—**Julie Stewart**, *University of Utah*

Social Theory Re-Wired

This social theory text combines the structure of a print reader with the ability to tailor the course via an extensive interactive website. Readings from important classical and contemporary theorists are placed in conversation with one another through core themes—the puzzle of social order, the dark side of modernity, identity, etc. The website includes videos, interactive commentaries, summaries of key concepts, exams and quizzes, annotated selections from key readings, classroom activities, and more. See the website at www.routledgesoc.com/theory

New to the second edition:

- Expanded web content.
- Teacher/student feedback employed to clarify difficult concepts.
- Reframed contemporary section now offers readings by Robert Merton, Bruno Latour, David Harvey, Zygmut Bauman, and Anthony Giddens.

Wesley Longhofer is Assistant Professor of Organization and Management at Emory University.

Daniel Winchester is Assistant Professor of Sociology at Purdue University.

Contemporary Sociological Perspectives

Edited by **Douglas Hartmann**, *University of Minnesota* and **Jodi O'Brien**, *Seattle University*

This innovative series is for all readers interested in books that provide frameworks for making sense of the complexities of contemporary social life. Each of the books in this series uses a sociological lens to provide current critical and analytical perspectives on significant social issues, patterns, and trends. The series consists of books that integrate the best ideas in sociological thought with an aim toward public education and engagement. These books are designed for use in the classroom as well as for scholars and socially curious general readers.

Published:

Political Justice and Religious Values by Charles F. Andrain

GIS and Spatial Analysis for the Social Sciences by Robert Nash Parker and Emily K. Asencio

Hoop Dreams on Wheels: Disability and the Competitive Wheelchair Athlete by Ronald J. Berger

The Internet and Social Inequalities by James C. Witte and Susan E. Mannon

Media and Middle Class Mom: Images and Realities of Work and Family by Lara Descartes and Conrad Kottak

Watching T.V. Is Not Required: Thinking about Media and Thinking about Thinking by Bernard McGrane and John Gunderson

Violence Against Women: Vulnerable Populations by Douglas Brownridge

State of Sex: Tourism, Sex and Sin in the New American Heartland by Barbara G. Brents, Crystal A. Jackson & Kate Hausbeck

Sociologists Backstage: Answers to 10 Questions About What They Do by Sarah Fenstermaker and Nikki Jones

Surviving the Holocaust: A Life Course Perspective by Ronald Berger

Stargazing: Celebrity, Fame, and Social Interaction by Kerry Ferris and Scott Harris

The Senses in Self, Society, and Culture by Phillip Vannini, Dennis Waskul and Simon Gottschalk

Surviving Dictatorship by Jacqueline Adams

The Womanist Idea by Layli Maparyan

Religion in Today's World: Global Issues, Sociological Perspectives, by Melissa Wilcox

Understanding Deviance: Connecting Classical and Contemporary Perspectives edited by Tammy L. Anderson

Social Statistics: Managing Data, Conducting Analyses, Presenting Results, Second Edition by Thomas J. Linneman

Transforming Scholarship: Why Women's and Gender Studies Students are Changing Themselves and the World, Second Edition by Michele Tracy Berger and Cheryl Radeloff

Who Lives, Who Dies, Who Decides? Abortion, Neonatal Care, Assisted Dying, and Capital Punishment, Second Edition by Sheldon Ekland-Olson

Life and Death Decisions: The Quest for Morality and Justice in Human Societies, Second Edition by Sheldon Ekland-Olson

Gender Circuits: Bodies and Identities in a Technological Age, Second Edition by Eve Shapiro

Migration, Incorporation, and Change in an Interconnected World by Syed Ali and Douglas Hartmann

Sociological Perspectives on Sport: The Games Outside the Games by David Karen and Robert E. Washington

Social Theory Re-Wired: New Connections to Classical and Contemporary Perspectives, Second Edition edited by Wesley Longhofer and Daniel Winchester

Forthcoming:

Social Worlds of Imagination by Chandra Mukerji

All Media are Social by Andrew Lindner

Social Theory Re-Wired

New Connections to Classical and Contemporary Perspectives

Second Edition

Edited by

Wesley Longhofer
Emory University

Daniel Winchester
Purdue University

Routledge
Taylor & Francis Group

NEW YORK AND LONDON

Please visit the companion website for this title at:
www.routledgesoc.com/theory

Second edition published 2016
by Routledge
711 Third Avenue, New York, NY 10017

and by Routledge
2 Park Square, Milton Park, Abingdon, Oxon, OX14 4RN

Routledge is an imprint of the Taylor & Francis Group, an informa business

First edition published by Routledge 2012

Library of Congress Cataloging in Publication Data
Names: Longhofer, Wesley, editor. | Winchester, Daniel, editor.
Title: Social theory re-wired : new connections to classical and contemporary perspectives / edited by Wesley Longhofer and Daniel Winchester.
Description: Second Edition. | New York : Routledge — Taylor & Francis, 2016. | Revised edition of Social theory re-wired, 2012.
Identifiers: LCCN 2015035852
Subjects: LCSH: Sociology. | Social sciences—Philosophy.
Classification: LCC HM585 .S577 2016 | DDC 301—dc23
LC record available at http://lccn.loc.gov/2015035852

ISBN: 978-1-138-01579-1 (hbk)
ISBN: 978-1-138-01580-7 (pbk)
ISBN: 978-1-315-77535-7 (ebk)

Typeset in StoneSerif
by Swales & Willis Ltd, Exeter, Devon, UK

Printed and bound in the United States of America by Sheridan

Contents

INTRODUCTORY ESSAY: THIS DESERTED ISLAND IS OUT OF ORDER

The classic novel The Lord of the Flies *helps us see that social order is both a product of our own making and something much more powerful than the sum of its parts. We move from the social facts of Durkheim to more contemporary takes on the enigma of social order.*

Section II NETWORKS OF CAPITAL: Dimensions of Global Capitalism   123

INTRODUCTORY ESSAY: SALVAGING WHAT WALL STREET LEFT BEHIND

Today's global financial crisis reminds us that economic troubles have profound consequences for social relationships. Marx sets the stage for a lively discussion of the role the economy plays in our global age, and Wallerstein, Bourdieu, and Harvey provide contemporary visions of the many links between the economic and the social.

Section III PATHWAY TO MELTDOWN: Theorizing the Dark Side of Modernity   221

INTRODUCTORY ESSAY: YOUR SMART PHONE MIGHT BE AN EVIL GENIUS

Smart phones are but one example of how our social world is becoming more and more shaped by technology. From the pious Puritans of Weber to the one-dimensional men of the Frankfurt School, we explore the pitfalls and promises of a rationalized, modern society.

Section IV SHIFTING THE PARADIGM: Excluded Voices, Alternative Knowledges

INTRODUCTORY ESSAY: WEBS OF KNOWLEDGE IN THE DIGITAL DIVIDE
The production of knowledge on the Internet is not as democratic as we might think. Du Bois, Beauvoir, and more contemporary voices within critical race, postcolonial, and feminist thought remind us the same is true in social theory.

Section V RISE OF THE AVATAR: Connecting Self and Society 445

INTRODUCTORY ESSAY: THROUGH THE LOOKING GLASS OF FACEBOOK

Our Facebook profiles provide a glimpse of the collective foundations of our individual selves. Mead and Simmel lay the foundations for thinking about the social origins of the self, and Goffman, Foucault, and others provide provocative takes on what identity means in today's complicated world.

Classical Connections: George Herbert Mead and Georg Simmel 453

Contemporary Extensions: Identity Re-Wired 482

Alternate Table of Contents by Tradition or Theorist

Series Foreword

THIS INNOVATIVE SERIES IS for all readers interested in books that provide frameworks for making sense of the complexities of contemporary social life. Each of the books in this series uses a sociological lens to provide current critical and analytical perspectives on the best ideas in sociological thought with an aim toward publication education and engagement. These books are designed for use in the classroom as well as for scholars and socially curious general readers.

In *Social Theory Re-Wired* Wesley Longhofer and Daniel Winchester apply these principles to the ideas, concepts, and writings at the core of all sociological research and thought. The volume covers all of the classic authors and works in the cannon, highlights the work of several under-appreciated or even forgotten contributors, and introduces (judiciously) the most provocative and important of contemporary theories and theorists. These pieces are organized into sections that are fresh yet familiar, and framed with brief introductory essays that are down-to-earth without being dumbed-down, chock full of insightful points and examples from the latest in social media, popular culture, and politics in the U.S. and all over the globe. This impressive volume also offers a unique set of original interactive exercises and teaching tools that are guaranteed to enrich both the teaching and the learning of sociological theory.

It has been said that every generation of sociology researchers and students must win its theoretical inheritance anew. We believe this to be true, and expect that *Social Theory Re-Wired* will not only be an important resource for teaching and learning social theory, but should help shape how theory is understood and used in the field for years to come.

Douglas Hartmann
Valerie Jenness
Jodi O'Brien
Series Editors

Preface

SOCIAL THEORY IS ABOUT making connections—connections between abstraction and observation, concepts and evidence, the knowable and the unknown. It is about connecting our curiosities about the social world with concepts and frameworks to help make sense of them. Social theory is a lot like the thousands of copper cables and optical fibers that together bring a computer network to life. When its connections are hidden, we too often take the network for granted, and we are completely befuddled when the network changes, jams, or has a system error. But, when we untangle the network and understand its connections, we can begin to see how things work, what is running smoothly or going wrong, and how to plug old components into new ones with greater ease and with better results.

Social theory is also about conversations. Contrary to popular belief, theory is not about dusty tomes of esoteric garbling about capitalism and the division of labor. Social theory is a response to the big and important questions of our time. And, the theorists in this book are not just responding to their own social condition; they are also talking to each other, answering each other's questions and posing new ones. At the risk of sounding trite, social theory is more than a network of ideas—it is a *social network* connecting the creators of those ideas to each other and to us.

So this book is about connections and conversations. It is a re-wiring of social theory that makes it fresh again for the world of Instagram and Twitter. We have tried to re-wire it in a way that revisits classical conversations and connects them to contemporary ones in interesting and sometimes surprising ways. As you peruse the main table of contents, you will see a lot of familiar folks, both classical and contemporary, but they might be arranged in ways that are less recognizable, lumped together under categories like convergence, capital, shift, and meltdown. We did this because we wanted the ideas and conversations to travel across and beyond any individual theorist, even though some theorists were foundational in creating them. We have not hit the reset button on social theory, but we may have tapped the refresh button once or twice.

The book is designed for teaching social theory in creative ways, integrating original, printed texts with modern, digital applications. In addition to our unique collection of original excerpts, we have developed new interactive online content for the second edition. This web-based material is chock full of additional information, activities, and teaching tips. The combination of print and digital makes this book a great addition to almost any social theory course. It's a blended format that comes out of our conviction that social theory courses often flounder not because the ideas are stale, but because the ideas haven't been presented in the best possible relationship to one another. In organizing the book in the way we do—making connections between classical and contemporary, print and digital—we think we can help social theory instructors take a step toward a better way. We hope that you will find it as fun to read and use as we did to make.

Organization of the Second Edition

Like the first edition, we have organized the book around five themes or conversations. Each theme includes an introductory essay by us as well as original readings from classical and contemporary theorists. The essays include vignettes on topics ranging from smart phones and social networking sites to the global financial crisis and the digital divide, as well as overviews of key concepts and ideas found in the readings. In the margins of each essay you will find "connections" to ideas introduced in other parts of the book or supplementary materials found on the website. We encourage students to read these essays before diving into the readings, as they help bring to life the complicated ideas found in the original texts. While, for the sake of clarity, we have kept the readings themselves free of marginal commentary, we also include "Connections" at the *end* of each reading with more tailored activities for students, including writing exercises, discussion questions, and additional online content.

The readings themselves are taken from the original sources. We have made an attempt, when possible, to select longer readings than are often found in a theory reader, keeping in mind that finding the right length is a difficult balance to achieve. Those of you familiar with the first edition may notice we subtracted a few readings and added others, including new selections from Robert Merton, Bruno Latour, David Harvey, Zygmunt Bauman, and Anthony Giddens. In adding these new selections, we think the second edition is both more balanced and more readable. We have summarized the readings and essays for each section below.

Section I—Emergence Through Convergence: The Puzzles of Social Order

We begin with the issue and enigma of social order and, in particular, Durkheim's ideas about solidarity and social facts. The introductory essay,

"This Deserted Island Is Out of Order," reflects on William Golding's brilliant *Lord of the Flies* and, in particular, how social order was created and later destroyed by the boys on the island. Excerpts from Durkheim include selections from his most famous works: *The Division of Labor in Society*, *Suicide*, *The Rules of Sociological Method*, and *The Elementary Forms of Religious Life*. Also included in this section are pieces from Robert Merton on manifest and latent functions, Harold Garfinkel on the ordering of moment-to-moment interactions, Peter Berger and Thomas Luckmann on the "social construction of reality" and the institutionalization of everyday life, and Bruno Latour on the role of nonhuman actors in the construction of social order. These contemporary pieces extend Durkheim's ideas on how social institutions that get constructed by individuals eventually take on lives of their own, whether it is at the largest of scales like law and religion or at a scale much smaller, such as our day-to-day routines and conversations.

Section II—Networks of Capital: Dimensions of Global Capitalism

The second section begins with Karl Marx coming to grips with capitalism and the emerging class-based social order. The introductory essay, titled "Salvaging What Wall Street Left Behind," invites students to ponder what Marx might have said about the recent global financial crisis and one of its key culprits—credit default swaps. Excerpts from *The German Ideology* and *Manifesto of the Communist Party* (both written with Friedrich Engels), along with pieces from *Capital* and the *Manuscripts of 1844*, introduce Marx's ideas on historical materialism, commodity fetishism, and alienation. Contemporary extensions include Immanuel Wallerstein's work on the capitalist world system, Pierre Bourdieu's takes on forms of capital beyond the economic, David Harvey's materialist critique of postmodernity, and a piece from Manuel Castells on the rise of the network society. The Wallerstein, Harvey, and Castells readings update Marx for the age of globalization, while Bourdieu brings us back down to the role cultural capital plays in shaping the *habitus* of the individual.

Section III—Pathway to Meltdown: Theorizing the Dark Side of Modernity

Max Weber sets the stage for the third section, which moves attention away from class and order to the entrenchment of new forms of power, control, and rationality in modern society. "Your Smart Phone Might Be an Evil Genius" is the apropos title for the introductory essay, which discusses how the advancement of technology constrains us as much as it liberates us, not unlike Weber's notion of the "iron cage." The pathway toward increased rationality, Weber warned long ago, might also lead to meltdown. We include excerpts from his *The Protestant Ethic and the Spirit of Capitalism* as well as essays on social action, authority and domination, and bureaucracy. We then introduce two pieces from the Frankfurt School of Critical Theory—Herbert Marcuse's *One-Dimensional Man* and Jurgen Habermas' *Toward a Rational Society*—and an excerpt from Michel Foucault's *Discipline and Punish*, all of which look at the subtle ways new kinds of power and surveillance become ingrained in modern society. Finally, we include a piece from Zygmunt Bauman on rationalization's sordid role in the organization and carrying out of modern genocide.

Section IV—Shifting the Paradigm: Excluded Voices, Alternative Knowledges

This section presents challenges to the supposedly stable categories of classical theory by introducing the work of critical race, feminist, and postcolonial scholars, beginning with an essay looking at how the digital divide shapes the knowledge we find on the Internet ("Webs of Knowledge in the Digital Divide"). The essay asks readers to consider questions about the social contexts of knowledge creation, and how unequal access to *what* we know and, more fundamentally, *how* we know about reality helps perpetuate social inequality and injustice. We set the stage with selections from two foundational scholars of race and feminist theory: W.E.B. Du Bois' *The Souls of Black Folks* and Simone de Beauvoir's *The Second Sex*. Additional excerpts include Frantz Fanon's powerful work on the racial discourses of colonialism, a selection from Edward Said's groundbreaking *Orientalism*, Michael Omi and Howard Winant on racial formation in the contemporary United States, Dorothy Smith's work on feminist standpoint theory, and Patricia Hill Collins' brilliant work on black feminist epistemology. Each of these contemporary theorists continues to unpack the place of lived experience and oppression in shaping social life and social theory, just as Du Bois and Beauvoir had decades earlier.

Section V—Rise of the Avatar: Connecting Self and Society

Finally, we turn to ideas on the construction and expression of identity in modern society, beginning with our introductory essay for this section titled "Through the Looking Glass of Facebook." Our essay asks an important question not just for social theory, but also for many college students today, whether they are enrolled in a theory course or not: Who would we be individually without the many communities—both online and offline—that support our identities and senses of self? And what are the social and individual consequences of the different versions (or avatars) of ourselves that we present to others on a daily basis? To dig deeper into these questions, we begin with George Herbert Mead's classic work on the self as a social object and two pieces by the great Georg Simmel on individuality and society: "The Metropolis and Mental Life" and "The Stranger." We then move on to Erving Goffman's more contemporary but no less pioneering "The Presentation of Self in Everyday Life." The final three selections address more poststructuralist and postmodern takes on the issue of identity with excerpts from Foucault's *The History of Sexuality*, Judith Butler's *Gender Trouble*, and Anthony Giddens' *Modernity and Self-Identity*. From the modern to the postmodern, these readings uncover the social origins of identity and that which we often take for granted most—our own sense of self.

Additional Table of Contents

The readings are organized by the themes above and should be viewed as collections of conversations between theorists and ideas. However, we also include a more traditional table of contents to assist instructors in designing a course to their liking. This additional table of contents is arranged according to theorist and theoretical tradition. Much of the companion website can also be organized along these dimensions to allow for greater fluidity between the printed pages and the digital ones.

Organization of the Website

We have recruited a stellar group of scholars to help bolster the web content for the second edition. It is now overflowing with student content as well as password-protected teaching materials and supplementary sources that instructors can use to design their courses. The web content provides opportunities for the student and instructor to engage one-on-one through written activities and assignments, and grades for assignments can be exported to most course management systems. Features of the website include:

Profile Pages

In the spirit of contemporary social networking sites, we have designed individual "profiles" for each theorist (e.g. Weber) or school of thought (e.g. Frankfurt School). These pages include a wealth of information ranging from biographical details and key concepts to external web content and learning activities, including short quizzes to help evaluate comprehension of key ideas and tips for reading the printed excerpts.

Interactive Readings

Reading social theory is no easy task. To make things easier, we have selected abbreviated excerpts of select passages for each section, put them online, and inserted interactive annotations linking key phrases or words to additional content, such as definitions, examples, short assignments, and web content. These interactive readings extend the vision of *Social Theory Re-Wired* by helping make challenging theoretical ideas more relevant and understandable to contemporary students. We have created interactive versions of one classical and one contemporary reading from each section—check the "Connections" following each reading to see if it has an interactive version available.

Writing Out Loud

We have found in our own courses that freeform writing about difficult passages in the text increases comprehension and student engagement with the material. The website thus includes a space for students to engage freely with the excerpts by writing their own responses to questions and prompts about the readings. These responses can be saved and, if the instructor wishes, responded to and graded within the *Social Theory Re-Wired* website itself. Grades can then be exported to a course management system.

Assignments

Assignments are scattered throughout the *profile pages, annotated readings,* and *writing spaces*. Assignments can also be organized to match the two tables of contents presented in this reader so that students and instructors can easily view which ones have been assigned and completed.

Supplementary Sources (instructors only)

We also include an annotated collection of supplementary materials that instructors may draw upon to design their syllabus or lectures. These include summaries of written work from academic and popular presses; suggestions for additional readings, films, television shows, and websites that help illustrate key concepts; and classroom activities such as discussion topics and games. We also include nearly a dozen full-text excerpts from additional theoretical works that instructors may wish to assign or paste into their own course management systems, including work from Theodor Adorno, Anthony Giddens, Donna Haraway, Patricia Hill Collins, Michel Foucault, Georg Simmel, and others.

Test Materials (instructors only)

We have designed written exams and answer keys based on the content of the reader and the website, including multiple-choice questions and essay prompts. These materials are presented in a downloadable form so that instructors can reference them when designing their own exams.

Why This Book?

This book is intended for instructors constantly in search of new ways to make theory relevant for their students. The combination of a website and an anthology of original texts provides flexibility for instructors to design the course they have always wanted to teach. We have organized the content around what we think are the key conversations motivating social theory, but we invite instructors to come up with additional conversations of their own. This intellectual flexibility and rigor make *Social Theory Re-Wired* perfect for any social theory class, whether it is online, offline, or a hybrid course.

Whether students have come to the study of social theory with enthusiasm or trepidation, this interactive text will guide them through the webs and networks of social theory from its classic halcyon days to the vibrant and complex world of now. They should feel free to dig into the nitty-gritty of the original texts, grapple with the interactive readings online, and take notes in the margins (whether on the printed pages or the digital ones). To instructors and students both: Welcome to *Social Theory Re-Wired*. Plug in and start making connections.

Acknowledgments

W E WOULD LIKE TO EXTEND A heartfelt thanks to the teachers, mentors, and colleagues that continue to inspire our quest for a deeper theoretical understanding of the social world. In particular, we would like to thank the following individuals who were instrumental in bringing this project to realization: Doug Hartmann, Chris Uggen, Letta Page, and the best collection of reviewers two young authors could ask for when compiling a book like this one. We would also like to thank Steve Rutter, Dean Birkenkamp, Samantha Barbaro, Margaret Moore, and the rest of the staff at Routledge and Taylor & Francis, without whom this project would have remained on our shelves as a stack of loose papers and tangled ideas. Finally, and most importantly, we would like to thank our families and our partners, Sonya and Christie, who believed in not only this gig, but also our decision to drop everything and join the band for good.

Emergence Through Convergence

The Puzzles of Social Order

Introductory Essay:
This Deserted Island Is Out of Order

In William Golding's famous novel, *Lord of the Flies*, a group of young boys are marooned on a deserted island, the only survivors of a terrible plane crash. Stranded, scared, and with no adult supervision, the boys quickly assemble themselves and make plans for living on—and hopefully being rescued from—the island.

The beginning of the novel depicts how they organize themselves into a miniature society. They establish a division of labor with specific tasks and roles, some boys hunting for food, while others build shelters, and still others maintain a fire signal to alert potential rescuers of their whereabouts. They also organize themselves according to age, with the older boys—called "biguns"—taking charge and looking after the younger, smaller "littluns." They also choose leaders. A level-headed and democratic-minded boy named Ralph is elected leader of the group, a chubby, unpopular intellectual nicknamed "Piggy" becomes his trusted advisor, and the charismatic (and dangerous, as it turns out) Jack is appointed leader of the hunters.

The remainder of the novel details how this once nicely ordered society of tweeners falls apart. Ralph begins to lose political authority and control, Jack makes a dictatorial grab for power, and Piggy—well, in the interest of not being a total plot spoiler, let's just say Piggy and some other boys meet less than fortunate ends.

If you were one of the many students assigned Golding's gripping tale of "boys gone wild" as required reading in middle or high school, you know that it is a novel that hits on many themes: civilization and savagery, democracy and dictatorship, conformity and individuality, morality and the will to power. But, from a sociological point of view, *Lord of the Flies* is also a profound literary example of one of social theory's most fundamental themes—the problem, and puzzle, of social order.

For a "true life" *Lord of the Flies* story, check out the famous "Robbers Cave Experiment" by social psychologist Muzafer Sherif, listed in the Supplementary Sources section of the *Social Theory Re-Wired* website.

The plot of *Lord of the Flies* lays bare some of the most elementary features of social order, features that all of the social theorists in this section are trying in some way to understand and explain. One of the most important of these features is the paradoxical "dual nature" of social order. By this we mean, on one hand, social order is the creation of individuals. The stranded boys in Golding's novel devised their own social order; they elected their leaders, organized who would do what tasks when, and so forth. Yet, on the other hand, once this social order was created, it quickly took on a life of its own, exerting influence over the identities and actions of the very individuals who created it. Schoolboys became "leaders" and "hunters," a seashell became a sign of democracy, a pig's head became a religious sacrifice and, later on, the dreaded "Lord of the Flies" itself. Out of the *convergence* of individuals, we see the *emergence* of a social order far more complex, meaningful, and powerful than the sum of its individual parts.

While, fortunately, most of us will never be stranded on an island with spear-wielding preteens, the basic dual nature of social order is something we confront in every aspect of our lives—in our families, schools, workplaces, governments, on the web, even in our leisure activities.

To use just one example, think of the classroom you may be sitting in right now while reading this book. This social order that we label and recognize as a "classroom" would cease to exist without the ongoing and coordinated activities of thousands of people, including you. For the classroom to be a classroom, you and your classmates have to act like students; the person who assigned you this book like a professor; the people in the registrar's office need to make sure that you are "officially enrolled" as a student; the university administration has to monitor the performance of the many colleges and departments to maintain government accreditation; the state and federal governments need to allocate sizeable amounts of their budgets to higher education so schools can pay their employees and you can apply for student loans; the authors of this book need to make sure they continue to write about sociological matters like social order instead of a recipe for chocolate chip cookies—you see how much work all of this is?

Yet, simultaneously, the social order that makes up a classroom has an existence over and above the activities of all of the many individuals who comprise it. The "classroom" as a social form has been around well before any of us was born. And after well over a dozen years of acting like a student from kindergarten through college, you have internalized your role as a student and implicitly know how to act in a classroom. Unlike the kindergartener, no one has to tell you what's going on here. The classroom just simply exists as a fact of your everyday life. It is there, and remains so even if you decide to sleep in, skip class, drop out, or join a cult. It is what Emile Durkheim would call a "social fact," and what many other sociologists call a "social structure" or "institution." How social orders get constantly created by individuals, but at the same time exist and have influences over and above the power of individuals, is one of the most intriguing puzzles of social order, and one with which each of the theorists in this section tries to come to grips.

Along with the intriguing dual nature of social order, *Lord of the Flies* also vividly demonstrates what happens when social order fails or falls apart. While social theorists don't think that social orders are always necessarily good (just see the next two sections of this book for some pretty scathing critiques of modern social orders), they almost always see them as necessary. Without social order, life becomes chaotic, meaningless, and directionless. Just think of what happens to communities after a natural disaster or war. For many of the theorists in this section, the necessity of social order for making sense of our lives is most evident when the social order starts to break down or weaken (see, for example, Durkheim's famous study of suicide in the following pages, or, for more humorous but no less telling examples, Garfinkel's famous "breaching" experiments). In fact, what may be most surprising about social order is that it is so ubiquitous and that its absence or breakdown is not more common.

Emergence only through convergence, individual meaning only through collective activity—such are the fascinating puzzles of social order that the theorists in the following pages help us better understand.

Classical Connections: Emile Durkheim

You can't talk social order without talking Emile Durkheim. A nineteenth-century French sociologist and one of the founders of the discipline, Durkheim's fundamental preoccupation was investigating and theorizing how societies hold—or fail to hold—together. Teaching and writing during a time of great political and economic change in France and the rest of Europe, Durkheim studied the structure and development of numerous social institutions, including law, crime and deviance, work, religion, politics, public morality, and education. For Durkheim, each of these played an essential role in the creation and maintenance of social order, or what Durkheim often called "social solidarity." Likening modern society to a vast and complex organism, a bit like a vast coral reef, Durkheim saw social structures as functioning to hold society together. This idea characterizes the whole of Durkheim's sociology, and makes him the foundational classical theorist of social order.

Log in to Durkheim's Profile Page on the *Social Theory Re-Wired* website to learn more about his life and work.

In the first part of this section, we present key excerpts from some of Durkheim's most famous and widely read works on social order, including *The Division of Labor in Society*, *Suicide*, and *The Elementary Forms of Religious Life*. But, before you plug in to these classic readings and learn about Durkheim's thoughts on social solidarity, anomie, collective representations, and more, it might be best to begin with the short excerpt from his *The Rules of Sociological*

Method. Here, Durkheim deals with what for him was the most fundamental question for sociology, namely "What is a Social Fact?"

For Durkheim, social facts are much more than simply facts about society. Rather, they expressed the emergent and constraining power of social order that we talked about earlier. In *The Rules*, Durkheim straightaway tells us that social facts are "manners of acting, thinking, and feeling external to the individual, which are invested with a coercive power by virtue of which they exercise control over him." In other words, social facts are things external to us, collective entities that have power over us, enabling us to do some things but constraining our ability to do others.

Social facts can take many shapes and forms, ranging from the legal system and churches to social norms, languages, and family values. One of Durkheim's most famous books concerns the social fact of work and, more specifically, the social development of the division of labor. In the reading from *The Division of Labor in Society*, Durkheim asks how an advanced and complex division of labor affects the solidarity of societies. How can a modern social order continue to "hang together" once we have moved from a more "traditional" and "simple" division of labor to a hugely complex, industrialized system in which we all have our own specialized and differentiated roles and responsibilities? In a new capitalist world that celebrated individualism (Durkheim himself called it "the cult of the individual"), many worried that the social order was withering away or, like Karl Marx, thought it was becoming divided into the two opposing and increasingly antagonistic camps of capitalists and laborers.

Durkheim saw things differently. Rather than understanding the transition from a traditional to modern economic system as signifying a movement away from social order and toward increasing disintegration and conflict, Durkheim theorized that what we were witnessing was a move from one form of social solidarity to another. According to Durkheim, as societies grow and become more complex, they move along a path from "mechanical solidarity" (a form of social order and cohesion characterized by the sameness of individuals connected through common forms of work, religion, values, and education), to "organic solidarity," based on the differentiation of individuals who are connected through interdependence. Durkheim argued that in a modern, complex division of labor, solidarity was maintained not so much through shared labor, interests, and values, but through individuals' mutual reliance on others to perform their own specialized tasks (for example, while workers rely on factory owners to provide them with jobs, factory owners simultaneously rely on workers to produce the goods that they sell).

While Durkheim was more optimistic than many social theorists about the capacity for modern, capitalist societies to maintain social order and cohesion, he was not entirely sanguine about the matter. In the reading we have chosen from *Suicide*, Durkheim argues that many modern societies lack the kind of social integration and solidarity necessary to stave off "anomie," the inability of social ties and norms to regulate what he sees as the otherwise insatiable passions and aspirations of individuals left to their own devices. Without sufficient regulation of our desires, Durkheim believes, we remain constantly disillusioned and unsatisfied with our lives. Societies with lower levels of moral regulation, in turn, have higher suicide rates. In *Suicide*, Durkheim demonstrates how paying theoretical attention to social order can help us discern the social causes behind even the most seemingly individual actions.

In the final selection from Durkheim, you'll read an excerpt from one of the most widely-read and influential works in all of social theory, *The Elementary Forms of Religious Life*. In *Elementary Forms*, Durkheim develops an extremely creative (and controversial) theory of the social origins of religion. For him, religion is nothing more than the collective representations of a society, or, as Durkheim says elsewhere, religion is society first becoming dimly aware and conscious of itself. There are no gods or deities in Durkheim's definition of religion—there is only society. That is, when religious groups worship their gods, they are really, without fully knowing it, worshipping the social order that binds them together. Despite being skeptical of the supernatural claims of religion, Durkheim, an atheist, was not anti-religion. He saw religion as a powerful and necessary social force, capable of establishing the cohesiveness of society by providing a set of shared symbols, beliefs, and rituals through which individuals could affirm their common bonds. In this way, for Durkheim, religion was and remains a very *real* thing—a preeminent social fact.

For a disturbing, contemporary example of anomie and social disintegration, check out the documentary film, *The Lost Children of Rockdale County*, listed in the Supplementary Sources section.

Check out the full-text excerpt from Mary Douglas on "Natural Symbols" (available in the "Additional Readings" section of the website) to give your students an idea of how Durkheim's theory of religion and ritual has been used by one of contemporary social theory's most prominent scholars.

Contemporary Extensions: Social Order Re-Wired

While Emile Durkheim provides the starting point for any theoretical conversation on social order, he is certainly not the last word. Contemporary theoretical perspectives on the puzzles of social order abound, and we have selected four readings from five profound (and more recent) social theorists to give you a flavor of how this discussion has been taken up and re-worked in recent times.

The first reading comes from an intellectual titan of mid-twentieth-century American sociology, Robert Merton. Merton was a student of Talcott Parsons and George Sarton at Harvard University in the 1930s, where Parsons and his colleagues developed the theory of structural functionalism. A central tenet of structural functionalism is that societies require particular "functions" in order to operate as stable systems. (For Durkheim, the division of labor functioned to generate social solidarity among its members.) In his piece, "Manifest and Latent Functions," Merton elaborates on this idea by distinguishing between those functions that are obvious and intended versus those that are more invisible and unexpected. As an example, Merton gives us the case of Hopi rain dances, which are ostensibly intended to bring about rain if we were to gauge their function based on motivations alone. However, as Merton notes, meteorologists know that no such function is possible, and Merton concludes the rain dances function latently to fulfill the needs of the group instead. It is in this same reading that we learn of "unintended consequences," perhaps one of the central concepts in sociology writ large. According to Merton, identifying the unintended consequences of social action is the cornerstone of sociological inquiry, and is through such identification that the latent functions of a seemingly irrational act become known.

In the second reading, you will continue this exploration into the functions of everyday life with the founder of ethnomethodology, Harold Garfinkel. Garfinkel understood ethnomethodology as a distinct approach to sociological inquiry, one that painstakingly analyzes and describes the various methods by which members of a social group maintain the orderliness and sensibility of their everyday worlds. If, for Durkheim, the reality of social facts was sociology's fundamental object of study, Garfinkel took it as his job to understand how this objective reality was constantly being produced, managed, and negotiated in the everyday activities and routines of ordinary people. In an excerpt from his *Studies in Ethnomethodology*, you'll learn about the many ways people (including yourself) maintain a sense of the social order and read humorous scenarios about what happens when that sense of everyday order is disrupted (if you've ever been asked as part of an Introduction to Sociology course to break a social norm by, say, singing in a crowded elevator, congratulations, you're a burgeoning ethnomethodologist!). More than any other social theorist, Garfinkel shows us how social order is an "ongoing accomplishment."

In the next reading, French anthropologist, sociologist, and philosopher Bruno Latour introduces you to a door-closer. A prominent figure in the sociology of science, Latour (under a pseudonym, James Johnson) asks whether something as simple and overlooked as a door-closer plays a role in constructing society. According to Latour, the specific nonhuman system used to close the door to the room you are sitting in right now not only allows the door to function but also prescribes to us our social order. It allows people to enter without getting bloody noses and signals to the room's occupants the norms for who should or should not be in the room. For example, imagine how your current social situation might be defined differently if the door closed with a tight spring or didn't close at all? The article is a seminal work in actor-network theory developed by Latour and his colleagues in the 1980s, a theoretical perspective which called for a closer examination of the role of nonhuman actors in social relations. You may find connections to Garfinkel's ethnomethodology in Latour's exposition, as both readings expose the role of semiotics and small-scale interactions in the creation of social order. But,

Learn more about ethnomethodology by connecting to the Mid-Twentieth-Century American Theory Profile Page.

For vivid examples of breaching experiments (with a Marxist twist), watch some clips from Michael Moore's television series, "The Awful Truth," listed in Supplementary Sources.

Interested in thinking about how the advent of electronic media has changed our sense of social reality? Consider assigning portions of Joshua Meyrowitz's *No Sense of Place*, referenced in the Supplementary Sources section.

for Latour, it is not just humans who are doing the work here. Nonhuman actors—whether simple technologies like door-closers or complex ones like social media platforms—play an equally important, but often neglected, role. Latour asks us to open our eyes to the many ways nonhuman actors make our commonsense realities possible.

In the final reading, you'll find a sample from one of the most influential theories of how the reality of social orders comes into being. In *The Social Construction of Reality*, Peter Berger and Thomas Luckmann ask how an objective social order—a shared sense of factual reality—can emerge from the convergence of the minds, bodies, and interactions of individuals. Laying out a scheme that includes brilliant insights on human consciousness, habit, institutionalization, and the multiplicity of social realities, Berger and Luckmann give us a compelling way to understand how society actually becomes the objective reality of our everyday experience.

Students, apply your knowledge of Berger and Luckmann's theory to how the "reality" of online social networking sites like Facebook and MySpace gets constructed in the Writing Out Loud section of the website.

Plug In

Emergence and convergence, solidarity and anomie, social facts and social constructions—these are the terms of reference for understanding social order. Whether you want to better understand something as complex as the global capitalist market or something as mundane as that awkward conversation you had with your neighbor last week, whether you want to know more about how people can come together through the powers of modern technologies or how a primitive island society of English schoolboys can devolve into a murderous cult, you'll benefit from plugging in to these classical and contemporary perspectives on one of sociology's most persistent and important themes.

1

The Rules of Sociological Method

Emile Durkheim

BEFORE BEGINNING THE SEARCH FOR the method appropriate to the study of social facts it is important to know what are the facts termed 'social'.

The question is all the more necessary because the term is used without much precision. It is commonly used to designate almost all the phenomena that occur within society, however little social interest of some generality they present. Yet under this heading there is, so to speak, no human occurrence that cannot be called social. Every individual drinks, sleeps, eats, or employs his reason, and society has every interest in seeing that these functions are regularly exercised. If therefore these facts were social ones, sociology would possess no subject matter peculiarly its own, and its domain would be confused with that of biology and psychology.

However, in reality there is in every society a clearly determined group of phenomena separable, because of their distinct characteristics, from those that form the subject matter of other sciences of nature.

When I perform my duties as a brother, a husband or a citizen and carry out the commitments I have entered into, I fulfil obligations which are defined in law and custom and which are external to myself and my actions. Even when they conform to my own sentiments and when I feel their reality within me, that reality does not cease to be objective, for it is not I who have prescribed these duties; I have received them through education. Moreover, how often does it happen that we are ignorant of the details of the obligations that we must assume, and that, to know them, we must consult the legal code and its authorised interpreters! Similarly the believer has discovered from birth, ready fashioned, the beliefs and practices of his religious life; if they existed before he did, it follows that they exist outside him. The system of signs that I employ to express my thoughts, the monetary system I use to pay my debts, the credit instruments I utilise in my commercial relationships, the practices I follow in my profession, etc., all function independently of the use I make of them. Considering in turn each member of society, the foregoing remarks can be repeated for each single one of them. Thus there are ways of acting, thinking and feeling which possess the remarkable property of existing outside the consciousness of the individual.

Not only are these types of behaviour and thinking external to the individual, but they are endued with a compelling and coercive power by virtue of which, whether he wishes it or not, they impose themselves upon him. Undoubtedly when I conform to them of my own free will, this coercion is not felt or felt hardly at all, since it is unnecessary. None the less it is intrinsically a characteristic of these facts; the proof of this is that it asserts itself as soon as I try to resist. If I attempt to violate the rules of law they react against me so as to forestall my action, if there is still time. Alternatively, they annul it or make my action conform to the norm if it is already accomplished but capable of being reversed; or they cause me to pay the penalty for it if it is irreparable. If purely moral rules are at stake, the public conscience restricts any act which infringes them by the surveillance it exercises over the conduct of citizens and by the special punishments it has at its disposal. In other cases the constraint is less violent; nevertheless, it does not cease to exist. If I do not conform to ordinary conventions, if in my mode of dress I pay no heed to what is customary in my country and in my social class, the laughter I provoke, the social distance at which I am kept, produce, although in a more mitigated form, the same results as any real penalty. In other cases, although it may be indirect, constraint is no less effective. I am not forced to speak French with my compatriots, nor to use the legal currency, but it is impossible for me to do otherwise. If I tried to escape the necessity, my attempt would fail miserably. As an industrialist nothing prevents me from working with the processes and methods of the previous century, but if I do I will most certainly ruin myself. Even when in fact I can struggle free from these rules and successfully break them, it is never without being forced to fight against them. Even if in the end they are overcome, they make their constraining power sufficiently felt in the resistance that they afford. There is no innovator, even a fortunate one, whose ventures do not encounter opposition of this kind.

Here, then, is a category of facts which present very special characteristics: they consist of manners of acting, thinking and feeling external to the individual, which are invested with a coercive power by virtue of which they exercise control over him. Consequently, since they consist of representations and actions, they cannot be confused with organic phenomena, nor with psychical phenomena, which have no existence save in and through the individual consciousness. Thus they constitute a new species and to them must be exclusively assigned the term *social*. It is appropriate, since it is clear that, not having the individual as their substratum, they can have none other than society, either political society in its entirety or one of the partial groups that it includes—religious denominations, political and literary schools, occupational corporations, etc. Moreover, it is for such as these alone that the term is fitting, for the word 'social' has the sole meaning of designating those phenomena which fall into none of the categories of facts already constituted and labelled. They are consequently the proper field of sociology. It is true that this word 'constraint', in terms of which we define them, is in danger of infuriating those who zealously uphold out-and-out individualism. Since they maintain that the individual is completely autonomous, it seems to them that he is diminished every time he is made aware that he is not dependent on himself alone. Yet since it is indisputable today that most of our ideas and tendencies are not developed by ourselves, but come to us from outside, they can only penetrate us by imposing themselves upon us. This is all that our definition implies. Moreover, we know that all social constraints do not necessarily exclude the individual personality.[1]

Yet since the examples just cited (legal and moral rules, religious dogmas, financial systems, etc.) consist wholly of beliefs and practices already well established, in view of what has been said it might be maintained that no social fact can exist except where there is a well defined social organisation. But there are other facts which do not present themselves in this already crystallised form but which also possess the same objectivity and ascendancy over the individual. These are what are called social 'currents'. Thus in a public gathering the great waves of enthusiasm, indignation and pity that are produced have their seat in no one individual consciousness. They come to each one of us from outside and can sweep us along in spite of ourselves. If perhaps I abandon myself to them I may not be conscious of the pressure that they are exerting upon me, but that pressure makes its presence felt immediately I attempt to struggle against them. If an individual tries to pit himself against one of these collective manifestations, the sentiments that he is rejecting will be turned against him. Now if this external coercive power asserts itself so acutely in cases of resistance, it must be because it exists in the other instances cited above without our being conscious of it. Hence we are the victims of an illusion which leads us to believe we have ourselves produced what has been imposed upon us externally. But if the willingness with which we let ourselves be carried along disguises the pressure we have undergone, it does not eradicate it. Thus air does not cease to have weight, although we no longer feel that weight. Even when we have individually and spontaneously shared in the common emotion, the impression we have experienced is utterly different from what we would have felt if we had been alone. Once the assembly has broken up and these social influences have ceased to act upon us, and we are once more on our own, the emotions we have felt seem an alien phenomenon, one in which we no longer recognise ourselves. It is then we perceive that we have undergone the emotions much more than generated them. These emotions may even perhaps fill us with horror, so much do they go against the grain. Thus individuals who are normally perfectly harmless may, when gathered together in a crowd, let themselves be drawn into acts of atrocity. And what we assert about these transitory outbreaks likewise applies to those more lasting movements of opinion which relate to religious, political, literary and artistic matters, etc., and which are constantly being produced around us, whether throughout society or in a more limited sphere.

Moreover, this definition of a social fact can be verified by examining an experience that is characteristic. It is sufficient to observe how children are brought up. If one views the facts as they are and indeed as they have always been, it is patently obvious that all education consists of a continual effort to impose upon the child ways of seeing, thinking and acting which he himself would not have arrived at spontaneously. From his earliest years we oblige him to eat, drink and sleep at regular hours, and to observe cleanliness, calm and obedience; later we force him to learn how to be mindful of others, to respect customs and conventions, and to work, etc. If this constraint in time ceases to be felt it is because it gradually gives rise to habits, to inner tendencies which render it superfluous; but they supplant the constraint only because they are derived from it. It is true that, in Spencer's view, a rational education should shun such means and allow the child complete freedom to do what he will. Yet as this educational theory has never been put into practice among any known people, it can only be the personal expression of a *desideratum* and not a fact which can be established in contradiction to the other facts given above. What renders these latter facts particularly illuminating is that education sets out precisely with the object of creating a social being. Thus there can be seen, as in an abbreviated form, how the social being has been fashioned historically. The pressure to which the child is subjected unremittingly is the same pressure of the social environment which seeks to shape him in its own image, and in which parents and teachers are only the representatives and intermediaries.

Thus it is not the fact that they are general which can serve to characterise sociological phenomena. Thoughts to be found in the consciousness of each individual and movements which are repeated by all individuals are not for this reason social facts. If some have been content with using this characteristic in order to define them it is because they have been confused, wrongly, with what might be termed their individual incarnations. What constitutes social facts are the beliefs, tendencies and practices of the group taken collectively. But the forms that these collective states may assume when they are 'refracted' through individuals are things of a different kind. What irrefutably demonstrates this duality of kind is that these two categories of facts frequently are manifested dissociated from each other. Indeed some of these ways of acting or thinking acquire, by dint of repetition, a sort of consistency which, so to speak, separates them out, isolating them from the particular events which reflect them. Thus they assume a shape, a tangible form peculiar to them and constitute a reality *sui generis* vastly distinct from the individual facts which manifest that reality. Collective custom does not exist only in a state of immanence in the successive actions which it determines, but, by a privilege without example in the biological kingdom, expresses itself once and for all in a formula repeated by word of mouth, transmitted by education and even enshrined in the written word. Such are the origins and nature of legal and moral rules, aphorisms and popular sayings, articles of faith in which religious or political sects epitomise their beliefs, and standards of taste drawn up by literary schools, etc. None of these modes of acting and thinking are to be found wholly in the application made of them by individuals, since they can even exist without being applied at the time.

Undoubtedly this state of dissociation does not always present itself with equal distinctiveness. It is sufficient for dissociation to exist unquestionably in the numerous important instances cited, for us to prove that the social fact exists separately from its individual effects. Moreover, even when the dissociation is not immediately observable, it can often be made so with the help of certain metho-dological devices. Indeed it is essential to embark on such procedures if one wishes to refine out the social fact from any amalgam and so observe it in its pure state. Thus certain currents of opinion, whose intensity varies according to the time and country in which they occur, impel us, for example, towards marriage or suicide, towards higher or lower birth-rates, etc. Such currents are plainly social facts. At first sight they seem inseparable from the forms they assume in individual cases. But statistics afford us a means of isolating them. They are indeed not inaccurately represented by rates of births, marriages and suicides, that is, by the result obtained after dividing the average annual total of marriages, births, and voluntary homicides by the number of persons of an age to marry, produce children, or commit suicide.[2] Since each one of these statistics includes without distinction all individual cases, the

individual circumstances which may have played some part in producing the phenomenon cancel each other out and consequently do not contribute to determining the nature of the phenomenon. What it expresses is a certain state of the collective mind.

That is what social phenomena are when stripped of all extraneous elements. As regards their private manifestations, these do indeed having something social about them, since in part they reproduce the collective model. But to a large extent each one depends also upon the psychical and organic constitution of the individual, and on the particular circumstances in which he is placed. Therefore they are not phenomena which are in the strict sense sociological. They depend on both domains at the same time, and could be termed socio-psychical. They are of interest to the sociologist without constituting the immediate content of sociology. The same characteristic is to be found in the organisms of those mixed phenomena of nature studied in the combined sciences such as biochemistry.

It may be objected that a phenomenon can only be collective if it is common to all the members of society, or at the very least to a majority, and consequently, if it is general. This is doubtless the case, but if it is general it is because it is collective (that is, more or less obligatory); but it is very far from being collective because it is general. It is a condition of the group repeated in individuals because it imposes itself upon them. It is in each part because it is in the whole, but far from being in the whole because it is in the parts. This is supremely evident in those beliefs and practices which are handed down to us ready fashioned by previous generations. We accept and adopt them because, since they are the work of the collectivity and one that is centuries old, they are invested with a special authority that our education has taught us to recognise and respect. It is worthy of note that the vast majority of social phenomena come to us in this way. But even when the social fact is partly due to our direct co-operation, it is no different in nature. An outburst of collective emotion in a gathering does not merely express the sum total of what individual feelings share in common, but is something of a very different order, as we have demonstrated. It is a product of shared existence, of actions and reactions called into play between the consciousnesses of individuals. If it is echoed in each one of them it is precisely by virtue of the special energy derived from its collective origins. If all hearts beat in unison, this is not as a consequence of a spontaneous, pre-established harmony; it is because one and the same force is propelling them in the same direction. Each one is borne along by the rest.

We have therefore succeeded in delineating for ourselves the exact field of sociology. It embraces one single, well defined group of phenomena. A social fact is identifiable through the power of external coercion which it exerts or is capable of exerting upon individuals. The presence of this power is in turn recognisable because of the existence of some pre-determined sanction, or through the resistance that the fact opposes to any individual action that may threaten it. However, it can also be defined by ascertaining how widespread it is within the group, provided that, as noted above, one is careful to add a second essential characteristic; this is, that it exists independently of the particular forms that it may assume in the process of spreading itself within the group. In certain cases this latter criterion can even be more easily applied than the former one. The presence of constraint is easily ascertainable when it is manifested externally through some direct reaction of society, as in the case of law, morality, beliefs, customs and even fashions. But when constraint is merely indirect, as with that exerted by an economic organisation, it is not always so clearly discernible. Generality combined with objectivity may then be easier to establish. Moreover, this second definition is simply another formulation of the first one: if a mode of behaviour existing outside the consciousnesses of individuals becomes general, it can only do so by exerting pressure upon them.[3]

However, one may well ask whether this definition is complete. Indeed the facts which have provided us with its basis are all *ways of functioning:* they are 'physiological' in nature. But there are also collective *ways of being*, namely, social facts of an 'anatomical' or morphological nature. Sociology cannot dissociate itself from what concerns the substratum of collective life. Yet the number and nature of the elementary parts which constitute society, the way in which they are articulated, the degree of coalescence they have attained, the distribution of population over the earth's surface, the extent and nature of the network of communications, the design of dwellings, etc., do not at first sight seem relatable to ways of acting, feeling or thinking.

Yet, first and foremost, these various phenomena present the same characteristic which has served us in defining the others. These ways of being impose themselves upon the individual just as do the ways of acting we have dealt with. In fact, when we wish to learn how a society is divided up politically, in what its divisions consist and the degree of solidarity that exists between them, it is not through physical inspection and geographical observation that we may come to find this out: such divisions are social, although they may have some physical basis. It is only through public law that we can study such political organisation, because this law is what determines its nature, just as it determines our domestic and civic relationships. The organisation is no less a form of compulsion. If the population clusters together in our cities instead of being scattered over the rural areas, it is because there exists a trend of opinion, a collective drive which imposes this concentration upon individuals. We can no more choose the design of our houses than the cut of our clothes—at least, the one is as much obligatory as the other. The communication network forcibly prescribes the direction of internal migrations or commercial exchanges, etc., and even their intensity. Consequently, at the most there are grounds for adding one further category to the list of phenomena already enumerated as bearing the distinctive stamp of a social fact. But as that enumeration was in no wise strictly exhaustive, this addition would not be indispensable.

Moreover, it does not even serve a purpose, for these ways of being are only ways of acting that have been consolidated. A society's political structure is only the way in which its various component segments have become accustomed to living with each other. If relationships between them are traditionally close, the segments tend to merge together; if the contrary, they tend to remain distinct. The type of dwelling imposed upon us is merely the way in which everyone around us and, in part, previous generations, have customarily built their houses. The communication network is only the channel which has been cut by the regular current of commerce and migrations, etc., flowing in the same direction. Doubtless if phenomena of a morphological kind were the only ones that displayed this rigidity, it might be thought that they constituted a separate species. But a legal rule is no less permanent an arrangement than an architectural style, and yet it is a 'physiological' fact. A simple moral maxim is certainly more malleable, yet it is cast in forms much more rigid than a mere professional custom or fashion. Thus there exists a whole range of gradations which, without any break in continuity, join the most clearly delineated structural facts to those free currents of social life which are not yet caught in any definite mould. This therefore signifies that the differences between them concern only the degree to which they have become consolidated. Both are forms of life at varying stages of crystallisation. It would undoubtedly be advantageous to reserve the term 'morphological' for those social facts which relate to the social substratum, but only on condition that one is aware that they are of the same nature as the others. Our definition will therefore subsume all that has to be defined it if states:

> *A social fact is any way of acting, whether fixed or not, capable of exerting over the individual an external constraint;*

or:

> *which is general over the whole of a given society whilst having an existence of its own, independent of its individual manifestations.*[4]

NOTES

1. Moreover, this is not to say that all constraint is normal. We shall return to this point later.
2. Suicides do not occur at any age, nor do they occur at all ages of life with the same frequency.
3. It can be seen how far removed this definition of the social fact is from that which serves as the basis for the ingenious system of Tarde. We must first state that our research has nowhere led us to corroboration of the preponderant influence that Tarde attributes to imitation in the genesis of collective facts. Moreover, from this definition, which is not a theory but a mere résumé of the immediate data observed, it seems clearly to follow that imitation does not always express, indeed never expresses, what is essential and characteristic in the social fact. Doubtless every social fact is imitated and has, as we have just shown, a tendency to become generalised, but this is because it is social, i.e. obligatory. Its capacity for expansion is not the cause but the consequence of its sociological character. If social facts were unique in bringing about this effect, imitation might serve, if not to explain them, at least to define them. But an individual state which impacts on others none the less remains individual. Moreover, one may speculate whether the term 'imitation' is indeed appropriate to designate a proliferation which occurs through some coercive influence. In such a single term very different phenomena, which need to be distinguished, are confused.
4. This close affinity of life and structure, organ and function, can be readily established in sociology because there exists between these two extremes a whole series of intermediate stages, immediately observable, which reveal the link between them. Biology lacks this methodological resource. But one may believe legitimately that sociological inductions on this subject are applicable to biology and that, in organisms as in societies, between these two categories of facts only differences in degree exist.

COMPANION WEBSITE

1. Go online to Write Out Loud about some contemporary social facts that are bigger than the sum of their parts.
2. Log on to Durkheim's Profile Page to learn more about the key role he played in establishing sociology as a discipline.
3. Check out the Profile Page for Mid-Century American Theory to learn more about Durkheim's functionalist legacy.

2

The Division of Labor in Society

Emile Durkheim

THE PROBLEM

Although the division of labour is not of recent origin, it was only at the end of the last century that societies began to become aware of this law, to which up to then they had submitted almost unwittingly. Undoubtedly even from antiquity several thinkers had perceived its importance.[1] Yet Adam Smith was the first to attempt to elaborate the theory of it. Moreover, it was he who first coined the term, which social science later lent to biology.

Nowadays the phenomenon has become so widespread that it catches everyone's attention. We can no longer be under any illusion about the trends in modern industry. It involves increasingly powerful mechanisms, large-scale groupings of power and capital, and consequently an extreme division of labour. Inside factories, not only are jobs demarcated, becoming extremely specialised, but each product is itself a speciality entailing the existence of others. Adam Smith and John Stuart Mill persisted in hoping that agriculture at least would prove an exception to the rule, seeing in it the last refuge of small-scale ownership. Although in such a matter we must guard against generalising unduly, nowadays it appears difficult to deny that the main branches of the agricultural industry are increasingly swept along in the general trend.[2] Finally, commerce itself contrives ways to follow and reflect, in all their distinctive nuances, the boundless diversity of industrial undertakings. Although this evolution occurs spontaneously and unthinkingly, those economists who study its causes and evaluate its results, far from condemning such diversification or attacking it, proclaim its necessity. They perceive in it the higher law of human societies and the condition for progress.

Yet the division of labour is not peculiar to economic life. We can observe its increasing influence in the most diverse sectors of society. Functions, whether political, administrative or judicial, are becoming more and more specialised. The same is true in the arts and sciences. The time lies far behind us when philosophy constituted the sole science. It has become fragmented into a host of special disciplines, each having its purpose, method and ethos. 'From one half-century to another the men who have left their mark upon the sciences have become more specialized.'[3]

[...]

FUNCTION OF THE DIVISION OF LABOR

Everybody knows that we like what resembles us, those who think and feel as we do. But the opposite phenomenon is no less frequently encountered. Very often we happen to feel drawn to people who do not resemble us, precisely because they do *not* do so. These facts are seemingly so much at odds that in every age moralists have hesitated about the true nature of friendship and have traced it now to the one cause, now to the other. The Greeks had already posed the question. 'Friendship,' says Aristotle, 'gives rise to much argument. For some it consists in a certain resemblance, and those who resemble each other like each other: hence the proverbs, "like goes with like", and "birds of a feather flock together", and other similar sayings. But on the contrary, according to others, all those who resemble one another grate upon one another. Other explanations are sought at a higher level which are taken from a consideration of nature. Thus Euripides says that the parched earth is in love with the rain, and that the overcast sky heavy with rain pours down upon the earth in a fury of love. Heraclitus claims that one only accommodates to what one opposes, that the finest harmony is born from differences, and that discord is the law of all becoming'.[4]

What demonstrates these opposing doctrines is the fact that both forms of friendship exist in nature. Dissimilarity, just like resemblance, can be a cause of mutual attraction. However, not every kind of dissimilarity is sufficient to bring this about. We find no pleasure in meeting others whose nature is merely different from our own. Prodigals do not seek the company of the miserly, nor upright and frank characters that of the hypocritical and underhand. Kind and gentle spirits feel no attraction for those of harsh and evil disposition. Thus only differences of a certain kind incline us towards one another. These are those which, instead of mutually opposing and excluding one another, complement one another. Bain says, 'There is a kind of disparity that repels and a kind that attracts; a kind that tends to rivalry, and a kind that tends to friendship … if what the one has, the other has not, but desires, there is a basis of positive attraction.'[5]

Thus the theorist with a reasoning and subtle mind has often a very special sympathy for practical men who are direct and whose intuition is swift. The fearful are attracted to those who are decisive and resolute, the weak to the strong, and vice versa. However richly endowed we may be, we always lack something, and the best among us feel our own inadequacy. This is why we seek in our friends those qualities we lack, because in uniting with them we share in some way in their nature, feeling ourselves then less incomplete. In this way small groups of friends grow up in which each individual plays a role in keeping with his character, in which a veritable exchange of services occurs. The one protects, the other consoles; one advises, the other executes, and it is this distribution of functions or, to use the common expression, this division of labour, that determines these relations of friendship.

We are therefore led to consider the division of labour in a new light. In this case, indeed, the economic services that it can render are insignificant compared with the moral effect that it produces, and its true function is to create between two or more people a feeling of solidarity. However this result is accomplished, it is this that gives rise to these associations of friends and sets its mark upon them.

The history of marital relationships affords an even more striking example of the same phenomenon.

Doubtless, sexual attraction is never felt save between individuals of the same species, and fairly generally love presumes a certain harmony of thought and feeling. It is nevertheless true that what imparts its specific character to this tendency and generates its specific force is not the similarity but the dissimilarity of the natures that it links together. It is because men and women differ from one another that they seek out one another with such passion. However, as in the previous case, it is not purely and simply contrast that causes reciprocal feelings to arise: only those differences that are assumed and that complement one another possess this power. In fact, men and women in isolation from each other are only different parts of the same concrete whole, which they reconstitute by uniting with each other. In other words, it is the sexual division of labour which is the source of conjugal solidarity, and this is why psychologists have very aptly remarked that the separation of the sexes was an event of prime importance in the evolution of the sentiments. This is because it has made possible perhaps the strongest of all disinterested tendencies.

There is something else. The division of labour between the sexes is capable of being more, and capable of being less. It can relate only to the sexual organs and some secondary traits that depend on them, or, on the contrary, can extend to all organic and social functions. It can be seen historically as having developed precisely along the same lines and in the same way as marital solidarity.

The further we go back into the past, the more we see that the division of labour between the sexes is reduced to very little. In those distant times woman was not at all the weak creature that she has become as morality has progressed. Prehistoric bone remains attest to the fact that the difference between the strength of a man and a woman was relatively much less than it is today.[6] Even nowadays, in infancy and up to puberty, the skeletal frame of the two sexes is not appreciably different: its characteristics are principally female. If one accepts that the development of the individual reproduces in abridged form that of the species, we may justifiably conjecture that the same homogeneity was to be found at the beginnings of human evolution, and see in the female form a close image of what was originally that single, common type from which the male sex has gradually become distinct. Moreover, travellers report that among a certain number of South American tribes man and woman show in their general build and appearance a similarity greater than that found elsewhere.[7] Finally, Dr Lebon has been able to establish directly, with mathematical precision, this original resemblance between the sexes, in regard to the preeminent organ of physical and mental life, the brain. By comparing a large number of skulls selected from among different races and societies, he arrived at the following conclusion:

> The volume of the skull of a man or woman, even when subjects of the same age, size and weight are being compared, presents considerable differences in favour of the man, and this disparity likewise

increases with the advance of civilization, so that, as regards the mass of the brain, and consequently of the intelligence, woman tends increasingly to become different from man. For example, the difference which exists between the average size of the brain between present-day Parisian men and women is almost double that observed between male and female skulls in ancient Egypt.[8]

A German anthropologist, Bischoff, has arrived at the same result in this respect.[9]

These anatomical similarities are concomitant with functional ones. In fact, in these same societies the female functions are not very clearly distinguished from the masculine ones, but the two sexes lead roughly the same kind of existence. Even now there is still a very large number of savage peoples where the woman takes part in political life. This has been observed especially among the Indian tribes of America, such as the Iroquois and the Natchez,[10] in Hawaii where she shares in the life of the man in countless ways,[11] in New Zealand and Samoa. Similarly we see very frequently the women going off to war with the men, stimulating them to fight, and even participating very actively in the fighting. In Cuba and Dahomey they are as warlike as the men, fighting side by side with them.[12] One of the distinctive attributes of a woman today, that of gentleness, does not originally appear to have been characteristic of her. Already among certain animal species the female is, on the contrary, noted for the opposite characteristic.

Among these same peoples marriage exists only in a very rudimentary state. Even if not yet demonstrated with certainty, it is even very likely that there was an era in the history of the family when marriage did not exist. Sexual relationships were made and unmade at will, the partners being bound by no legal tie. In any case we know of a family type relatively close to us[13] in which marriage is still only in a distinctly embryonic state, that is, the matriarchal family. The relationships between mother and children are very clearly defined, but those between the two partners are very lax. They can cease as soon as the parties wish, or indeed may be entered into only for a limited period.[14] Marital fidelity is still not required. Marriage, or what is so termed, comprises solely obligations of a strictly limited nature, and these are very often of short duration, linking the husband to the wife's relations. Thus it amounts to very little. In any given society the set of legal rules that constitute marriage only symbolises the state of conjugal solidarity. If this is very strong, the bonds uniting husband and wife are numerous and complex, and consequently the marriage rules, whose purpose is to define them, are themselves very elaborate. If, on the other hand, the marital state lacks cohesiveness, if the relations between the man and the woman are unstable and sporadic, they cannot assume a very fixed form. Consequently marriage comes down to a small number of rules lacking rigour and preciseness. The state of marriage in societies where the two sexes are only slightly differentiated thus bears witness to the fact that conjugal solidarity is itself very weak.

On the other hand, as we approach modern times, we see marriage developing. The network of ties that it creates becomes ever more extensive, the obligations that it imposes increase. The conditions on which it may be entered into, and those on which it may be dissolved are stipulated with increasing precision, as are the consequences of such a dissolution. The duty of fidelity takes on an organised form; at first laid upon the wife alone, it later becomes reciprocal. When the institution of the dowry makes its appearance, very complex rules emerge fixing the respective rights of each partner regarding their individual fortunes. Moreover, we need only cast a glance through our legal codes to see how important is the place of marriage. The union of the two spouses has ceased to be ephemeral; no longer is it an external, temporary and partial contact, but an intimate association, one that is lasting, often even indissoluble, between two lives throughout their whole existence.

Beyond question, over the same period of time labour became increasingly divided up as between the sexes. At first limited to the sexual functions alone, it gradually extended to many other functions. The woman had long withdrawn from warfare and public affairs, and had centred her existence entirely round the family. Since then her role has become even more specialised. Nowadays, among civilised peoples the woman leads an existence entirely different from the man's. It might be said that the two great functions of psychological life had become as if dissociated from each other, one sex having taken over the affective, the other the intellectual function. Noticing how, among certain social classes the women are taken up with art and literature, just as are the men, one might, it is true, believe that the activities of both sexes are tending once more to become homogeneous. But even in this sphere of activity, the woman brings to bear her own nature, and her role remains very special, one very different from that of the man. What is more, if art and letters are beginning to become matters that occupy women, the other sex appears to be abandoning them so as to devote itself more especially to science. Thus it might well happen that this apparent reversion to a primeval homogeneity is no more than the beginning of a fresh differentiation.

[...]

We have not merely to investigate whether, in these kinds of societies, there exists a social solidarity arising from the division of labour. This is a self-evident truth, since in them the division of labour is highly developed and it engenders solidarity. But above all we must determine the degree to which the solidarity it produces contributes generally to the integration of society. Only then shall we learn to what extent it is necessary, whether it is an essential factor in social cohesion, or whether, on the contrary, it is only an ancillary and secondary condition for it. To answer this question we must therefore compare this social bond to others, in order to measure what share in the total effect must be attributed to it. To do this it is indispensable to begin by classifying the different species of social solidarity.

However, social solidarity is a wholly moral phenomenon which by itself is not amenable to exact observation and especially not to measurement. To arrive at this classification, as well as this comparison, we must therefore substitute for this internal datum, which escapes us, an external one which symbolises it, and then study the former through the latter.

That visible symbol is the law. Indeed where social solidarity exists, in spite of its non-material nature, it does not remain in a state of pure potentiality, but shows its presence through perceptible effects. Where it is strong it attracts men strongly to one another, ensures frequent contacts between them, and multiplies the opportunities available to them to enter into mutual relationships. To state the position precisely, at the point we have now reached it is not easy to say whether it is social solidarity that produces these phenomena or, on the contrary, whether it is the result of them. Likewise it is a moot point whether men draw closer to one another because of the strong effects of social solidarity, or whether it is strong because men *have* come closer together. However, for the moment we need not concern ourselves with clarifying this question. It is enough to state that these two orders of facts are linked, varying with each other simultaneously and directly. The more closely knit the members of a society, the more they maintain various relationships either with one another or with the group collectively. For if they met together rarely, they would not be mutually dependent, except sporadically and somewhat weakly. Moreover, the number of these relationships is necessarily proportional to that of the legal rules that determine them. In fact, social life, wherever it becomes lasting, inevitably tends to assume a definite form and become organised. Law is nothing

more than this very organisation in its most stable and precise form.[15] Life in general within a society cannot enlarge in scope without legal activity simultaneously increasing in proportion. Thus we may be sure to find reflected in the law all the essential varieties of social solidarity.

[...]

Thus our method is clearly traced out for us. Since law reproduces the main forms of social solidarity, we have only to classify the different types of law in order to be able to investigate which types of social solidarity correspond to them. It is already likely that one species of law exists which symbolises the special solidarity engendered by the division of labour. Once we have made this investigation, in order to judge what part the division of labour plays it will be enough to compare the number of legal rules which give it expression with the total volume of law.

To undertake this study we cannot use the habitual distinctions made by jurisprudents. Conceived for the practice of law, from this viewpoint they can be very convenient, but science cannot be satisfied with such empirical classifications and approximations. The most widespread classification is that which divides law into public and private law. Public law is held to regulate the relationships of the individual with the state, private law those of individuals with one another. Yet when we attempt to define these terms closely, the dividing line, which appeared at first sight to be so clear-cut, disappears. All law is private, in the sense that always and everywhere individuals are concerned and are its actors. Above all, however, all law is public, in the sense that it is a social function, and all individuals are, although in different respects, functionaries of society. The functions of marriage and parenthood, etc. are not spelt out or organised any differently from those of ministers or legislators. Not without reason did Roman law term guardianship a *munus publicum*. Moreover; what is the state? Where does it begin, where does it end? The controversial nature of this question is well known. It is unscientific to base such a fundamental classification on such an obscure and inadequately analysed idea.

In order to proceed methodically, we have to discover some characteristic which, whilst essential to juridical phenomena, is capable of varying as they vary. Now, every legal precept may be defined as a rule of behaviour to which sanctions apply. Moreover, it is clear that the sanctions change according to the degree of seriousness attached to the precepts, the place they occupy in the public consciousness, and the role they play in society. Thus it is appropriate to classify legal rules according to the different sanctions that are attached to them.

These are of two kinds. The first consist essentially in some injury, or at least some disadvantage imposed upon the perpetrator of a crime. Their purpose is to do harm to him through his fortune, his honour, his life, his liberty, or to deprive him of some object whose possession he enjoys. These are said to be repressive sanctions, such as those laid down in the penal code. It is true that those that appertain to purely moral rules are of the same character. Yet such sanctions are administered in a diffuse way by everybody without distinction, whilst those of the penal code are applied only through the mediation of a definite body—they are organised. As for the other kind of sanctions, they do not necessarily imply any suffering on the part of the perpetrator, but merely consist in *restoring the previous state of affairs*, re-establishing relationships that have been disturbed from their normal form. This is done either by forcibly redressing the action impugned, restoring it to the type from which it has deviated, or by annulling it, that is depriving it of all social value. Thus legal rules must be divided into two main species, according to whether they relate to repressive, organised sanctions, or to ones that are purely restitutory. The first group covers all penal law; the second, civil law, commercial law, procedural law, administrative and constitutional law, when any penal rules which may be attached to them have been removed.

Let us now investigate what kind of social solidarity corresponds to each of these species.

MECHANICAL SOLIDARITY, OR SOLIDARITY BY SIMILARITIES

The totality of beliefs and sentiments common to the average members of a society forms a determinate system with a life of its own. It can be termed the collective or common consciousness. Undoubtedly the substratum of this consciousness does not consist of a single organ. By definition it is diffused over society as a whole, but nonetheless possesses specific characteristics that make it a distinctive reality. In fact it is independent of the particular conditions in which individuals find themselves. Individuals pass on, but it abides. It is the same in north and south, in large towns and in small, and in different professions. Likewise it does not change with every generation but, on the contrary, links successive generations to one another. Thus it is something totally different from the consciousnesses of individuals, although it is only realised in individuals. It is the psychological type of society, one which has its properties, conditions for existence and mode of development, just as individual types do, but in a different fashion. For this reason it has the right to be designated by a special term. It is true that the one we have employed above is not without ambiguity. Since the terms 'collective' and 'social' are often taken as synonyms, one is inclined to believe that the collective consciousness is the entire social consciousness, that is, co-terminous with the psychological life of society, whereas, particularly in higher societies, it constitutes only a very limited part of it. Those functions that are judicial, governmental, scientific or industrial— in short, all the specific functions—appertain to the psychological order, since they consist of systems of representation and action. However, they clearly lie outside the common consciousness. To avoid a confusion[16] that has occurred it would perhaps be best to invent a technical expression which would specifically designate the sum total of social similarities. However, since the use of a new term, when it is not absolutely necessary, is not without its disadvantages, we shall retain the more generally used expression, 'collective (or common) consciousness', but always keeping in mind the restricted sense in which we are employing it.

Thus, summing up the above analysis, we may state that an act is criminal when it offends the strong, well-defined states of the collective consciousness.[17]

This proposition, taken literally, is scarcely disputed, although usually we give it a meaning very different from the one it should have. It is taken as if it expressed, not the essential characteristics of the crime, but one of its repercussions. We well know that crime offends very general sentiments, but ones that are strongly held. But it is believed that their generality and strength spring from the criminal nature of the act, which consequently still remains wholly to be defined. It is not disputed that any criminal act excites universal disapproval, but it is taken for granted that this results from its criminal nature. Yet one is then hard put to it to state what is the nature of this criminality. Is it in a particularly serious form of immorality? I would concur, but this is to answer a question by posing another, by substituting one term for another. For what *is* immorality is precisely what we want to know—and particularly that special form of immorality which society represses by an organised system of punishments, and which constitutes criminality. Clearly it can only derive from one or several characteristics common to all varieties of crime. Now the only characteristic to satisfy that condition refers to the opposition that exists between crime of any kind and certain collective sentiments. It is thus this opposition which, far from deriving from the crime, constitutes the crime. In other words, we should not say that an act offends the common consciousness because it is criminal, but that it is criminal because it offends that consciousness. We do not condemn it because

it is a crime, but it is a crime because we condemn it. As regards the intrinsic nature of these feelings, we cannot specify what that is. They have very diverse objects, so that they cannot be encompassed within a single formula. They cannot be said to relate to the vital interests of society or to a minimum of justice. All such definitions are inadequate. But by the mere fact that a sentiment, whatever may be its origin and purpose, is found in every consciousness and endowed with a certain degree of strength and precision, every act that disturbs it is a crime. Present-day psychology is increasingly turning back to Spinoza's idea that things are good because we like them, rather than that we like them because they are good. What is primary is the tendency and disposition: pleasure and pain are only facts derived from this. The same holds good for social life. An act is socially evil because it is rejected by society. But, it will be contended, are there no collective sentiments that arise from the pleasure or pain that society feels when it comes into contact with their objects? This is doubtless so, but all such sentiments do not originate in this way. Many, if not the majority, derive from utterly different causes. Anything that obliges our activity to take on a definite form can give rise to habits that result in dispositions which then have to be satisfied. Moreover, these dispositions alone are truly fundamental. The others are only special forms of them and are more determinate. Thus to find charm in a particular object, collective sensibility must already have been constituted in such a way as to be able to appreciate it. If the corresponding sentiments are abolished, an act most disastrous for society will not only be capable of being tolerated, but honoured and held up as an example. Pleasure cannot create a disposition out of nothing; it can only link to a particular end those dispositions that already exist, provided that end is in accordance with their original nature.

[...]

We can therefore see what kind of solidarity the penal law symbolises. In fact we all know that a social cohesion exists whose cause can be traced to a certain conformity of each individual consciousness to a common type, which is none other than the psychological type of society. Indeed under these conditions all members of the group are not only individually attracted to one another because they resemble one another, but they are also linked to what is the condition for the existence of this collective type, that is, to the society that they form by coming together. Not only do fellow-citizens like one another, seeking one another out in preference to foreigners, but they love their country. They wish for it what they would wish for themselves, they care that it should be lasting and prosperous, because without it a whole area of their psychological life would fail to function smoothly. Conversely, society insists upon its citizens displaying all these basic resemblances because it is a condition for its own cohesion. Two consciousnesses exist within us: the one comprises only states that are personal to each one of us, characteristic of us as individuals, whilst the other comprises states that are common to the whole of society.[18] The former represents only our individual personality, which it constitutes; the latter represents the collective type and consequently the society without which it would not exist. When it is an element of the latter determining our behaviour, we do not act with an eye to our own personal interest, but are pursuing collective ends. Now, although distinct, these two consciousnesses are linked to each other, since in the end they constitute only one entity, for both have one and the same organic basis. Thus they are solidly joined together. This gives rise to a solidarity *sui generis* which, deriving from resemblances, binds the individual directly to society. In the next chapter we shall be better able to demonstrate why we propose to term this solidarity mechanical. It does not consist merely in a general, indeterminate attachment of the individual to the group, but is also one that concerts their detailed actions. Indeed, since such collective motives are the same everywhere, they produce everywhere the same effects. Consequently, whenever they are brought into play all wills spontaneously move as one in the same direction.

It is this solidarity that repressive law expresses, at least in regard to what is vital to it. Indeed the acts which such law forbids and stigmatises as crimes are of two kinds: either they manifest directly a too violent dissimilarity between the one who commits them and the collective type; or they offend the organ of the common consciousness. In both cases the force shocked by the crime and that rejects it is thus the same. It is a result of the most vital social similarities, and its effect is to maintain the social cohesion that arises from these similarities. It is that force which the penal law guards against being weakened in any way. At the same time it does this by insisting upon a minimum number of similarities from each one of us, without which the individual would be a threat to the unity of the body social, and by enforcing respect for the symbol which expresses and epitomises these resemblances, whilst simultaneously guaranteeing them.

By this is explained why some acts have so frequently been held to be criminal, and punished as such, without in themselves being harmful to society. Indeed, just like the individual type, the collective type has been fashioned under the influence of very diverse causes, and even of random events. A product of historical development, it bears the mark of those circumstances of every kind through which society has lived during its history. It would therefore be a miracle if everything to be found in it were geared to some useful end. Some elements, more or less numerous, cannot fail to have been introduced into it which are unrelated to social utility. Among the dispositions and tendencies the individual has received from his ancestors or has developed over time there are certainly many that serve no purpose, or that cost more than the benefits they bring. Undoubtedly most of these are not harmful, for if they were, in such conditions the individual could not live. But there are some that persist although lacking in all utility. Even those that do undisputedly render a service are frequently of an intensity disproportionate to their usefulness, because that intensity derives in part from other causes. The same holds good for collective emotions. Every act that disturbs them is not dangerous in itself, or at least is not so perilous as the condemnation it earns. However, the reprobation such acts incur is not without reason. For, whatever the origin of these sentiments, once they constitute a part of the collective type, and particularly if they are essential elements in it, everything that serves to undermine them at the same time undermines social cohesion and is prejudicial to society. In their origin they had no usefulness but, having survived, it becomes necessary for them to continue despite their irrationality. This is generally why it is good that acts that offend these sentiments should not be tolerated. Doubtless, by reasoning in the abstract it can indeed be shown that there are no grounds for a society to prohibit the eating of a particular kind of meat, an action inoffensive in itself. But once an abhorrence of this food has become an integral part of the common consciousness it cannot disappear without social bonds becoming loosened, and of this the healthy individual consciousness is vaguely aware.[19]

The same is true of punishment. Although it proceeds from an entirely mechanical reaction and from an access of passionate emotion, for the most part unthinking, it continues to play a useful role. But that role is not the one commonly perceived. It does not serve, or serves only very incidentally, to correct the guilty person or to scare off any possible imitators. From this dual viewpoint its effectiveness may rightly be questioned; in any case it is mediocre. Its real function is to maintain inviolate the cohesion of society by sustaining the common consciousness in all its vigour. If that consciousness were thwarted so categorically, it would necessarily lose some of its power, were an emotional reaction from the community not forthcoming to make good that loss. Thus there would result a relaxation in the bonds of social solidarity. The consciousness must therefore be conspicuously reinforced the moment it meets with opposition. The sole means of doing

so is to give voice to the unanimous aversion that the crime continues to evoke, and this by an official act, which can only mean suffering inflicted upon the wrongdoer. Thus, although a necessary outcome of the causes that give rise to it, this suffering is not a gratuitous act of cruelty. It is a sign indicating that the sentiments of the collectivity are still unchanged, that the communion of minds sharing the same beliefs remains absolute, and in this way the injury that the crime has inflicted upon society is made good. This is why it is right to maintain that the criminal should suffer in proportion to his crime, and why theories that deny to punishment any expiatory character appear, in the minds of many, to subvert the social order. In fact such theories could only be put into practice in a society from which almost every trace of the common consciousness has been expunged. Without this necessary act of satisfaction what is called the moral consciousness could not be preserved. Thus, without being paradoxical, we may state that punishment is above all intended to have its effect upon honest people. Since it serves to heal the wounds inflicted upon the collective sentiments, it can only fulfil this role where such sentiments exist, and in so far as they are active. Undoubtedly, by forestalling in minds already distressed any further weakening of the collective psyche, punishment can indeed prevent such attacks from multiplying. But such a result, useful though it is, is merely a particular side-effect. In short, to visualise an exact idea of punishment, the two opposing theories that have been advanced must be reconciled: the one sees in punishment an expiation, the other conceives it as a weapon for the defence of society. Certainly it does fulfil the function of protecting society, but this is because of its expiatory nature. Moreover, if it must be expiatory, this is not because suffering redeems error by virtue of some mystic strength or another, but because it cannot produce its socially useful effect save on this one condition.[20]

[...]

SOLIDARITY ARISING FROM THE DIVISION OF LABOR, OR ORGANIC SOLIDARITY

The very nature of the restitutory sanction is sufficient to show that the social solidarity to which that law corresponds is of a completely different kind.

The distinguishing mark of this sanction is that it is not expiatory, but comes down to a mere *restoration of the 'status quo ante'*. Suffering in proportion to the offence is not inflicted upon the one who has broken the law or failed to acknowledge it; he is merely condemned to submit to it. If certain acts have already been performed, the judge restores them to what they should be. He pronounces what the law is, but does not talk of punishment. Damages awarded have no penal character: they are simply a means of putting back the clock so as to restore the past, so far as possible, to its normal state. It is true that Tarde believed that he had discovered a kind of civil penal law in the awarding of costs, which are always borne by the losing party.[21] Yet taken in this sense the term has no more than a metaphorical value. For there to be punishment there should at least be some proportionality between the punishment and the wrong, and for this one would have to establish exactly the degree of seriousness of the wrong. In fact the loser of the case pays its costs even when his intentions were innocent and he is guilty of nothing more than ignorance. The reasons for this rule therefore seem to be entirely different. Since justice is not administered free, it seems equitable that the costs should be borne by the one who has occasioned them. Moreover, although it is possible that the prospect of such costs may stop the overhasty litigant, this is not enough for them to be considered a punishment. The fear of ruin that is normally consequent upon idleness and neglect may cause the businessman to be energetic and diligent. Yet ruin, in the exact connotation of the term, is not the penal sanction for his shortcomings.

Failure to observe these rules is not even sanctioned by a diffused form of punishment. The plaintiff who has lost his case is not disgraced, nor is his honour impugned. We can even envisage these rules being different from what they are without any feeling of repugnance. The idea that murder can be tolerated sets us up in arms, but we very readily accept that the law of inheritance might be modified, and many even conceive that it could be abolished. At least it is a question that we are not unwilling to discuss. Likewise, we agree without difficulty that the laws regarding easements or usufruct might be framed differently, or that the mutual obligations of buyer and vendor might be determined in another way, and that administrative functions might be allocated according to different principles. Since these prescriptions do not correspond to any feeling within us, and as generally we do not know their scientific justification, since this science does not yet exist, they have no deep roots in most of us. Doubtless there are exceptions: We do not tolerate the idea that an undertaking entered into that is contrary to morals or obtained either by violence or fraud can bind the contracting parties. Thus when public opinion is faced with cases of this kind it shows itself less indifferent than we have just asserted, and it adds its disapprobation to the legal sanction, causing it to weigh more heavily. This is because there are no clear-cut partitions between the various domains of moral life. On the contrary, they form a continuum, and consequently adjacent areas exist where different characteristics may be found at one and the same time. Nevertheless the proposition we have enunciated remains true in the overwhelming majority of cases. It demonstrates that rules where sanctions are restitutory either constitute no part at all of the collective consciousness, or subsist in it in only a weak state. Repressive law corresponds to what is the heart and centre of the common consciousness. Purely moral rules are already a less central part of it. Lastly, restitutory law springs from the farthest zones of consciousness and extends well beyond them. The more it becomes truly itself, the more it takes its distance.

This characteristic is moreover evinced in the way that it functions. Whereas repressive law tends to stay diffused throughout society, restitutory law sets up for itself ever more specialized bodies: consular courts, and industrial and administrative tribunals of every kind. Even in its most general sector, that of civil law, it is brought into use only by special officials—magistrates, lawyers, etc., who have been equipped for their role by a very special kind of training.

But although these rules are more or less outside the collective consciousness, they do not merely concern private individuals. If this were the case, restitutory law would have nothing in common with social solidarity, for the relationships it regulates would join individuals to one another without their being linked to society. They would be mere events of private life, as are, for instance, relationships of friendship. Yet it is far from the case that society is absent from this sphere of legal activity. Generally it is true that it does not intervene by itself and of its own volition: it must be solicited to do so by the parties concerned. Yet although it has to be invoked, its intervention is none the less the essential cog in the mechanism, since it alone causes that mechanism to function. It is society that declares what the law is, through its body of representatives.

However, it has been maintained that this role is in no way an especially social one, but comes down to being that of a conciliator of private interests. Consequently it has been held that any private individual could fulfil it, and that if society adopted it, this was solely for reasons of convenience. Yet it is wholly inaccurate to make society a kind of third-party arbitrator between the other parties. When it is induced to intervene it is not to reconcile the interests of individuals. It does not investigate what may be the most advantageous solution for the protagonists, nor does it suggest a compromise. But it does apply to the particular case submitted to it the general and traditional rules of the law. Yet the law is pre-eminently a social matter, whose object is absolutely different from the interests of the litigants. The judge who examines a divorce petition is not concerned to know whether this form of separation is really desirable for the husband and wife, but whether the causes invoked for it fall into one of the categories stipulated by law.

Yet to assess accurately the importance of the intervention by society it must be observed not only at the moment when the sanction is applied, or when the relationship that has been upset is restored, but also when it is instituted.

Social action is in fact necessary either to lay a foundation for, or to modify, a number of legal relationships regulated by this form of law, and which the assent of the interested parties is not adequate enough either to institute or alter. Of this nature are those relationships in particular that concern personal status. Although marriage is a contract, the partners can neither draw it up nor rescind it at will. The same holds good for all other domestic relationships, and *a fortiori* for all those regulated by administrative law. It is true that obligations that are properly contractual can be entered into or abrogated by the mere will to agreement of the parties. Yet we must bear in mind that, if a contract has binding force, it is society which confers that force. Let us assume that it does not give its blessing to the obligations that have been contracted; these then become pure promises possessing only moral authority.[22] Every contract therefore assumes that behind the parties who bind each other, society is there, quite prepared to intervene and to enforce respect for any undertakings entered into. Thus it only bestows this obligatory force upon contracts that have a social value in themselves, that is, those that are in conformity with the rules of law. We shall even occasionally see that its intervention is still more positive. It is therefore present in every relationship determined by restitutory law, even in ones that appear the most completely private, and its presence, although not felt, at least under normal conditions, is no less essential.[23]

Since the rules where sanctions are restitutory do not involve the common consciousness, the relationships that they determine are not of the sort that affect everyone indiscriminately. This means that they are instituted directly, not between the individual and society, but between limited and particular elements in society, which they link to one another. Yet on the other hand, since society is not absent it must necessarily indeed be concerned to some extent, and feel some repercussions. Then, depending upon the intensity with which it feels them, it intervenes at a greater or lesser distance, and more or less actively, through the mediation of special bodies whose task it is to represent it. These relationships are therefore very different from those regulated by repressive law, for the latter join directly, without any intermediary, the individual consciousness to that of society, that is, the individual himself to society.

[...]

IV

Since negative solidarity on its own brings about no integration; and since, moreover, there is nothing specific in it, we shall identify only two kinds of positive solidarity, distinguished by the following characteristics:

(1) The first kind links the individual directly to society without any intermediary. With the second kind he depends upon society because he depends upon the parts that go to constitute it.

(2) In the two cases, society is not viewed from the same perspective. In the first, the term is used to denote a more or less organised society composed of beliefs and sentiments common to all the members of the group: this is the collective type. On the contrary, in the second case the society to which we are solidly joined is a system of different and special functions united by definite relationships. Moreover, these two societies are really one. They are two facets of one and the same reality, but which none the less need to be distinguished from each other.

(3) From this second difference there arises another which will serve to allow us to characterise and delineate the features of these two kinds of solidarity.

The first kind can only be strong to the extent that the ideas and tendencies common to all members of the society exceed in number and intensity those that appertain personally to each one of those members. The greater this excess, the more active this kind of society is. Now what constitutes our personality is that which each one of us possesses that is peculiar and characteristic, what distinguishes it from others. This solidarity can therefore only increase in inverse relationship to the personality. As we have said, there is in the consciousness of each one of us two consciousnesses: one that we share in common with our group in its entirety, which is consequently not ourselves, but society living and acting within us; the other that, on the contrary, represents us alone in what is personal and distinctive about us, what makes us an individual.[24] The solidarity that derives from similarities is at its *maximum* when the collective consciousness completely envelops our total consciousness, coinciding with it at every point. At that moment our individuality is zero. That individuality cannot arise until the community fills us less completely. Here there are two opposing forces, the one centripetal, the other centrifugal, which cannot increase at the same time. We cannot ourselves develop simultaneously in two so opposing directions. If we have a strong inclination to think and act for ourselves we cannot be strongly inclined to think and act like other people. If the ideal is to create for ourselves a special, personal image, this cannot mean to be like everyone else. Moreover, at the very moment when this solidarity exerts its effect, our personality, it may be said by definition, disappears, for we are no longer ourselves, but a collective being.

The social molecules that can only cohere in this one manner cannot therefore move as a unit save in so far as they lack any movement of their own, as do the molecules of inorganic bodies. This is why we suggest that this kind of solidarity should be called mechanical. The word does not mean that the solidarity is produced by mechanical and artificial means. We only use this term for it by analogy with the cohesion that links together the elements of raw materials, in contrast to that which encompasses the unity of living organisms. What finally justifies the use of this term is the fact that the bond that thus unites the individual with society is completely analogous to that which links the thing to the person. The individual consciousness, considered from this viewpoint, is simply a dependency of the collective type, and follows all its motions, just as the object possessed follows those which its owner imposes upon it. In societies where this solidarity is highly developed the individual, as we shall see later, does not belong to himself; he is literally a thing at the disposal of society. Thus, in these same social types, personal rights are still not yet distinguished from 'real' rights.

The situation is entirely different in the case of solidarity that brings about the division of labour. Whereas the other solidarity implies that individuals resemble one another, the latter assumes that they are different from one another. The former type is only possible in so far as the individual personality is absorbed into the collective personality; the latter is only possible if each one of us has a sphere of action that is peculiarly our own, and consequently a personality. Thus the collective consciousness leaves uncovered a part of the individual consciousness, so that there may be established in it those special functions that it cannot regulate. The more extensive this free area is, the stronger the cohesion that arises

from this solidarity. Indeed, on the one hand each one of us depends more intimately upon society the more labour is divided up, and on the other, the activity of each one of us is correspondingly more specialised, the more personal it is. Doubtless, however circumscribed that activity may be, it is never completely original. Even in the exercise of our profession we conform to usages and practices that are common to us all within our corporation. Yet even in this case, the burden that we bear is in a different way less heavy than when the whole of society bears down upon us, and this leaves much more room for the free play of our initiative. Here, then, the individuality of the whole grows at the same time as that of the parts. Society becomes more effective in moving in concert, at the same time as each of its elements has more movements that are peculiarly its own. This solidarity resembles that observed in the higher animals. In fact each organ has its own special characteristics and autonomy, yet the greater the unity of the organism, the more marked the individualisation of the parts. Using this analogy, we propose to call 'organic' the solidarity that is due to the division of labour.

THE CAUSES

Thus it is in certain variations of the social environment that we must seek the cause that explains the progress of the division of labour. The results outlined in the preceding book allow us to induce immediately what these variations consist of.

In fact we have seen that the organised structure, and consequently the division of labour, develops regularly as the segmentary structure vanishes. It is therefore this disappearance that is the cause of this development; alternatively, the latter may be the cause of the former. This last hypothesis is not acceptable, for we know that the segmentary arrangement is an insurmountable obstacle to the division of labour and that the arrangement must have disappeared, at least in part, for the division of labour to be able to appear. It can only do so when that arrangement no longer exists. Undoubtedly once the division of labour exists it can contribute to speeding up its disappearance, but it only becomes apparent after the segmentary arrangement has partly receded. The effect reacts upon the cause, but does not in consequence cease to be an effect. Thus the reaction that it exerts is a secondary one. The increase in the division of labour is therefore due to the fact that the social segments lose their individuality, that the partitions dividing them become more permeable. In short, there occurs between them a coalescence that renders the social substance free to enter upon new combinations.

But the disappearance of this type can only bring about this result for the following reason. It is because there occurs a drawing together of individuals who were separated from one another, or at least they draw more closely together than they had been. Hence movements take place between the parts of the social mass which up to then had no reciprocal effect upon one another. The more the alveolar system is developed, the more the relationships in which each one of us is involved become enclosed within the limits of the alveola to which we belong. There are, as it were, moral vacuums between the various segments. On the other hand these vacuums fill up as the system levels off. Social life, instead of concentrating itself in innumerable small foci that are distinct but alike, becomes general. Social relationships—more exactly we should say intrasocial relationships—consequently become more numerous, since they push out beyond their original boundaries on all sides. Thus the division of labour progresses the more individuals there are who are sufficiently in contact with one another to be able mutually to act and react upon one another. If we agree to call dynamic or moral density this drawing together and the active exchanges that result from it, we can say that the progress of the division of labour is in direct proportion to the moral or dynamic density of society.

But this act of drawing together morally can only bear fruit if the real distance between individuals has itself diminished, in whatever manner. Moral density cannot therefore increase without physical density increasing at the same time, and the latter can serve to measure the extent of the former. Moreover, it is useless to investigate which of the two has influenced the other; it suffices to realise that they are inseparable.

The progressive increase in density of societies in the course of their historical development occurs in three main ways:

(1) Whilst lower societies spread themselves over areas that are relatively vast in comparison with the number of individuals that constitute them, amongst more advanced peoples the population is continually becoming more concentrated. Spencer says: 'If we contrast the populousness of regions inhabited by wild tribes with the populousness of equal regions in Europe; or if we contrast the density of population in England under the Heptarchy with its present density; we see that besides the growth produced by union of groups there has gone an interstitial growth.'[25]

The changes wrought successively in the industrial life of nations demonstrate how general this transformation is. The activity of nomadic tribes, whether hunters or shepherds, entails in fact the absence of any kind of concentration and dispersion over as wide an area as possible. Agriculture, because it is of necessity a settled existence, already presumes a certain drawing together of the social tissues, but one still very incomplete, since between each family tracts of land are interposed.[26] In the city, although the condensation process was greater, yet houses did not adjoin one another, for joined building was not known in Roman law.[27] This was invented on our own soil and demonstrates that the social ties have become tighter.[28] Moreover, from their origins

European societies have seen their density increase continuously in spite of a few cases of temporary regression.[29]

(2) The formation and development of towns are a further symptom, even more characteristic, of the same phenomenon. The increase in average density can be due solely to the physical increase in the birth rate and can consequently be reconciled with a very weak concentration of people, and the very marked maintenance of the segmentary type of society. But towns always result from the need that drives individuals to keep constantly in the closest possible contact with one another. They are like so many points where the social mass is contracting more strongly than elsewhere. They cannot therefore multiply and spread out unless the moral density increases. Moreover, we shall see that towns recruit their numbers through migration to them, which is only possible to the extent that the fusion of social segments is far advanced.

So long as the social organisation is essentially segmentary, towns do not exist. There are none in lower societies; they are not met with among the Iroquois, nor among the primitive German tribes.[30] The same was true for the primitive populations of Italy. 'The peoples of Italy,' states Marquardt, 'originally used not to live in towns, but in family or village communities (*pagi*), over which farms (*vici*, οίχοί) were scattered.'[31] Yet after a fairly short period of time the town made its appearance. Athens and Rome were or became towns, and the same transformation was accomplished throughout Italy. In our Christian societies the town appears from the very beginning, for those that the Roman Empire had left behind did not disappear with it. Since then, they have not ceased to grow and multiply. The tendency of country dwellers to flow into the towns, so general in the civilised world,[32] is only a consequence of this movement. But this phenomenon does not date from the present day: from the seventeenth century onwards it preoccupied statesmen.[33]

Because societies generally start with an agricultural period we have occasionally been tempted to regard the development of urban centres as a sign of old age and decadence.[34] But we must not lose sight of the fact that this agricultural phase is the shorter the more societies belong to a higher type. Whilst in Germany, among the American Indians and among all primitive peoples, it lasts as long as do these peoples themselves, in Rome or Athens it ceases fairly early on, and in France we may say that this agricultural state has never existed in a pure form. Conversely, urban life begins very early on, and consequently extends itself more. The regularly quicker acceleration of this development demonstrates that, far from constituting a kind of pathological phenomenon, it derives from the very nature of the higher social species. Even supposing therefore that today this movement has reached threatening proportions for our societies, which perhaps have no longer sufficient flexibility to adapt to it, it will not cease to continue, either through them, or after them, and the social types to be formed after our own will probably be distinguished by a more rapid and more complete regression of agricultural society.

(3) Finally, there is the number and speed of the means of communication and transmission. By abolishing or lessening the vacuums separating social segments, these means increase the density of society. Moreover, there is no need to demonstrate that they are the more numerous and perfect the higher the type of society.

Since this visible and measurable symbol reflects the variations in what we have termed moral density,[35] we can substitute this symbol for the latter in the formula that we have put forward. We must, moreover, repeat here what we were saying earlier.

If society, in concentrating itself, determines the development of the division of labour, the latter in its turn increases the concentration of society. But this is of no consequence, for the division of labour remains the derived action, and consequently the advances it makes are due to a parallel progress in social density, whatever may be the cause of this progress. This all we wished to establish.

But this factor is not the only one.

If the concentration of society produces this result, it is because it multiplies intra-social relationships. But these will be even more numerous if the total number of members in a society also becomes larger. If it includes more individuals, as well as their being in closer contact, the effect will necessarily be reinforced. Social volume has therefore the same influence over the division of labour as density.

In fact, societies are generally more voluminous the more advanced they are and consequently labour is more divided up in them. Spencer says that, 'Societies, like living bodies, begin as germs— originate from masses which are extremely minute in comparison with the masses some of them eventually reach. That out of small wandering hordes such as the lowest races now form, have arisen the largest societies, is a conclusion not to be contested.'[36]

What we have said about the segmentary constitution makes this unquestionably true. We know in fact that societies are formed by a certain number of segments of unequal size that overlap with one another. These moulds are not artificial creations, particularly in the beginning. Even when they have become conventional they imitate and reproduce so far as possible the forms of natural arrangement that preceded them. Many ancient societies are maintained in this form. The largest among these subdivisions, those that include the others, correspond to the nearest lower social type. Likewise, among the segments of which they in turn are made up, the most extensive are the remains of the type that comes directly below the preceding one, and so on. Among the most advanced

peoples we find traces of the most primitive social organisation.[37] Thus the tribe is made up of an aggregate of hordes or clans; the nation (the Jewish nation, for example) and the city, of an aggregate of tribes; the city, in its turn, with the villages that are subordinate to it, is one element that enters into the most complex societies, etc. The social volume therefore cannot fail to grow, since each species is made up of a replication of societies of the immediately preceding species.

Yet there are exceptions. The Jewish nation, before the conquest, was probably more voluminous than the Roman city of the fourth century; yet it was of a lower species. China and Russia are much more populous than the most civilised nations of Europe. Consequently among these same peoples the division of labour did not develop in proportion to the social volume. This is because the growth in volume is not necessarily a mark of superiority if the density does not grow at the same time and in the same proportion. A society can reach very large dimensions because it contains a very large number of segments, whatever may be the nature of these. If therefore the largest of them only reproduces societies of a very inferior type, the segmentary structure will remain very pronounced, and in consequence the social organisation will be little advanced. An aggregate of clans, even if immense, ranks below the smallest society that is organised, since the latter has already gone through those stages of evolution below which the aggregate has remained. Likewise if the number of social units has some influence over the division of labour, it is not through itself and of necessity, but because the number of social relationships increases generally with the number of individuals. To obtain this result it is not enough for the society to comprise a large number of persons, but they must be in fairly intimate contact so as to act and react upon one another. If on the other hand they are separated by environments that are mutually impenetrable, only very rarely, and with difficulty, can they establish relationships, and everything occurs as if the number of people was small. An increase in social volume therefore does not always speed up the progress of the division of labour, but only when the mass condenses at the same time and to the same degree. Consequently it is, one may say, only an additional factor. Yet, when joined to the first factor, it extends the effects by an action peculiarly its own, and thus requires to be distinguished from it.

We can therefore formulate the following proposition:

> The division of labour varies in direct proportion to the volume and density of societies and if it progresses in a continuous manner over the course of social development it is because societies become regularly more dense and generally more voluminous.

At all times, it is true, it has been clearly understood that there was a relationship between these two orders of facts. This is because, for functions to specialise even more, there must be additional co-operating elements, which must be grouped close enough together to be able to co-operate. Yet in societies in this condition we usually see hardly more than the means by which the division of labour is developed, and not the cause of this development. The cause is made to depend upon individual aspirations towards wellbeing and happiness, which can be the better satisfied when societies are more extensive and more condensed. The law we have just established is completely different. We state, not that the growth and condensation of societies *permit* a greater division of labour, but that they *necessitate* it. It is not the instrument whereby that division is brought about; but it is its determining cause.[38]

[...]

THE ANOMIC DIVISION OF LABOR

Although Auguste Comte recognised that the division of labour is a source of solidarity, he does not appear to have perceived that this solidarity is

sui generis and is gradually substituted for that which social similarities engender. This is why, noticing that these similarities are very blurred where the functions are very specialised, he saw in this process of disappearance a morbid phenomenon, a threat to social cohesion, due to excessive specialisation. He explained in this way the fact of the lack of co-ordination which sometimes accompanies the development of the division of labour. Yet since we have established that the weakening of the collective consciousness is a normal phenomenon, we could not make it the cause of the abnormal phenomena we are at present studying. If in certain cases organic solidarity is not all that is needful, it is certainly not because mechanical solidarity has lost ground, but because all the conditions of existence for the former have not been realised.

Indeed we know that wherever it is to be observed, we meet at the same time a regulatory system sufficiently developed to determine the mutual relationships between functions.[39] For organic solidarity to exist it is not enough for there to be a system of organs necessary to one another that feel their solidarity in a general way. The manner in which they should co-operate, if not on every kind of occasion when they meet, at least in the most common circumstances, must be predetermined. Otherwise, a fresh struggle would be required each time in order to bring them into a state of equilibrium with one another, for the conditions for this equilibrium can only be found by a process of trial and error, in the course of which each party treats the other as an opponent as much as an auxiliary. Such conflicts would therefore break out continually, and in consequence solidarity would be hardly more than virtual, and the mutual obligations would have to be negotiated anew in their entirety for each individual case. It will be objected that contracts exist. But firstly, not every social relationship is capable of assuming this legal form. Moreover, we know that a contract is not sufficient in itself, but supposes a regulatory system that extends and grows more complicated just as does contractual life itself. Moreover, the ties originating in this way are always of short duration. The contract is only a truce, and a fairly precarious one at that; it suspends hostilities only for a while. Doubtless, however precise the regulatory system may be, it will always leave room for much dispute. But it is neither necessary nor even possible for social life to be without struggle. The role of solidarity is not to abolish competition but to moderate it.

Moreover, in the normal state, these rules emerge automatically from the division of labour; they are, so to speak, its prolongation. Certainly if the division of labour only brought together individuals who unite for a brief space of time with a view to the exchange of personal services, it could not give rise to any regulatory process. But what it evokes are functions, that is, definite ways of acting that are repeated identically in given circumstances, since they relate to the general, unchanging conditions of social life. The relationships entertained between these functions cannot therefore fail to arrive at the same level of stability and regularity. There are certain ways of reacting upon one another which, being more in accordance with the nature of things, are repeated more often and become habits. Then the habits, as they grow in strength, are transformed into rules of conduct. The past predetermines the future. In other words, there exists a certain allocation of rights and duties that is established by usage and that ends up by becoming obligatory. Thus the rule does not set up the state of mutual dependence in which the solidly linked organs are to be found, but only serves to express it in a perceptible, definite way, as a function of a given situation. Likewise the nervous system, far from dominating the evolution of the organism, as was once believed,[40] is a result of it. The nerve tracts are probably only the paths along which have passed the wave-like movements and stimuli exchanged between the various organs. They are the channels that life has dug for itself by always flowing in the same direction, and the ganglions would only be the place where several

of these paths intersect.[41] It is because they have failed to recognise this aspect of the phenomenon that certain moralists have charged the division of labour with not producing real solidarity. They have seen in it only individual exchanges, ephemeral combinations, without a past, just as they also have no tomorrow, in which the individual is abandoned to his own devices. They have not perceived that slow task of consolidation, that network of ties that gradually becomes woven of its own accord and that makes organic solidarity something that is permanent.

Now, in all the cases we have described above, this regulatory process either does not exist or is not related to the degree of development of the division of labour. Nowadays there are no longer any rules that fix the number of economic undertakings, and in each branch of industry production is not regulated in such a way that it remains exactly at the level of consumption. Moreover, we do not wish to draw from this fact any practical conclusion. We do not maintain that restrictive legislation is necessary. We have not to weigh here the advantages and disadvantages. What is certain is that this lack of regulation does not allow the functions to perform regularly and harmoniously. The economists show, it is true, that harmony is re-established by itself when necessary, thanks to the increase or decrease in prices, which, according to the need, stimulates or slows production. But in any case it is not re-established in this way until after breaks in equilibrium and more or less prolonged disturbances have occurred. Moreover, such disturbances are naturally all the more frequent the more specialised the functions, for the more complex an organisation is, the more the necessity for extensive regulation is felt.

The relationships between capital and labour have up to now remained in the same legal state of indeterminacy. The contract for the hiring of services occupies in our legal codes a very small place, particularly when we consider the diversity and complexity of the relationships it is called upon to regulate. Moreover, we need emphasise no further the deficiencies that all peoples feel at the present time and that they are attempting to remedy.[42]

Methodological rules are to science what rules of law and morality are to conduct. They direct the thinking of the scientist just as the latter govern the actions of men. Yet if every science has its method, the order that is established is entirely an internal one. The method co-ordinates the procedures followed by scientists who are studying the same science, but not their relationships externally. There are hardly any disciplines that harmonise the efforts of the different sciences towards a common goal. This is especially true of the moral and social sciences, for the mathematical, physical, chemical and even biological sciences do not seem to such an extent foreign to one another. But the jurist, the psychologist, the anthropologist, the economist, the statistician, the linguist, the historian—all these go about their investigations as if the various orders of facts that they are studying formed so many independent worlds. Yet in reality these facts interlock with one another at every point. Consequently the same should occur for the corresponding sciences. This is how there has arisen the anarchy that has been pinpointed—moreover, not without some exaggeration—in science generally, but that is above all true for these special sciences. Indeed they afford the spectacle of an aggregate of disconnected parts that fail to co-operate with one another. If they therefore form a whole lacking in unity, it is not because there is no adequate view of their similarities, it is because they are not organised.

These various examples are therefore varieties of a same species. In all these cases, if the division of labour does not produce solidarity it is because the relationships between the organs are not regulated; it is because they are in a state of *anomie.*

But from where does this state spring?

Since a body of rules is the definite form taken over time by the relationships established spontaneously between the social functions, we may say *a priori* that a state of *anomie* is impossible

wherever organs solidly linked to one another are in sufficient contact, and in sufficiently lengthy contact. Indeed, being adjacent to one another, they are easily alerted in every situation to the need for one another and consequently they experience a keen, continuous feeling of their mutual dependence. For the same reason, exchanges between them occur easily; being regular, they occur frequently; they regulate themselves and time gradually effects the task of consolidation. Finally, because the slightest reaction can be felt throughout, the rules formed in this way bear the mark of it, that is, they foresee and fix in some detail the conditions of equilibrium. Yet if, on the other hand, some blocking environment is interposed between them, only stimuli of a certain intensity can communicate from one organ to another. Contacts being rare, they are not repeated often enough to take on a determinate form. Each time the procedure is again one of trial and error. The paths along which pass the wave-like movements can no longer become definite channels because the waves themselves are too intermittent. If at least some rules are successfully constituted, these are general and vague, for in these conditions only the most general outlines of the phenomena can be fixed. The same is true of closeness of contact: whilst it is sufficient, it is too recent or has lasted too short a while.[43]

Very generally this condition of contiguity is realised by the nature of things. For a function cannot distribute itself between two or more parts of an organism unless these parts are more or less in contact. Moreover, once labour is divided up, as they have need of one another, they tend naturally to reduce the distance that separates them. This is why, as one rises in the animal scale, one sees organs growing closer together and, as Spencer puts it, insinuating themselves into one another's interstices. But a coincidence of exceptional circumstances can cause it to be otherwise.

This is what occurs in the cases with which we are dealing at present. So long as the segmentary type of society is strongly marked, there are roughly as many economic markets as there are different segments. In consequence, each one of them is very limited. The producers, being very close to the consumers, can easily estimate the extent of the needs that have to be satisfied. The equilibrium is therefore established without difficulty and production is regulated by itself. On the contrary, as the organised type of society develops, the fusion of the various segments entails the fusion of the markets into one single market, which embraces almost all of society. It even extends beyond and tends to become universal, for the barriers between peoples are lowered at the same time as those that separate the segments within each one of them. The result is that each industry produces for consumers who are dispersed over the length and breadth of the country, or even the whole world. The contact is therefore no longer sufficient. The producer can no longer keep the whole market within his purview, not even mentally. He can no longer figure out to himself its limits, since it is, so to speak, unlimited. Consequently production lacks any check or regulation. It can only proceed at random, and in the course of so doing it is inevitable that the yardstick is wrong, either in one way or the other. Hence the crises that periodically disturb economic functions. The increase in those local and limited crises represented by bankruptcies is likely to be an effect of the same cause.

As the market becomes more extensive, large-scale industry appears. The effect of it is to transform the relationship between employers and workers. The greater fatigue occasioned to the nervous system, linked to the contagious influence of large urban areas, causes the needs of the workers to increase. Machine work replaces that of the man, manufacturing that of the small workshop. The worker is regimented, removed for the whole day from his family. He lives ever more apart from the person who employs him, etc. These new conditions of industrial life naturally require a new organisation. Yet because these transformations have been accomplished with extreme rapidity the

conflicting interests have not had time to strike an equilibrium.[44]

[...]

THE FORCED DIVISION OF LABOR

However, it is not enough for rules to exist, for occasionally it is these very rules that are the cause of evil. This is what happens in the class war. The institution of classes or castes constitutes one organisation of the division of labour, one that is closely regulated. Yet it is often a source of dissension. Since the lower classes are not, or no longer are, satisfied with the role that has fallen to them by custom or law, they aspire to functions that are prohibited to them and seek to dispossess those who exercise them. Hence civil wars, which arise from the way in which labour is shared out.

No similar phenomenon is to be observed within the organism. Doubtless in moments of crisis its different elements war with one another, feeding at the expense of one another. But a cell or an organ never attempts to usurp any role other than that which is rightfully its own. The reason for this being the case is that each anatomical element proceeds mechanically towards its goal. Its constitution and place in the organism determine its vocation; its task is a consequence of its nature. It can perform it badly, but it cannot assume that of another, unless the latter abandons it, as happens in the rare cases of substitution about which we have spoken. The same does not hold good for societies. Here the chance factor is greater. There is a larger gap between the hereditary tendencies of the individual and the social function he will fulfil. Hereditary tendencies do not signify with such direct necessity any set function. The field is open to trial and error and discussion, as well as being open to the free play of a host of causes that may make the individual nature deviate from its normal path, thus creating a pathological state. Since the organisation is more flexible, it is also more delicate and amenable to change. We are certainly not predestined from birth to any particular form of employment, but we nevertheless possess tastes and aptitudes that limit our choice. If no account is taken of them, if they are constantly frustrated in our daily occupation, we suffer, and seek the means of bringing that suffering to an end. There is no solution other than to change the established order and create a new one. For the division of labour to engender solidarity, it is thus not sufficient for everyone to have his task: it must also be agreeable to him.

This condition is not realised in the instance we are examining. Indeed, if the institution of class or caste sometimes gives rise to miserable squabbling instead of producing solidarity, it is because the distribution of social functions on which it rests does not correspond, or rather no longer corresponds, to the distribution of natural abilities. For, whatever may have been asserted,[45] it is not solely the spirit of imitation that makes the lower classes end up by having ambitions for an upper-class life. To tell the truth, imitation of itself cannot even explain anything, for it supposes something other than itself. Imitation is only possible between creatures who already resemble one another, and according also to the degree of resemblance. It does not occur between different species or varieties. The same is true for moral contagion as is true for physical contagion: it only manifests itself in fields favourable to it. For needs to spread from one class to another, the differences originally separating these classes must have disappeared or grown less. As a result of the changes that have occurred in society, one group must have become capable of carrying out functions that were originally beyond its capacity, at the same time as another group was losing its original superiority. When the plebeians began to dispute with the patricians the honour of performing religious and administrative functions, it was not merely to imitate them, but it was because they [the plebeians] had become more intelligent, more wealthy and more numerous, and their tastes and ambitions had in consequence

been modified. Through these transformations the congruence in a whole sector of society was broken between the aptitudes of individuals and the kind of activity allocated to them. Constraint alone, more or less violent, more or less direct, henceforth binds them to these functions. In consequence only an imperfect, troubled form of solidarity can exist.

Such an outcome is therefore not a necessary sequel to the division of labour. It only occurs in very special circumstances, that is, when it is the result of some external constraint. Matters are very different when it is established through some purely internal and spontaneous action, without anything arising to hinder individual initiatives. On this condition, in fact, a harmony between individual natures and social functions cannot fail to occur, at least over the average number of cases. If nothing hampers or favours unduly rivals who are disputing the tasks they perform, inevitably only those most fitted for each type of activity will succeed in obtaining it. The sole cause then determining how labour is divided up is the diversity of abilities. In the nature of things this allocation is made according to aptitude, since there is no reason for it to happen otherwise. Thus a harmony is automatically realised between the constitution of each individual and his condition. It will be argued that this is not always sufficient to satisfy men, for there are some whose desires overreach their abilities. This is true, but these are exceptional cases and may be termed of a morbid kind. Normally a man finds happiness in fulfilling his nature; his needs are proportionate to his means. Thus in the organism each organ claims only that quantity of food consistent with its position.

The forced division of labour is thus a second morbid type that we can distinguish. But we must not mistake the meaning of the term. What causes constraint is not any kind of regulation, since on the contrary the division of labour, as we have just seen, cannot do without this. Even when functions are allocated in accordance with set rules, the distribution is not necessarily the result of constraint. This is what takes place even under a caste regime, so long as it is based upon the nature of society. Indeed the institution of caste is not at all times and places an arbitrary one. When it functions regularly in a society, meeting with no opposition, it is because it at least approximately expresses the immutable way in which professional abilities are distributed throughout society. This is why, although tasks are to a certain extent allocated by law, each organ performs its own spontaneously. Constraint begins only when regulation, no longer corresponding to the true state of affairs and consequently without any moral foundation, is only maintained by force.

CONCLUSION

Yet does not the division of labour, by rendering each one of us an incomplete being, not entail some curtailment of the individual personality? This criticism has often been made.

Firstly, let us note that it is difficult to see why it might be more in accord with the logic of human nature to develop more superficially rather than in depth. Why should a more extensive activity, one that is more dispersed, be superior to one more concentrated and circumscribed? Why should more dignity attach to being complete and mediocre than in leading a more specialised kind of life but one more intense, particularly if we can recapture in this way what we have lost, through our association with others who possess what we lack and who make us complete beings? We start from the principle that man must realise his nature as man—as Aristotle said, accomplish his οἰχέιον ἔργον. But at different moments in history this nature does not remain constant; it is modified with societies. Among lower peoples, the act that connotes a man is to resemble his fellows, to realise within himself all the characteristics of the collective type which, even more than today, was then confused with the human type. In more advanced societies man's

nature is mainly to be a part of society; consequently the act that connotes a man is for him to play his part as one organ of society.

There is something more: far from the progress of specialisation whittling away the individual personality, this develops with the division of labour.

Indeed to be a person means to be an autonomous source of action. Thus man only attains this state to the degree that there is something within him that is his and his alone, that makes him an individual, whereby he is more than the mere embodiment of the generic type of his race and group. It will in any case be objected that he is endowed with free will, and that this is sufficient upon which to base his personality. But whatever this freedom may consist of—and it is the subject of much argument—it is not this impersonal, invariable, metaphysical attribute that can serve as the sole basis for the empirical, variable and concrete personality of individuals. That personality cannot be formed by the entirely abstract capacity to choose between two opposites. This faculty must be exercised in relation to ends and motives that are peculiar to the person acting. In other words the stuff of which his consciousness is made up must have a personal character. Now we have seen in the second book of this study that is an outcome that occurs progressively as the division of labour itself progresses. The disappearance of the segmentary type of society, at the same time as it necessitates greater specialisation, frees the individual consciousness in part from the organic environment that supports it, as it does from the social environment that envelops it. This dual emancipation renders the individual more independent in his own behaviour. The division of labour itself contributes to this liberating effect. Individual natures become more complex through specialising; by this very fact they are partly shielded against the effects of the collectivity and the influences of heredity, which can scarcely enforce themselves except in simple, general matters.

NOTES

1. Οὐ γάρ εχ δύο ἰατρων γιγνεται χοινωία, αλλ᾿ εξ ἰατρου χαὶ δεωργου χαὶ δ λωζ ξ τέρων οὐχ ισων, *Nichomachean Ethics*, E. 1133a, 16.
2. *Journal des économistes* (November 1884) p. 211.
3. De Candolle, *Histoire des Sciences et des Savants*, 2nd edn, p. 263.
4. *Nichomachean Ethics*, vol. VIII, no. 1, 115a, 32.
5. A. Bain, *The Emotions and the Will* (London, 1889).
6. Topinard, *Anthropologie*, p. 146.
7. H. Spencer, *Essays: Scientific, Political, and Speculative* (London, 1858). Waitz, in his *Anthropologie der Naturvölker*, vol. I, p. 76, reports many facts of the same kind.
8. Lebon, *L'homme et les sociétés*, vol. II, p. 154.
9. Bischoff, *Das Herngewicht der Menschen. Eine Studie* (Bonn, 1880).
10. Waitz, *Anthropologie*, vol. III, pp. 101–2.
11. Ibid., vol. VI, p. 121.
12. H. Spencer, *The Principles of Sociology* (London, 1876) vol. I, pp. 753–4.
13. The matriarchal family certainly existed among the Germanic tribes. Cf. Dargun, *Mutterrecht und Raubehe im germanischen Rechte* (Breslau, 1883).
14. W. Robertson Smith, *Marriage and Kinship in Early Arabia* (Cambridge, 1885) p. 67.
15. Cf. *infra*, Book III, Chapter I.
16. Such a confusion is not without its dangers. Thus it is occasionally asked whether the individual consciousness varies with the collective consciousness. Everything depends on the meaning assigned to the term. If it represents social similarities, the variation, as will be seen, is one of inverse relationship. If it designates the entire psychological life of society, the relationship is direct. Hence the need to draw a distinction.
17. We shall not go into the question as to whether the collective consciousness is like that of the individual. For us this term merely designates the sum total of social similarities, without prejudice to the category by which this system of phenomena must be defined.
18. In order to simplify our exposition we assume that the individual belongs to only one society. In fact we form a part of several groups and there exist in us several collective consciousnesses; but this complication does not in any way change the relationship we are establishing.
19. This does not mean that a penal rule should nonetheless be retained because at some given moment it corresponded to a particular collective feeling. The rule has no justification unless the feeling is still alive and active. If it has disappeared or grown weak nothing is so vain or even counter-productive as to attempt to preserve it artificially by force. It may even happen to become necessary to fight against a practice that was common once, but is no longer so, one that militates against the establishment of new and essential practices. But we need not enter into this problem of a casuistic nature.
20. In saying that punishment, as it is, has a reason for its existence we do not mean that it is perfect and cannot be improved upon. On the contrary, it is only too plain that, since it is produced by purely mechanical causes, it can only be very imperfectly attuned to its role. The justification can only be a rough and ready one.
21. Tarde, *Criminalité comparee* (Alcan, Paris) p. 113.
22. Even the moral authority derives from the custom, and hence from society.
23. We must confine ourselves here to these general remarks, common to every form of restitutory law. Numerous demonstrations of this truth will be found later (Chapter VII) for that part of law that corresponds to the solidarity engendered by the division of labour.
24. It has sometimes been stated that the status of father or son, etc. was the object of 'real' rights (cf. Ortolan, *Instituts*, vol. 1, p. 660). But such forms of status are only abstract symbols of various rights, some 'real' (for example, a father's right over the fortune of his under-age children), others personal.
25. H. Spencer, *Principles of Sociology* (London, 1855) vol. I, p. 487.
26. 'Colunt diversi ac discreti,' says Tacitus of the Germans; 'suam quisque domum spatio circumdat' (*Germania*, vol. XVI).
27. Cf. in Accarias, *Précis*, vol. I, p. 640, the list of urban charges. Cf. Fustel de Coulanges, *La cité antique*, p. 65.
28. By reasoning in this way we do not mean that the increase in density is the result of economic changes. The two facts have a mutual conditioning effect upon each other, and this suffices for the presence of the one to attest to the presence of the other.
29. Cf. Levasseur, *La population française, passim*.
30. Tacitus, *Germania*, vol. XVI; Sohm, *Über die Entstehung der Städte*.
31. Marquardt, *Römische Altertümer*, vol. IV, p. 3.
32. Cf. on this point, Dumont, *Dépopulation et civilisation* (Paris, 1890) ch. 8; and Oettingen, *Moralstatistik*, pp. 273 ff.
33. Cf. Levasseur, *La population française*, p. 200.

34. This seems to us to be the opinion of Tarde in his *Lois de l'Imitation.*
35. However, there are special cases of an exceptional kind, where material density and moral density are perhaps not entirely in proportion. Cf. note 31 below.
36. Spencer, *Principles of Sociology*, vol. I, p. 481.
37. The village, which originally was only a clan whose abode was fixed.
38. On this point we can again rely upon the authority of Comte. 'I need only,' he says, 'point now to the progressive increase in density of our species as an ultimate general factor helping to regulate the effective rapidity of social movement. First, therefore, one may freely recognise that this influence contributes a great deal, above all at the beginning; in determining for human labour as a whole its increasingly specialised division, which is necessarily incompatible with a small number of people co-operating together. *Moreover, by a more intimate and less well-known property, although of even greater importance, such a densifying process directly and very powerfully stimulates the swifter development in social evolution*, either by stimulating individuals to put forth fresh efforts using refined methods, in order to ensure for themselves an existence which otherwise would become more difficult, or by obliging society also to react with greater energy and persistence, and in more concerted fashion, struggling against the increasedly powerful upsurge of particular divergences. On both counts we see that here it is not a question of the absolute increase in the number of individuals, but above all of the more intense competition between them in a given area' (*Cours de philosophie positive*, vol. IV, p. 455).
39. Cf. *supra*, Book I, Chapter VII.
40. Cf. Perrier, *Colonies animales*, p. 746.
41. Cf. H. Spencer, *Principles of Biology* (London, 1884) vol. I.
42. This was written in 1893. Since then industrial legislation has assumed a more important place in our law. This demonstrates how serious the gap was, and it is far from having been filled.
43. There is, however, one case where *anomie* can occur, although the contiguity is sufficient. This is when the necessary regulation can only be established at the expense of transformations that the social structure is no longer capable of carrying out, for the malleability of societies is not indefinite. When it has reached its limit, even necessary changes are impossible.
44. Let us nevertheless remember that, as we shall see in the next chapter, this antagonism is not due wholly to the speed of these transformations, but to a considerable extent to the still too great inequality in the external conditions of the struggle. Over this factor time has no effect.
45. H. Spencer, *Principles of Biology* (London, 1884) vol. I.

COMPANION WEBSITE

1. Go online to Write Out Loud about the pathologies of the division of labor.
2. Log on to Durkheim's Profile Page to learn more about how the division of labor functions as an important source of social solidarity.
3. Check out the film *Pleasantville* for an example of how a community responds to the breakdown of social norms, listed online in the *Emergence Through Convergence* Supplementary Sources.

3

Suicide

Emile Durkheim

I

It is a well-known fact that economic crises have an aggravating effect on the suicidal tendency.

In Vienna, in 1873 a financial crisis occurred which reached its height in 1874; the number of suicides immediately rose. From 141 in 1872, they rose to 153 in 1873 and 216 in 1874. The increase in 1874 is 53 per cent[1] above 1872 and 41 per cent above 1873. What proves this catastrophe to have been the sole cause of the increase is the special prominence of the increase when the crisis was acute, or during the first four months of 1874. From January 1 to April 30 there had been 48 suicides in 1871, 44 in 1872, 43 in 1873; there were 73 in 1874. The increase is 70 per cent.[2] The same crisis occurring at the same time in Frankfurt-on-Main produced the same effects there. In the years before 1874, 22 suicides were committed annually on the average; in 1874 there were 32, or 45 per cent more.

The famous crash is unforgotten which took place on the Paris Bourse during the winter of 1882. Its consequences were felt not only in Paris but throughout France. From 1874 to 1886 the average annual increase was only 2 per cent; in 1882 it was 7 per cent. Moreover, it was unequally distributed among the different times of year, occurring principally during the first three months or at the very time of the crash. Within these three months alone 59 per cent of the total rise occurred.

So distinctly is the rise the result of unusual circumstances that it not only is not encountered in 1881 but has disappeared in 1883, although on the whole the latter year had a few more suicides than the preceding one:

	1881	1882	1883
Annual total	6,741	7,213 (plus 7%)	7,267
First three months	1,589	1,770 (plus 11%)	1,604

This relation is found not only in some exceptional cases, but is the rule. The number of bankruptcies is a barometer of adequate sensitivity, reflecting the variations of economic life. When they increase abruptly from year to year, some serious disturbance has certainly occurred. From 1845 to 1869 there were sudden rises, symptomatic of crises, on three occasions. While the annual increase in the number of bankruptcies during this period is 3.2 per cent, it is 26 per cent in 1847, 37 per cent in 1854 and 20 per cent in 1861. At these three moments, there is also to be observed an unusually rapid rise in the number of suicides. While the average annual increase during these 24 years was only 2 per cent, it was 17 per cent in 1847, 8 per cent in 1854 and 9 per cent in 1861.

But to what do these crises owe their influence? Is it because they increase poverty by causing public wealth to fluctuate? Is life more readily renounced as it becomes more difficult? The explanation is seductively simple; and it agrees with the popular idea of suicide. But it is contradicted by facts.

Actually, if voluntary deaths increased because life was becoming more difficult, they should diminish perceptibly as comfort increases. Now, although when the price of the most necessary foods rises excessively, suicides generally do the same, they are not found to fall below the average in the opposite case. In Prussia, in 1850 wheat was quoted at the lowest point it reached during the entire period of 1848–81; it was at 6.91 marks per 50 kilograms; yet at this very time suicides rose from 1,527 where they were in 1849 to 1,736, or an increase of 13 per cent, and continued to increase during the years 1851, 1852 and 1853 although the cheap market held. In 1858–59 a new fall took place; yet suicides rose from 2,038 in 1857 to 2,126 in 1858, and to 2,146 in 1859. From 1863 to 1866 prices which had reached 11.04 marks in 1861 fell progressively to 7.95 marks in 1864 and remained very reasonable for the whole period; suicides during the same time increased 17 per cent (2,112 in 1862, 2,485 in 1866).[3] Similar facts are observed in Bavaria. According to a curve constructed by Mayr[4] for the period 1835–61, the price of rye was lowest during the years 1857–58 and 1858–59; now suicides, which in 1857 numbered only 286, rose to 329 in 1858, to 387 in 1859. The same phenomenon had already occurred during the years 1848–50; at that time wheat had been very cheap in Bavaria as well as throughout Europe. Yet, in spite of a slight temporary drop due to political events, which we have mentioned, suicides remained at the same level. There were 217 in 1847, there were still 215 in 1848, and if they dropped for a moment to 189 in 1849, they rose again in 1850 and reached 250.

So far is the increase in poverty from causing the increase in suicide that even fortunate crises, the effect of which is abruptly to enhance a country's prosperity, affect suicide like economic disasters.

The conquest of Rome by Victor-Emmanuel in 1870, by definitely forming the basis of Italian unity, was the starting point for the country of a process of growth which is making it one of the great powers of Europe. Trade and industry received a sharp stimulus from it and surprisingly rapid changes took place. Whereas in 1876, 4,459 steam boilers with a total of 54,000 horse-power were enough for industrial needs, the number of machines in 1887 was 9,983 and their horse-power of 167,000 was threefold more. Of course the amount of production rose proportionately during the same time.[5] Trade followed the same rising course; not only did the merchant marine, communications and transportation develop, but the number of persons and things transported doubled.[6] As this generally heightened activity caused an increase in salaries (an increase of 35 per cent is estimated to have taken place from 1873 to 1889), the material comfort of workers rose, especially since the price of bread was falling at the same time.[7] Finally, according to calculations by Bodio, private wealth rose from 45 and a half billions on the average during the period 1875–80 to 51 billions during the years 1880–85 and 54 billions and a half in 1885–90.[8]

Now, an unusual increase in the number of suicides is observed parallel with this collective renaissance. From 1866 to 1870 they were roughly stable; from 1871 to 1877 they increased 36 per cent. There were in

1864–70	29 suicides per million	1874	37 suicides per million
1871	31 suicides per million	1875	34 suicides per million
1872	33 suicides per million	1876	36.5 suicides per million
1873	36 suicides per million	1877	40.6 suicides per million

And since then the movement has continued. The total figure, 1,139 in 1877, was 1,463 in 1889, a new increase of 28 per cent.

In Prussia the same phenomenon occurred on two occasions. In 1866 the kingdom received a first enlargement. It annexed several important provinces, while becoming the head of the Confederation of the North. Immediately this growth in glory and power was accompanied by a sudden rise in the number of suicides. There had been 123 suicides per million during the period 1856–60 per average year and only 122 during the years 1861–65. In the five years, 1866–70, in spite of the drop in 1870, the average rose to 133. The year 1867, which immediately followed victory, was that in which suicide achieved the highest point it had reached since 1816 (1 suicide per 5,432 inhabitants, while in 1864 there was only one case per 8,739).

On the morrow of the war of 1870 a new accession of good fortune took place. Germany was unified and placed entirely under Prussian hegemony. An enormous war indemnity added to the public wealth; commerce and industry made great strides. The development of suicide was never so rapid. From 1875 to 1886 it increased 90 per cent, from 3,278 cases to 6,212.

World expositions, when successful, are considered favorable events in the existence of a society. They stimulate business, bring more money into the country and are thought to increase public prosperity, especially in the city where they take place. Yet, quite possibly, they ultimately take their toll in a considerably higher number of suicides. Especially does this seem to have been true of the Exposition of 1878. The rise that year was the highest occurring between 1874 and 1886. It was 8 per cent, that is, higher than the one caused by the crash of 1882. And what almost proves the Exposition to have been the cause of this increase is that 86 per cent of it took place precisely during the six months of the Exposition.

In 1889 things were not identical all over France. But quite possibly the Boulanger crisis neutralized the contrary effects of the Exposition by its depressive influence on the growth of suicides. Certainly at Paris, although the political feeling aroused must have had the same effect as in the rest of the country, things happened as in 1878. For the 7 months of the Exposition, suicides increased almost 10 per cent, 9.66 to be exact, while through the remainder of the year they were below what they had been in 1888 and what they afterwards were in 1890.

	1888	1889	1890
The seven months of the Exposition	517	567	540
The five other months	319	311	356

It may well be that but for the Boulanger influence the rise would have been greater.

What proves still more conclusively that economic distress does not have the aggravating influence often attributed to it, is that it tends rather to produce the opposite effect. There is very little suicide in Ireland, where the peasantry leads so wretched a life. Poverty-stricken Calabria has almost no suicides; Spain has a tenth as many as France. Poverty may even be considered a protection. In the various French departments the more people there are who have independent means, the more numerous are suicides.

Departments Where, per 100,000 Inhabitants, Suicides Were Committed (1878–1887) Suicides	Number of Departments	Average Number of Persons of Independent Means per 1,000 Inhabitants in Each Group of Departments (1886)
From 48 to 43	5	127
From 38 to 31	6	73
From 30 to 24	6	69
From 23 to 18	15	59
From 17 to 13	18	49
From 12 to 8	26	49
From 7 to 3	10	42

Comparison of the maps confirms that of the averages.

If therefore industrial or financial crises increase suicides, this is not because they cause poverty, since crises of prosperity have the same result; it is because they are crises, that is, disturbances of the collective order.[9] Every disturbance of equilibrium, even though it achieves greater comfort and a heightening of general vitality, is an impulse to voluntary death. Whenever serious readjustments take place in the social order, whether or not due to a sudden growth or to an unexpected catastrophe, men are more inclined to self-destruction. How is this possible? How can something considered generally to improve existence serve to detach men from it?

For the answer, some preliminary considerations are required.

II

No living being can be happy or even exist unless his needs are sufficiently proportioned to his means. In other words, if his needs require more than can be granted, or even merely something of a different sort, they will be under continual friction and can only function painfully. Movements incapable of production without pain tend not to be reproduced. Unsatisfied tendencies atrophy, and as the impulse to live is merely the result of all the rest, it is bound to weaken as the others relax.

In the animal, at least in a normal condition, this equilibrium is established with automatic spontaneity because the animal depends on purely material conditions. All the organism needs is that the supplies of substance and energy constantly employed in the vital process should be periodically renewed by equivalent quantities; that replacement be equivalent to use. When the void created by existence in its own resources is filled, the animal, satisfied, asks nothing further. Its power of reflection is not sufficiently developed to imagine other ends than those implicit in its physical nature. On the other hand, as the work demanded of each organ itself depends on the general state of vital energy and the needs of organic equilibrium, use is regulated in turn by replacement and the balance is automatic. The limits of one are those of the other; both are fundamental to the constitution of the existence in question, which cannot exceed them.

This is not the case with man, because most of his needs are not dependent on his body or not to the same degree. Strictly speaking, we may consider that the quantity of material supplies necessary to the physical maintenance of a human life is subject to computation, though this be less exact than in the preceding case and a wider margin left for the free combinations of the will; for beyond the indispensable minimum which satisfies nature when instinctive, a more awakened reflection suggests better conditions, seemingly desirable ends craving fulfillment. Such appetites, however, admittedly sooner or later reach a limit which they cannot pass. But how determine the quantity of well-being, comfort or luxury legitimately to be craved by a human being? Nothing appears in man's organic nor in his psychological constitution which sets a limit to such tendencies. The functioning of individual life does not require them to cease at one point rather than at another; the proof being that they have constantly increased since the beginnings of history, receiving more and more complete satisfaction, yet with no weakening of average health. Above all, how establish their proper variation with different conditions of life, occupations, relative importance of services, etc.? In no society are they equally satisfied in the different stages of the social hierarchy. Yet human nature is substantially the same among all men, in its essential qualities. It is not human nature which can assign the variable limits necessary to our needs. They are thus unlimited so far as they depend on the individual alone. Irrespective of any external regulatory force, our capacity for feeling is in itself an insatiable and bottomless abyss.

But if nothing external can restrain this capacity, it can only be a source of torment to itself.

Unlimited desires are insatiable by definition and insatiability is rightly considered a sign of morbidity. Being unlimited, they constantly and infinitely surpass the means at their command; they cannot be quenched. Inextinguishable thirst is constantly renewed torture. It has been claimed, indeed, that human activity naturally aspires beyond assignable limits and sets itself unattainable goals. But how can such an undetermined state be any more reconciled with the conditions of mental life than with the demands of physical life? All man's pleasure in acting, moving and exerting himself implies the sense that his efforts are not in vain and that by walking he has advanced. However, one does not advance when one walks toward no goal, or—which is the same thing—when his goal is infinity. Since the distance between us and it is always the same, whatever road we take, we might as well have made the motions without progress from the spot. Even our glances behind and our feeling of pride at the distance covered can cause only deceptive satisfaction, since the remaining distance is not proportionately reduced. To pursue a goal which is by definition unattainable is to condemn oneself to a state of perpetual unhappiness. Of course, man may hope contrary to all reason, and hope has its pleasures even when unreasonable. It may sustain him for a time; but it cannot survive the repeated disappointments of experience indefinitely. What more can the future offer him than the past, since he can never reach a tenable condition nor even approach the glimpsed ideal? Thus, the more one has, the more one wants, since satisfactions received only stimulate instead of filling needs. Shall action as such be considered agreeable? First, only on condition of blindness to its uselessness. Secondly, for this pleasure to be felt and to temper and half veil the accompanying painful unrest, such unending motion must at least always be easy and unhampered. If it is interfered with only restlessness is left, with the lack of ease which it, itself, entails. But it would be a miracle if no insurmountable obstacle were never encountered. Our thread of life

on these conditions is pretty thin, breakable at any instant.

To achieve any other result, the passions first must be limited. Only then can they be harmonized with the faculties and satisfied. But since the individual has no way of limiting them, this must be done by some force exterior to him. A regulative force must play the same role for moral needs which the organism plays for physical needs. This means that the force can only be moral. The awakening of conscience interrupted the state of equilibrium of the animal's dormant existence; only conscience, therefore, can furnish the means to re-establish it. Physical restraint would be ineffective; hearts cannot be touched by physio-chemical forces. So far as the appetites are not automatically restrained by physiological mechanisms, they can be halted only by a limit that they recognize as just. Men would never consent to restrict their desires if they felt justified in passing the assigned limit. But, for reasons given above, they cannot assign themselves this law of justice. So they must receive it from an authority which they respect, to which they yield spontaneously. Either directly and as a whole, or through the agency of one of its organs, society alone can play this moderating role; for it is the only moral power superior to the individual, the authority of which he accepts. It alone has the power necessary to stipulate law and to set the point beyond which the passions must not go. Finally, it alone can estimate the reward to be prospectively offered to every class of human functionary, in the name of the common interest.

As a matter of fact, at every moment of history there is a dim perception, in the moral consciousness of societies, of the respective value of different social services, the relative reward due to each, and the consequent degree of comfort appropriate on the average to workers in each occupation. The different functions are graded in public opinion and a certain coefficient of well-being assigned to each, according to its place in the hierarchy. According to accepted ideas, for example, a certain way of living is considered the upper limit to which a workman may aspire in his efforts to improve his existence, and there is another limit below which he is not willingly permitted to fall unless he has seriously bemeaned himself. Both differ for city and country workers, for the domestic servant and the day-laborer, for the business clerk and the official, etc. Likewise the man of wealth is reproved if he lives the life of a poor man, but also if he seeks the refinements of luxury overmuch. Economists may protest in vain; public feeling will always be scandalized if an individual spends too much wealth for wholly superfluous use, and it even seems that this severity relaxes only in times of moral disturbance.[10] A genuine regimen exists, therefore, although not always legally formulated, which fixes with relative precision the maximum degree of ease of living to which each social class may legitimately aspire. However, there is nothing immutable about such a scale. It changes with the increase or decrease of collective revenue and the changes occurring in the moral ideas of society. Thus what appears luxury to one period no longer does so to another; and the well-being which for long periods was granted to a class only by exception and supererogation, finally appears strictly necessary and equitable.

Under this pressure, each in his sphere vaguely realizes the extreme limit set to his ambitions and aspires to nothing beyond. At least if he respects regulations and is docile to collective authority, that is, has a wholesome moral constitution, he feels that it is not well to ask more. Thus, an end and goal are set to the passions. Truly, there is nothing rigid nor absolute about such determination. The economic ideal assigned each class of citizens is itself confined to certain limits, within which the desires have free range. But it is not infinite. This relative limitation and the moderation it involves, make men contented with their lot while stimulating them moderately to improve it; and this average contentment causes the feeling of calm, active happiness, the pleasure in existing and living which characterizes health for societies as well as for individuals. Each person

is then at least, generally speaking, in harmony with his condition, and desires only what he may legitimately hope for as the normal reward of his activity. Besides, this does not condemn man to a sort of immobility. He may seek to give beauty to his life; but his attempts in this direction may fail without causing him to despair. For, loving what he has and not fixing his desire solely on what he lacks, his wishes and hopes may fail of what he has happened to aspire to, without his being wholly destitute. He has the essentials. The equilibrium of his happiness is secure because it is defined, and a few mishaps cannot disconcert him.

But it would be of little use for everyone to recognize the justice of the hierarchy of functions established by public opinion, if he did not also consider the distribution of these functions just. The workman is not in harmony with his social position if he is not convinced that he has his deserts. If he feels justified in occupying another, what he has would not satisfy him. So it is not enough for the average level of needs for each social condition to be regulated by public opinion, but another, more precise rule, must fix the way in which these conditions are open to individuals. There is no society in which such regulation does not exist. It varies with times and places. Once it regarded birth as the almost exclusive principle of social classification; today it recognizes no other inherent inequality than hereditary fortune and merit. But in all these various forms its object is unchanged. It is also only possible, everywhere, as a restriction upon individuals imposed by superior authority, that is, by collective authority. For it can be established only by requiring of one or another group of men, usually of all, sacrifices and concessions in the name of the public interest.

Some, to be sure, have thought that this moral pressure would become unnecessary if men's economic circumstances were only no longer determined by heredity. If inheritance were abolished, the argument runs, if everyone began life with equal resources and if the competitive struggle were fought out on a basis of perfect equality, no one could think its results unjust. Each would instinctively feel that things are as they should be.

Truly, the nearer this ideal equality were approached, the less social restraint will be necessary. But it is only a matter of degree. One sort of heredity will always exist, that of natural talent. Intelligence, taste, scientific, artistic, literary or industrial ability, courage and manual dexterity are gifts received by each of us at birth, as the heir to wealth receives his capital or as the nobleman formerly received his title and function. A moral discipline will therefore still be required to make those less favored by nature accept the lesser advantages which they owe to the chance of birth. Shall it be demanded that all have an equal share and that no advantage be given those more useful and deserving? But then there would have to be a discipline far stronger to make these accept a treatment merely equal to that of the mediocre and incapable.

But like the one first mentioned, this discipline can be useful only if considered just by the peoples subject to it. When it is maintained only by custom and force, peace and harmony are illusory; the spirit of unrest and discontent are latent; appetites superficially restrained are ready to revolt. This happened in Rome and Greece when the faiths underlying the old organization of the patricians and plebeians were shaken, and in our modern societies when aristocratic prejudices began to lose their old ascendancy. But this state of upheaval is exceptional; it occurs only when society is passing through some abnormal crisis. In normal conditions the collective order is regarded as just by the great majority of persons. Therefore, when we say that an authority is necessary to impose this order on individuals, we certainly do not mean that violence is the only means of establishing it. Since this regulation is meant to restrain individual passions, it must come from a power which dominates individuals; but this power must also be obeyed through respect, not fear.

It is not true, then, that human activity can be released from all restraint. Nothing in the world can enjoy such a privilege. All existence being a part of the universe is relative to the remainder; its nature and method of manifestation accordingly depend not only on itself but on other beings, who consequently restrain and regulate it. Here there are only differences of degree and form between the mineral realm and the thinking person. Man's characteristic privilege is that the bond he accepts is not physical but moral; that is, social. He is governed not by a material environment brutally imposed on him, but by a conscience superior to his own, the superiority of which he feels. Because the greater, better part of his existence transcends the body, he escapes the body's yoke, but is subject to that of society.

But when society is disturbed by some painful crisis or by beneficent but abrupt transitions, it is momentarily incapable of exercising this influence; thence come the sudden rises in the curve of suicides which we have pointed out above.

In the case of economic disasters, indeed, something like a declassification occurs which suddenly casts certain individuals into a lower state than their previous one. Then they must reduce their requirements, restrain their needs, learn greater self-control. All the advantages of social influence are lost so far as they are concerned; their moral education has to be recommenced. But society cannot adjust them instantaneously to this new life and teach them to practice the increased self-repression to which they are unaccustomed. So they are not adjusted to the condition forced on them, and its very prospect is intolerable; hence the suffering which detaches them from a reduced existence even before they have made trial of it.

It is the same if the source of the crisis is an abrupt growth of power and wealth. Then, truly, as the conditions of life are changed, the standard according to which needs were regulated can no longer remain the same; for it varies with social resources, since it largely determines the share of each class of producers. The scale is upset; but a new scale cannot be immediately improvised. Time is required for the public conscience to reclassify men and things. So long as the social forces thus freed have not regained equilibrium, their respective values are unknown and so all regulation is lacking for a time. The limits are unknown between the possible and the impossible, what is just and what is unjust, legitimate claims and hopes and those which are immoderate. Consequently, there is no restraint upon aspirations. If the disturbance is profound, it affects even the principles controlling the distribution of men among various occupations. Since the relations between various parts of society are necessarily modified, the ideas expressing these relations must change. Some particular class especially favored by the crisis is no longer resigned to its former lot, and, on the other hand, the example of its greater good fortune arouses all sorts of jealousy below and about it. Appetites, not being controlled by a public opinion become disoriented, no longer recognize the limits proper to them. Besides, they are at the same time seized by a sort of natural erethism simply by the greater intensity of public life. With increased prosperity desires increase. At the very moment when traditional rules have lost their authority, the richer prize offered these appetites stimulates them and makes them more exigent and impatient of control. The state of de-regulation or anomy is thus further heightened by passions being less disciplined, precisely when they need more disciplining.

But then their very demands make fulfillment impossible. Overweening ambition always exceeds the results obtained, great as they may be, since there is no warning to pause here. Nothing gives satisfaction and all this agitation is uninterruptedly maintained without appeasement. Above all, since this race for an unattainable goal can give no other pleasure but that of the race itself, if it is one, once it is interrupted the participants are left empty-handed. At the same time the struggle grows more violent and painful, both from being less controlled and because competition is greater. All classes contend among themselves because no established classification any longer exists. Effort grows, just when it becomes less productive. How could the desire to live not be weakened under such conditions?

This explanation is confirmed by the remarkable immunity of poor countries. Poverty protects against suicide because it is a restraint in itself. No matter how one acts, desires have to depend upon resources to some extent; actual possessions are partly the criterion of those aspired to. So the less one has the less he is tempted to extend the range of his needs indefinitely. Lack of power, compelling moderation, accustoms men to it, while nothing excites envy if no one has superfluity. Wealth, on the other hand, by the power it bestows, deceives us into believing that we depend on ourselves only. Reducing the resistance we encounter from objects, it suggests the possibility of unlimited success against them. The less limited one feels, the more intolerable all limitation appears. Not without reason, therefore, have so many religions dwelt on the advantages and moral value of poverty. It is actually the best school for teaching self-restraint. Forcing us to constant self-discipline, it prepares us to accept collective discipline with equanimity, while wealth, exalting the individual, may always arouse the spirit of rebellion which is the very source of immorality. This, of course, is no reason why humanity should not improve its material condition. But though the moral danger involved in every growth of prosperity is not irremediable, it should not be forgotten.

III

If anomy never appeared except, as in the above instances, in intermittent spurts and acute crisis, it might cause the social suicide-rate to vary from time to time, but it would not be a regular, constant factor. In one sphere of social life, however—the sphere of trade and industry—it is actually in a chronic state.

For a whole century, economic progress has mainly consisted in freeing industrial relations from all regulation. Until very recently, it was the function of a whole system of moral forces to exert this discipline. First, the influence of religion was felt alike by workers and masters, the poor and the rich. It consoled the former and taught them contentment with their lot by informing them of the providential nature of the social order, that the share of each class was assigned by God himself, and by holding out the hope for just compensation in a world to come in return for the inequalities of this world. It governed the latter, recalling that worldly interests are not man's entire lot, that they must be subordinate to other and higher interests, and that they should therefore not be pursued without rule or measure. Temporal power, in turn, restrained the scope of economic functions by its supremacy over them and by the relatively subordinate role it assigned them. Finally, within the business world proper, the occupational groups by regulating salaries, the price of products and production itself, indirectly fixed the average level of income on which needs are partially based by the very force of circumstances. However, we do not mean to propose this organization as a model. Clearly it would be inadequate to existing societies without great changes. What we stress is its existence, the fact of its useful influence, and that nothing today has come to take its place.

Actually, religion has lost most of its power. And government, instead of regulating economic life, has become its tool and servant. The most opposite schools, orthodox economists and extreme socialists, unite to reduce government to the role of a more or less passive intermediary among the various social functions. The former wish to make it simply the guardian of individual contracts; the latter leave it the task of doing the collective bookkeeping, that is, of recording the demands of consumers, transmitting them to producers, inventorying the total revenue and distributing it according to a fixed formula. But both refuse it any power to subordinate other social organs to itself and to make them converge toward one dominant aim. On both sides nations are declared to have the single or chief purpose of achieving industrial prosperity; such is the implication of the dogma of economic materialism, the basis of both apparently opposed systems. And as these theories merely express the state of opinion, industry, instead of being still regarded as a means to an end transcending itself, has become the supreme end of individuals and societies alike. Thereupon the appetites thus excited have become freed of any limiting authority. By sanctifying them, so to speak, this apotheosis of well-being has placed them above all human law. Their restraint seems like a sort of sacrilege. For this reason, even the purely utilitarian regulation of them exercised by the industrial world itself through the medium of occupational groups has been unable to persist. Ultimately, this liberation of desires has been made worse by the very development of industry and the almost infinite extension of the market. So long as the producer could gain his profits only in his immediate neighborhood, the restricted amount of possible gain could not much overexcite ambition. Now that he may assume to have almost the entire world as his customer, how could passions accept their former confinement in the face of such limitless prospects?

Such is the source of the excitement predominating in this part of society, and which has thence extended to the other parts. There, the state of crisis and anomy is constant and, so to speak, normal. From top to bottom of the ladder, greed is aroused without knowing where to find ultimate foothold. Nothing can calm it, since its goal is far beyond all it can attain. Reality seems valueless by comparison with the dreams of fevered imaginations; reality is therefore abandoned, but so too is possibility abandoned when it in turn becomes reality. A thirst arises for novelties, unfamiliar pleasures, nameless sensations, all of which lose their savor once known. Henceforth one has no strength to endure the least reverse. The whole fever subsides and the sterility of all the tumult is apparent, and it is seen that all these new sensations in their infinite quantity cannot form a solid foundation of happiness to support one during days of trial. The wise man, knowing how to enjoy achieved results without having constantly to replace them with others, finds in them an attachment to life in the hour of difficulty. But the man who has always pinned all his hopes on the future and lived with his eyes fixed upon it, has nothing in the past as a comfort against the present's afflictions, for the past was nothing to him but a series of hastily experienced stages. What blinded him to himself was his expectation always to find further on the happiness he had so far missed. Now he is stopped in his tracks; from now on nothing remains behind or ahead of him to fix his gaze upon. Weariness alone, moreover, is enough to bring disillusionment, for he cannot in the end escape the futility of an endless pursuit.

We may even wonder if this moral state is not principally what makes economic catastrophes of our day so fertile in suicides. In societies where a man is subjected to a healthy discipline, he submits more readily to the blows of chance. The necessary effort for sustaining a little more discomfort costs him relatively little, since he is used to discomfort and constraint. But when every constraint is hateful in itself, how can closer constraint not seem intolerable? There is no tendency to resignation in the feverish impatience of men's lives. When there is no other aim but to outstrip constantly the point arrived at, how painful to be thrown back! Now this very lack of organization characterizing our economic condition throws the door wide to every sort of adventure.

Since imagination is hungry for novelty, and ungoverned, it gropes at random. Setbacks necessarily increase with risks and thus crises multiply, just when they are becoming more destructive.

Yet these dispositions are so inbred that society has grown to accept them and is accustomed to think them normal. It is everlastingly repeated that it is man's nature to be eternally dissatisfied, constantly to advance, without relief or rest, toward an indefinite goal. The longing for infinity is daily represented as a mark of moral distinction, whereas it can only appear within unregulated consciences which elevate to a rule the lack of rule from which they suffer. The doctrine of the most ruthless and swift progress has become an article of faith. But other theories appear parallel with those praising the advantages of instability, which, generalizing the situation that gives them birth, declare life evil, claim that it is richer in grief than in pleasure and that it attracts men only by false claims. Since this disorder is greatest in the economic world, it has most victims there.

Industrial and commercial functions are really among the occupations which furnish the greatest number of suicides (see Table 3.1). Almost on a level with the liberal professions, they sometimes surpass them; they are especially more afflicted than agriculture, where the old regulative forces still make their appearance felt most and where the fever of business has least penetrated. Here is best recalled what was once the general constitution of the economic order. And the divergence would be yet greater if, among the suicides of industry, employers were distinguished from workmen, for the former are probably most stricken by the state of anomy. The enormous rate of those with independent means (720 per million) sufficiently shows that the possessors of most comfort suffer most. Everything that enforces subordination attenuates the effects of this state. At least the horizon of the lower classes is limited by those above them, and for this same reason their desires are more modest. Those who

TABLE 3.1

Suicides per Million Persons of Different Occupations

	TRADE	TRANSPORTATION	INDUSTRY	AGRICULTURE	LIBERAL* PROFESSIONS
France (1878–87)[†]	440	. . . . .	340	240	300
Switzerland (1876)	664	1,514	577	304	558
Italy (1866–76)	277	152.6	80.4	26.7	618[‡]
Prussia (1883–90)	754	. . . . .	456	315	832
Bavaria (1884–91)	465	. . . . .	369	153	454
Belgium (1886–90)	421	. . . . .	160	160	100
Wurttemberg (1873–78)	273	. . . . .	190	206	...
Saxony (1878)		341.59 §		71.17	...

*When statistics distinguish several different sorts of liberal occupations, we show as a specimen the one in which the suicide-rate is highest.

[†]From 1826 to 1880 economic functions seem less affected (see Compte-rendu of 1880); but were occupational statistics very accurate?

[‡]This figure is reached only by men of letters.

§Figure represents Trade, Transportation and Industry combined for Saxony. Ed.

have only empty space above them are almost inevitably lost in it, if no force restrains them.

Anomy, therefore, is a regular and specific factor in suicide in our modern societies; one of the springs from which the annual contingent feeds. So we have here a new type to distinguish from the others. It differs from them in its dependence, not on the way in which individuals are attached to society, but on how it regulates them. Egoistic suicide results from man's no longer finding a basis for existence in life; altruistic suicide, because this basis for existence appears to man situated beyond life itself. The third sort of suicide, the existence of which has just been shown, results from man's activities lacking regulation and his consequent sufferings. By virtue of its origin we shall assign this last variety the name of *anomic suicide*.

Certainly, this and egoistic suicide have kindred ties. Both spring from society's insufficient presence in individuals. But the sphere of its absence is not the same in both cases. In egoistic suicide it is deficient in truly collective activity, thus depriving the latter of object and meaning. In anomic suicide, society's influence is lacking in the basically individual passions, thus leaving them without a check-rein. In spite of their relationship, therefore, the two types are independent of each other. We may offer society everything social in us, and still be unable to control our desires; one may live in an anomic state without being egoistic, and vice versa. These two sorts of suicide therefore do not draw their chief recruits from the same social environments; one has its principal field among intellectual careers, the world of thought—the other, the industrial or commercial world.

NOTES

1. Durkheim incorrectly gives this figure as 51 per cent.—Ed.
2. In 1874 over 1873.—Ed.
3. See Starck, *Verbrechen und Vergehen in Preussen*, Berlin, 1884, p. 55.
4. *Die Gesetzmässigkeit im Gesellschaftsleben*, p. 345.
5. See Fornasari di Verce, *La criminalita e le vicende economiche d'Italia*, Turin 1894, pp. 77–83.

6. *Ibid.*, pp. 108–117.
7. *Ibid.*, pp. 86–104.
8. The increase is less during the period 1885–90 because of a financial crisis.
9. To prove that an increase in prosperity diminishes suicides, the attempt has been made to show that they become less when emigration, the escape-valve of poverty, is widely practiced (see Legoyt, pp. 257–259). But cases are numerous where parallelism instead of inverse proportions exist between the two. In Italy from 1876 to 1890 the number of emigrants rose from 76 per 100,000 inhabitants to 335, a figure itself exceeded between 1887 and 1889. At the same time suicides did not cease to grow in numbers.
10. Actually, this is a purely moral reprobation and can hardly be judicially implemented. We do not consider any reestablishment of sumptuary laws desirable or even possible.

COMPANION WEBSITE

1. Go online to Write Out Loud about how economic booms, and not just crises, can lead to higher levels of suicide.
2. Log on to the *Emergence Through Convergence* Supplementary Sources to learn more about the PBS documentary, *The Suicide Tourist*, and other related material.
3. Check out the Interactive Reading and discuss the "suicide paradox" today with the Freakonomics guys, economist Steven Levitt, and journalist Stephen Dubner.

4

The Elementary Forms of Religious Life

Emile Durkheim

FIRST OF ALL, WE CANNOT ARRIVE at an understanding of the most modern religions without tracing historically the manner in which they have gradually taken shape. Indeed, history is the only method of explanatory analysis that can be applied to them. History alone enables us to break down an institution into its component parts, because it shows those parts to us as they are born in time, one after the other. Second, by situating each part of the institution within the totality of circumstances in which it was born, history puts into our hands the only tools we have for identifying the causes that have brought it into being. Thus, whenever we set out to explain something human at a specific moment in time—be it a religious belief, a moral rule, a legal principle, an aesthetic technique, or an economic system—we must begin by going back to its simplest and most primitive form. We must seek to account for the features that define it at that period of its existence and then show how it has gradually developed, gained in complexity, and become what it is at the moment under consideration.

It is easy to see how important the determination of the initial starting point is for this series of progressive explanations. A cartesian principle had it that the first link takes precedence in the chain of scientific truths. To be sure, it is out of the question to base the science of religions on a notion elaborated in the cartesian manner—that is, a logical concept, pure possibility constructed

solely by force of intellect. What we must find is a concrete reality that historical and ethnographic observation alone can reveal to us. But if that primary conception must be arrived at by other methods, the fact remains that it is destined to have an important influence on all the subsequent propositions that science establishes. Biological evolution was conceived altogether differently from the moment the existence of unicellular organisms was discovered. Likewise, the particulars of religious facts are explained differently if naturism is placed at the beginning of religious evolution than if animism, or some other form, is placed there. Indeed, even the most specialized scholars must choose a hypothesis and take their inspiration from it if they want to try to account for the facts they analyze—unless they mean to confine themselves to a task of pure erudition. Willy-nilly, the questions they ask take the following form: What has caused naturism or animism to take on such and such a particular aspect here or there, and to be enriched or impoverished in such and such a way? Since taking a position on the initial problem is unavoidable, and since the solution given will affect the science as a whole, the problem is best confronted at the outset. This is what I propose to do.

Besides, apart from those indirect consequences, the study of primitive religions in itself has immediate interest of the first importance.

If it is useful to know what a given religion consists of; it is far more important to examine what religion is in general. This is a problem that has always intrigued philosophers, and not without reason: It is of interest to all humanity. Unfortunately, the method philosophers ordinarily use to solve it is purely one of dialectic: All they do is analyze the idea they have of religion, even if they have to illustrate the results of that mental analysis with examples borrowed from those religions that best suit their model. But while this method must be abandoned, the problem of definition remains; and philosophy's great service has been to prevent it from being settled once and for all[1] by the disdain of the savants. The problem can in fact be approached in another way. Since all religions may be compared, all being species within the same genus, some elements are of necessity common to them all. By that I mean not only the outward and visible features that they all equally exhibit and that make it possible to define religion in a provisional way at the beginning of research. The discovery of these apparent signs is relatively easy, for the observation required does not go beyond the surface of things. But these external resemblances presuppose deeper ones. At the foundation of all systems of belief and all cults, there must necessarily be a certain number of fundamental representations and modes of ritual conduct[2] that, despite the diversity of forms that the one and the other may have taken on, have the same objective meaning everywhere and everywhere fulfill the same functions. It is these enduring elements that constitute what is eternal and human in religion. They are the whole objective content of the idea that is expressed when *religion* in general is spoken of.

How, then, can those elements be uncovered?

Surely it is not by observing the complex religions that have arisen in the course of history. Each of those religions is formed from such a variety of elements that it is very hard to distinguish what is secondary to them from what is primary, and what is essential from what is accessory. Simply consider religions like those of Egypt, India, or classical antiquity! Each is a dense tangle of many cults that can vary according to localities, temples, generations, dynasties, invasions, and so on. Popular superstitions intermingle in them with the most sophisticated dogmas. Neither religious thinking nor religious practice is shared equally among the mass of the faithful. The beliefs as well as the rites are taken in different ways, depending on men, milieux, and circumstances. Here it is priests, there monks, elsewhere the laity; here, mystics and rationalists, theologians and prophets, and so on. Under such conditions, it is difficult to perceive what might be common to all. It is indeed possible to find ways of studying some particular phenomenon fruitfully—such as prophetism, monasticism, or the mysteries—through one or another of those systems in which it is especially well developed. But how can one find the common basis of religious life under the luxuriant vegetation that grows over it? How can one find the fundamental states characteristic of the religious mentality in general through the clash of theologies, the variations of ritual, the multiplicity of groupings, and the diversity of individuals?

The case is altogether different in the lower societies. The lesser development of individuality, the smaller scale of the group, and the homogeneity of external circumstances all contribute to reducing the differences and variations to a minimum. The group regularly produces an intellectual and moral uniformity of which we find only rare examples in the more advanced societies. Everything is common to everyone. The movements are stereotyped; everyone executes the same ones in the same circumstances; and this conformity of conduct merely translates that of thought. Since all the consciousnesses are pulled along in the same current, the individual type virtually confounds itself with the generic type. At the same time that all is uniform, all is simple. What could be more basic than those myths composed of a single theme, repeated endlessly, or than those rites composed of a small number of movements, repeated until the participants can do no more. Neither the popular nor the priestly imagination has yet had the time or the means to refine and transform the basic material of ideas and religious practices; reduced to essentials, that material spontaneously presents itself to examination, and discovering it calls for only a minimal effort. Inessential, secondary, and luxurious developments have not yet come to hide what is primary.[3] Everything is boiled down to what is absolutely indispensable, to that without which there would be no religion. But the indispensable is also the fundamental, in other words, that which it is above all important for us to know.

Thus, primitive civilizations are prime cases because they are simple cases. This is why, among all the orders of facts, the observations of ethnographers have often been veritable revelations that have breathed new life into the study of human institutions. Before the middle of the nineteenth century, for example, it was generally believed that the father was the essential element of the family; it was not even imaginable that there could be a family organization of which paternal power was not the keystone. Bachofen's discovery toppled that old notion. Until quite recent times, it was thought obvious that the moral and legal relations that constitute kinship were only another aspect of the physiological relations that result from shared descent. Bachofen and his successors, McLennan, Morgan, and many others, were still operating under the influence of that preconception. But, quite the contrary, we have known ever since we became acquainted with the nature of the primitive clan that kinship cannot be defined by common blood.[4] To return to religions: Exclusive consideration of the religious forms that are the most familiar to us long led us to believe that the idea of god was characteristic of all that is religious. The religion I will study below is largely a stranger to any notion of divinity. In it, the forces to which the rites are addressed differ greatly from those that are of paramount importance in our modern religions, and yet they will help us to understand our modern religions better. Nothing is more unjust, therefore, than the

disdain with which too many historians still regard ethnographers' work. In point of fact, ethnography has often brought about the most fertile revolutions in the various branches of sociology. For the same reason, moreover, the discovery of unicellular creatures, which I noted earlier, transformed the idea of life that was widely held. Since life is down to its fundamental features among very simple beings, those features may be less easily misread.

But primitive religions do not merely allow us to isolate the constituent elements of religion; their great advantage is also that they aid in its explanation. Because the facts are simpler, the relations between them are more apparent. The reasons men invoke to explain their actions to themselves have not yet been refined and revamped by sophisticated thought: They are closer and more akin to the motives that caused those actions.

[...]

It has long been known that the first systems of representations that man made of the world and himself were of religious origin. There is no religion that is not both a cosmology and a speculation about the divine. If philosophy and the sciences were born in religion, it is because religion itself began by serving as science and philosophy. Further, and less often noted, religion has not merely enriched a human intellect already formed but in fact has helped to form it. Men owe to religion not only the content of their knowledge, in significant part, but also the form in which that knowledge is elaborated.

At the root of our judgments, there are certain fundamental notions that dominate our entire intellectual life. It is these ideas that philosophers, beginning with Aristotle, have called the categories of understanding: notions of time, space,[5] number, cause, substance, personality.[6] They correspond to the most universal properties of things. They are like solid frames that confine thought. Thought does not seem to be able to break out of them without destroying itself, since it seems we cannot think of objects that are not in time or space, that cannot be counted, and so forth. The other ideas are contingent and changing, and we can conceive of a man, a society, or an epoch that lacks them; but these fundamental notions seem to us as almost inseparable from the normal functioning of the intellect. They are, as it were, the skeleton of thought. Now, when one analyzes primitive religious beliefs methodically, one naturally finds the principal categories among them. They are born in and from religion; they are a product of religious thought. This is a point that I will make again and again in the course of this book.

Even now that point has a certain interest of its own, but here is what gives it its true significance.

The general conclusion of the chapters to follow is that religion is an eminently social thing. Religious representations are collective representations that express collective realities; rites are ways of acting that are born only in the midst of assembled groups and whose purpose is to evoke, maintain, or recreate certain mental states of those groups. But if the categories are of religious origin, then they must participate in[7] what is common to all religion: They, too, must be social things, products of collective thought. At the very least—since with our present understanding of these matters, radical and exclusive these are to be guarded against—it is legitimate to say that they are rich in social elements.

This, it must be added, is something one can begin to see even now for certain of the categories. For example, what if one tried to imagine what the notion of time would be in the absence of the methods we use to divide, measure, and express it with objective signs, a time that was not a succession of years, months, weeks, days, and hours? It would be nearly impossible to conceive of. We can conceive of time only if we differentiate between moments. Now, what is the origin of that differentiation? Undoubtedly, states of consciousness that we have already experienced can be reproduced in us in the same order in which they originally occurred; and, in this way, bits of our past become

immediate again, even while spontaneously distinguishing themselves from the present. But however important this distinction might be for our private experience, it is far from sufficient to constitute the notion or category of time. The category of time is not simply a partial or complete commemoration of our lived life. It is an abstract and impersonal framework that contains not only our individual existence but also that of humanity. It is like an endless canvas on which all duration is spread out before the mind's eye and on which all possible events are located in relation to points of reference that are fixed and specified. It is not *my time* that is organized in this way; it is time that is conceived of objectively by all men of the same civilization. This by itself is enough to make us begin to see that any such organization would have to be collective. And indeed, observation establishes that these indispensable points, in reference to which all things are arranged temporally, are taken from social life. The division into days, weeks, months, years, etc., corresponds to the recurrence of rites, festivals, and public ceremonies at regular intervals.[8] A calendar expresses the rhythm of collective activity while ensuring that regularity.[9]

The same applies to space. As Hamelin[10] has shown, space is not the vague and indeterminate medium that Kant imagined. If purely and absolutely homogeneous, it would be of no use and would offer nothing for thought to hold on to. Spatial representation essentially consists in a primary coordination of given sense experience. But this coordination would be impossible if the parts of space were qualitatively equivalent, if they really were mutually interchangeable. To have a spatial ordering of things is to be able to situate them differently: to place some on the right, others on the left, these above, those below, north or south, east or west, and so forth, just as, to arrange states of consciousness temporally, it must be possible to locate them at definite dates. That is, space would not be itself if, like time, it was not divided and differentiated. But where do these divisions that are essential to space come from? In itself it has no right, no left, no high or low, no north or south, etc. All these distinctions evidently arise from the fact that different affective colorings have been assigned to regions. And since all men of the same civilization conceive of space in the same manner, it is evidently necessary that these affective colorings and the distinctions that arise from them also be held in common—which implies almost necessarily that they are of social origin.[11]

Besides, in some instances this social character is made manifest. There are societies in Australia and North America in which space is conceived in the form of an immense circle, because the camp itself is circular[12] and the spatial circle is divided in exactly the same way as the tribal circle and in its image. As many regions are distinguished as there are clans in the tribe, and it is the place the clans occupy in the encampment that determines the orientation of the regions. Each region is defined by the totem of the clan to which it is assigned. Among the Zuñi, for example, the pueblo is made up of seven sections; each of these sections is a group of clans that has acquired its own unity. In all likelihood, it was originally a single clan that later subdivided. Space similarly contains seven regions, and each of these seven sections of the world is in intimate relationship with a section of the pueblo, that is, with a group of clans.[13] "Thus," says Cushing, "one division is considered to be in relation with the north; another represents the west, another the south,[14] etc." Each section of the pueblo has its distinctive color, which symbolizes it; each region has its own color, which is that of the corresponding section. Over the course of history, the number of basic clans has varied, and the number of regions has varied in the same way. Thus, spatial organization was modeled on social organization and replicates it. Far from being built into human nature, no idea exists, up to and including the distinction between right and left, that is not, in all probability, the product of religious, hence collective, representations.[15]

Analogous demonstrations concerning the notions of genus, force, personality, and efficacy will be found below. One might even ask whether the notion of contradiction does not also arise from social conditions. What tends to make this plausible is the fact that the hold the notion of contradiction has had over thought has varied with times and societies. Today the principle of identity governs scientific thought; but there are vast systems of representation that have played a major role in the history of ideas, in which it is commonly ignored: These systems are the mythologies, from the crudest to the most sophisticated.[16] Mythologies deal with beings that have the most contradictory attributes at the same time, that are one and many, material and spiritual, and capable of subdividing themselves indefinitely without losing that which makes them what they are. These historical variations of the rule that seems to govern our present logic show that, far from being encoded from eternity in the mental constitution of man, the rule depends at least in part upon historical, hence social, factors. We do not know exactly what these factors are, but we can presume that they exist.[17]

Once this hypothesis is accepted, the problem of knowledge can be framed in new terms.

Up to the present, only two doctrines have opposed one another. For some, the categories cannot be derived from experience. They are logically prior to experience and condition it. They are thought of as so many simple data that are irreducible and immanent in the human intellect by virtue of its natural makeup. They are thus called *a priori*. For others, by contrast, the categories are constructed, made out of bits and pieces, and it is the individual who is the artisan of that construction.[18]

Both solutions give rise to grave difficulties.

Is the empiricist thesis adopted? Then the categories must be stripped of their characteristic properties. In fact, they are distinguished from all other knowledge by their universality and their necessity. They are the most general concepts that exist, because they are applied to all that is real;

and just as they are not attached to any particular object, they are independent of any individual subject. They are the common ground where all minds meet. What is more, minds meet there of necessity: Reason, which is none other than the fundamental categories taken together, is vested with an authority that we cannot escape at will. When we try to resist it, to free ourselves from some of these fundamental notions, we meet sharp resistance. Hence, far from merely depending upon us, they impose themselves upon us. But the characteristics of empirical data are diametrically opposite. A sensation or an image is always linked to a definite object or collection of definite objects, and it expresses the momentary state of a particular consciousness. It is fundamentally individual and subjective. Moreover, we can do as we wish with representations that are of this origin. Of course, when sensations are present to us, they impose themselves on us *in fact. By right,* however, we remain free to conceive them otherwise than they are and to picture them as occurring in an order different from the one in which they occurred. In regard to them, nothing is binding on us unless considerations of a different sort intervene. Here, then, are two sorts of knowledge that are like opposite poles of the intellect. Under these conditions, to reduce reason to experience is to make reason disappear—because it is to reduce the universality and necessity that characterize reason to mere appearances, illusions that might be practically convenient but that correspond to nothing in things. Consequently, it is to deny all objective reality to that logical life which the function of the categories is to regulate and organize. Classical empiricism leads to irrationalism; perhaps it should be called by that name.

Notwithstanding the sense we ordinarily attach to the labels, it is the apriorists who are more attentive to the facts. Since they do not take it as self-evident truth that the categories are made of the same elements as our sense representations, they are not committed to impoverishing the categories systematically, emptying them of all real content

and reducing them to mere verbal artifices. Quite the contrary, apriorists leave the categories with all their distinctive characteristics. The apriorists are rationalists; they believe that the world has a logical aspect that reason eminently expresses. To do this, however, they have to ascribe to the intellect a certain power to transcend experience and add to what is immediately given. But for this singular power, they offer neither explanation nor warrant. Merely to say it is inherent in the nature of human intellect is not to explain that power. It would still be necessary to see where we acquire this astounding prerogative and how we are able to see relationships in things that mere spectating cannot reveal to us. To confine oneself to saying that experience itself is possible only on that condition is to shift the problem, perhaps, but not to solve it. The point is to know how it happens that experience is not enough, but presupposes conditions that are external and prior to experience, and how it happens that these conditions are met at the time and in the manner needed. To answer these questions, it has sometimes been imagined that, beyond the reason of individuals, there is a superior and perfect reason from which that of individuals emanated and, by a sort of mystic participation, presumably acquired its marvelous faculty: That superior and perfect reason is divine reason. But, at best, this hypothesis has the grave disadvantage of being shielded from all experimental control, so it does not meet the requirements of a scientific hypothesis. More than that, the categories of human thought are never fixed in a definite form; they are ceaselessly made, unmade, and remade; they vary according to time and place. By contrast, divine reason is immutable. How could this invariance account for such constant variability?

Such are the two conceptions that have competed for centuries. And if the debate has gone on and on, it is because the arguments back and forth are in fact more or less equivalent. If reason is but a form of individual experience, then reason is no more. On the other hand, if the capacities with which it is credited are recognized but left unaccounted for, then reason apparently is placed outside nature and science. Faced with these opposite objections, the intellect remains uncertain. But if the social origin of the categories is accepted, a new stance becomes possible, one that should enable us, I believe, to avoid these opposite difficulties.

The fundamental thesis of apriorism is that knowledge is formed from two sorts of elements that are irreducible one to the other—two distinct, superimposed layers, so to speak.[19] My hypothesis keeps this principle intact. The knowledge that people speak of as empirical—all that theorists of empiricism have ever used to construct reason—is the knowledge that the direct action of objects calls forth in our minds. Thus they are individual states that are wholly[20] explained by the psychic nature of the individual. But if the categories are essentially collective representations, as I think they are, they translate states of the collectivity, first and foremost. They depend upon the way in which the collectivity is organized, upon its morphology, its religious, moral, and economic institutions, and so on. Between these two kinds of representations, then, is all the distance that separates the individual from the social; one can no more derive the second from the first than one can deduce the society from the individual, the whole from the part, or the complex from the simple.[21] Society is a reality *sui generis*; it has its own characteristics that are either not found in the rest of the universe or are not found there in the same form. The representations that express society therefore have an altogether different content from the purely individual representations, and one can be certain in advance that the former add something to the latter.

PRELIMINARY QUESTIONS

Whether simple or complex, all known religious beliefs display a common feature: They presuppose a classification of the real or ideal things that men conceive of into two classes—two opposite genera—that are widely designated by two distinct terms, which the words *profane* and *sacred* translate fairly well. The division of the world into two domains, one containing all that is sacred and the other all that is profane—such is the distinctive trait of religious thought. Beliefs, myths, dogmas, and legends are either representations or systems of representations that express the nature of sacred things, the virtues and powers attributed to them, their history, and their relationships with one another as well as with profane things. Sacred things are not simply those personal beings that are called gods or spirits. A rock, a tree, a spring, a pebble, a piece of wood, a house, in a word anything, can be sacred. A rite can have sacredness; indeed there is no rite that does not have it to some degree. There are words, phrases, and formulas that can be said only by consecrated personages; there are gestures and movements that cannot be executed by just anyone. If Vedic sacrifice has had such great efficacy—if, indeed, sacrifice was far from being a method of gaining the gods' favor but, according to mythology, actually generated the gods—that is because the virtue it possessed was comparable to that of the most sacred beings. The circle of sacred objects cannot be fixed once and for all; its scope can vary infinitely from one religion to another. What makes Buddhism a religion is that, in the absence of gods, it accepts the existence of sacred things, namely, the Four Noble Truths and the practices that are derived from them.[22]

But I have confined myself thus far to enumerating various sacred things as examples: I must now indicate the general characteristics by which they are distinguished from profane things.

One might be tempted to define sacred things by the rank that is ordinarily assigned to them in the hierarchy of beings. They tend to be regarded as superior in dignity and power to profane things, and particularly to man, in no way sacred when he is only a man. Indeed, he is portrayed as occupying a rank inferior to and dependent upon them. While that portrayal is certainly not without truth, nothing about it is truly characteristic of the sacred. Subordination of one thing to another is not enough to make one sacred and the other not. Slaves are subordinate to their masters, subjects to their king, soldiers to their leaders, lower classes to ruling classes, the miser to his gold, and the power seeker to the power holders. If a man is sometimes said to have the religion of beings or things in which he recognizes an eminent value and a kind of superiority to him, it is obvious that, in all such cases, the word is taken in a metaphorical sense, and there is nothing in those relations that is religious in a strict sense.[23]

On the other hand, we should bear in mind that there are things with which man feels relatively at ease, even though they are sacred to the highest degree. An amulet has sacredness, and yet there is nothing extraordinary about the respect it inspires. Even face to face with his gods, man is not always in such a marked state of inferiority, for he very often uses physical coercion on them to get what he wants. He beats the fetish when he is displeased, only to be reconciled with it if, in the end, it becomes more amenable to the wishes of its worshipper.[24] To get rain, stones are thrown into the spring or the sacred lake where the god of the rain is presumed to reside; it is believed that he is forced by this means to come out and show himself.[25] Furthermore, while it is true that man is a dependent of his gods, this dependence is mutual. The gods also need man; without offerings and sacrifices, they would die. I will have occasion to show that this dependence of gods on their faithful is found even in the most idealistic[26] religions.

However, if the criterion of a purely hierarchical distinction is at once too general and too imprecise, nothing but their heterogeneity is left to define the relation between the sacred and the profane. But what makes this heterogeneity sufficient to characterize that classification of things and to distinguish it from any other is that it has a very particular feature: *It is absolute*. In the history of

human thought, there is no other example of two categories of things as profoundly differentiated or as radically opposed to one another. The traditional opposition between good and evil is nothing beside this one: Good and evil are two opposed species of the same genus, namely morals, just as health and illness are nothing more than two different aspects of the same order of facts, life; by contrast, the sacred and the profane are always and everywhere conceived by the human intellect as separate genera, as two worlds with nothing in common. The energies at play in one are not merely those encountered in the other, but raised to a higher degree; they are different in kind. This opposition has been conceived differently in different religions. Here, localizing the two kinds of things in different regions of the physical universe has appeared sufficient to separate them; there, the sacred is thrown into an ideal and transcendent milieu, while the residuum is abandoned as the property of the material world. But while the forms of the contrast are variable,[27] the fact of it is universal.

This is not to say that a being can never pass from one of these worlds to the other. But when this passage occurs, the manner in which it occurs demonstrates the fundamental duality of the two realms, for it implies a true metamorphosis. Rites of initiation, which are practiced by a great many peoples, demonstrate this especially well. Initiation is a long series of rites to introduce the young man into religious life. For the first time, he comes out of the purely profane world, where he has passed his childhood, and enters into the circle of sacred things. This change of status is conceived not as a mere development of preexisting seeds but as a transformation *totius substantiae*.[28] At that moment, the young man is said to die, and the existence of the particular person he was, to cease—instantaneously to be replaced by another. He is born again in a new form. Appropriate ceremonies are held to bring about the death and the rebirth, which are taken not merely in a symbolic sense but literally.[29] Is this not proof that there is a rupture between the profane being that he was and the religious being that he becomes?

Indeed, this heterogeneity is such that it degenerates into real antagonism. The two worlds are conceived of not only as separate but also as hostile and jealous rivals. Since the condition of belonging fully to one is fully to have left the other, man is exhorted to retire completely from the profane in order to live an exclusively religious life. From thence comes monasticism, which artificially organizes a milieu that is apart from, outside of, and closed to the natural milieu where ordinary men live a secular life, and that tends almost to be its antagonist. From thence as well comes mystic asceticism, which seeks to uproot all that may remain of man's attachment to the world. Finally, from thence come all forms of religious suicide, the crowning logical step of this asceticism, since the only means of escaping profane life fully and finally is escaping life altogether.

The opposition of these two genera is expressed outwardly by a visible sign that permits ready recognition of this very special classification, wherever it exists. The mind experiences deep repugnance about mingling, even simple contact, between the corresponding things, because the notion of the sacred is always and everywhere separate from the notion of the profane in man's mind, and because we imagine a kind of logical void between them. The state of dissociation in which the ideas are found in consciousness is too strongly contradicted by such mingling, or even by their being too close to one another. The sacred thing is, par excellence, that which the profane must not and cannot touch with impunity. To be sure, this prohibition cannot go so far as to make all communication between the two worlds impossible, for if the profane could in no way enter into relations with the sacred, the sacred would be of no use. This placing in relationship in itself is always a delicate operation that requires precautions and a more or less complex initiation.[30] Yet such an operation is impossible if the profane does not lose its specific traits, and if it does not

become sacred itself in some measure and to some degree. The two genera cannot, at the same time, both come close to one another and remain what they were.

Now we have a first criterion of religious beliefs. No doubt, within these two fundamental genera, there are secondary species that are themselves more or less incompatible with each other.[31] But characteristically, the religious phenomenon is such that it always assumes a bipartite division of the universe, known and knowable, into two genera that include all that exists but radically exclude one another. Sacred things are things protected and isolated by prohibitions; profane things are those things to which the prohibitions are applied and that must keep at a distance from what is sacred. Religious beliefs are those representations that express the nature of sacred things and the relations they have with other sacred things or with profane things. Finally, rites are rules of conduct that prescribe how man must conduct himself with sacred things.

When a certain number of sacred things have relations of coordination and subordination with one another, so as to form a system that has a certain coherence and does not belong to any other system of the same sort, then the beliefs and rites, taken together, constitute a religion. By this definition, a religion is not necessarily contained within a single idea and does not derive from a single principle that may vary with the circumstances it deals with, while remaining basically the same everywhere. Instead, it is a whole formed of separate and relatively distinct parts. Each homogeneous group of sacred things, or indeed each sacred thing of any importance, constitutes an organizational center around which gravitates a set of beliefs and rites, a cult of its own. There is no religion, however unified it may be, that does not acknowledge a plurality of sacred things. Even Christianity, at least in its Catholic form, accepts the Virgin, the angels, the saints, the souls of the dead, etc.—above and beyond the divine personality (who, besides, is both three and one). As a rule, furthermore, religion is not merely a single cult either but is made up of a system of cults that possess a certain autonomy. This autonomy is also variable. Sometimes the cults are ranked and subordinated to some dominant cult into which they are eventually absorbed; but sometimes as well they simply exist side by side in confederation. The religion to be studied in this book will provide an example of this confederate organization.

At the same time, we can explain why groups of religious phenomena that belong to no constituted religion can exist: because they are not or are no longer integrated into a religious system. If, for specific reasons, one of those cults just mentioned should manage to survive while the whole to which it belonged has disappeared, it will survive only in fragments. This is what has happened to so many agrarian cults that live on in folklore. In certain cases, what persists in that form is not even a cult, but a mere ceremony or a particular rite.[32]

Although this definition is merely preliminary, it indicates the terms in which the problem that dominates the science of religions must be posed. If sacred beings are believed to be distinguished from the others solely by the greater intensity of the powers attributed to them, the question of how men could have imagined them is rather simple: Nothing more is needed than to identify those forces that, through their exceptional energy, have managed to impress the human mind forcefully enough to inspire religious feelings. But if, as I have tried to establish, sacred things are different in nature from profane things, if they are different in their essence, the problem is far more complex. In that case, one must ask what led man to see the world as two heterogeneous and incomparable worlds, even though nothing in sense experience seems likely to have suggested the idea of such a radical duality.

CONCLUSION

It may be asked, Exactly what society is it that in this way becomes the substrate of religious life? Is it the real society, such as it exists and functions before our eyes, with the moral and juridical organization that it has toiled to fashion for itself over the course of history? But that society is full of flaws and imperfections. In that society, good rubs shoulders with evil, injustice is ever on the throne, and truth is continually darkened by error. How could a being so crudely made inspire the feelings of love, ardent enthusiasm, and willing self-sacrifice that all the religions demand of their faithful? Those perfect beings that are the gods cannot have taken their traits from such a mediocre, sometimes even base, reality.

Would it not be instead the perfect society, in which justice and truth reigned, and from which evil in all its forms was uprooted? No one disputes that this perfect society has a close relationship to religious sentiment, for religions are said to aim at realizing it. However, this society is not an empirical fact, well defined and observable; it is a fancy, a dream with which men have lulled their miseries but have never experienced in reality. It is a mere idea that expresses in consciousness our more or less obscure aspirations toward the good, the beautiful, and the ideal. These aspirations have their roots in us; since they come from the very depths of our being, nothing outside us can account for them. Furthermore, in and of themselves, they are already religious; hence, far from being able to explain religion, the ideal society presupposes it.[33]

But to see only the idealistic side of religion is to simplify arbitrarily. In its own way, religion is realistic. There is no physical or moral ugliness, no vice, and no evil that has not been deified. There have been gods of theft and trickery, lust and war, sickness and death. As uplifted as its idea of divinity is, Christianity itself was obliged to make a place in its mythology for the spirit of evil. Satan is an essential component of the Christian machinery; yet, even if he is an impure being, he is not a profane being. The anti-god is a god—lower and subordinate, it is true, yet invested with broad powers; he is even the object of rites, at the very least negative ones. Far from ignoring and disregarding the real society, religion is its image, reflecting all its features, even the most vulgar and repellent. Everything is to be found in it, and if we most often see good triumphing over evil, life over death, and the forces of light over the forces of darkness, this is because it is no different in reality. If the relationship between these forces was reversed, life would be impossible, whereas in fact, life maintains itself and even tends to develop.

But it is quite true that even if the mythologies and theologies allow a clear glimpse of the reality, the reality we find in them has been enlarged, transformed, and idealized. The most primitive religions are no different in this respect from the most modern and the most refined. We have seen, for example, how the Arunta place at the beginning of time a mythical society whose organization exactly replicates the one that still exists today. It is made up of the same clans and phratries, it is subject to the same marriage rules, and it practices the same rites. But the personages that comprise it are ideal beings endowed with capacities to which mere mortals cannot lay claim. Belonging to animality and humanity at the same time, their nature is not only higher but also different. The evil powers undergo a similar metamorphosis in that religion. It is as though evil itself undergoes refinement and idealization. The question that arises is where this idealization comes from.

One proposed answer is that man has a natural capacity to idealize, that is, to replace the real world with a different one to which he travels in thought. But such an answer changes the terms of the problem, neither solving nor even advancing it. This persistent idealization is a fundamental feature of religions. So to explain religions in terms of an innate capacity to idealize is simply to replace one word with its equivalent; it is like saying that man created religion because he has a religious nature. Yet the animal knows only one world: the world it perceives through experience, internal as well as external. Man alone has the capacity to conceive of the ideal and add it to the real. Where, then, does this remarkable distinction come from? Before

taking it to be a primary fact or a mysterious virtue that eludes science, one should first have made sure that this remarkable distinction does not arise from conditions that can be determined empirically.

My proposed explanation of religion has the specific advantage of providing an answer to this question, since what defines the sacred is that the sacred is added to the real. And since the ideal is defined in the same way, we cannot explain the one without explaining the other. We have seen, in fact, that if collective life awakens religious thought when it rises to a certain intensity, that is so because it brings about a state of effervescence that alters the conditions of psychic activity. The vital energies become hyperexcited, the passions more intense, the sensations more powerful; there are indeed some that are produced only at this moment. Man does not recognize himself; he feels somehow transformed and in consequence transforms his surroundings. To account for the very particular impressions he receives, he imputes to the things with which he is most directly in contact properties that they do not have, exceptional powers and virtues that the objects of ordinary experience do not possess. In short, upon the real world where profane life is lived, he superimposes another that, in a sense, exists only in his thought, but one to which he ascribes a higher kind of dignity than he ascribes to the real world of profane life. In two respects, then, this other world is an ideal one.

Thus the formation of an ideal is by no means an irreducible datum that eludes science. It rests on conditions that can be uncovered through observation. It is a natural product of social life. If society is to be able to become conscious of itself and keep the sense it has of itself at the required intensity, it must assemble and concentrate. This concentration brings about an uplifting of moral life that is expressed by a set of ideal conceptions in which the new life thus awakened is depicted. These ideal conceptions correspond to the onrush of psychic forces added at that moment to those we have at our disposal for the everyday tasks of life. A society can neither create nor recreate itself without creating some kind of ideal by the same stroke. This creation is not a sort of optional extra step by which society, being already made, merely adds finishing touches; it is the act by which society makes itself, and remakes itself, periodically. Thus, when we set the ideal society in opposition to the real society, like two antagonists supposedly leading us in opposite directions, we are reifying and opposing abstractions. The ideal society is not outside the real one but is part of it. Far from our being divided between them as though between two poles that repel one another, we cannot hold to the one without holding to the other. A society is not constituted simply by the mass of individuals who comprise it, the ground they occupy, the things they use, or the movements they make, but above all by the idea it has of itself. And there is no doubt that society sometimes hesitates over the manner in which it must conceive itself. It feels pulled in all directions. When such conflicts break out, they are not between the ideal and the reality but between different ideals, between the ideal of yesterday and that of today, between the ideal that has the authority of tradition and one that is only coming into being. Studying how ideals come to evolve certainly has its place, but no matter how this problem is solved, the fact remains that the whole of it unfolds in the world of the ideal.

Therefore the collective ideal that religion expresses is far from being due to some vague capacity innate to the individual; rather, it is in the school of collective life that the individual has learned to form ideals. It is by assimilating the ideals worked out by society that the individual is able to conceive of the ideal. It is society that, by drawing him into its sphere of action, has given him the need to raise himself above the world of experience, while at the same time furnishing him the means of imagining another. It is society that built this new world while building itself, because it is society that the new world expresses. There is nothing mysterious about the faculty of idealization, then, whether in the individual or in the group. This faculty is not a sort of luxury, which man could do without, but a condition of his existence. If he had not acquired it, he would not be a social being, which is to say that he would not be man. To be sure, collective ideals tend to become individualized as they become incarnate in individuals. Each person understands them in his own way and gives them an individual imprint, some elements being taken out and others being added. As the individual personality develops and becomes an autonomous source of action, the personal ideal diverges from the social one. But if we want to understand that aptitude for living outside the real, which is seemingly so remarkable, all we need to do is relate it to the social conditions on which it rests.

But the last thing to do is to see this theory of religion as merely a refurbishment of historical materialism. That would be a total misunderstanding of my thought. In pointing out an essentially social thing in religion, I in no way mean to say that religion simply translates the material forms and immediate vital necessities of society into another language. I do indeed take it to be obvious that social life depends on and bears the mark of its material base, just as the mental life of the individual depends on the brain and indeed on the whole body. But collective consciousness is something other than a mere epiphenomenon of its morphological base just as individual consciousness is something other than a mere product of the nervous system. If collective consciousness is to appear, a *sui generis* synthesis of individual consciousnesses must occur. The product of this synthesis is a whole world of feelings, ideas, and images that follow their own laws once they are born. They mutually attract one another, repel one another, fuse together, subdivide, and proliferate; and none of these combinations is directly commanded and necessitated by the state of the underlying reality. Indeed, the life thus unleashed enjoys such great independence that it sometimes plays about in forms that have no aim or utility of any kind, but only for the pleasure of affirming itself. I have shown that precisely this is often true of ritual activity and mythological thought.[34]

[...]

II

Thus there is something eternal in religion that is destined to outlive the succession of particular symbols in which religious thought has clothed itself. There can be no society that does not experience the need at regular intervals to maintain and strengthen the collective feelings and ideas that provide its coherence and its distinct individuality. This moral remaking can be achieved only through meetings, assemblies, and congregations in which the individuals, pressing close to one another, reaffirm in common their common sentiments. Such is the origin of ceremonies that, by their object, by their results, and by the techniques used, are not different in kind from ceremonies that are specifically religious. What basic difference is there between Christians' celebrating the principal dates of Christ's life, Jews' celebrating the exodus from Egypt or the promulgation of the Decalogue, and a citizens' meeting commemorating the advent of a new moral charter or some other great event of national life?

If today we have some difficulty imagining what the feasts and ceremonies of the future will be, it is because we are going through a period of transition and moral mediocrity. The great things of the past that excited our fathers no longer arouse the same zeal among us, either because they have passed so completely into common custom that we lose awareness of them or because they no longer suit our aspirations. Meanwhile, no replacement for them has yet been created. We are no longer electrified by those principles in whose name Christianity exhorted the masters to treat their slaves humanely; and besides, Christianity's idea of human equality and fraternity seems to us today

to leave too much room for unjust inequalities. Its pity for the downcast seems to us too platonic. We would like one that is more vigorous but do not yet see clearly what it should be or how it might be realized in fact.

In short, the former gods are growing old or dying, and others have not been born. This is what voided Comte's attempt to organize a religion using old historical memories, artificially revived. It is life itself, and not a dead past, that can produce a living cult. But that state of uncertainty and confused anxiety cannot last forever. A day will come when our societies once again will know hours of creative effervescence during which new ideals will again spring forth and new formulas emerge to guide humanity for a time. And when those hours have been lived through, men will spontaneously feel the need to relive them in thought from time to time—that is, to preserve their memory by means of celebrations that regularly recreate their fruits. We have already seen how the [French] Revolution instituted a whole cycle of celebrations in order to keep the principles that inspired it eternally young. If that institution quickly perished, it is because the revolutionary faith lasted only briefly, and because disappointments and discouragements quickly replaced the first moment of enthusiasm. But although that work miscarried, it helps us to imagine what might have come to be under other conditions; and everything leads us to believe that the work will sooner or later be taken up again. There are no immortal gospels, and there is no reason to believe that humanity is incapable of conceiving new ones in the future. As to knowing what the symbols will be in which the new faith will come to express itself, whether they will resemble those of the past, whether they will better suit the reality to be expressed—that is a question that exceeds human faculties of prediction and that, moreover, is beside the point.

But feasts and rites—in a word, the cult—are not the whole of religion. Religion is not only a system of practices but also a system of ideas whose object is to express the world; even the humblest have their own cosmologies, as we have seen. No matter how these two elements of religious life may be related, they are nonetheless quite different. One is turned toward action, which it elicits and regulates; the other toward thought, which it enriches and organizes. Since they do not rest on the same conditions, then, there is reason to ask whether the ideas correspond to needs as universal and as permanent as the practices do.

NOTES

1. Swain rendered Durkheim's *prescrit* as "suppressed," as if he had written *proscrit*.
2. *Attitudes rituelles*. On this phrase, see below, p. 301n.
3. This is not to say, of course, that primitive cults do not go beyond bare essentials. Quite the contrary, as we will see, religious beliefs and practices that do not have narrowly utilitarian aims are found in every religion (Bk. III, chap. 4, §2). This nonutilitarian richness is indispensable to religious life, and of its very essence. But it is by far less well developed in the lower religions than in the others, and this fact will put us in a better position to determine its raison d'être.
4. Jacob Johann Bachofen (1815–1887) postulated the existence of matriliny (reckoning descent through the female line) and matriarchy or mother right, a stage he envisaged as standing between primitive promiscuity and patriarchy. Ethnographic study worldwide has borne out the first and discredited the second. Like Bachofen, John Ferguson McLennan (1827–1881) and Lewis Henry Morgan (1818–1881) were lawyers interested in the rules that govern family and property. Among other achievements, Morgan pioneered the study of kin statuses distinct from blood relationship; McLennan is credited with having drawn attention to totemism. See below, Bk. I. chap. 4, p. 85.
5. I call time and space categories because there is no difference between the role these notions play in intellectual life and that which falls to notions of kind and cause. (See on this point [Octave] Hamelin, *Essai sur les éléments principaux de la représentation*, Paris, Alcan [1907], pp. 63, 76.)
6. Usually referred to in Kantian circles as the "categories of understanding" or the "categories of the understanding," technically these are called "pure concepts of understanding"—that is, concepts, or rules for organizing the variety of sense perceptions, that lie ready in the mind and are brought into play by our efforts to make sense of our sensations. For clarifying correspondence on these points, I thank Professor Robert Paul Wolff.
7. The phrase "participate in," which occurs frequently, has usually not been replaced with simpler possibilities such as "partakes of" or "shares in" because the notion of participation that can be seen in the sentence "Jesus participated in divine and human nature" must be borne in mind, together with an argument in which Durkheim was engaged. Lucien Lévy-Bruhl, whose book *Les Fonctions mentales dans les sociétés inférieures* Durkheim criticizes, considered "participations" to exemplify the inherent illogic of "primitive" thought. Durkheim held just the opposite.
8. In support of this assertion, see Henri Hubert and Marcel Mauss, *Mélanges d'histoire des religions,* the chapter on "La Représentation du temps dans la religion," Paris, Alcan [1909].
9. Through this we see how completely different are the complexus of sensations and images that serves to orient us in duration, and the category of time. The first are the summary of individual experiences, which hold only for the individual who has had them. By contrast, the category of time expresses a time common to the group—social time, so to speak. This category itself is a true social institution. Thus it is peculiar to man; animals have no representation of this kind.

    This distinction between the category of time and the corresponding individual sensations could easily be made in regard to space and cause. This may perhaps help clear up certain confusions, which have fed controversies on these questions. I will return to this point at the Conclusion of the present work.
10. Hamelin, *Essai sur les éléments principaux de la représentation*, pp. 75ff.
11. Otherwise, in order to explain this agreement, one would have to accept the idea that all individuals, by virtue of their organico-psychic constitution, are affected in the same manner by the different parts of space—which is all the more improbable since the different regions have no affective coloring. Moreover, the divisions of space vary among

societies—proof that they are not based exclusively on the inborn nature of man.

12. See Emile Durkheim and Marcel Mauss, "De Quelques formes primitives de la classification," *AS,* vol. VI, 1903, pp. 47ff.

13. Ibid., pp. 34ff.

14. [Frank Hamilton] Cushing, "Outlines of Zuni Creation Myths," *Thirteenth Report*, BAE, Washington, DC, Government Printing Office, 1896, pp. 367ff. [Throughout, quoted material is translated into English from Durkheim's French renderings.]

15. See Robert Hertz, "La Prééminence de la main droite: Etude de polarité religieuse," *RP,* December, 1909. On this question of the relations between the representation of space and the form of the group, see the chapter in [Friedrich] Ratzel, *Politische Geographie* [Leipzig, R. Oldenbourg, 1897], titled "Der Raum im Geiste der Völker" [pp. 261–262].

16. I do not mean to say that it is unknown to mythological thinking but that mythological thinking departs from this principle more often and more overtly than scientific thought. Conversely, I will show that science cannot help but violate it, even while following it more scrupulously than religion does. In this respect and many others, there are only differences of degree between science and religion; but if these should not be overstated, it is important to notice them, for they are significant.

17. This hypothesis has already been advanced by the founders of *Völkerpsychologie*. It is referred to, for example, in a short article by Wilhelm Windelband titled, "Die Erkenntnislehre unter dem Völkerpsychologischen Geschichtspunkte," in *ZV* [Lichtenstein, Kraus Reprints, Ltd., 1968], VIII, pp. 166ff. Cf. a note by [Heymann] Steinthal on the same subject, ibid., pp. 178ff.

18. Even in the theory of [Herbert] Spencer, the categories are constructed from experience. The only difference in this respect between ordinary and evolutionary empiricism is that, according to the latter, the results of individual experience are consolidated by heredity. But that consolidation adds nothing essential; no element enters into their composition that does not originate in the experience of the individual. Also, according to that theory, the necessity with which the categories impose themselves upon us in the present is itself the product of an illusion, a superstitious prejudice that is deeply rooted in the organism but without foundation in the nature of things.

19. It is perhaps surprising that I should not define apriorism by the hypothesis of innateness. But that idea actually has only a secondary role in the doctrine. It is a simplistic way of portraying the irreducibility of rational cognition to empirical data. To call it innate is no more than a positive way of saying that it is not a product of experience as usually conceived.

20. At least to the extent that there are individual, and thus fully empirical, representations. But in fact there probably is no case in which those two sorts of elements are not found closely bound up together.

21. Furthermore, this irreducibility should not be understood in an absolute sense. I do not mean that there is nothing in the empirical representations that announces the rational ones, or that there is nothing in the individual that can be considered the harbinger of social life. If experience was completely foreign to all that is rational, reason would not be applicable to it. Likewise, if the psychic nature of the individual was absolutely resistant to social life, society would be impossible. Therefore a full analysis of the categories would look for the seeds of rationality in individual consciousness. I shall have occasion to return to this point in my Conclusion. All I wish to establish here is that there is a distance between the indistinct seeds of reason and reason properly so-called that is comparable to the distance between the properties of mineral elements, from which the living being is made, and the characteristic properties of life, once constituted.

22. Not to mention the sage or the saint who practices these truths, and who is for this reason sacred.

23. This is not to say that the relations cannot take on a religious character, but that they do not necessarily.

24. [Fritz] Schultze, [*Der*] *Fetichismus* [*Ein Beitrag zur Anthropologie und Religionsgeschichte,* Leipzig, C. Wilfferodt, 1871], p. 129.

25. Examples of these customs will be found in [James George] Frazer, *Golden Bough,* 2d ed., vol. I [New York, Macmillan, 1894], pp. 81ff.

26. For the meaning of "idealistic," bear in mind Durkheim's contrast (above, p. 2) between religions that contain more concepts and fewer sensations and images.

27. The conception according to which the profane is opposed to the sacred as the rational is to the irrational; the intelligible to the mysterious, is only one of the forms in which this opposition is expressed. Science, once constituted, has taken on

a profane character, especially in the eyes of the Christian religions; in consequence, it has seemed that science could not be applied to sacred things.

28. Of the whole essence.

29. See James George Frazer, "On Some Ceremonies of the Central Australian Tribes," in *AAAS* [Melbourne, Victoria, published by the association], 1901 [vols. VIII–IX], pp. 313ff. The concept is, moreover, very common. In India, mere participation in the sacrificial act has the same effects; the sacrificer, by the very fact of entering into the circle of sacred things, changes personality. (See Henri Hubert and Marcel Mauss, "Essai sur [la nature et fonction du] sacrifice," *AS,* vol. II [1897], p. 101.)

30. See what I say about initiation on

31. Later I will show how, for example sacred things between which there exclude one another as the sa profane (Bk. III, chap. 5, §4).

32. This is the case, for example, of certain marriage and funeral rites.

33. [Emile] Boutroux, *Science et religion* [*dans la philosophie contemporaine,* Paris, E. Flammarion, 1907], pp. 206–207.

34. See above, pp. 382ff. Cf. my article on the same question: "Représentations individuelles et représentations collectives," *RMM,* vol. VI, 1898 [pp. 273ff.]

COMPANION WEBSITE

1. Go online to Write Out Loud about a time when you felt a sense of collective effervescence attached to something sacred.
2. Log on to Durkheim's Profile Page to learn more about his theory of the sacred and the profane.
3. Check out the documentary *Devil's Playground* for an example of how tight-knit religious communities exert moral pressure on their members, listed online in the *Emergence Through Convergence* Supplementary Sources.

5

Manifest and Latent Functions

Robert Merton

As HAS BEEN IMPLIED IN earlier sections, the distinction between manifest and latent functions was devised to preclude the inadvertent confusion, often found in the sociological literature, between conscious *motivations* for social behavior and its *objective consequences*. Our scrutiny of current vocabularies of functional analysis has shown how easily, and how unfortunately, the sociologist may identify *motives* with *functions*. It was further indicated that the motive and the function vary independently and that the failure to register this fact in an established terminology has contributed to the unwitting tendency among sociologists to confuse the subjective categories of motivation with the objective categories of function. This, then, is the central purpose of our succumbing to the not-always-commendable practice of introducing new terms into the rapidly growing technical vocabulary of sociology, a practice regarded by many laymen as an affront to their intelligence and an offense against common intelligibility.

As will be readily recognized, I have adapted the terms "manifest" and "latent" from their use in another context by Freud (although Francis Bacon had long ago spoken of "latent process" and "latent configuration" in connection with processes which are below the threshold of superficial observation).

The distinction itself has been repeatedly drawn by observers of human behavior at irregular intervals over a span of many centuries.[1] Indeed, it would be disconcerting to find that a distinction which we have come to regard as central to

functional analysis had not been made by any of that numerous company who have in effect adopted a functional orientation. We need mention only a few of those who have, in recent decades, found it necessary to distinguish in their specific interpretations of behavior between the end-in-view and the functional consequences of action.

George H. Mead[2]: "that attitude of hostility toward the law-breaker has the unique advantage [read: latent function] of uniting all members of the community in the emotional solidarity of aggression. While the most admirable of humanitarian efforts are sure to run counter to the individual interests of very many in the community, or fail to touch the interest and imagination of the multitude and to leave the community divided or indifferent, the cry of thief or murderer is attuned to profound complexes, lying below the surface of competing individual efforts, and citizens who have [been] separated by divergent interests stand together against the common enemy."

Emile Durkheim's[3] similar analysis of the social functions of punishment is also focused on its latent functions (consequences for the community) rather than confined to manifest functions (consequences for the criminal).

W. G. Sumner[4]: "from the first acts by which men try to satisfy needs, each act stands by itself, and looks no further than the immediate satisfaction. From recurrent needs arise habits for the individual and customs for the group, but these results are consequences which were never conscious, and never foreseen or intended. They are not noticed until they have long existed, and it is still longer before they are appreciated." Although this fails to locate the latent functions of standardized social actions for a designated social structure, it plainly makes the basic distinction between ends-in-view and objective consequences.

R. M. MacIver[5]: In addition to the direct effects of institutions, "there are further effects by way of control which lie outside the direct purposes of men ... this type of reactive form of control ... may, though unintended, be of profound service to society."

W. I. Thomas and F. Znaniecki[6]: "Although all the new [Polish peasant cooperative] institutions are thus formed with the definite purpose of satisfying certain specific needs, their social function is by no means limited to their explicit and conscious purpose ... every one of these institutions—commune or agricultural circle, loan and savings bank, or theater—is not merely a mechanism for the management of certain values but also an association of people, each member of which is supposed to participate in the common activities as a living, concrete individual. Whatever is the predominant, official common interest upon which the institution is founded, the association as a concrete group of human personalities unofficially involves many other interests; the social contacts between its members are not limited to their common pursuit, though the latter, of course, constitutes both the main reason for which the association is formed and the most permanent bond which holds it together. Owing to this combination of an abstract political, economic, or rather rational mechanism for the satisfaction of specific needs with the concrete unity of a social group, the new institution is also the best intermediary link between the peasant primary-group and the secondary national system."

These and numerous other sociological observers have, then, from time to time distinguished between categories of subjective disposition ("needs, interests, purposes") and categories of generally unrecognized but objective functional consequences ("unique advantages," "never conscious" consequences, "unintended ... service to society," "function not limited to conscious and explicit purpose").

Since the occasion for making the distinction arises with great frequency, and since the purpose of a conceptual scheme is to direct observations toward salient elements of a situation and to prevent the inadvertent oversight of these elements, it would seem justifiable to designate this distinction by an appropriate set of terms. This is the rationale for the distinction between manifest functions and latent functions; the first referring to those objective consequences for a specified unit (person, subgroup, social or cultural system) which contribute to its adjustment or adaptation and were so intended; the second referring to unintended and unrecognized consequences of the same order.

There are some indications that the christening of this distinction may serve a heuristic purpose by becoming incorporated into an explicit conceptual apparatus, thus aiding both systematic observation and later analysis. In recent years, for example, the distinction between manifest and latent functions has been utilized in analyses of racial intermarriage,[7] social stratification,[8] affective frustration,[9] Veblen's sociological theories,[10] prevailing American orientations toward Russia,[11] propaganda as a means of social control,[12] Malinowski's anthropological theory,[13] Navajo witchcraft,[14] problems in the sociology of knowledge,[15] fashion,[16] the dynamics of personality,[17] national security measures,[18] the internal social dynamics of bureaucracy,[19] and a great variety of other sociological problems.

The very diversity of these subject-matters suggests that the theoretic distinction between manifest and latent functions is not bound up with a limited and particular range of human behavior. But there still remains the large task of ferreting out the specific uses to which this distinction can be put, and it is to this large task that we devote the remaining pages of this chapter.

HEURISTIC PURPOSES OF THE DISTINCTION

Clarifies the analysis of seemingly irrational social patterns. In the first place, the distinction aids the sociological interpretation of many social practices which persist even though their manifest purpose is clearly not achieved. The time-worn procedure in such instances has been for diverse, particularly lay, observers to refer to these practices as "superstitions," irrationalities," "mere inertia of tradition," *etc.* In other words, when group behavior does not—and, indeed, often cannot—attain its ostensible purpose there is an inclination to attribute its occurrence to lack of intelligence, sheer ignorance, survivals, or so-called inertia. Thus, the Hopi ceremonials designed to produce abundant rainfall may be labelled a superstitious practice of primitive folk and that is assumed to conclude the matter. It should be noted that this in no sense accounts for the group behavior. It is simply a case of name-calling; it substitutes the epithet "superstition" for an analysis of the actual role of this behavior in the life of the group. Given the concept of latent function, however, we are reminded that this behavior *may* perform a function for the group, although this function may be quite remote from the avowed purpose of the behavior.

The concept of latent function extends the observer's attention beyond the question of whether or not the behavior attains its avowed purpose. Temporarily ignoring these explicit purposes, it directs attention *toward* another range of consequences: those bearing, for example, upon the individual personalities of Hopi involved in the ceremony and upon the persistence and continuity of the larger group. Were one to confine himself to the problem of whether a manifest (purposed) function occurs, it becomes a problem, not for the sociologist, but for the meteorologist. And to be sure, our meteorologists agree that the rain ceremonial does not produce rain; but this is hardly to the point. It is merely to say that the ceremony does not have this technological use; that this purpose of the ceremony and its actual consequences do not coincide. But with the concept of latent function, we continue our inquiry, examining the consequences of the ceremony not for the rain gods or for meteorological phenomena, but for the groups which conduct the ceremony. And here it may be found, as many observers indicate, that the ceremonial does indeed have functions—but functions which are non-purposed or latent.

Ceremonials may fulfill the latent function of reinforcing the group identity by providing a periodic occasion on which the scattered members of a group assemble to engage in a common activity. As Durkheim among others long since indicated, such ceremonials are a means by which collective expression is afforded the sentiments which, in a further analysis, are found to be a basic source of group unity. Through the systematic application of the concept of latent function, therefore, *apparently* irrational behavior may *at times* be found to be positively functional for the group. Operating with the concept of latent function, we are not too quick to conclude that if an activity of a group does not achieve its nominal purpose, then its persistence can be described only as an instance of "inertia," "survival," or "manipulation by powerful subgroups in the society."

In point of fact, some conception like that of latent function has very often, almost invariably, been employed by social scientists observing *a standardized practice designed to achieve an objective which one knows from accredited physical science cannot be thus achieved.* This would plainly be the case, for example, with Pueblo rituals dealing with rain or fertility. *But with behavior which is not directed toward a clearly unattainable objective, sociological observers are less likely to examine the collateral or latent functions of the behavior.*

Directs attention to theoretically fruitful fields of inquiry. The distinction between manifest and latent functions serves further to direct the attention of the sociologist to precisely those realms of behavior, attitude and belief where he can most fruitfully apply his special skills. For what is his task if he confines himself to the study of manifest functions? He is then concerned very largely with determining whether a practice instituted for a particular purpose does, in fact, achieve this purpose. He will then inquire, for example, whether a new system of wage-payment achieves its avowed purpose of reducing labor turnover or of increasing output. He will ask whether a propaganda campaign has indeed gained its objective of increasing "willingness to fight" or "willingness to buy war bonds," or "tolerance toward other ethnic groups." Now, these are important, and complex, types of inquiry. But, so long as sociologists *confine* themselves to the study of manifest functions, their inquiry is set for them by practical men of affairs (whether a captain of industry, a trade union leader, or, conceivably, a Navaho chieftain, is for the moment immaterial), rather than by the theoretic problems which are at the core of the discipline. By dealing primarily with the realm of manifest functions, with the key problem of whether deliberately instituted practices or organizations succeed in achieving their objectives, the sociologist becomes converted into an industrious and skilled recorder of the altogether familiar pattern of behavior. *The terms of appraisal are fixed and limited by the question put to him by the non-theoretic men of affairs, e.g., has the new wage-payment program achieved such-and-such purposes?*

But armed with the concept of latent function, the sociologist extends his inquiry in those very directions which promise most for the theoretic development of the discipline. He examines the familiar (or planned) social practice to ascertain the latent, and hence generally unrecognized, functions (as well, of course, as the manifest functions). He considers, for example, the consequences of the new wage plan for, say, the trade union in which

the workers are organized or the consequences of a propaganda program, not only for increasing its avowed purpose of stirring up patriotic fervor, but also for making large numbers of people reluctant to speak their minds when they differ with official policies, *etc.* In short, it is suggested that the *distinctive* intellectual contributions of the sociologist are found primarily in the study of unintended consequences (among which are latent functions) of social practices, as well as in the study of anticipated consequences (among which are manifest functions).[20]

There is some evidence that it is precisely at the point where the research attention of sociologists has shifted from the plane of manifest to the plane of latent functions that they have made their *distinctive* and major contributions. This can be extensively documented but a few passing illustrations must suffice.

THE HAWTHORNE WESTERN ELECTRIC STUDIES:[21] As is well known, the early stages of this inquiry were concerned with the problem of the relations of "illumination to efficiency" of industrial workers. For some two and a half years, attention was focused on problems such as this: do variations in the intensity of lighting affect production? The initial results showed that within wide limits there was no uniform relation between illumination and output. Production output increased *both* in the experimental group where illumination was increased (or *decreased*) *and* in the control group where no changes in illumination were introduced. In short, the investigators confined themselves wholly to a search for the manifest functions. Lacking a concept of latent social function, no attention whatever was initially paid to the social consequences *of the experiment* for relations among members of the test and control groups or for relations between workers and the test room authorities. In other words, the investigators lacked a sociological frame of reference and operated merely as "engineers" (just as a group of meteorologists might have explored the "effects" upon rainfall of the Hopi ceremonial).

Only after continued investigation, did it occur to the research group to explore the consequences of the new "experimental situation" for the self-images and self-conceptions of the workers taking part in the experiment, for the interpersonal relations among members of the group, for the coherence and unity of the group. As Elton Mayo reports it, "the illumination fiasco had made them alert to the need that very careful records should be kept of everything that happened in the room in addition to the obvious engineering and industrial devices. Their observations therefore included not only records of industrial and engineering changes but also records of physiological or medical changes, and, *in a sense,* of social and anthropological. This last took the form of a 'log' that gave as full an account as possible of the actual events of every day …"[22] In short, it was only after a long series of experiments which wholly neglected the latent social functions of the experiment (as a contrived social situation) that this distinctly sociological framework was introduced. "With this realization," the authors write, "the inquiry changed its character. No longer were the investigators interested in testing for the effects of single variables. In the place of a controlled experiment, they substituted the notion of a social situation which needed to be described and understood as a system of interdependent elements." Thereafter, as is now widely known, inquiry was directed very largely toward ferreting out the latent functions of standardized practices among the workers, of informal organization developing among workers, of workers' games instituted by "wise administrators," of large programs of worker counselling and interviewing, *etc.* The new conceptual scheme entirely altered the range and types of data gathered in the ensuing research.

One has only to return to the previously quoted excerpt from Thomas and Znaniecki in their classical work of some thirty years ago, to recognize the correctness of Shils' remark:

indeed the history of the study of primary groups in American sociology is a supreme instance of the *discontinuities of the development of this discipline:* a problem is stressed by one who is an acknowledged founder of the discipline, the problem is left unstudied, then, some years later, it is taken up with enthusiasm as if no one had ever thought of it before.[23]

For Thomas and Znaniecki had repeatedly emphasized the sociological view that, whatever its major purpose, "the association as a concrete group of human personalities unofficially involves many other interests; the social contacts between its members are not limited to their common pursuit …" In effect, then, it had taken years of experimentation to turn the attention of the Western Electric research team to the latent social functions of primary groups emerging in industrial organizations. It should be made clear that this case is not cited here as an instance of defective experimental design; that is not our immediate concern. It is considered only as an illustration of the pertinence for *sociological* inquiry of the concept of latent function, and the associated concepts of functional analysis. It illustrates how the inclusion of this concept (whether the term is used or not is inconsequential) can sensitize sociological investigators to a range of significant social variables which are otherwise easily overlooked. The explicit ticketing of the concept may perhaps lessen the frequency of such occasions of discontinuity in future sociological research.

The discovery of latent functions represents significant increments in sociological knowledge. There is another respect in which inquiry into latent functions represents a distinctive contribution of the social scientist. It is precisely the latent functions of a practice or belief which are *not* common knowledge, for these are unintended and generally unrecognized social and psychological consequences. As a result, findings concerning latent functions represent a greater increment in knowledge than findings concerning manifest functions. They represent, also, greater departures from "common-sense" knowledge about social life. Inasmuch as the latent functions depart, more or less, from the avowed manifest functions, the research which uncovers latent functions very often produces "paradoxical" results. The seeming paradox arises from the sharp modification of a familiar popular preconception which regards a standardized practice or belief *only* in terms of its manifest functions by indicating some of its subsidiary or collateral latent functions. The introduction of the concept of latent function in social research leads to conclusions which show that "social life is not as simple as it first seems." For as long as people confine themselves to *certain* consequences (e.g. manifest consequences), it is comparatively simple for them to pass moral judgments upon the practice or belief in question. Moral evaluations, generally based on these manifest consequences, tend to be polarized in terms of black or white. But the perception of further (latent) consequences often complicates the picture. Problems of moral evaluation (which are not our immediate concern) and problems of social engineering (which are our concern[24]) both take on the additional complexities usually involved in responsible social decisions.

An example of inquiry which implicitly uses the notion of latent function will illustrate the sense in which "paradox"—discrepancy between the apparent, merely manifest, function and the actual, which also includes latent functions—tends to occur as a result of including this concept. Thus, to revert to Veblen's well-known analysis of conspicuous consumption, it is no accident that he has been recognized as a social analyst gifted with an eye for the paradoxical, the ironic, the satiric. For these are frequent, if not inevitable, outcomes of applying the concept of latent function (or its equivalent).

THE PATTERN OF CONSPICUOUS CONSUMPTION. The manifest purpose of buying consumption goods is, of course, the satisfaction of the needs for which these goods are explicitly designed. Thus,

automobiles are obviously intended to provide a certain kind of transportation; candles, to provide light; choice articles of food to provide sustenance; rare art products to provide aesthetic pleasure. Since these products *do* have these uses, it was largely assumed that these encompass the range of socially significant functions. Veblen indeed suggests that this was ordinarily the prevailing view (in the pre-Veblenian era, of course): "The end of acquisition and accumulation is conventionally held to be the consumption of the goods accumulated. ... This is at least felt to be the economically legitimate end of acquisition, *which alone it is incumbent on the theory to take account of.*"[25]

However, says Veblen in effect, as sociologists we must go on to consider the latent functions of acquisition, accumulation and consumption, and these latent functions are remote indeed from the manifest functions. "But, it is only when taken in a sense far removed from its naive meaning [*i.e.* manifest function] that the consumption of goods can be said to afford the incentive from which accumulation invariably proceeds." And among these latent functions, which help explain the persistence and the social location of the pattern of conspicuous consumption, is its symbolization of "pecuniary strength and so of gaining or retaining a good name." The exercise of "punctilious discrimination" in the excellence of "food, drink, shelter, service, ornaments, apparel, amusements" results not merely in direct gratifications derived from the consumption of "superior" to "inferior" articles, but also, and Veblen argues, more importantly, it results in a *heightening or reaffirmation of social status.*

The Veblenian paradox is that people buy expensive goods not so much because they are superior but because they are expensive. For it is the latent equation ("costliness = mark of higher social status") which he singles out in his functional analysis, rather than the manifest equation ("costliness = excellence of the goods"). Not that he denies manifest functions *any* place in buttressing the pattern of conspicuous consumption. These, too, are operative. "What has just been said must not be taken to mean that there are no other incentives to acquisition and accumulation than this desire to excel in pecuniary standing and so gain the esteem and envy of one's fellow men. The desire for added comfort and security from want is present as a motive at every stage ..." Or again: "It would be hazardous to assert that a useful purpose is ever absent from the utility of any article or of any service, however obviously its prime purpose and chief element is conspicuous waste" and derived social esteem.[26] It is only that *these direct, manifest functions do not fully account for the prevailing patterns of consumption. Otherwise put, if the latent functions of status-enhancement or status-reaffirmation were removed from the patterns of conspicuous consumption, these patterns would undergo severe changes of a sort which the "conventional" economist could not foresee.*

In these respects, Veblen's analysis of latent functions departs from the common-sense notion that the end-product of consumption is "of course, the direct satisfaction which it provides": "People eat caviar because they're hungry; buy Cadillacs because they want the best car they can get; have dinner by candlelight because they like the peaceful atmosphere." The common-sense interpretation in terms of selected manifest motives gives way, in Veblen's analysis, to the collateral latent functions which are also, and perhaps more significantly, fulfilled by these practices. To be sure, the Veblenian analysis has, in the last decades, entered so fully into popular thought, that these latent functions are now widely recognized. [This raises the interesting problem of the changes occurring in a prevailing pattern of behavior when its *latent* functions become generally recognized (and are thus no longer latent). There will be no occasion for discussing this important problem in the present publication.]

The discovery of latent functions does not merely render conceptions of the functions served by certain social patterns more precise (as is the case also with studies of manifest functions), but introduces a *qualitatively different increment in the previous state of knowledge.*

Precludes the substitution of naive moral judgments for sociological analysis. Since moral evaluations in a society tend to be largely in terms of the manifest consequences of a practice or code, we should be prepared to find that analysis in terms of latent functions at times runs counter to prevailing moral evaluations. For it does not follow that the latent functions will operate in the same fashion as the manifest consequences which are ordinarily the basis of these judgments. Thus, in large sectors of the American population, the political machine or the "political racket" are judged as unequivocally "bad" and "undesirable." The grounds for such moral judgment vary somewhat, but they consist substantially in pointing out that political machines violate moral codes: political patronage violates the code of selecting personnel on the basis of impersonal qualifications rather than on grounds of party loyalty or contributions to the party war-chest; bossism violates the code that votes should be based on individual appraisal of the qualifications of candidates and of political issues, and not on abiding loyalty to a feudal leader; bribery, and "honest graft" obviously offend the proprieties of property; "protection" for crime clearly violates the law and the mores; and so on.

In view of the manifold respects in which political machines, in varying degrees, run counter to the mores and at times to the law, it becomes pertinent to inquire how they manage to continue in operation. The familiar "explanations" for the continuance of the political machine are not here in point. To be sure, it may well be that if "respectable citizenry" would live up to their political obligations, if the electorate were to be alert and enlightened; if the number of elective officers were substantially reduced from the dozens, even hundreds, which the average voter is now expected to appraise in the course of town, county, state and national elections;

if the electorate were activated by the "wealthy and educated classes without whose participation," as the not-always democratically oriented Bryce put it, "the best-framed government must speedily degenerate";—if these and a plethora of similar changes in political structure were introduced, perhaps the "evils" of the political machine would indeed be exorcized.[27] But it should be noted that these changes are often not introduced, that political machines have had the phoenix-like quality of arising strong and unspoiled from their ashes, that, in short, this structure has exhibited a notable vitality in many areas of American political life.

Proceeding from the functional view, therefore, that we should *ordinarily* (not invariably) expect persistent social patterns and social structures to perform positive functions *which are at the time not adequately fulfilled by other existing patterns and structures,* the thought occurs that perhaps this publicly maligned organization is, *under present conditions,* satisfying basic latent functions.[28] A brief examination of current analyses of this type of structure may also serve to illustrate additional problems of functional analysis.

SOME FUNCTIONS OF THE POLITICAL MACHINE. Without presuming to enter into the variations of detail marking different political machines—a Tweed, Vare, Crump, Flynn, Hague are by no means identical types of bosses—we can briefly examine the functions more or less common to the political machine, as a generic type of social organization. We neither attempt to itemize all the diverse functions of the political machine nor imply that all these functions are similarly fulfilled by each and every machine.

The key structural function of the Boss is to organize, centralize and maintain in good working condition "the scattered fragments of power" which are at present dispersed through our political organization. By this centralized organization of political power, the boss and his apparatus can satisfy the needs of diverse subgroups in the larger community which are not adequately satisfied by legally devised and culturally approved social structures.

To understand the role of bossism and the machine, therefore, we must look at two types of sociological variables: (1) the *structural context* which makes it difficult, if not impossible, for morally approved structures to fulfill essential social functions, thus leaving the door open for political machines (or their structural equivalents) to fulfill these functions and (2) the subgroups whose distinctive needs are left unsatisfied, except for the latent functions which the machine in fact fulfills.[29]

Structural Context: The constitutional framework of American political organization specifically precludes the legal possibility of highly centralized power and, it has been noted, thus "discourages the growth of effective and responsible leadership. The framers of the Constitution, as Woodrow Wilson observed, set up the check and balance system 'to keep government at a sort of mechanical equipoise by means of a standing amicable contest among its several organic parts.' They distrusted power as dangerous to liberty: and therefore they spread it thin and erected barriers against its concentration." This dispersion of power is found not only at the national level but in local areas as well. "As a consequence," Sait goes on to observe, "when *the people or particular groups* among them demanded positive action, no one had adequate authority to act. The machine provided an antidote."[30]

The constitutional dispersion of power not only makes for difficulty of effective decision and action but when action does occur it is defined and hemmed in by legalistic considerations. In consequence, there developed "a much *more human system* of partisan government, whose chief object soon became the circumvention of government by law. ... The lawlessness of the extra-official democracy was merely the counterpoise of the legalism of the official democracy. The lawyer having been permitted to subordinate democracy to the Law, the Boss had to be called in to extricate the victim, which he did after a fashion and for a consideration."[31]

Officially, political power is dispersed. Various well-known expedients were devised for this manifest objective. Not only was there the familiar separation of powers among the several branches of the government but, in some measure, tenure in each office was limited, rotation in office approved. And the scope of power inherent in each office was severely circumscribed. Yet, observes Sait in rigorously functional terms, "Leadership is necessary; and *since* it does not develop readily within the constitutional framework, the Boss provides it in a crude and irresponsible form from the outside."[32]

Put in more generalized terms, *the functional deficiencies of the official structure generate an alternative (unofficial) structure to fulfill existing needs somewhat more effectively.* Whatever its specific historical origins, the political machine persists as an apparatus for satisfying otherwise unfulfilled needs of diverse groups in the population. By turning to a few of these subgroups and their characteristic needs, we shall be led at once to a range of latent functions of the political machine.

Functions of the Political Machine for Diverse Subgroups. It is well known that one source of strength of the political machine derives from its roots in the local community and the neighborhood. The political machine does not regard the electorate as an amorphous, undifferentiated mass of voters. With a keen sociological intuition, the machine recognizes that the voter is a person living in a specific neighborhood, with specific personal problems and personal wants. Public issues are abstract and remote; private problems are extremely concrete and immediate. It is not through the generalized appeal to large public concerns that the machine operates, but through the direct, quasi-feudal relationships between local representatives of the machine and voters in their neighborhood. Elections are won in the precinct.

The machine welds its link with ordinary men and women by elaborate networks of personal relations. Politics is transformed into personal ties. The precinct captain "must be a friend to every man, assuming if he does not feel sympathy with the unfortunate, and utilizing in his good works the resources which the boss puts at his disposal."[33] The precinct captain is forever a friend in need. In our prevailingly impersonal society, the machine, through its local agents, fulfills the important social *function of humanizing and personalizing all manner of assistance* to those in need. Foodbaskets and jobs, legal and extra-legal advice, setting to rights minor scrapes with the law, helping the bright poor boy to a political scholarship in a local college, looking after the bereaved—the whole range of crises when a feller needs a friend, and, above all, a friend who knows the score and who can do something about it,—all these find the ever-helpful precinct captain available in the pinch.

To assess this function of the political machine adequately, it is important to note not only that aid *is* provided but *the manner in which it is provided.* After all, other agencies do exist for dispensing such assistance. Welfare agencies, settlement houses, legal aid clinics, medical aid in free hospitals, public relief departments, immigration authorities—these and a multitude of other organizations are available to provide the most varied types of assistance. But in contrast to the professional techniques of the welfare worker which may typically represent in the mind of the recipient the cold, bureaucratic dispensation of limited aid following upon detailed investigation of *legal* claims to aid of the "client" are the unprofessional techniques of the precinct captain who asks no questions, exacts no compliance with legal rules of eligibility and does not "snoop" into private affairs.[34]

For many, the loss of "self-respect" is too high a price for legalized assistance. In contrast to the gulf between the settlement house workers who so often come from a different social class, educational background and ethnic group, the precinct worker is "just one of us," who understands what it's all about. The condescending lady bountiful can hardly compete with the understanding friend in need. In *this struggle between alternative structures for fulfilling the nominally same function* of providing aid and support to those who need it, it is clearly the machine politician who is better integrated with the groups which he serves than the impersonal, professionalized, socially distant and legally constrained welfare worker. And since the politician can at times influence and manipulate the official organizations for the dispensation of assistance, whereas the welfare worker has practically no influence on the political machine, this only adds to his greater effectiveness. More colloquially and also, perhaps, more incisively, it was the Boston ward-leader, Martin Lomasny, who described this essential function to the curious Lincoln Steffens: "I think," said Lomasny, "that there's got to be in every ward somebody that any bloke can come to— no matter what he's done—and get help. *Help, you understand; none of your law and justice, but help.*"[35]

The "deprived classes," then, constitute one subgroup for whom the political machine satisfies wants not adequately satisfied in the same fashion by the legitimate social structure.

For a second subgroup, that of business (primarily "big" business but also "small"), the political boss serves the function of providing those political privileges which entail immediate economic gains. Business corporations, among which the public utilities (railroads, local transportation and electric light companies, communications corporations) are simply the most conspicuous in this regard, seek special political dispensations which will enable them to stabilize their situation and to near their objective of maximizing profits. Interestingly enough, corporations often want to avoid a chaos of uncontrolled competition. They want the greater security of an economic czar who controls, regulates and organizes competition, providing that this czar is not a public official with his decisions subject to public scrutiny and public control. (The latter would be "government control," and hence taboo.) The political boss fulfills these requirements admirably.

Examined for a moment apart from any moral considerations, the political apparatus operated by the Boss is effectively designed to perform these functions with a minimum of inefficiency. Holding the strings of diverse governmental divisions, bureaus and agencies in his competent hands, the Boss rationalizes the relations between public and private business. He serves as the business community's ambassador in the otherwise alien (and sometimes unfriendly) realm of government. And, in strict business-like terms, he is well-paid for his economic services to his respectable business clients. In an article entitled, "An Apology to Graft," Lincoln Steffens suggested that "Our economic system, which held up riches, power and acclaim as prizes to men bold enough and able enough to buy corruptly timber, mines, oil fields and franchises and 'get away with it,' was at fault."[36] And, in a conference with a hundred or so of Los Angeles business leaders, he described a fact well known to all of them: the Boss and his machine were an *integral part* of the organization of the economy. "You cannot build or operate a railroad, or a street railway, gas, water, or power company, develop and operate a mine, or get forests and cut timber on a large scale, or run any privileged business, without corrupting or joining in the corruption of the government. You tell me privately that you must, and here I am telling you semi-publicly that you must. And that is so all over the country. And that means that we have an organization of society in which, *for some reason,* you and your kind, the ablest, most intelligent, most imaginative, daring, and resourceful leaders of society, are and must be against society and its laws and its all-around growth."[37]

Since the demand for the services of special privileges are built into the structure of the society, the Boss fulfills diverse functions for this second subgroup of business-seeking-privilege. These "needs" of business, as presently constituted, are not adequately provided for by conventional and culturally approved social structures; consequently, the extra-legal but more-or-less efficient organization of the political machine comes to provide these services. To adopt an *exclusively* moral attitude toward the "corrupt political machine" is to lose sight of the very structural conditions which generate the "evil" that is so bitterly attacked. To adopt a functional outlook is to provide not an apologia for the political machine but a more solid basis for modifying or eliminating the machine, *providing* specific structural arrangements are introduced either for eliminating these effective demands of the business community or, if that is the objective, of satisfying these demands through alternative means.

A third set of distinctive functions fulfilled by the political machine for a special subgroup is that of providing alternative channels of social mobility for those otherwise excluded from the more conventional avenues for personal "advancement." Both the sources of this special "need" (for social mobility) and the respect in which the political machine comes to help satisfy this need can be understood by examining the structure of the larger culture and society. As is well known, the American culture lays enormous emphasis on money and power as a "success" goal legitimate for all members of the society. By no means alone in our inventory of cultural goals, it still remains among the most heavily endowed with positive affect and value. However, certain subgroups and certain ecological areas are notable for the relative absence of opportunity for achieving these (monetary and power) types of success. They constitute, in short, sub-populations where "the cultural emphasis upon pecuniary success has been absorbed, but where there is *little access to conventional and legitimate* means for attaining such success. The conventional occupational opportunities of persons in (such areas) are almost completely limited to manual labor. Given our cultural stigmatization of manual labor,[38] and its correlate, the prestige of white-collar work, it is clear that the result is a tendency to achieve these culturally approved objectives *through whatever means are possible*. These people are on the one hand, "asked to orient their conduct toward

the prospect of accumulating wealth [and power] and, on the other, they are largely denied effective opportunities to do so institutionally."

It is within this context of social structure that the political machine fulfills the basic function of providing avenues of social mobility for the otherwise disadvantaged. Within this context, even the corrupt political machine and the racket "represent the triumph of amoral intelligence over morally prescribed 'failure' when the channels of vertical mobility are closed or narrowed *in a society which places a high premium on economic affluence, [power] and social ascent for all its members.*"[39] As one sociologist has noted on the basis of several years of close observation in a slum area:

The sociologist who dismisses racket and political organizations as deviations from desirable standards thereby neglects some of the major elements of slum life. ... *He does not discover the functions they perform for the members* [of the groupings in the slum]. The Irish and later immigrant peoples have had the greatest difficulty in finding places for themselves in our urban social and economic structure. Does anyone believe that the immigrants and their children could have achieved their present degree of social mobility without gaining control of the political organization of some of our largest cities? The same is true of the racket organization. *Politics and the rackets have furnished an important means of social mobility for individuals, who, because of ethnic background and low class position,* are blocked from advancement in the "respectable" channels.[40]

This, then, represents a third type of function performed for a distinctive subgroup. This function, it may be noted in passing, is fulfilled by the *sheer* existence and operation of the political machine, for it is in the machine itself that these individuals and subgroups find their culturally induced needs more or less satisfied. It refers to the services which the political apparatus provides for its own personnel. But seen in the wider social context we have set forth, it no longer appears as *merely* a means of self-aggrandizement for profit-hungry and power-hungry *individuals,* but as an organized provision for *subgroups* otherwise excluded from or handicapped in the race for "getting ahead."

Just as the political machine performs services for "legitimate" business, so it operates to perform not dissimilar services for "illegitimate" business: vice, crime and rackets. Once again, the basic sociological role of the machine in this respect can be more fully appreciated only if one temporarily abandons attitudes of moral indignation, to examine in all moral innocence the actual workings of the organization. In this light, it at once appears that the subgroup of the professional criminal, racketeer or gambler has basic similarities of organization, demands and operation to the subgroup of the industrialist, man of business or speculator. If there is a Lumber King or an Oil King, there is also a Vice King or a Racket King. If expansive legitimate business organizes administrative and financial syndicates to "rationalize" and to "integrate" diverse areas of production and business enterprise, so expansive rackets and crime organize syndicates to bring order to the otherwise chaotic areas of production of illicit goods and services. If legitimate business regards the proliferation of small business enterprises as wasteful and inefficient, substituting, for example, the giant chain stores for hundreds of corner groceries, so illegitimate business adopts the same businesslike attitude and syndicates crime and vice.

Finally, and in many respects, most important, is the basic similarity, if not near-identity, of the economic role of "legitimate" business and of "illegitimate" business. *Both are in some degree concerned with the provision of goods and services for which there is an economic demand.* Morals aside, they are both business, industrial and professional enterprises, dispensing goods and services which some people want, for which there is a market in which goods and services are transformed into commodities. And, in a prevalently market society, we should expect appropriate enterprises to arise whenever there is a market demand for certain goods or services.

As is well known, vice, crime and the rackets *are* "big business." Consider only that there have been estimated to be about 500,000 professional prostitutes in the United States of 1950, and compare this with the approximately 200,000 physicians and 350,000 professional registered nurses. It is difficult to estimate which have the larger clientele: the professional men and women of medicine or the professional men and women of vice. It is, of course, difficult to estimate the economic assets, income, profits and dividends of illicit gambling in this country and to compare it with the economic assets, income, profits and dividends of, say, the shoe industry, but it is altogether possible that the two industries are about on a par. No precise figures exist on the annual expenditures on illicit narcotics, and it is probable that these are less than the expenditures on candy, but it is also probable that they are larger than the expenditure on books.

It takes but a moment's thought to recognize that, *in strictly economic terms,* there is no relevant difference between the provision of licit and of illicit goods and services. The liquor traffic illustrates this perfectly. It would be peculiar to argue that prior to 1920 (when the 18th amendment became effective), the provision of liquor constituted an economic service, that from 1920 to 1933, its production and sale no longer constituted an economic service dispensed in a market, and that from 1934 to the present, it once again took on a serviceable aspect. Or, it would be *economically* (not morally) absurd to suggest that the sale of bootlegged liquor in the dry state of Kansas is less a response to a market demand than the sale of publicly manufactured liquor in the neighboring wet state of Missouri. Examples of this sort can of course be multiplied many times over. Can it be held that in European countries, with registered and legalized prostitution, the prostitute contributes an economic service, whereas in this country, lacking legal sanction, the prostitute provides no such service? Or that the professional abortionist is in the economic market where he has approved legal status and that he is out of the economic market where he is legally taboo? Or that gambling satisfies a specific demand for entertainment in Nevada, where it constitutes the largest business enterprise of the larger cities in the state, but that it differs essentially in this respect from motion pictures in the neighboring state of California?[41]

The failure to recognize that these businesses are only *morally* and not *economically* distinguishable from "legitimate" businesses has led to badly scrambled analysis. Once the economic identity of the two is recognized, we may anticipate that if the political machine performs functions for "legitimate big business" it will be all the more likely to perform not dissimilar functions for "illegitimate big business." And, of course, such is often the case.

The distinctive function of the political machine for their criminal, vice and racket clientele is to enable them to operate in satisfying the economic demands of a large market without due interference from the government. Just as big business may contribute funds to the political party war-chest to ensure a minimum of governmental interference, so with big rackets and big crime. In both instances, the political machine can, in varying degrees, provide "protection." In both instances, many features of the structural context are identical: (1) market demands for goods and services; (2) the operators' concern with maximizing gains from their enterprises; (3) the need for partial control of government which might otherwise interfere with these activities of businessmen; (4) the need for an efficient, powerful and centralized agency to provide an effective liaison of "business" with government.

Without assuming that the foregoing pages exhaust either the range of functions or the range of subgroups served by the political machine, we can at least see that *it presently fulfills some functions for these diverse subgroups which are not adequately fulfilled by culturally approved or more conventional structures.*

Several additional implications of the functional analysis of the political machine can be mentioned here only in passing, although they obviously require to be developed at length. First, the foregoing analysis has direct implications for *social engineering*. It helps explain why the periodic efforts at "political reform," "turning the rascals out" and "cleaning political house" are typically (though not necessarily) short-lived and ineffectual. It exemplifies a basic theorem: *any attempt to eliminate an existing social structure without providing adequate alternative structures for fulfilling the functions previously fulfilled by the abolished organization is doomed to failure.* (Needless to say, this theorem has much wider bearing than the one instance of the political machine.) When "political reform" confines itself to the manifest task of "turning the rascals out," it is engaging in little more than sociological magic. The reform may for a time bring new figures into the political limelight; it may serve the casual social function of re-assuring the electorate that the moral virtues remain intact and will ultimately triumph; it may actually effect a turnover in the personnel of the political machine; it may even, for a time, so curb the activities of the machine as to leave unsatisfied the many needs it has previously fulfilled. But, inevitably, unless the reform also involves a "re-forming" of the social and political structure such that the existing needs are satisfied by alternative structures or unless it involves a change which eliminates these needs altogether, the political machine will return to its integral place in the social scheme of things. *To seek social change, without due recognition of the manifest and latent functions performed by the social organization undergoing change, is to indulge in social ritual rather than social engineering.* The concepts of manifest and latent functions (or their equivalents) are indispensable elements in the theoretic repertoire of the social engineer. In this crucial sense, these concepts are not "merely" theoretical (in the abusive sense of the term), but are eminently practical. In the deliberate enactment of social change, they can be ignored only at the price of considerably heightening the risk of failure.

A second implication of this analysis of the political machine also has a bearing upon areas wider than the one we have considered. The paradox has often been noted that the supporters of the political machine include both the "respectable" business class elements who are, of course, opposed to the criminal or racketeer and the distinctly "unrespectable" elements of the underworld. And, at first appearance, this is cited as an instance of very strange bedfellows. The learned judge is not infrequently called upon to sentence the very racketeer beside whom he sat the night before at an informal dinner of the political bigwigs. The district attorney jostles the exonerated convict on his way to the back room where the Boss has called a meeting. The big business man may complain almost as bitterly as the big racketeer about the "extortionate" contributions to the party fund demanded by the Boss. Social opposites meet—in the smoke-filled room of the successful politician.

In the light of a functional analysis all this of course no longer seems paradoxical. Since the machine serves both the businessman and the criminal man, the two seemingly antipodal groups intersect. This points to a more general theorem: *the social functions of an organization help determine the structure (including the recruitment of personnel involved in the structure), just as the structure helps determine the effectiveness with which the functions are fulfilled.* In terms of social status, the business group and the criminal group are indeed poles apart. But status does not fully determine behavior and the inter-relations between groups. Functions modify these relations. Given their distinctive needs, the several subgroups in the large society are "integrated," whatever their personal desires or intentions, by the centralizing structure which serves these several needs. In a phrase with many implications which require further study, *structure affects function and function affects structure.*

CONCLUDING REMARKS

This review of some salient considerations in structural and functional analysis has done little more than indicate some of the principal problems and potentialities of this mode of sociological interpretation. Each of the items codified in the paradigm require sustained theoretic clarification and cumulative empirical research. But it is clear that in functional theory, stripped of those traditional postulates which have fenced it in and often made it little more than a latter-day rationalization of existing practices, sociology has one beginning of a systematic and empirically relevant mode of analysis. It is hoped that the direction here indicated will suggest the feasibility and the desirability of further codification of functional analysis. In due course each section of the paradigm will be elaborated into a documented, analyzed and codified chapter in the history of functional analysis.

NOTES

1. References to some of the more significant among these earlier appearances of the distinction will be found in Merton, "Unanticipated consequences …," *op. cit.*
2. George H. Mead, "The psychology of punitive justice," *American Journal of Sociology,* 1918, 23, 577–602, esp. 591.
3. As suggested earlier in this chapter, Durkheim adopted a functional orientation throughout his work, and he operates, albeit often without explicit notice, with concepts equivalent to that of latent function in all of his researches. The reference in the text at this point is to his "Deux lois de l'évolution penale," *L'année sociologique,* 1899–1900, 4, 55–95, as well as to his *Division of Labor in Society* (Glencoe, Illinois: The Free Press, 1947).
4. This one of his many such observations is of course from W. G. Sumner's *Folkways,* (Boston: Ginn & Co., 1906), 3. His collaborator, Albert G. Keller retained the distinction in his own writings; see, for example, his *Social Evolution,* (New York: Macmillan, 1927), at 93–95.
5. This is advisedly drawn from one of MacIver's earlier works, *Community,* (London: Macmillan, 1915). The distinction takes on greater importance in his later writings, becoming a major element in his *Social Causation,* (Boston: Ginn & Co., 1942), esp. at 314–321, and informs the greater part of his *The More Perfect Union,* (New York: Macmillan, 1948).

6. The single excerpt quoted in the text is one of scores which have led to *The Polish Peasant in Europe and America* being deservedly described as a "sociological classic." See pages 1426–7 and 1523 ff. As will be noted later in this chapter, the insights and conceptual distinctions contained in this one passage, and there are many others like it in point of richness of content, were forgotten or never noticed by those industrial sociologists who recently came to develop the notion of "formal organization" in industry.

7. Merton, "Intermarriage and the social structure," *op. cit.*

8. Kingsley Davis, "A conceptual analysis of stratification," *American Sociological Review,* 1942, 7, 309–321.

9. Thonier, *op. cit.*, esp. at 165.

10. A. K. Davis, *Thorstein Veblen's Social Theory,* Harvard Ph.D. dissertation, 1941 and "Veblen on the decline of the Protestant Ethic," *Social Forces,* 1944, 22, 282–86; Louis Schneider, *The Freudian Psychology and Veblen's Social Theory*, New York: King's Crown Press, 1948), esp. Chapter 2.

11. A. K. Davis, "Some sources of American hostility to Russia," *American Journal of Sociology,* 1947, 53, 174–183.

12. Talcott Parsons, "Propaganda and social control," in his *Essays in Sociological Theory.*

13. Clyde Kluckhohn, "Bronislaw Malinowski, 1884–1942," *Journal of American Folklore,* 1943, 56, 208–219.

14. Clyde Kluckhohn, *Navaho Witchcraft, op. cit.,* esp. at 46–47 and ff.

15. Merton, Chapter XIV of this volume.

16. Bernard Barber and L. S. Lobel, "'Fashion' in women's clothes and the American social system," *Social Forces,* 1952, 31, 124–131.

17. O. H. Mowrer and C. Kluckhohn, "Dynamic theory of personality," in J. M. Hunt, ed., *Personality and the Behavior Disorders,* (New York: Ronald Press, 1944), 1, 69–135, esp. at 72.

18. Marie Jahoda and S. W. Cook, "Security measures and freedom of thought: an exploratory study of the impact of loyalty and security programs," *Yale Law Journal,* 1952, 61, 296–333.

19. Philip Selznick, *TVA and the Grass Roots* (University of California Press, 1949); A. W. Gouldner, *Patterns of Industrial Bureaucracy* (Glencoe, Illinois: The Free Press, 1954); P. M. Blau, *The Dynamics of Bureaucracy* (University of Chicago Press, 1955); A. K. Davis,

"Bureaucratic patterns in Navy officer corps," *Social Forces* 1948, 27, 142–153.

20. For a brief illustration of this general proposition, see Robert K. Merton, Marjorie Fiske and Alberta Curtis, *Mass Persuasion,* (New York: Harper, 1946), 185–189; Jahoda and Cook, *op. cit.*

21. This is cited as a case study of how *an elaborate research was wholly changed in theoretic orientation and in the character of its research findings by the introduction of a concept approximating the concept of latent function.* Selection of the case for this purpose does not, of course, imply full acceptance of the *interpretations* which the authors give their findings. Among the several volumes reporting the Western Electric research, see particularly F. J. Roethlisberger and W. J. Dickson, *Management and the Worker,* (Harvard University Press, 1939).

22. Elton Mayo, *The Social Problems of an Industrial Civilization,* (Harvard University Press, 1945), 70.

23. Edward Shils, *The Present State of American Sociology,* (Glencoe, Illinois The Free Press, 1948), 42 [italics supplied].

24. This is not to deny that social engineering has direct moral implications or that technique and morality are inescapably intertwined, but I do not intend to deal with this range of problems in the present chapter. For some discussion of these problems see chapters VIII, XVII and XIX; also Merton, Fiske and Curtis, *Mass Persuasion,* Chapter 7.

25. Veblen, *Theory of Leisure Class, op. cit.*, p. 25.

26. *Ibid.*, 32, 101. It will be noted throughout that Veblen is given to loose terminology. In the marked passages (and repeatedly elsewhere) he uses "incentive," "desire," "purpose," and "function" interchangeably. Since the context usually makes clear the denotation of these terms, no great harm is done. But it is clear that the expressed purposes of conformity to a culture pattern are by no means identical with the latent functions of the conformity. Veblen occasionally recognizes this. For example, "In strict accuracy nothing should be included under the head of conspicuous waste but such expenditure as is incurred on the ground of an invidious pecuniary comparison. But in order to bring any given item or element in under this head *it is not necessary that it should be recognized as waste in this sense by the person incurring the expenditure.*" (*Ibid.* 99; italics supplied). *Cf.* A. K. Davis, "Veblen on the decline of the Protestant Ethic," *op. cit.*

27. These "explanations" are "causal" in design. They profess to indicate the social conditions under which

political machines come into being. In so far as they are empirically confirmed, these explanations of course add to our knowledge concerning the problem: how is it that political machines operate in certain areas and not in others? How do they manage to continue? *But these causal accounts are not sufficient.* The functional consequences of the machine, as we shall see, go far toward supplementing the causal interpretation.

28. I trust it is superfluous to add that this hypothesis is not "in support of the political machine." The question whether the dysfunctions of the machine outweigh its functions, the question whether alternative structures are not available which may fulfill its functions without necessarily entailing its social dysfunctions, still remain to be considered at an appropriate point. We are here concerned with documenting the statement that moral judgments based *entirely* on an appraisal of manifest functions of a social structure are "unrealistic" in the strict sense, *i.e.*, they do not take into account other actual consequences of that structure, consequences which may provide basic social support for the structure. As will be indicated later, "social reforms" or "social engineering" which ignore latent functions do so on pain of suffering acute disappointments and boomerang effects.

29. Again, as with preceding cases, we shall not consider the possible dysfunctions of the political machine.

30. Edward M. Sait, "Machine, Political," *Encyclopedia of the Social Sciences*, IX, 658 b [italics supplied]; *cf.* A. F. Bentley, *The Process of Government* (Chicago, 1908), Chap. 2.

31. Herbert Croly, *Progressive Democracy*, (New York, 1914), p. 254, cited by Sait, *op. cit.*, 658 b.

32. Sait, *op. cit.*, 659 a. [italics supplied].

33. *Ibid.*, 659 a.

34. Much the same contrast with official welfare policy is found in Harry Hopkins' open-handed and non-political distribution of unemployment relief in New York State under the governorship of Franklin Delano Roosevelt. As Sherwood reports: "Hopkins was harshly criticized for these irregular activities by the established welfare agencies, which claimed it was 'unprofessional conduct' to hand out work tickets without thorough investigation of each applicant, his own or his family's financial resources and probably his religious affiliations. 'Harry told the agency to go to hell,' said [Hopkins' associate, Dr. Jacob A.] Goldberg." Robert E. Sherwood, *Roosevelt*

and Hopkins, An Intimate History, (New York: Harper, 1948), 30.

35. *The Autobiography of Lincoln Steffens,* (Chautauqua, New York: Chautauqua Press, 1931), 618. Deriving largely from Steffens, as he says, F. Stuart Chapin sets forth these functions of the political machine with great clarity. See his *Contemporary American Institutions*, (New York: Harper, 1934), 40–54.

36. *Autobiography of Lincoln Steffens,* 570.

37. *Ibid.*, 572–3 [italics supplied]. This helps explain, as Steffens noted after Police Commissioner Theodore Roosevelt, "the prominence and respectability of the men and women who intercede for crooks" when these have been apprehended in a periodic effort to "clean up the political machine." *Cf.* Steffens, 371, and *passim*.

38. See the National Opinion Research Center survey of evaluation of occupations which firmly documents the general impression that the manual occupations rate very low indeed in the social scale of values, *even among those who are themselves engaged in manual labor.* Consider this latter point in its full implications. In effect, the cultural and social structure exacts the values of pecuniary and power success even among those who find themselves confined to the stigmatized manual occupations. Against this background, consider the powerful motivation for achieving this type of "success" by any means whatsoever. A garbage-collector who joins with other Americans in the view that the garbage-collector is "the lowest of the low" occupations can scarcely have a self-image which is pleasing to him; he is in a "pariah" occupation in the very society where he is assured that "all who have genuine merit can get ahead." Add to this, his occasional recognition that "he didn't have the same chance as others, no matter what they say," and one perceives the enormous psychological pressure upon him for "evening up the score" by finding some means, whether strictly legal or not, for moving ahead. All this provides the structural and derivatively psychological background for the "socially induced need" in *some* groups to find some accessible avenue for social mobility.

39. Merton, "Social structure and anomie," Chapter VI of this volume.

40. William F. Whyte, "Social organization in the slums," *American Sociological Review*, Feb. 1943, 8, 34–39 (italics supplied). Thus, the political machine and the racket represent a special case of the type of organizational adjustment to the conditions described in

Chapter VI. It represents, note, an *organizational* adjustment: definite structures arise and operate to reduce somewhat the acute tensions and problems of individuals caught up in the described conflict between the "cultural accent on success-for-all" and the "socially structured fact of unequal opportunities for success." As Chapter VI indicates, other types of *individual* "adjustment" are possible: lone-wolf crime, psychopathological states, rebellion, retreat by abandoning the culturally approved goals, etc. Likewise, other types of *organizational adjustment* sometimes occur; the racket or the political machine are not *alone* available as organized means for meeting this socially induced problem. Participation in revolutionary organizations, for example, can be seen within this context, as an alternative mode of organizational adjustment. All this bears theoretic notice here, since we might otherwise overlook the basic functional concepts of functional substitutes and functional equivalents, which are to be discussed at length in a subsequent publication.

41. Perhaps the most perceptive statement of this view has been made by Hawkins and Waller. "The prostitute, the pimp, the peddler of dope, the operator of the gambling hall, the vendor of obscene pictures, the bootlegger, the abortionist, all are productive, all produce services or goods which people desire and for which they are willing to pay. It happens that society has put these goods and services under the ban, but people go on producing them and people go on consuming them, and an act of the legislature does not make them any less a part of the economic system." "Critical notes on the cost of crime," *Journal of Criminal Law and Criminology*, 1936, 26, 679–94, at 684.

COMPANION WEBSITE

1. Go online to Write Out Loud about your own thoughts on how unintended consequences emerge in everyday life.
2. Log on to the Mid-Twentieth-Century American Theory Profile Page to learn more about structural-functionalism and its import for social theory today.
3. Check out more readings in the structural-functionalist tradition in the *Emergence Through Convergence* Supplementary Sources.

6

Studies in Ethnomethodology

Harold Garfinkel

THE FOLLOWING STUDIES SEEK to treat practical activities, practical circumstances, and practical sociological reasoning as topics of empirical study, and by paying to the most commonplace activities of daily life the attention usually accorded extraordinary events, seek to learn about them as phenomena in their own right. Their central recommendation is that the activities whereby members produce and manage settings of organized everyday affairs are identical with members' procedures for making those settings "account-able." The "reflexive," or "incarnate" character of accounting practices and accounts makes up the crux of that recommendation. When I speak of accountable my interests are directed to such matters as the following. I mean observable-and-reportable, *i.e.* available to members as situated practices of looking-and-telling. I mean, too, that such practices consist of an endless, on-going, contingent accomplishment; that they are carried on under the auspices of, and are made to happen as events in, the same ordinary affairs that in organizing they describe; that the practices are done by parties to those settings whose skill with, knowledge of, and entitlement to the detailed work of that accomplishment—whose competence—they obstinately depend upon, recognize, use, and take for granted; and *that* they take their competence for granted itself furnishes parties with a setting's distinguishing and particular features, and of course it furnishes them as well as resources, troubles, projects, and the rest.

Some structurally equivocal features of the methods and results by persons doing sociology, lay and professional, of making practical activities observable were epitomized by Helmer and Rescher.[1] When members' accounts of everyday activities are used as prescriptions with which to locate, to identify, to analyze, to classify, to make recognizable, or to find one's way around in comparable occasions, the prescriptions, they observe, are law-like, spatio-temporally restricted, and "loose." By "loose" is meant that though they are intendedly conditional in their logical form, "the nature of the conditions is such that they can often not be spelled out completely or fully." The authors cite as an example a statement about sailing fleet tactics in the 18th century. They point out the statement carries as a test condition reference to the state of naval ordnance.

> In elaborating conditions (under which such a statement would hold) the historian delineates what is typical of the place and period. The full implications of such reference may be vast and inexhaustible; for instance … ordnance soon ramifies via metal working technology into metallurgy, mining, etc. Thus, the conditions which are operative in the formulation of an historical law may only be indicated in a general way, and are not necessarily, indeed, in most cases cannot be expected to be exhaustively articulated. This characteristic of such laws is here designed as *looseness*.…

A consequence of the looseness of historical laws is that they are not universal, but merely quasi-general in that they admit of exceptions. Since the conditions delimiting the area of application of the law are often not exhaustively articulated, a supposed violation of the law may be explicable by showing that a legitimate, but as yet unformulated, precondition of the law's applicability is not fulfilled in the case under consideration.

Consider that this holds in every *particular* case, and holds not by reason of the meaning of "quasi-law," but because of investigators' actual, particular practices.

Further, Helmer and Rescher point out,

The laws may be taken to contain a tacit caveat of the "usually" or "other things being equal" type. An historical law is thus not strictly universal in that it must be taken as applicable to all cases falling within the scope of its explicitly formulated or formulable conditions; rather, it may be thought to formulate relationships which obtain generally, or better, which obtain "as a rule."

Such a "law" we will term *quasi-law*. In order for the law to be valid it is not necessary that no apparent exceptions occur. It is only necessary that, if an apparent exception should occur, an adequate explanation be forthcoming, an explanation demonstrating the exceptional characteristic of the case in hand by establishing the violation of an appropriate, if hitherto unformulated, condition of the law's applicability.

These and other features can be cited for the cogency with which they describe members' accounting practices. Thus: (1) Whenever a member is required to demonstrate that an account analyzes an actual situation, he invariably makes use of the practices of "et cetera," "unless," and "let it pass" to demonstrate the rationality of his achievement. (2) The definite and sensible character of the matter that is being reported is settled by an assignment that reporter and auditor make to each other that each will have furnished whatever unstated understandings are required. Much therefore of what is actually reported is not mentioned. (3) Over the time for their delivery accounts are apt to require that "auditors" be willing to wait for what will have been said in order that the present significance of what has been said will have become clear. (4) Like conversations, reputations, and careers, the particulars of accounts are built up step by step over the actual uses of and references to them. (5) An account's materials are apt to depend heavily for sense upon their serial placement, upon their relevance to the auditor's projects, or upon the developing course of the organizational occasions of their use.

In short, *recognizable* sense, or fact, or methodic character, or impersonality, or objectivity of accounts are not independent of the socially organized occasions of their use. Their rational features *consist* of what members do with, what they "make of" the accounts in the socially organized actual occasions of their use. Members' accounts are reflexively and essentially tied for their rational features to the socially organized occasions of their use for they are *features* of the socially organized occasions of their use.

That tie establishes the central topic of our studies: the rational accountability of practical actions as an ongoing, practical accomplishment. I want to specify the topic by reviewing three of its constituent, problematic phenomena. Wherever studies of practical action and practical reasoning are concerned, these consist of the following: (1) the unsatisfied programmatic distinction between and substitutability of objective (context free) for indexical expressions; (2) the "uninteresting" essential reflexivity of accounts of practical actions; and (3) the analyzability of actions-in-context as a practical accomplishment.

[...]

THE PROBLEM

For Kant the moral order "within" was an awesome mystery; for sociologists the moral order "without" is a technical mystery. From the point of view of sociological theory the moral order consists of the rule governed activities of everyday life. A society's members encounter and know the moral order as perceivedly normal courses of action—familiar scenes of everyday affairs, the world of daily life known in common with others and with others taken for granted.

They refer to this world as the "natural facts of life" which, for members, are through and through moral facts of life. For members not only are matters so about familiar scenes, but they are so because it is morally right or wrong that they are so. Familiar scenes of everyday activities, treated by members as the "natural facts of life," are massive facts of the members' daily existence both as a real world and as the product of activities in a real world. They furnish the "fix," the "this is it" to which the waking state returns one, and are the points of departure and return for every modification of the world of daily life that is achieved in play, dreaming, trance, theater, scientific theorizing, or high ceremony.

In every discipline, humanistic or scientific, the familiar common sense world of everyday life is a matter of abiding interest. In the social sciences, and in sociology particularly, it is a matter of essential preoccupation. It makes up sociology's problematic subject matter, enters the very constitution of the sociological attitude, and exercises an odd and obstinate sovereignty over sociologists' claims to adequate explanation.

Despite the topic's centrality, an immense literature contains little data and few methods with which the essential features of socially recognized "familiar scenes" may be detected and related to dimensions of social organization. Although sociologists take socially structured scenes of everyday life as a point of departure they rarely see,[2] as a task of sociological inquiry in its own right, the general question of how any such common sense world is possible. Instead, the possibility of the everyday world is either settled by theoretical representation or merely assumed. As a topic and methodological ground for sociological inquiries, the definition of the common sense world of everyday life, though it is appropriately a project of sociological inquiry, has been neglected. My purposes in this paper are to demonstrate the essential relevance, to sociological inquiries, of a concern for common sense activities as a topic of inquiry in its own right and, by reporting a series of studies, to urge its "rediscovery."

MAKING COMMONPLACE SCENES VISIBLE

In accounting for the stable features of everyday activities sociologists commonly select familiar settings such as familial households or work places and ask for the variables that contribute to their stable features. Just as commonly, one set of considerations are unexamined: the socially standardized and standardizing, "seen but unnoticed," expected, background features of everyday scenes. The member of the society uses background expectancies as a scheme of interpretation. With their use actual appearances are for him recognizable and intelligible as the appearances-of-familiar-events. Demonstrably he is responsive to this background, while at the same time he is at a loss to tell us specifically of what the expectancies consist. When we ask him about them he has little or nothing to say.

For these background expectancies to come into view one must either be a stranger to the "life as usual" character of everyday scenes, or become estranged from them. As Alfred Schutz pointed out, a "special motive" is required to make them problematic. In the sociologists' case this "special motive" consists in the programmatic task of treating a societal member's practical circumstances, which include from the member's point of view the morally necessary character of many of its background features, as matters of theoretic interest.

The seen but unnoticed backgrounds of everyday activities are made visible and are described from a perspective in which persons live out the lives they do, have the children they do, feel the feelings, think the thoughts, enter the relationships they do, all in order to permit the sociologist to solve his theoretical problems.

Almost alone among sociological theorists, the late Alfred Schutz, in a series of classical studies[3] of the constitutive phenomenology of the world of everyday life, described many of these seen but unnoticed background expectancies. He called them the "attitude of daily life." He referred to their scenic attributions as the "world known in common and taken for granted." Schutz' fundamental work makes it possible to pursue further the tasks of clarifying their nature and operation, of relating them to the processes of concerted actions, and assigning them their place in an empirically imaginable society.

The studies reported in this paper attempt to detect some expectancies that lend commonplace scenes their familiar, life-as-usual character, and to relate these to the stable social structures of everyday activities. Procedurally it is my preference to start with familiar scenes and ask what can be done to make trouble. The operations that one would have to perform in order to multiply the senseless features of perceived environments; to produce and sustain bewilderment, consternation, and confusion; to produce the socially structured affects of anxiety, shame, guilt, and indignation; and to produce disorganized interaction should tell us something about how the structures of everyday activities are ordinarily and routinely produced and maintained.[4]

A word of reservation. Despite their procedural emphasis, my studies are not properly speaking experimental. They are demonstrations, designed, in Herbert Spiegelberg's phrase, as "aids to a sluggish imagination." I have found that they produce reflections through which the strangeness of an obstinately familiar world can be detected.

SOME ESSENTIAL FEATURES OF COMMON UNDERSTANDINGS

Various considerations dictate that common understandings cannot possibly consist of a measured amount of shared agreement among persons on certain topics. Even if the topics are limited in number and scope and every practical difficulty of assessment is forgiven, the notion that we are dealing with an amount of shared agreement remains essentially incorrect. This may be demonstrated as follows.

Students were asked to report common conversations by writing on the left side of a sheet what the parties actually said and on the right side what they and their partners understood that they were talking about. A student reported the following colloquy between himself and his wife [see p. 89].

An examination of the colloquy reveals the following. (a) There were many matters that the partners understood they were talking about that they did not mention. (b) Many matters that the partners understood were understood on the basis not only of what was actually said but what was left unspoken. (c) Many matters were understood through a process of attending to the temporal series of utterances as documentary evidences of a developing conversation rather than as a string of terms. (d) Matters that the two understood in common were understood only in and through a course of understanding work that consisted of treating an actual linguistic event as "the document of," as "pointing to," as standing on behalf of an underlying pattern of matters that each already supposed to be the matters that the person, by his speaking, could be telling the other about. The underlying pattern was not only derived from a course of individual documentary evidences but the documentary evidences in their turn were interpreted on the basis of "what was known" and anticipatorily knowable about the underlying patterns.[5] Each was used to elaborate the other.

HUSBAND:	Dana succeeded in putting a penny in a parking meter today without being picked up.	This afternoon as I was bringing Dana, our four-year-old son, home from the nursery school, he succeeded in reaching high enough to put a penny in a parking meter when we parked in a meter parking zone, whereas before he has always had to be picked up to reach that high.
WIFE:	Did you take him to the record store?	Since he put a penny in a meter that means that you stopped while he was with you. I know that you stopped at the record store either on the way to get him or on the way back. Was it on the way back, so that he was with you or did you stop there on the way to get him and somewhere else on the way back?
HUSBAND:	No, to the shoe repair shop.	No, I stopped at the record store on the way to get him and stopped at the shoe repair shop on the way home when he was with me.
WIFE:	What for?	I know of one reason why you might have stopped at the shoe repair shop. Why did you in fact?
HUSBAND:	I got some new shoe laces for my shoes.	As you will remember I broke a shoe lace on one of my brown oxfords the other day so I stopped to get some new laces.
WIFE:	Your loafers need new heels badly.	Something else you could have gotten that I was thinking of. You could have taken in your black loafers which need heels badly. You'd better get them taken care of pretty soon.

(e) In attending to the utterances as events-in-the-conversation each party made references to the biography and prospects of the present interaction which each used and attributed to the other as a common scheme of interpretation and expression. (f) Each waited for something more to be said in order to hear what had previously been talked about, and each seemed willing to wait.

Common understandings would consist of a measured amount of shared agreement if the common understandings consisted of events co-ordinated with the successive positions of the hands of the clock, i.e., of events in standard time. The foregoing results, because they deal with the exchanges of the colloquy as events-in-a-conversation, urge that one more time parameter, at least, is required: the role of time as it is constitutive of "the matter talked about" as a developing and developed event over the course of action that produced it, as both the process and product were known *from within* this development by both parties, each for himself as well as on behalf of the other.

The colloquy reveals additional features. (1) Many of its expressions are such that their sense cannot be decided by an auditor unless he knows or assumes something about the biography and the purposes of the speaker, the circumstances of the utterance, the previous course of the conversation, or the particular relationship of actual or potential interaction that exists between user and auditor. The expressions do not have a sense that remains identical through the changing occasions of their use. (2) The events that were talked about were specifically vague. Not only do they not frame a clearly restricted set of possible determinations but the depicted events include as their essentially intended and sanctioned features an accompanying "fringe" of determinations that are open with respect to internal relationships, relationships to other events, and relationships to retrospective and prospective possibilities. (3) For the sensible character of an expression, upon its occurrence each of the conversationalists as auditor of his own as well as the other's productions had to assume as of any present accomplished point in the exchange that by waiting for what he or the other person might have said at a later time the present significance of what had already been said would have been clarified. Thus many expressions had the property of being progressively realized and realizable through the further course of the conversation. (4) It hardly needs to be pointed out that the sense of the expressions depended upon where the expression occurred in serial order, the expressive character of the terms that comprised it, and the importance to the conversationalists of the events depicted.

These properties of common understandings stand in contrast to the features they would have if we disregarded their temporally constituted character and treated them instead as precoded entries on a memory drum, to be consulted as a definite set of alternative meanings from among which one was to select, under predecided conditions that specified in which of some set of alternative ways one was to understand the situation upon the occasion that the necessity for a decision arose. The latter properties are those of strict rational discourse as these are idealized in the rules that define an adequate logical proof.

For the purposes of *conducting their everyday affairs* persons refuse to permit each other to understand "what they are really talking about" in this way. The anticipation that persons *will* understand, the occasionality of expressions, the specific vagueness of references, the retrospective-prospective sense of a present occurrence, waiting for something later in order to see what was meant before, are sanctioned properties of common discourse. They furnish a background of seen but unnoticed features of common discourse whereby actual utterances are recognized as events of common, reasonable, understandable, plain talk. Persons require these properties of discourse as conditions under which they are themselves entitled and entitle others to claim that they know what they are talking about, and that what they are saying is understandable and ought to be understood. In short, their seen but unnoticed presence is used to entitle persons to conduct their common conversational affairs without interference. Departures from such usages call forth immediate attempts to restore a right state of affairs.

The sanctioned character of these properties is demonstrable as follows. Students were instructed to engage an acquaintance or a friend in an ordinary conversation and, without indicating that what the experimenter was asking was in any way unusual, to insist that the person clarify the sense of his commonplace remarks. Twenty-three students reported twenty-five instances of such encounters. The following are typical excerpts from their accounts.

Case 1

The subject was telling the experimenter, a member of the subject's car pool, about having had a flat tire while going to work the previous day.

(S)   I had a flat tire.

(E)   What do you mean, you had a flat tire?

She appeared momentarily stunned. Then she answered in a hostile way: "What do you mean, 'What do you mean?' A flat tire is a flat tire. That is what I meant. Nothing special. What a crazy question!"

Case 2

(S)   Hi, Ray. How is your girl friend feeling?

(E)   What do you mean, "How is she feeling?" Do you mean physical or mental?

(S)   I mean how is she feeling? What's the matter with you? (He looked peeved.)

(E)   Nothing. Just explain a little clearer what do you mean?

(S)   Skip it. How are your Med School applications coming?

(E) What do you mean, "How are they?"

(S) You know what I mean.

(E) I really don't.

(S) What's the matter with you? Are you sick?

Case 3

"On Friday night my husband and I were watching television. My husband remarked that he was tired. I asked, 'How are you tired? Physically, mentally, or just bored?' "

(S) I don't know, I guess physically, mainly.

(E) You mean that your muscles ache or your bones?

(S) I guess so. Don't be so technical. (*After more watching*)

(S) All these old movies have the same kind of old iron bedstead in them.

(E) What do you mean? Do you mean all old movies, or some of them, or just the ones you have seen?

(S) What's the matter with you? You know what I mean.

(E) I wish you would be more specific.

(S) You know what I mean! Drop dead!

Case 4

During a conversation (with the E's female fiancée) the E questioned the meaning of various words used by the subject …

> For the first minute and a half the subject responded to the questions as if they were legitimate inquiries. Then she responded with "Why are you asking me those questions?" and repeated this two or three times after each question. She became nervous and jittery, her face and hand movements … uncontrolled. She appeared bewildered and complained that I was making her nervous and demanded that I "Stop it". … The subject picked up a magazine and covered her face. She put down the magazine and pretended to be engrossed. When asked why she was looking at the magazine she closed her mouth and refused any further remarks.

Case 5

My friend said to me, "Hurry or we will be late." I asked him what did he mean by late and from what point of view did it have reference. There was a look of perplexity and cynicism on his face. "Why are you asking me such silly questions? Surely I don't have to explain such a statement. What is wrong with you today? Why should I have to stop to analyze such a statement? Everyone understands my statements and you should be no exception!"

Case 6

The victim waved his hand cheerily.

(S) How are you?

(E) How am I in regard to what? My health, my finances, my school work, my peace of mind, my …?

(S) (Red in the face and suddenly out of control.) Look! I was just trying to be polite. Frankly, I don't give a damn how you are.

Case 7

My friend and I were talking about a man whose overbearing attitude annoyed us. My friend expressed his feeling.

(S) I'm sick of him.

(E) Would you explain what is wrong with you that you are sick?

(S) Are you kidding me? You know what I mean.

(E) Please explain your ailment.

(S) (He listened to me with a puzzled look.) What came over you? We never talk this way, do we?

[…]

BACKGROUND UNDERSTANDINGS AND BEWILDERMENT

Earlier the argument was made that the possibility of common understanding does not consist in demonstrated measures of shared knowledge of social structure, but consists instead and entirely in the enforceable character of actions in compliance with the expectancies of everyday life as a morality. Common sense knowledge of the facts of social life for the members of the society is institutionalized knowledge of the real world. Not only does common sense knowledge portray a real society for members, but in the manner of a self fulfilling prophecy the features of the real society are produced by persons' motivated compliance with these background expectancies. Hence the stability of concerted actions should vary directly with whatsoever are the real conditions of social organization that guarantee persons' motivated compliance with this background texture of relevances as a legitimate order of beliefs about life in society seen "from within" the society. Seen from the person's point of view, his commitments to motivated compliance consist of his grasp of and subscription to the "natural facts of life in society."

Such considerations suggest that the firmer a societal member's grasp of What Anyone Like Us Necessarily Knows, the more severe should be his disturbance when "natural facts of life" are impugned for him as a depiction of his real circumstances. To test this suggestion a procedure would need to modify the *objective* structure of the familiar, known-in-common environment by rendering the background expectancies inoperative. Specifically, this modification would consist of subjecting a person to a breach of the background expectancies of everyday life while (a) making it difficult for the person to interpret his situation as a game, an experiment, a deception, a play, *i.e.*, as something other than the one known according to the attitude of everyday life as a matter of enforceable morality and action,

(b) making it necessary that he reconstruct the "natural facts" but giving him insufficient time to manage the reconstruction with respect to required mastery of practical circumstances for which he must call upon his knowledge of the "natural facts," and (c) requiring that he manage the reconstruction of the natural facts by himself and without consensual validation.

Presumably he should have no alternative but to try to normalize the resultant incongruities within the order of events of everyday life. Under the developing effort itself, events should lose their perceivedly normal character. The member should be unable to recognize an event's status as typical. Judgments of likelihood should fail him. He should be unable to assign present occurrences to similar orders of events he has known in the past. He should be unable to assign, let alone to "see at a glance," the conditions under which the events can be reproduced. He should be unable to order these events to means-ends relationships. The conviction should be undermined that the moral authority of the familiar society compels their occurrence. Stable and "realistic" matchings of intentions and objects should dissolve, by which I mean that the ways, otherwise familiar to him, in which the objective perceived environment serves as both the motivating grounds of feelings and is motivated by feelings directed to it, should become obscure. In short, the members' real perceived environment on losing its known-in-common background should become "specifically senseless."[6] Ideally speaking, behaviors directed to such a senseless environment should be those of bewilderment, uncertainty, internal conflict, psycho-social isolation, acute, and nameless anxiety along with various symptoms of acute depersonalization. Structures of interaction should be correspondingly disorganized.

This is expecting quite a lot of a breach of the background expectancies. Obviously we would settle for less if the results of a procedure for their breach was at all encouraging about this formulation. As it happens, the procedure produced convincing and easily detected bewilderment and anxiety.

To begin with, it is necessary to specify just what expectancies we are dealing with. Schutz reported that the feature of a scene, "known in common with others," was compound and consisted of several constituents. Because they have been discussed elsewhere[7] I shall restrict discussion to brief enumeration.

According to Schutz, the person assumes, assumes that the other person assumes as well, and assumes that as he assumes it of the other person the other person assumes the same for him:

1. That the determinations assigned to an event by the witness are required matters that hold on grounds that specifically disregard personal opinion or socially structured circumstances of particular witnesses, *i.e.*, that the determinations are required as matters of "objective necessity" or "facts of nature."
2. That a relationship of undoubted correspondence is the sanctioned relationship between the-presented-appearance-of-the-object and the-intended-object-that-presents-itself-in-the-perspective-of-the-particular-appearance.
3. That the event that is known in the manner that it is known can actually and potentially affect the witness and can be affected by his action.
4. That the meanings of events are products of a socially standardized process of naming, reification, and idealization of the user's stream of experience, *i.e.*, are the products of a language.
5. That present determinations of an event, whatsoever these may be, are determinations that were intended on previous occasions and that may be again intended in identical fashion on an indefinite number of future occasions.
6. That the intended event is retained as the temporally identical event throughout the stream of experience.
7. That the event has as its context of interpretation: (a) a commonly entertained scheme of interpretation consisting of a standardized system of symbols, and (b) "What Anyone Knows," *i.e.*, a preestablished corpus of socially warranted knowledge.
8. That the actual determinations that the event exhibits for the witness are the potential determinations that it would exhibit for the other person were they to exchange positions.
9. That to each event there corresponds its determinations that originate in the witness's and in the other person's particular biography. From the witness's point of view such determinations are irrelevant for the purposes at hand of either, and both he and the other have selected and interpreted the actual and potential determinations of events in an empirically identical manner that is sufficient for all their practical purposes.
10. That there is a characteristic disparity between the publicly acknowledged determinations and the personal, withheld determinations of events, and this private knowledge is held in reserve, *i.e.*, that the event means for both the witness and the other more than the witness can say.
11. That alterations of this characteristic disparity remain within the witness's autonomous control.

It is *not* the case that what an event exhibits as a distinctive determination is a condition of its membership in a known-in-the-manner-of-common-sense-environment. Instead the conditions of its membership are the attributions that its determinations, *whatever they might substantively consist of*, could be seen by the other person if their positions were exchanged, or that its features are not assigned as matters of personal preference but are to be seen by anyone, *i.e.*, the previously enumerated features. These and only these enumerated features *irrespective* of any other determinations of an event define the common sense character of an event. Whatever other determinations an event of everyday life may exhibit—whether its determinations are those of persons' motives, their life histories, the distributions of income in the population, kinship obligations, the organization of an industry, or what ghosts do when night falls—if and only if the event has for the witness the enumerated determinations is it an event in an environment "known in common with others."

Such attributions are features of witnessed events that are seen without being noticed. They are demonstrably relevant to the common sense that the actor makes of what is going on about him. They inform the witness about any particular appearance of an interpersonal environment. They inform the witness as to the real objects that actual appearances are the appearances of, but without these attributed features necessarily being recognized in a deliberate or conscious fashion.

Since each of the expectancies that make up the attitude of daily life assigns an expected feature to the actor's environment, it should be possible to breach these expectancies by deliberately modifying scenic events so as to disappoint these attributions. By definition, surprise is possible with respect to each of these expected features. The nastiness of surprise should vary directly with the extent to which the person as a matter of moral necessity complies with their use as a scheme for assigning witnessed appearances their status as events in a perceivedly normal environment. In short, the realistic grasp by a collectivity member of the natural facts of life, and his commitment to a knowledge of them as a condition of self-esteem as a bona-fide and competent collectivity member,[8] is the condition that we require in order to maximize his confusion upon the occasion that the grounds of this grasp are made a source of irreducible incongruity.

[...]

CONCLUDING REMARKS

I have been arguing that a concern for the nature, production, and recognition of reasonable, realistic, and analyzable actions is not the monopoly of philosophers and professional sociologists. Members of a society are concerned as a matter of course and necessarily with these matters both as features and for the socially managed production of their everyday affairs. The study of common sense knowledge and common sense activities consists of treating as problematic phenomena the actual methods whereby members of a society, doing sociology, lay or professional, make the social structures of everyday activities observable. The "rediscovery" of common sense is possible perhaps because professional sociologists, like members, have had too much to do with common sense knowledge of social structures as both a topic and a resource for their inquiries and not enough to do with it only and exclusively as sociology's programmatic topic.

NOTES

1. Olaf Helmer and Nicholas Rescher, *On the Epistemology of the Inexact Sciences*, P-1513 (Santa Monica, California: RAND Corporation, October 13, 1958), pp. 8–14.
2. The work of Alfred Schutz, cited in footnote 3, is a magnificent exception. Readers who are acquainted with his writings will recognize how heavily this paper is indebted to him.
3. Alfred Schutz, *Der Sinnhafte Aufbau Der Sozialen Welt* (Wein: Verlag von Julius Springer, 1932); *Collected Papers I: The Problem of Social Reality*, ed. Maurice Natanson (The Hague: Martinus Nijhoff, 1962); *Collected Papers II: Studies in Social Theory*, ed. Arvid Broderson (The Hague: Martinus *Nijhoff*, 1964); *Collected Papers III: Studies in Phenomenological Philosophy*, ed. I. Schutz (The Hague: Martinus Nijhoff, 1966).
4. Obversely, a knowledge of how the structures of everyday activities are routinely produced should permit us to tell how we might proceed for the effective production of desired disturbances.
5. Karl Mannheim, in his essay "On the Interpretation of 'Weltanschauung' " (in *Essays on the Sociology of Knowledge*, trans, and ed. Paul Kecskemeti [New York: Oxford University Press, 1952], pp. 33–83), referred

to this work as the "documentary method of interpretation." Its features are detailed in Chapter Three.

6. The term is borrowed from Max Weber's essay, "The Social Psychology of the World Religions," in *From Max Weber: Essays in Sociology*, trans. H. H. Gerth and C. Wright Mills (New York: Oxford University Press, 1946), pp. 267–301. I have adapted its meaning.

7. Schutz, "Common Sense and Scientific Interpretations of Human Action," in *Collected Papers I: The Problem of Social Reality*, pp. 3–96; and "On Multiple Realities," pp. 207–259. Garfinkel, Chapter Eight, and "Common Sense Knowledge of Social Structures," *Transactions of the Fourth World Congress of Sociology*, 4 (Milan, 1959), 51–65.

8. I use the term "competence" to mean the claim that a collectivity member is entitled to exercise that he is capable of managing his everyday affairs without interference. That members can take such claims for granted I refer to by speaking of a person as a "bona-fide" collectivity member. More extensive discussion of the relationships between "competence" and "common sense knowledge of social structures" will be found in the Ph.D. dissertation by Egon Bittner, "Popular Interests in Psychiatric Remedies: A Study in Social Control," University of California, Los Angeles, 1961. The terms, "collectivity" and "collectivity membership" are intended in strict accord with Talcott Parsons' usage in *The Social System* (New York: The Free Press of Glencoe, Inc., 1951) and in the general introduction to *Theories of Society*, by Talcott Parsons, Edward Shils, Kaspar D. Naegele, and Jesse R. Pitts (New York: The Free Press of Glencoe, Inc., 1961).

COMPANION WEBSITE

1. Go online to Write Out Loud about a moment when you relied on background expectancies to make your own conversation "happen."
2. Log on to the Mid-Twentieth-Century American Theory Profile Page to learn more about Garfinkel and his thoughts on how members of social groups maintain order in their everyday worlds.
3. Check out the Interactive Reading and go "Garfinkeling" yourself!

7

Mixing Humans and Nonhumans Together: The Sociology of a Door-Closer*

Bruno Latour[1]

THE MOST LIBERAL SOCIOLOGIST often discriminates against nonhumans. Ready to study the most bizarre, exotic, or convoluted social behavior, he or she balks at studying nuclear plants, robots, or pills. Although sociology is expert at dealing with human groupings, when it comes to nonhumans, it is less sure of itself. The temptation is to leave the nonhuman to the care of technologists or to study the impact of black-boxed techniques upon the evolution of social groups. In spite of the works of Marx or Lewis Mumford and the more recent development of a sociology of techniques (MacKenzie and Wacjman, 1985; Bijker, Hughes, and Pinch, 1986; Winner, 1986; Latour, 1987), sociologists still feel estranged when they fall upon the bizarre associations of humans with nonhumans. Part of their uneasiness has to do with the technicalities of complex objects and with the absence of a convenient vocabulary allowing them to move freely from studying associations of human to associations of nonhumans. In this paper I want to contribute to the reinsertion of nonhumans into the mainstream of American sociology by examining an extremely simple technique and offering a coherent vocabulary that could be applied to more complex imbroglios of humans and nonhumans.

REINVENTING THE DOOR

On a freezing day in February, posted on the door of the Sociology Department at Walla Walla University, Washington, could be seen a small hand-written notice: "The door-closer is on strike, for God's sake, keep the door closed." This fusion of labor relations, religion, advertisement, semiotics, and technique in one single insignificant fact is exactly the sort of thing I want to help describe. As a technologist teaching in an engineering school in Columbus, Ohio, I want to challenge some of the assumptions sociologists often hold about the "social context" of machines.

Walls are a nice invention, but if there were no holes in them, there would be no way to get in or out; they would be mausoleums or tombs. The problem is that, if you make holes in the walls, anything and anyone can get in and out (bears, visitors, dust, rats, noise). So architects invented this hybrid: a hole-wall, often called a *door,* which, although common enough, has always struck me as a miracle of technology. The cleverness of the invention hinges upon the hinge-pin: instead of driving a hole through walls with a sledge hammer or a pick, you simply gently push the door (I am supposing here that the lock has not been invented; this would over-complicate the already highly complex story of this door). Furthermore, and here is the real trick, once you have passed through the door, you do not have to find trowel and cement to rebuild the wall you have just destroyed; you simply push the door gently back (I ignore for now the added complication of the "pull" and "push" signs).

So, to size up the work done by hinges, you simply have to imagine that every time you want to get in or out of the building you have to do the same work as a prisoner trying to escape or a gangster trying to rob a bank, plus the work of those who rebuild either the prison's or the bank's walls.

If you do not want to imagine people destroying walls and rebuilding them every time they wish to leave or enter a building, then imagine the work that would have to be done in order to keep inside or to keep outside all the things and people that, left to themselves, would go the wrong way. As Maxwell could have said, imagine his demon working *without* a door. Anything could escape from or penetrate into the department, and there would soon be complete equilibrium between the depressing and noisy surrounding area and the inside of the building. Techniques are always involved when asymmetry or irreversibility is the goal; it might appear that doors are a striking counter example since they maintain the hole-wall in a reversible state, but the allusion to Maxwell's demon clearly shows that such is not the case. The reversible door is the only way to irreversibly trap inside a differential accumulation of warm sociologists, knowledge, papers, and also, alas, paperwork; the hinged door allows a selection of what gets in and what gets out so as to locally increase order or information. If you let the drafts get inside, the drafts will never get outside to the publishers.

Now, draw two columns (if I am not allowed to give orders to the reader of *Social Problems* then take it as a piece of strongly worded advice). In the right column, list the work people would have to do if they had no door; in the left column write down the gentle pushing (or pulling) they have to do in order to fulfill the same tasks. Compare the two columns; the enormous effort on the right is balanced by the little one on the left, and this thanks to hinges. I will define this transformation of a major effort into a minor one by the word *translation* or *delegation;* I will say that we have delegated (or translated or displaced or shifted out) to the hinge the work of reversibly solving the hole-wall dilemma. Calling on a sociologist friend, I do not have to do this work nor even to think about it; it was delegated by the carpenter to a character, the hinge, that I will call a nonhuman (notice that I did not say "inhuman"). I simply enter the department of sociology. As a more general descriptive rule, every time you want to know what a nonhuman does, simply imagine what other humans or other nonhumans would have to do were this character not present. This imaginary substitution exactly sizes up the role, or function, of this little figure.

Before going on, let me cash out one of the side benefits of this table: in effect, we have drawn a scale balance where tiny efforts balance out mighty weights. The scale we drew (at least the one that you drew if you have obeyed my orders—I mean, followed my advice) reproduces the very leverage allowed by hinges. That the small be made stronger than the large is a very moral story indeed (think of David and Goliath). By the same token, this is also, since at least Archimedes' days, a very good definition of a lever and of power: the minimum you need to hold and deploy astutely in order to produce the maximum effect. Am I alluding to machines or to Syracuse's King? I don't know, and it does not matter since the King and Archimedes fused the two "minimaxes" into one single story told by Plutarch: the defense of Syracuse. I contend that this reversal of forces is what sociologists should look at in order to understand the "social construction" of techniques and not at a hypothetical social context they are not equipped to grasp. This little point having been made, let me go on with the story (we will understand later why I do not really need your permission to go on and why, nevertheless, you are free not to go on, although only *relatively* so).

DELEGATING TO HUMANS

There is a problem with doors. Visitors push them to get in or pull on them to get out (or vice versa), but then the door remains open. That is, instead of the door you have a gaping hole in the wall through which, for instance, cold rushes in and heat rushes out. Of course, you could imagine that people living in the building or visiting the department of sociology would be a well disciplined lot (after all, sociologists are meticulous people). They will learn to close the door behind them and retransform the momentary hole into a well-sealed wall. The problem is that discipline is not the main characteristic of people. Are they going to be so well-behaved? Closing a door would appear to be a simple enough piece of know-how once hinges have been invented; but, considering the amount of work, innovations, sign-posts, recriminations that go on endlessly everywhere to keep them closed (at least in Northern regions), it seems to be rather poorly disseminated.

This is where the age-old choice, so well analyzed by Mumford (1966), is offered to you: either to discipline the people or to *substitute* for the unreliable people another *delegated human character* whose only function is to open and close the door. This is called a groom or a porter (from the French word for door) or a gatekeeper, or a janitor, or a concierge, or a turnkey, or a gaoler. The advantage is that you now have to discipline only one human and may safely leave the others to their erratic behavior. No matter who these others are and where they come from, the groom will always take care of the door. A nonhuman (the hinges) plus a human (the groom) have solved the hole-wall dilemma.

Solved? Not quite. First of all, if the department pays for a porter, they will have no money left to buy coffee or books or to invite eminent foreigners to give lectures. If they give the poor little boy other duties besides that of porter, then he will not be present most of the time, and the damned door will stay open. Even if they had money to keep him there, we are now faced with a problem that two hundred years of capitalism has not completely solved: how to discipline a youngster to reliably fulfill a boring and underpaid duty. Although there is now only one human to be disciplined instead of hundreds (in practice only dozens because Walla Walla is rather difficult to locate), the weak point of the tactic is now revealed: if this one lad is unreliable then the whole chain breaks down. If he falls asleep on the job or goes walkabout, there will be no appeal; the damned door will stay open (remember that locking it is no solution since this would turn it into a wall, and then providing every visitor with the right key is an impossible task). Of course, the little rat may be punished or even flogged. But imagine the headlines: "Sociologists of science flog porter from poor working class background." And what if he is black, which might very well be the case, given the low pay? No, disciplining a groom is an enormous and costly task that only Hilton Hotels can tackle, and that for other reasons that have nothing to do with keeping the door properly closed.

If we compare the work of disciplining the groom with the work he substitutes for, according to the list defined above, we see that this delegated character has the opposite effect to that of the hinge. A simple task, forcing people to close the door, is now performed at an incredible cost; the minimum effect is obtained with maximum spending and spanking. We also notice, when drawing the two lists, an interesting difference. In the first relationship (hinges vis-à-vis work of many people), you not only had a reversal of forces (the lever allows gentle manipulations to heavy weights) but also a reversal of *time*. Once the hinges are in place, nothing more has to be done apart from maintenance (oiling them from time to time). In the second set of relations (groom's work versus many people's work), not only do you fail to reverse the forces, but you also fail to modify the time schedule. Nothing can be done to prevent the groom who has been reliable for two months from failing on the sixty-second day; at this point it is not maintenance work that has to be done, but the same work as on the first day—apart from the few habits that you might have been able to *incorporate* into his body. Although they appear to be two similar delegations, the first one is concentrated in time, whereas the other is continuous; more exactly, the first one creates a clear-cut distinction between production and maintenance, whereas in the other the distinction between training and keeping in operation is either fuzzy or nil. The first one evokes the past perfect ("once hinges had been installed"); the second the present tense ("when the groom is at his post"). There is a built-in inertia in the first that is largely lacking in the second. A profound temporal shift takes place when nonhumans are appealed to: time is folded.

DISCIPLINING THE DOOR-CLOSER

It is at this point that you have this relatively new choice: either to discipline the people or to substitute for the unreliable humans a delegated nonhuman character whose only function is to open and close the door. This is called a door-closer or a "groom." The advantage is that you now have to discipline only one nonhuman and may safely leave the others (bellboys included) to their erratic behavior. No matter who they are and where they come from—polite or rude, quick or slow, friends or foes—the nonhuman groom will always take care of the door in any weather and at any time of the day. A nonhuman (hinges) plus another nonhuman (groom) have solved the hole-wall dilemma.

Solved? Well, not quite. Here comes the deskilling question so dear to social historians of technology: thousands of human grooms have been put on the dole by their nonhuman brethren. Have they been replaced? This depends on the kind of action that has been translated or delegated to them. In other words, when humans are displaced and deskilled, nonhumans have to be upgraded and reskilled. This is not an easy task, as we shall now see.

We have all experienced having a door with a powerful spring mechanism slam in our face. For sure, springs do the job of replacing grooms, but they play the role of a very rude, uneducated porter who obviously prefers the wall version of the door to its hole version. They simply slam the door shut. The interesting thing with such impolite doors is

this: if they slam shut so violently, it means that you, the visitor, *have* to be very quick in passing through and that you *should* not be at someone else's heels; otherwise your nose will get shorter and bloody. An unskilled nonhuman groom thus presupposes a skilled human user. It is always a trade-off. I will call, after Madeleine Akrich, the behavior imposed back onto the human by nonhuman delegates *prescription* (Akrich, 1987). How can these prescriptions be brought out? By replacing them by strings of sentences (usually in the imperative) that are uttered (silently and continuously) by the mechanisms for the benefit of those who are mechanized: do this, do that, behave this way, don't go that way. Such sentences look very much like a programming language. This substitution of words for silence can be made in the analyst's thought experiments, but also by instruction booklets or explicitly in any training session through the voice of a demonstrator or instructor or teacher. The military are especially good at shouting them out through the mouthpiece of human instructors who delegate back to themselves the task of explaining, in the rifle's name, the characteristics of the rifle's ideal user. As Akrich notes, prescription is the moral and ethical dimension of mechanisms. In spite of the constant weeping of moralists, no human is as relentlessly moral as a machine, especially if it is (she is, he is, they are) as "user friendly" as my computer.

The results of such distributions of skills between humans and nonhumans is well known: members of the department of sociology will safely pass through the slamming door at a good distance from one another; visitors, unaware of the *local cultural condition,* will crowd through the door and will get bloody noses. This story is of the same form as that about the buses loaded with poor blacks that could not pass under driveways leading to Manhattan parks (Winner, 1980). So, inventors get back to their drawing board and try to imagine a nonhuman character that will not prescribe the same rare local cultural skills to its human users.

A weak spring might appear to be a good solution. Such is not the case because it would substitute for another type of very unskilled and undecided groom who is never sure about the door's (or his own) status: is it a hole or a wall? Am I a closer or an opener? If it is both at once, you can forget about the heat. In computer parlance, a door is an OR, not an AND *gate.*

I am a great fan of hinges, but I must confess that I admire hydraulic door-closers much more, especially the old copper plated heavy one that slowly closed the main door of our house in Columbus, Ohio. I am enchanted by the addition to the spring of an hydraulic piston which easily draws up the energy of those who open the door and retains it, then gives it back slowly with a subtle variety of implacable firmness that one could expect from a well trained butler. Especially clever is its way of extracting energy from each and every unwilling, unwitting passer-by. My military friends at the academy call such a clever extraction an "obligatory passage point," which is a very fitting name for a door; no matter what you feel, think, or do, you have to leave a bit of your energy, literally, at the door. This is as clever as a toll booth.

This does not quite solve all the problems, though. To be sure the hydraulic door-closer does not bang the noses of those who are not aware of local conditions, so its prescriptions may be said to be less restrictive. But it still leaves aside segments of human populations. Neither my little nephews nor my grandmother could get in unaided because our groom needed the force of an able-bodied person to accumulate enough energy to close the door. To use the classic Langdon Winner's motto (1980), because of their prescriptions these doors *discriminate* against very little and very old persons. Also, if there is no way to keep them open for good, they discriminate against furniture removers and in general everyone with packages, which usually means, in our late capitalist society, working or lower-middle class employees (who, even coming from a higher strata, has not been cornered by an automated butler when

he or she had their hands full of packages?). There are solutions though: the groom's delegation may be written off (usually by blocking its arm) or, more prosaically, its delegated action may be opposed by a foot (salesman are said to be expert at this). The foot may in turn be delegated to a carpet or anything that keeps the butler in check (although I am always amazed by the number of objects that fail this trial of force, and I have very often seen the door I just wedged open politely closing when I turned my back to it).

As a technologist, I could claim that, provided you put aside maintenance and the few sectors of population that are discriminated against, the groom does its job well, closing the door behind you constantly, firmly, and slowly. It shows in its humble way how three rows of delegated nonhuman actants (hinges, springs, and hydraulic pistons) replace, 90 percent of the time, either an undisciplined bell-boy who is never there when needed or, for the general public, the program instructions that have to do with remembering-to-close-the-door-when-it-is-cold. The hinge plus the groom is the technologist's dream of efficient action, at least it was until the sad day when I saw the note posted on Walla Walla Sociology Department's door with which I started this article: "the groom is on strike." So not only have we been able to delegate the act of closing the door from the human to the nonhuman, we have also been able to delegate the little rat's lack of discipline (and maybe the union that goes with it). On strike. Fancy that! Nonhumans stopping work and claiming what? Pension payments? Time off? Landscaped offices? Yet it is no use being indignant because it is very true that nonhumans are not so reliable that the irreversibility we would like to grant them is complete. We did not want ever to have to think about this door again—apart from regularly scheduled routine maintenance (which is another way of saying that we did not have to bother about it)—and here we are, worrying again about how to keep the door closed and drafts outside.

What is interesting in the note on the door is the humor of attributing a human character to a failure that is usually considered as "purely technical." This humor, however, is more profound than the synonymous notice they could have posted "the groom is not working." I constantly talk with my computer, who answers back; I am sure you swear at your old car; we are constantly granting mysterious faculties to gremlins inside every conceivable home appliance, not to mention cracks in the concrete belt of our nuclear plants. Yet, this behavior is considered by moralists, I mean sociologists, as a scandalous breach of natural barriers. When you write that a groom is "on strike," this is only seen as a "projection," as they say, of a human behavior onto a nonhuman cold technical object, one by nature impervious to any feeling. They call such a projection anthropomorphism, which for them is a sin akin to zoophily but much worse.

It is this sort of moralizing that is so irritating for technologists because the automatic groom is already anthropomorphic through and through. "Anthropos" and "morphos" together mean either what has human shape or what gives shape to humans. Well the groom is indeed anthropomorphic, and in three senses: first, it has been made by men, it is a construction; second it substitutes for the actions of people, and is a delegate that permanently occupies the position of a human; and third, it shapes human action by prescribing back what sort of people should pass through the door. And yet some would forbid us to ascribe feelings to this thoroughly anthropomorphic creature, to delegate labor relations, to "project"—that is to say, to translate—*other* human properties to the groom. What of those many other innovations that have endowed much more sophisticated doors with the ability to see you arrive in advance (electronic eyes), or to ask for your identity (electronic passes), or to slam shut—or open—in case of danger? But anyway, who are you, you the sociologists, to decide forever the real and final shape of humans, to trace with confidence the boundary between what is a "real" delegation and what is a "mere" projection, to sort out forever and without due inquiry the

three different kinds of anthropomorphism I listed above? Are we not shaped by nonhuman grooms, although, I admit, only a very little bit? Are they not our brethren? Do they not deserve consideration? With your self-serving and self-righteous social problems, you always plead against machines and for deskilled workers; are you aware of *your* discriminatory biases? You discriminate between the human and the inhuman. I do not hold this bias but see only actors—some human, some nonhuman, some skilled, some unskilled—that exchange their properties.

So the note posted on the door is an accurate one. It gives a humorous but exact rendering of the groom's behavior: it is not working; it is on strike (notice, that the word "strike" is also an anthropomorphism carried from the nonhuman repertoire to the human one, which proves again that the divide is untenable). What happens is that sociologists confuse the dichotomy human/inhuman with another one: *figurative/non-figurative*. If I say that Hamlet is the figuration of "depression among the aristocratic class," I move from a personal figure to a less personal one (class). If I say that Hamlet stands for doom and gloom, I use less figurative entities; and if I claim that he represents western civilization, I use non-figurative abstractions. Still, they all are equally actants, that is to say entities that *do* things, either in Shakespeare's artful plays or in the commentators' more tedious tomes. The choice of granting actants figurativity or not is left entirely to the authors. It is exactly the same for techniques. We engineers are the authors of these subtle plots or *scenariis,* as Madeleine Akrich (1987) calls them, of dozens of delegated and interlocking characters so few people know how to appreciate. The label "inhuman" applied to techniques simply overlooks translation mechanisms and the many choices that exist for figuring or de-figuring, personifying or abstracting, embodying or disembodying actors.

For instance, on the freeway the other day, I slowed down because there was a guy in a yellow suit and a red helmet waving a red flag. Well, the guy's moves were so regular and he was located so dangerously and had such a pale although smiling face that, when I passed by, I recognized it to be a machine (it failed the Turing test, a cognitivist would say). Not only was the red flag delegated, not only was the arm waving the flag also delegated, but the body appearance was also added to the machine. We engineers could move much further in the direction of figuration, although at a cost; we could have given him/her (careful here, no sexual discrimination of robots) electronic eyes to wave only when there is a car approaching or regulated the movement so that it is faster when cars do not obey. Also we could have added—why not?—a furious stare or a recognizable face like a mask of President Reagan, which would have certainly slowed drivers down very efficiently. But we could also have moved the other way, to a *less* figurative delegation; the flag by itself could have done the job. And why a flag? Why not simply a sign: "work in progress"? And why a sign at all? Drivers, if they are circumspect, disciplined, and watchful will see for themselves that there is work in progress and will slow down.

The *enunciator* (a general word for the author of a text or for the mechanics who devised the machine) is free to place or not a representation of himself or herself in the script (texts or machines). The engineer may delegate or not in the flag-mover a shape that is similar to him/ herself. This is exactly the same operation as the one I did in pretending that the author of this article was a hardcore technologist from Columbus, Ohio. If I say "we, the technologists," I propose a picture of the author-of-the-text which has only a vague relation with the author-in-the-flesh, in the same way as the engineer delegates in his flag-mover a picture of him that bears little resemblance to him/her.[2] But it would have been perfectly possible for me and for the mechanics to position no figurated character at all as the author *in* the scripts *of* our scripts (in semiotic parlance there would be no narrator). I would just have had to say things like "recent developments

in sociology of science have shown that" instead of "I," and the mechanics would simply have had to take out the dummy worker and replace it by cranks and pullies.

APPEALING TO GODS

Here comes the most interesting and saddest lesson of the note posted on the door: people are not circumspect, disciplined, and watchful, especially not Walla Walla drivers after the happy-hour on Friday night. Well, that's exactly the point that the note made: "The groom is on strike, *for God's sake,* keep the door closed." In our societies, they are two systems of appeal: nonhuman and super-human, that is machines and gods. This note indicates how desperate its frozen and anonymous authors were (I have never been able to trace them back and to honor them as they deserved). They first relied on the inner morality and common sense of humans. This failed; the door was always left open. Then they appealed to what we technologists consider the supreme court of appeal, that is, to a nonhuman who regularly and conveniently does the job in place of unfaithful humans. To our shame, we must confess that it also failed after a while. The door was again always left open. How poignant their line of thought is! They moved up and backward to the oldest and firmest court of appeal there is, there was, and ever will be. If human and nonhuman have failed, certainly God will not deceive them. I am ashamed to say that, when I crossed the hallway this fatal February day, the door *was* open. Do not accuse God, though, because the note did not appeal directly to Him (I know I should have added "Her" for affirmative action reasons, but I wonder how theologians would react). God is not accessible without mediators. The anonymous authors knew their catechisms well, so instead of asking for a direct miracle (God Him/Herself holding the door firmly closed or doing so through the mediation of an angel, as has happened in several occasions, for instance when Paul was delivered from his prison), they appeal to the respect for God in human hearts. This was their mistake. In our secular times, this is no longer enough.

Nowadays nothing seems to do the job of disciplining men and women and forcing them simply to close doors in cold weather. It is a similar despair that pushed the road engineer to add a Golem to the red flag to force drivers to beware—although the only way to slow drivers is still a good traffic-jam. You seem to always need more and more of these figurated delegates aligned in rows. It is the same with delegates as with drugs; you start with soft ones and end by shooting up. There is an inflation for delegated characters too. After a while they weaken. In the old days it might have been enough just to have a door for people to know how to close it. But then, the embodied skills somehow disappeared; people had to be reminded of their training. Still, the simple inscription "keep the door closed" might have been sufficient in the good old days. But you know people; they no longer pay attention to such notices and need to be reminded by stronger devices. It is then that you install automatic grooms, since electric shocks are not as acceptable for men as for cows. In the old times, when quality was still good, it might have been enough just to oil it from time to time, but nowadays even automatisms go on strike.

It is not, however, that the movement is always from softer to harder devices, that is, from an autonomous body of knowledge to force through the intermediary situation of worded injunctions, as the Walla Walla door would suggest. It also goes the other way. Although the deskilling thesis appears to be the general case (always go from intra-somatic to extra-somatic skills; never rely on undisciplined men, but always on safe delegated nonhumans), this is far from true. For instance, red lights are usually respected, at least when they are sophisticated enough to integrate traffic flows through sensors. The delegated policemen standing there day and night is respected even though it has no whistles, gloved hands, and body to enforce this respect. Imagined collisions with the other cars or with the absent policemen are enough to keep drivers and cars in check. The thought experiment "what would happen if the delegated character was not there," is the same as the one I recommended above to size up its function. The same incorporation from written injunction to body skills is at work with car user manuals. No one, I guess, will cast more than a cursory glance at the manual before igniting the engine. There is a large body of skills that we have now so well embodied or incorporated that the mediations of the written instructions are useless. From extra-somatic they have become intra-somatic. Incorporation in human or in nonhuman bodies is also left to the authors/engineers.

OFFERING A COHERENT VOCABULARY

It is because humans, nonhumans, and even angels are never sufficient in themselves and because there is no one direction going from one type of delegation to the other, that it is so useless to impose a priori divisions between which skills are human and which ones are not human, which characters are personified and which remain abstract, which delegation is forbidden and which is permissible, which type of delegation is stronger or more durable than the other. In place of these many cumbersome distinctions why not take up a few simple descriptive tools?

Following Madeleine Akrich's lead, we will speak only in terms of *scripts* or scenes or scenarios played by human or nonhuman actors, which may be either figurative or non-figurative. Humans are not necessarily figurative; for instance you are not allowed to take the highway policeman as an individual chum. He/she is the representative of authority, and if he/she is really dumb, he/she will reject any individualizing efforts from you, like smiles, jokes, bribes, or fits of anger. He/she will fully play the administrative *machinery*.

Following Akrich, I will call the retrieval of the script from the situation *description*. These descriptions are always in words and appear very much like semiotic commentaries on a text or like a programming language. They define actors, endow them with competences and make them do things, and evaluate the sanction of these actions very much like the narrative program of semioticians.

Although most of the scripts are in practice silent either because they are intra- or extra-somatic, the written descriptions are not an artifact of the analyst (technologist, sociologist, or semiotician) because there exist many states of affairs in which they are *explicitly* uttered. The gradient going from intra-somatic to extra-somatic skills through discourse is never fully stabilized and allows many entries revealing the process of translation. I have already listed several entries: user manuals, instruction, demonstration or drilling situations (in this case a human or a speech-synthesizer speaks out the user manual), practical thought experiments ("what would happen if instead of the red light a policemen were there"). To this should be added the innovator's workshop where most of the objects to be devised are still at the stage of projects committed to paper ("if we had a device doing this and that, we could then do this and that"); market analysis in which consumers are confronted with the new device; and, naturally, the training situation studied by anthropologists where people faced with a foreign device talk to themselves while trying out various combinations ("what will happen if I attach this lead here to the mains?"). The analyst has to capture these situations in order to write down the scripts. The analyst makes a thought experiment by comparing presence/absence tables and collating all the actions done by actants: if I take this one away, this and that other action will be modified.

I will call the translation of any script from one repertoire to a more durable one *transcription* or *inscription* or encoding. Translation does not have here only its linguistic meaning but also the religious one, "translation of the remains of St Christel," and

the artistic one, "translating the feelings of Calder into bronze." This definition does not imply that the direction always goes from soft bodies to hard machines, but simply that it goes from a provisional less reliable one to a longer-lasting, more faithful one. For instance, the embodiment in cultural tradition of the user manual of a car is a transcription, but so is the replacement of a policeman by a traffic-light. One goes from machines to bodies, whereas the other goes the other way. Specialists of robotics have very much abandoned the pipe dream of total automation; they learned the hard way that many skills are better delegated to humans than to nonhumans, whereas others may be moved away from incompetent humans.

I will call *prescription* whatever a scene presupposes from its *transcribed* actors and authors (this is very much like "role expectation" in sociology, except that it may be inscribed or encoded in the machine). For instance, a Renaissance Italian painting is designed to be viewed from a specific angle of view prescribed by the vanishing lines, exactly like a traffic light expects that its users will watch it from the street and not sideways. In the same way as they presuppose a user, traffic lights presuppose that there is someone who has regulated the lights so that they have a regular rhythm. When the mechanism is stuck it is very amusing to see how long it takes drivers before deciding that the traffic light is no longer mastered by a reliable author. "User input" in programming language is another very telling example of this inscription in the automatism of a living character whose behavior is both free and predetermined.

This inscription of author and users in the scene is very much the same as that of a text. I already showed how the author of this article was ascribed (wrongly) to be a technologist in Ohio. It is the same for the reader. I have many times used "you" and even "you sociologists." If you remember well, I even ordered you to draw up a table (or advised you to do so). I also asked your permission to go on with the story. In doing so, I built up an *inscribed reader* to whom I prescribed qualities and behavior as surely as the traffic light or the painting prepared a position for those looking at them. Did you *subscribe* to this definition of yourself? Or worse, is there any one at all to read this text and occupy the position prepared for the reader? This question is a source of constant difficulties for those who do not grasp the basics of semiotics. Nothing in a given scene can prevent the inscribed user or reader from behaving differently from what was expected (nothing, that is, until the next paragraph). The reader-in-the-flesh may totally ignore my definition of him or her. The user of the traffic light may well cross on the red. Even visitors to the department of sociology may never show up because Walla Walla is too far away, *in spite of* the fact that their behavior and trajectory have been perfectly anticipated by the groom. As for the computer user input, the cursor might flash for ever without the user being there or knowing what to do. There might be an enormous gap between the prescribed user and the user-in-the-flesh, a difference as big as the one between the "I" of a novel and the novelist. It is exactly this difference that so much upset the authors of the anonymous appeal posted on the door. It is because they could not discipline people with words, notes, and grooms, that they had to appeal to God. On another occasion, however, the gap between the two may be nil: the prescribed user is so well anticipated, so carefully nested inside the scenes, so exactly dovetailed, that it does what is expected. To stay within the same etymological root, I would be tempted to call the way actors (human or nonhuman) tend to extirpate themselves from the prescribed behavior *des-inscription* and the way they accept or happily acquiesce to their lot *subscription*.

The problem with scenes is that they are usually well prepared for anticipating users or readers who are at close quarter. For instance, the groom is quite good in its anticipation that people will push the door open and give it the energy to reclose it. It is very bad at doing anything to help people arrive there. After fifty centimeters, it is helpless and cannot act, for example, to bring people to Washington State.

Still, no scene is prepared without a preconceived idea of what sort of actors will come to occupy the prescribed positions. This is why I said that, although *you* were free not to go on with this paper, *you* were only "relatively" so. Why? Because I know you are hard-working, serious American sociologists, reading a serious issue of *Social Problems* on sociology of science and technology. So, I can safely bet that I have a good chance of having you read the paper thoroughly! So my injunction "read the paper up to the end, you sociologist" is not very risky. I will call *pre-inscription* all the work that has to be done upstream of the scene and all the things assimilated by an actor (human or nonhuman) before coming to the scene as a user or as an author. For instance, how to drive a car is basically pre-inscribed in any (western) youth years before he or she comes to passing the driving licence test; hydraulic pistons were also pre-inscribed for slowly giving back the energy gathered years before innovators brought them to bear on automated grooms. Engineers can bet on this pre-determination when they draw up their prescriptions. This is what Gerson and his colleagues call "articulation work" (Fujimura, 1987). A lovely example of efforts at pre-inscription is provided by Orson Welles in *Citizen Kane,* where the hero not only bought a theater for his singing wife to be applauded in, but also bought the journals that were to do the reviews, bought off the art critics themselves, and paid the audience to show up—all to no avail, since the wife eventually quit. Humans and nonhumans are very, very undisciplined no matter what you do and how many predeterminations you are able to control upstream of the action.

Drawing a side-conclusion in passing, we can call *sociologism* the claim that, given the competence and pre-inscription of human users and authors, you can read out the scripts nonhuman actors have to play; and *technologism* the symmetric claim that, given the competence and pre-inscription of the nonhuman actors, you can easily read out and deduce the behavior prescribed to authors and users. From now on, these two absurdities will, I hope, disappear from the scene, since the actors at any point may be human or nonhuman and since the displacement (or translation, or transcription) makes the easy reading-out of one repertoire into the next impossible. The bizarre idea that society might be made up of human relations is a mirror image of the other no less bizarre idea that techniques might be made up of nonhuman relations. We deal with characters, delegates, representatives, or, more nicely, lieutenants (from the French "lieu" "tenant," i.e., holding the place of, for, someone else); some figurative, others nonfigurative; some human, others nonhuman; some competent, others incompetent. You want to cut through this rich diversity of delegates and artificially create two heaps of refuse: "society" on one side and "technology" on the other? That's your privilege, but I have a less messy task in mind.

A scene, a text, an automatism can do a lot of things to their prescribed users at close range, but most of the effect finally ascribed to them depends on a range of other set-ups being aligned. For instance, the groom closes the door only if there are people reaching the Sociology Department of Walla Walla. These people arrive in front of the door only if they have found maps and only if there are roads leading to it; and, of course, people will start bothering about reading the maps, getting to Washington State and pushing the door open only if they are convinced that the department is worth visiting. I will call this *gradient* of aligned set-ups that endow actors with the pre-inscribed competences to find its users a *chreod* (a "necessary path" in the biologist Waddington's Greek): people effortlessly flow through the door, and the groom, hundreds of times a day, recloses the door—when it is not stuck. The result of such an alignment of set-ups is to decrease the number of occasions in which words are used; most of the actions become silent, familiar, incorporated (in human or in nonhuman bodies)—making the analyst's job so much harder. Even the classic debates about freedom, determination, predetermination, brute force, or

efficient will—debates which are the twentieth century version of seventeenth century discussions on grace—will be slowly eroded away. (Since *you* have reached this point, it means I was right in saying earlier that you were not at all free to stop reading the paper. Positioning myself cleverly along a chreod, and adding a few other tricks of my own, I led you *here* … or did I? Maybe you skipped most of it; maybe you did not understand a word of it, oh you undisciplined American sociologist readers!)

There is one loose end in my story: why did the little (automatic) rat go on strike? The answer to this is the same as for the question earlier of why few people show up in Walla Walla. It is not because a piece of behavior is prescribed by an inscription that the predetermined characters will show up on time and do the job expected of them. This is true of humans, but it is truer of nonhumans. In this case the hydraulic piston did its job, but not the spring that collaborated with it. Any of the words above may be used to describe a set-up at any level and not only at the simple one I chose for the sake of clarity. It does not have to be limited to the case where a human deals with a series of nonhuman delegates; it can also be true of relations among nonhumans. In other words, when we get into a more complicated lash-up than the groom, we do not have to stop doing sociology; we go on studying "role expectation," behavior, social relations. The non-figurative character of the actors should not intimidate us.

THE LIEUTENANTS OF OUR SOCIETIES

I used the story of the door-closer to make a nonhuman delegate familiar to the ears and eyes of sociologists. I also used reflexively the semiotic of a story to explain the relations between inscription, prescription, pre-inscription, and chreods. There is, however, a crucial difference between texts and machines that I have to point out. Machines are lieutenants; they hold the places and the roles delegated to them, but this way of shifting is very different from other types (Latour, 1988b).

In story-telling, one calls *shifting out* any displacement of a character either to another space or to another time or to another character. If I tell you "Millikan entered the aula," I translate the present setting—you and me—and shift it to another space, another time, and to other characters (Millikan and his audience). "I," the enunciator, may decide to appear or to disappear or to be represented by a narrator who tells the story ("that day, I was sitting on the upper row of the aula"); "I" may also decide to position you and any reader inside the story ("had you been there, you would have been convinced by Millikan's experiments"). There is no limit to the number of shiftings out a story may be built with. For instance, "I" may well stage a dialogue inside the aula between two characters who are telling a story about what happened at the Academy of Science in Washington, DC. In that case, the aula is the place *from which* narrators shift out to tell a story about the Academy, and they may or may not *shift back in* the aula to resume the first story about Millikan. "I" may also *shift in* the entire series of nested stories to close mine and come back to the situation I started from: you and me. All these displacements are well-known in literature departments and make up the craft of talented writers.

No matter how clever and crafty are our novelists, they are no match for engineers. Engineers constantly shift out characters in other spaces and other times, devise positions for human and nonhuman users, break down competences that they then redistribute to many different actants, build complicated narrative programs and sub-programs that are evaluated and judged. Unfortunately, there are many more literary critiques than there are technologists and the subtle beauties of techno-social imbroglios escape the attention of the literate public. One of the reasons for this lack of concern may be the peculiar nature of the shifting-out that generates machines and devices. Instead of sending the listener of a story into another world, the technical shifting-out inscribes the words into another matter. Instead of allowing the reader of the story to be at the same time away (in the story's frame of reference) and here (in his armchair), the technical shifting-out forces him to choose between frames of reference. Instead of allowing enunciators and enunciatees a sort of simultaneous presence and communion with other actors, technics allow both of them to ignore the delegated actors and to walk away without even feeling their presence.[3]

To understand this difference in the two directions of shifting out, let us venture out once more onto a Columbus freeway. For the umpteenth time I have screamed to Robin, "don't sit on the middle of the rear seat; if I brake too hard, you're dead." In an auto shop further along the freeway I come across a device *made for* tired-and-angry-parents-driving-cars-with-kids-between-two-and-five (that is too old for a baby seat and not old enough for a seat belt) and-from-small-families (that is without other persons to hold them safely) and-having-cars-with-two-separated-front-seats-and-head-rests. It is a small market but nicely analyzed by these Japanese fellows and, given the price, it surely pays off handsomely. This description of myself and the small category into which I am happy to *subscribe* is *transcribed* in the device—a steel bar with strong attachments to the head rests—and in the advertisement on the outside of the box. It is also *pre-inscribed* in about the only place where I could have realized that I needed it, the freeway. Making a short story already too long, I no longer scream at Robin and I no longer try to foolishly stop him with my extended right arm: he firmly holds the bar that protects him—or so I believe—against my braking. I have delegated the continuous injunction of my voice and extension of my right arm (with diminishing results as we know from Feschner's law) to a reinforced, padded, steel bar. Of course, I had to make two detours: one to my wallet, the second to my tool box. Thirty bucks and five minutes later I had fixed the device (after making sense of the instructions encoded with Japanese ideograms). The detour plus the translation of words and extended arm to steel is a shifting out to be sure, but not of the same type as that of a story. The steel bar has now taken over my competence as far as keeping my son at arm's length is concerned.

If in our societies, there are thousands of such lieutenants to which we have delegated competences, it means that what defines our social relations is, for the most part, prescribed back to us by nonhumans. Knowledge, morality, craft, force, sociability are not properties of humans but of humans *accompanied by* their retinue of delegated characters. Since each of those delegates ties together part of our social world, it means that studying social relations without the nonhumans is impossible (Latour, 1988a) or adapted only to complex primate societies like those of baboons (Strum and Latour, 1987). One of the tasks of sociology is to do for the masses of nonhumans that make up our modern societies what it did so well for the masses of ordinary and despised humans that make up our society. To the people and ordinary folks should now be added the lively, fascinating, and honorable ordinary mechanism. If the concepts, habits, and preferred fields of sociologists have to be modified a bit to accommodate these new masses, it is small price to pay.

NOTES

* A version of this paper was delivered at Twente, Holland, in September, 1987. This paper owes a lot to Madeleine Akrich's work.

1. See note below for the social deconstruction of the authors.

2. The author-in-the-text is Jim Johnson, technologist in Columbus, Ohio, who went to Walla Walla University, whereas the author-in-the-flesh is Bruno Latour, sociologist, from Paris, France, who never went to Columbus nor to Walla Walla University. The distance between the two is great but similar to that between Steven Jobs, the inventor of Macintosh, and the figurative nonhuman character who/which says "welcome to Macintosh" when you switch on your computer. The reason for this use of pseudonym was the opinion of the editors that no American sociologist is willing to read things that refer to specific places and times which are not American. Thus I inscribed in my text American scenes so as to decrease the gap between the prescribed reader and the pre-inscribed one. (*Editors' Note:* Since we believed these locations to be unimportant to Bruno Latour's argument, we urged him to remove specific place references that might have been unfamiliar to U.S. readers and thus possibly distracting. His solution seems to have proven our point. Correspondence to the author-in-the-flesh should go to Centre de Sociologie de l'Innovation, Ecole Nationale Supérieure des Mines, 62 boulevard Saint-Michel, 75006 Paris, France.)

3. To the shame of our trade, it is an art historian, Michael Baxandall (1985), who offers the most precise description of a technical artifact (a Scottish Iron Bridge) and who shows in most detail the basic distinctions between delegated actors which remain silent (black-boxed) and the rich series of mediators who remain *present* in a work of art.

REFERENCES

Akrich, Madeleine
1987 "Comment décrite les objects techniques." Technique et Culture 5:49–63.

Baxandall, Michael
1985 Patterns of Invention. On the Historical Explanation of Pictures. New Haven, CT: Yale University Press.

Bijker, Wiebe, Thomas Hughes, and Trevor Pinch, eds.
1986 New Developments in the Social Studies of Technology. Cambridge, MA: MIT Press.

Fujimura, Joan
1987 "Constructing 'do-able' problems in cancer research: articulating alignment." Social Studies of Science 17:257–93.

Latour, Bruno
1987 Science in Action. Cambridge, MA: Harvard University Press.
1988a "How to write *The Prince* for machines as well as for machinations." Pp. 20–63 in Brian Elliot (ed.), Technology and Social Change. Edinburgh: Edinburgh University Press.
1988b "A relativistic account of Einstein's relativity." Social Studies of Science 18:3–44.

MacKenzie, Donald and Judy Wacjman, eds.
1985   The Social Shaping of Technology. A Reader. Philadelphia: Milton Keynes and Open University Press.

Mumford, Lewis
1966   The Myth of the Machine. New York: Harcourt.

Strum, Shirley and Bruno Latour
1987   "Redefining the social link: from baboons to humans." Social Science Information 26:783–802.

Winner, Langdon
1986   The Whale and the Reactor: A Search for the Limits in an Age of High Technology. Chicago: University of Chicago Press.
1980   "Do artefacts have politics?" Daedalus 109:121–36.

COMPANION WEBSITE

1. Go online to Write Out Loud about the role nonhuman actors "play" in the construction of social life.
2. Log on to the Profile Pages to learn more about Latour and other contemporary French theorists.
3. Check out the *Emergence Through Convergence* Supplementary Sources for more resources on actor-network theory.

8

The Social Construction of Reality

Peter Berger and Thomas Luckmann

THE REALITY OF EVERYDAY LIFE

Since our purpose in this treatise is a sociological analysis of the reality of everyday life, more precisely, of knowledge that guides conduct in everyday life, and we are only tangentially interested in how this reality may appear in various theoretical perspectives to intellectuals, we must begin by a clarification of that reality as it is available to the commonsense of the ordinary members of society. How that commonsense reality may be influenced by the theoretical constructions of intellectuals and other merchants of ideas is a further question. Ours is thus an enterprise that, although theoretical in character, is geared to the understanding of a reality that forms the subject matter of the empirical science of sociology, that is, the world of everyday life.

It should be evident, then, that our purpose is *not* to engage in philosophy. All the same, if the reality of everyday life is to be understood, account must be taken of its intrinsic character before we can proceed with sociological analysis proper. Everyday life presents itself as a reality interpreted by men and subjectively meaningful to them as a coherent world. As sociologists we take this reality as the object of our analyses. Within the frame of reference of sociology as an empirical science it is possible to take this reality as given, to take as data particular phenomena arising within it, without further inquiring about the foundations of this reality, which is a philosophical task. However, given the particular purpose of the present treatise, we cannot completely bypass the philosophical problem. The world of everyday life is not only taken for granted as reality by the ordinary members of society in the subjectively meaningful conduct of their lives. It is a world that originates in their thoughts and actions, and is maintained as real by these. Before turning to our main task we must, therefore, attempt to clarify the foundations of knowledge in everyday life, to wit, the objectivations of subjective processes (and meanings) by which the *inter*subjective commonsense world is constructed.

For the purpose at hand, this is a preliminary task, and we can do no more than sketch the main features of what we believe to be an adequate solution to the philosophical problem—adequate, let us hasten to add, only in the sense that it can serve as a starting point for sociological analysis. The considerations immediately following are, therefore, of the nature of philosophical prolegomena and, in themselves, presociological. The method we consider best suited to clarify the foundations of knowledge in everyday life is that of phenomenological analysis, a purely descriptive method and, as such, "empirical" but not "scientific"—as we understand the nature of the empirical sciences.[1]

The phenomenological analysis of everyday life, or rather of the subjective experience of everyday life, refrains from any causal or genetic hypotheses, as well as from assertions about the ontological status of the phenomena analyzed. It is important to remember this. Commonsense contains innumerable pre and quasi-scientific interpretations about everyday reality, which it takes for granted. If we are to describe the reality of commonsense we must refer to these interpretations, just as we must take account of its taken-for-granted character—but we do so within phenomenological brackets.

Consciousness is always intentional; it always intends or is directed toward objects. We can never apprehend some putative substratum of consciousness as such, only consciousness of something or other. This is so regardless of whether the object of consciousness is experienced as belonging to an external physical world or apprehended as an element of an inward subjective reality. Whether I (the first person singular, here as in the following illustrations, standing for ordinary self-consciousness in everyday life) am viewing the panorama of New York City or whether I become conscious of an inner anxiety, the processes of consciousness involved are intentional in both instances. The point need not be belabored that the consciousness of the Empire State Building differs from the awareness of anxiety. A detailed phenomenological analysis would uncover the various layers of experience, and the different structures of meaning involved in, say, being bitten by a dog, remembering having been bitten by a dog, having a phobia about all dogs, and so forth. What interests us here is the common intentional character of all consciousness.

Different objects present themselves to consciousness as constituents of different spheres of reality. I recognize the fellowmen I must deal with in the course of everyday life as pertaining to a reality quite different from the disembodied figures that appear in my dreams. The two sets of objects introduce quite different tensions into my consciousness and I am attentive to them in quite different ways. My consciousness, then, is capable of moving through different spheres of reality. Put differently, I am conscious of the world as consisting of multiple realities. As I move from one reality to another, I experience the transition as a kind of shock. This shock is to be understood as caused by the shift in attentiveness that the transition entails. Waking up from a dream illustrates this shift most simply.

Among the multiple realities there is one that presents itself as the reality par excellence. This is the reality of everyday life. Its privileged position entitles it to the designation of paramount reality. The tension of consciousness is highest in everyday life, that is, the latter imposes itself upon consciousness in the most massive, urgent and intense manner. It is impossible to ignore, difficult even to weaken in its imperative presence. Consequently, it forces me to be attentive to it in the fullest way. I experience everyday life in the state of being wide-awake. This wide-awake state of existing in and apprehending the reality of everyday life is taken by me to be normal and self-evident, that is, it constitutes my natural attitude.

I apprehend the reality of everyday life as an ordered reality. Its phenomena are prearranged in patterns that seem to be independent of my apprehension of them and that impose themselves upon the latter. The reality of everyday life appears already objectified, that is, constituted by an order of objects that have been designated *as* objects before my appearance on the scene. The language used in everyday life continuously provides me with the necessary objectifications and posits the order within which these make sense and within which everyday life has meaning for me. I live in a place that is geographically designated; I employ tools, from can openers to sports cars, which are designated in the technical vocabulary of my society; I live within a web of human relationships, from my chess club to the United States of America, which are also ordered by means of vocabulary. In this manner language marks the co-ordinates of my life in society and fills that life with meaningful objects.

The reality of everyday life is organized around the "here" of my body and the "now" of my present.

This "here and now" is the focus of my attention to the reality of everyday life. What is "here and now" presented to me in everyday life is the *realissimum* of my consciousness. The reality of everyday life is not, however, exhausted by these immediate presences, but embraces phenomena that are not present "here and now." This means that I experience everyday life in terms of differing degrees of closeness and remoteness both spatially and temporally. Closest to me is the zone of everyday life that is directly accessible to my bodily manipulation. This zone contains the world within my reach, the world in which I act so as to modify its reality, or the world in which I work. In this world of working my consciousness is dominated by the pragmatic motive, that is, my attention to this world is mainly determined by what I am doing, have done or plan to do in it. In this way it is *my* world par excellence. I know, of course, that the reality of everyday life contains zones that are not accessible to me in this manner. But either I have no pragmatic interest in these zones or my interest in them is indirect insofar as they may be, potentially, manipulative zones for me. Typically, my interest in the far zones is less intense and certainly less urgent. I am intensely interested in the cluster of objects involved in my daily occupation—say, the world of the garage, if I am a mechanic. I am interested, though less directly, in what goes on in the testing laboratories of the automobile industry in Detroit—I am unlikely ever to be in one of these laboratories, but the work done there will eventually affect my everyday life. I may also be interested in what goes on at Cape Kennedy or in outer space, but this interest is a matter of private, "leisure-time" choice rather than an urgent necessity of my everyday life.

The reality of everyday life further presents itself to me as an intersubjective world, a world that I share with others. This intersubjectivity sharply differentiates everyday life from other realities of which I am conscious. I am alone in the world of my dreams, but I know that the world of everyday life is as real to others as it is to myself. Indeed, I cannot exist in everyday life without continually interacting and communicating with others. I know that my natural attitude to this world corresponds to the natural attitude of others, that they also comprehend the objectifications by which this world is ordered, that they also organize this world around the "here and now" of *their* being in it and have projects for working in it. I also know, of course, that the others have a perspective on this common world that is not identical with mine. My "here" is their "there." My "now" does not fully overlap with theirs. My projects differ from and may even conflict with theirs. All the same, I know that I live with them in a common world. Most importantly, I know that there is an ongoing correspondence between *my* meanings and *their* meanings in this world, that we share a common sense about its reality. The natural attitude is the attitude of commonsense consciousness precisely because it refers to a world that is common to many men. Commonsense knowledge is the knowledge I share with others in the normal, self-evident routines of everyday life.

The reality of everyday life is taken for granted *as* reality. It does not require additional verification over and beyond its simple presence. It is simply *there*, as self-evident and compelling facticity. I *know* that it is real. While I am capable of engaging in doubt about its reality, I am obliged to suspend such doubt as I routinely exist in everyday life. This suspension of doubt is so firm that to abandon it, as I might want to do, say, in theoretical or religious contemplation, I have to make an extreme transition. The world of everyday life proclaims itself and, when I want to challenge the proclamation, I must engage in a deliberate, by no means easy effort. The transition from the natural attitude to the theoretical attitude of the philosopher or scientist illustrates this point. But not all aspects of this reality are equally unproblematic. Everyday life is divided into sectors that are apprehended routinely, and others that present me with problems of one kind or another. Suppose that I am an automobile mechanic who is highly knowledgeable about all American-made cars. Everything that pertains to the latter is a routine, unproblematic facet of my everyday life. But one day someone appears in the garage and asks me to repair his Volkswagen. I am now compelled to enter the problematic world of foreign-made cars. I may do so reluctantly or with professional curiosity, but in either case I am now faced with problems that I have not yet routinized. At the same time, of course, I do not leave the reality of everyday life. Indeed, the latter becomes enriched as I begin to incorporate into it the knowledge and skills required for the repair of foreign-made cars. The reality of everyday life encompasses both kinds of sectors, as long as what appears as a problem does not pertain to a different reality altogether (say, the reality of theoretical physics, or of nightmares). As long as the routines of everyday life continue without interruption they are apprehended as unproblematic.

But even the unproblematic sector of everyday reality is so only until further notice, that is, until its continuity is interrupted by the appearance of a problem. When this happens, the reality of everyday life seeks to integrate the problematic sector into what is already unproblematic. Commonsense knowledge contains a variety of instructions as to how this is to be done.

[...]

ORIGINS OF INSTITUTIONALIZATION

All human activity is subject to habitualization. Any action that is repeated frequently becomes cast into a pattern, which can then be reproduced with an economy of effort and which, *ipso facto*, is apprehended by its performer *as* that pattern. Habitualization further implies that the action in question may be performed again in the future in the same manner and with the same economical effort. This is true of non-social as well as of social activity. Even the solitary individual on the proverbial desert island habitualizes his activity. When he wakes up in the morning and resumes his attempts to construct a canoe out of matchsticks, he may mumble to himself, "There I go again," as he starts on step one of an operating procedure consisting of, say, ten steps. In other words, even solitary man has at least the company of his operating procedures.

Habitualized actions, of course, retain their meaningful character for the individual although the meanings involved become embedded as routines in his general stock of knowledge, taken for granted by him and at hand for his projects into the future.[2] Habitualization carries with it the important psychological gain that choices are narrowed. While in theory there may be a hundred ways to go about the project of building a canoe out of matchsticks, habitualization narrows these down to one. This frees the individual from the burden of "all those decisions," providing a psychological relief that has its basis in man's undirected instinctual structure. Habitualization provides the direction and the specialization of activity that is lacking in man's biological equipment, thus relieving the accumulation of tensions that result from undirected drives.[3]

[...]

Institutionalization occurs whenever there is a reciprocal typification of habitualized actions by types of actors. Put differently, any such typification is an institution.[4] What must be stressed is the reciprocity of institutional typifications and the typicality of not only the actions but also the actors in institutions. The typifications of habitualized actions that constitute institutions are always shared ones. They are *available* to all the members of the particular social group in question, and the institution itself typifies individual actors as well as individual actions. The institution posits that actions of type X will be performed by actors of type X. For example, the institution of the law posits that heads shall be chopped off in specific ways under specific circumstances, and that specific types of individuals shall do the chopping (executioners, say, or members of an impure caste, or virgins under a certain age, or those who have been designated by an oracle).

Institutions further imply historicity and control. Reciprocal typifications of actions are built up in the course of a shared history. They cannot be created instantaneously. Institutions always have a history, of which they are the products. It is impossible to understand an institution adequately without an understanding of the historical process in which it was produced. Institutions also, by the very fact of their existence, control human conduct by setting up predefined patterns of conduct, which channel it in one direction as against the many other directions that would theoretically be possible. It is important to stress that this controlling character is inherent in institutionalization as such, prior to or apart from any mechanisms of sanctions specifically set up to support an institution. These mechanisms (the sum of which constitute what is generally called a system of social control) do, of course, exist in many institutions and in all the agglomerations of institutions that we call societies. Their controlling efficacy, however, is of a secondary or supplementary kind. As we shall see again later, the primary social control is given in the existence of an institution as such. To say that a segment of human activity has been institutionalized is already to say that this segment of human activity has been subsumed under social control. Additional control mechanisms are required only insofar as the processes of institutionalization are less than completely successful. Thus, for instance, the law may provide that anyone who breaks the incest taboo will have his head chopped off. This provision may be necessary because there have been cases when individuals offended against the taboo. It is

unlikely that this sanction will have to be invoked continuously (unless the institution delineated by the incest taboo is itself in the course of disintegration, a special case that we need not elaborate here). It makes little sense, therefore, to say that human sexuality is socially controlled by beheading certain individuals. Rather, human sexuality is socially controlled by its institutionalization in the course of the particular history in question. One may add, of course, that the incest taboo itself is nothing but the negative side of an assemblage of typifications, which define in the first place which sexual conduct is incestuous and which is not.

In actual experience institutions generally manifest themselves in collectivities containing considerable numbers of people. It is theoretically important, however, to emphasize that the institutionalizing process of reciprocal typification would occur even if two individuals began to interact *de novo*. Institutionalization is incipient in every social situation continuing in time. Let us assume that two persons from entirely different social worlds begin to interact. By saying "persons" we presuppose that the two individuals have formed selves, something that could, of course, have occurred only in a social process. We are thus for the moment excluding the cases of Adam and Eve, or of two "feral" children meeting in a clearing of a primeval jungle. But we are assuming that the two individuals arrive at their meeting place from social worlds that have been historically produced in segregation from each other, and that the interaction therefore takes place in a situation that has not been institutionally defined for either of the participants. It may be possible to imagine a Man Friday joining our matchstick-canoe builder on his desert island, and to imagine the former as a Papuan and the latter as an American. In that case, however, it is likely that the American will have read or at least have heard about the story of Robinson Crusoe, which will introduce a measure of predefinition of the situation at least for him. Let us, then, simply call our two persons *A* and *B*.

As *A* and *B* interact, in whatever manner, typifications will be produced quite quickly. *A* watches *B* perform. He attributes motives to *B's* actions and, seeing the actions recur, typifies the motives as recurrent. As *B* goes on performing, *A* is soon able to say to himself, "Aha, there he goes again." At the same time, *A* may assume that *B* is doing the same thing with regard to him. From the beginning, both *A* and *B* assume this reciprocity of typification. In the course of their interaction these typifications will be expressed in specific patterns of conduct. That is, *A* and *B* will begin to play roles *vis-à-vis* each other. This will occur even if each continues to perform actions different from those of the other. The possibility of taking the role of the other will appear with regard to the same actions performed by both. That is, A will inwardly appropriate *B's* reiterated roles and make them the models for his own role-playing. For example, *B's* role in the activity of preparing food is not only typified as such by *A*, but enters as a constitutive element into *A's* own food-preparation role. Thus a collection of reciprocally typified actions will emerge, habitualized for each in roles, some of which will be performed separately and some in common.[5] While this reciprocal typification is not yet institutionalization (since, there only being two individuals, there is no possibility of a typology of actors), it is clear that institutionalization is already present *in nucleo*.

At this stage one may ask what gains accrue to the two individuals from this development. The most important gain is that each will be able to predict the other's actions. Concomitantly, the interaction of both becomes predictable. The "There he goes again" becomes a "There *we* go again." This relieves both individuals of a considerable amount of tension. They save time and effort, not only in whatever external tasks they might be engaged in separately or jointly, but in terms of their respective psychological economies. Their life together is now defined by a widening sphere of taken-for-granted routines. Many actions are possible on a low level of attention. Each action of one is no longer a source of astonishment and potential danger to the other. Instead, much of what goes on takes on the triviality of what, to both, will be everyday life. This means that the two individuals are constructing a background, in the sense discussed before, which will serve to stabilize both their separate actions and their interaction. The construction of this background of routine in turn makes possible a division of labor between them, opening the way for innovations, which demand a higher level of attention. The division of labor and the innovations will lead to new habitualizations, further widening the background common to both individuals. In other words, a social world will be in process of construction, containing within it the roots of an expanding institutional order.

Generally, all actions repeated once or more tend to be habitualized to some degree, just as all actions observed by another necessarily involve some typification on his part. However, for the kind of reciprocal typification just described to occur there must be a continuing social situation in which the habitualized actions of two or more individuals interlock. Which actions are likely to be reciprocally typified in this manner?

The general answer is, those actions that are relevant to both *A* and *B* within their common situation. The areas likely to be relevant in this way will, of course, vary in different situations. Some will be those facing *A* and *B* in terms of their previous biographies, others may be the result of the natural, presocial circumstances of the situation. What will in all cases have to be habitualized is the communication process between *A* and *B*. Labor, sexuality and territoriality are other likely foci of typification and habitualization. In these various areas the situation of *A* and *B* is paradigmatic of the institutionalization occurring in larger societies.

Let us push our paradigm one step further and imagine that *A* and *B* have children. At this point the situation changes qualitatively. The appearance of a third party changes the character of the ongoing social interaction between *A* and *B*, and it will change even further as additional individuals continue to be added.[6] The institutional world, which existed *in statu nascendi* in the original situation of *A* and *B*, is now passed on to others. In this process institutionalization perfects itself. The habitualizations and typifications undertaken in the common life of *A* and *B*, formations that until this point still had the quality of *ad hoc* conceptions of two individuals, now become historical institutions. With the acquisition of historicity, these formations also acquire another crucial quality, or, more accurately, perfect a quality that was incipient as soon as *A* and *B* began the reciprocal typification of their conduct: this quality is objectivity. This means that the institutions that have now been crystallized (for instance, the institution of paternity as it is encountered by the children) are experienced as existing over and beyond the individuals who "happen to" embody them at the moment. In other words, the institutions are now experienced as possessing a reality of their own, a reality that confronts the individual as an external and coercive fact.[7]

As long as the nascent institutions are constructed and maintained only in the interaction of *A* and *B*, their objectivity remains tenuous, easily changeable, almost playful, even while they attain a measure of objectivity by the mere fact of their formation. To put this a little differently, the routinized background of *A's* and *B's* activity remains fairly accessible to deliberate intervention by *A* and *B*. Although the routines, once established, carry within them a tendency to persist, the possibility of changing them or even abolishing them remains at hand in consciousness. *A* and *B* alone are responsible for having constructed this world. *A* and *B* remain capable of changing or abolishing it. What is more, since they themselves have shaped this world in the course of a shared biography which they can remember, the world thus shaped appears fully

transparent to them. They understand the world that they themselves have made. All this changes in the process of transmission to the new generation. The objectivity of the institutional world "thickens" and "hardens," not only for the children, but (by a mirror effect) for the parents as well. The "There we go again" now becomes "This is how these things are done." A world so regarded attains a firmness in consciousness; it becomes real in an ever more massive way and it can no longer be changed so readily. For the children, especially in the early phase of their socialization into it, it becomes *the* world. For the parents, it loses its playful quality and becomes "serious." For the children, the parentally transmitted world is not fully transparent. Since they had no part in shaping it, it confronts them as a given reality that, like nature, is opaque in places at least.

Only at this point does it become possible to speak of a social world at all, in the sense of a comprehensive and given reality confronting the individual in a manner analogous to the reality of the natural world. Only in this way, *as an objective world*, can the social formations be transmitted to a new generation. In the early phases of socialization the child is quite incapable of distinguishing between the objectivity of natural phenomena and the objectivity of the social formations.[8] To take the most important item of socialization, language appears to the child as inherent in the nature of things, and he cannot grasp the notion of its conventionality. A thing *is* what it is called, and it could not be called anything else. All institutions appear in the same way, as given, unalterable and self-evident. Even in our empirically unlikely example of parents having constructed an institutional world *de novo*, the objectivity of this world would be increased for them by the socialization of their children, because the objectivity experienced by the children would reflect back upon their own experience of this world. Empirically, of course, the institutional world transmitted by most parents already has the character of historical and objective reality. The process of transmission simply strengthens the parents' sense of reality, if only because, to put it crudely, if one says, "This is how these things are done," often enough one believes it oneself.[9]

An institutional world, then, is experienced as an objective reality. It has a history that antedates the individual's birth and is not accessible to his biographical recollection. It was there before he was born, and it will be there after his death. This history itself, as the tradition of the existing institutions, has the character of objectivity. The individual's biography is apprehended as an episode located within the objective history of the society. The institutions, as historical and objective facticities, confront the individual as undeniable facts. The institutions are *there*, external to him, persistent in their reality, whether he likes it or not. He cannot wish them away. They resist his attempts to change or evade them. They have coercive power over him, both in themselves, by the sheer force of their facticity, and through the control mechanisms that are usually attached to the most important of them. The objective reality of institutions is not diminished if the individual does not understand their purpose or their mode of operation. He may experience large sectors of the social world as incomprehensible, perhaps oppressive in their opaqueness, but real nonetheless. Since institutions exist as external reality, the individual cannot understand them by introspection. He must "go out" and learn about them, just as he must to learn about nature. This remains true even though the social world, as a humanly produced reality, is potentially understandable in a way not possible in the case of the natural world.[10]

It is important to keep in mind that the objectivity of the institutional world, however massive it may appear to the individual, is a humanly produced, constructed objectivity. The process by which the externalized products of human activity attain the character of objectivity is objectivation.[11] The institutional world is objectivated human activity, and so is every single institution. In other words,

despite the objectivity that marks the social world in human experience, it does not thereby acquire an ontological status apart from the human activity that produced it. The paradox that man is capable of producing a world that he then experiences as something other than a human product will concern us later on. At the moment, it is important to emphasize that the relationship between man, the producer, and the social world, his product, is and remains a dialectical one. That is, man (not, of course, in isolation but in his collectivities) and his social world interact with each other. The product acts back upon the producer. Externalization and objectivation are moments in a continuing dialectical process. The third moment in this process, which is internalization (by which the objectivated social world is retrojected into consciousness in the course of socialization), will occupy us in considerable detail later on. It is already possible, however, to see the fundamental relationship of these three dialectical moments in social reality. Each of them corresponds to an essential characterization of the social world. *Society is a human product. Society is an objective reality. Man is a social product.* It may also already be evident that an analysis of the social world that leaves out any one of these three moments will be distortive.[12] One may further add that only with the transmission of the social world to a new generation (that is, internalization as effectuated in socialization) does the fundamental social dialectic appear in its totality. To repeat, only with the appearance of a new generation can one properly speak of a social world.

At the same point, the institutional world requires legitimation, that is, ways by which it can be "explained" and justified. This is not because it appears less real. As we have seen, the reality of the social world gains in massivity in the course of its transmission. This reality, however, is a historical one, which comes to the new generation as a tradition rather than as a biographical memory. In our paradigmatic example, *A* and *B*, the original creators of the social world, can always reconstruct the circumstances under which their world and any part of it was established. That is, they can arrive at the meaning of an institution by exercising their powers of recollection. *A's* and *B's* children are in an altogether different situation. Their knowledge of the institutional history is by way of "hearsay." The original meaning of the institutions is inaccessible to them in terms of memory. It, therefore, becomes necessary to interpret this meaning to them in various legitimating formulas. These will have to be consistent and comprehensive in terms of the institutional order, if they are to carry conviction to the new generation. The same story, so to speak, must be told to all the children. It follows that the expanding institutional order develops a corresponding canopy of legitimations, stretching over it a protective cover of both cognitive and normative interpretation. These legitimations are learned by the new generation during the same process that socializes them into the institutional order. This, again, will occupy us in greater detail further on.

The development of specific mechanisms of social controls also becomes necessary with the historicization and objectivation of institutions. Deviance from the institutionally "programmed" courses of action becomes likely once the institutions have become realities divorced from their original relevance in the concrete social processes from which they arose. To put this more simply, it is more likely that one will deviate from programs set up for one by others than from programs that one has helped establish oneself. The new generation posits a problem of compliance, and its socialization into the institutional order requires the establishment of sanctions. The institutions must and do claim authority over the individual, independently of the subjective meanings he may attach to any particular situation. The priority of the institutional definitions of situations must be consistently maintained over individual temptations at redefinition. The children must be "taught to behave" and, once taught,

must be "kept in line." So, of course, must the adults. The more conduct is institutionalized, the more predictable and thus the more controlled it becomes. If socialization into the institutions has been effective, outright coercive measures can be applied economically and selectively. Most of the time, conduct will occur "spontaneously" within the institutionally set channels. The more, on the level of meaning, conduct is taken for granted, the more possible alternatives to the institutional "programs" will recede, and the more predictable and controlled conduct will be.

In principle, institutionalization may take place in any area of collectively relevant conduct. In actual fact, sets of institutionalization processes take place concurrently. There is no *a priori* reason for assuming that these processes will necessarily "hang together" functionally, let alone as a logically consistent system. To return once more to our paradigmatic example, slightly changing the fictitious situation, let us assume this time, not a budding family of parents and children, but a piquant triangle of a male *A*, a bisexual female *B*, and a Lesbian *C*. We need not belabor the point that the sexual relevances of these three individuals will not coincide. Relevance *A-B* is not shared by *C*. The habitualizations engendered as a result of relevance *A-B* need bear no relationship to those engendered by relevances *B-C* and *C-A*. There is, after all, no reason why two processes of erotic habitualization, one heterosexual and one Lesbian, cannot take place side by side without functionally integrating with each other or with a third habitualization based on a shared interest in, say, the growing of flowers (or whatever other enterprise might be jointly relevant to an active heterosexual male and an active Lesbian). In other words, three processes of habitualization or incipient institutionalization may occur without their being functionally or logically integrated as social phenomena. The same reasoning holds if *A*, *B* and *C* are posited as collectivities rather than individuals, regardless of what content their relevances might have. Also, functional or logical integration cannot be assumed *a priori* when habitualization or institutionalization processes are limited to the same individuals or collectivities, rather than to the discrete ones assumed in our example.

Nevertheless, the empirical fact remains that institutions do tend to "hang together." If this phenomenon is not to be taken for granted, it must be explained. How can this be done? First, one may argue that *some* relevances will be common to all members of a collectivity. On the other hand, many areas of conduct will be relevant only to certain types. The latter involves an incipient differentiation, at least in the way in which these types are assigned some relatively stable meaning. This assignment may be based on presocial differences, such as sex, or on differences brought about in the course of social interaction, such as those engendered by the division of labor. For example, only women may be concerned with fertility magic and only hunters may engage in cave painting. Or, only the old men may perform the rain ceremonial and only weapon makers may sleep with their maternal cousins. In terms of their external social functionality, these several areas of conduct need not be integrated into *one* cohesive system. They can continue to coexist on the basis of segregated performances. But while performances can be segregated, meanings tend toward at least minimal consistency. As the individual reflects about the successive moments of his experience, he tries to fit their meanings into a consistent biographical framework. This tendency increases as the individual shares with others his meanings and their biographical integration. It is possible that this tendency to integrate meanings is based on a psychological need, which may in turn be physiologically grounded (that is, that there may be a built-in "need" for cohesion in the psycho-physiological constitution of man). Our argument, however, does not rest on such anthropological assumptions, but rather on the analysis of meaningful reciprocity in processes of institutionalization.

It follows that great care is required in any statements one makes about the "logic" of institutions. The logic does not reside in the institutions and their external functionalities, but in the way these are treated in reflection about them. Put differently, reflective consciousness superimposes the quality of logic on the institutional order.[13]

Language provides the fundamental superimposition of logic on the objectivated social world. The edifice of legitimations is built upon language and uses language as its principal instrumentality. The "logic" thus attributed to the institutional order is part of the socially available stock of knowledge and taken for granted as such. Since the well-socialized individual "knows" that his social world is a consistent whole, he will be constrained to explain both its functioning and malfunctioning in terms of this "knowledge." It is very easy, as a result, for the observer of any society to assume that its institutions do indeed function and integrate as they are "supposed to."[14]

De facto, then, institutions *are* integrated. But their integration is not a functional imperative for the social processes that produce them; it is rather brought about in a derivative fashion. Individuals perform discrete institutionalized actions within the context of their biography. This biography is a reflected-upon whole in which the discrete actions are thought of not as isolated events, but as related parts in a subjectively meaningful universe whose meanings are not specific to the individual, but socially articulated and shared. Only by way of this detour of socially shared universes of meaning do we arrive at the need for institutional integration.

This has far-reaching implications for any analysis of social phenomena. If the integration of an institutional order can be understood only in terms of the "knowledge" that its members have of it, it follows that the analysis of such "knowledge" will be essential for an analysis of the institutional order in question. It is important to stress that this does not exclusively or even primarily involve a preoccupation with complex theoretical systems serving as legitimations for the institutional order. Theories also have to be taken into account, of course. But theoretical knowledge is only a small and by no means the most important part of what passes for knowledge in a society. Theoretically sophisticated legitimations appear at particular moments of an institutional history. The primary knowledge about the institutional order is knowledge on the pretheoretical level. It is the sum total of "what everybody knows" about a social world, an assemblage of maxims, morals, proverbial nuggets of wisdom, values and beliefs, myths, and so forth, the theoretical integration of which requires considerable intellectual fortitude in itself, as the long line of heroic integrators from Homer to the latest sociological system-builders testifies. On the pretheoretical level, however, every institution has a body of transmitted recipe knowledge, that is, knowledge that supplies the institutionally appropriate rules of conduct.[15]

Such knowledge constitutes the motivating dynamics of institutionalized conduct. It defines the institutionalized areas of conduct and designates all situations falling within them. It defines and constructs the roles to be played in the context of the institutions in question. *Ipso facto*, it controls and predicts all such conduct. Since this knowledge is socially objectivated *as* knowledge, that is, as a body of generally valid truths about reality, any radical deviance from the institutional order appears as a departure from reality. Such deviance may be designated as moral depravity, mental disease, or just plain ignorance. While these fine distinctions will have obvious consequences for the treatment of the deviant, they all share an inferior cognitive status within the particular social world. In this way, the particular social world becomes the world *tout court*. What is taken for granted as knowledge in the society comes to be coextensive with the knowable, or at any rate provides the framework within which anything not yet known will come

to be known in the future. This is the knowledge that is learned in the course of socialization and that mediates the internalization within individual consciousness of the objectivated structures of the social world. Knowledge, in this sense, is at the heart of the fundamental dialectic of society. It "programs" the channels in which externalization produces an objective world. It objectifies this world through language and the cognitive apparatus based on language, that is, it orders it into objects to be apprehended as reality.[16] It is internalized again *as* objectively valid truth in the course of socialization. Knowledge about society is thus a *realization* in the double sense of the word, in the sense of apprehending the objectivated social reality, and in the sense of ongoingly producing this reality.

For example, in the course of the division of labor a body of knowledge is developed that refers to the particular activities involved. In its linguistic basis, this knowledge is already indispensable to the institutional "programming" of these economic activities. There will be, say, a vocabulary designating the various modes of hunting, the weapons to be employed, the animals that serve as prey, and so on. There will further be a collection of recipes that must be learned if one is to hunt correctly. This knowledge serves as a channeling, controlling force in itself, an indispensable ingredient of the institutionalization of this area of conduct. As the institution of hunting is crystallized and persists in time, the same body of knowledge serves as an objective (and, incidentally, empirically verifiable) description of it. A whole segment of the social world is objectified by this knowledge. There will be an objective "science" of hunting, corresponding to the objective reality of the hunting economy. The point need not be belabored that here "empirical verification" and "science" are not understood in the sense of modern scientific canons, but rather in the sense of knowledge that may be borne out in experience and that can subsequently become systematically organized as a body of knowledge.

Again, the same body of knowledge is transmitted to the next generation. It is learned as objective truth in the course of socialization and thus internalized as subjective reality. This reality in turn has power to shape the individual. It will produce a specific type of person, namely the hunter, whose identity and biography *as* a hunter have meaning only in a universe constituted by the aforementioned body of knowledge as a whole (say, in a hunters' society) or in part (say, in our own society, in which hunters come together in a sub-universe of their own). In other words, no part of the institutionalization of hunting can exist without the particular knowledge that has been socially produced and objectivated with reference to this activity. To hunt and to be a hunter implies existence in a social world defined and controlled by this body of knowledge. *Mutatis mutandis*, the same applies to any area of institutionalized conduct.

NOTES

1. This entire section of our treatise is based on Alfred Schutz and Thomas Luckmann, *Die Strukturen der Lebenswelt*, now being prepared for publication. In view of this, we have refrained from providing individual references to the places in Schutz's published work where the same problems are discussed. Our argument here is based on Schutz, as developed by Luckmann in the afore-mentioned work, *in toto*. The reader wishing to acquaint himself with Schutz's work published to date may consult Alfred Schutz, *Der sinnhafte Aufbau der sozialen Welt* (Vienna, Springer, 1960); *Collected Papers*, Vols. I and II. The reader interested in Schutz's adaptation of the phenomenological method to the analysis of the social world may consult especially his *Collected Papers*, Vol. I, pp. 99 ff., and Maurice Natanson (ed.), *Philosophy of the Social Sciences* (New York, Random House, 1963), pp. 183 ff.
2. The term "stock of knowledge" is taken from Schutz.
3. Gehlen refers to this point in his concepts of *Triebüberschuss* and *Entlastung*.
4. We are aware of the fact that this concept of institution is broader than the prevailing one in contemporary sociology. We think that such a broader concept is useful for a comprehensive analysis of basic social processes. On social control, *cf.* Friedrich Tenbruck, "Soziale Kontrolle," *Staatslexikon der Goerres-Gesellschaft* (1962), and Heinrich Popitz, "Soziale Normen," *European Journal of Sociology*.
5. The term "taking the role of the other" is taken from Mead. We are here taking Mead's paradigm of socialization and applying it to the broader problem of institutionalization. The argument combines key features of both Mead's and Gehlen's approaches.
6. Simmel's analysis of the expansion from the dyad to the triad is important in this connection. The following argument combines Simmel's and Durkheim's conceptions of the objectivity of social reality.
7. In Durkheim's terms this means that, with the expansion of the dyad into a triad and beyond, the original formations become genuine "social facts," that is, they attain *choséité*.
8. Jean Piaget's concept of infantile "realism" may be compared here.
9. For an analysis of this process in the contemporary family, *cf.* Peter L. Berger and Hansfried Kellner, "Marriage and the Construction of Reality," *Diogenes* 46 (1964), 1 ff.
10. The preceding description closely follows Durkheim's analysis of social reality. This does *not* contradict the Weberian conception of the meaningful character of society. Since social reality always originates in meaningful human actions, it continues to carry meaning even if it is opaque to the individual at a given time. The original may be *reconstructed*, precisely by means of what Weber called *Verstehen*.
11. The term "objectivation" is derived from the Hegelian/Marxian *Versachlichung*.
12. Contemporary American sociology tends towards leaving out the first moment. Its perspective on society thus tends to be what Marx called a reification (*Verdinglichung*), that is, an undialectical distortion of social reality that obscures the latter's character as an ongoing human production, viewing it instead in thing-like categories appropriate only to the world of nature. That the dehumanization implicit in this is mitigated by values deriving from the larger tradition of the society is, presumably, morally fortunate, but is irrelevant theoretically.
13. Pareto's analysis of the "logic" of institutions is relevant here. A point similar to ours is made by Friedrich Tenbruck, *op. cit.* He too insists that

the "strain towards consistency" is rooted in the meaningful character of human action.

14. This, of course, is the fundamental weakness of any functionalistically oriented sociology. For an excellent critique of this, *cf.* the discussion of Bororo society in Claude Lévi-Strauss, *Tristes tropiques* (New York, Atheneum, 1964), pp. 183 ff.

15. The term "recipe knowledge" is taken from Schutz.

16. The term "objectification" is derived from the Hegelian *Vergegenständlichung*.

COMPANION WEBSITE

1. Go online to Write Out Loud about how social reality is constructed through social networking sites and other online mediums.

2. Log on to the Mid-Twentieth-Century American Theory Profile Page to learn more about the reciprocal process of social construction.

3. Check out the *Emergence Through Convergence* Supplementary Sources for more resources on social construction, including Peter Berger's provocative book on religion, *The Sacred Canopy*.

Networks of Capital

Dimensions of Global Capitalism

Introductory Essay:
Salvaging What Wall Street Left Behind

Global economic quakes shook the world in the summer of 2007. Rumblings about troubled assets, zombie banks, and "naked shorts" (yes, that is a real thing) all hinted at deeper fault lines in something bigger, something with more layers than the earth and more questions than answers. As news reports about rising unemployment and government bailouts hinted at a catastrophe on the level of the Great Depression, it became apparent to many that the structure on which our modern economy operates had suddenly revealed its fragility. Yet, despite the doomsday predictions and the real life struggles many people experienced, many of us still lined up around the block for the latest iPad or biked to the co-op for some organic (and more expensive) apples. Perhaps it goes back to that old saying: the more things change, the more they stay the same.

This is to say that where we fit into the big economic picture is complicated. Or, that's the easy answer, but we're more interested in the difficult one. A good place to start for making sense of the global financial crisis is to think about how our economic choices relate to the bigger picture through a series of relationships, much like a network. Take, for example, the subprime mortgage crisis, a major culprit in the global financial meltdown. The problem with subprime mortgages—loans given at high rates to people with less favorable credit histories—was not just that mortgages were given to people who couldn't afford them. Rather, subprime mortgages were simply one layer in a complex system of debt and credit that spanned across the globe through something called "credit default swaps."

Credit default swaps were the hottest thing to hit Wall Street since the power lunch. In the late 1990s, investment banks like Morgan Stanley realized that keeping money on hand as a way to protect themselves against the risk of defaults on the loans they were handing out simply wasn't going to work (after all, money sitting in the bank couldn't make nearly as much as money invested in new markets). So, they began selling those risks, called "credit swaps," to third parties who would assume the risk in exchange for regular payments from the banks, sort of like an insurance policy. For the bank and the investors, this made a lot of sense so long as the original loans were eventually paid off—until then, the money being traded was practically imaginary. According to *Newsweek*, the credit default market was so successful that it doubled annually until reaching more than $6 trillion by 2004.

The problem was that much of this market was based in mortgage-backed securities. For years hopeful homeowners had been purchasing mortgages that were then sold by brokers and banks to investors and insured through these credit default swaps. One homeowner's decision to take out a mortgage suddenly became embedded within largely bogus financial packages that were then traded in a risky global marketplace. Credit default swappers were dealing in thousands and thousands of these mortgage-backed securities, and when the housing bubble burst and homeowners could no longer pay their mortgages, the entire multi-trillion dollar system began to quake and crumble. Financial packages like credit default swaps are what Karl Marx called "insane forms of money" because they obscure, hide, and reconstitute the social relationships that created them in the first place. When the market collapsed, some homeowners realized they didn't even know whom they owed money! If you happened to be one of the homebuyers looking to track where your mortgage went after you took it out to pay for your new three-bedroom rambler, good luck.

This section of readings is all about how our individual decisions to buy a house, an iPad, or an organic apple relate to an entire economic structure that is bigger than the sum of its parts. Our economic lives are comprised of thousands of wages, purchases, gifts, savings, and investments, but they are also social lives comprised of complex human relationships—relationships between our bosses and co-workers, relationships between the products of our labor and ourselves, and relationships between us and the material world. Indeed, how we relate to the economic world shapes how we relate to one another in more ways than we can imagine. It is the reason why we bargain for higher pay, seek out the best deal, and define ourselves through our clothing styles and indie rock collections. Networks of capital are social networks as much as economic ones.

Classical Connections: Karl Marx

Imagine if Karl Marx were to scan the headlines today (on his smart phone, probably). Economy on the brink! Beware the credit crunch! Thousands of jobs disappear! A specter is haunting Europe! Okay, that last one was actually his copy. The specter that Marx and his colleague, Friedrich Engels, referred to was the introduction of a new mode of economic production making its way onto the European scene—communism. But, Marx wasn't so much a theorist of communism as an expert in the inner-workings of capitalism. He was constantly amazed at the ability of capitalism to reinvent itself when confronted with crisis and disarray. Years of progress and growth had also brought poverty and disease to the streets of 1850s Paris and London, yet the economy and all of its fortunes continually marched onward. These contradictory images of success on the one hand and struggle on the other suggested to Marx that something endemic to capitalism could not last, something that would eventually lead to its downfall or, if not that, its magnificent reincarnation.

For Marx, social change is a lot like a chemical reaction. Two or more elements, along with the requisite amounts of fizz, heat, and light, collide to apparently create new substances out of seemingly nothing. Marx argued that the spontaneous collision of social and economic events is actually not spontaneous at all, but is driven by underlying contradictions in how we create, manufacture, and manipulate the material necessities of life. Think about all of the material things that are required in your own life: the fertilizers used to grow that apple you just ate, the chemicals used to flavor your toothpaste, and the computer chips embedded in the back of your cell phone. In the selection from *The German Ideology*, Marx and Engels describe in detail how history begins with material production and progresses as that production process undergoes change and transformation. Marx also argued that along with these material necessities comes a social relationship—more specifically, a relationship based on labor—that becomes repackaged and reallocated to the point where it no longer exists as a social thing to us. It becomes something called *capital* and, to quote Shakespeare, there's the rub.

At a basic level, capital is nothing more than money—money we earn, money we spend, and money we owe. But, for Marx, capital is more than this; for Marx, *capital has become the basis of our entire being*. It is the node that connects us to the rest of the material and social world—and it's the source of instability in the capitalist order.

Let's break down why capital is so unstable. According to Marx's labor theory of value, the exchange value of any single commodity is equal to the amount of labor it takes to produce it. However, when that commodity rolls off the factory floor and into the marketplace, it gets sold for much more than the cost of the original labor. The surplus made from the sale of the commodity gives the appearance that capital can grow and accumulate on its own, not unlike the mortgages that generated boatloads of new money when repackaged as credit swaps.

This smoke-and-mirrors process of capital accumulation through the exploitation of labor power creates havoc for the capitalist system. When work is cheap and the technology swift, too many commodities flood the market, and the workers themselves cannot afford to buy them. So the capitalist searches

For a vivid insight into the living and working conditions in 1840s England, check out Friedrich Engel's "Working-Class Manchester" and Steven Johnson's *The Ghost Map*, both listed in the Supplementary Sources section of the website.

Log onto Marx's Profile Page to learn more about Hegel's dialectical method and Marx's involvement in the Young Hegelians while studying at the University of Berlin.

For a breakdown of how the labor theory of value works and how surplus is generated through the exchange of commodities, go to the interactive reading for Marx's *Capital*.

for new markets in which to sell those commodities or, in some cases, lays off workers to slow down production. This conflict between overproduction and capital accumulation starts as a deal made between a worker and an employer, but it quickly gets scaled up to the level of a town, country, or even the world and its fragility reveals itself, leading to the class antagonisms that Marx and Engels describe in the selection from *Manifesto of the Communist Party*. And it all starts when the social relationship of capital gets repackaged as a magical one.

This is why capital is remarkably resilient despite its volatility. How often do we think about the social relationships that are responsible for the things we buy and consume? Think back to a time when we wanted something that we could not afford or when something we bought seemed so much bigger or more important than life itself. Maybe it was those sneakers that promised Olympic-qualifying leaping ability or those out-of-season mangos that took us back to that Caribbean vacation last winter (or, for most of us, that commercial for a Caribbean resort we watched on TV late last night). The idea that simple commodities have qualities beyond their labor value is what Marx meant by fetishism, which he describes in the selection from his magnum opus, *Capital*. We might call it the "white earbud" effect today. When iPods were released in 2001, it didn't take long for those iconic white earbuds to become more than a portal for transmitting sound waves from a machine to a listener's ears. They instantly became a status marker, a symbol of someone's place in the hip (and expensive) subculture of the new millennium in which Apple is a key trendsetter. And, yet, somewhere in a factory on the other side of the globe, someone or something was putting those earbuds together. Commodity fetishism can manifest itself in myriad ways so long as it obscures the social relationships necessary to produce the commodity itself.

Marx thought the commodification of nearly everything was unavoidable. So long as commodities are just out of our reach, we will want them. In the *Economic and Philosophic Manuscripts of 1844*, Marx describes how the process of producing those commodities eventually alienates us from our desire to creatively produce our material world on our own accord. For Marx, the whole production process—from the labor process to the commodity itself—is one that tears us further and further away from our human nature and, just as importantly, tears us away from our social relationships. As Marx and Engels tell us in *The German Ideology*, our ideas, values, politics, and relationships with each other emanate from how we go about producing the material necessities of life. And, because we take the underlying economic order for granted, thinking of it more as the natural flow of capital and less as a social invention, we collectively search for ways to right the ship, bail out the banks, and rescue the flailing hedge funds when the system begins to quake.

Plug into the Supplementary Sources for some contemporary examples of how class operates today, such as the stellar New York Times' *Class Matters* series.

Ian Cook et al.'s brilliant portrait of the "papaya fetish," listed in the Supplementary Sources of the *Social Theory Re-Wired* website, really brings Marx's idea to life.

Contemporary Extensions: Capital Re-Wired

The uneven development of capitalism across the globe was most certainly in the back of Marx's mind when he was writing in the mid-nineteenth century, but it is hard to imagine he would have predicted the extent to which globalization has captured our imagination today. To many, globalization represents the expansion of capital gone into overdrive, characterized by malicious multinational corporations and dimly lit sweatshops where exploitation happens just as Marx described it. To others, the buzz of Bangalore call centers and the excitement of cargo ships carrying giant containers across oceans come to mind. But, to many of us, we can't quite grasp what globalization is yet; we just know that it is happening.

For suggestions on excellent films on the topic of globalization, including the provocative documentary *Life and Debt,* log on to the Supplementary Sources section for "Networks of Capital."

According to Immanuel Wallerstein, globalization has been happening long before we had a word for it. In "The Rise and Future Demise of the World Capitalist System," Wallerstein outlines what he calls the world-system, which has emerged since the 1500s through a series of economic transitions and now connects all countries through a single division of labor. Much like Marx argued that exploitation happens through the relationship between a laborer and a member of the bourgeoisie, Wallerstein paints an elaborate picture in which core countries extract labor and raw materials from peripheral ones. In other words, capital now accumulates through an ever-expanding network of trade routes, property rights, and labor agreements that simultaneously connect the world while reinforcing its inequalities. And, like Marx, Wallerstein and other world-systems scholars believe that the world-system is fragile and unstable. At some point, the world economy will expand to the limits of the globe, push the boundaries until they can no longer budge, and eventually burst.

Want to *see* how unbalanced and unequal the world is in terms of income, population, or life expectancy? Check out the global "balloon maps" from NPR, available on the Supplementary Sources of the *Re-Wired* website.

Not all scholars agree that increased global connectedness is purely economic. In the next reading, "Materials for an Exploratory Theory of Network Society," Manuel Castells argues that globalization is a network of production, culture, and power that is constantly shaped by advances in technology, which range from communications technologies to genetic engineering and happen faster than Facebook changes its privacy settings. While he agrees with Wallerstein that the entire world has become capitalist to some extent, Castells suggests that the rules of the global network have changed to embrace these new technologies. Power now flows not from corporations or states, but through the informational flows and codes that connect those corporations and states to each other and the world. To go back to the example of the credit default swaps, power did not rest in the investors themselves but rather in the credit swappers who managed those investments, gobbling them up and reallocating them in a virtual marketplace from their individual computer terminals. However, the advancement of the Information Age does not mean that the world has become more flat; rather, with technological advance comes exclusion and inclusion, fragmentation and integration.

Both Wallerstein and Castells give us a bird's eye view on how capital flows through the networks of the modern world. Next, French sociologist Pierre Bourdieu offers a different take on capital, expanding its definition to encompass more than its economic aspects and articulating how capital at the level of the individual is relational. According to Bourdieu, the social space each of us occupies is determined by our economic and cultural capital, both of which are described in "The Forms of Capital." Economic capital is simply capital that can be converted into money, such as land or a trust fund, but cultural capital is much more complex. It is a collection of habits and tastes that can be used to acquire both economic and non-economic advantages only when those around us grant our habits and tastes symbolic importance. Thus, cultural capital is typically acquired through education and can be embodied in how we talk or objectified by what we wear or hang on our walls.

For a different take on cultural capital in American consumerist society, take a look at John Seabrook's *New Yorker* article on "nobrow culture" in the Supplementary Sources.

In the reading from *Distinction*, Bourdieu provides an effective example of cultural capital as embodied in the ways French people talk about art: high-capital aficionados describe the art as "aesthetically beautiful" while low-capital novices label the same piece of art a "mystery." Like Marx, Bourdieu argues that this type of capital is closely connected with inequality; that is, cultural capital reproduces inequality by conferring advantages to children with high cultural capital through the education system. Cultural capital is also important for Bourdieu's concept of *habitus*. Think of *habitus* as a set of dispositions structured by our social position, ranging from what we like and don't like to our actual physicality. That is, how we walk our walk and talk our talk is formed through prior experiences and the types of capital we pick up along the way. *Habitus* is what jazz legend Miles Davis talked about when he told an interviewer how he chose fellow musicians to play with: it wasn't about their talent, Davis said, but rather how they carried themselves and whether their horn was an extension of their body. Bourdieu's concept of *habitus* is different than Marx's thoughts on commodification, but both are describing how capital becomes entrenched and taken for granted in our daily lives.

Visit the Supplementary Sources for examples of cultural capital and habitus in action, including clips from the popular TV drama, *The Wire*, and the popular PBS film, *People Like Us*.

Finally, we include "Capitalism: The Factory of Fragmentation," a piece by geographer David Harvey. Again, like Marx, Harvey is concerned about the crisis of accumulation endemic to modern capitalism, including how much of this accumulation occurs through the dispossession of land and wealth from the public through government-initiated policies and processes. Harvey also has a lot to say about postmodernism, the intellectual and artistic movement in the late twentieth century that, according to Harvey, "tended to jumble together images and thoughts as if criteria of coherence did not matter." (It did much more than this, but Harvey concerns himself here with the postmodern point that nothing is knowable.) Things like culture and lifestyles, although they seem both fragmented and fleeting in modern society, are rooted in this process of accumulation, according to Harvey. Take, for example, our relationship with time and space. We can communicate in nanoseconds with friends and coworkers around the globe, share with them files via Dropbox, Google Hangout, and dozens of related technologies, and, if needed should all of the available technologies fail, catch a plane to see them in just a few hours. Some might argue that our identities have simply become more fluid and, ahem, postmodern, but Harvey uncovers the underlying process of accumulation that allows such identities to happen. If there wasn't capital required to create a modern technological marvel, if capital didn't flow through it, and if more capital wasn't produced as a consequence of it, then the marvel itself probably wouldn't last.

Plug In

As you read the selections by Marx (and don't forget about Engels!), pay close attention to his method of historical materialism, his articulation of how capital generates surplus, and his arguments for how the economic order induces various forms of alienation. But also think about how social relationships in today's world get repackaged into "insane forms of money" and the networks through which those social relationships move and flow. Do the same for Wallerstein, Castells, and Harvey as they scale up the notion of networks and capital to capture the buzz of globalization, and for Bourdieu as he extends the definition of capital to encompass its symbolic and relational aspects. For all the theorists in this section, capital and the networks it flows through—whether those networks traverse the globe or our own social space—are fundamentally social. In order to fully understand monumental events like the recent financial meltdown, we should first understand its social origins.

9

The German Ideology

Karl Marx and Friedrich Engels

T HE PREMISES FROM WHICH we begin are not arbitrary ones, not dogmas, but real premises from which abstraction can only be made in the imagination. They are the real individuals, their activity and the material conditions under which they live, both those which they find already existing and those produced by their activity. These premises can thus be verified in a purely empirical way.

The first premise of all human history is, of course, the existence of living human individuals. Thus the first fact to be established is the physical organisation of these individuals and their consequent relation to the rest of nature. Of course, we cannot here go either into the actual physical nature of man, or into the natural conditions in which man finds himself—geological, orohydrographical, climatic and so on. The writing of history must always set out from these natural bases and their modification in the course of history through the action of men.

Men can be distinguished from animals by consciousness, by religion or anything else you like. They themselves begin to distinguish themselves from animals as soon as they begin to *produce* their means of subsistence, a step which is conditioned by their physical organisation. By producing their means of subsistence men are indirectly producing their actual material life.

The way in which men produce their means of subsistence depends first of all on the nature of the actual means of subsistence they find in existence and have to reproduce. This mode of production must not be considered simply as being the reproduction of the physical existence of the individuals. Rather it is a definite form of activity of these individuals, a definite form of expressing their life, a definite *mode of life* on their part. As individuals express their life, so they are. What they are, therefore, coincides with their production, both with *what* they produce and with *how* they produce. The nature of individuals thus depends on the material conditions determining their production.

[...]

The fact is, therefore, that definite individuals who are productively active in a definite way enter into these definite social and political relations. Empirical observation must in each separate instance bring out empirically, and without any mystification and speculation, the connection of the social and political structure with production. The social structure and the State are continually evolving out of the life process of definite individuals, but of individuals, not as they may appear in their own or other people's imagination, but as they *really* are; i.e., as they operate, produce materially, and hence as they work under definite material limits, presuppositions and conditions independent of their will.

The production of ideas, of conceptions, of consciousness, is at first directly interwoven with the material activity and the material intercourse of men, the language of real life. Conceiving, thinking, the mental intercourse of men, appear at this stage as the direct efflux of their material behaviour. The same applies to mental production as expressed in the language of politics, laws, morality, religion, metaphysics, etc., of a people. Men are the producers of their conceptions, ideas, etc.—real, active men, as they are conditioned by a definite development of their productive forces and of the intercourse corresponding to these, up to its furthest forms. Consciousness can never be anything else than conscious existence, and the existence of men is their actual life-process. If in all ideology men and their circumstances appear upside-down as in a *camera obscura*, this phenomenon arises just as much from their historical life-process as the inversion of objects on the retina does from their physical life-process.

In direct contrast to German philosophy which descends from heaven to earth, here we ascend from earth to heaven. That is to say, we do not set out from what men say, imagine, conceive, nor from men as narrated, thought of, imagined, conceived, in order to arrive at men in the flesh. We set out from real, active men, and on the basis of their real life-process we demonstrate the development of the ideological reflexes and echoes of this life-process. The phantoms formed in the human brain are also, necessarily, sublimates of their material life-process, which is empirically verifiable and bound to material premises. Morality, religion, metaphysics, all the rest of ideology and their corresponding forms of consciousness, thus no longer retain the semblance of independence. They have no history, no development; but men, developing their material production and their material intercourse, alter, along with this their real existence, their thinking and the products of their thinking. Life is not determined by consciousness, but consciousness by life. In the first method of approach the starting-point is consciousness taken as the living individual; in the second method, which conforms to real life, it is the real living individuals themselves, and consciousness is considered solely as *their* consciousness.

This method of approach is not devoid of premises. It starts out from the real premises and does not abandon them for a moment. Its premises are men, not in any fantastic isolation and rigidity, but in their actual, empirically perceptible process of development under definite conditions. As soon as this active life-process is described, history ceases to be a collection of dead facts as it is with the empiricists (themselves still abstract), or an imagined activity of imagined subjects, as with the idealists.

Where speculation ends—in real life—there real, positive science begins: the representation of the practical activity, of the practical process of development of men. Empty talk about consciousness ceases, and real knowledge has to take its place. When reality is depicted, philosophy as an independent branch of knowledge loses its medium of existence. At the best its place can only be taken by a summing-up of the most general results, abstractions which arise from the observation of the historical development of men. Viewed apart from real history, these abstractions have in themselves no value whatsoever. They can only serve to facilitate the arrangement of historical material, to indicate the sequence of its separate strata. But they by no means afford a recipe or schema, as does philosophy, for neatly trimming the epochs of history. On the contrary, our difficulties begin only when we set about the observation and the arrangement—the real depiction—of our historical material, whether of a past epoch or of the present. The removal of these difficulties is governed by premises which it is quite impossible to state here, but which only the study of the actual life-process and the activity of the individuals of each epoch will make evident. We shall select here some of these abstractions, which we use in contradistinction to the ideologists, and shall illustrate them by historical examples.

[...]

The production of life, both of one's own in labour and of fresh life in procreation, now appears as a double relationship: on the one hand as a natural, on the other as a social relationship. By social we understand the co-operation of several individuals, no matter under what conditions, in what manner and to what end. It follows from this that a certain mode of production, or industrial stage, is always combined with a certain mode of co-operation, or social stage, and this mode of co-operation is itself a "productive force." Further, that the multitude of productive forces accessible to men determines the nature of society, hence, that the "history of humanity" must always be studied and treated in relation to the history of industry and exchange. But it is also clear how in Germany it is impossible to write this sort of history, because the Germans lack not only the necessary power of comprehension and the material but also the "evidence of their senses," for across the Rhine you cannot have any experience of these things since history has stopped happening. Thus it is quite obvious from the start that there exists a materialistic connection of men with one another, which is determined by their needs and their mode of production, and which is as old as men themselves. This connection is ever taking on new forms, and thus presents a "history" independently of the existence of any political or religious nonsense which would especially hold men together.

Only now, after having considered four moments, four aspects of the primary historical relationships, do we find that man also possesses "consciousness";[1] but, even so, not inherent, not "pure" consciousness. From the start the "spirit" is afflicted with the curse of being "burdened" with matter, which here makes its appearance in the form of agitated layers of air, sounds, in short, of language. Language is as old as consciousness, language *is* practical consciousness that exists also for other men, and for that reason alone it really exists for me personally as well; language, like consciousness, only arises from the need, the necessity, of intercourse with other men. Where there exists a relationship, it exists for me: the animal does not enter into *"relations"* with anything, it does not enter into any relation at all. For the animal, its relation to others does not exist as a relation. Consciousness is, therefore, from the very beginning a social product, and remains so as long as men exist at all. Consciousness is at first, of course, merely consciousness concerning the *immediate* sensuous environment and consciousness of the limited connection with other persons and things outside the individual who is growing self-conscious. At the same time it is consciousness of nature, which first appears to men as a completely alien, all-powerful and unassailable force, with which men's relations are purely animal and by which they are overawed like beasts; it is thus a purely animal consciousness of nature (natural religion).

We see here immediately: this natural religion or this particular relation of men to nature is determined by the form of society and vice versa. Here, as everywhere, the identity of nature and man appears in such a way that the restricted relation of men to nature determines their restricted relation to one another, and their restricted relation to one another determines men's restricted relation to nature, just because nature is as yet hardly modified historically; and, on the other hand, man's consciousness of the necessity of associating with the individuals around him is the beginning of the consciousness that he is living in society at all. This beginning is as animal as social life itself at this stage. It is mere herd-consciousness, and at this point man is only distinguished from sheep by the fact that with him consciousness takes the place of instinct or that his instinct is a conscious one. This sheep-like or tribal consciousness receives its further development and extension through increased productivity, the increase of needs, and, what is fundamental to both of these, the increase of population. With these there develops the division of labour, which was originally nothing but the division of labour in the sexual act, then that division of labour which develops spontaneously or "naturally" by virtue of natural predisposition (e.g., physical strength), needs, accidents, etc.,

etc. Division of labour only becomes truly such from the moment when a division of material and mental labour appears.[2] From this moment onwards consciousness *can* really flatter itself that it is something other than consciousness of existing practice, that it *really* represents something without representing something real; from now on consciousness is in a position to emancipate itself from the world and to proceed to the formation of "pure" theory, theology, philosophy, ethics, etc. But even if this theory, theology, philosophy, ethics, etc., comes into contradiction with the existing relations, this can only occur because existing social relations have come into contradiction with existing forces of production....

[...]

The ideas of the ruling class are in every epoch the ruling ideas: i.e., the class which is the ruling *material* force of society, is at the same time its ruling *intellectual* force. The class which has the means of material production at its disposal, has control at the same time over the means of mental production, so that thereby, generally speaking, the ideas of those who lack the means of mental production are subject to it. The ruling ideas are nothing more than the ideal expression of the dominant material relationships, the dominant material relationships grasped as ideas; hence of the relationships which make the one class the ruling one, therefore, the ideas of its dominance. The individuals composing the ruling class possess among other things consciousness, and therefore think. Insofar, therefore, as they rule as a class and determine the extent and compass of an epoch, it is self-evident that they do this in its whole range, hence among other things rule also as thinkers, as producers of ideas, and regulate the production and distribution of the ideas of their age: thus their ideas are the ruling ideas of the epoch. For instance, in an age and in a country where royal power, aristocracy and bourgeoisie are contending for mastery and where, therefore, mastery is shared, the doctrine of the separation of powers proves to be the dominant idea and is expressed as an "eternal law."

The division of labour, which we have already seen above as one of the chief forces of history up till now, manifests itself also in the ruling class as the division of mental and material labour, so that inside this class one part appears as the thinkers of the class (its active, conceptive ideologists, who make the perfecting of the illusion of the class about itself their chief source of livelihood), while the others' attitude to these ideas and illusions is more passive and receptive, because they are in reality the active members of this class and have less time to make up illusions and ideas about themselves. Within this class this cleavage can even develop into a certain opposition and hostility between the two parts, which, however, in the case of a practical collision, in which the class itself is endangered, automatically comes to nothing, in which case there also vanishes the semblance that the ruling ideas were not the ideas of the ruling class and had a power distinct from the power of this class. The existence of revolutionary ideas in a particular period presupposes the existence of a revolutionary class; about the premises for the latter sufficient has already been said above.

If now in considering the course of history we detach the ideas of the ruling class from the ruling class itself and attribute to them an independent existence, if we confine ourselves to saying that these or those ideas were dominant at a given time, without bothering ourselves about the conditions of production and the producers of these ideas, if we thus ignore the individuals and world conditions which are the source of the ideas, we can say, for instance, that during the time that the aristocracy was dominant, the concepts honour, loyalty, etc., were dominant, during the dominance of the bourgeoisie the concepts freedom, equality, etc. The ruling class itself on the whole imagines this to be so. This conception of history, which is common to all historians, particularly since the eighteenth century, will necessarily come up against the phenomenon that increasingly abstract ideas hold sway, i.e., ideas which increasingly take on the form of universality. For each new class which puts itself in the place of one ruling before it, is compelled, merely in order to carry through its aim, to represent its interest as the common interest of all the members of society, that is, expressed in ideal form: it has to give its ideas the form of universality, and represent them as the only rational, universally valid ones. The class making a revolution appears from the very start, if only because it is opposed to a *class*, not as a class but as the representative of the whole of society; it appears as the whole mass of society confronting the one ruling class.[3] It can do this because, to start with, its interest really is more connected with the common interest of all other non-ruling classes, because under the pressure of hitherto existing conditions its interest has not yet been able to develop as the particular interest of a particular class. Its victory, therefore, benefits also many individuals of the other classes which are not winning a dominant position, but only insofar as it now puts these individuals in a position to raise themselves into the ruling class. When the French bourgeoisie overthrew the power of the aristocracy, it thereby made it possible for many proletarians to raise themselves above the proletariat, but only insofar as they became bourgeois. Every new class, therefore, achieves its hegemony only on a broader basis than that of the class ruling previously, whereas the opposition of the non-ruling class against the new ruling class later develops all the more sharply and profoundly. Both these things determine the fact that the struggle to be waged against this new ruling class, in its turn, aims at a more decided and radical negation of the previous conditions of society than could all previous classes which sought to rule.

This whole semblance, that the rule of a certain class is only the rule of certain ideas, comes to a natural end, of course, as soon as class rule in general ceases to be the form in which society is organised, that is to say, as soon as it is no longer necessary to represent a particular interest as general or the "general interest" as ruling.

NOTES

1. Marginal note by Marx: "Men have history because they must *produce* their life, and because they must produce it moreover in a *certain* way: this is determined by their physical organisation; their consciousness is determined in just the same way."
2. Marginal note by Marx: "The first form of ideologists, *priests*, is concurrent."
3. Marginal note by Marx: "Universality corresponds to (1) the class versus the estate, (2) the competition, world-wide intercourse, etc., (3) the great numerical strength of the ruling class, (4) the illusion of the *common* interests (in the beginning this illusion is true), (5) the delusion of the ideologists and the division of labour."

COMPANION WEBSITE

1. Go online to Write Out Loud about ruling ideas that govern contemporary society and where those ideas might come from.
2. For an excerpt from Engels' eulogy for his friend Karl Marx, log on to Marx's Profile Page.
3. To learn more about the legacy of Marx, check out Jonathan Wolff's *Why Read Marx Today?*, listed in the *Networks of Capital* Supplementary Sources.

10

Manifesto of the Communist Party

Karl Marx and Friedrich Engels

A SPECTRE IS HAUNTING Europe—the spectre of Communism. All the Powers of old Europe have entered into a holy alliance to exorcise this spectre: Pope and Czar, Metternich and Guizot, French Radicals and German police-spies.

Where is the party in opposition that has not been decried as Communistic by its opponents in power? Where the Opposition that has not hurled back the branding reproach of Communism, against the more advanced opposition parties, as well as against its reactionary adversaries?

Two things result from this fact.

I. Communism is already acknowledged by all European Powers to be itself a Power.
II. It is high time that Communists should openly, in the face of the whole world, publish their views, their aims, their tendencies, and meet this nursery tale of the Spectre of Communism with a Manifesto of the party itself.

To this end, Communists of various nationalities have assembled in London, and sketched the following Manifesto, to be published in the English, French, German, Italian, Flemish and Danish languages.

BOURGEOIS AND PROLETARIANS[1]

The history of all hitherto existing society[2] is the history of class struggles.

Freeman and slave, patrician and plebeian, lord and serf, guild-master[3] and journeyman, in a word, oppressor and oppressed, stood in constant opposition to one another, carried on an uninterrupted, now hidden, now open fight, a fight that each time ended, either in a revolutionary re-constitution of society at large, or in the common ruin of the contending classes.

In the earlier epochs of history, we find almost everywhere a complicated arrangement of society into various orders, a manifold gradation of social rank. In ancient Rome we have patricians, knights, plebeians, slaves; in the Middle Ages, feudal lords, vassals, guild-masters, journeymen, apprentices, serfs; in almost all of these classes, again, subordinate gradations.

The modern bourgeois society that has sprouted from the ruins of feudal society has not done away with clash antagonisms. It has but established new classes, new conditions of oppression, new forms of struggle in place of the old ones.

Our epoch, the epoch of the bourgeoisie, possesses, however, this distinctive feature: it has simplified the class antagonisms: Society as a whole is more and more splitting up into two great hostile camps, into two great classes directly facing each other: Bourgeoisie and Proletariat.

From the serfs of the Middle Ages sprang the chartered burghers of the earliest towns. From these burgesses the first elements of the bourgeoisie were developed.

The discovery of America, the rounding of the Cape, opened up fresh ground for the rising bourgeoisie. The East-Indian and Chinese markets, the colonisation of America, trade with the colonies, the increase in the means of exchange and in commodities generally, gave to commerce, to navigation, to industry, an impulse never before known, and thereby, to the revolutionary element in the tottering feudal society, a rapid development.

The feudal system of industry, under which industrial production was monopolised by closed guilds, now no longer sufficed for the growing wants of the new markets. The manufacturing system took its place. The guild-masters were pushed on one side by the manufacturing middle class; division of labour between the different corporate guilds vanished in the face of division of labour in each single workshop.

Meantime the markets kept ever growing, the demand ever rising. Even manufacture no longer sufficed. Thereupon, steam and machinery revolutionised industrial production. The place of manufacture was taken by the giant, Modern Industry, the place of the industrial middle class, by industrial millionaires, the leaders of whole industrial armies, the modern bourgeois.

Modern industry has established the world-market, for which the discovery of America paved the way. This market has given an immense development to commerce, to navigation, to communication by land. This development has, in its turn, reacted on the extension of industry; and in proportion as industry, commerce, navigation, railways extended, in the same proportion the bourgeoisie developed, increased its capital, and pushed into the background every class handed down from the Middle Ages.

We see, therefore, how the modern bourgeoisie is itself the product of a long course of development, of a series of revolutions in the modes of production and of exchange.

Each step in the development of the bourgeoisie was accompanied by a corresponding political advance of that class. An oppressed class under the sway of the feudal nobility, an armed and self-governing association in the mediaeval commune;[4] here independent urban republic (as in Italy and Germany), there taxable "third estate" of the monarchy (as in France), afterwards, in the period of manufacture proper, serving either the semi-feudal or the absolute monarchy as a counterpoise against the nobility, and, in fact, corner-stone of the great monarchies in general, the bourgeoisie has at last, since the establishment of Modern Industry and of the world-market, conquered for itself, in the modern representative State, exclusive political sway. The executive of the modern State is but a committee for managing the common affairs of the whole bourgeoisie.

The bourgeoisie, historically, has played a most revolutionary part.

The bourgeoisie, wherever it has got the upper hand, has put an end to all feudal, patriarchal, idyllic relations. It has pitilessly torn asunder the motley feudal ties that bound man to his "natural superiors," and has left remaining no other nexus between man and man than naked self-interest, than callous "cash payment." It has drowned the most heavenly ecstasies of religious fervour, of chivalrous enthusiasm, of philistine sentimentalism, in the icy water of egotistical calculation. It has resolved personal worth into exchange value, and in place of the numberless indefeasible chartered freedoms, has set up that single, unconscionable freedom— Free Trade. In one word, for exploitation, veiled by religious and political illusions, it has substituted naked, shameless, direct, brutal exploitation.

The bourgeoisie has stripped of its halo every occupation hitherto honoured and looked up to with reverent awe. It has converted the physician, the lawyer, the priest, the poet, the man of science, into its paid wage-labourers.

The bourgeoisie has torn away from the family its sentimental veil, and has reduced the family relation to a mere money relation.

The bourgeoisie has disclosed how it came to pass that the brutal display of vigour in the Middle

Ages, which Reactionists so much admire, found its fitting complement in the most slothful indolence. It has been the first to show what man's activity can bring about. It has accomplished wonders far surpassing Egyptian pyramids, Roman aqueducts, and Gothic cathedrals; it has conducted expeditions that put in the shade all former Exoduses of nations and crusades.

The bourgeoisie cannot exist without constantly revolutionising the instruments of production, and thereby the relations of production, and with them the whole relations of society. Conservation of the old modes of production in unaltered form, was, on the contrary, the first condition of existence for all earlier industrial classes. Constant revolutionising of production, uninterrupted disturbance of all social conditions, everlasting uncertainty and agitation distinguish the bourgeois epoch from all earlier ones. All fixed, fast-frozen relations, with their train of ancient and venerable prejudices and opinions, are swept away, all new-formed ones become antiquated before they can ossify. All that is solid melts into air, all that is holy is profaned, and man is at last compelled to face with sober senses, his real conditions of life, and his relations with his kind.

The need of a constantly expanding market for its products chases the bourgeoisie over the whole surface of the globe. It must nestle everywhere, settle everywhere, establish connexions everywhere.

The bourgeoisie has through its exploitation of the world-market given a cosmopolitan character to production and consumption in every country. To the great chagrin of Reactionists, it has drawn from under the feet of industry the national ground on which it stood. All old-established national industries have been destroyed or are daily being destroyed. They are dislodged by new industries, whose introduction becomes a life and death question for all civilised nations, by industries that no longer work up indigenous raw material, but raw material drawn from the remotest zones; industries whose products are consumed, not only at home,

but in every quarter of the globe. In place of the old wants, satisfied by the productions of the country, we find new wants, requiring for their satisfaction the products of distant lands and climes. In place of the old local and national seclusion and self-sufficiency, we have intercourse in every direction, universal inter-dependence of nations. And as in material, so also in intellectual production. The intellectual creations of individual nations become common property. National one-sidedness and narrow-mindedness become more and more impossible, and from the numerous national and local literatures, there arises a world literature.

The bourgeoisie, by the rapid improvement of all instruments of production, by the immensely facilitated means of communication, draws all, even the most barbarian, nations into civilisation. The cheap prices of its commodities are the heavy artillery with which it batters down all Chinese walls, with which it forces the barbarians' intensely obstinate hatred of foreigners to capitulate. It compels all nations, on pain of extinction, to adopt the bourgeois mode of production; it compels them to introduce what it calls civilisation into their midst, *i.e.*, to become bourgeois themselves. In one word, it creates a world after its own image.

The bourgeoisie has subjected the country to the rule of the towns. It has created enormous cities, has greatly increased the urban population as compared with the rural, and has thus rescued a considerable part of the population from the idiocy of rural life. Just as it has made the country dependent on the towns, so it has made barbarian and semi-barbarian countries dependent on the civilised ones, nations of peasants on nations of bourgeois, the East on the West.

The bourgeoisie keeps more and more doing away with the scattered state of the population, of the means of production, and of property. It has agglomerated population, centralised means of production, and has concentrated property in a few hands. The necessary consequence of this was political centralisation. Independent, or but loosely connected provinces, with separate interests, laws, governments and systems of taxation, became lumped together into one nation, with one government, one code of laws, one national class-interest, one frontier and one customs-tariff.

The bourgeoisie, during its rule of scarce one hundred years, has created more massive and more colossal productive forces than have all preceding generations together. Subjection of Nature's forces to man, machinery, application of chemistry to industry and agriculture, steam-navigation, railways, electric telegraphs, clearing of whole continents for cultivation, canalisation of rivers, whole populations conjured out of the ground—what earlier century had even a presentiment that such productive forces slumbered in the lap of social labour?

We see then: the means of production and of exchange, on whose foundation the bourgeoisie built itself up, were generated in feudal society. At a certain stage in the development of these means of production and of exchange, the conditions under which feudal society produced and exchanged, the feudal organisation of agriculture and manufacturing industry, in one word, the feudal relations of property became no longer compatible with the already developed productive forces; they became so many fetters. They had to be burst asunder; they were burst asunder.

Into their place stepped free competition, accompanied by a social and political constitution adapted to it, and by the economical and political sway of the bourgeois class.

A similar movement is going on before our own eyes. Modern bourgeois society with its relations of production, of exchange and of property, a society that has conjured up such gigantic means of production and of exchange, is like the sorcerer, who is no longer able to control the powers of the nether world whom he has called up by his spells. For many a decade past the history of industry and commerce is but the history of the revolt of modern productive forces against modern conditions of production, against the property relations that are the conditions for the existence of the bourgeoisie and of its rule. It is enough to mention the commercial crises that by their periodical return put on its trial, each time more threateningly, the existence of the entire bourgeois society. In these crises a great part not only of the existing products, but also of the previously created productive forces, are periodically destroyed. In these crises there breaks out an epidemic that, in all earlier epochs, would have seemed an absurdity—the epidemic of overproduction. Society suddenly finds itself put back into a state of momentary barbarism; it appears as if a famine, a universal war of devastation had cut off the supply of every means of subsistence; industry and commerce seem to be destroyed; and why? Because there is too much civilisation, too much means of subsistence, too much industry, too much commerce. The productive forces at the disposal of society no longer tend to further the development of the conditions of bourgeois property; on the contrary, they have become too powerful for these conditions, by which they are fettered, and so soon as they overcome these fetters, they bring disorder into the whole of bourgeois society, endanger the existence of bourgeois property. The conditions of bourgeois society are too narrow to comprise the wealth created by them. And how does the bourgeoisie get over these crises? On the one hand by enforced destruction of a mass of productive forces; on the other, by the conquest of new markets, and by the more thorough exploitation of the old ones. That is to say, by paving the way for more extensive and more destructive crises, and by diminishing the means whereby crises are prevented.

The weapons with which the bourgeoisie felled feudalism to the ground are now turned against the bourgeoisie itself.

But not only has the bourgeoisie forged the weapons that bring death to itself; it has also called into existence the men who are to wield those weapons—the modern working class—the proletarians.

In proportion as the bourgeoisie, *i.e.*, capital, is developed, in the same proportion is the proletariat, the modern working class, developed—a class of labourers, who live only so long as they find work, and who find work only so long as their labour increases capital. These labourers, who must sell themselves piece-meal, are a commodity, like every other article of commerce, and are consequently exposed to all the vicissitudes of competition, to all the fluctuations of the market.

Owing to the extensive use of machinery and to division of labour, the work of the proletarians has lost all individual character, and consequently, all charm for the workman. He becomes an appendage of the machine, and it is only the most simple, most monotonous, and most easily acquired knack, that is required of him. Hence, the cost of production of a workman is restricted, almost entirely, to the means of subsistence that he requires for his maintenance, and for the propagation of his race. But the price of a commodity, and therefore also of labour,[5] is equal to its cost of production. In proportion, therefore, as the repulsiveness of the work increases, the wage decreases. Nay more, in proportion as the use of machinery and division of labour increases, in the same proportion the burden of toil also increases, whether by prolongation of the working hours, by increase of the work exacted in a given time or by increased speed of the machinery, etc.

Modern industry has converted the little workshop of the patriarchal master into the great factory of the industrial capitalist. Masses of labourers, crowded into the factory, are organised like soldiers. As privates of the industrial army they are placed under the command of a perfect hierarchy of officers and sergeants. Not only are they slaves of the bourgeois class, and of the bourgeois State; they are daily and hourly enslaved by the machine, by the over-looker, and, above all, by the individual bourgeois manufacturer himself. The more openly this despotism proclaims gain to be its end and aim, the more petty, the more hateful and the more embittering it is.

The less the skill and exertion of strength implied in manual labour, in other words, the more modern industry becomes developed, the more is the labour of men superseded by that of women. Differences of age and sex have no longer any distinctive social validity for the working class. All are instruments of labour, more or less expensive to use, according to their age and sex.

No sooner is the exploitation of the labourer by the manufacturer, so far, at an end, that he receives his wages in cash, than he is set upon by the other portions of the bourgeoisie, the landlord, the shopkeeper, the pawnbroker, etc.

The lower strata of the middle class—the small tradespeople, shopkeepers, and retired tradesmen generally, the handicraftsmen and peasants—all these sink gradually into the proletariat, partly because their diminutive capital does not suffice for the scale on which Modern Industry is carried on, and is swamped in the competition with the large capitalists, partly because their specialised skill is rendered worthless by new methods of production. Thus the proletariat is recruited from all classes of the population.

The proletariat goes through various stages of development. With its birth begins its struggle with the bourgeoisie. At first the contest is carried on by individual labourers, then by the workpeople of a factory, then by the operatives of one trade, in one locality, against the individual bourgeois who directly exploits them. They direct their attacks not against the bourgeois conditions of production, but against the instruments of production themselves; they destroy imported wares that compete with their labour, they smash to pieces machinery, they set factories ablaze, they seek to restore by force the vanished status of the workman of the Middle Ages.

At this stage the labourers still form an incoherent mass scattered over the whole country, and broken up by their mutual competition. If anywhere they unite to form more compact bodies, this is not yet the consequence of their own active union, but of the union of the bourgeoisie, which class, in order to attain its own political ends, is compelled to set the whole proletariat in motion, and is moreover yet, for a time, able to do so. At this stage, therefore, the proletarians do not fight their enemies, but the enemies of their enemies, the remnants of absolute monarchy, the landowners, the non-industrial bourgeois, the petty bourgeoisie. Thus the whole historical movement is concentrated in the hands of the bourgeoisie; every victory so obtained is a victory for the bourgeoisie.

But with the development of industry the proletariat not only increases in number; it becomes concentrated in greater masses, its strength grows, and it feels that strength more. The various interests and conditions of life within the ranks of the proletariat are more and more equalised, in proportion as machinery obliterates all distinctions of labour, and nearly everywhere reduces wages to the same low level. The growing competition among the bourgeois, and the resulting commercial crises, make the wages of the workers ever more fluctuating. The unceasing improvement of machinery, ever more rapidly developing, makes their livelihood more and more precarious; the collisions between individual workmen and individual bourgeois take more and more the character of collisions between two classes. Thereupon the workers begin to form combinations (Trades Unions) against the bourgeois; they club together in order to keep up the rate of wages; they found permanent associations in order to make provision beforehand for these occasional revolts. Here and there the contest breaks out into riots.

Now and then the workers are victorious, but only for a time. The real fruit of their battles lies, not in the immediate result, but in the ever-expanding union of the workers. This union is helped on by the improved means of communication that are created by modern industry and that place the workers of different localities in contact with one another. It was just this contact that was needed to centralise the numerous local struggles, all of the same character, into one national struggle between classes. But every class struggle is a political struggle. And that union, to attain which the burghers of the Middle Ages, with their miserable highways, required centuries, the modern proletarians, thanks to railways, achieve in a few years.

This organisation of the proletarians into a class, and consequently into a political party, is continually being upset again by the competition between the workers themselves. But it ever rises up again, stronger, firmer, mightier. It compels legislative recognition of particular interests of the workers, by taking advantage of the divisions among the bourgeoisie itself. Thus the ten-hours' bill in England was carried.

Altogether collisions between the classes of the old society further, in many ways, the course of development of the proletariat. The bourgeoisie finds itself involved in a constant battle. At first with the aristocracy; later on, with those portions of the bourgeoisie itself, whose interests have become antagonistic to the progress of industry; at all times, with the bourgeoisie of foreign countries. In all these battles it sees itself compelled to appeal to the proletariat, to ask for its help, and thus, to drag it into the political arena. The bourgeoisie itself, therefore, supplies the proletariat with its own elements of political and general education, in other words, it furnishes the proletariat with weapons for fighting the bourgeoisie.

Further, as we have already seen, entire sections of the ruling classes are, by the advance of industry, precipitated into the proletariat, or are at least threatened in their conditions of existence. These also supply the proletariat with fresh elements of enlightenment and progress.

Finally, in times when the class struggle nears the decisive hour, the process of dissolution going on within the ruling class, in fact within the whole range of society, assumes such a violent, glaring character, that a small section of the ruling class cuts itself adrift, and joins the revolutionary class, the class that holds the future in its hands. Just as, therefore, at an earlier period, a section of the nobility went over to the bourgeoisie, so now a portion of the bourgeoisie goes over to the proletariat, and in particular, a portion of the bourgeois ideologists, who have raised themselves to the level of comprehending theoretically the historical movement as a whole.

Of all the classes that stand face to face with the bourgeoisie today, the proletariat alone is a really revolutionary class. The other classes decay and finally disappear in the face of Modern Industry; the proletariat is its special and essential product.

The lower middle class, the small manufacturer, the shopkeeper, the artisan, the peasant, all these fight against the bourgeoisie, to save from extinction their existence as fractions of the middle class. They are therefore not revolutionary, but conservative. Nay more, they are reactionary, for they try to roll back the wheel of history. If by chance they are revolutionary, they are so only in view of their impending transfer into the proletariat, they thus defend not their present, but their future interests, they desert their own standpoint to place themselves at that of the proletariat.

The "dangerous class," the social scum, that passively rotting mass thrown off by the lowest layers of old society, may, here and there, be swept into the movement by a proletarian revolution; its conditions of life, however, prepare it far more for the part of a bribed tool of reactionary intrigue.

In the conditions of the proletariat, those of old society at large are already virtually swamped. The proletarian is without property; his relation to his wife and children has no longer anything in common with the bourgeois family-relations; modern industrial labour, modern subjection to capital, the same in England as in France, in America as in Germany, has stripped him of every trace of national character. Law, morality, religion, are to him so many bourgeois prejudices, behind which lurk in ambush just as many bourgeois interests.

All the preceding classes that got the upper hand, sought to fortify their already acquired status by subjecting society at large to their conditions of appropriation. The proletarians cannot become masters of the productive forces of society, except by abolishing their own previous mode of appropriation, and thereby also every other previous mode of appropriation. They have nothing of their own to secure and to fortify; their mission is to destroy all previous securities for, and insurances of, individual property.

All previous historical movements were movements of minorities, or in the interests of minorities. The proletarian movement is the self-conscious, independent movement of the immense majority, in the interests of the immense majority. The proletariat, the lowest stratum of our present society, cannot stir, cannot raise itself up, without the whole superincumbent strata of official society being sprung into the air.

Though not in substance, yet in form, the struggle of the proletariat with the bourgeoisie is at first a national struggle. The proletariat of each country must, of course, first of all settle matters with its own bourgeoisie.

In depicting the most general phases of the development of the proletariat, we traced the more or less veiled civil war, raging within existing society, up to the point where that war breaks out into open revolution, and where the violent overthrow of the bourgeoisie lays the foundation for the sway of the proletariat.

Hitherto, every form of society has been based, as we have already seen, on the antagonism of oppressing and oppressed classes. But in order to oppress a class, certain conditions must be assured to it under which it can, at least, continue its slavish existence. The serf, in the period of serfdom, raised himself to membership in the commune, just as the petty bourgeois, under the yoke of feudal absolutism, managed to develop into a bourgeois. The modern labourer, on the contrary, instead of rising with the progress of industry, sinks deeper and deeper below the conditions of existence of his own class. He becomes a pauper, and pauperism develops more rapidly than population and wealth. And here it becomes evident, that the bourgeoisie is unfit any longer to be the ruling class in society, and to impose its conditions of existence upon society as an over-riding law. It is unfit to rule because it is incompetent to assure an existence to its slave within his slavery, because it cannot help letting him sink into such a state, that it has to feed him, instead of being fed by him. Society can no longer live under this bourgeoisie, in other words, its existence is no longer compatible with society.

The essential condition for the existence, and for the sway of the bourgeois class, is the formation and augmentation of capital; the condition for capital is wage-labour. Wage-labour rests exclusively on competition between the labourers. The advance of industry, whose involuntary promoter is the bourgeoisie, replaces the isolation of the labourers, due to competition, by their revolutionary combination, due to association. The development of Modern Industry, therefore, cuts from under its feet the very foundation on which the bourgeoisie produces and appropriates products. What the bourgeoisie, therefore, produces, above all, is its own grave-diggers. Its fall and the victory of the proletariat are equally inevitable.

[...]

The proletariat will use its political supremacy to wrest, by degrees, all capital from the bourgeoisie, to centralise all instruments of production in the hands of the State, *i.e.*, of the proletariat organised as the ruling class; and to increase the total of productive forces as rapidly as possible.

Of course, in the beginning, this cannot be effected except by means of despotic inroads on the rights of property, and on the conditions of bourgeois production; by means of measures, therefore, which appear economically insufficient and untenable, but which, in the course of the movement, outstrip themselves, necessitate further inroads upon the old social order, and are unavoidable as a means of entirely revolutionising the mode of production.

These measures will of course be different in different countries.

Nevertheless in the most advanced countries, the following will be pretty generally applicable.

1. Abolition of property in land and application of all rents of land to public purposes.
2. A heavy progressive or graduated income tax.
3. Abolition of all right of inheritance.
4. Confiscation of the property of all emigrants and rebels.
5. Centralisation of credit in the hands of the State, by means of a national bank with State capital and an exclusive monopoly.
6. Centralisation of the means of communication and transport in the hands of the State.
7. Extension of factories and instruments of production owned by the State; the bringing into cultivation of waste-lands, and the improvement of the soil generally in accordance with a common plan.
8. Equal liability of all to labour. Establishment of industrial armies, especially for agriculture.
9. Combination of agriculture with manufacturing industries; gradual abolition of the distinction between town and country, by a more equable distribution of the population over the country.
10. Free education for all children in public schools. Abolition of children's factory labour in its present form. Combination of education with industrial production, &c., &c.

When, in the course of development, class distinctions have disappeared, and all production has been concentrated in the hands of a vast association of the whole nation, the public power will lose its political character. Political power, properly so called, is merely the organised power of one class for oppressing another. If the proletariat during its contest with the bourgeoisie is compelled, by the force of circumstances, to organise itself as a class, if, by means of a revolution, it makes itself the ruling class, and, as such, sweeps away by force the old conditions of production, then it will, along with these conditions, have swept away the conditions for the existence of class antagonisms and of classes generally, and will thereby have abolished its own supremacy as a class.

In place of the old bourgeois society, with its classes and class antagonisms, we shall have an association, in which the free development of each is the condition for the free development of all.

NOTES

1. By bourgeoisie is meant the class of modern Capitalists, owners of the means of social production and employers of wage-labour. By proletariat, the class of modern wage-labourers who, having no means of production of their own, are reduced to selling their labour-power in order to live. [*Engels, English edition of 1888*]

2. That is, all *written* history. In 1847, the pre-history of society, the social organisation existing previous to recorded history, was all but unknown. Since then, Haxthausen discovered common ownership of land in Russia, Maurer proved it to be the social foundation from which all Teutonic races started in history, and by and by village communities were found to be, or to have been the primitive form of society everywhere from India to Ireland. The inner organisation of this primitive Communistic society was laid bare, in its typical form, by Morgan's crowning discovery of the true nature of the *gens* and its relation to the *tribe*. With the dissolution of these primaeval communities society begins to be differentiated into separate and finally antagonistic classes. I have attempted to retrace this process of dissolution in: "Der Ursprung der Familie, des Privateigenthums und des Staats" [*The Origin of the Family, Private Property and the State*], 2nd edition, Stuttgart 1886. [*Engels, English edition of 1888*]

3. Guild-master, that is, a full member of a guild, a master within, not a head of a guild. [*Engels, English edition of 1888*]

4. "Commune" was the name taken, in France, by the nascent towns even before they had conquered from their feudal lords and masters local self-government and political rights as the "Third Estate." Generally speaking, for the economical development of the bourgeoisie, England is here taken as the typical country; for its political development, France. [*Engels, English edition of 1888*]

   This was the name given their urban communities by the townsmen of Italy and France, after they had purchased or wrested their initial rights of self-government from their feudal lords. [*Engels, German edition of 1890*]

5. Subsequently Marx pointed out that the worker sells not his labour but his labour power.

COMPANION WEBSITE

1. Go online to Write Out Loud about how the bourgeoisie "forged the weapons that bring death to itself."

2. Log on to Marx's Profile Page for more on his theory of historical materialism and class struggle.

3. Take a look at renowned Marxist scholar Erik Olin Wright's Real Utopias Project, listed in the *Networks of Capital* Supplementary Sources.

11

Capital

Karl Marx

PART I. COMMODITIES AND MONEY

CHAPTER I. COMMODITIES

Section 1. The two factors of a commodity: use-value and value (the substance of value and the magnitude of value)

The wealth of those societies in which the capitalist mode of production prevails, presents itself as "an immense accumulation of commodities,"[1] its unit being a single commodity. Our investigation must therefore begin with the analysis of a commodity.

A commodity is, in the first place, an object outside us, a thing that by its properties satisfies human wants of some sort or another. The nature of such wants, whether, for instance, they spring from the stomach or from fancy, makes no difference.[2] Neither are we here concerned to know how the object satisfies these wants, whether directly as means of subsistence, or indirectly as means of production.

Every useful thing, as iron, paper, &c., may be looked at from the two points of view of quality and quantity. It is an assemblage of many properties, and may therefore be of use in various ways. To discover the various uses of things is the work of history.[3] So also is the establishment of socially-recognised standards of measure for the quantities of these useful objects. The diversity of these measures has its origin partly in the diverse nature of the objects to be measured, partly in convention.

The utility of a thing makes it a use-value.[4] But this utility is not a thing of air. Being limited by the physical properties of the commodity, it has no existence apart from that commodity. A commodity, such as iron, corn, or a diamond, is therefore, so far as it is a material thing, a use-value, something useful. This property of a commodity is independent of the amount of labour required to appropriate its useful qualities. When treating of use-value, we always assume to be dealing with definite quantities, such as dozens of watches, yards of linen, or tons of iron. The use-values of commodities furnish the material for a special study, that of the commercial knowledge of commodities.[5] Use-values become a reality only by use or consumption: they also constitute the substance of all wealth, whatever may be the social form of that wealth. In the form of society we are about to consider, they are, in addition, the material depositories of exchange-value.

Exchange-value, at first sight, presents itself as a quantitative relation, as the proportion in which values in use of one sort are exchanged for those of another sort,[6] a relation constantly changing with time and place. Hence exchange-value appears to be something accidental and purely relative, and consequently an intrinsic value, *i.e.*, an exchange-value that is inseparably connected with, inherent in commodities, seems a contradiction in terms.[7] Let us consider the matter a little more closely.

A given commodity, *e.g.*, a quarter of wheat is exchanged for x blacking, y silk, or z gold, &c.—in

short, for other commodities in the most different proportions. Instead of one exchange-value, the wheat has, therefore, a great many. But since x blacking, y silk, or z gold, &c., each represent the exchange-value of one quarter of wheat, x blacking, y silk, z gold, &c., must, as exchange-values, be replaceable by each other, or equal to each other. Therefore, first: the valid exchange-values of a given commodity express something equal; secondly, exchange-value, generally, is only the mode of expression, the phenomenal form, of something contained in it, yet distinguishable from it.

Let us take two commodities, *e.g.*, corn and iron. The proportions in which they are exchangeable, whatever those proportions may be, can always be represented by an equation in which a given quantity of corn is equated to some quantity of iron: *e.g.*, 1 quarter corn = x cwt. iron. What does this equation tell us? It tells us that in two different things—in 1 quarter of corn and x cwt. of iron, there exists in equal quantities something common to both. The two things must therefore be equal to a third, which in itself is neither the one nor the other. Each of them, so far as it is exchange-value, must therefore be reducible to this third.

A simple geometrical illustration will make this clear. In order to calculate and compare the areas of rectilinear figures, we decompose them into triangles. But the area of the triangle itself is expressed by something totally different from its visible figure, namely, by half the product of the base into the altitude. In the same way the exchange-values of commodities must be capable of being expressed in terms of something common to them all, of which thing they represent a greater or less quantity.

This common "something" cannot be either a geometrical, a chemical, or any other natural property of commodities. Such properties claim our attention only in so far as they affect the utility of those commodities, make them use-values. But the exchange of commodities is evidently an act characterised by a total abstraction from use-value. Then one use-value is just as good as another,

provided only it be present in sufficient quantity. Or, as old Barbon says, "one sort of wares are as good as another, if the values be equal. There is no difference or distinction in things of equal value. ... An hundred pounds' worth of lead or iron, is of as great value as one hundred pounds' worth of silver or gold." As use-values, commodities are, above all, of different qualities, but as exchange-values they are merely different quantities, and consequently do not contain an atom of use-value.

If then we leave out of consideration the use-value of commodities, they have only one common property left, that of being products of labour. But even the product of labour itself has undergone a change in our hands. If we make abstraction from its use-value, we make abstraction at the same time from the material elements and shapes that make the product a use-value; we see in it no longer a table, a house, yarn, or any other useful thing. Its existence as a material thing is put out of sight. Neither can it any longer be regarded as the product of the labour of the joiner, the mason, the spinner, or of any other definite kind of productive labour. Along with the useful qualities of the products themselves, we put out of sight both the useful character of the various kinds of labour embodied in them, and the concrete forms of that labour; there is nothing left but what is common to them all; all are reduced to one and the same sort of labour, human labour in the abstract.

Let us now consider the residue of each of these products; it consists of the same unsubstantial reality in each, a mere congelation of homogeneous human labour, of labour-power expended without regard to the mode of its expenditure. All that these things now tell us is, that human labour-power has been expended in their production, that human labour is embodied in them. When looked at as crystals of this social substance, common to them all, they are—Values.

We have seen that when commodities are exchanged, their exchange-value manifests itself as something totally independent of their use-value.

But if we abstract from their use-value, there remains their Value as defined above. Therefore, the common substance that manifests itself in the exchange-value of commodities, whenever they are exchanged, is their value. The progress of our investigation will show that exchange-value is the only form in which the value of commodities can manifest itself or be expressed. For the present, however, we have to consider the nature of value independently of this, its form.

A use-value, or useful article, therefore, has value only because human labour in the abstract has been embodied or materialised in it. How, then, is the magnitude of this value to be measured? Plainly, by the quantity of the value-creating substance, the labour, contained in the article. The quantity of labour, however, is measured by its duration, and labour-time in its turn finds its standard in weeks, days, and hours.

Some people might think that if the value of a commodity is determined by the quantity of labour spent on it, the more idle and unskillful the labourer, the more valuable would his commodity be, because more time would be required in its production. The labour, however, that forms the substance of value, is homogeneous human labour, expenditure of one uniform labour-power. The total labour-power of society, which is embodied in the sum total of the values of all commodities produced by that society, counts here as one homogeneous mass of human labour-power, composed though it be of innumerable individual units. Each of these units is the same as any other, so far as it has the character of the average labour-power of society, and takes effect as such; that is, so far as it requires for producing a commodity, no more time than is needed on an average, no more than is socially necessary. The labour-time socially necessary is that required to produce an article under the normal conditions of production, and with the average degree of skill and intensity prevalent at the time. The introduction of power-looms into England probably reduced by one-half the labour required

to weave a given quantity of yarn into cloth. The handloom weavers, as a matter of fact, continued to require the same time as before; but for all that, the product of one hour of their labour represented after the change only half an hour's social labour, and consequently fell to one-half its former value.

We see then that that which determines the magnitude of the value of any article is the amount of labour socially necessary, or the labour-time socially necessary for its production.[8] Each individual commodity, in this connexion, is to be considered as an average sample of its class.[9] Commodities, therefore, in which equal quantities of labour are embodied, or which can be produced in the same time, have the same value. The value of one commodity is to the value of any other, as the labour-time necessary for the production of the one is to that necessary for the production of the other. "As values, all commodities are only definite masses of congealed labour-time."

The value of a commodity would therefore remain constant, if the labour-time required for its production also remained constant. But the latter changes with every variation in the productiveness of labour. This productiveness is determined by various circumstances, amongst others, by the average amount of skill of the workmen, the state of science, and the degree of its practical application, the social organisation of production, the extent and capabilities of the means of production, and by physical conditions. For example, the same amount of labour in favourable seasons is embodied in 8 bushels of corn, and in unfavourable, only in four. The same labour extracts from rich mines more metal than from poor mines. Diamonds are of very rare occurrence on the earth's surface, and hence their discovery costs, on an average, a great deal of labour-time. Consequently much labour is represented in a small compass. Jacob doubts whether gold has ever been paid for at its full value. This applies still more to diamonds. According to Eschwege, the total produce of the Brazilian diamond mines for the eighty years, ending in 1823, had not realised the price of one-and-a-half years' average produce of the sugar and coffee plantations of the same country, although the diamonds cost much more labour, and therefore represented more value. With richer mines, the same quantity of labour would embody itself in more diamonds, and their value would fall. If we could succeed at a small expenditure of labour, in converting carbon into diamonds, their value might fall below that of bricks. In general, the greater the productiveness of labour, the less is the labour-time required for the production of an article, the less is the amount of labour crystallised in that article, and the less is its value; and *vice versa*, the less the productiveness of labour, the greater is the labour-time required for the production of an article, and the greater is its value. The value of a commodity, therefore, varies directly as the quantity, and inversely as the productiveness, of the labour incorporated in it.

A thing can be a use-value, without having value. This is the case whenever its utility to man is not due to labour. Such are air, virgin soil, natural meadows, &c. A thing can be useful, and the product of human labour, without being a commodity. Whoever directly satisfies his wants with the produce of his own labour, creates, indeed, use-values, but no commodities. In order to produce the latter, he must not only produce use-values, but use-values for others, social use-values. (And not only for others, without more. The mediaeval peasant produced quit-rent-corn for his feudal lord and tithe-corn for his parson. But neither the quit-rent-corn nor the tithe-corn became commodities by reason of the fact that they had been produced for others. To become a commodity a product must be transferred to another, whom it will serve as a use-value, by means of an exchange.)[10] Lastly nothing can have value, without being an object of utility. If the thing is useless, so is the labour contained in it; the labour does not count as labour, and therefore creates no value.

[...]

Section 4. The fetishism of commodities and the secret thereof

A commodity appears, at first sight, a very trivial thing, and easily understood. Its analysis shows that it is, in reality, a very queer thing, abounding in metaphysical subtleties and theological niceties. So far as it is a value in use, there is nothing mysterious about it, whether we consider it from the point of view that by its properties it is capable of satisfying human wants, or from the point that those properties are the product of human labour. It is as clear as noon-day, that man, by his industry, changes the forms of the materials furnished by Nature, in such a way as to make them useful to him. The form of wood, for instance, is altered, by making a table out of it. Yet, for all that, the table continues to be that common, every-day thing, wood. But, so soon as it steps forth as a commodity, it is changed into something transcendent. It not only stands with its feet on the ground, but, in relation to all other commodities, it stands on its head, and evolves out of its wooden brain grotesque ideas, far more wonderful than "table-turning" ever was.

The mystical character of commodities does not originate, therefore, in their use-value. Just as little does it proceed from the nature of the determining factors of value. For, in the first place, however varied the useful kinds of labour, or productive activities, may be, it is a physiological fact, that they are functions of the human organism, and that each such function, whatever may be its nature or form, is essentially the expenditure of human brain, nerves, muscles, &c. Secondly, with regard to that which forms the ground-work for the quantitative determination of value, namely, the duration of that expenditure, or the quantity of labour, it is quite clear that there is a palpable difference between its quantity and quality. In all states of society, the labour-time that it costs to produce the means of subsistence, must necessarily be an object of interest to mankind, though not of equal interest in different stages of development.[11] And lastly, from the moment that men in any way work for one another, their labour assumes a social form.

Whence, then, arises the enigmatical character of the product of labour, so soon as it assumes the form of commodities? Clearly from this form itself. The equality of all sorts of human labour is expressed objectively by their products all being equally values; the measure of the expenditure of labour-power by the duration of that expenditure, takes the form of the quantity of value of the products of labour; and finally, the mutual relations of the producers, within which the social character of their labour affirms itself; take the form of a social relation between the products.

A commodity is therefore a mysterious thing, simply because in it the social character of men's labour appears to them as an objective character stamped upon the product of that labour; because the relation of the producers to the sum total of their own labour is presented to them as a social relation, existing not between themselves, but between the products of their labour. This is the reason why the products of labour become commodities, social things whose qualities are at the same time perceptible and imperceptible by the senses. In the same way the light from an object is perceived by us not as the subjective excitation of our optic nerve, but as the objective form of something outside the eye itself. But, in the act of seeing, there is at all events; an actual passage of light from one thing to another, from the external object to the eye. There is a physical relation between physical things. But it is different with commodities. There, the existence of the things *quâ* commodities, and the value-relation between the products of labour which stamps them as commodities, have absolutely no connexion with their physical properties and with the material relations arising therefrom. There it is a definite social relation between men, that assumes, in their eyes, the fantastic form of a relation between things. In order, therefore, to find an analogy, we must have recourse to the mist-enveloped regions of the religious world. In that world the productions of the human brain appear as independent beings endowed with life, and entering into relation both with one another and the human race. So it is in the world of commodities with the products of men's hands. This I call the Fetishism which attaches itself to the products of labour, so soon as they are produced as commodities, and which is therefore inseparable from the production of commodities.

This Fetishism of commodities has its origin, as the foregoing analysis has already shown, in the peculiar social character of the labour that produces them.

As a general rule, articles of utility become commodities, only because they are products of the labour of private individuals or groups of individuals who carry on their work independently of each other. The sum total of the labour of all these private individuals forms the aggregate labour of society. Since the producers do not come into social contact with each other until they exchange their products, the specific social character of each producer's labour does not show itself except in the act of exchange. In other words, the labour of the individual asserts itself as a part of the labour of society, only by means of the relations which the act of exchange establishes directly between the products, and indirectly, through them, between the producers. To the latter, therefore, the relations connecting the labour of one individual with that of the rest appear, not as direct social relations between individuals at work, but as what they really are, material relations between persons and social relations between things. It is only by being exchanged that the products of labour acquire, as values, one uniform social status, distinct from their varied forms of existence as objects of utility. This division of a product into a useful thing and a value becomes practically important, only when exchange has acquired such an extension that useful articles are produced for the purpose of being exchanged, and their character as values has therefore to be taken into account, beforehand, during production.

From this moment the labour of the individual producer acquires socially a two-fold character. On the one hand, it must, as a definite useful kind of labour, satisfy a definite social want, and thus hold its place as part and parcel of the collective labour of all, as a branch of a social division of labour that has sprung up spontaneously. On the other hand, it can satisfy the manifold wants of the individual producer himself, only in so far as the mutual exchangeability of all kinds of useful private labour is an established social fact, and therefore the private useful labour of each producer ranks on an equality with that of all others. The equalisation of the most different kinds of labour can be the result only of an abstraction from their inequalities, or of reducing them to their common denominator, viz., expenditure of human labour-power or human labour in the abstract. The two-fold social character of the labour of the individual appears to him, when reflected in his brain, only under those forms which are impressed upon that labour in every-day practice by the exchange of products. In this way, the character that his own labour possesses of being socially useful takes the form of the condition, that the product must be not only useful, but useful for others, and the social character that his particular labour has of being the equal of all other particular kinds of labour, takes the form that all the physically different articles that are the products of labour, have one common quality, viz., that of having value.

Hence, when we bring the products of our labour into relation with each other as values, it is not because we see in these articles the material receptacles of homogeneous human labour. Quite the contrary: whenever, by an exchange, we equate as values our different products, by that very act, we also equate, as human labour, the different kinds of labour expended upon them. We are not aware of this, nevertheless we do it. Value, therefore, does not stalk about with a label describing what it is. It is value, rather, that converts every product into a social hieroglyphic. Later on, we try to decipher the hieroglyphic, to get behind the secret of our own social products; for to stamp an object of utility as a value, is just as much a social product as language. The recent scientific discovery, that the products of labour, so far as they are values, are but material expressions of the human labour spent in their production, marks, indeed, an epoch in the history of the development of the human race, but, by no means, dissipates the mist through which the social character of labour appears to us to be an objective character of the products themselves. The fact, that in the particular form of production with which we are dealing, viz., the production of commodities, the specific social character of private labour carried on independently, consists in the equality of every kind of that labour, by virtue of its being human labour, which character, therefore, assumes in the product the form of value—this fact appears to the producers, notwithstanding the discovery above referred to, to be just as real and final, as the fact, that, after the discovery by science of the component gases of air, the atmosphere itself remained unaltered.

NOTES

1. Karl Marx, "Zur Kritik der Politischen Oekonomie." Berlin, 1859, p. 3. [*Marx*]
2. "Desire implies want; it is the appetite of the mind, and as natural as hunger to the body. ... The greatest number (of things) have their value from supplying the wants of the mind." Nicholas Barbon: "A Discourse Concerning Coining the New Money Lighter. In Answer to Mr. Locke's Considerations," &c., London, 1696, pp. 2, 3. [*Marx*]
3. "Things have an intrinsick vertue" (this is Barbon's special term for value in use) "which in all places have the same vertue; as the loadstone to attract iron" (1. c., p. 6). The property which the magnet possesses of attracting iron, became of use only after by means of that property the polarity of the magnet had been discovered. [*Marx*]
4. "The natural worth of anything consists in its fitness to supply the necessities, or serve the conveniences

of human life." (John Locke, "Some Considerations on the Consequences of the Lowering of Interest, 1691," in Works Edit. Lond., 1777, Vol. II., p. 28.) In English writers of the 17th century we frequently find "worth" in the sense of value in use, and "value" in the sense of exchange-value. This is quite in accordance with the spirit of a language that likes to use a Teutonic word for the actual thing, and a Romance word for its reflexion. [*Marx*]

5. In bourgeois societies the economic fictio juris prevails, that every one, as a buyer, possesses an encyclopaedic knowledge of commodities. [*Marx*]

6. "La valeur consiste dans le rapport d'échange qui se trouve entre telle chose et telle autre, entre telle mesure d'une production, et telle mesure d'une autre." (Le Trosne: "De l'Intérêt Social." Physiocrates, Ed. Daire. Paris, 1846. p. 889.) [*Marx*]

7. "Nothing can have an intrinsick value." (N. Barbon, 1. c., p. 6); or as Butler says—
    "The value of a thing is just as much as it will bring."
    [*Marx*]

8. "The value of them (the necessaries of life), when they are exchanged the one for another, is regulated by the quantity of labour necessarily required and commonly taken in producing them." ("Some Thoughts on the Interest of Money in General, and Particularly in the Publick Funds, &c." Lond., p. 36.) This remarkable anonymous work, written in the last century, bears no date. It is clear, however, from internal evidence, that it appeared in the reign of George II. about 1739 or 1740. [*Marx*]

9. "Toutes les productions d'un même genre ne forment proprement qu'une masse, dont le prix se détermine en général et sans égard aux circonstances particulières." (Le Trosne, 1. c., p. 893.) [*Marx*]

10. I am inserting parentheses because its omission has often given rise to the misunderstanding that every product that is consumed by some one other than its producer is considered in Marx a commodity. [*Engels, 4th German edition*]

11. Among the ancient Germans the unit for measuring land was what could be harvested in a day, and was called Tagwerk, Tagwanne (jurnale, or terra jurnalis, or diornalis), Mannsmaad, &c. (See G. L. von Maurer. "Einleitung zur Geschichte der Mark—, &c. Verfassung," München, 1854, p. 129 sq.) [*Marx*]

COMPANION WEBSITE

1. Go online to Write Out Loud about how a commodity that you think has become fetishized in modern society (and how we might de-fetishize it).
2. Log on to the *Networks of Capital* Supplementary Sources for a list of episodes from the radio program *This American Life* about the "invention of money."
3. Check out the Interactive Reading and discuss ways in which "collaborative consumption" might be able to bring "the social" back in to our economic activities.

12

Economic and Philosophic Manuscripts of 1844

Karl Marx

ESTRANGED LABOUR[1]

We have proceeded from the premises of political economy. We have accepted its language and its laws. We presupposed private property, the separation of labour, capital and land, and of wages, profit of capital and rent of land—likewise division of labour, competition, the concept of exchange-value, etc. On the basis of political economy itself, in its own words, we have shown that the worker sinks to the level of a commodity and becomes indeed the most wretched of commodities; that the wretchedness of the worker is in inverse proportion to the power and magnitude of his production; that the necessary result of competition is the accumulation of capital in a few hands, and thus the restoration of monopoly in a more terrible form; that finally the distinction between capitalist and land-rentier, like that between the tiller of the soil and the factory-worker, disappears and that the whole of society must fall apart into the two classes—the property-*owners* and the propertyless *workers*.

[...]

Now, therefore, we have to grasp the essential connection between private property, avarice, and the separation of labour, capital and landed property; between exchange and competition, value and the devaluation of men, monopoly and competition, etc.; the connection between this whole estrangement and the *money*-system.

Do not let us go back to a fictitious primordial condition as the political economist does, when he tries to explain. Such a primordial condition explains nothing. He merely pushes the question away into a grey nebulous distance. He assumes in the form of fact, of an event, what he is supposed to deduce—namely, the necessary relationship between two things—between, for example, division of labour and exchange. Theology in the same way explains the origin of evil by the fall of man: that is, it assumes as a fact, in historical form, what has to be explained.

We proceed from an *actual* economic fact.

The worker becomes all the poorer the more wealth he produces, the more his production increases in power and range. The worker becomes an ever cheaper commodity the more commodities he creates. With the *increasing value* of the world of things proceeds in direct proportion the *devaluation* of the world of men. Labour produces not only commodities; it produces itself and the worker as a *commodity*—and does so in the proportion in which it produces commodities generally.

This fact expresses merely that the object which labour produces—labour's product—confronts it as *something alien*, as a *power independent* of the producer. The product of labour is labour which has been congealed in an object, which has become material: it is the *objectification* of labour. Labour's realization is its objectification. In the conditions dealt with by political economy this realization of labour appears as *loss of reality* for the workers; objectification as *loss of the object* and *object-bondage*; appropriation as *estrangement*, as *alienation*.[2]

So much does labour's realization appear as loss of reality that the worker loses reality to the point of starving to death. So much does objectification appear as loss of the object that the worker is robbed of the objects most necessary not only for his life but for his work. Indeed, labour itself becomes an object which he can get hold of only with the greatest effort and with the most irregular interruptions. So much does the appropriation of the object appear as estrangement that the more objects the worker produces the fewer can he possess and the more he falls under the dominion of his product, capital.

All these consequences are contained in the definition that the worker is related to the *product of his labour* as to an *alien* object. For on this premise it is clear that the more the worker spends himself, the more powerful the alien objective world becomes which he creates over-against himself, the poorer he himself—his inner world—becomes, the less belongs to him as his own. It is the same in religion. The more man puts into God, the less he retains in himself. The worker puts his life into the object; but now his life no longer belongs to him but to the object. Hence, the greater this activity, the greater is the worker's lack of objects. Whatever the product of his labour is, he is not. Therefore the greater this product, the less is he himself. The *alienation* of the worker in his product means not only that his labour becomes an object, an *external* existence, but that it exists *outside him*, independently, as something alien to him, and that it becomes a power of its own confronting him; it means that the life which he has conferred on the object confronts him as something hostile and alien.

Let us now look more closely at the *objectification*, at the production of the worker; and therein at the *estrangement*, the *loss* of the object, his product.

The worker can create nothing without *nature*, without the *sensuous external world*. It is the material on which his labor is manifested, in which it is active, from which and by means of which it produces.

But just as nature provides labor with the *means of life* in the sense that labour cannot *live* without objects on which to operate, on the other hand, it also provides the *means of life* in the more restricted sense—i.e., the means for the physical subsistence of the *worker* himself.

Thus the more the worker by his labour *appropriates* the external world, sensuous nature, the more he deprives himself of *means of life* in the double respect: first, that the sensuous external world more and more ceases to be an object belonging to his labour—to be his labour's *means of life*; and secondly, that it more and more ceases to be *means of life* in the immediate sense, means for the physical subsistence of the worker.

Thus in this double respect the worker becomes a slave of his object, first, in that he receives an *object of labour*, i.e., in that he receives *work*; and secondly, in that he receives *means of subsistence*. Therefore, it enables him to exist, first, as a *worker*; and, second, as a *physical subject*. The extremity of this bondage is that it is only as a *worker* that he continues to maintain himself as a *physical subject*, and that it is only as a *physical subject* that he is a *worker*.

(The laws of political economy express the estrangement of the worker in his object thus: the more the worker produces, the less he has to consume; the more values he creates, the more valueless, the more unworthy he becomes; the better formed his product, the more deformed becomes the worker; the more civilized his object, the more barbarous becomes the worker; the mightier labour becomes, the more powerless becomes the worker; the more ingenious labour becomes, the duller becomes the worker and the more he becomes nature's bondsman.)

Political economy conceals the estrangement inherent in the nature of labour by not considering the direct relationship between the worker (labour) *and production*. It is true that labour produces for the rich wonderful things—but for the worker it produces privation. It produces palaces—but for the worker, hovels. It produces beauty—but for the worker, deformity. It replaces labour by machines—but some of the workers it throws back to a barbarous type of labour, and the other workers it turns into machines. It produces intelligence—but for the worker idiocy, cretinism.

The direct relationship of labour to its produce is the relationship of the worker to the objects of his production. The relationship of the man of means to the objects of his production and to production itself is only a *consequence* of this first relationship—and confirms it. We shall consider this other aspect later.

When we ask, then, what is the essential relationship of labour we are asking about the relationship of the *worker* to production.

Till now we have been considering the estrangement, the alienation of the worker only in one of its aspects, i.e., the worker's *relationship to the products of his labour*. But the estrangement is manifested not only in the result but in the *act of production—* within the *producing activity* itself. How would the worker come to face the product of his activity as a stranger, were it not that in the very act of production he was estranging himself from himself? The product is after all but the summary of the activity of production. If then the product of labour is alienation, production itself must be active alienation, the alienation of activity, the activity of alienation. In the estrangement of the object of labour is merely summarized the estrangement, the alienation, in the activity of labour itself.

What, then, constitutes the alienation of labour?

First, the fact that labour is *external* to the worker, i.e., it does not belong to his essential being; that in his work, therefore, he does not affirm himself but denies himself, does not feel content but unhappy, does not develop freely his physical and mental energy but mortifies his body and ruins his mind. The worker therefore only feels himself outside his work, and in his work feels outside himself. He is at home when he is not working, and when he is working he is not at home. His labour

is therefore not voluntary, but coerced; it is *forced labour*. It is therefore not the satisfaction of a need; it is merely a *means* to satisfy needs external to it. Its alien character emerges clearly in the fact that as soon as no physical or other compulsion exists, labour is shunned like the plague. External labour, labour in which man alienates himself, is a labour of self-sacrifice, of mortification. Lastly, the external character of labour for the worker appears in the fact that it is not his own, but someone else's, that it does not belong to him, that in it he belongs, not to himself, but to another. Just as in religion the spontaneous activity of the human imagination, of the human brain and the human heart, operates independently of the individual—that is, operates on him as an alien, divine or diabolical activity— in the same way the worker's activity is not his spontaneous activity. It belongs to another; it is the loss of his self.

As a result, therefore, man (the worker) no longer feels himself to be freely active in any but his animal functions—eating, drinking, procreating, or at most in his dwelling and in dressing-up, etc.; and in his human functions he no longer feels himself to be anything but an animal. What is animal becomes human and what is human becomes animal.

Certainly eating, drinking, procreating, etc., are also genuinely human functions. But in the abstraction which separates them from the sphere of all other human activity and turns them into sole and ultimate ends, they are animal.

We have considered the act of estranging practical human activity, labour, in two of its aspects. (1) The relation of the worker to the *product of labour* as an alien object exercising power over him. This relation is at the same time the relation to the sensuous external world, to the objects of nature as an alien world antagonistically opposed to him. (2) The relation of labour to the *act of production* within the *labour* process. This relation is the relation of the worker to his own activity as an alien activity not belonging to him; it is activity as suffering, strength as weakness, begetting as emasculating, the worker's *own* physical and mental energy, his personal life or what is life other than activity—as an activity which is turned against him, neither depends on nor belongs to him. Here we have *self-estrangement*, as we had previously the estrangement of the *thing*.

We have yet a third aspect of *estranged labour* to deduce from the two already considered.

Man is a species being, not only because in practice and in theory he adopts the species as his object (his own as well as those of other things), but—and this is only another way of expressing it—but also because he treats himself as the actual, living species; because he treats himself as a *universal* and therefore a free being.

The life of the species, both in man and in animals, consists physically in the fact that man (like the animal) lives on inorganic nature; and the more universal man is compared with an animal, the more universal is the sphere of inorganic nature on which he lives. Just as plants, animals, stones, the air, light, etc., constitute a part of human consciousness in the realm of theory, partly as objects of natural science, partly as objects of art— his spiritual inorganic nature, spiritual nourishment which he must first prepare to make it palatable and digestible—so too in the realm of practice they constitute a part of human life and human activity. Physically man lives only on these products of nature, whether they appear in the form of food, heating, clothes, a dwelling, or whatever it may be. The universality of man is in practice manifested precisely in the universality which makes all nature his *inorganic* body—both inasmuch as nature is (1) his direct means of life, and (2) the material, the object, and the instrument of his life-activity. Nature is man's *inorganic body*—nature, that is, in so far as it is not itself the human body. Man *lives* on nature—means that nature is his *body*, with which he must remain in continuous intercourse if he is not to die. That man's physical and spiritual life is linked to nature means simply that nature is linked to itself, for man is a part of nature.

In estranging from man (1) nature, and (2) himself, his own active functions, his life-activity, estranged labour estranges the *species* from man. It turns for him the *life of the species* into a means of individual life. First it estranges the life of the species and individual life, and secondly it makes individual life in its abstract form the purpose of the life of the species, likewise in its abstract and estranged form.

For in the first place labour, *life-activity, productive life* itself, appears to man merely as a *means* of satisfying a need—the need to maintain the physical existence. Yet the productive life is the life of the species. It is life-engendering life. The whole character of a species—its species character— is contained in the character of its life-activity; and free, conscious activity is man's species character. Life itself appears only as *a means to life*.

The animal is immediately identical with its life-activity. It does not distinguish itself from it. It is *its life-activity*. Man makes his life-activity itself the object of his will and of his consciousness. He has conscious life-activity. It is not a determination with which he directly merges. Conscious life-activity directly distinguishes man from animal life-activity. It is just because of this that he is a species being. Or it is only because he is a species being that he is a Conscious Being, i.e., that his own life is an object for him. Only because of that is his activity free activity. Estranged labour reverses this relationship, so that it is just because man is a conscious being that he makes his life-activity, his *essential* being, a mere means to his *existence*.

In creating an *objective world* by his practical activity, in *working-up* inorganic nature, man proves himself a conscious species being, i.e., as a being that treats the species as its own essential being, or that treats itself as a species being. Admittedly animals also produce. They build themselves nests, dwellings, like the bees, beavers, ants, etc. But an animal only produces what it immediately needs for itself or its young. It produces one-sidedly, whilst man produces universally. It produces only under the dominion of immediate physical need, whilst man produces even when he is free from physical need and only truly produces in freedom therefrom. An animal produces only itself, whilst man reproduces the whole of nature. An animal's product belongs immediately to its physical body, whilst man freely confronts his product. An animal forms things in accordance with the standard and the need of the species to which it belongs, whilst man knows how to produce in accordance with the standard of every species, and knows how to apply everywhere the inherent standard to the object. Man therefore also forms things in accordance with the laws of beauty.

It is just in the working-up of the objective world, therefore, that man first really proves himself to be a *species being*. This production is his active species life. Through and because of this production, nature appears as *his* work and his reality. The object of labour is, therefore, the *objectification of man's species life*: for he duplicates himself not only, as in consciousness, intellectually, but also actively, in reality, and therefore he contemplates himself in a world that he has created. In tearing away from man the object of his production, therefore, estranged labour tears from him his *species life*, his real species objectivity, and transforms his advantage over animals into the disadvantage that his inorganic body, nature, is taken from him.

Similarly, in degrading spontaneous activity, free activity, to a means, estranged labour makes man's species life a means to his physical existence.

The consciousness which man has of his species is thus transformed by estrangement in such a way that the species life becomes for him a means.

Estranged labour turns thus:

(3) *Man's species being*, both nature and his spiritual species property, into a being *alien* to him, into a *means* to his *individual existence*. It estranges man's own body from him, as it does external nature and his spiritual essence, his *human* being.

(4) An immediate consequence of the fact that man is estranged from the product of his labour, from his life-activity, from his species being is the *estrangement of man* from *man*. If a man is confronted by himself, he is confronted by the *other* man. What applies to a man's relation to his work, to the product of his labour and to himself, also holds of a man's relation to the other man, and to the other man's labour and object of labour.

In fact, the proposition that man's species nature is estranged from him means that one man is estranged from the other, as each of them is from man's essential nature.[3]

The estrangement of man, and in fact every relationship in which man stands to himself, is first realized and expressed in the relationship in which a man stands to other men.

Hence within the relationship of estranged labour each man views the other in accordance with the standard and the position in which he finds himself as a worker.

We took our departure from a fact of political economy—the estrangement of the worker and his production. We have formulated the concept of this fact—*estranged, alienated* labour. We have analysed this concept—hence analysing merely a fact of political economy.

Let us now see, further, how in real life the concept of estranged, alienated labour must express and present itself.

If the product of labour is alien to me, if it confronts me as an alien power, to whom, then, does it belong?

If my own activity does not belong to me, if it is an alien, a coerced activity, to whom, then, does it belong?

To a being *other* than me.

Who is this being?

The *gods*? To be sure, in the earliest times the principal production (for example, the building of temples, etc., in Egypt, India and Mexico) appears to be in the service of the gods, and the product belongs to the gods. However, the gods on their own were never the lords of labour. No more was *nature*. And what a contradiction it would be if, the more man subjugated nature by his labour and the more the miracles of the gods were rendered superfluous by the miracles of industry, the more man were to renounce the joy of production and the enjoyment of the produce in favour of these powers.

The *alien* being, to whom labour and the produce of labour belongs, in whose service labour is done and for whose benefit the produce of labour is provided, can only be *man* himself.

If the product of labour does not belong to the worker, if it confronts him as an alien power, this can only be because it belongs to some *other man than the worker*. If the worker's activity is a torment to him, to another it must be *delight* and his life's joy. Not the gods, not nature, but only man himself can be this alien power over man.

We must bear in mind the above-stated proposition that man's relation to himself only becomes *objective* and *real* for him through his relation to the other man. Thus, if the product of his labour, his labour *objectified*, is for him an *alien*, hostile, powerful object independent of him, then his position towards it is such that someone else is master of this object, someone who is alien, hostile, powerful, and independent of him. If his own activity is to him an unfree activity, then he is treating it as activity performed in the service, under the dominion, the coercion and the yoke of another man.

Every self-estrangement of man from himself and from nature appears in the relation in which he places himself and nature to men other than and differentiated from himself. For this reason religious self-estrangement necessarily appears in the relationship of the layman to the priest, or again to a mediator, etc., since we are here dealing with the intellectual world. In the real practical world self-estrangement can only become manifest through the real practical relationship to other men. The medium through which estrangement takes place is itself *practical*. Thus through estranged labour man not only engenders his relationship to the object and to the act of production as to powers that are alien and hostile to him; he also engenders

the relationship in which other men stand to his production and to his product, and the relationship in which he stands to these other men. Just as he begets his own production as the loss of his reality, as his punishment; just as he begets his own product as a loss, as a product not belonging to him; so he begets the dominion of the one who does not produce over production and over the product. Just as he estranges from himself his own activity, so he confers to the stranger activity which is not his own.

Till now we have only considered this relationship from the standpoint of the worker and later we shall be considering it also from the standpoint of the non-worker.

Through *estranged, alienated labour*, then, the worker produces the relationship to this labour of a man alien to labour and standing outside it. The relationship of the worker to labour engenders the relation to it of the capitalist, or whatever one chooses to call the master of labour. *Private property* is thus the product, the result, the necessary consequence, of *alienated labour*, of the external relation of the worker to nature and to himself.

Private property thus results by analysis from the concept of *alienated labour*—i.e., of *alienated man*, of estranged labour, of estranged life, of *estranged* man.

True, it is as a result of the *movement of private property* that we have obtained the concept of *alienated labour* (*of alienated life*) from political economy. But on analysis of this concept it becomes clear that though private property appears to be the source, the cause of alienated labour, it is really its consequence, just as the gods *in the beginning* are not the cause but the effect of man's intellectual confusion. Later this relationship becomes reciprocal.

Only at the very culmination of the development of private property does this, its secret, re-emerge, namely, that on the one hand it is the *product* of alienated labour, and that secondly it is the *means* by which labour alienates itself, the *realization of this alienation*.

This exposition immediately sheds light on various hitherto unsolved conflicts.

(1) Political economy starts from labour as the real soul of production; yet to labour it gives nothing, and to private property everything. From this contradiction Proudhon has concluded in favour of labour and against private property. We understand, however, that this apparent contradiction is the contradiction of *estranged labour* with itself, and that political economy has merely formulated the laws of estranged labour.

We also understand, therefore, that *wages* and *private property* are identical: where the product, the object of labour pays for labour itself, the wage is but a necessary consequence of labour's estrangement, for after all in the wage of labour, labour does not appear as an end in itself but as the servant of the wage. We shall develop this point later, and meanwhile will only deduce some conclusions.

A *forcing-up of wages* (disregarding all other difficulties, including the fact that it would only be by force, too, that the higher wages, being an anomaly, could be maintained) would therefore be nothing but *better payment for the slave*, and would not conquer either for the worker or for labour their human status and dignity.

Indeed, even the *equality of wages* demanded by Proudhon only transforms the relationship of the present-day worker to his labour into the relationship of all men to labour. Society is then conceived as an abstract capitalist.

Wages are a direct consequence of estranged labour, and estranged labour is the direct cause of private property. The downfall of the one aspect must therefore mean the downfall of the other.

(2) From the relationship of estranged labour to private property it further follows that the emancipation of society from private property, etc., from servitude, is expressed in the *political* form of the *emancipation of the workers*; not that *their* emancipation alone was at stake but because the emancipation of the workers contains universal human emancipation—and it contains this, because the whole of human servitude is involved in the relation of the worker to production, and every relation of servitude is but a modification and consequence of this relation.

NOTES

1. *Die Entfremdete Arbeit*. See the Note on Texts and Terminology, p. xli, above, for a discussion of this term. [*R.T.*]
2. "Alienation"—*Entäusserung*.
3. "Species nature" (and, earlier, "species being")—*Gattungswesen*; "man's essential nature"—*menschlichen Wesen*.

COMPANION WEBSITE

1. Go online to Write Out Loud about how some of the most hated jobs in America might be due to alienation.
2. Log on to Marx's Profile Page for more on his theory of alienation.
3. For more on what Marx might think if he were around today, check out Howard Zinn's play *Marx in Soho*, listed in the *Networks of Capital* Supplementary Sources.

13

The Rise and Future Demise of the World Capitalist System

Immanuel Wallerstein

NOTHING ILLUSTRATES THE DISTORTIONS of ahistorical models of social change better than the dilemmas to which the concept of stages gives rise. If we are to deal with social transformations over long historical time (Braudel's 'the long term'), and if we are to give an explanation of both continuity and transformation, then we must logically divide the long term into segments in order to observe the structural changes from time A to time B. These segments are however not discrete but continuous in reality; *ergo* they are 'stages' in the 'development' of a social structure, a development which we determine however not *a priori* but *a posteriori*. That is, we cannot predict the future concretely, but we can predict the past.

The crucial issue when comparing 'stages' is to determine the units of which the 'stages' are synchronic portraits (or 'ideal types', if you will). And the fundamental error of ahistorical social science (including ahistorical versions of Marxism) is to reify parts of the totality into such units and then to compare these reified structures.

For example, we may take modes of disposition of agricultural production, and term them subsistence-cropping and cash-cropping. We may then see these as entities which are 'stages' of a development. We may talk about decisions of groups of peasants to shift from one to the other. We may describe other partial entities, such as states, as having within them two separate 'economies', each based on a different mode

of disposition of agricultural production. If we take each of these successive steps, all of which are false steps, we will end up with the misleading concept of the 'dual economy' as have many liberal economists dealing with the so-called underdeveloped countries of the world. Still worse, we may reify a misreading of British history into a set of universal 'stages' as Rostow does.

Marxist scholars have often fallen into exactly the same trap. If we take modes of payment of agricultural labor and contrast a 'feudal' mode wherein the laborer is permitted to retain for subsistence a part of his agricultural production with a 'capitalist' mode wherein the same laborer turns over the totality of his production to the landowner, receiving part of it back in the form of wages, we may then see these two modes as 'stages' of a development. We may talk of the interests of 'feudal' landowners in preventing the conversion of their mode of payment to a system of wages. We may then explain the fact that in the twentieth century a partial entity, say a state in Latin America, has not yet industrialized as the consequence of its being dominated by such landlords. If we take each of these successive steps, all of which are false steps, we will end up with the misleading concept of a 'state dominated by feudal elements', as though such a thing could possibly exist in a capitalist world-economy. But, as André Gunder Frank has clearly spelled out, such a myth dominated for a long time 'traditional Marxist' thought in Latin America.[1]

Not only does the misidentification of the entities to be compared lead us into false concepts, but it creates a non-problem: can stages be skipped? This question is only logically meaningful if we have 'stages' that 'co-exist' within a single empirical framework. If within a capitalist world-economy, we define one state as feudal, a second as capitalist, and a third as socialist, then and only then can we pose the question: can a country 'skip' from the feudal stage to the socialist stage of national development without 'passing through capitalism'?

But if there is no such thing as 'national development' (if by that we mean a natural history), and if the proper entity of comparison is the world-system, then the problem of stage-skipping is nonsense. If a stage can be skipped, it isn't a stage. And we know this *a posteriori*.

If we are to talk of stages, then—and we should talk of stages—it must be stages of social systems, that is, of totalities. And the only totalities that exist or have historically existed are mini-systems and world-systems, and in the nineteenth and twentieth centuries there has been only one world-system in existence, the capitalist world-economy.

We take the defining characteristic of a social system to be the existence within it of a division of labor, such that the various sectors or areas within are dependent upon economic exchange with others for the smooth and continuous provisioning of the needs of the area. Such economic exchange can clearly exist without a common political structure and even more obviously without sharing the same culture.

A mini-system is an entity that has within it a complete division of labor, and a single cultural framework. Such systems are found only in very simple agricultural or hunting and gathering societies. Such mini-systems no longer exist in the world. Furthermore, there were fewer in the past than is often asserted, since any such system that became tied to an empire by the payment of tribute

as 'protection costs'[2] ceased by that fact to be a 'system', no longer having a self-contained division of labor. For such an area, the payment of tribute marked a shift, in Polanyi's language, from being a reciprocal economy to participating in a larger redistributive economy.[3]

Leaving aside the now defunct mini-systems, the only kind of social system is a world-system, which we define quite simply as a unit with a single division of labor and multiple cultural systems. It follows logically that there can, however, be two varieties of such world-systems, one with a common political system and one without. We shall designate these respectively as world-empires and world-economies.

It turns out empirically that world-economies have historically been unstable structures leading either towards disintegration or conquest by one group and hence transformation into a world-empire. Examples of such world-empires emerging from world-economies are all the so-called great civilizations of pre-modern times, such as China, Egypt, Rome (each at appropriate periods of its history). On the other hand, the so-called nineteenth-century empires, such as Great Britain or France, were not world-empires at all, but nation-states with colonial appendages operating within the framework of a world-economy.

World-empires were basically redistributive in economic form. No doubt they bred clusters of merchants who engaged in economic exchange (primarily long-distance trade), but such clusters, however large, were a minor part of the total economy and not fundamentally determinative of its fate. Such long-distance trade tended to be, as Polanyi argues, 'administered trade' and not market trade, utilizing 'ports of trade'.

It was only with the emergence of the modern world-economy in sixteenth-century Europe that we saw the full development and economic predominance of market trade. This was the system called capitalism. Capitalism and a world-economy (that is, a single division of labor but multiple polities and cultures) are obverse sides of the same coin. One does not cause the other. We are merely defining the same indivisible phenomenon by different characteristics.

How and why it came about that this particular European world-economy of the sixteenth century did not become transformed into a redistributive world-empire but developed definitively as a capitalist world-economy I have explained elsewhere.[4] The genesis of this world-historical turning-point is marginal to the issues under discussion in this paper, which is rather what conceptual apparatus one brings to bear on the analysis of developments within the framework of precisely such a capitalist world-economy.

Let us therefore turn to the capitalist world-economy. We shall seek to deal with two pseudo-problems, created by the trap of not analyzing totalities: the so-called persistence of feudal forms, and the so-called creation of socialist systems. In doing this, we shall offer an alternative model with which to engage in comparative analysis, one rooted in the historically specific totality which is the world capitalist economy. We hope to demonstrate thereby that to be historically specific is not to fail to be analytically universal. On the contrary, the only road to nomothetic propositions is through the historically concrete, just as in cosmology the only road to a theory of the laws governing the universe is through the concrete analysis of the historical evolution of this same universe.[5]

On the 'feudalism' debate, we take as a starting-point Frank's concept of 'the development of under-development', that is, the view that the economic structures of contemporary underdeveloped countries is not the form which a 'traditional' society takes upon contact with 'developed' societies, not an earlier stage in the 'transition' to industrialization. It is rather the result of being involved in the world-economy as a peripheral, raw material producing area, or as Frank puts it for Chile, 'under-development ... is the necessary product of four centuries of capitalism itself'.[6]

This formulation runs counter to a large body of writing concerning the underdeveloped countries that was produced in the period 1950–70, a literature which sought the factors that explained 'development' within non-systems such as 'states' or 'cultures' and, once having presumably discovered these factors, urged their reproduction in underdeveloped areas as the road to salvation.[7]

[...]

What was happening in Europe from the sixteenth to the eighteenth centuries is that over a large geographical area going from Poland in the northeast westwards and southwards throughout Europe and including large parts of the Western Hemisphere as well, there grew up a world-economy with a single division of labor within which there was a world market, for which men produced largely agricultural products for sale and profit. I would think the simplest thing to do would be to call this agricultural capitalism.

This then resolves the problems incurred by using the pervasiveness of *wage*-labor as a defining characteristic of capitalism. An individual is no less a capitalist exploiting labor because the state assists him to pay his laborers low wages (including wages in kind) and denies these laborers the right to change employment. Slavery and so-called 'second serfdom' are not to be regarded as anomalies in a capitalist system. Rather the so-called serf in Poland or the Indian on a Spanish *encomienda* in New Spain in this sixteenth-century world-economy were working for landlords who 'paid' them (however euphemistic this term) for cash-crop production. This is a relationship in which labor-power is a commodity (how could it ever be more so than under slavery?), quite different from the relationship of a feudal serf to his lord in eleventh-century Burgundy, where the economy was not oriented to a world market, and where labor-power was (therefore?) in no sense bought or sold.

Capitalism thus means labor as a commodity to be sure. But in the era of agricultural capitalism, wage-labor is only one of the modes in which labor is recruited and recompensed in the labor market. Slavery, coerced cash-crop production (my name for the so-called 'second feudalism'), share-cropping, and tenancy are all alternative modes. It would be too long to develop here the conditions under which differing regions of the world-economy tend to specialize in different agricultural products. I have done this elsewhere.[8]

What we must notice now is that this specialization occurs in specific and differing geographic regions of the world-economy. This regional specialization comes about by the attempts of actors in the market to avoid the normal operation of the market whenever it does not maximize their profit. The attempts of these actors to use non-market devices to ensure short-run profits makes them turn to the political entities which have in fact power to affect the market—the nation-states. (Again, why at this stage they could not have turned to city-states would take us into a long discursus, but it has to do with the state of military and shipping technology, the need of the European land-mass to expand overseas in the fifteenth century if it was to maintain the level of income of the various aristocracies, combined with the state of political disintegration to which Europe had fallen in the Middle Ages.)

In any case, the local capitalist classes—cash-crop landowners (often, even usually, nobility) and merchants—turned to the state, not only to liberate them from non-market constraints (as traditionally emphasized by liberal historiography) but to create new constraints on the new market, the market of the European world-economy.

By a series of accidents—historical, ecological, geographic—northwest Europe was better situated in the sixteenth century to diversify its agricultural specialization and add to it certain industries (such as textiles, shipbuilding, and metal wares) than were other parts of Europe. Northwest Europe emerged as the core area of this world-economy, specializing in agricultural production of higher skill levels, which favored (again for reasons too complex to develop)

tenancy and wage-labor as the modes of labor control. Eastern Europe and the Western Hemisphere became peripheral areas specializing in export of grains, bullion, wood, cotton, sugar—all of which favored the use of slavery and coerced cash-crop labor as the modes of labor control. Mediterranean Europe emerged as the semi-peripheral area of this world-economy specializing in high-cost industrial products (for example, silks) and credit and specie transactions, which had as a consequence in the agricultural arena share-cropping as the mode of labor control and little export to other areas.

The three structural positions in a world-economy—core, periphery, and semi-periphery—had become stabilized by about 1640. How certain areas became one and not the other is a long story.[9] The key fact is that given slightly different starting-points, the interests of various local groups converged in northwest Europe, leading to the development of strong state mechanisms, and diverged sharply in the peripheral areas, leading to very weak ones. Once we get a difference in the strength of the state-machineries, we get the operation of 'unequal exchange'[10] which is enforced by strong states on weak ones, by core states on peripheral areas. Thus capitalism involves not only appropriation of the surplus-value by an owner from a laborer, but an appropriation of surplus of the whole world-economy by core areas. And this was as true in the stage of agricultural capitalism as it is in the stage of industrial capitalism.

In the early Middle Ages, there was to be sure trade. But it was largely either 'local', in a region that we might call the 'extended' manor, or 'long-distance', primarily of luxury goods. There was no exchange of 'bulk' goods, of 'staples' across intermediate-size areas, and hence no production for such markets. Later on in the Middle Ages, world-economies may be said to have come into existence, one centering on Venice, a second on the cities of Flanders and the Hanse. For various reasons, these structures were hurt by the retractions (economic, demographic, and ecological) of the period

1300–1450. It is only with the creating of a *European* division of labor after 1450 that capitalism found firm roots.

Capitalism was from the beginning an affair of the world-economy and not of nation-states. It is a misreading of the situation to claim that it is only in the twentieth century that capitalism has become 'world-wide', although this claim is frequently made in various writings, particularly by Marxists. Typical of this line of argument is Charles Bettelheim's response to Arghiri Emmanuel's discussion of unequal exchange:

> The tendency of the capitalist mode of production to become worldwide is manifested not only through the constitution of a group of national economies forming a complex and hierarchical structure, including an imperialist pole and a dominated one, and not only through the antagonistic relations that develop between the different 'national economies' and the different states, but also through the constant 'transcending' of 'national limits' by big capital (the formation of 'international big capital', 'world firms', etc... .).[11]

The whole tone of these remarks ignores the fact that capital has never allowed its aspirations to be determined by national boundaries in a capitalist world-economy, and that the creation of 'national' barriers—generically, mercantilism—has historically been a defensive mechanism of capitalists located in states which are one level below the high point of strength in the system. Such was the case of England *vis-à-vis* the Netherlands in 1660–1715, France *vis-à-vis* England in 1715–1815, Germany *vis-à-vis* Britain in the nineteenth century, the Soviet Union *vis-à-vis* the U.S. in the twentieth. In the process a large number of countries create national economic barriers whose consequences often last beyond their initial objectives. At this later point in the process the very same capitalists who pressed their national governments to impose the restrictions now find these restrictions constraining. This is not an 'internationalization' of 'national' capital. This is

simply a new political demand by certain sectors of the capitalist classes who have at all points in time sought to maximize their profits within the real economic market, that of the world-economy.

If this is so, then what meaning does it have to talk of structural positions within this economy and identify states as being in one of these positions? And why talk of three positions, inserting that of 'semi-periphery' in between the widely-used concepts of core and periphery? The state-machineries of the core states were strengthened to meet the needs of capitalist landowners and their merchant allies. But that does not mean that these state-machineries were manipulable puppets. Obviously any organization, once created, has a certain autonomy from those who pressed it into existence for two reasons. It creates a stratum of officials whose own careers and interests are furthered by the continued strengthening of the organization itself, however the interests of its capitalist backers may vary. Kings and bureaucrats wanted to stay in power and increase their personal gain constantly. Secondly, in the process of creating the strong state in the first place, certain 'constitutional' compromises had to be made with other forces within the state-boundaries and these institutionalized compromises limit, as they are designed to do, the freedom of maneuver of the managers of the state-machinery. The formula of the state as 'executive committee of the ruling class' is only valid, therefore, if one bears in mind that executive committees are never mere reflections of the wills of their constituents, as anyone who has ever participated in any organization knows well.

The strengthening of the state-machineries in core areas has as its direct counterpart the decline of the state-machineries in peripheral areas. The decline of the Polish monarchy in the sixteenth and seventeenth centuries is a striking example of this phenomenon.[12] There are two reasons for this. In peripheral countries, the interests of the capitalist landowners lie in an opposite direction from those of the local commercial bourgeoisie. Their interests lie in maintaining an open economy to maximize their profit from world-market trade (no restrictions in exports and access to lower-cost industrial products from core countries) and in elimination of the commercial bourgeoisie in favor of outside merchants (who pose no local political threat). Thus, in terms of the state, the coalition which strengthened it in core countries was precisely absent.

The second reason, which has become ever more operative over the history of the modern world-system, is that the strength of the state-machinery in core states is a function of the weakness of other state-machineries. Hence intervention of outsiders via war, subversion, and diplomacy is the lot of peripheral states.

All this seems very obvious. I repeat it only in order to make clear two points. One cannot reasonably explain the strength of various state-machineries at specific moments of the history of the modern world-system primarily in terms of a genetic-cultural line of argumentation, but rather in terms of the structural role a country plays in the world-economy at that moment in time. To be sure, the initial eligibility for a particular role is often decided by an accidental edge a particular country has, and the 'accident' of which one is talking is no doubt located in part in past history, in part in current geography. But once this relatively minor accident is given, it is the operations of the world-market forces which accentuate the differences, institutionalize them, and make them impossible to surmount over the short run.

The second point we wish to make about the structural differences of core and periphery is that they are not comprehensible unless we realize that there is a third structural position: that of the semi-periphery. This is not the result merely of establishing arbitrary cutting-points on a continuum of characteristics. Our logic is not merely inductive, sensing the presence of a third category from a comparison of indicator curves. It is also deductive. The semi-periphery is needed to make a capitalist world-economy run smoothly. Both kinds of world-system,

the world-empire with a redistributive economy and the world-economy with a capitalist market economy, involve markedly unequal distribution of rewards. Thus, logically, there is immediately posed the question of how it is possible politically for such a system to persist. Why do not the majority who are exploited simply overwhelm the minority who draw disproportionate benefits? The most rapid glance at the historic record shows that these world-systems have been faced rather rarely by fundamental system-wide insurrection. While internal discontent has been eternal, it has usually taken quite long before the accumulation of the erosion of power has led to the decline of a world-system, and as often as not, an external force has been a major factor in this decline.

There have been three major mechanisms that have enabled world-systems to retain relative political stability (not in terms of the particular groups who will play the leading roles in the system, but in terms of systemic survival itself). One obviously is the concentration of military strength in the hands of the dominant forces. The modalities of this obviously vary with the technology, and there are to be sure political prerequisites for such a concentration, but nonetheless sheer force is no doubt a central consideration.

A second mechanism is the pervasiveness of an ideological commitment to the system as a whole. I do not mean what has often been termed the 'legitimation' of a system, because that term has been used to imply that the lower strata of a system feel some affinity with or loyalty towards the rulers, and I doubt that this has ever been a significant factor in the survival of world-systems. I mean rather the degree to which the staff or cadres of the system (and I leave this term deliberately vague) feel that their own well-being is wrapped up in the survival of the system as such and the competence of its leaders. It is this staff which not only propagates the myths; it is they who believe them.

But neither force nor the ideological commitment of the staff would suffice were it not for the division of the majority into a larger lower stratum and a smaller middle stratum. Both the revolutionary call for polarization as a strategy of change and the liberal encomium to consensus as the basis of the liberal polity reflect this proposition. The import is far wider than its use in the analysis of contemporary political problems suggests. It is the normal condition of either kind of world-system to have a three-layered structure. When and if this ceases to be the case, the world-system disintegrates.

In a world-empire, the middle stratum is in fact accorded the role of maintaining the marginally-desirable long-distance luxury trade, while the upper stratum concentrates its resources on controlling the military machinery which can collect the tribute, the crucial mode of redistributing surplus. By providing, however, for an access to a limited portion of the surplus to urbanized elements who alone, in pre-modern societies, could contribute political cohesiveness to isolated clusters of primary producers, the upper stratum effectively buys off the potential leadership of co-ordinated revolt. And by denying access to political rights for this commercial-urban middle stratum, it makes them constantly vulnerable to confiscatory measures whenever their economic profits become sufficiently swollen so that they might begin to create for themselves military strength.

In a world-economy, such 'cultural' stratification is not so simple, because the absence of a single political system means the concentration of economic roles vertically rather than horizontally throughout the system. The solution then is to have three *kinds* of states, with pressures for cultural homogenization within each of them—thus, besides the upper stratum of core-states and the lower stratum of peripheral states, there is a middle stratum of semi-peripheral ones.

This semi-periphery is then assigned as it were a specific economic role, but the reason is less economic than political. That is to say, one might make a good case that the world-economy as an economy would function every bit as well without a semi-periphery.

But it would be far less *politically* stable, for it would mean a polarized world-system. The existence of the third category means precisely that the upper stratum is not faced with the *unified* opposition of all the others because the *middle* stratum is both exploited and exploiter. It follows that the specific economic role is not all that important, and has thus changed through the various historical stages of the modern world-system. We shall discuss these changes shortly.

Where then does class analysis fit in all of this? And what in such a formulation are nations, nationalities, peoples, ethnic groups? First of all, without arguing the point now,[13] I would contend that all these latter terms denote variants of a single phenomenon which I will term 'ethno-nations'.

Both classes and ethnic groups, or status-groups, or ethno-nations are phenomena of world-economies and much of the enormous confusion that has surrounded the concrete analysis of their functioning can be attributed quite simply to the fact that they have been analyzed as though they existed within the nation-states of this world-economy, instead of within the world-economy as a whole. This has been a Procrustean bed indeed.

The range of economic activities being far wider in the core than in the periphery, the range of syndical interest groups is far wider there.[14] Thus, it has been widely observed that there does not exist in many parts of the world today a proletariat of the kind which exists in, say, Europe or North America. But this is a confusing way to state the observation. Industrial activity being disproportionately concentrated in certain parts of the world-economy, industrial wage-workers are to be found principally in certain geographic regions. Their interests as a syndical group are determined by their collective relationship to the world-economy. Their ability to influence the political functioning of this world-economy is shaped by the fact that they command larger percentages of the population in one sovereign entity than another. The form their organizations take have, in large part, been governed too by these political boundaries. The same might be said about industrial capitalists. Class analysis is perfectly capable of accounting for the political position of, let us say, French skilled workers if we look at their structural position and interests in the world-economy. Similarly with ethno-nations. The meaning of ethnic consciousness in a core area is considerably different from that of ethnic consciousness in a peripheral area precisely because of the different class position such ethnic groups have in the world-economy.[15]

Political struggles of ethno-nations or segments of classes within national boundaries of course are the daily bread and butter of local politics. But their significance or consequences can only be fruitfully analyzed if one spells out the implications of their organizational activity or political demands for the functioning of the world-economy. This also incidentally makes possible more rational assessments of these politics in terms of some set of evaluative criteria such as 'left' and 'right'.

The functioning then of a capitalist world-economy requires that groups pursue their economic interests within a single world market while seeking to distort this market for their benefit by organizing to exert influence on states, some of which are far more powerful than others but none of which controls the world-market in its entirety. Of course, we shall find on closer inspection that there are periods where one state is relatively quite powerful and other periods where power is more diffuse and contested, permitting weaker states broader ranges of action. We can talk then of the relative tightness or looseness of the world-system as an important variable and seek to analyze why this dimension tends to be cyclical in nature, as it seems to have been for several hundred years.

[...]

What then have been the consequences for the world-system of the emergence of many states in which there is no private ownership of the basic means of production? To some extent, this has meant an internal reallocation of consumption. It has certainly undermined the ideological justifications in world capitalism, both by showing the political vulnerability of capitalist entrepreneurs and by demonstrating that private ownership is irrelevant to the rapid expansion of industrial productivity. But to the extent that it has raised the ability of the new semi-peripheral areas to enjoy a larger share of the world surplus, it has once again depolarized the world, recreating the triad of strata that has been a fundamental element in the survival of the world-system.

Finally, in the peripheral areas of the world-economy, both the continued economic expansion of the core (even though the core is seeing some reallocation of surplus internal to it) and the new strength of the semi-periphery has led to a further weakening of the political and hence economic position of the peripheral areas. The pundits note that 'the gap is getting wider', but thus far no-one has succeeded in doing much about it, and it is not clear that there are very many in whose interests it would be to do so. Far from a strengthening of state authority, in many parts of the world we are witnessing the same kind of deterioration Poland knew in the sixteenth century, a deterioration of which the frequency of military coups is only one of many signposts. And all of this leads us to conclude that stage four has been the stage of the *consolidation* of the capitalist world-economy.

Consolidation, however, does not mean the absence of contradictions and does not mean the likelihood of long-term survival. We thus come to projections about the future, which has always been man's great game, his true *hybris*, the most convincing argument for the dogma of original sin. Having read Dante, I will therefore be brief.

There are two fundamental contradictions, it seems to me, involved in the workings of the capitalist world-system. In the first place, there is the contradiction to which the nineteenth-century

Marxian corpus pointed, which I would phrase as follows: whereas in the short-run the maximization of profit requires maximizing the withdrawal of surplus from immediate consumption of the majority, in the long-run the continued production of surplus requires a mass demand which can only be created by redistributing the surplus withdrawn. Since these two considerations move in opposite directions (a 'contradiction'), the system has constant crises which in the long-run both weaken it and make the game for those with privilege less worth playing.

The second fundamental contradiction, to which Mao's concept of socialism as process points, is the following: whenever the tenants of privilege seek to co-opt an oppositional movement by including them in a minor share of the privilege, they may no doubt eliminate opponents in the short-run; but they also up the ante for the next oppositional movement created in the next crisis of the world-economy. Thus the cost of 'co-option' rises ever higher and the advantages of co-option seem ever less worthwhile.

There are today no socialist systems in the world-economy any more than there are feudal systems because there is only *one* world-system. It is a world-economy and it is by definition capitalist in form. Socialism involves the creation of a new kind of *world*-system, neither a redistributive world-empire nor a capitalist world-economy but a socialist world-government. I don't see this projection as being in the least utopian but I also don't feel its institution is imminent. It will be the outcome of a long struggle in forms that may be familiar and perhaps in very new forms, that will take place in *all* the areas of the world-economy (Mao's continual 'class struggle'). Governments may be in the hands of persons, groups or movements sympathetic to this transformation but *states* as such are neither progressive nor reactionary. It is movements and forces that deserve such evaluative judgments.

Having gone as far as I care to in projecting the future, let me return to the present and to the scholarly enterprise which is never neutral but does have its own logic and to some extent its own priorities. We have adumbrated as our basic unit of observation a concept of world-systems that have structural parts and evolving stages. It is within such a frame work, I am arguing, that we can fruitfully make comparative analyses—of the wholes and of parts of the whole. Conceptions precede and govern measurements. I am all for minute and sophisticated quantitative indicators. I am all for minute and diligent archival work that will trace a concrete historical series of events in terms of all its immediate complexities. But the point of either is to enable us to see better what has happened and what is happening. For that we need glasses with which to discern the dimensions of difference, we need models with which to weigh significance, we need summarizing concepts with which to create the knowledge which we then seek to communicate to each other. And all this because we are men with hybris and original sin and therefore seek the good, the true, and the beautiful.

NOTES

1. See André Gunder Frank, Ch. IV (A), 'The Myth of Feudalism' in *Capitalism and Underdevelopment in Latin America* (New York: Monthly Review Press, 1967), pp. 221–42.

2. See Frederic Lane's discussion of 'protection costs' which is reprinted as Part Three of *Venice and History* (Baltimore: Johns Hopkins Press, 1966). For the specific discussion of tribute, see pp. 389–90, 416–20.

3. See Karl Polanyi, 'The Economy as Instituted Process', in Karl Polanyi, Conrad M. Arsenberg and Harry W. Pearson (eds.), *Trade and Market in the Early Empire* (Glencoe: Free Press, 1957), pp. 243–70.

4. See my *The Modern World-System: Capitalist Agriculture and the Origins of the European World-Economy in the Sixteenth Century* (New York: Academic Press, 1974).

5. Philip Abrams concludes a similar plea with this admonition: 'The academic and intellectual

dissociation of history and sociology seems, then, to have had the effect of deterring both disciplines from attending seriously to the most important issues involved in the understanding of social transition'. 'The Sense of the Past and the Origins of Sociology', *Past and Present*, No. 55, May 1972, 32.

6. Frank, *op. cit.*, p. 3.

7. Frank's critique, now classic, of these theories is entitled 'Sociology of Development and Underdevelopment of Sociology' and is reprinted in *Latin America: Underdevelopment or Revolution* (New York: Monthly Review Press, 1969), pp. 21–94.

8. See my *The Modern World-System, op. cit.*, Chap. 2.

9. I give a brief account of this in 'Three Paths of National Development in the Sixteenth Century', *Studies in Comparative International Development*, VII, 2, Summer 1972, 95–101.

10. See Arghiri Emmanuel, *Unequal Exchange* (New York: Monthly Review Press, 1972).

11. Charles Bettelheim, 'Theoretical Comments' in Emmanuel, *op. cit.*, p. 295.

12. See J. Siemenski, 'Constitutional Conditions in the Fifteenth and Sixteenth Centuries', *Cambridge History of Poland*, I, W. F. Reddaway *et al.* (eds.), *From the Origins to Sobieski (to 1696)* (Cambridge: At the

University Press, 1950), pp. 416–40; Janusz Tazbir, 'The Commonwealth of the Gentry', in Aleksander Gieysztor *et al.*, *History of Poland* (Warszawa: PWN—Polish Scientific Publ., 1968), pp. 169–271.

13. See my fuller analysis in 'Social Conflict in Post-Independence Black Africa: The Concepts of Race and Status-Group Reconsidered' in Ernest W. Campbell (ed.), *Racial Tensions and National Identity* (Nashville: Vanderbilt Univ. Press, 1972), pp. 207–26.

14. Range in this sentence means the number of different occupations in which a significant proportion of the population is engaged. Thus peripheral society typically is overwhelmingly agricultural. A core society typically has its occupations well-distributed over all of Colin Clark's three sectors. If one shifted the connotation of range to talk of style of life, consumption patterns, even income distribution, quite possibly one might reverse the correlation. In a typical peripheral society, the differences between a subsistence farmer and an urban professional are probably far greater than those which could be found in a typical core state.

15. See my 'The Two Modes of Ethnic Consciousness: Soviet Central Asia in Transition?' in Edward Allworth (ed.), *The Nationality Question in Soviet Central Asia* (New York: Praeger, 1973), pp. 168–75.

COMPANION WEBSITE

1. Go online to Write Out Loud about some of the negative and positive consequences of globalization.

2. For more on theories of globalization, including the work of David Harvey and Saskia Sassen, log on to the Globalization Theory Profile Page.

3. For a list of documentaries about globalization, including *Life and Debt*, a powerful film about the lives of Jamaicans as they struggle to survive under the constraints of foreign economic agendas, check out the *Networks of Capital* Supplementary Sources.

14

Materials for an Exploratory Theory of the Network Society[1]

Manuel Castells

THE NETWORK SOCIETY IS a specific form of social structure tentatively identified by empirical research as being characteristic of the Information Age. By social structure I understand the organizational arrangements of humans in relationships of production/consumption, experience, and power, as expressed in meaningful interaction framed by culture. By Information Age I refer to a historical period in which human societies perform their activities in a technological paradigm constituted around microelectronics-based information communication technologies, and genetic engineering. It replaces/subsumes the technological paradigm of the Industrial Age, organized primarily around the production and distribution of energy.

In this article I aim at clarifying the theoretical implications that can be induced from my observation of contemporary social structures and social change, proposed in my trilogy *The Information Age: Economy, Society, and Culture* (see the updated, and revised 'New Millennium edition' of this work: Castells 2000a). Since, in my view, theory is simply a research tool, and not the end product of research, the purpose of this exercise is to help the construction of an analytical framework that could inform, and better organize, further research. However, given the difficulty of the task, and the necessarily collective character of this endeavour, what is presented here should be considered, literally, as materials to be used in the building of a sociological theory able to grasp emerging forms of social organization and

conflict. This theory is still in its exploratory stage, and should remain, like all relevant theories, as a work in progress open to rectification by empirical research.

Because I am trying to distill theory from observation, I will not discuss here the many important, and fruitful, theoretical contributions that exist in sociology and related disciplines, which could anchor the categories and analyses proposed in this article. I will present an argument as schematic, and simplified as possible, so that it could be useful to sociologists' collective investigation, without spending space and time in reminding the reader of well-established theoretical contributions. A short bibliography indicates the works that have helped me in theorizing my investigation. Similarly, the statements on current social trends cannot be empirically substantiated in this paper: they rely on data and sources presented in the updated version of my trilogy (Castells 2000a).

For the sake of clarity, I will first present the conceptual framework I use in my analysis of social structure. I will then proceed to enumerate the main transformations taking place in social structures around the world, in the Information Age. Since a trend common to many of these transformations refers to the prevalence of information networking as the organizational form of dominant activities, I will then define information networks, and elaborate on the implications of networking in social morphology. Finally, I will present how, specifically, information networks affect social structures (as conceptualized in this article) to induce the kind of transformations we are observing. Within the limits of tentative elaboration, this exercise intends to open the way for a theoretically meaningful codification of current processes of social transformation, thus providing theoretical meaning to the ideal type of the network society. I hope the reader will be benevolent enough to use what s/he finds useful in this effort, and discard the rest. I also hope that we all end up adopting the notion of disposable theory.

CONCEPTUALIZING SOCIAL STRUCTURE

Human societies are made from the conflictive interaction between humans organized in and around a given social structure. This social structure is formed by the interplay between relationships of production/consumption; relationships of experience; and relationships of power. Meaning is constantly produced and reproduced through symbolic interaction between actors framed by this social structure, and, at the same time, acting to change it or to reproduce it. By meaning, I understand the symbolic identification by an actor of the purpose of her/his/their action. The consolidation of shared meaning through crystallization of practices in spatio–temporal configurations creates cultures, that is systems of values and beliefs informing codes of behaviour. There is no systemic dominance in this matrix of relationships. There are all layers of social structure and social causation, folded into each other, distinguishable only in analytical terms. Thus, meaning is not produced in the cultural realm: it is the cultural realm that is produced by the consolidation of meaning. Meaning results from symbolic interaction between brains which are socially and ecologically constrained, and, at the same time, biologically and culturally able of innovation. Meaning is produced, reproduced, and fought over in all layers of social structure, in production as in consump-

tion, in experience as in power. What makes sense to anyone is defined by the endless reconstruction by humans of the sources and purpose of their action, always constrained but never pre-scripted. So, production can be oriented towards glorifying God (and punishing the infidels), as well as religious belief can be twisted to the service of capital accumulation. What actually happens, when, and where (usually by random combination of social events in a pre-existing, historically determined, social structure), makes specific societies, such as now the 'network society'.

Production is the action of humankind on matter (nature), to appropriate it and transform it for its benefit by obtaining a product, consuming (unevenly) part of it, and accumulating the surplus for investment, according to socially decided goals. Consumption is the appropriation of the product by humans for their individual benefit. Analytically, it is a component of the production process, seen from the reverse side.

Experience is the action of humans on themselves, determined by the interplay between their biological and cultural identities, and in relationship to their social and natural environment. It is constructed around the endless search for the fulfilment of human needs and desires.

Power is the action of humans on other humans to impose their will on others, by the use, potential or actual, of symbolic or physical violence. Institutions of society are built to enforce power relationships existing in each historical period, including the controls, limits, and social contracts, achieved in the power struggles.

More particularly, production is organized in class relationships (or relationships of production) that define the process by which some humans, on the basis of their position in the production process decide the organization of production, the sharing and uses of the product vis-à-vis consumption, and investment, as well as the differential appropriation of the product (consumption). The structural principle under which surplus is appropriated and controlled characterizes a mode of production, such as capitalism or statism. The concept of mode of production belongs exclusively to the relationships of production. In this view, the notion, for instance, of a capitalist state, is void of theoretical meaning, although it can usefully characterize an empirical observation, when a given state is primarily geared toward the preservation and promotion of capitalist social relationships of production.

Experience is structured around sexual/gender relationships, historically organized around the family, and characterized hitherto by the domination of men over women and children. Family relationships and sexuality are the foundations of personality systems, understanding by personality the individuation of social relationships in specific brains, in interaction with the brain's biological features.

Power is founded upon the ability to exercise violence. Historically, it is the monopoly of physical violence, embodied in the state, which has been the main expression of power relationships. Outside the direct sphere of the state, the exercise of power within production organizations or in apparatuses of experience (such as the family) ultimately relied on the ability of these apparatuses to call upon the state (or para-states, such as the Church) to enforce violently the dominant rules on restive subjects. However, symbolic violence has always been a fundamental dimension of power, and it increases in importance over time, as societies make progress in establishing institutional limits to the arbitrary exercise of physical violence. By symbolic violence I mean the capacity of a given symbolic code to delete a different code from the individual brain upon whom power is exercised.

Symbolic communication between humans, and the relationship between humans and nature through production/consumption, experience, and power, crystallize over history in specific territories, thus generating cultures which go on to live a life on their own. Individuals may adopt/adapt to cultures, so building their identities. Or else, they may construct their own, individual identities through the interaction between available cultures, and their own symbolic recombinant capacity, influenced by their specific experience.

There is another layer that is folded in production/consumption, experience, power, and culture. This is technology. By technology I mean 'the use of scientific knowledge to specify ways of doing things in a reproducible manner'. Technology is embodied in technical relationships, which are socially conditioned, so in itself it is not an independent, non-human dimension. In principle, because it is the application of knowledge to obtain a product of some kind, it could be assigned primarily to the process of production, in which we could then distinguish social relationships of production, and technical relationships of production, as proposed in the Marxian model, and as I had proposed in my own work. I now think this is questionable. Because technology is as decisive in the realm of power (military technology, for instance) as in the realm of production. Similarly, technology plays an essential role in framing the relationships of experience: for instance, human reproductive technology frames family relationships and sexuality. Therefore, we must integrate technology, on its own ground, as a specific layer of the social structure, following an old tradition in human ecology. I would like to use for conceptualizing technology as a layer of the social structure, the Tourainian concept of 'mode of development' (also consistent with Bell's analytical framework), that I will define, in my own terms, as: 'the technological arrangements through which humans act upon matter (nature), upon themselves, and upon other humans'. By technological arrangements I mean the set of tools, rules, and procedures, through which scientific knowledge is applied to a given task in a reproducible manner. Modes of development are defined by their central technological paradigm and by their principle of performance. Following, and adapting to sociology, Christopher Freeman's definition of a techno-economic paradigm, I would characterize as a technological paradigm a cluster of inter-related technical, organizational, and managerial innovations, whose advantages are to be found in their superior productivity and efficiency in accomplishing an assigned goal, as a result of synergy between its components (1982). Each paradigm is constituted around a fundamental set of technologies, specific to the paradigm, and whose coming together into a synergistic set establishes the paradigm. Thus, energy for the Industrial Paradigm, Information/communication technologies (including genetic engineering) for the Informational Paradigm.

Technology as a material tool, and meaning as symbolic construction, through relationships of production/consumption, experience, and power, are the fundamental ingredients of human action—an action that ultimately produces and modifies social structure.

THE NETWORK SOCIETY: AN OVERVIEW

In the last two decades of the twentieth century a related set of social transformations has taken place around the world. While cultures, institutions, and historical trajectories introduce a great deal of diversity in the actual manifestations of each one of these transformations, it can be shown that, overall, the vast majority of societies are affected in a fundamental way by these transformations. All together they constitute a new type of social structure that I call the network society for reasons that hopefully will become apparent. I shall summarize below the main features of these transformations, in a sequential order that does not imply hierarchy of causation in any way.

We have entered *a new technological paradigm*, centred around microelectronics-based, information/communication technologies, and genetic engineering. In this sense what is characteristic of the network society is not the critical role of knowledge and information, because knowledge and information were central in all societies. Thus, we should abandon the notion of 'Information Society', which I have myself used some times, as unspecific and misleading. What is new in our age is a new set of information technologies. I contend they represent a greater change in the history of technology than the technologies associated with the Industrial Revolution, or with the previous Information Revolution (printing). Furthermore, we are only at the beginning of this technological revolution, as the Internet becomes a universal tool of interactive communication, as we shift from computer-centred technologies to network-diffused technologies, as we make progress in nanotechnology (and thus in the diffusion capacity of information devices), and, even more importantly, as we unleash the biology revolution, making possible for the first time, the design and manipulation of living organisms, including human parts. What is also characteristic of this technological paradigm is the use of knowledge-based, information technologies to enhance and accelerate the production of knowledge and information, in a self-expanding, virtuous circle. Because information processing is at the source of life, and of social action, every domain of our eco-social system is thereby transformed.

We live in *a new economy*, characterized by three fundamental features. First, it is *informational*, that is, the capacity of generating knowledge and processing/managing information determine the productivity and competitiveness of all kinds of economic units, be they firms, regions, or countries. While it took two decades for the new technological system to yield its productivity dividend, we are now observing substantial productivity growth in the most advanced economies and sectors, in spite of the difficulty in measuring informational productivity with the categories of the industrial era.

Second, this new economy is *global* in the precise sense that its core, strategic activities, have the capacity to work as a unit on a planetary scale in real time or chosen time. By core activities I mean financial markets, science and technology, international trade of goods and services, advanced business services, multinational production firms and their ancillary networks, communication media, and highly skilled speciality labour. Most jobs are in fact not global, but all economies are under the influence of the movements of their globalized core. Globalization is highly selective. It proceeds by linking up all that, according to dominant interests, has value anywhere in the planet, and discarding anything (people, firms, territories, resources) which has no value or becomes devalued, in a variable geometry of creative destruction and destructive creation of value.

Third, the new economy is *networked*. At the heart of the connectivity of the global economy and of the flexibility of informational production, there is a new form of economic organization, the *network enterprise*. This is not a network of enterprises. It is a network made from either firms or segments of firms, and/or from internal segmentation of firms. Large corporations are internally de-centralized as networks. Small and medium businesses are connected in networks. These networks connect among themselves on specific business projects, and switch to another network as soon as the project is finished. Major corporations work in a strategy of changing alliances and partnerships, specific to a given product, process, time, and space. Furthermore, these co-operations are based increasingly on sharing of information. These are information networks, which, in the limit, link up suppliers and customers through one firm, with this firm being essentially an intermediary of supply and demand, collecting a fee for its ability to process information.

The unit of this production process is not the firm, but the business project. The firm continues to be the legal unit of capital accumulation. But since the value of the firm ultimately depends on its valuation in the stock market, the unit of capital

accumulation (the firm) itself becomes a node in a global network of financial flows. In this economy, the dominant layer is the global financial market, where all earnings from all activities and countries end up being traded. This global financial market works only partly according to market rules. It is shaped and moved by information turbulences of various origins, processed and transmitted almost instantly by tele-communicated, information systems, in the absence of the institutional regulation of global capital flows.

This new economy (informational, global, networked) is certainly capitalist. Indeed, for the first time in history, the whole planet is capitalist, for all practical purposes (except North Korea, but not Cuba or Myanmar, and certainly not China). But it is a new brand of capitalism, in which rules for investment, accumulation, and reward, have substantially changed (see Giddens and Hutton 2000). Besides, since nothing authorizes capitalism as eternal, it is essential to focus on the characteristics of the new economy because it may well outlast the mode of production where it was born, once capitalism comes under decisive challenge and/ or plunges into a structural crisis derived from its internal contradictions (after all, statism died from its self-inflicted flaws).

Work and employment are substantially transformed in/by the new economy. But, against a persistent myth, there is no mass unemployment as a consequence of new information technologies. The empirical record is conclusive on this matter (Carnoy 2000). Yet, there is a serious unemployment problem in Europe, unrelated to technology, and there are dramatic problems of underemployment in the developing world, caused by economic and institutional backwardness, including the insufficient diffusion and inefficient use of information technologies. There is a decisive transformation of work and employment. Induced by globalization, and the network enterprise, and facilitated by information/communication technologies, the most important transformation in employment patterns concerns the development of flexible work, as the predominant form of working arrangements. Part-time work, temporary work, self-employment, work by contract, informal or semi-formal labour arrangements, and relentless occupational mobility, are the key features of the new labour market. Feminization of paid labour leads to the rise of the 'flexible woman', gradually replacing the 'organization man', as the harbinger of the new type of worker. The key transformation is the individualization of labour, reversing the process of socialization of production characteristic of the industrial era, still at the roots of our current system of industrial relations.

The work process is interconnected between firms, regions, and countries, in a stepped up spatial division of labour, in which networks of locations are more important than hierarchies of places. Labour is fundamentally divided in two categories: self-programmable labour, and generic labour. Self-programmable labour is equipped with the ability to retrain itself, and adapt to new tasks, new processes and new sources of information, as technology, demand, and management speed up their rate of change. Generic labour, by contrast, is exchangeable and disposable, and co-exists in the same circuits with machines and with unskilled labour from around the world. Beyond the realm of employable labour, legions of discarded, devalued people form the growing planet of the irrelevant, from where perverse connections are made, by fringe capitalist business, through to the booming, global criminal economy. Because of this structural divide in terms of informational capacities, and because of the individualization of the reward system, in the absence of a determined public policy aimed at correcting structural trends, we have witnessed in the last 20 years a dramatic surge of inequality, social polarization, and social exclusion in the world at large, and in most countries, particularly, among advanced societies, in the USA and in the

UK (see UNDP 1999; Hutton 1996; Castells 2000b, for sources).

Shifting to the *cultural realm*, we see the emergence of a similar pattern of networking, flexibility, and ephemeral symbolic communication, in a culture organized primarily around an integrated system of electronic media, obviously including the Internet. Cultural expressions of all kinds are increasingly enclosed in or shaped by this electronic hypertext. But the new media system is not characterized by one-way, undifferentiated messages through a limited number of channels that constituted the world of mass media. And it is not a global village. Media are extraordinarily diverse, and send targeted messages to specific segments of audiences responding to specific moods of audiences. They are increasingly inclusive, bridging from one another, from network TV to cable TV or satellite TV, radio, VCR, video, portable devices, and the Internet. The whole set is coming together in the multimedia system, computer-operated by the digitalized set-top box that opens up hundreds of channels of interactive communication, reaching from the global from the local. While there is oligopolistic concentration of multimedia groups, there is, at the same time, market segmentation, and the rise of an interactive audience, superseding the uniformity of the mass audience. Because of the inclusiveness and flexibility of this system of symbolic exchange, most cultural expressions are enclosed in it, thus inducing the formation of what I call a culture of 'real virtuality'. Our symbolic environment is, by and large, structured by this flexible, inclusive hypertext, in which many people surf each day. The virtuality of this text is in fact a fundamental dimension of reality, providing the symbols and icons from which we think and thus exist.

This growing enclosure of communication in the space of a flexible, interactive, electronic hypertext does not only concern culture. It has a fundamental effect on *politics*. In almost all countries, media have become the space of politics. To an overwhelming extent people receive their information, on the basis of which they form their political opinion and structure their behaviour, through the media and particularly television and radio. Media politics needs to convey very simple messages. The simplest message is an image. The simplest, individualized image is a person. Political competition increasingly revolves around the personalization of politics. The most effective political weapons are negative messages. The most effective negative message is character assassination of opponents' personalities, and/or of their supporting organizations. Political marketing is an essential means to win political competition, including, in the information age, media presence, media advertising, telephone banks, targeted mailing, image making and unmaking. Thus, politics becomes a very expensive business, way beyond the means of traditional sources of political financing, at a time when citizens resist giving more of their tax money to politicians. Thus, parties and leaders use access to power as ways to obtain resources for their trade. Political corruption becomes a systemic feature of information age politics. Since character assassination needs some substance from time to time, systemic political corruption provides ample opportunity, as a market of intermediaries is created to leak and counter-leak damaging information. The politics of scandal takes centre stage in political competition, in close interaction with the media system, and with the co-operation of judges and prosecutors, the new stars of our political soap operas. Politics becomes a horse race, and a tragicomedy motivated by greed, backstage manoeuvres, betrayals, and, often, sex and violence—a genre increasingly indistinguishable from TV scripts.

As with all historical transformations, the emergence of a new social structure is linked to a redefinition of the material foundations of our life, of *time and space*, as Giddens (1984), Adam (see chapter below), Lash and Urry (1994), Thrift (1990), and Harvey (1990), among others, have argued. I pro-pose the hypothesis that two emergent social forms of time and space characterize the network society, while coexisting with prior forms of time and space. These are timeless time and the space of flows. In contrast to the rhythm of biological time characteristic of most of human existence, and to clock time characterizing the industrial age, timeless time is defined by the use of new information/communication technologies in a relentless effort to annihilate time. On the one hand, time is compressed (as in split second global financial transactions, or in the attempt to fight 'instant wars'), and on the other hand, time is de-sequenced, including past, present, and future occurring in a random sequence (as in the electronic hypertext or in the blurring of life-cycle patterns, both in work and parenting).

The space of flows refers to the technological and organizational possibility of organizing the simultaneity of social practices without geographical contiguity. Most dominant functions in our societies (financial markets, transnational production networks, media systems etc.) are organized around the space of flows. And so to do an increasing number of alternative social practices (such as social movements) and personal interaction networks. However, the space of flows does include a territorial dimension, as it requires a technological infrastructure that operates from certain locations, and as it connects functions and people located in specific places. Yet, the meaning and function of the space of flows depend on the flows processed within the networks, by contrast with the space of places, in which meaning, function, and locality are closely interrelated.

The central power-holding institution of human history, *the state*, is also undergoing a process of dramatic transformation. On the one hand, its sovereignty is called into question by global flows of wealth, communication, and information. On the other hand, its legitimacy is undermined by the politics of scandal and its dependence on media politics. The weakening of its power and credibility induce people to build their own systems of defence and representation around their identities, further de-legitimizing the state. However, the state does not disappear. It adapts and transforms itself. On the one hand, it builds partnerships between nation-states and shares sovereignty to retain influence. The European Union is the most obvious case, but around the world there is a decisive shift of power toward multi-national and transnational institutions, such as NATO, IMF/World Bank, United Nations agencies, World Trade Organization, regional trade associations, and the like. On the other hand, to regain legitimacy, most states have engaged in a process of devolution of power, decentralizing responsibilities and resources to nationalities, regions, and local governments, often extending this de-centralization to non-governmental organizations. The international arena is also witnessing a proliferation of influential, resourceful non-governmental organizations that interact with governments, and multinational political institutions. Thus, overall the new state is not any longer a nation-state. The state in the information age is a network state, a state made out of a complex web of power-sharing, and negotiated decision-making between international, multinational, national, regional, local, and non-governmental, political institutions.

There are two common trends in these processes of transformation that, together, signal a new historical landscape. First, none of them could have taken place without new information/communication technologies. Thus, while technology is not the cause of the transformation, it is indeed the indispensable medium. And in fact, it is what constitutes the historical novelty of this multidimensional transformation. Second, all processes are enacted by organizational forms that are built upon networks, or to be more specific, upon information networks. Thus, to analyse the emerging social structure in theoretically meaningful terms, we have to define what information networks are, and elaborate on their strategic role in fostering and shaping current processes of social transformation.

SOCIAL STRUCTURE AND SOCIAL MORPHOLOGY: FROM NETWORKS TO INFORMATION NETWORKS

A network is a set of interconnected nodes. A node is the point where the curve intersects itself. Networks are very old forms of social organization. But they have taken on a new life in the Information Age by becoming information networks, powered by new information technologies. Indeed, networks had traditionally a major advantage and a major problem, in contrast to other configurations of social morphology, such as centralized hierarchies. On the one hand, they are the most flexible, and adaptable forms of organization, able to evolve with their environment and with the evolution of the nodes that compose the network. On the other hand, they have considerable difficulty in co-ordinating functions, in focusing resources on specific goals, in managing the complexity of a given task beyond a certain size of the network. Thus, while they were the natural forms of social expression, they were generally outperformed as tools of instrumentality. For most of human history, and unlike biological evolution, networks were outperformed by organizations able to master resources around centrally defined goals, achieved through the implementation of tasks in rationalized, vertical chains of command and control. But for the first time, the introduction of new information/communication technologies allows networks to keep their flexibility and adaptability, thus asserting their evolutionary nature. While, at the same time, these technologies allow for co-ordination and management of complexity, in an interactive system which features feedback effects, and communication patterns from anywhere to everywhere within the networks. It follows an unprecedented combination of flexibility and task implementation, of co-ordinated decision making, and decentralized execution, which provide a superior social morphology for all human action.

Networks de-centre performance and share decision-making. By definition, a network has no centre. It works on a binary logic: inclusion/exclusion. All there is in the network is useful and necessary for the existence of the network. What is not in the network does not exist from the network's perspective, and thus must be either ignored (if it is not relevant to the network's task), or eliminated (if it is competing in goals or in performance). If a node in the network ceases to perform a useful function it is phased out from the network, and the network rearranges itself—as cells do in biological processes. Some nodes are more important than others, but they all need each other as long as they are within the network. And no nodal domination is systemic. Nodes increase their importance by absorbing more information and processing it more efficiently. If they decline in their performance, other nodes take over their tasks. Thus, the relevance, and relative weight of nodes does not come from their specific features, but from their ability to be trusted by the network with an extra-share of information. In this sense, the main nodes are not centres, but switchers, following a networking logic rather than a command logic, in their function vis-à-vis the overall structure.

Networks, as social forms, are value-free or neutral. They can equally kill or kiss: nothing personal. They process the goals they are programmed to perform. All goals contradictory to the programmed goals will be fought off by the network components. In this sense, a network is an automaton. But, who programmes the network? Who decides the rules that the automaton will follow? Social actors, naturally. Thus, there is a social struggle to assign goals to the network. But once the network is programmed, it imposes its logic to all its members (actors). Actors will have to play their strategies within the rules of the network. To assign different goals to the programme of the network (in contrast to perfect the programme within the same set of goals), actors will have to challenge the network from the outside and in fact destroy it by building an alternative network around alternative values. Or else, building a defensive, non-network structure (a commune) which does not allow connections outside its own set of values. Networks may communicate, if they are compatible in their goals. But for this they need actors who possess compatible access codes to operate the switches. They are the switchers or power-holders in our society (as in the connections between media and politics, financial markets and technology, science and the military, and drug traffic and global finance through money laundering).

The speed and shape of structural transformations in our society, ushering in a new form of social organization, come from the widespread introduction of information networks as the predominant organizational form. Why now? The answer lies in the simultaneous availability of new, flexible information technologies and a set of historical events, which came together by accident, around the late 1960s, and 1970s. These events include the restructuring of capitalism with its emphasis on deregulation and liberalization; the failed restructuring of statism unable to adapt itself to informationalism; the influence of libertarian ideology arising from the countercultural social movements of the 1960s; and the development of a new media system, enclosing cultural expressions in a global/local, interactive hypertext. All processes, interacting with each other, favoured the adoption of information networks as a most efficient form of organization. Once introduced, and powered by information technology, information networks, through competition, gradually eliminate other organizational forms, rooted in a different social logic. In this sense, they tend to assert the predominance of social morphology over social action. Let me clarify the meaning of this statement by entering into the heart of the argument, that is, by examining how specifically the introduction of information networks into the social structure accounts for the set of observable transformations as presented in the preceding section. Or, in other words, how and why information networks constitute the backbone of the network society.

THE ROLE OF INFORMATION NETWORKS IN SHAPING RELATIONSHIPS OF PRODUCTION, CONSUMPTION, POWER, EXPERIENCE, AND CULTURE

Information networks, as defined above, contribute, to a large extent, to the transformation of social structure in the information age. To be sure, this multidimensional transformation has other sources that interact with the specific effect of information networks, as mentioned above. Yet, in this analysis, I will focus on the specificity of the interaction between this new social morphology and the evolution of social structure. I will be as parsimonious as possible, trying to avoid repetition of arguments and observations already presented in this text.

A social structure is transformed when there is simultaneous and systemic transformation of relationships of production/consumption, power, and experience, ultimately leading to a transformation of culture. Information networks play a substantial role in the set of transformations I have analysed in my work and summarized here. This is how and why.

Relationships of production

Although I suppose information networks will shape, eventually, other modes of production, for the time being we can only assess their effect in the capitalist mode of production. Networks change the two terms of the relationship (capital, labour), and their relationship. They transform capital by organizing its circulation in global networks and making it the dominant sphere of capital—the one where value, from whichever origin, increases (or decreases) and is ultimately realized. Global financial markets are information networks. They constitute themselves into a collective 'capitalist', independent from any specific capitalist (but not indifferent to), and activated by rules that are only partly market rules. In this sense, capital in the Information Age has become a human-made automaton, which, through mediations, imposes its structural determination to relationships of production. More specifically, global financial markets and their management networks constitute an automated network, governed by interactions between its multiple nodes, propelled by a combination of market logic, information turbulences, and actors' strategies and bets (see Castells 2000b).

Relationships between capital and labour (all kinds of capital, all kinds of labour) are organized around the network enterprise form of production. This network enterprise is also globalized at its core, through telecommunications and transportation networks. Thus, the work process is globally integrated, but labour tends to be locally fragmented. There is simultaneous integration of production and specification of labour's contribution to the production process. Value in the production process depends essentially on the position occupied by each specific labour or each specific firm in the value chain. The rule is individualization of the relationship between capital and labour. In a growing number of cases, self-employment, or payment in stocks, leads to workers becoming holders of their own capital—however, any individual capital is submitted to the movements of the global automaton. As labour comes to be defined by a network of production and individualized in its relationship to capital, the critical cleavage within labour becomes that between networked labour and switched-off labour which ultimately becomes non-labour. Within networked labour, it is the capacity to contribute to the value-producing chain that determines the individual bargaining position. Thus labour's informational capacity, by ensuring the possibility of strategic positioning in the network, leads to a second, fundamental cleavage, between self-programmable labour and generic labour. For self-programmable labour, its individual interest is better served by enhancing its role in performing the goals of the network, thus establishing competition between labour and co-operation between capital (the network enterprise) as the structural rule of the game. Indeed game theory and rational choice theory seem to be adequate intellectual tools to understand socio-economic behaviour in the networked economy. While for generic labour, its strategy is survival: the key issue becomes not be degraded to the realm of discarded or devalued labour, either by automation or globalization, or both.

In the last analysis, the networking of relationships of production leads to the blurring of class relationships. This does not preclude exploitation, social differentiation and social resistance. But production-based, social classes, as constituted, and enacted in the Industrial Age, cease to exist in the network society.

Relationships of consumption

Relationships of consumption (that is, the culturally meaningful, differential appropriation of the product) are determined by the interplay between relationships of production and culture. Who does what, in a given value production system, determines who gets what. What is valued as appropriation is framed by culture. The networking of production relationships, and the consequent individualization of labour, leads on the one hand to increasing differentiation and thus inequality in consumption. It also leads to social polarization and social exclusion following the opposition between self-programmable labour and generic labour, and between labour and devalued labour. The ability of networks to connect valuable labour and territories, and to discard dispensable labour and territories, so

enhancing their performance through reconfiguration, leads to cumulative growth and cumulative decline. The winner-takes-all system is, in the consumption sphere, the expression of value creation by/in the networks.

On the other hand, the fragmentation of culture, and the individualization of positions in relationships of production, lead jointly to a growing diversification of consumption patterns. Mass consumption was predicated upon standardized production, stable relationships of production, and a mass culture organized around predictable senders and identifiable sets of values. In a world of networks, self-programmable individuals constantly redefine their life styles and thus their consumption patterns; while generic labour just strives for survival.

As culture is similarly fragmented and constantly recombined in the networks of a kaleidoscopic hypertext, consumption patterns follow the variable geometry of symbolic appropriation. Thus, in the interplay between relationships of production and cultural framing, relationships of production define levels of consumption, and culture induces consumption patterns and life styles.

Relationships of power

The most direct impact of information networks on social structure concerns power relationships. Historically, power was embedded in organizations and institutions, organized around a hierarchy of centres. Networks dissolve centres, they disorganize hierarchy, and make materially impossible the exercise of hierarchical power without processing instructions in the network, according to the network's morphological rules. Thus, contemporary information networks of capital, production, trade, science, communication, human rights, and crime, bypass the nation-state, which, by and large, has stopped being a sovereign entity, as I argued above. A similar process, in different ways, takes place in other hierarchical organizations that used to embody power ('power apparatuses' in the old Marxist terminology), such as churches, schools, hospitals, bureaucracies of all kinds. Just to illustrate this diversity, churches see their privilege as senders of belief called into question by the ubiquitous sending and receiving of messages in the interactive hypertext. While religions are flourishing, churches have to enter the new media world in order to promote their gospel. So doing, they survive, and even prosper, but they open themselves up to constant challenges to their authority. In a sense, they are secularized by their co-existence with profanity in the hypertext, except when/if they anchor themselves in fundamentalism by refusing to bend to the network, thus building self-contained, cultural communes.

The state reacts to its bypassing by information networks, by transforming itself into a network state. So doing, its former centres fade away as centres becoming nodes of power-sharing, and forming institutional networks. Thus, in the war against Yugoslavia, in spite of US military hegemony, decision-making was shared in various degrees by NATO governments, including regular video-conferences between the leaders of the main countries where key decisions were taken. This example goes beyond the former instances of traditional military alliances, by introducing joint war-making in real time. NATO was reinforced by NATO's state members, when these states, including the USA, entered the new world of shared sovereignty. But individual states became weakened in their autonomous decision making. The network became the unit.

Thus, while there are still power relationships in society, the bypassing of centres by flows of information circulating in networks creates a new, fundamental hierarchy: the power of flows takes precedence over the flows of power.

Relationships of experience

If power relationships are the ones most directly affected by the prevailing networking logic, the role of networks in the transformation of relationships of experience is more subtle. I will not force the logic of the analysis. I do not believe that we must see networks everywhere for the sake of coherence. Yet, I think it could be intriguing to elaborate tentatively on the links between networking and the transformation of relationships of experience.

This transformation, empirically speaking, revolves around the crisis of patriarchalism, and its far-reaching consequences for family, sexuality and personality. The fundamental source of this crisis is women's cultural revolution, and men's resistance to reverse their millennial privileges. Additional sources are the feminization of labour markets (undermining male domination in the family and in society at large), the revolution in reproductive technology, the self-centring of culture, the individualization of life patterns and the weakening of the state's authority to enforce patriarchalism. What networks have to do with all this?

There is one direct connection between the networking of work and the individualization of labour, and the mass incorporation of women to paid labour, under conditions of structural discrimination. Thus, new social relationships of production, translate into a good fit between the 'flexible woman' (forced to flexibility to cope with her multiple roles) and the network enterprise. Networks of information, and global communication are also critical in diffusing alternative life styles, role models and, more importantly, critical information, for instance about self-control of biological reproduction. Then, there is an additional, meaningful connection. The disintegration of the patriarchal family does not let people, and children, isolated. They reconfigure life-sharing forms through networking. This is particularly true of women and their children, relying on a form of sociability and solidarity tested by millennia of living 'underground'. But also men, and men and women after going their own ways, come to rely on networks (sometimes around children of multiple marriages) to both survive and reinvent forms of togetherness. This trend shifts the basis of interpersonal relationships from nuclei to networks: networks of individuals and their children—which, by the way, are also individuals. What is left of families are transformed in partnerships which are nodes of networks. Sexuality is de-coupled from the family, and transformed into consumption/images, stimulated and simulated from the electronic hypertext. The body, as proposed by Giddens some time ago, becomes an expression of identity (1991). It is individualized and consumed in sexual networks. At the level of personality, the process of socialization becomes customized, individualized, and made out of composite models. The autonomous ability to reprogramme one's own personality, in interaction with an environment of networks, becomes the crucial feature for psychological balance, replacing the strengthening of a set personality, embedded in established values. In this 'risk society' (Beck 1992), the management of anxiety is the most useful personal skill. Two conflicting modes of interpersonal interaction emerge: on the one hand, self-reliant communes, anchored in their non-negotiable sets of beliefs; and on the other hand, networks of ever shifting individuals.

These are social networks, not information networks. So, in a way, they are a fundamental part of our societies, but not necessarily a feature of the network society—unless we extend the meaning of the concept beyond what I propose: information networks-based social structure. However, as communication technology, biological technology, transgender networking, and networks of individuals, develop in parallel, as key elements of social practice, they are interacting, and influencing each other. Thus, the Internet is becoming a very instrumental tool of management of new forms of life, including the building of on-line communities of support and collective learning.

I see, however, a much stronger connection between networks and relationships of experience through the cultural transformations induced by communication networks, as experience becomes practice by its rooting in cultural codes.

Networks and cultural transformation

Culture was historically produced by symbolic interaction in a given space/time. With time being annihilated and space becoming a space of flows, where all symbols coexist without reference to experience, culture becomes the culture of real virtuality. It takes the form of an interactive network in the electronic hypertext, mixing everything, and voiding the meaning of any specific message out of this context, except that is for fundamental, non-communicable values external to the hypertext. So, culture is unified in the hypertext but interpreted individually (in line with the 'interactive audience' school of thought in media theory). Culture is constructed by the actor, self-produced and self-consumed. Thus, because there are few common codes, there is systemic misunderstanding. It is this structurally induced cacophony that is celebrated as postmodernity. However, there is one common language, the language of the hypertext. Cultural expressions left out of the hypertext are purely individual experiences. The hypertext is the vehicle of communication, thus the provider of shared cultural codes. But these codes are formal, voided of specific meaning. Their only shared meaning is to be a node, or a blip, in the network of communication flows. Their communicative power comes from their capacity to be interpreted and re-arranged in a multi-vocality of meanings, depending on the receiver, and on the interactor. Any assigned meaning becomes instantly obsolete, reprocessed by a myriad of different views and alternative codes. The fragmentation of culture and the recurrent circularity of the hypertext, leads to the individualization of cultural meaning in the communication networks. The networking of production, the differentiation of consumption, the decentring of power, and the individualization of experience, are reflected, amplified, and codified by the fragmentation of meaning in the broken mirror of the electronic hypertext—where the only shared meaning is the meaning of sharing the network.

CONCLUSION: SOCIAL CHANGE IN THE NETWORK SOCIETY

Social structures are sets of organizational regularities historically produced by social actors, and constantly challenged, and ultimately transformed by deliberate social action. The network society is no exception to this sociological law. Yet, the characteristics of specific social structures impose constraints on the characteristics of their transformation process. Thus, the recurrence and flexibility of information networks, their embedded ability to bypass, ignore or eliminate, instructions alien to their programmed goals, make social change in the network society a very tricky task. This is because, apparently, nothing must be changed—any new input can theoretically be added to the network, like free expression in the global media system. Yet, the price for the addition is to accept implicitly the programmed goal of the network, its ancillary language and operating procedures. Thus, my hypothesis is that there is little chance of social change within a given network, or network of networks. Understanding by social change, the transformation of the programme of the network, to assign to the network a new goal, following a different set of values and beliefs. This is in contrast to reprogramming the network by adding instructions compatible with the overarching goal.

Because of the capacity of the network to find new avenues of performance by switching off any non-compatible node, I think social change, under these circumstances, happens primarily through two mechanisms, both external to dominant networks. The first is the denial of the networking logic through the affirmation of values that cannot be processed in any network, only obeyed and followed. This is what I call cultural communes, that are not necessarily linked to fundamentalism, but which are always centred around their self-contained meaning. The second is alternative networks, that is networks built around alternative projects, which compete, from network to network, to build bridges of communication to other networks in society, in opposition to the codes of the currently dominant networks. Religious, national, territorial, and ethnic communes are examples of the first type of challenge. Ecologism, feminism, human rights movements are examples of alternative networks. All use the Internet and electronic media hypertext, as dominant networks do. This is not what makes them networks or communes. The critical divide lies in the communicability or non-communicability of their codes beyond their specific self-definition. The fundamental dilemma in the network society is that political institutions are not the site of power any longer. The real power is the power of instrumental flows, and cultural codes, embedded in networks. Therefore, the assault to these immaterial power sites, from outside their logic, requires either the anchoring in eternal values, or the projection of alternative, communicative codes that expand through networking of alternative networks. That social change proceeds through one way or another will make the difference between fragmented communalism and new history making.

NOTE

1. The elaboration presented in this text has been greatly helped, indirectly, by the scholarly reviews of my book on *The Information Age*, particularly those by Anthony Giddens, Alain Touraine, Anthony Smith, Benjamin Barber, Peter Hall, Roger-Pol Droit, Sophie Watson, Frank Webster, Krishan Kumar, David Lyon, Craig Calhoun, Jeffrey Henderson, Ramon Ramos, Jose E. Rodrigues-Ibanez, Jose F. Tezanos, Mary Kaldor, Stephen Jones and Christopher Freeman. In tightening, and rectifying my argument, I am trying to respond to the intellectual dialogue engaged by these, and many other colleagues. I am most grateful for their interest and collegial criticism.

BIBLIOGRAPHY

Arquilla, John and Rondfeldt, David 1999 *The Emergence of Noopolitik*, Santa Monica, CA: Rand, National Defense Research Institute.

Barber, Benjamin 1995 *Jihad vs. McWorld*, New York: Times Books.

Beck, Ulrich 1992 *Risk Society: Towards a New Modernity*, London: Sage.

Calhoun, Craig (ed.) 1994 *Social Theory and the Politics of Identity*, Oxford: Blackwell.

Carnoy, Martin 2000 *Work, Family and Community in the Information Age*, New York: Russell Sage.

Castells, Manuel 2000a *The Information Age: Economy, Society and Culture*, Updated edition, Oxford: Blackwell, 3 volumes.

—— 2000b 'Information technology and global capitalism', in A. Giddens and W. Hutton (eds) 2000 *On the Edge*, London: Jonathan Cape.

Croteau, David and Hoynes, William 1997 *Media/Society: Industries, Images, and Audiences*, Thousand Oaks, CA: Pine Forge Press.

De Kerckhove, Derrick 1997 *'Connected intelligence'*, Toronto: Somerville House.

Dutton, William H. 1999 *Society on the Line: Information Politics in the Digital Age*, Oxford: Oxford University Press.

Freeman, Christopher 1982 *The Economics of Industrial Innovation*, London: Pinter.

Giddens, Anthony 1984 *The Constitution of Society: Outline of a Theory of Structuration*, Cambridge: Polity Press.

—— 1991 *Modernity and Self-Identity. Self and Society in the Late Modern Age*, Stanford: Stanford University Press.

Giddens, Anthony and Hutton, Will (eds) 2000 *On the Edge*, London: Jonathan Cape.

Graham, Stephen, and Marvin, Simon 1996 *Telecommunications and the City: Electronic Spaces, Urban Places*, London: Routledge.

Hage, Jerald, and Powers, Charles 1992 *Postindustrial Lives: Roles and Relationships in the 21st Century*, London: Sage.

Hall, Peter (Sir) 1998 *Cities in Civilization,* New York: Pantheon.

Harvey, David 1990 *The Condition of Post-modernity*, Oxford: Blackwell.

Held, David, and Mc Grew, Anthony, Goldblatt, David and Perraton, Jonathan 1999 *Global Transformations: Politics, Economics, and Culture*, Stanford: Stanford University Press.

Hutton, Will 1996[1995] *The State We're In,* London: Jonathan Cape.

Lash, Scott, and Urry, John 1994 *Economies of Signs and Space*, London: Sage.

Lyon, David 1999 *Postmodernity*, Buckingham: Open University Press.

Mansell, Robin and Silverstone, Roger (eds) 1996 *Communication By Design: The Politics of Information and Communication Technologies*, Oxford: Oxford University Press.

Scott, Allen 1998 *Regions and the World Economy. The Coming Shape of Global Production, Competition, and Political Order*, New York: Oxford University Press.

Subirats, Marina 1998 'Con diferencia: las mujeres frente al reto de la autonomia', Barcelona: Icaria.

Thrift, Nigel J. 1990 'The making of capitalism in time consciousness', in J. Hassard (ed.) *The Sociology of Time,* London: Macmillan.

Touraine, Alain 1993[1973] *Production de la societé*, Paris: Seuil.

—— 1997 *Pourrons-nous vivre ensemble? Egaux et differents*, Paris: Fayard.

Turkle, Sherry 1995 *Life On the Screen. Identity In the Age of Internet*, New York: Simon and Schuster.

United Nations Development Programme 1999 *1999 Human Development Report: Globalization with a Human Face*, New York: UNDP-United Nations.

Webster, Juliet 1996 *Shaping Women's Work. Gender, Employment, and Information Technology*, London: Longman.

Wellman, Barry (ed.) 1999 *Networks in the Global Village*, Boulder, Colorado: Westview Press.

COMPANION WEBSITE

1. Go online to Write Out Loud about how the rise of the network society and its associated technologies have transformed your own social world.
2. For a brief overview of the buzz surrounding globalization, log on to the Globalization Theory Profile Page.
3. Check out the Supplementary Sources for a list of helpful websites depicting global networks and global inequality in vivid detail.

15

The Forms of Capital[1]

Pierre Bourdieu

THE SOCIAL WORLD IS accumulated history, and if it is not to be reduced to a discontinuous series of instantaneous mechanical equilibria between agents who are treated as interchangeable particles, one must reintroduce into it the notion of capital and with it, accumulation and all its effects. Capital is accumulated labor (in its materialized form or its "incorporated," embodied form) which, when appropriated on a private, i.e., exclusive, basis by agents or groups of agents, enables them to appropriate social energy in the form of reified or living labor. It is a *vis insita*, a force inscribed in objective or subjective structures, but it is also a *lex insita*, the principle underlying the immanent regularities of the social world. It is what makes the games of society—not least, the economic game—something other than simple games of chance offering at every moment the possibility of a miracle. Roulette, which holds out the opportunity of winning a lot of money in a short space of time, and therefore of changing one's social status quasi-instantaneously, and in which the winning of the previous spin of the wheel can be staked and lost at every new spin, gives a fairly accurate image of this imaginary universe of perfect competition or perfect equality of opportunity, a world without inertia, without accumulation, without heredity or acquired properties, in which every moment is perfectly independent of the previous one, every soldier has a marshal's baton in his knapsack, and every prize can be attained, instantaneously, by everyone, so that at each moment anyone can become anything. Capital, which, in its objectified or embodied forms, takes time to accumulate and which, as a potential capacity to produce profits and to reproduce itself in identical or expanded form, contains a tendency to persist in its being, is a force inscribed in the objectivity of things so that everything is not equally possible or impossible.[2] And the structure of the distribution of the different types and subtypes of capital at a given moment in time represents the immanent structure of the social world, i.e., the set of constraints, inscribed in the very reality of that world, which govern its functioning in a durable way, determining the chances of success for practices.

It is in fact impossible to account for the structure and functioning of the social world unless one reintroduces capital in all its forms and not solely in the one form recognized by economic theory. Economic theory has allowed to be foisted upon it a definition of the economy of practices which is the historical invention of capitalism; and by reducing the universe of exchanges to mercantile exchange, which is objectively and subjectively oriented toward the maximization of profit, i.e., (economically) *self-interested*, it has implicitly defined the other forms of exchange as noneconomic, and therefore *disinterested*. In particular, it defines as disinterested those forms of exchange which ensure the *transubstantiation* whereby the most material types of capital—those which are economic in the restricted sense—can present themselves in the immaterial form of cultural capital or social capital and vice versa. Interest; in the restricted sense it is given in economic theory, cannot be produced without producing its negative counterpart, disinterestedness. The class of practices whose explicit purpose is to maximize monetary profit cannot be defined as such without producing the purposeless finality of cultural or artistic practices and their products; the world of bourgeois man, with his double-entry accounting, cannot be invented without producing the pure, perfect universe of the artist and the intellectual and the gratuitous activities of art-for-art's sake and pure theory. In other words, the constitution of a science of mercantile relationships which, inasmuch as it takes for granted the very foundations of the order it claims to analyze—private property, profit, wage labor, etc.—is not even a science of the field of economic production, has prevented the constitution of a general science of the economy of practices, which would treat mercantile exchange as a particular case of exchange in all its forms.

It is remarkable that the practices and assets thus salvaged from the "icy water of egotistical calculation" (and from science) are the virtual monopoly of the dominant class—as if economism had been able to reduce everything to economics only because the reduction on which that discipline is based protects from sacrilegious reduction everything which needs to be protected. If economics deals only with practices that have narrowly economic interest as their principle and only with goods that are directly and immediately convertible into money (which makes them quantifiable), then the universe of bourgeois production and exchange becomes an exception and can see itself and present itself as a realm of disinterestedness. As everyone knows, priceless things have their price, and the extreme difficulty of converting certain practices and certain objects into money is only due to the fact that this conversion is refused in the very intention that produces them, which is nothing other than the denial (*Verneinung*) of the economy. A general

science of the economy of practices, capable of reappropriating the totality of the practices which, although objectively economic, are not and cannot be socially recognized as economic, and which can be performed only at the cost of a whole labor of dissimulation or, more precisely, *euphemization*, must endeavor to grasp capital and profit in all their forms and to establish the laws whereby the different types of capital (or power, which amounts to the same thing) change into one another.[3]

Depending on the field in which it functions, and at the cost of the more or less expensive transformations which are the precondition for its efficacy in the field in question, capital can present itself in three fundamental guises: as *economic capital*, which is immediately and directly convertible into money and may be institutionalized in the form of property rights; as *cultural capital*, which is convertible, on certain conditions, into economic capital and may be institutionalized in the form of educational qualifications; and as *social capital*, made up of social obligations ("connections"), which is convertible, in certain conditions, into economic capital and may be institutionalized in the form of a title of nobility.[4]

CULTURAL CAPITAL

Cultural capital can exist in three forms: in the *embodied* state, i.e., in the form of long-lasting dispositions of the mind and body; in the *objectified* state, in the form of cultural goods (pictures, books, dictionaries, instruments, machines, etc.), which are the trace or realization of theories or critiques of these theories, problematics, etc.; and in the *institutionalized* state, a form of objectification which must be set apart because, as will be seen in the case of educational qualifications, it confers entirely original properties on the cultural capital which it is presumed to guarantee.

The reader should not be misled by the somewhat peremptory air which the effort at axiomization may give to my argument.[5] The notion of cultural capital initially presented itself to me, in the course of research, as a theoretical hypothesis which made it possible to explain the unequal scholastic achievement of children originating from the different social classes by relating academic success, i.e., the specific profits which children from the different classes and class fractions can obtain in the academic market, to the distribution of cultural capital between the classes and class fractions. This starting point implies a break with the presuppositions inherent both in the commonsense view, which sees academic success or failure as an effect of natural aptitudes, and in human capital theories. Economists might seem to deserve credit for explicitly raising the question of the relationship between the rates of profit on educational investment and on economic investment (and its evolution). But their measurement of the yield from scholastic investment takes account only of *monetary* investments and profits, or those directly convertible into money, such as the costs of schooling and the cash equivalent of time devoted to study; they are unable to explain the different proportions of their resources which different agents or different social classes allocate to economic investment and cultural investment because they fail to take systematic account of the structure of the differential chances of profit which the various markets offer these agents or classes as a function of the volume and the composition of their assets (see esp. Becker 1964b). Furthermore, because they neglect to relate scholastic investment strategies to the whole set of educational strategies and to the system of reproduction strategies, they inevitably, by a necessary paradox, let slip the best hidden and socially most determinant educational investment, namely, the domestic transmission of cultural capital. Their studies of the relationship between academic ability and academic investment show that they are unaware that ability or talent is itself the product of an investment of time and cultural capital (Becker 1964a, pp. 63–66). Not

surprisingly, when endeavoring to evaluate the profits of scholastic investment, they can only consider the profitability of educational expenditure for society as a whole, the "social rate of return," or the "social gain of education as measured by its effects on national productivity" (Becker 1964b, pp. 121, 155). This typically functionalist definition of the functions of education ignores the contribution which the educational system makes to the reproduction of the social structure by sanctioning the hereditary transmission of cultural capital. From the very beginning, a definition of human capital, despite its humanistic connotations, does not move beyond economism and ignores, *inter alia*, the fact that the scholastic yield from educational action depends on the cultural capital previously invested by the family. Moreover, the economic and social yield of the educational qualification depends on the social capital, again inherited, which can be used to back it up.

The Embodied State. Most of the properties of cultural capital can be deduced from the fact that, in its fundamental state, it is linked to the body and presupposes embodiment. The accumulation of cultural capital in the embodied state, i.e., in the form of what is called culture, cultivation, *Bildung*, presupposes a process of embodiment, incorporation, which, insofar as it implies a labor of inculcation and assimilation, costs time, time which must be invested personally by the investor. Like the acquisition of a muscular physique or a suntan, it cannot be done at second hand (so that all effects of delegation are ruled out).

The work of acquisition is work on oneself (self-improvement), an effort that presupposes a personal cost (*on paie de sa personne*, as we say in French), an investment, above all of time, but also of that socially constituted form of libido, *libido sciendi*, with all the privation, renunciation, and sacrifice that it may entail. It follows that the least inexact of all the measurements of cultural capital are those which take as their standard the length of acquisition—so long, of course, as this is not reduced to length of schooling and allowance is made for early domestic education by giving it a positive value (a gain in time, a head start) or a negative value (wasted time, and doubly so because more time must be spent correcting its effects), according to its distance from the demands of the scholastic market.[6]

This embodied capital, external wealth converted into an integral part of the person, into a habitus, cannot be transmitted instantaneously (unlike money, property rights, or even titles of nobility) by gift or bequest, purchase or exchange. It follows that the use or exploitation of cultural capital presents particular problems for the holders of economic or political capital, whether they be private patrons or, at the other extreme, entrepreneurs employing executives endowed with a specific cultural competence (not to mention the new state patrons). How can this capital, so closely linked to the person, be bought without buying the person and so losing the very effect of legitimation which presupposes the dissimulation of dependence? How can this capital be concentrated—as some undertakings demand—without concentrating the possessors of the capital, which can have all sorts of unwanted consequences?

Cultural capital can be acquired, to a varying extent, depending on the period, the society, and the social class, in the absence of any deliberate inculcation, and therefore quite unconsciously. It always remains marked by its earliest conditions of acquisition which, through the more or less visible marks they leave (such as the pronunciations characteristic of a class or region), help to determine its distinctive value. It cannot be accumulated beyond the appropriating capacities of an individual agent; it declines and dies with its bearer (with his biological capacity, his memory, etc.). Because it is thus linked in numerous ways to the person in his biological singularity and is subject to a hereditary transmission which is always heavily disguised, or even invisible, it defies the old, deep-rooted distinction the Greek jurists made between inherited properties (*ta patroa*) and acquired properties (*epikteta*), i.e., those which an individual adds to his heritage. It thus manages to combine the prestige of innate property with the merits of acquisition. Because the social conditions of its transmission and acquisition are more disguised than those of economic capital, it is predisposed to function as symbolic capital, i.e., to be unrecognized as capital and recognized as legitimate competence, as authority exerting an effect of (mis)recognition, e.g., in the matrimonial market and in all the markets in which economic capital is not fully recognized, whether in matters of culture, with the great art collections or great cultural foundations, or in social welfare, with the economy of generosity and the gift. Furthermore, the specifically symbolic logic of distinction additionally secures material and symbolic profits for the possessors of a large cultural capital: any given cultural competence (e.g., being able to read in a world of illiterates) derives a scarcity value from its position in the distribution of cultural capital and yields profits of distinction for its owner. In other words, the share in profits which scarce cultural capital secures in class-divided societies is based, in the last analysis, on the fact that all agents do not have the economic and cultural means for prolonging their children's education beyond the minimum necessary for the reproduction of the labor-power least valorized at a given moment.[7]

Thus the capital, in the sense of the means of appropriating the product of accumulated labor in the objectified state which is held by a given agent, depends for its real efficacy on the form of the distribution of the means of appropriating the accumulated and objectively available resources; and the relationship of appropriation between an agent and the resources objectively available, and hence the profits they produce, is mediated by the relationship of (objective and/or subjective) competition between himself and the other possessors of capital competing for the same goods, in which scarcity—and through it social value—is generated. The structure of the field, i.e., the unequal distribution of capital, is the source of the specific effects of capital, i.e., the appropriation of profits and the power to impose the laws of functioning of the field most favorable to capital and its reproduction.

But the most powerful principle of the symbolic efficacy of cultural capital no doubt lies in the logic of its transmission. On the one hand, the process of appropriating objectified cultural capital and the time necessary for it to take place mainly depend on the cultural capital embodied in the whole family—through (among other things) the generalized Arrow effect and all forms of implicit transmission.[8] On the other hand, the initial accumulation of cultural capital, the precondition for the fast, easy accumulation of every kind of useful cultural capital, starts at the outset, without delay, without wasted time, only for the offspring of families endowed with strong cultural capital; in this case, the accumulation period covers the whole period of socialization. It follows that the transmission of cultural capital is no doubt the best hidden form of hereditary transmission of capital, and it therefore receives proportionately greater weight in the system of reproduction strategies, as the direct, visible forms of transmission tend to be more strongly censored and controlled.

It can immediately be seen that the link between economic and cultural capital is established through the mediation of the time needed for acquisition. Differences in the cultural capital possessed by the family imply differences first in the age at which the work of transmission and accumulation begins—the limiting case being full use of the time biologically available, with the maximum free time being harnessed to maximum cultural capital—and then in the capacity, thus defined, to satisfy the specifically cultural demands of a prolonged process of acquisition. Furthermore, and in correlation with this, the length of time for which a given individual can prolong his acquisition process depends on the length of time for which his family can provide him with the free time, i.e., time free from economic necessity, which is the precondition for the initial accumulation (time which can be evaluated as a handicap to be made up).

The Objectified State. Cultural capital, in the objectified state, has a number of properties which are defined only in the relationship with cultural capital in its embodied form. The cultural capital objectified in material objects and media, such as writings, paintings, monuments, instruments, etc., is transmissible in its materiality. A collection of paintings, for example, can be transmitted as well as economic capital (if not better, because the capital transfer is more disguised). But what is transmissible is legal ownership and not (or not necessarily) what constitutes the precondition for specific appropriation, namely, the possession of the means of "consuming" a painting or using a machine, which, being nothing other than embodied capital, are subject to the same laws of transmission.[9]

Thus cultural goods can be appropriated both materially—which presupposes economic capital— and symbolically—which presupposes cultural capital. It follows that the owner of the means of production must find a way of appropriating either the embodied capital which is the precondition of specific appropriation or the services of the holders of this capital. To possess the machines, he only needs economic capital; to appropriate them and use them in accordance with their specific purpose (defined by the cultural capital, of scientific or technical type, incorporated in them), he must have access to embodied cultural capital, either in person or by proxy. This is no doubt the basis of the ambiguous status of cadres (executives and engineers). If it is emphasized that they are not the possessors (in the strictly economic sense) of the means of production which they use, and that they derive profit from their own cultural capital only by selling the services and products which it makes possible, then they will be classified among the dominated groups; if it is emphasized that they draw their profits from the use of a particular form of capital, then they will be classified among the dominant groups. Everything suggests that as the cultural capital incorporated in the means of production increases (and with it the period of embodiment needed to acquire the means of appropriating it), so the collective strength of the holders of cultural capital would tend to increase—if the holders of the dominant type of capital (economic capital) were not able to set the holders of cultural capital in competition with one another. (They are, moreover, inclined to competition by the very conditions in which they are selected and trained, in particular by the logic of scholastic and recruitment competitions.)

Cultural capital in its objectified state presents itself with all the appearances of an autonomous, coherent universe which, although the product of historical action, has its own laws, transcending individual wills, and which, as the example of language well illustrates, therefore remains irreducible to that which each agent, or even the aggregate of the agents, can appropriate (i.e., to the cultural capital embodied in each agent or even in the aggregate of the agents). However, it should not be forgotten that it exists as symbolically and materially active, effective capital only insofar as it is appropriated by agents and implemented and invested as a weapon and a stake in the struggles which go on in the fields of cultural production (the artistic field, the scientific field, etc.) and, beyond them, in the field of the social classes—struggles in which the agents wield strengths and obtain profits proportionate to their mastery of this objectified capital, and therefore to the extent of their embodied capital.[10]

The Institutionalized State. The objectification of cultural capital in the form of academic qualifications is one way of neutralizing some of the properties it derives from the fact that, being embodied, it has the same biological limits as its bearer. This objectification is what makes the difference between the capital of the autodidact, which may be called into question at any time, or even the cultural capital of the courtier, which can yield only ill-defined profits, of fluctuating value, in the market of high-society exchanges, and the cultural capital academically sanctioned by legally guaranteed

qualifications, formally independent of the person of their bearer. With the academic qualification, a certificate of cultural competence which confers on its holder a conventional, constant, legally guaranteed value with respect to culture, social alchemy produces a form of cultural capital which has a relative autonomy vis-à-vis its bearer and even vis-à-vis the cultural capital he effectively possesses at a given moment in time. It institutes cultural capital by collective magic, just as, according to Merleau-Ponty, the living institute their dead through the ritual of mourning. One has only to think of the *concours* (competitive recruitment examination) which, out of the continuum of infinitesimal differences between performances, produces sharp, absolute, lasting differences, such as that which separates the last successful candidate from the first unsuccessful one, and institutes an essential difference between the officially recognized, guaranteed competence and simple cultural capital, which is constantly required to prove itself. In this case, one sees clearly the performative magic of the power of instituting, the power to show forth and secure belief or, in a word, to impose recognition.

By conferring institutional recognition on the cultural capital possessed by any given agent, the academic qualification also makes it possible to compare qualification holders and even to exchange them (by substituting one for another in succession). Furthermore, it makes it possible to establish conversion rates between cultural capital and economic capital by guaranteeing the monetary value of a given academic capital.[11] This product of the conversion of economic capital into cultural capital establishes the value, in terms of cultural capital, of the holder of a given qualification relative to other qualification holders and, by the same token, the monetary value for which it can be exchanged on the labor market (academic investment has no meaning unless a minimum degree of reversibility of the conversion it implies is objectively guaranteed). Because the material and symbolic profits which the academic qualification guarantees also depend on its scarcity, the investments made (in time and effort) may turn out to be less profitable than was anticipated when they were made (there having been a *de facto* change in the conversion rate between academic capital and economic capital). The strategies for converting economic capital into cultural capital, which are among the short-term factors of the schooling explosion and the inflation of qualifications, are governed by changes in the structure of the chances of profit offered by the different types of capital.

SOCIAL CAPITAL

Social capital is the aggregate of the actual or potential resources which are linked to possession of a durable network of more or less institutionalized relationships of mutual acquaintance and recognition—or in other words, to membership in a group[12]—which provides each of its members with the backing of the collectivity-owned capital, a "credential" which entitles them to credit, in the various senses of the word. These relationships may exist only in the practical state, in material and/or symbolic exchanges which help to maintain them. They may also be socially instituted and guaranteed by the application of a common name (the name of a family, a class, or a tribe or of a school, a party, etc.) and by a whole set of instituting acts designed simultaneously to form and inform those who undergo them; in this case, they are more or less really enacted and so maintained and reinforced, in exchanges. Being based on indissolubly material and symbolic exchanges, the establishment and maintenance of which presuppose reacknowledgment of proximity, they are also partially irreducible to objective relations of proximity in physical (geographical) space or even in economic and social space.[13]

The volume of the social capital possessed by a given agent thus depends on the size of the network of connections he can effectively mobilize and on the volume of the capital (economic, cultural or symbolic) possessed in his own right by each of those to whom he is connected.[14] This means that, although it is relatively irreducible to the economic and cultural capital possessed by a given agent, or even by the whole set of agents to whom he is connected, social capital is never completely independent of it because the exchanges instituting mutual acknowledgment presuppose the reacknowledgment of a minimum of objective homogeneity, and because it exerts a multiplier effect on the capital he possesses in his own right.

The profits which accrue from membership in a group are the basis of the solidarity which makes them possible.[15] This does not mean that they are consciously pursued as such, even in the case of groups like select clubs, which are deliberately organized in order to concentrate social capital and so to derive full benefit from the multiplier effect implied in concentration and to secure the profits of membership—material profits, such as all the types of services accruing from useful relationships, and symbolic profits, such as those derived from association with a rare, prestigious group.

The existence of a network of connections is not a natural given, or even a social given, constituted once and for all by an initial act of institution, represented, in the case of the family group, by the genealogical definition of kinship relations, which is the characteristic of a social formation. It is the product of an endless effort at institution, of which institution rites—often wrongly described as rites of passage—mark the essential moments and which is necessary in order to produce and reproduce lasting, useful relationships that can secure material or symbolic profits (see Bourdieu 1982). In other words, the network of relationships is the product of investment strategies, individual or collective, consciously or unconsciously aimed at establishing or reproducing social relationships that are directly usable in the short or long term, i.e., at transforming contingent relations, such as those of neighborhood, the workplace, or even kinship, into relationships that are at once necessary and elective, implying durable obligations subjectively felt (feelings of gratitude, respect, friendship, etc.) or institutionally guaranteed (rights). This is done through the alchemy of *consecration*, the symbolic constitution produced by social institution (institution as a relative—brother, sister, cousin, etc.—or as a knight, an heir, an elder, etc.) and endlessly reproduced in and through the exchange (of gifts, words, women, etc.) which it encourages and which presupposes and produces mutual knowledge and recognition. Exchange transforms the things exchanged into signs of recognition and, through the mutual recognition and the recognition of group membership which it implies, re-produces the group. By the same token, it reaffirms the limits of the group, i.e., the limits beyond which the constitutive exchange—trade, commensality, or marriage—cannot take place. Each member of the group is thus instituted as a custodian of the limits of the group: because the definition of the criteria of entry is at stake in each new entry, he can modify the group by modifying the limits of legitimate exchange through some form of misalliance. It is quite logical that, in most societies, the preparation and conclusion of marriages should be the business of the whole group, and not of the agents directly concerned. Through the introduction of new members into a family, a clan, or a club, the whole definition of the group, i.e., its fines, its boundaries, and its identity, is put at stake, exposed to redefinition, alteration, adulteration. When, as in modern societies, families lose the monopoly of the establishment of exchanges which can lead to lasting relationships, whether socially sanctioned (like marriage) or not, they may continue to control these exchanges, while remaining within the logic of laissez-faire, through all the institutions which are designed to favor legitimate exchanges and exclude illegitimate ones by producing occasions (rallies, cruises, hunts, parties, receptions, etc.), places (smart neighborhoods, select schools, clubs, etc.), or practices (smart sports, parlor games, cultural ceremonies, etc.) which bring together, in a seemingly fortuitous way, individuals as homogeneous as possible in all the pertinent respects in terms of the existence and persistence of the group.

The reproduction of social capital presupposes an unceasing effort of sociability, a continuous series of exchanges in which recognition is endlessly affirmed and reaffirmed. This work, which implies expenditure of time and energy and so, directly or indirectly, of economic capital, is not profitable or even conceivable unless one invests in it a specific competence (knowledge of genealogical relationships and of real connections and skill at using them, etc.) and an acquired disposition to acquire and maintain this competence, which are themselves integral parts of this capital.[16] This is one of the factors which explain why the profitability of this labor of accumulating and maintaining social capital rises in proportion to the size of the capital. Because the social capital accruing from a relationship is that much greater to the extent that the person who is the object of it is richly endowed with capital (mainly social, but also cultural and even economic capital), the possessors of an inherited social capital, symbolized by a great name, are able to transform all circumstantial relationships into lasting connections. They are sought after for their social capital and, because they are well known, are worthy of being known ("I know him well"); they do not need to "make the acquaintance" of all their "acquaintances"; they are known to more people than they know, and their work of sociability, when it is exerted, is highly productive.

Every group has its more or less institutionalized forms of delegation which enable it to concentrate the totality of the social capital, which is the basis of the existence of the group (a family or a nation, of course, but also an association or a party), in the hands of a single agent or a small group of agents and to mandate this plenipotentiary, charged with *plena potestas agendi et loquendi*,[17] to represent the group, to speak and act in its name and so, with the aid of this collectively owned capital, to exercise a power incommensurate with the agent's personal contribution. Thus, at the most elementary degree of institutionalization, the head of the family, the *pater familias*, the eldest, most senior member, is tacitly recognized as the only person entitled to speak on behalf of the family group in all official circumstances. But whereas in this case, diffuse delegation requires the great to step forward and defend the collective honor when the honor of the weakest members is threatened. The institutionalized delegation, which ensures the concentration of social capital, also has the effect of limiting the consequences of individual lapses by explicitly delimiting responsibilities and authorizing the recognized spokesmen to shield the group as a whole from discredit by expelling or excommunicating the embarrassing individuals.

If the internal competition for the monopoly of legitimate representation of the group is not to threaten the conservation and accumulation of the capital which is the basis of the group, the members of the group must regulate the conditions of access to the right to declare oneself a member of the group and, above all, to set oneself up as a representative (delegate, plenipotentiary, spokesman, etc.) of the whole group, thereby committing the social capital of the whole group. The title of nobility is the form *par excellence* of the institutionalized social capital which guarantees a particular form of social relationship in a lasting way. One of the paradoxes of delegation is that the mandated agent can exert on (and, up to a point, against) the group the power which the group enables him to concentrate. (This is perhaps especially true in the limiting cases in which the mandated agent creates the group which creates him but which only exists through him.) The mechanisms of delegation and representation (in both the theatrical and the legal senses) which fall into place—that much more strongly, no doubt, when the group is large and its members weak—as one of the conditions for the concentration of social capital (among other reasons, because it enables numerous, varied, scattered agents to act as one man and to overcome the limitations of space and time) also contain the seeds of an embezzlement or misappropriation of the capital which they assemble.

This embezzlement is latent in the fact that a group as a whole can be represented, in the various meanings of the word, by a subgroup, clearly delimited and perfectly visible to all, known to all, and recognized by all, that of the *nobiles*, the "people who are known," the paradigm of whom is the nobility, and who may speak on behalf of the whole group, represent the whole group, and exercise authority in the name of the whole group. The noble is the group personified. He bears the name of the group to which he gives his name (the metonymy which links the noble to his group is clearly seen when Shakespeare calls Cleopatra "Egypt" or the King of France "France," just as Racine calls Pyrrhus "Epirus"). It is by him, his name, the difference it proclaims, that the members of his group, the liegemen, and also the land and castles, are known and recognized. Similarly, phenomena such as the "personality cult" or the identification of parties, trade unions, or movements with their leader are latent in the very logic of representation. Everything combines to cause the signifier to take the place of the signified, the spokesmen that of the group he is supposed to express, not least because his distinction, his "outstandingness," his visibility constitute the essential part, if not the essence, of this power, which, being entirely set within the logic of knowledge and acknowledgment, is fundamentally a symbolic power; but also because the representative, the sign, the emblem, may be, and create, the whole reality of groups which receive effective social existence only in and through representation.[18]

CONVERSIONS

The different types of capital can be derived from *economic capital*, but only at the cost of a more or less great effort of transformation, which is needed to produce the type of power effective in the field in question. For example, there are some goods and services to which economic capital gives immediate access, without secondary costs; others can be obtained only by virtue of a social capital of relationships (or social obligations) which cannot act instantaneously, at the appropriate moment, unless they have been established and maintained for a long time, as if for their own sake, and therefore outside their period of use, i.e., at the cost of an investment in sociability which is necessarily long-term because the time lag is one of the factors of the transmutation of a pure and simple debt into that recognition of nonspecific indebtedness which is called gratitude.[19] In contrast to the cynical but also economical transparency of economic exchange, in which equivalents change hands in the same instant, the essential ambiguity of social exchange, which presupposes misrecognition, in other words, a form of faith and of bad faith (in the sense of self-deception), presupposes a much more subtle economy of time.

So it has to be posited simultaneously that economic capital is at the root of all the other types of capital and that these transformed, disguised forms of economic capital, never entirely reducible to that definition, produce their most specific effects only to the extent that they conceal (not least from their possessors) the fact that economic capital is at their root, in other words—but only in the last analysis—at the root of their effects. The real logic of the functioning of capital, the conversions from one type to another, and the law of conservation which governs them cannot be understood unless two opposing but equally partial views are superseded: on the one hand, economism, which, on the grounds that every type of capital is reducible in the last analysis to economic capital, ignores what makes the specific efficacy of the other types of capital, and on the other hand, semiologism (nowadays represented by structuralism, symbolic interactionism, or ethnomethodology), which reduces social exchanges to phenomena of communication and ignores the brutal fact of universal reducibility to economics.[20]

In accordance with a principle which is the equivalent of the principle of the conservation of energy, profits in one area are necessarily paid for by costs in another (so that a concept like wastage has no meaning in a general science of the economy of practices). The universal equivalent, the measure of all equivalences, is nothing other than labor-time (in the widest sense); and the conservation of social energy through all its conversions is verified if, in each case, one takes into account both the labor-time accumulated in the form of capital and the labor-time needed to transform it from one type into another.

It has been seen, for example, that the transformation of economic capital into social capital presupposes a specific labor, i.e., an apparently gratuitous expenditure of time, attention, care, concern, which, as is seen in the endeavor to personalize a gift, has the effect of transfiguring the purely monetary import of the exchange and, by the same token, the very meaning of the exchange. From a narrowly economic standpoint, this effort is bound to be seen as pure wastage, but in the terms of the logic of social exchanges, it is a solid investment, the profits of which will appear, in the long run, in monetary or other form. Similarly, if the best measure of cultural capital is undoubtedly the amount of time devoted to acquiring it, this is because the transformation of economic capital into cultural capital presupposes an expenditure of time that is made possible by possession of economic capital. More precisely, it is because the cultural capital that is effectively transmitted within the family itself depends not only on the quantity of cultural capital, itself accumulated by spending time, that the domestic group possess, but also on the usable time (particularly in the form of the mother's free time) available to it (by virtue of its economic capital, which enables it to purchase the time of others) to ensure the transmission of this capital and to delay entry into the labor market through prolonged schooling, a credit which pays off, if at all, only in the very long term.[21]

The convertibility of the different types of capital is the basis of the strategies aimed at ensuring the reproduction of capital (and the position occupied in social space) by means of the conversions least costly in terms of conversion work and of the losses inherent in the conversion itself (in a given state of the social power relations). The different types of capital can be distinguished according to their reproducibility or, more precisely, according to how easily they are transmitted, i.e., with more or less loss and with more or less concealment; the rate of loss and the degree of concealment tend to vary in inverse ratio. Everything which helps to disguise the economic aspect also tends to increase the risk of loss (particularly the intergenerational transfers). Thus the (apparent) incommensurability of the different types of capital introduces a high degree of uncertainty into all transactions between holders of different types. Similarly, the declared refusal of calculation and of guarantees which characterizes exchanges tending to produce a social capital in the form of a capital of obligations that are usable in the more or less long term (exchanges of gifts, services, visits, etc.) necessarily entails the risk of ingratitude, the refusal of that recognition of nonguaranteed debts which such exchanges aim to produce. Similarly, too, the high degree of concealment of the transmission of cultural capital has the disadvantage (in addition to its inherent risks of loss) that the academic qualification which is its institutionalized form is neither transmissible (like a title of nobility) nor negotiable (like stocks and shares). More precisely, cultural capital, whose diffuse, continuous transmission within the family escapes observation and control (so that the educational system seems to award its honors solely to natural qualities) and which is increasingly tending to attain full efficacy, at least on the labor market, only when validated by the educational system, i.e., converted into a capital of qualifications, is subject to a more disguised but more risky transmission than economic capital. As the educational qualification, invested with the specific force of the official, becomes the condition for legitimate access to a growing number of positions, particularly the dominant ones, the educational system tends increasingly to dispossess the domestic group of the monopoly of the transmission of power and privileges—and, among other things, of the choice of its legitimate heirs from among children of different sex and birth rank.[22] And economic capital itself poses quite different problems of transmission, depending on the particular form it takes. Thus, according to Grassby (1970), the liquidity of commercial capital, which gives immediate economic power and favors transmission, also makes it more vulnerable than landed property (or even real estate) and does not favor the establishment of long-lasting dynasties.

Because the question of the arbitrariness of appropriation arises most sharply in the process of transmission—particularly at the time of succession, a critical moment for all power—every reproduction strategy is at the same time a legitimation strategy aimed at consecrating both an exclusive appropriation and its reproduction. When the subversive critique which aims to weaken the dominant class through the principle of its perpetuation by bringing to light the arbitrariness of the entitlements transmitted and of their transmission (such as the critique which the Enlightenment *philosophes* directed, in the name of nature, against the arbitrariness of birth) is incorporated in institutionalized mechanisms (for example, laws of inheritance) aimed at controlling the official, direct transmission of power and privileges, the holders of capital have an ever greater interest in resorting to reproduction strategies capable of ensuring better-disguised transmission, but at the cost of greater loss of capital, by exploiting the convertibility of the types of capital. Thus the more the official transmission of capital is prevented or hindered, the more the effects of the clandestine circulation of capital in the form of cultural capital become determinant in the reproduction of the social structure. As an instrument of reproduction capable of disguising its own function, the scope of the educational system tends to increase, and together with this increase is the unification of the market in social qualifications which gives rights to occupy rare positions.

NOTES

1. Originally published as *"Ökonomisches Kapital, kulturelles Kapital, soziales Kapital,"* in *Soziale Ungleichheiten* (Soziale Welt, Sonderheft 2), edited by Reinhard Kreckel. Goettingen: Otto Schartz & Co., 1983, pp. 183–98. The article appears here for the first time in English, translated by Richard Nice.

2. This inertia, entailed by the tendency of the structures of capital to reproduce themselves in institutions or in dispositions adapted to the structures of which they are the product, is, of course, reinforced by a specifically political action of concerted conservation, i.e., of demobilization and depoliticization. The latter tends to keep the dominated agents in the state of a practical group, united only by the orchestration of their dispositions and condemned to function as an aggregate repeatedly performing discrete, individual acts (such as consumer or electoral choices).

3. This is true of all exchanges between members of different fractions of the dominant class, possessing different types of capital. These range from sales of expertise, treatment, or other services which take the form of gift exchange and dignify themselves with the most decorous names that can be found (honoraria, emoluments, etc.) to matrimonial exchanges, the prime example of a transaction that can only take place insofar as it is not perceived or defined as such by the contracting parties. It is remarkable that the apparent extensions of economic theory beyond the limits constituting the discipline have left intact the asylum of the sacred, apart from a few sacrilegious incursions. Gary S. Becker, for example, who was one of the first to take explicit account of the types of capital that are usually ignored, never considers anything other than monetary costs and profits, forgetting the nonmonetary investments (*inter alia*, the affective ones) and the material and symbolic profits that education provides in a deferred, indirect way, such as the added value which the dispositions produced or reinforced by schooling (bodily or verbal manners, tastes, etc.) or the relationships established with fellow students can yield in the matrimonial market (Becker 1964a).

4. *Symbolic capital*, that is to say, capital—in whatever form—insofar as it is represented, i.e., apprehended symbolically, in a relationship of knowledge or, more precisely, of misrecognition and recognition, presupposes the intervention of the habitus, as a socially constituted cognitive capacity.

5. When talking about concepts for their own sake, as I do here, rather than using them in research, one always runs the risk of being both schematic and formal, i.e., theoretical in the most usual and most usually approved sense of the word.

6. This proposition implies no recognition of the value of scholastic verdicts; it merely registers the relationship which exists in reality between a certain cultural capital and the laws of the educational market. Dispositions that are given a negative value in the educational market may receive very high value in other markets—not least, of course, in the relationships internal to the class.

7. In a relatively undifferentiated society, in which access to the means of appropriating the cultural heritage is very equally distributed, embodied culture does not function as cultural capital, i.e., as a means of acquiring exclusive advantages.

8. What I call the generalized Arrow effect, i.e., the fact that all cultural goods—paintings, monuments, machines, and any objects shaped by man, particularly all those which belong to the childhood environment—exert an educative effect by their mere existence, is no doubt one of the structural factors behind the "schooling explosion," in the sense that a growth in the quantity of cultural capital accumulated in the objectified state increases the educative effect automatically exerted by the environment. If one adds to this the fact that embodied cultural capital is constantly increasing, it can be seen that, in each generation, the educational system can take more for granted. The fact that the same educational investment is increasingly productive is one of the structural factors of the inflation of qualifications (together with cyclical factors linked to effects of capital conversion).

9. The cultural object, as a living social institution, is, simultaneously, a socially instituted material object and a particular class of habitus, to which it is addressed. The material object—for example, a work of art in its materiality—may be separated by space (e.g., a Dogon statue) or by time (e.g., a Simone Martini painting) from the habitus for which it was intended. This leads to one of the most fundamental biases of art history. Understanding the effect (not to be confused with the function) which the work tended to produce—for example, the form of belief it tended to induce—and which is the true basis of the conscious or unconscious choice of the means used (technique, colors, etc.), and therefore of the form itself, is possible only if one at least raises the question of the habitus on which it "operated."

10. The dialectical relationship between objectified cultural capital—of which the form *par excellence* is writing—and embodied cultural capital has generally been reduced to an exalted description of the degradation of the spirit by the letter, the living by the inert, creation by routine, grace by heaviness.

11. This is particularly true in France, where in many occupations (particularly the civil service) there is a very strict relationship between qualification, rank, and remuneration (translator's note).

12. Here, too, the notion of cultural capital did not spring from pure theoretical work, still less from an analogical extension of economic concepts. It arose from the need to identify the principle of social effects which, although they can be seen clearly at the level of singular agents—where statistical inquiry inevitably operates—cannot be reduced to the set of properties individually possessed by a given agent. These effects, in which spontaneous sociology readily perceives the work of "connections," are particularly visible in all cases in which different individuals obtain very unequal profits from virtually equivalent (economic or cultural) capital, depending on the extent to which they can mobilize by proxy the capital of a group (a family, the alumni of an elite school, a select club, the aristocracy, etc.) that is more or less constituted as such and more or less rich in capital.

13. Neighborhood relationships may, of course, receive an elementary form of institutionalization, as in the Bearn—or the Basque region—where neighbors, *lous besis* (a word which, in old texts, is applied to the legitimate inhabitants of the village, the rightful members of the assembly), are explicitly designated, in accordance with fairly codified rules, and are assigned functions which are differentiated according to their rank (there is a "first neighbor," a "second neighbor," and so on), particularly for the major social ceremonies (funerals, marriages, etc.). But even in this case, the relationships actually used by no means always coincide with the relationships socially instituted.

14. Manners (bearing, pronunciation, etc.) may be included in social capita insofar as, through the mode of acquisition they point to, they indicate initial membership of a more or less prestigious group.

15. National liberation movements or nationalist ideologies cannot be accounted for solely by reference to strictly economic profits, i.e., anticipation of the profits which may be derived from redistribution of a proportion of wealth to the advantage of the nationals (nationalization) and the recovery of highly paid jobs (see Breton 1964). To these specifically economic anticipated profits, which would only explain the nationalism of the privileged classes, must be added the very real and very immediate profits derived from membership (social capital) which are proportionately greater for those who are lower down the social hierarchy ("poor whites") or, more precisely, more threatened by economic and social decline.

16. There is every reason to suppose that socializing, or, more generally, relational, dispositions are very unequally distributed among the social classes and, within a given class, among fractions of different origin.

17. A "full power to act and speak" (translator).

18. It goes without saying that social capital is so totally governed by the logic of knowledge and acknowledgment that it always functions as symbolic capital.

19. It should be made clear, to dispel a likely misunderstanding, that the investment in question here is not necessarily conceived as a calculated pursuit of gain, but that it has every likelihood of being experienced in terms of the logic of emotional investment, i.e., as an involvement which is both necessary and disinterested. This has not always been appreciated by historians, who (even when they are as alert to symbolic effects as E. P. Thompson) tend to conceive symbolic practices—powdered wigs and the whole paraphernalia of office—as explicit strategies of domination, intended to be seen (from below), and to interpret generous or charitable conduct as "calculated acts of class appeasement." This naively Machiavellian view forgets that the most sincerely disinterested acts may be those best corresponding to objective interest. A number of fields, particularly those which most tend to deny interest and every sort of calculation, like the fields of cultural production, grant full recognition, and with it the consecration which guarantees success, only to those who distinguish themselves by the immediate conformity of their investments, a token of sincerity and attachment to the essential principles of the field. It would be thoroughly erroneous to describe the choices of the habitus which lead an artist, writer, or researcher toward his natural place (a subject, style, manner, etc.) in terms of rational strategy and cynical calculation. This is despite the fact that, for example, shifts from one genre, school, or speciality to another, quasi-religious conversions that are performed "in all sincerity," can be understood as capital conversions, the direction and moment of which (on which their success often depends) are

determined by a "sense of investment" which is the less likely to be seen as such the more skillful it is. Innocence is the privilege of those who move in their field of activity like fish in water.

20. To understand the attractiveness of this pair of antagonistic positions which serve as each other's alibi, one would need to analyze the unconscious profits and the profits of unconsciousness which they procure for intellectuals. While some find in economism a means of exempting themselves by excluding the cultural capital and all the specific profits which place them on the side of the dominant, others can abandon the detestable terrain of the economic, where everything reminds them that they can be evaluated, in the last analysis, in economic terms, for that of the symbolic. (The latter merely reproduce, in the realm of the symbolic, the strategy whereby intellectuals and artists endeavor to impose the recognition of their values, i.e., their value, by inverting the law of the market in which what one has or what one earns completely defines what one is worth and what one is—as is shown by the practice of banks which, with techniques such as the personalization of credit, tend to subordinate the granting of loans and the fixing of interest rates to an exhaustive inquiry into the borrower's present and future resources.)

21. Among the advantages procured by capital in all its types, the most precious is the increased volume of useful time that is made possible through the various methods of appropriating other people's time (in the form of services). It may take the form either of increased spare time, secured by reducing the time consumed in activities directly channeled toward producing the means of reproducing the existence of the domestic group, or of more intense use of the time so consumed, by recourse to other people's labor or to devices and methods which are available only to those who have spent time learning how to use them and which (like better transport or living close to the place of work) make it possible to save time. (This is in contrast to the cash savings of the poor, which are paid for in time—do-it-yourself, bargain hunting, etc.) None of this is true of mere economic capital; it is possession of cultural capital that makes it possible to derive greater profit not only from labor-time, by securing a higher yield from the same time, but also from spare time, and so to increase both economic and cultural capital.

22. It goes without saying that the dominant fractions, who tend to place ever greater emphasis on educational investment, within an overall strategy of asset diversification and of investments aimed at combining security with high yield, have all sorts of ways of evading scholastic verdicts. The direct transmission of economic capital remains one of the principal means of reproduction, and the effect of social capital ("a helping hand," "string-pulling," the "old boy network") tends to correct the effect of academic sanctions. Educational qualifications never function perfectly as currency. They are never entirely separable from their holders: their value rises in proportion to the value of their bearer, especially in the least rigid areas of the social structure.

REFERENCES

Becker, Gary S. *A Theoretical and Empirical Analysis with Special Reference to Education*. New York: National Bureau of Economic Research, 1964a.

———. *Human Capital*. New York: Columbia University Press, 1964b.

Bourdieu, Pierre. "Les rites d'institution." *Actes de la recherche en sciences sociales* 43 (1982): 58–63.

Breton, A. "The Economics of Nationalism." *Journal of Political Economy* 72 (1964): 376–86.

Grassby, Richard. "English Merchant Capitalism in the Late Seventeenth Century: The Composition of Business Fortunes." *Past and Present* 46 (1970): 87–107.

COMPANION WEBSITE

1. Go online to Write Out Loud about how, according to Bourdieu, inequality is reproduced through the education system.
2. Log on to Bourdieu's Profile Page to learn more about his life as a public intellectual in France.
3. Check out the Interactive Reading and explore how consumer goods, such as digital music players and coffeemakers, relate to the reproduction of inequality.

16

Distinction

Pierre Bourdieu

AESTHETICS, ETHICS AND AESTHETICISM When faced with legitimate works of art, people most lacking the specific competence apply to them the perceptual schemes of their own ethos, the very ones which structure their everyday perception of everyday existence. These schemes, giving rise to products of an unwilled, unselfconscious systematicity, are opposed to the more or less fully stated principles of an aesthetic.[1] The result is a systematic 'reduction' of the things of art to the things of life, a bracketing of form in favour of 'human' content, which is barbarism par excellence from the standpoint of the pure aesthetic.[2] Everything takes place as if the emphasis on form could only be achieved by means of a neutralization of any kind of affective or ethical interest in the object of representation which accompanies (without any necessary cause-effect relation) mastery of the means of grasping the distinctive properties which this particular form takes on in its relations with other forms (i.e., through reference to the universe of works of art and its history).

> Confronted with a photograph of an old woman's hands, the culturally most deprived express a more or less conventional emotion or an ethical complicity but never a specifically aesthetic judgement (other than a negative one): 'Oh, she's got terribly deformed hands! ... There's one thing I don't get (the left hand)—it's as if her left thumb was about to come away from her hand. Funny

way of taking a photo. The old girl must've worked hard. Looks like she's got arthritis. She's definitely crippled, unless she's holding her hands like that (imitates gesture)? Yes, that's it, she's got her hand bent like that. Not like a duchess's hands or even a typist's! ... I really feel sorry seeing that poor old woman's hands, they're all knotted, you might say' (manual worker, Paris). With the lower middle classes, exaltation of ethical virtues comes to the forefront ('hands worn out by toil'), sometimes tinged with populist sentimentality ('Poor old thing! Her hands must really hurt her. It really gives a sense of pain'); and sometimes even concern for aesthetic properties and references to painting make their appearance: 'It's as if it was a painting that had been photographed ... Must be really beautiful as a painting' (clerical worker, Paris). 'That reminds me of a picture I saw in an exhibition of Spanish paintings, a monk with his hands clasped in front of him and deformed fingers' (technician, Paris). 'The sort of hands you see in early Van Goghs, an old peasant woman or people eating potatoes' (junior executive, Paris). At higher levels in the social hierarchy, the remarks become increasingly abstract, with (other people's) hands, labour and old age functioning as allegories or symbols which serve as pretexts for general reflections on general problems: 'Those are the hands of someone who has worked too much, doing very hard manual work ... As a matter of fact it's very unusual to see hands like that' (engineer, Paris). 'These two hands unquestionably evoke a poor and unhappy

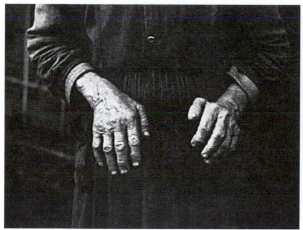 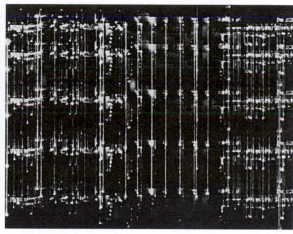

The Lacq gasworks by night

old age' (teacher, provinces). An aestheticizing reference to painting, sculpture or literature, more frequent, more varied and more subtly handled, resorts to the neutralization and distancing which bourgeois discourse about the social world requires and performs. 'I find this a very beautiful photograph. It's the very symbol of toil. It puts me in mind of Flaubert's old servant-woman … That woman's gesture, at once very humble … It's terrible that work and poverty are so deforming' (engineer, Paris).

A portrait of a heavily made-up woman, taken from an unusual angle with unusual lighting, provokes very similar reactions. Manual workers, and even more so craftsmen and small shop-keepers, react with horror and disgust: 'I wouldn't like that photo in my house, in my room. It isn't very nice to look at. It's rather painful' (manual worker, provinces). 'Is she dead? Ghastly, enough to keep you awake at night … ghastly, horrible, I don't want to look at it' (shopkeeper, provinces). While most of the office workers and junior executives reject a photo which they can only describe as 'frightful' or 'unpleasant to look at', some of them try to characterize the technique: 'The photo is very well taken, very beautiful, but horrible' (clerical worker, Paris). 'What gives the impression of something monstrous is the expression on the face of the man or woman who is the subject of the photo and the angle from which it has been taken, that's to say looking up from below' (junior executive, Paris). Others appeal to aesthetic references, mainly drawn from the cinema: 'A rather fantastic sort of character, or at least rather bizarre … it could be a Dreyer character, Bergman at a pinch, or perhaps even Eisenstein, in *Ivan the Terrible* … I like it a lot' (technician, Paris). Most of the senior executives and members of the professions find the photograph 'beautiful' and 'expressive' and make reference not only to the films of Bergman, Orson Welles, Dreyer, and others, but also to the theatre, invoking Hamlet, Macbeth or Racine's Athalie.

When confronted with a photograph of the Lacq gas refinery, which is likely to disconcert realist expectations both by its subject, an industrial complex, normally excluded from the world of legitimate representation, and by the treatment it receives (night photography), manual workers perplexed, hesitate, and eventually, in most cases, admit defeat: 'At first sight it's a construction in metal but I can't make head or tail of it. It might be something used in an electric power station … I can't make out what it is, it's a mystery to me' (manual worker, provinces). 'Now, that one really bothers me, I haven't got anything to say about it …

I can't see what it could be, apart from the lighting. It isn't car headlights, it wouldn't be all straight lines like that. Down here I can see a railing and a goods lift, no, really, I can't say' (manual worker, Paris). 'That's something to do with electronics, I don't know anything about that' (manual worker, Paris). Among small employers, who tend to be hostile to modern art experiments and, more generally, to all art in which they cannot see the marks and traces of work, a sense of confusion often leads to simple refusal: 'That is of no interest, it may be all very fine, but not for me. It's always the same thing. Personally that stuff leaves me cold' (craftsman, provinces). 'I've tried to work out if it really is a photo. Perhaps it's a reproduction of a drawing done with a few pencil lines ... I wouldn't know what to do with a photo like that. Perhaps it suits modern tastes. Up and down with the pencil and they like it. And as for the photo and the photographer, they don't deserve any credit, they've done nothing at all. The artist did it all, he's the one who ought to take the credit, he's the one who drew it' (shopkeeper, provinces). Office workers and junior executives, who are just as disconcerted as the manual workers and small employers, but are less inclined to admit it than the former and less inclined than the latter to challenge the legitimacy of what challenges them, less often decline to give a verdict:[3] I like it as a photo ... because it's all drawn out; they're just lines, it seems immense to me ... A vast piece of scaffolding ... It's just light, captured by the camera' (clerical worker, Paris). 'Buffet likes doing things like that' (technician, Paris). But only among members of the dominant class, who most often recognize the object represented, does judgement of form take on full autonomy vis-à-vis judgement of content ('It's inhuman but aesthetically beautiful because of the contrasts'), and the representation is apprehended as such, without reference to anything other than itself or realities of the same class ('abstract painting', 'avant-garde plays' etc.).

The variations in the attitude to a very comparable object, a metal frame, provide a numerical proof of this: the proportion of respondents who think it could make a beautiful photo is 6 percent among manual workers and domestic servants, 9 percent among craftsmen and small shopkeepers, 9.5 percent among the clerical workers and junior administrative executives, 24 percent among the primary teachers and technicians, 24.5 percent in the dominant class—and 50 percent among the secondary and higher-education teachers. (One may assume that the reactions aroused by the architecture of the Beaubourg Centre obey the same principles.)

A THREE-DIMENSIONAL SPACE

Endeavouring to reconstitute the units most homogeneous from the point of view of the conditions of production of habitus, i.e., with respect to the elementary conditions of existence and the resultant conditionings, one can construct a space whose three fundamental dimensions are defined by volume of capital, composition of capital, and change in these two properties over time (manifested by past and potential trajectory in social space).[4]

The primary differences, those which distinguish the major classes of conditions of existence, derive from the overall volume of capital, understood as the set of actually usable resources and powers—economic capital, cultural capital and also social capital. The distribution of the different classes (and class fractions) thus runs from those who are best provided with both economic and cultural capital to those who are most deprived in both respects (see figure 16.1, later in this section). The members of the professions, who have high incomes and high qualifications, who very often (52.9 percent) originate from the dominant class (professions or senior executives), who receive and consume a large quantity of both material and cultural goods, are opposed in almost all respects to the office workers, who have low qualifications, often originate from the working or middle classes, who receive little and consume little, devoting a high proportion of their time to car maintenance and home improvement; and they are even more opposed to the skilled or semi-skilled workers, and still more to unskilled workers or farm labourers, who have the lowest incomes, no qualifications, and originate almost exclusively (90.5 percent of farm labourers, 84.5 percent of unskilled workers) from the working classes.[5]

The differences stemming from the total volume of capital almost always conceal, both from common awareness and also from 'scientific' knowledge, the secondary differences which, within each of the classes defined by overall volume of capital, separate class fractions, defined by different asset structures, i.e., different distributions of their total capital among the different kinds of capital.

Among the difficulties which this model aims to account for in a unitary and systematic way, the most visible is the observation, which others have often made (e.g., C.S. VII), that the hierarchies, both in the dominant class, between the executives and the employers, and in the middle class, between the junior executives and the craftsmen or shopkeepers, vary according to the activity or asset in question. This effect seems to support the relativistic critique of the social classes until it is seen that there is a relationship between the nature of these activities or assets, for example, theatre-going or possession of a colour TV, and the structure of each group's capital.

Once one takes account of the structure of total assets—and not only, as has always been done implicitly, of the dominant kind in a given structure, 'birth', 'fortune' or 'talents', as the nineteenth century put it—one has the means of making more precise divisions and also of observing the specific effects of the structure of distribution between the different kinds of capital. This may, for example, be symmetrical (as in the case of the professions, which combine very high income with very high cultural capital) or asymmetrical (in the case of higher-education and secondary teachers or employers,

with cultural capital dominant in one case, economic capital in the other). One thus discovers two sets of homologous positions. The fractions whose reproduction depends on economic capital, usually inherited—industrial and commercial employers at the higher level, craftsmen and shopkeepers at the intermediate level—are opposed to the fractions which are least endowed (relatively, of course) with economic capital, and whose reproduction mainly depends on cultural capital—higher-education and secondary teachers at the higher level, primary teachers at the intermediate level.

The industrialists, who are grouped with the commercial employers in surveys by representative sample because of their small number, declare considerably higher incomes than the latter (33.6 percent say they earn more than 100,000 French francs, as against 14.5 percent of the commercial employers). Those classified as industrialists in the INSEE survey (C.S. I) are much closer to the new bourgeoisie than are the commercial employers: many more of them declare salaries and investment income, many fewer declare industrial, commercial or non-commercial profits. For the working classes, who are strongly ranked by overall capital volume, the data available do not enable one to grasp the differences in the second dimension (composition of capital). However, differences such as those between semi-skilled, educationally unqualified, provincial factory workers of rural origin, living in an inherited farmhouse, and skilled workers in the Paris region who have been in the working class for generations, who possess a 'trade' or technical qualifications, must be the source of differences in life-style and religious and political opinion.

Given that, as one moves from the artists to the industrial and commercial employers, volume of economic capital rises and volume of cultural capital falls, it can be seen that the dominant class is organized in a chiastic structure. To establish this, it is necessary to use various indicators borrowed from a survey which has the advantage of distinguishing between public-sector and private-sector executives (C.S. V) to examine, successively, the distribution of economic capital and the distribution of cultural capital among the fractions; the structures of these distributions must then be correlated.

Although it is self-evident when one considers indicators of wealth (as will be done later), the hierarchy of the class fractions as regards possession of economic capital, running from industrial and commercial employers to teachers, is already less visible when, as here, one is only dealing with indices of consumption (cars, boats, hotels) which are neither entirely adequate nor entirely unambiguous (see table 16.1). The first (cars) also depends on the type of professional activity, and the other two depend on spare time, which, as one learns in other ways, varies inversely with economic capital. Home ownership also depends on stability in the same place of residence (lower among executives, engineers and teachers). Incomes are very unevenly underestimated (the rate of non-declaration may be considered an indicator of the tendency to under-declare) and very unequally accompanied by fringe benefits such as expense-account meals and business trips (which are known to rise as one moves from teachers to private-sector executives and employers).

As regards cultural capital, except for a few inversions, which reflect secondary variables such as place of residence, with the corresponding supply of culture, and income, with the means it provides, the different fractions are organized in an opposite hierarchy (see table 16.2). (Differentiation according to the type of capital possessed, literary, scientific or economic and political, is mainly seen in the fact that engineers show more interest in music and 'intellectual' games such as bridge or chess than in literary activities—theatre-going or reading Le Figaro Littéraire.)

These indicators no doubt tend to minimize the gaps between the different fractions. Most cultural consumption also entails an economic cost: theatre-going, for example, depends on income as well as education. Moreover, equipment such as FM radios or hi-fi systems can be used in very different ways (e.g., classical music or dance music), whose values, in terms of the dominant hierarchy of possible uses, may vary as much as the different types of reading-matter or theatre. In fact, the position of the different fractions ranked according to their interest in the different types of reading-matter tends to correspond to their position when ranked according to volume of cultural capital as one moves towards the rarer types of reading, which are known to be those most linked to educational level and highest in the hierarchy of cultural legitimacy (see table 16.3).

One also finds (C.S. XIV, table 215a) that the over-representation of teachers (and students) in the audience of the different theatres steadily declines and the over-representation of the other fractions (employers, senior executives and members of the professions, unfortunately not distinguished in the statistics) increases as one moves from avant-garde or reputedly avant-garde theatre to classical theatre and especially from classical to boulevard theatre, which draws between a third and a quarter of its audience from the least 'intellectual' fractions of the dominant class.

Having established that the structure of the distribution of economic capital is symmetrical and opposite to that of cultural capital, we can turn to the question of the hierarchy of the two principles of hierarchization (without forgetting that this hierarchy is at all times a stake in struggles and that, in certain conjunctures, as in present-day France, cultural capital may be one of the conditions for access to control of economic capital). We may take as an indicator of the state of the power relation between these two principles of domination the frequency of intergenerational movements between the fractions.

If we use as indices of the rarity of a position (or, which amounts to the same thing, its degree of closure) the proportion of its occupants who originate from the dominant class as a whole and from the fraction in question, we find that the

TABLE 16.1

Some Indicators of Economic Capital in Different Fractions of the Dominant Class, 1966.[a]

INDICATORS OF ECONOMIC CAPITAL	TEACHERS (HIGHER AND SECONDARY)	PUBLIC-SECTOR EXECS.	PROFESSIONS	ENGINEERS	PRIVATE-SECTOR EXECS.	INDUSTRIAL EMPLOYERS	COMMERCIAL EMPLOYERS
Homeowner	51%	38%	54%	44%	40%	70%	70%
Luxury car owner	12%	20%	28%	21%	22%	34%	33%
Boat owner	8%	8%	44%	10%	12%	14%	13%
Hotel holidays	15%	17%	23%	17%	21%	26%	32%
Median annual income (thousands of francs)	33	32	41	36	37	36	33
Rate of undeclared income	6	8	27	9	13	28	24

Source: C.S. V (1966).
a. In each row the italic figures indicate the strongest tendency.

TABLE 16.2

Some Indicators of Cultural Practice in Different Fractions of the Dominant Class, 1966.[a]

INDICATORS	TEACHERS (HIGHER AND SECONDARY)	PUBLIC SECTOR EXECS.	PROFESSIONS	ENGINEERS	PRIVATE-SECTOR EXECS.	INDUSTRIAL EMPLOYERS	COMMERCIAL EMPLOYERS
Reading books other than for job[b]	21%	18%	18%	16%	16%	10%	10%
Theatre-going[c]	38%	29%	29%	28%	34%	16%	20%
Listening to classical music	83%	89%	86%	89%	89%	75%	73%
Museum visits	75%	66%	68%	58%	69%	47%	52%
Art gallery visits	58%	54%	57%	45%	47%	37%	34%
Own FM radio	59%	54%	57%	56%	53%	48%	48%
No TV	46%	30%	28%	33%	28%	14%	24%
Reading *Le Monde*[d]	410	235	230	145	151	82	49
Reading *Le Figaro Littéraire*[d]	168	132	131	68	100	64	24

Source: C.S. V (1966).
a. In each row the italic figures indicate the strongest tendency.
b. 15 hours or more per week.
c. At least once every two or three months.
d. Per thousand.

TABLE 16.3

Types of Books Preferred by Different Fractions of the Dominant Class (%), 1966.[a]

TYPE OF BOOK	TEACHERS (HIGHER AND SECONDARY)	PUBLIC-SECTOR EXECS.	PROFESSIONS	ENGINEERS	PRIVATE-SECTOR EXECS.	INDUSTRIAL EMPLOYERS	COMMERCIAL EMPLOYERS
Detective stories	25 (6)	29 (1)	27 (4)	28 (3)	29 (1)	27 (4)	25 (6)
Adventure stories	17 (7)	20 (3)	18 (6)	24 (1)	22 (2)	19 (4)	19 (4)
Historical	44 (4)	47 (2)	49 (1)	47 (2)	44 (4)	36 (6)	27 (7)
Illustrated art books	28 (2)	20 (3)	31 (1)	19 (5)	20 (3)	17 (6)	14 (7)
Novels	64 (2)	68 (1)	59 (5)	62 (3)	62 (3)	45 (6)	42 (7)
Philosophy	20 (1)	13 (3)	12 (5)	13 (3)	15 (2)	10 (7)	12 (5)
Politics	15 (1)	12 (2)	9 (4)	7 (5)	10 (3)	5 (6)	4 (7)
Economics	10 (1)	8 (3)	5 (6)	7 (5)	9 (2)	8 (3)	5 (6)
Science	15 (3)	14 (4)	18 (2)	21 (1)	9 (7)	10 (6)	11 (5)

Source: C.S. V (1966).

a. The figures in a given row show the percentage of each category of respondents who included that type of book among their favourite types (italic figures indicate the strongest tendency in the row). The figures in parentheses show the rank of each class fraction in that row. Books on economics and science are set apart on the grounds that interest in these types of reading-matter depends on secondary factors, in one case occupational activity (hence the rank of the private-sector executives and employers) and in the other, academic training (hence the rank of the engineers).

resulting hierarchy corresponds fairly exactly, for both indices, to the hierarchy by volume of economic capital (see table 16.4). The proportion of members of each fraction who originated from the dominant class, and the proportion of individuals who originated from the fraction to which they now belong, decline in parallel as one moves from the industrial employers to the teachers, with a clear break between the three higher-ranking fractions (industrial and commercial employers and the professions) and the three lower-ranking fractions (engineers, public-sector executives and teachers).

The use of these indicators may be contested on the grounds that the different fractions have very unequal control over the conditions of their social reproduction, so that the high proportion of endogenous employers may express nothing other than the capacity of these fractions (or at least of a proportion of their members) to transmit their powers and privileges without mediation or control. Indeed, this capacity is itself one of the rarest privileges, which, by giving greater freedom vis-à-vis academic verdicts, reduces the necessity or urgency of making the cultural investments which cannot be avoided by those who depend entirely on the education system for their reproduction. The fractions richest in cultural capital do in fact tend to invest in their children's education as well as in the cultural practices likely to maintain and increase their specific rarity; the fractions richest in economic capital set aside cultural and educational investments in favour of economic investments— industrial and commercial employers more so, however, than the new bourgeoisie of private-sector executives, who manifest the same concern for rational investment both in economic and in educational matters. The members of the professions (especially doctors and lawyers), relatively well endowed with both forms of capital, but too little integrated into economic life to use their capital in it actively, invest in their children's education but also and especially in cultural practices which symbolize possession of the material and cultural

means of maintaining a bourgeois life-style and which provide a social capital, a capital of social connections, honourability and respectability that is often essential in winning and keeping the confidence of high society, and with it a clientele, and may be drawn on, for example, in making a political career.

Given that scholastic success mainly depends on inherited cultural capital and on the propensity to invest in the educational system (and that the latter varies with the degree to which maintained or improved social position depends on such success), it is clear why the proportion of pupils in a given school or college who come from the culturally richest fractions rises with the position of that school in the specifically academic hierarchy (measured, for example, by previous academic success), reaching its peak in the institution responsible for reproducing the professorial corps (the Ecole Normale Supérieure). In fact, like the dominant class which they help to reproduce, higher-education institutions are organized in accordance with two opposing principles of hierarchy. The hierarchy dominant within the educational system, i.e., the one which ranks institutions by specifically academic criteria, and, correlatively, by the proportion of their students drawn from the culturally richest fractions, is diametrically opposed to the hierarchy dominant outside the educational system, i.e., the one which ranks institutions by the proportion of their students drawn from the fractions richest in economic capital or in power and by the position in the economic or power hierarchy of the occupations they lead to. If the offspring of the dominated fractions are less represented in the economically highest institutions (such as ENA or HEC) than might be expected from their previous academic success and the position of these schools in the specifically scholastic hierarchy, this is, of course, because these schools refuse to apply purely scholastic criteria, but it is also because the scholastic hierarchy is most faithfully respected (so that the science section of the ENS is preferred to Polytechnique, or the Arts faculty to

TABLE 16.4

Social Origin of Members of the Dominant Class, by Class Fraction (%), 1970.[a]

FATHER'S CLASS FRACTION	SON'S CLASS FRACTION					
	INDUSTRIAL EMPLOYERS	COMMERCIAL EMPLOYERS	PROFESSIONS	ENGINEERS	PUBLIC-SECTOR EXECUTIVES	TEACHERS (HIGHER AND SECONDARY)
Industrial employers	33.5	2.8	2.3	6.1	4.4	1.5
Commercial employers	1.9	31.0	0	1.8	5.0	0.8
Professions	0.6	0.9	20.0	0.9	2.4	7.6
Engineers	0	0	6.4	6.7	2.3	4.6
Public-sector executives	1.9	3.3	9.9	13.2	14.2	7.6
Teachers (higher and secondary)	0.6	0	2.9	2.7	0.3	6.1
Whole class	38.5	38.0	41.5	31.4	28.7	28.2

Source: C.S. II (1970).
a. In each row the italic figure indicates the strongest tendency.

Sciences Po), by those who are most dependent on the educational system. (Blindness to alternative ranking principles is most nearly complete in the case of teachers, children, whose whole upbringing inclines them to identify all success with academic success.)

The same chiastic structure is found at the level of the middle classes, where volume of cultural capital again declines, while economic capital increases, as one moves from primary teachers to small industrial and commercial employers, with junior executives, technicians and clerical workers in an intermediate position, homologous to that of engineers and executives at the higher level. Artistic craftsmen and art-dealers, who earn their living from industrial and commercial profits, and are close in those respects to other small businessmen, are set apart from them by their relatively high cultural capital, which brings them closer to the new petite bourgeoisie. The medical and social services, drawn to a relatively large extent from the dominant class,[6] are in a central position, roughly homologous to that of the professions (although slightly more tilted towards the pole of cultural capital); they are the only ones who receive not only wages or salaries but also, in some cases, non-commercial profits (like the professions).

It can immediately be seen that the homology between the space of the dominant class and that of the middle classes is explained by the fact that their structure is the product of the same principles. In each case, there is an opposition between owners (of their own home, of rural or urban property, of stocks and shares), often older, with little spare time, often the children of industrial or agricultural employers, and non-owners, chiefly endowed with educational capital and spare time, originating from the wage-earning fractions of the middle and upper classes or from the working class. The occupants of homologous positions, primary teachers and professors, for example, or small shopkeepers and commercial entrepreneurs, are mainly separated by the volume of the kind of capital that is dominant in the structure of their assets, i.e., by differences of degree which separate individuals unequally endowed with the same scarce resources. The lower positions—and, correlatively, the dispositions of their occupants—derive some of their characteristics from the fact that they are objectively related to the corresponding positions at the higher level, towards which they tend and 'pre-tend'. This is clearly seen in the case of the wage-earning petite bourgeoisie, whose ascetic virtues and cultural good intentions—which it manifests in all sorts of ways, taking evening classes, enrolling in libraries, collecting stamps etc.—very clearly express the aspiration to rise to the higher position, the objective destiny of the occupants of the lower position who manifest such dispositions.

To reconstruct the social conditions of production of the habitus as fully as possible, one also has to consider the social trajectory of the class or class fraction the agent belongs to, which, through the probable slope of the collective future, engenders progressive or regressive dispositions towards the future; and the evolution, over several generations, of the asset structure of each lineage, which is perpetuated in the habitus and introduces divisions even within groups that are as homogeneous as the fractions. To give an idea of the range of possibilities, it need only be pointed out that an individual's social trajectory represents the combination of: the lifelong evolution of the volume of his capital, which can be described, very approximately, as increasing, decreasing or stationary; the volume of each sort of capital (amenable to the same distinctions), and therefore the composition of his capital (since constant volume can conceal a change in structure); and, in the same way, the father's and mother's asset volume and structure and their respective weights in the different kinds of capital (e.g., father stronger in economic capital and mother in cultural capital, or vice versa, or equivalence); and therefore the volume and structure of the capital of both sets of grandparents.

To account more fully for the differences in lifestyle between the different fractions—especially as regards culture—one would have to take account of their distribution in a *socially ranked geographical space*. A group's chances of appropriating any given class of rare assets (as measured by the mathematical probability of access) depend partly on its capacity for the specific appropriation, defined by the economic, cultural and social capital it can deploy in order to appropriate materially or symbolically the assets in question, that is, its position in social space, and partly on the relationship between its distribution in geographical space and the distribution of the scarce assets in that space.[7] (This relationship can be measured in average distances from goods or facilities, or in travelling time—which involves access to private or public transport.) In other words, a group's real social distance from certain assets must integrate the geographical distance, which itself depends on the group's spatial distribution and, more precisely, its distribution with respect to the 'focal point' of economic and cultural values, i.e., Paris or the major regional centres (in some careers—e.g., in the postal banking system—employment or promotion entails a period of exile).[8] Thus, the distance of farm workers from legitimate culture would not be so vast if the specifically cultural distance implied by their low cultural capital were not compounded by their spatial dispersion. Similarly, many of the differences observed in the (cultural and other) practices of the different fractions of the dominant class are no doubt attributable to the size of the town they live in. Consequently, the opposition between engineers and private-sector executives on the one hand, and industrial and commercial employers on the other, partly stems from the fact that the former mostly live in Paris and work for relatively large firms (only 7 percent of private-sector executives work in firms employing from 1 to 5 people, as against 34 percent in medium-sized firms and 40 percent in firms employing more than 50 people), whereas the latter mainly run small firms (in the 1966 survey by SOFRES

[Société française d'enquêtes par sondages]—C.S. V—6 percent of the industrialists had from 1 to 5 employees; 70 percent, 6 to 49; 24 percent, more than 50; in commerce, the corresponding figures are 30 percent, 42 percent and 12 percent) and mostly live in the provinces and even in the country (according to the 1968 census, 22.3 percent of the industrialists and 15.5 percent of the commercial employers lived in a rural commune, 14.1 percent and 11.8 percent in communes of less than 10,000 inhabitants).

The model which emerges would not be so difficult to arrive at if it did not presuppose a break with the common-sense picture of the social world, summed up in the metaphor of the 'social ladder' and suggested by all the everyday language of 'mobility', with its 'rises' and 'falls'; and a no less radical break with the whole sociological tradition which, when it is not merely tacitly accepting the one-dimensional image of social space, as most research on 'social mobility' does, subjects it to a pseudo-scientific elaboration, reducing the social universe to a continuum of abstract strata ('upper middle class', 'lower middle class' etc.),[9] obtained by aggregating different forms of capital, thanks to the construction of indices (which are, par excellence, the destroyers of structures).[10] Projection onto a single axis, in order to construct the continuous, linear, homogeneous, one-dimensional series with which the social hierarchy is normally identified, implies an extremely difficult (and, if it is unwitting, extremely dangerous) operation, whereby the different types of capital are reduced to a single standard. This abstract operation has an objective basis in the possibility, which is always available, of converting one type of capital into another; however, the exchange rates vary in accordance with the power relation between the holders of the different forms of capital. By obliging one to formulate the principle of the convertibility of the different kinds of capital, which is the precondition for reducing the space to one dimension, the construction of a two-dimensional space makes it clear that the exchange rate of the different kinds of capital is one of the fundamental stakes in the struggles between class fractions whose power and privileges are linked to one or the other of these types. In particular, this exchange rate is a stake in the struggle over the dominant principle of domination (economic capital, cultural capital or social capital), which goes on at all times between the different fractions of the dominant class.

THE HABITUS AND THE SPACE OF LIFE-STYLES

The mere fact that the social space described here can be presented as a diagram indicates that it is an abstract representation, deliberately constructed, like a map, to give a bird's-eye view, a point of view on the whole set of points from which ordinary agents (including the sociologist and his reader, in their ordinary behaviour) see the social world. Bringing together in simultaneity, in the scope of a single glance—this is its heuristic value—positions which the agents can never apprehend in their totality and in their multiple relationships, social space is to the practical space of everyday life, with its distances which are kept or signalled, and neighbours who may be more remote than strangers, what geometrical space is to the 'travelling space' (*espace hodologique*) of ordinary experience, with its gaps and discontinuities.

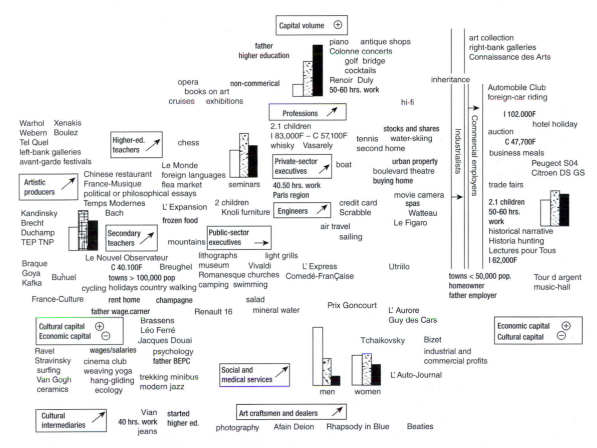

Figure 16.1 The Space of Social Positions and Life-styles.

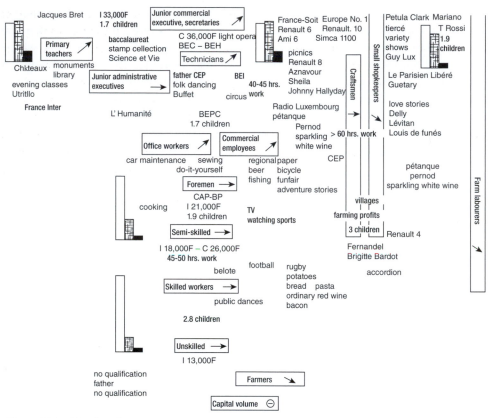

Figure 16.1   (Continued)

But the most crucial thing to note is that the question of this space is raised within the space itself—that the agents have points of view on this objective space which depend on their position within it and in which their will to transform or conserve it is often expressed. Thus many of the words which sociology uses to designate the classes it constructs are borrowed from ordinary usage, where they serve to express the (generally polemical) view that one group has of another. As if carried away by their quest for greater objectivity, sociologists almost always forget that the 'objects' they classify produce not only objectively classifiable practices but also classifying operations that are no less objective and are themselves classifiable. The division into classes performed by sociology leads to the common root of the classifiable practices which agents produce and of the classificatory judgements

they make of other agents' practices and their own. The habitus is both the generative principle of objectively classifiable judgements and the system of classification (*principium divisionis*) of these practices. It is in the relationship between the two capacities which define the habitus, the capacity to produce classifiable practices and works, and the capacity to differentiate and appreciate these practices and products (taste), that the represented social world, i.e., the space of life-styles, is constituted.

The relationship that is actually established between the pertinent characteristics of economic and social condition (capital volume and composition, in both synchronic and diachronic aspects) and the distinctive features associated with the corresponding position in the universe of life-styles only becomes intelligible when the habitus is constucted as the generative formula which makes it possible to account both for the classifiable practices and products and for the judgements, themselves classified, which make these practices and works into a system of distinctive signs. When one speaks of the aristocratic asceticism of teachers or the pretension of the petite bourgeoisie, one is not only describing these groups by one, or even the most important, of their properties, but also endeavouring to name the principle which generates all their properties and all their judgements of their, or other people's, properties. The habitus is necessity internalized and converted into a disposition that generates meaningful practices and meaning-giving perceptions; it is a general, transposable disposition which carries out a systematic, universal application—beyond the limits of what has been directly learnt—of the necessity inherent in the learning conditions. That is why an agent's whole set of practices (or those of a whole set of agents produced by similar conditions) are both systematic, inasmuch as they are the product of the application of identical (or interchangeable) schemes, and systematically distinct from the practices constituting another life-style.

Because different conditions of existence produce different habitus—systems of generative schemes applicable, by simple transfer, to the most varied areas of practice—the practices engendered by the different habitus appear as systematic configurations of properties expressing the differences objectively inscribed in conditions of existence in the form of systems of differential deviations which, when perceived by agents endowed with the schemes of perception and appreciation necessary in order to identify, interpret and evaluate their pertinent features, function as life-styles (see figure 16.2).[11]

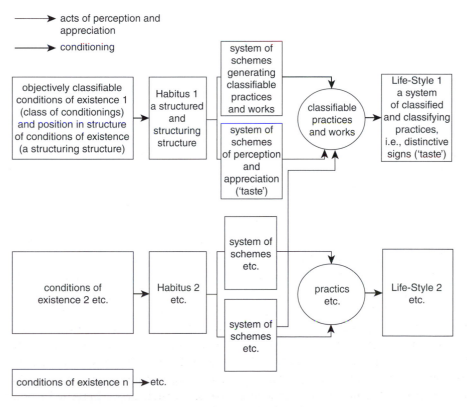

Figure 16.2 Conditions of Existence, Habitus and Life-style.

The habitus is not only a structuring structure, which organizes practices and the perception of practices, but also a structured structure: the principle of division into logical classes which organizes the perception of the social world is itself the product of internalization of the division into social classes. Each class condition is defined, simultaneously, by its intrinsic properties and by the relational properties which it derives from its position in the system of class conditions, which is also a system of differences, differential positions, i.e., by everything which distinguishes it from what it is not and especially from everything it is opposed to; social identity is defined and asserted through difference. This means that inevitably inscribed within the dispositions of the habitus is the whole structure of the system of conditions, as it presents itself in the experience of a life-condition occupying a particular position within that structure. The most fundamental oppositions in the structure (high/low, rich/poor etc.) tend to establish themselves as the fundamental structuring principles of practices and the perception of practices. As a system of practice-generating schemes which expresses systematically the necessity and freedom inherent in its class condition and the difference constituting that position, the habitus apprehends differences between conditions, which it grasps in the form of differences between classified, classifying practices (products of other habitus), in accordance with principles of differentiation which, being themselves the product of these differences, are objectively attuned to them and therefore tend to perceive them as natural.

> The observer who divides a population into classes performs an operation which has its equivalent in social practice. If he is not aware of this, he is likely to present a more or less modified form of a native classification as a scientific classification (a number of 'typologies' are precisely this). In addition, he has no chance of bringing to the level of consciousness the true status of his classifying operations which, like native knowledge, presuppose connections and comparisons and which, even when they seem

to belong to the realm of social physics, in fact produce and interpret signifying distinctions, in short, belong to the order of the symbolic.

While it must be reasserted, against all forms of mechanism, that ordinary experience of the social world is a cognition, it is equally important to realize—contrary to the illusion of the spontaneous generation of consciousness which so many theories of the 'awakening of class consciousness' (*prise de conscience*) amount to—that primary cognition is misrecognition, recognition of an order which is also established in the mind. Life-styles are thus the systematic products of habitus, which, perceived in their mutual relations through the schemes of the habitus, become sign systems that are socially qualified (as 'distinguished', 'vulgar' etc.) The dialectic of conditions and habitus is the basis of an alchemy which transforms the distribution of capital, the balance-sheet of a power relation, into a system of perceived differences, distinctive properties, that is, a distribution of symbolic capital, legitimate capital, whose objective truth is misrecognized.

As structured products (*opus operatum*) which a structuring structure (*modus operandi*) produces through retranslations according to the specific logic of the different *fields*, all the practices and products of a given agent are objectively harmonized among themselves, without any deliberate pursuit of coherence, and objectively orchestrated, without any conscious concertation, with those of all members of the same class. The habitus continuously generates practical metaphors, that is to say, transfers (of which the transfer of motor habits is only one example) or, more precisely, systematic transpositions required by the particular conditions in which the habitus is 'put into practice' (so that, for example, the ascetic ethos which might be expected always to express itself in saving may, in a given context, express itself in a particular way of using credit). The practices of the same agent, and, more generally, the practices of all agents of the same class, owe the stylistic affinity which makes each of them a metaphor of any of the others to the fact that they are the product of transfers of the same schemes of action from one field to another. An obvious paradigm would be the disposition called 'handwriting', a singular way of tracing letters which always produces the same writing, i.e., graphic forms which, in spite of all the differences of size, material or colour due to the surface (paper or blackboard) or the instrument (pen or chalk)—in spite, therefore, of the different use of muscles—present an immediately perceptible family resemblance, like all the features of style or manner whereby a painter or writer can be recognized as infallibly as a man by his walk.

> True pastiche, as Proust does it, for example, reproduces not the most striking features of a style— like parody or caricature—but the habitus, which Jacques Rivière calls 'the hearth of mental activity', in which the original discourse is generated: 'We are amused to see each writer "resurrected" with his whole personality and, faced with an event he has never experienced, react just as he did to those which life brought him. The hearth of his mental activity is rekindled, the lamp relit in his brain.'[12]

Systematicity is found in the opus operatum because it is in the modus operandi.[13] It is found in all the properties—and property—with which individuals and groups surround themselves, houses, furniture, paintings, books, cars, spirits, cigarettes, perfume, clothes, and in the practices in which they manifest their distinction, sports, games, entertainments, only because it is in the synthetic unity of the habitus, the unifying, generative principle of all practices. Taste, the propensity and capacity to appropriate (materially or symbolically) a given class of classified, classifying objects or practices, is the generative formula of life-style, a unitary set of distinctive preferences which express the same expressive intention in the specific logic of each of the symbolic sub-spaces, furniture, clothing, language or body hexis. Each dimension of life-style 'symbolizes with' the others, in Leibniz's phrase, and symbolizes them. An old cabinetmaker's world view, the way he manages his budget, his time or his body, his use of language and choice of clothing are fully present in his ethic of scrupulous, impeccable craftsmanship and in the aesthetic of work for work's sake which leads him to measure the beauty of his products by the care and patience that have gone into them.

The system of matching properties, which includes people—one speaks of a 'well-matched couple', and friends like to say they have the same tastes—is organized by taste, a system of classificatory schemes which may only very partially become conscious although, as one rises in the social hierarchy, lifestyle is increasingly a matter of what Weber calls the 'stylization of life'. Taste is the basis of the mutual adjustment of all the features associated with a person, which the old aesthetic recommended for the sake of the mutual reinforcement they give one another; the countless pieces of information a person consciously or unconsciously imparts endlessly underline and confirm one another, offering the alert observer the same pleasure an art-lover derives from the symmetries and correspondences produced by a harmonious distribution of redundancies. The over-determination that results from these redundancies is felt the more strongly because the different features which have to be isolated for observation or measurement strongly interpenetrate in ordinary perception; each item of information imparted in practice (e.g., a judgement of a painting) is contaminated—and, if it deviates from the probable feature, corrected— by the effect of the whole set of features previously or simultaneously perceived. That is why a survey which tends to isolate features—for example, by dissociating the things said from the way they are said—and detach them from the system of correlative features tends to minimize the deviation, on each point, between the classes, especially that between the petit bourgeois and the bourgeois. In the ordinary situations of bourgeois life, banalities about art, literature or cinema are inseparable from the steady tone, the slow, casual diction, the distant or self-assured smile, the measured gesture, the well-tailored suit and the bourgeois salon of the person who pronounces them.

> Thus, lacunae can turn into disdainful refusals and confusion into absent-mindedness. Bourgeois respondents particularly distinguish themselves by their ability to control the survey situation (and any analysis of survey data should take this into account). Control over the social situation in which culture operates is given to them by the very unequally distributed capacity to adopt the relation to language which is called for in all situations of polite conversation (e.g., chatter about cinema or travel), and which presupposes an art of skimming, sliding and masking, making abundant use of all the hinges, fillers and qualifiers identified by linguists as characteristic of bourgeois language.

Taste is the practical operator of the transmutation of things into distinct and distinctive signs, of continuous distributions into discontinuous oppositions; it raises the differences inscribed in the physical order of bodies to the symbolic order of significant distinctions. It transforms objectively classified practices, in which a class condition signifies itself (through taste), into classifying practices, that is, into a symbolic expression of class position, by perceiving them in their mutual relations and in terms of social classificatory schemes. Taste is thus the source of the system of distinctive features which cannot fail to be perceived as a systematic expression of a particular class of conditions of existence, i.e., as a distinctive life-style, by anyone who possesses practical knowledge of the relationships between distinctive signs and positions in the distributions—between the universe of objective properties, which is brought to light by scientific construction, and the no less objective universe of life-styles, which exists as such for and through ordinary experience.

This classificatory system, which is the product of the internalization of the structure of social space, in the form in which it impinges through the experience of a particular position in that space, is, within the limits of economic possibilities and impossibilities (which it tends to reproduce in its own logic), the generator of practices adjusted to the regularities inherent in a condition. It continuously transforms necessities into strategies, constraints into preferences, and, without any mechanical determination, it generates the set of 'choices' constituting life-styles, which derive their meaning, i.e., their value, from their position in a system of oppositions and correlations.[14] It is a virtue made of necessity which continuously transforms necessity into virtue by inducing 'choices' which correspond to the condition of which it is the product. As can be seen whenever a change in social position puts the habitus into new conditions, so that its specific efficacy can be isolated, it is taste—the taste of necessity or the taste of luxury—and not high or low income which commands the practices objectively adjusted to these resources. Through taste, an agent has what he likes because he likes what he has, that is, the properties actually given to him in the distributions and legitimately assigned to him in the classifications.[15]

NOTES

1. The populist image of the proletarian as an opaque, dense, hard 'in-itself', the perfect antithesis of the intellectual or aesthete, a self-transparent, insubstantial 'for-itself', has a certain basis here.
2. Interest in form, when it is expressed, is still rooted in the schemes of the ethos. It only takes on its true meaning when related to its real principle; the taste for neat, careful work which inspires it stems from the same dispositions as hyper-correction in language, strict correctness of dress and sobriety in interior decoration.
3. The posture of good intentions combined with insecurity which characterizes the rising petite bourgeoisie is expressed in the 'refuge' choice of saying that the objects could make an 'interesting'— as opposed to beautiful, ugly or meaningless— photograph. Thus, 40 percent of the junior executives and clerical workers consider that a snake would make an interesting photo (as against 22.5 percent of the new petite bourgeoisie, who are more inclined to say it could make a beautiful photo).

4. A fuller presentation of the fundamental principles of this construction, i.e., the theory of the different sorts of capital, their specific properties and the laws of conversion between these different forms of social energy, which is simultaneously a theory of the classes and class fractions defined by possession of a given volume and structure of capital, is reserved for another book, so as not to overcomplicate the present analysis of the judgement of taste.

5. The gaps are more clear-cut and certainly more visible as regards education than income, because information on incomes (based on tax declarations) is much less reliable than information on qualifications. This is especially true of industrial and commercial employers (who, in the CESP survey—C.S. V—provided, along with doctors, the highest rate of non-response to the questions about income), craftsmen, shopkeepers and farmers.

6. The category 'medical and social services' is characterized by the fact that it contains men mainly drawn from the working classes and women of whom a considerable proportion come from the upper classes (see the two histograms in figure 16.1).

7. A number of cultural properties are acquired by virtue of position in geographical space, partly through the quality of the social contacts favoured by spatial proximity. One of the most crucial is pronunciation, which unmistakably designates a stigmatized or prestigious origin.

8. The distribution of a class or class fraction in socially ranked geographical space—in particular its distance from the economic and cultural 'centres'—almost always manifests also its internal hierarchies. For example, secondary analysis of the 1967 INSEE survey on leisure activities shows that, in all socio-occupational categories, cultural activity increases with the size of the town (a good indicator of cultural supply): this is no doubt partly because the apparent homogeneity of the categories conceals differences, within the categories themselves, by size of town, especially with respect to cultural capital.

9. In English in the original text (translator).

10. Gerhard Lenski, who, to his credit, sees the problem of discrepancies between the different sorts of capital and points to some of the hidden effects they can produce (in particular, the tendency to 'liberalism' associated with strong 'decrystallization' of status), is no doubt prevented from developing all the consequences of his intuition by the positivist ritual of constructing an index. See G. Lenski, 'Status Crystallization: A Non-Vertical Dimension of Social Status', *American Sociological Review*, 19 (1954), 405–413.

11. It follows from this that the relationship between conditions of existence and practices or the meaning of practices is not to be understood in terms either of the logic of mechanism or of the logic of consciousness.

12. J. Rivière in M. Proust and J. Rivière, *Correspondence*, 1914–1922 (Paris, Gallimard, 1976), p. 326.

13. In contrast to the atomistic approach of social psychology, which breaks the unity of practice to establish partial 'laws' claiming to account for the products of practice, the opus operatum, the aim is to establish general laws reproducing the laws of production, the modus operandi.

14. Economic theory, which treats economic agents as interchangeable actors, paradoxically fails to take account of the economic dispositions, and is thereby prevented from really explaining the systems of preferences which define incommensurable and independent subjective use-values.

15. An ethic, which seeks to impose the principles of an ethos (i.e., the forced choices of a social condition) as a universal norm, is another, more subtle way of succumbing to *amor fati*, of being content with what one is and has. Such is the basis of the felt contradiction between ethics and revolutionary intent.

COMPANION WEBSITE

1. Go online to Write Out Loud about how your own *habitus* is embodied in how you talk, walk, and do most everything else.
2. For more on Bourdieu's concepts of *habitus* and fields, log on to his Profile Page.
3. Check out clips from the critically-acclaimed HBO drama *The Wire* that brilliantly illustrate Bourdieu's concept of *habitus*, listed in the *Networks of Capital* Supplementary Sources.

17

Capitalism: The Factory of Fragmentation*

David Harvey

The drive for capital accumulation is the central motif in the narrative of historical-geographical transformation of the western world in recent times and seems set to engulf the whole world into the twenty-first century. For the past 300 years it has been the fundamental force at work in reshaping the world's politics, economy and environment. This process of using money to make more money is not the only process at work, of course, but it is hard to make any sense of social changes these past 300 years without looking closely at it.

Contemporary historical materialism attempts to isolate the fundamental processes of capital accumulation that generate social, economic and political change and, through a careful study of them, get some understanding of the whys and hows of those changes. The focus is on *processes,* rather than on things and events. It is a bit like watching a potter at work on a wheel: the process may be simple to describe, but the outcomes can be infinitely varied in shape and size.

However, to say there is a simple process at work is not to say that everything ends up looking exactly the same, that events are easily predictable or that everything can be explained by reference to it alone. The drive for capital accumulation has helped create cities as diverse as Los Angeles, Edmonton, Atlanta and Boston, and transformed out of almost all recognition (though in quite different ways) ancient cities like Athens, Rome, Paris and London. It has

likewise led to a restless search for new product lines, new technologies, new lifestyles, new ways to move around, new places to colonize – an infinite variety of stratagems that reflect a boundless human ingenuity for coming up with new ways to make a profit. Capitalism has, in short, always thrived on the production of difference.

Yet the rules that govern the game of capital accumulation are relatively simple and knowable. Capitalism is always about growth, no matter what the ecological, social or geopolitical consequences (indeed, we define 'crisis' as low growth); it is always about technological and lifestyle changes ('progress' is inevitable); and it is always conflictual (class and other forms of struggle abound).

Above all, capitalism generates a lot of insecurity: it is always unstable and crisis-prone. The history of capitalist crisis formation and resolution is, I maintain, fundamental to understanding our history. Understanding the rules of capital accumulation helps us understand why our history and our geography take the forms they do.

THE WORSHIP OF FRAGMENTS

In *The Condition of Postmodernity,* I tried to put this style of thinking to work in explaining recent changes in economy and culture in the advanced capitalist world. I noticed that postmodern thought tended to deny anything systematic or general in history, and to jumble together images and thoughts as if criteria of coherence did not matter: It emphasized separation, fragmentation, ephemerality, difference and what is often now called 'otherness' (a strange term that is mainly used to indicate that I have no right to speak *for* or even, perhaps, *about* others or that when I do speak about them, I 'construct' them in my own image).

Furthermore, some postmodern theorists argued that the world was not knowable because there was no sure way of establishing truth and that even pretending to know or, worse still, holding to some version of 'universal truth' lay at the root of gulags, holocausts and other social disasters. The best that we could hope for, they said, was to let things flourish in their multiple and different ways, look for alliances where possible, but always to avoid peddling supposed universal solutions or pretending there were general, knowable truths. This sort of thinking carried over into architecture, the arts, popular culture, new lifestyles and gender politics.

Now, there is much that is refreshing about all of this, particularly the emphasis upon heterogeneity, diversity, multiple overlapping concerns of gender, class, ecology, and so on. But I just could not see why the sort of heterogeneity that postmodernism celebrates was in any way inconsistent with thinking the world was knowable through an appreciation, of, for example, processes of capital accumulation, which not only thrive upon but actively produce social difference and heterogeneity.

After 1973, for example, we find that working-class politics went on the defensive as unemployment and job insecurity rose, economic growth slackened, real wages stagnated, and all sorts of substitutes for real productive activity took over to compensate for wave after wave of deindustrialization. Merger manias, credit binges and all the other excesses of the 1980s, which we are now paying for, were the only vital activity at a time of gradual dismantling of the welfare state and the rise of *laissez-faire* and very conservative politics. Strong appeal to individualism, greed and entrepreneurial spirit characterized the Reagan-Thatcher years. Furthermore, the crisis of 1973 set in motion a frantic search for new products, new technologies, new lifestyles and new cultural gimmicks that could turn a profit. And these years also saw a radical reorganization of international power relations, with Europe and Japan challenging a dominant US power in economic and financial markets.

This general shift from old-style capital accumulation to a new style, I call the shift from Fordism (mass assembly line, mass political organization and welfare-state interventions) to flexible accumulation (the pursuit of niche markets, decentralization coupled with spatial dispersal of production, withdrawal of the nation-state from interventionist policies coupled with deregulation and privatization). It seemed to me quite plausible to argue, therefore, that capitalism, in undergoing this transition, had produced the conditions for the rise of postmodern ways of thinking and operating.

THE POSTMODERN PHOENIX

Since this shift in cultural sensibility paralleled some quite radical changes in the organization of capitalism after the capitalist crisis in 1973–5, it even seemed plausible to argue that postmodernism itself was a product of the process of capital accumulation.

TIME–SPACE COMPRESSION

But it is always dangerous to treat simultaneity as causation, so I set about looking for some sort of link between the two trends. The link I believed worked best was the one between time and space. Capital accumulation has always been about speed-up (consider the history of technological innovations in production processes, marketing, money exchanges) and revolutions in transport and communications (the railroad and telegraph, radio and automobile, jet transport and telecommunications), which have the effect of reducing spatial barriers.

The experience of time and space has periodically been radically transformed. We see a particularly strong example of this kind of radical transformation since around 1970: the impact of telecommunications, jet cargo transport, containerization of road, rail and ocean transport, the development of futures markets, electronic banking and computerized production systems. We have recently been going through a strong phase of what I call 'time–space compression': the world suddenly feels much smaller, and the time-horizons over which we can think about social action become much shorter.

Our sense of who we are, where we belong and what our obligations encompass – in short, our *identity* – is profoundly affected by our sense of location in space and time. In other words, we broadly locate our identity in terms of space (I belong *here*) and time (this is *my biography, my history*). Crises of identity (Where is my place in this world? What future can I have?) arise out of strong phases of time–space compression. Moreover, I think it plausible to argue that the most recent phase has so shaken up our sense of who and what we are that there had to be some kind of crisis of representation in general, a crisis that is manifest in the contemporary world primarily by postmodern ways of thinking.

Embracing ephemerality as a desired quality in cultural production, for example, matches the rapid shifts in fashion and production designs and techniques that evolved as part of the response to the crisis of accumulation that developed after 1973.

Interestingly, when we look back on other phases of rapid time–space compression – the period after 1848 in Europe, the period just before and during the First World War, for example – we find similar phases of rapid change in the arts and in cultural activities. From this I conclude that it is possible to arrive at a *general* interpretation of the rise of postmodernism and its relation to the new experience of space and time that new forms of capital accumulation have produced.

But, again, I want to enter a caveat: this is not to say that everything is simply deterministic. I repeat, capitalism thrives on and produces heterogeneity and difference, though only within certain bounds.

NICHE MARKETS

There is nothing about postmodernism in general that inhibits the further development of capital accumulation. Indeed, the postmodern turn has proved a perfect vehicle for the development of new fields and forms of profit-making.

Fragmentation and ephemerality, for example, open up abundant opportunities to explore quick-changing niche markets for new products. But this does not mean that there has been any radical inversion of the historical materialist view of reality, an inversion where culture, not economics, has become the driving force of history. I think such a view misinterprets rather than misrepresents what is happening.

Marx held that production of any sort requires the prior exercise of the human imagination; it is always about the mobilization of human desires, purposes and intentions to a given end. The problem under industrial capitalism is that most people are denied access to this process: a select few do the imagining and designing, make all the decisions and set up technologies that regulate the worker's actions, so that for the mass of the population the full play of human creativity is denied.

That is a profoundly alienating situation, and much of history recounts attempts to respond to this alienation. The rich and the privileged, themselves not enamored of industrialism, countered alienation by developing a distinctive field of *culture* – think of romanticism and the cultivation of aesthetic pleasures and values – as a kind of protected zone for creative activities outside of the crass materialism of industrial capitalism.

Workers likewise developed their own creative pleasures when they could: hunting, gardening, tinkering with cars. These activities, which went under the general name of 'culture,' high or low, were not so much superstructural as compensatory for what industrial capitalism denied to the mass of the people in the workplace.

Over time, those compensatory pleasures have gradually become absorbed into the processes of capital accumulation and turned into new spheres for making profit. As industrial capitalism became less and less profitable, at least in the US and Britain, so these new spheres of profit-making became much more important, particularly after 1945 and even more so after the crisis of 1973–5.

So, there is a sense in which culture no longer trails other forms of economic activity but has moved into the vanguard, not as a protected zone of non-economic activity, however, but as an arena of fierce competition for profit-making. The accumulation of market niches, of diverse preferences and the promotion of new heterogeneous lifestyles, all occur within the orbit of capital accumulation.

The latter, furthermore, has had the effect of breaking down distinctions between high and low culture – it commercializes aesthetics – at the same time as it has thrived, as it always does, on the production of diversity, heterogeneity and difference. What we generally think of as 'culture' has become a primary field of entrepreneurial and capitalistic activity.

THROUGH THE POSTMODERN DOOR

The picture I have so far painted probably looks very pessimistic, with capital accumulation, market materialism and entrepreneurial greed ruling the roost. So let me look now at the opportunities and dangers that attach to this postmodern condition.

I notice, first of all, that capitalism has not solved its crisis tendencies and that capital accumulation, economic growth and sustained development into the foreseeable future are, if anything, more remote now than they were twenty years ago. When the fundamental irrationality of capitalism becomes plainer for all to see – as in the present depression on both sides of the Atlantic – the conditions are set up in which some kind of new direction has to be taken (if only throwing the ruling party out of power).

Secondly, the frantic promotion of cultural heterogeneity and difference over the past twenty years has opened up all kinds of new spaces for the exploration of different lifestyles, different preferences and a more generalized debate about human potentialities and the sources of their frustration. This is the positive side of what much of postmodernism stands for: it produces openings for a critique of dominant values, including those that directly attach to the rules of capital accumulation, and therefore all kinds of opportunities for radical politics. The corollary is that contemporary radical politics has as much to do with culture as with traditional problems of class struggle in production.

But here we encounter as many dangers as opportunities. The crisis of identity provoked by time–space compression can lead to the acceptance of exclusionary religious doctrines (the promise of eternity in a world of rapid change) or exclusionary territorial practices (maintaining the security and position of the home, the locality, the nation against external and international pressures). The rise of fascist and exclusionary sentiments across Europe and the progress of the Buchanan campaign in the US provide good examples. The refusal to accept that there are some basic processes at work and that knowable truths can be established can all too easily lead to head-in-the-sand politics ('I will pursue my particular political interest and to hell with all the rest').

The fetishism of the image at the expense of any concern for the social reality of daily life can divert our gaze, our politics, our sensitivities away from the material world of experience and into the seemingly endless and intricate webs of representations. And while it is true that the 'personal is political', we do not have to look much further than the present presidential campaign to see how that principle can be abused. Above all, the promotion of cultural activities as a primary field of capital accumulation promotes a commodified and prepackaged form of aesthetics at the expense of concerns for ethics, social justice, fairness, and the local and international issues of exploitation of both nature and human nature.

So postmodernism opens a door to radical politics but for the most part has refused to pass through it. To pass to a thoroughly radical critique of contemporary capitalism, which is plainly languishing not only economically but culturally and spiritually, requires that we grapple with the central processes of capital accumulation that are so radical in their implications for our lives. Capitalism has transformed the face of the earth at an accelerating pace these past 200 years. It cannot possibly continue on that trajectory for another 200 years. Someone, somewhere, has to think about what kind of social system should replace it. There seems no alternative except to build some kind of socialist politics that will have as its central motif the question: What could life be about if capital accumulation no longer dominated? That question deserves the close attention of everyone.

NOTE

*   First published in *New Perspectives Quarterly*, 1992.

COMPANION WEBSITE

1. Walk through the postmodern door and Write Out Loud about your own experiences with time–space compression.
2. For more on how other contemporary theorists have thought about globalization, such as Anthony Giddens and Saskia Sassen, log on to the Globalization Theory Profile Page.
3. The Supplementary Sources are chock full of vivid examples of accumulation and time–space compression, check them out!

Pathway to Meltdown

Theorizing the Dark Side of Modernity

Introductory Essay:
Your Smart Phone Might Be an Evil Genius

Let's face it—smartphones are cool. With today's mobile technologies, you no longer have to be satisfied with just making phone calls or sending text messages (how 2001!), you can also download and listen to music from your favorite bands, go online to purchase a new e-book, or download the exact GPS coordinates of that new coffee shop you keep hearing about. Your phone can even help you bargain shop these days, with platforms like ShopSavvy and PriceGrabber that allow you to scan barcodes to compare prices at nearby competitors and online retailers.

While mobile technologies such as these may be the wave of the future, their allure is based on what seem like ageless human desires for greater choice, convenience, freedom, and individuality. And, in many ways, our technologically advanced world fits the bill (at least for those of us who can afford to pay for it). In the digital age, we can simultaneously download the entire Jay-Z discography, track down an espresso, and find the most affordable pair of stonewashed skinny jeans in town. How's that for multitasking?

But there's a catch, one even more ironic than those skinny jeans you're looking for. It turns out that while you're using your phone to watch out for music, books, directions, and clothes, your phone is also watching you.

A recent investigation by the *Wall Street Journal* found that 56 of the 101 most popular smartphone applications transmitted some form of their users' personal information—the phone user's age, gender, name, contacts, phone ID number, username and password, and even GPS coordinates of the user's physical location—to other companies. Pandora, one of the most popular free music apps on the market, for example, sent information about users' locations, demographic data, and phone IDs to eight separate companies. The point of all this data mining, critics point out, is for marketers to compile ever-more detailed information on the buying habits of consumers, transforming

Want to read the full *Wall Street Journal* investigation? Go to the Supplementary Sources section of the website for more information.

even their morning walks into sellable commodities. Karl Marx rolls in his grave.

While these spy-phones may just be the latest in a long line of scandals concerning privacy in our wired world, the social theorists in this section would likely see them as another instance of a much more general and disturbing contradiction that has haunted modern societies since the age of the Enlightenment. With each new freedom the modern world offers up, these theorists argue, comes a new kind of control; with each new promise of emancipation, an insidious form of domination.

As the thinkers in the following pages will demonstrate, modernity's road to reason could just as well be a pathway to meltdown. The Enlightenment, so it seems, has its dark side.

Classical Connections: Max Weber

For a good example of rationalization at work, see how French fries are meticulously made in Eric Schlosser's *Fast Food Nation*, listed in the Supplementary Sources.

No one understood this ambivalent character of modern life quite like Max Weber. One of the most wide-ranging social theorists of all time, the great German sociologist wrote on topics as varied as religion, politics, science, law, business, and economics. Yet integrating this impressive range of research topics was a theoretical focus on what Weber saw as the most characteristic feature of modern societies—the increasing *rationalization* of social life.

By "rationalization," Weber wasn't referring to the use of human reason to deliberate about important issues like ethics, morality, politics, and culture, but to the way forms of social action were becoming increasingly organized and motivated by concerns of efficiency and calculation. Weber distinguished between these two forms of rationality by referring to the first kind as "value rationality" and the second as "instrumental rationality" (see below in "Types of Social Action"). For Weber, the "rationalization" of modern societies meant that more and more of our lives were becoming organized by instrumental rationality—by questions of the most efficient and calculable ways to get things done.

While this focus on efficiency and control certainly had tangible benefits in that it allowed humans far greater control over and consistency within their day-to-day lives, Weber also felt rationalization had its pitfalls, often leading to the erosion of our more value-oriented forms of reason and to an overall loss of meaning in our lives (what Weber elsewhere termed the "disenchantment of the world").

Weber's interest in processes of rationalization began with his studies of the relationship between religion and modern capitalism, the most famous of which remains *The Protestant Ethic and the Spirit of Capitalism*, the first reading in this section. Still one of the most widely read works of sociology around,

The Protestant Ethic is Weber's attempt to understand why the most advanced, rationalized kind of capitalism—that is, the form in which the goal is to maximize profits in the most efficient way possible—was found in areas of Europe and the United States that were predominately Protestant.

In studying this question, Weber found that modern capitalism is unique in that it is infused with a legitimating ethos or "spirit" that regards labor and the acquisition of capital not only as a means to an end (an idea common in more ancient or "traditional" forms of capitalism), but as morally valuable in and of itself. Weber sees in this historically novel idea—epitomized in the writings of Benjamin Franklin—one of the driving forces behind the rise of modern capitalism, and he traces this idea to the religious beliefs of European and early-American Protestants.

Specifically, Weber argues that the Lutheran belief that each person, and not just clergy members, had a "calling" from God, coupled with the later Calvinist doctrine of "predestination"—in brief, the idea that each person's soul was already destined from before birth to go to heaven or hell—created fertile cultural grounds for modern, rationalized capitalism. In attempting to order their lives through a "calling" and constantly trying to ascertain whether their souls were destined for heaven or hell, Weber recognized these pious Puritans as the unwitting creators of the spirit of capitalism. Yet, for Weber, there was a disturbing irony connected to the religious origins of the spirit of capitalism. While the ethos certainly remained alive and well in Weber's day, its religious connotations had largely disappeared. While groups like the early Puritans had labored and acquired for a higher, religious purpose, in our day, the rationalized making of money has become the end itself. As Puritan religious values gave way to the instrumental rationality of capitalism, Weber wondered if we now occupied an "iron cage" from which there was no escape. "The Puritan wanted to work in a calling," Weber writes, but "we are forced to do so."

In reading Weber's rich descriptions of the ascetic and anxiety-ridden Puritan worldview, you'll also get a good sense of his ideas of what sociology is and how one should go about doing it. In the reading on "Basic Sociological Terms," Weber defines sociology as an interpretive science concerned in large part with the subjective meanings attached to social action. The sociologist must be able to at least partially grasp these meanings to hope to produce an adequate account of why people do what they do—for Weber, this implies that a sociologist's job involves *verstehen*, an empathic understanding of what an action means from the actor's point of view. Such a methodology certainly involves the sociologist drawing on her powers of imagination and empathy, but Weber argues that it should involve rigorous logic as well. This emphasis can most clearly be seen in Weber's use of *ideal types*, analytical constructs or logical "yardsticks" that allowed him (and can allow us) to fruitfully compare

Use Spike Lee's film, *Do the Right Thing*, to help illustrate Weber's types of social action (see the Supplementary Sources section).

and analyze multiple kinds of social phenomena. While Weber used ideal types in almost all of his work, the excerpt from "Basic Sociological Terms" introduces you to one of his most famous sets of ideal-typical concepts—his four types of social action.

While Weber saw antecedents for a fully rationalized society in the ascetic lifestyles of the Puritans, he observed the very embodiment of rationalization in that form of organization we call bureaucracy. Today we might associate bureaucratic organization with all things evil, but Weber was actually much more even-handed. Weber reminds us that, in their ideal-typical form, bureaucracies have fixed jurisdictional areas: officials within a bureaucracy have specific jobs and responsibilities for which they are specifically trained (e.g. sales, human resources, or marketing), and that leads to much greater efficiency and overall competence. Moreover, these jobs fall within a clear hierarchy and are assigned based on training and expertise, and there are standard rules that apply to everyone. Because of all these characteristics, Weber suggested that bureaucracies increased affluence and could actually level social and economic differences, as preferential treatment based on non-rational characteristics like family name, personal charisma, and even race or gender were much rarer in bureaucracies than in previous forms of organization. Of course, Weber was no naïve idealist. He also saw that bureaucracies emphasized efficient means over morally valued ends, and that the security and predictability they offered often came at the expense of creativity, individuality, and intrinsically meaningful work. He also argued that the increasing power of bureaucracy was at odds with a truly participatory form of democracy. For Weber, political bureaucracies govern us rather than the other way around.

Weber also observed the rising influence of rationalization in the type of legitimate domination or authority that governed people within bureaucracies and other areas of modern social life. In the reading on "The Types of Legitimate Domination," he lays out the differences between what he terms "traditional," "charismatic," and "rational-legal" forms of authority. In modern times, Weber writes, we rarely acquiesce to authority because of belief in long-standing customs (as in traditional authority) or the exceptional qualities of an individual (as in charismatic authority). Instead, we acquiesce because of our acceptance of abstract rules and laws that outline appropriate courses of action (the rational-legal form of authority).

The final reading from Max Weber also addresses issues of power and domination, but this time through a nuanced theory of social stratification and inequality. In contrast to Marx, who saw all forms of inequality and domination as arising from the economic conditions associated with class, Weber offers a three-part scheme that differentiates between economic class, social status, and party. Each of these types of positions or groups entails its own way of exercising power and creating social inequality.

Contemporary Extensions: The Rational Society Re-Wired

Weber, of course, was not the last social theorist to contemplate the more sinister side of modern life. While several contemporary theorists have taken up the conversation that Weber started, arguably no group of scholars has done it with as much sophistication and panache as the Frankfurt School of Critical Theory.

Learn more about the theorists of the Frankfurt School by visiting their Profile Page.

Originally established in 1920s Germany as the Frankfurt Institute for Social Research, the Frankfurt School is now associated with prominent social theorists such as Max Horkheimer, Theodore Adorno, Herbert Marcuse, Erich Fromm, and Jurgen Habermas. These German thinkers—many of them also Jewish—were strongly influenced by the ideas of Weber, Marx, and Sigmund Freud, and, just as importantly, by the rise of Nazism in Germany and the horrors of the Holocaust.

In the wake of the atrocities of the Holocaust and the continuing advancement of ever-more rationalized forms of capitalism, culture, and politics, the theorists of the Frankfurt School began writing some of the most provocative and critical theories of modern society. In the following pages, we present you with readings from two of the most profound theorists in this critical tradition—Herbert Marcuse and Jurgen Habermas.

In the excerpt from his unsettling *One-Dimensional Man*, Marcuse lays out a scathing indictment of the "advanced industrial societies" of the modern West. Whether living in a capitalist or communist society, Marcuse argued in the mid-1960s, modern persons were becoming almost thoroughly controlled by the rationalizing forces of the mass media, advertising, science, and technology. As a result, they were becoming increasingly "one dimensional" in their thoughts and activities. Such a one-dimensional person, though, is nothing but a by-product of a society governed by "technological" (what Weber called instrumental) rationality. She's not a value-rational being capable of developing her own needs and capabilities, democratically governing her own political destiny, or even noticing, let alone opposing, the many forces that seek to control her. In such a one-dimensional world, Marcuse writes, "society's domination over the individual is greater than ever before." It's an iron cage if there ever was one.

If Marcuse's writing personifies the Frankfurt School's most critical and pessimistic indictments of modern society, the next reading by Jurgen Habermas holds out hope that modernity can still grant us a truly Rational—and not merely rationalized—society. In this reading from *Toward a Rational Society*, Habermas echoes Marcuse's overriding concern that the increasing technological rationalization of the social world is supplanting instead of aiding people in meaningfully deciding how they want to live together. Habermas sees this as a fundamental tension in the relationship between the spheres of technology and democracy. In a truly rational society, Habermas argues, technological forms of rational control should be brought under the authority of the value-rational sphere of democracy. In other words, citizens should be able to deliberate over, decide on, and ultimately control how particular technologies are used in their societies. Yet Habermas is convinced it is often the other way around. He follows Weber's sentiments about the anti-democratic nature of bureaucracies: In our day and age, technological forms of rationality dictate how we are to live together. Despite this critique, Habermas remains optimistic that rationalization processes can be brought under the power of truly democratic deliberation.

Following the readings from the Frankfurt School, we have selected a reading from the French social theorist Michel Foucault (see the "Rise of the Avatar" section for another reading from this great thinker). As brilliant and provocative as any member of the Frankfurt School, Foucault was also keen to shed light in the dark corners of modern social life. Like Weber, he was extremely interested in how modern forms of social organization and control came to be. In seeking to answer this question, Foucault conducted brilliant analyses of the histories of modern institutions like the insane asylum, the medical clinic, and, in this reading, the modern prison.

In the excerpt from *Discipline and Punish*, Foucault begins with a vivid and gruesome description of the torture and execution of an eighteenth-century would-be political assassin—his flesh torn; boiling oil, lead, sulphur, and wax poured into his wounds; his body drawn and quartered by horses. After describing this brutal scenario, Foucault takes us a scant eight years into the future, where a schedule is being written for a juvenile prison-house. In this plan, instead of the spectacle of torture, there is a detailed, meticulous ordering of the prisoners' daily activities from sunrise to sunset, a schedule that doesn't order the distribution of pain, but organizes everyday practices of eating, working, bathing, and sleeping. Foucault sets out to understand the drastic movement from the spectacle of the scaffold to the tedious timetable of the penal institution.

We might be tempted to believe that this is a gradual, progressive process toward greater humanization of punishment, but Foucault argues that the establishment of the modern prison system is actually the harbinger of a new form of disciplinary power, exercised through a whole series of rationalized techniques, forms of organization, and modes of surveillance (most vividly illustrated by his description of Jeremy Bentham's "Panopticon"). In studying the birth of the prison, Foucault observes practices of organization and surveillance that characterize our society at large. If, for Weber, we live in a rationalized, disenchanted world, for Foucault, ours is the "disciplinary society." It is through the many techniques of discipline that our society has become so thoroughly ordered, homogenized, and controllable. Welcome to the Big House.

See the full-text excerpt of Theodore Adorno's "How to Look at Television" for a quintessential Frankfurt School theorist's take on one of our favorite leisure activities.

Instructors, find more full-text excerpts from Foucault's *Madness and Civilization* and *The Birth of the Clinic* in the Supplementary Sources.

To read more about the many institutions Foucault studied over his brilliant career, log on to his Profile Page.

The section concludes with a reading from one of sociology's most prolific and creative theorists, Zygmunt Bauman. Renowned for writing some of the most insightful theories of contemporary social life, the excerpt from Bauman's *Modernity and the Holocaust* illustrates his ability to shine theoretical light on one of modern society's darkest, most horrific events. Through the Holocaust, Bauman analyzes just what horrible things can be done through a highly rationalized system of organization. While mass murder has regrettably been part of human history for millennia, Bauman argues that genocide on the scale of the Holocaust is a distinctly modern accomplishment.

Bauman states that it is tempting (and perhaps comforting) to think of the Holocaust as a temporary breakdown of modern civilization. But, on the contrary, several familiar characteristics of modern society actually made the genocide more effective and efficient. First, Bauman argues that modernity has always been characterized by bold, optimistic (and many would say misguided) visions of creating a more perfectly organized and rational society. While some peoples' visions might be harmlessly utopian, others, like Adolph Hitler, have been much more willing to use violence in trying to translate their visions of a perfectly ordered society into reality. Second, the characteristics of modern bureaucracy make the carrying out of such violence much easier and more efficient. The highly rationalized, hierarchical, and specialized division of labor characteristic of modern bureaucracy, for example, allowed those engaging in genocide to distance themselves from the moral consequences of their actions. Disturbingly, Bauman argues that the majority of the many Germans who did the tasks necessary to keep the killing machine up and running were not enraged psychopaths or even necessarily that anti-Semitic toward Jewish people. Rather, they were the quintessential modern workers who followed orders and completed their tasks in the most efficient way possible.

The Nazis constructed and employed a highly rationalized, efficient, and calculated system of extermination: They used all of the powers of bureaucracy and rational-legal authority to implement one of the most notoriously immoral acts in human history. And nothing, Bauman concludes, about our modern civilization has changed to prevent this kind of atrocity from occurring again.

For suggestions on assigning portions of Bauman's book, *Modernity and the Holocaust*, see the Supplementary Sources.

For an apropos look at the disenchanting aspects of digital technologies, and their associated risks, check out Jaron Lanier's provocative *You Are Not a Gadget*: *A Manifesto* in the Supplementary Sources.

Plug In

In the readings to follow, you'll begin making connections with some of the most provocative thinking in all of social theory. In learning about the anxious lives of pious Puritans, the surveillance of the social order, and the rationalization of, well, just about everything, you'll be plugging into the deep, dark underbelly of modern society with a few of the most challenging theorists of our times. Take a flashlight … but maybe leave the smart phone behind.

18

The Protestant Ethic and the Spirit of Capitalism

Max Weber

A GLANCE AT THE OCCUPATIONAL statistics of any country of mixed religious composition brings to light with remarkable frequency[1] a situation which has several times provoked discussion in the Catholic press and literature,[2] and in Catholic congresses in Germany, namely, the fact that business leaders and owners of capital, as well as the higher grades of skilled labour, and even more the higher technically and commercially trained personnel of modern enterprises, are overwhelmingly Protestant.[3] This is true not only in cases where the difference in religion coincides with one of nationality, and thus of cultural development, as in Eastern Germany between Germans and Poles. The same thing is shown in the figures of religious affiliation almost wherever capitalism, at the time of its great expansion, has had a free hand to alter the social distribution of the population in accordance with its needs, and to determine its occupational structure. The more freedom it has had, the more clearly is the effect shown. It is true that the greater relative participation of Protestants in the ownership of capital,[4] in management, and the upper ranks of labour in great modern industrial and commercial enterprises,[5] may in part be explained in terms of historical circumstances[6] which extend far back into the past, and in which religious affiliation is not a cause of the economic conditions, but to a certain extent appears to be a result of them. Participation in the above economic functions usually involves some previous ownership of capital, and generally an expensive education; often both. These are to-day largely dependent on the possession of inherited wealth, or at least on a certain degree of material well-being. A number of those sections of the old Empire which were most highly developed economically and most favoured by natural resources and situation, in particular a majority of the wealthy towns, went over to Protestantism in the sixteenth century. The results of that circumstance favour the Protestants even to-day in their struggle for economic existence. There arises thus the historical question: why were the districts of highest economic development at the same time particularly favourable to a revolution in the Church? The answer is by no means so simple as one might think.

The emancipation from economic traditionalism appears, no doubt, to be a factor which would greatly strengthen the tendency to doubt the sanctity of the religious tradition, as of all traditional authorities. But it is necessary to note, what has often been forgotten, that the Reformation meant not the elimination of the Church's control over everyday life, but rather the substitution of a new form of control for the previous one. It meant the repudiation of a control which was very lax, at that time scarcely perceptible in practice, and hardly more than formal, in favour of a regulation of the whole of conduct which, penetrating to all departments of private and public life was infinitely burdensome and earnestly enforced. The rule of the Catholic

Church, "punishing the heretic, but indulgent to the sinner", as it was in the past even more than to-day, is now tolerated by peoples of thoroughly modern economic character, and was borne by the richest and economically most advanced peoples on earth at about the turn of the fifteenth century. The rule of Calvinism, on the other hand, as it was enforced in the sixteenth century in Geneva and in Scotland, at the turn of the sixteenth and seventeenth centuries in large parts of the Netherlands, in the seventeenth in New England, and for a time in England itself, would be for us the most absolutely unbearable form of ecclesiastical control of the individual which could possibly exist. That was exactly what large numbers of the old commercial aristocracy of those times, in Geneva as well as in Holland and England, felt about it. And what the reformers complained of in those areas of high economic development was not too much supervision of life on the part of the Church, but too little. Now how does it happen that at that time those countries which were most advanced economically, and within them the rising bourgeois middle classes, not only failed to resist this unexampled tyranny of Puritanism, but even developed a heroism in its defence? For bourgeois classes as such have seldom before and never since displayed heroism. It was "the last of our heroisms", as Carlyle, not without reason, has said.

But further, and especially important: it may be, as has been claimed, that the greater participation of Protestants in the positions of ownership and management in modern economic life may to-day be understood, in part at least, simply as a result of the greater material wealth they have inherited. But there are certain other phenomena which cannot be explained in the same way. Thus, to mention only a few facts: there is a great difference discoverable in Baden, in Bavaria, in Hungary, in the type of higher education which Catholic parents, as opposed to Protestant, give their children. That the percentage of Catholics among the students and graduates of higher educational institutions in general lags

behind their proportion of the total population,[7] may, to be sure, be largely explicable in terms of inherited differences of wealth. But among the Catholic graduates themselves the percentage of those graduating from the institutions preparing, in particular, for technical studies and industrial and commercial occupations, but in general from those preparing for middle-class business life, lags still farther behind the percentage of Protestants.[8] On the other hand, Catholics prefer the sort of training which the humanistic Gymnasium affords. That is a circumstance to which the above explanation does not apply, but which, on the contrary, is one reason why so few Catholics are engaged in capitalistic enterprise.

Even more striking is a fact which partly explains the smaller proportion of Catholics among the skilled labourers of modern industry. It is well known that the factory has taken its skilled labour to a large extent from young men in the handicrafts; but this is much more true of Protestant than of Catholic journeymen. Among journeymen, in other words, the Catholics show a stronger propensity to remain in their crafts, that is they more often become master craftsmen, whereas the Protestants are attracted to a larger extent into the factories in order to fill the upper ranks of skilled labour and administrative positions.[9] The explanation of these cases is undoubtedly that the mental and spiritual peculiarities acquired from the environment, here the type of education favoured by the religious atmosphere of the home community and the parental home, have determined the choice of occupation, and through it the professional career.

The smaller participation of Catholics in the modern business life of Germany is all the more striking because it runs counter to a tendency which has been observed at all times[10] including the present. National or religious minorities which are in a position of subordination to a group of rulers are likely, through their voluntary or involuntary exclusion from positions of political influence, to be driven with peculiar force into economic activity. Their ablest members seek to satisfy the desire for recognition of their abilities in this field, since there is no opportunity in the service of the State. This has undoubtedly been true of the Poles in Russia and Eastern Prussia, who have without question been undergoing a more rapid economic advance than in Galicia, where they have been in the ascendant. It has in earlier times been true of the Huguenots in France under Louis XIV, the Nonconformists and Quakers in England, and, last but not least, the Jew for two thousand years. But the Catholics in Germany have shown no striking evidence of such a result of their position. In the past they have, unlike the Protestants, undergone no particularly prominent economic development in the times when they were persecuted or only tolerated, either in Holland or in England. On the other hand, it is a fact that the Protestants (especially certain branches of the movement to be fully discussed later) both as ruling classes and as ruled, both as majority and as minority, have shown a special tendency to develop economic rationalism which cannot be observed to the same extent among Catholics either in the one situation or in the other.[11] Thus the principal explanation of this difference must be sought in the permanent intrinsic character of their religious beliefs, and not only in their temporary external historico-political situations.[12]

THE SPIRIT OF CAPITALISM

In the title of this study is used the somewhat pretentious phrase, the spirit of capitalism. What is to be understood by it? The attempt to give anything like a definition of it brings out certain difficulties which are in the very nature of this type of investigation.

If any object can be found to which this term can be applied with any understandable meaning, it can only be an historical individual, i.e. a complex of elements associated in historical reality which we unite into a conceptual whole from the standpoint of their cultural significance.

Such an historical concept, however, since it refers in its content to a phenomenon significant for its unique individuality, cannot be defined according to the formula *genus proximum, differentia specifica*, but it must be gradually put together out of the individual parts which are taken from historical reality to make it up. Thus the final and definitive concept cannot stand at the beginning of the investigation, but must come at the end. We must, in other words, work out in the course of the discussion, as its most important result, the best conceptual formulation of what we here understand by the spirit of capitalism, that is the best from the point of view which interests us here. This point of view (the one of which we shall speak later) is, further, by no means the only possible one from which the historical phenomena we are investigating can be analysed. Other standpoints would, for this as for every historical phenomenon, yield other characteristics as the essential ones. The result is that it is by no means necessary to understand by the spirit of capitalism only what it will come to mean to us for the purposes of our analysis. This is a necessary result of the nature of historical concepts which attempt for their methodological purposes not to grasp historical reality in abstract general formulæ, but in concrete genetic sets of relations which are inevitably of a specifically unique and individual character.[13]

Thus, if we try to determine the object, the analysis and historical explanation of which we are attempting, it cannot be in the form of a conceptual definition, but at least in the beginning only a provisional description of what is here meant by the spirit of capitalism. Such a description is, however, indispensable in order clearly to understand the object of the investigation. For this purpose we turn to a document of that spirit which contains what we are looking for in almost classical purity, and at the same time has the advantage of being free from all direct relationship to religion, being thus, for our purposes, free of preconceptions.

Remember, that *time* is money. He that can earn ten shillings a day by his labour, and goes abroad, or sits idle, one half of that day, though he spends but sixpence during his diversion or idleness, ought not to reckon *that* the only expense; he has really spent, or rather thrown away, five shillings besides.

Remember, that *credit* is money. If a man lets his money lie in my hands after it is due, he gives me the interest, or so much as I can make of it during that time. This amounts to a considerable sum where a man has good and large credit, and makes good use of it.

Remember, that money is of the prolific, generating nature. Money can beget money, and its offspring can beget more, and so on. Five shillings turned is six, turned again it is seven and threepence, and so on, till it becomes a hundred pounds. The more there is of it, the more it produces every turning, so that the profits rise quicker and quicker. He that kills a breeding-sow, destroys all her offspring to the thousandth generation. He that murders a crown, destroys all that it might have produced, even scores of pounds.

Remember this saying, *The good paymaster is lord of another man's purse.* He that is known to pay punctually and exactly to the time he promises, may at any time, and on any occasion, raise all the money his friends can spare. This is sometimes of great use. After industry and frugality, nothing contributes more to the raising of a young man in the world than punctuality and justice in all his dealings; therefore never keep borrowed money an hour beyond the time you promised, lest a disappointment shut up your friend's purse for ever.

The most trifling actions that affect a man's credit are to be regarded. The sound of your hammer at five in the morning, or eight at night, heard by a creditor, makes him easy six months longer; but if he sees you at a billiard-table, or hears your voice at a tavern, when you should be at work, he sends for his money the next day; demands it, before he can receive it, in a lump.

It shows, besides, that you are mindful of what you owe; it makes you appear a careful as well as an honest man, and that still increases your credit.

Beware of thinking all your own that you possess, and of living accordingly. It is a mistake that many people who have credit fall into. To prevent this, keep an exact account for some time both of your expenses and your income. If you take the pains at first to mention particulars, it will have this good effect: you will discover how wonderfully small, trifling expenses mount up to large sums; and will discern what might have been, and may for the future be saved, without occasioning any great inconvenience.

For six pounds a year you may have the use of one hundred pounds, provided you are a man of known prudence and honesty.

He that spends a groat a day idly, spends idly above six pounds a year, which is the price for the use of one hundred pounds.

He that wastes idly a groat's worth of his time per day, one day with another, wastes the privilege of using one hundred pounds each day.

He that idly loses five shillings' worth of time; loses five shillings, and might as prudently throw five shillings into the sea.

He that loses five shillings, not only loses that sum, but all the advantage that might be made by turning it in dealing, which by the time that a young man becomes old, will amount to a considerable sum of money.[14]

It is Benjamin Franklin who preaches to us in these sentences, the same which Ferdinand Kürnberger satirizes in his clever and malicious *Picture of American Culture*[15] as the supposed confession of faith of the Yankee. That it is the spirit of capitalism which here speaks in characteristic fashion, no one will doubt, however little we may wish to claim that everything which could be understood as pertaining to that spirit is contained in it. Let us pause a moment to consider this passage, the philosophy of which Kürnberger sums up in the words, "They make tallow out of cattle and money out of men". The peculiarity of this philosophy of avarice appears to be the ideal of the honest man of recognized credit, and above all the idea of a duty of the individual toward the increase of his capital, which is assumed as an end in itself. Truly what is here preached is not simply a means of making one's way in the world, but a peculiar ethic. The infraction of its rules is treated not as foolishness but as forgetfulness of duty. That is the essence of the matter. It is not mere business astuteness, that sort of thing is common enough, it is an ethos. This is the quality which interests us.

When Jacob Fugger, in speaking to a business associate who had retired and who wanted to persuade him to do the same, since he had made enough money and should let others have a chance, rejected that as pusillanimity and answered that "he (Fugger) thought otherwise, he wanted to make money as long as he could",[16] the spirit of his statement is evidently quite different from that of Franklin. What in the former case was an expression of commercial daring and a personal inclination morally neutral,[17] in the latter takes on the character of an ethically coloured maxim for the conduct of life. The concept spirit of capitalism is here used in this specific sense,[18] it is the spirit of modern capitalism. For that we are here dealing only with Western European and American capitalism is obvious from the way in which the problem was stated. Capitalism existed in China, India, Babylon, in the classic world, and in the Middle Ages. But in all these cases, as we shall see, this particular ethos was lacking.

Now, all Franklin's moral attitudes are coloured with utilitarianism. Honesty is useful, because it assures credit; so are punctuality, industry, frugality, and that is the reason they are virtues. A logical deduction from this would be that where, for instance, the appearance of honesty serves the same purpose, that would suffice, and an unnecessary surplus of this virtue would evidently appear to Franklin's eyes as unproductive waste. And as a

matter of fact, the story in his autobiography of his conversion to those virtues,[19] or the discussion of the value of a strict maintenance of the appearance of modesty, the assiduous belittlement of one's own deserts in order to gain general recognition later,[20] confirms this impression. According to Franklin, those virtues, like all others, are only in so far virtues as they are actually useful to the individual, and the surrogate of mere appearance is always sufficient when it accomplishes the end in view. It is a conclusion which is inevitable for strict utilitarianism. The impression of many Germans that the virtues professed by Americanism are pure hypocrisy seems to have been confirmed by this striking case. But in fact the matter is not by any means so simple. Benjamin Franklin's own character, as it appears in the really unusual candidness of his autobiography, belies that suspicion. The circumstance that he ascribes his recognition of the utility of virtue to a divine revelation which was intended to lead him in the path of righteousness, shows that something more than mere garnishing for purely egocentric motives is involved.

In fact, the *summum bonum* of this ethic, the earning of more and more money, combined with the strict avoidance of all spontaneous enjoyment of life, is above all completely devoid of any eudaemonistic, not to say hedonistic, admixture. It is thought of so purely as an end in itself, that from the point of view of the happiness of, or utility to, the single individual, it appears entirely transcendental and absolutely irrational.[21] Man is dominated by the making of money, by acquisition as the ultimate purpose of his life. Economic acquisition is no longer subordinated to man as the means for the satisfaction of his material needs. This reversal of what we should call the natural relationship, so irrational from a naive point of view, is evidently as definitely a leading principle of capitalism as it is foreign to all peoples not under capitalistic influence. At the same time it expresses a type of feeling which is closely connected with certain religious ideas. If we thus ask, why should "money be made out of men", Benjamin Franklin himself, although he was a colourless deist, answers in his autobiography with a quotation from the Bible, which his strict Calvinistic father drummed into him again and again in his youth: "Seest thou a man diligent in his business? He shall stand before kings" (Prov. xxii. 29). The earning of money within the modern economic order is, so long as it is done legally, the result and the expression of virtue and proficiency in a calling; and this virtue and proficiency are, as it is now not difficult to see, the real Alpha and Omega of Franklin's ethic, as expressed in the passages we have quoted, as well as in all his works without exception.[22]

And in truth this peculiar idea, so familiar to us to-day, but in reality so little a matter of course, of one's duty in a calling, is what is most characteristic of the social ethic of capitalistic culture, and is in a sense the fundamental basis of it. It is an obligation which the individual is supposed to feel and does feel towards the content of his professional[23] activity, no matter in what it consists, in particular no matter whether it appears on the surface as a utilization of his personal powers, or only of his material possessions (as capital).

Of course, this conception has not appeared only under capitalistic conditions. On the contrary, we shall later trace its origins back to a time previous to the advent of capitalism. Still less, naturally, do we maintain that a conscious acceptance of these ethical maxims on the part of the individuals, entrepreneurs or labourers, in modern capitalistic enterprises, is a condition of the further existence of present-day capitalism. The capitalistic economy of the present day is an immense cosmos into which the individual is born, and which presents itself to him, at least as an individual, as an unalterable order of things in which he must live. It forces the individual, in so far as he is involved in the system of market relationships, to conform to capitalistic rules of action. The manufacturer who in the long run acts counter to these norms, will just as

inevitably be eliminated from the economic scene as the worker who cannot or will not adapt himself to them will be thrown into the streets without a job.

Thus the capitalism of to-day, which has come to dominate economic life, educates and selects the economic subjects which it needs through a process of economic survival of the fittest. But here one can easily see the limits of the concept of selection as a means of historical explanation. In order that a manner of life so well adapted to the peculiarities of capitalism could be selected at all, i.e. should come to dominate others, it had to originate somewhere, and not in isolated individuals alone, but as a way of life common to whole groups of men. This origin is what really needs explanation. Concerning the doctrine of the more naive historical materialism, that such ideas originate as a reflection or superstructure of economic situations, we shall speak more in detail below. At this point it will suffice for our purpose to call attention to the fact that without doubt, in the country of Benjamin Franklin's birth (Massachusetts), the spirit of capitalism (in the sense we have attached to it) was present before the capitalistic order. There were complaints of a peculiarly calculating sort of profit-seeking in New England, as distinguished from other parts of America, as early as 1632. It is further undoubted that capitalism remained far less developed in some of the neighbouring colonies, the later Southern States of the United States of America, in spite of the fact that these latter were founded by large capitalists for business motives, while the New England colonies were founded by preachers and seminary graduates with the help of small bourgeois, craftsmen and yoe-men, for religious reasons. In this case the causal relation is certainly the reverse of that suggested by the materialistic standpoint.

But the origin and history of such ideas is much more complex than the theorists of the superstructure suppose. The spirit of capitalism, in the sense in which we are using the term, had to fight its way to supremacy against a whole world of hostile forces. A state of mind such as that expressed in the passages we have quoted from Franklin, and which called forth the applause of a whole people, would both in ancient times and in the Middle Ages[24] have been proscribed as the lowest sort of avarice and as an attitude entirely lacking in self-respect. It is, in fact, still regularly thus looked upon by all those social groups which are least involved in or adapted to modern capitalistic conditions. This is not wholly because the instinct of acquisition was in those times unknown or undeveloped, as has often been said. Nor because the *auri sacra fames,* the greed for gold, was then, or now, less powerful outside of bourgeois capitalism than within its peculiar sphere, as the illusions of modern romanticists are wont to believe. The difference between the capitalistic and pre-capitalistic spirits is not to be found at this point. The greed of the Chinese Mandarin, the old Roman aristocrat, or the modern peasant, can stand up to any comparison. And the *auri sacra fames* of a Neapolitan cab-driver or *barcaiuolo*, and certainly of Asiatic representatives of similar trades, as well as of the craftsmen of southern European or Asiatic countries, is, as anyone can find out for himself, very much more intense, and especially more unscrupulous than that of, say, an Englishman in similar circumstances.[25]

[...]

One of the technical means which the modern employer uses in order to secure the greatest possible amount of work from his men is the device of piece-rates. In agriculture, for instance, the gathering of the harvest is a case where the greatest possible intensity of labour is called for, since, the weather being uncertain, the difference between high profit and heavy loss may depend on the speed with which the harvesting can be done. Hence a system of piece-rates is almost universal in this case. And since the interest of the employer in a speeding-up of harvesting increases with the increase of the results and the intensity of the work, the attempt has again and again been made, by increasing the piece-rates of the workmen, thereby giving them an opportunity to earn what is for them a very high wage, to interest them in increasing their own efficiency. But a peculiar difficulty has been met with surprising frequency: raising the piece-rates has often had the result that not more but less has been accomplished in the same time, because the worker reacted to the increase not by increasing but by decreasing the amount of his work. A man, for instance, who at the rate of 1 mark per acre mowed $2^1/_2$ acres per day and earned $2^1/_2$ marks, when the rate was raised to 1.25 marks per acre mowed, not 3 acres, as he might easily have done, thus earning 3.75 marks, but only 2 acres, so that he could still earn the $2^1/_2$ marks to which he was accustomed. The opportunity of earning more was less attractive than that of working less. He did not ask: how much can I earn in a day if I do as much work as possible? but: how much must I work in order to earn the wage, $2^1/_2$ marks, which I earned before and which takes care of my traditional needs? This is an example of what is here meant by traditionalism. A man does not "by nature" wish to earn more and more money, but simply to live as he is accustomed to live and to earn as much as is necessary for that purpose. Wherever modern capitalism has begun its work of increasing the productivity of human labour by increasing its intensity, it has encountered the immensely stubborn resistance of this leading trait of pre-capitalistic labour. And to-day it encounters it the more, the more backward (from a capitalistic point of view) the labouring forces are with which it has to deal.

Another obvious possibility, to return to our example, since the appeal to the acquisitive instinct through higher wage-rates failed, would have been to try the opposite policy, to force the worker by reduction of his wage-rates to work harder to earn the same amount than he did before. Low wages and high profits seem even to-day to a superficial observer to stand in correlation; everything which is paid out in wages seems to involve a corresponding reduction of profits. That road capitalism has taken again and again since its beginning. For centuries it was an article of faith, that low wages were productive, i.e. that they increased the material results of labour so that, as Pieter de la Cour, on this point, as we shall see, quite in the spirit of the old Calvinism, said long ago, the people only work because and so long as they are poor.

But the effectiveness of this apparently so efficient method has its limits.[26] Of course the presence of a surplus population which it can hire cheaply in the labour market is a necessity for the development of capitalism. But though too large a reserve army may in certain cases favour its quantitative expansion, it checks its qualitative development, especially the transition to types of enterprise which make more intensive use of labour. Low wages are by no means identical with cheap labour.[27] From a purely quantitative point of view the efficiency of labour decreases with a wage which is physiologically insufficient, which may in the long run even mean a survival of the unfit. The present-day average Silesian mows, when he exerts himself to the full, little more than two-thirds as much land as the better paid and nourished Pomeranian or Mecklenburger, and the Pole, the further East he comes from, accomplishes progressively less than the German. Low wages fail even from a purely business point of view wherever it is a question of producing goods which require any sort of skilled labour, or the use of expensive machinery which is easily damaged, or in general wherever any great amount of sharp attention or of initiative is required. Here low wages do not pay, and their effect is the opposite of what was intended. For not only is a developed sense of responsibility absolutely indispensable, but in general also an attitude which, at least during working hours, is freed from continual calculations of how the customary wage may be earned with a maximum of comfort and a minimum of exertion.

Labour must, on the contrary, be performed as if it were an absolute end in itself, a calling. But such an attitude is by no means a product of nature. It cannot be evoked by low wages or high ones alone, but can only be the product of a long and arduous process of education. Today, capitalism, once in the saddle, can recruit its labouring force in all industrial countries with comparative ease. In the past this was in every case an extremely difficult problem.[28] And even today it could probably not get along without the support of a powerful ally along the way, which, as we shall see below, was at hand at the time of its development.

[...]

Some moralists of that time, especially of the nominalistic school, accepted developed capitalistic business forms as inevitable, and attempted to justify them, especially commerce, as necessary. The *industria* developed in it they were able to regard, though not without contradictions, as a legitimate source of profit, and hence ethically unobjectionable. But the dominant doctrine rejected the spirit of capitalistic acquisition as *turpitudo*, or at least could not give it a positive ethical sanction. An ethical attitude like that of Benjamin Franklin would have been simply unthinkable. This was, above all, the attitude of capitalistic circles themselves. Their life-work was, so long as they clung to the tradition of the Church, at best something morally indifferent. It was tolerated, but was still, even if only on account of the continual danger of collision with the Church's doctrine on usury, somewhat dangerous to salvation. Quite considerable sums, as the sources show, went at the death of rich people to religious institutions as conscience money, at times even back to former debtors as *usura* which had been unjustly taken from them. It was otherwise, along with heretical and other tendencies looked upon with disapproval, only in those parts of the commercial aristocracy which were already emancipated from the tradition. But even sceptics and people indifferent to the Church often reconciled themselves with it by gifts, because it was a sort of insurance against the uncertainties of what might come after death, or because (at least according to the very widely held latter view) an external obedience to the commands of the Church was sufficient to insure salvation.[29] Here the either non-moral or immoral character of their action in the opinion of the participants themselves comes clearly to light.

Now, how could activity, which was at best ethically tolerated, turn into a calling in the sense of Benjamin Franklin? The fact to be explained historically is that in the most highly capitalistic centre of that time, in Florence of the fourteenth and fifteenth centuries, the money and capital market of all the great political Powers, this attitude was considered ethically unjustifiable, or at best to be tolerated. But in the backwoods small bourgeois circumstances of Pennsylvania in the eighteenth century, where business threatened for simple lack of money to fall back into barter, where there was hardly a sign of large enterprise, where only the earliest beginnings of banking were to be found, the same thing was considered the essence of moral conduct, even commanded in the name of duty. To speak here of a reflection of material conditions in the ideal superstructure would be patent nonsense. What was the background of ideas which could account for the sort of activity apparently directed toward profit alone as a calling toward which the individual feels himself to have an ethical obligation? For it was this idea which gave the way of life of the new entrepreneur its ethical foundation and justification.

THE RELIGIOUS FOUNDATIONS OF WORLDLY ACETICISM

With Calvin the *decretum horribile* is derived not, as with Luther, from religious experience, but from the logical necessity of his thought; therefore its importance increases with every increase in the logical consistency of that religious thought. The interest of it is solely in God, not in man; God does not exist for men, but men for the sake of God.[30] All creation, including of course the fact, as it undoubtedly was for Calvin, that only a small proportion of men are chosen for eternal grace, can have any meaning only as means to the glory and majesty of God. To apply earthly standards of justice to His sovereign decrees is meaningless and an insult to His Majesty,[31] since He and He alone is free, i.e. is subject to no law. His decrees can only be understood by or even known to us in so far as it has been His pleasure to reveal them. We can only hold to these fragments of eternal truth. Everything else, including the meaning of our individual destiny, is hidden in dark mystery which it would be both impossible to pierce and presumptuous to question.

For the damned to complain of their lot would be much the same as for animals to bemoan the fact they were not born as men. For everything of the flesh is separated from God by an unbridgeable gulf and deserves of Him only eternal death, in so far as He has not decreed otherwise for the glorification of His Majesty. We know only that a part of humanity is saved, the rest damned. To assume that human merit or guilt play a part in determining this destiny would be to think of God's absolutely free decrees, which have been settled from eternity, as subject to change by human influence, an impossible contradiction. The Father in heaven of the New Testament, so human and understanding, who rejoices over the repentance of a sinner as a woman over the lost piece of silver she has found, is gone. His place has been taken by a transcendental being, beyond the reach of human understanding, who with His quite incomprehensible decrees has decided the fate of every individual and regulated the tiniest details of the cosmos from eternity.[32] God's grace is, since His decrees cannot change, as impossible for those to whom He has granted it to lose as it is unattainable for those to whom He has denied it.

In its extreme inhumanity this doctrine must above all have had one consequence for the life of a generation which surrendered to its magnificent consistency. That was a feeling of unprecedented inner loneliness of the single individual.[33] In what was for the man of the age of the Reformation the most important thing in life, his eternal salvation, he was forced to follow his path alone to meet a destiny which had been decreed for him from eternity. No one could help him. No priest, for the chosen one can understand the word of God only in his own heart. No sacraments, for though the sacraments had been ordained by God for the increase of His glory, and must hence be scrupulously observed, they are not a means to the attainment of grace, but only the subjective *externa subsidia* of faith. No Church, for though it was held that *extra ecclesiam nulla salus* in the sense that whoever kept away from the true Church could never belong to God's chosen band,[34] nevertheless the membership of the external Church included the doomed. They should belong to it and be subjected to its discipline, not in order thus to attain salvation, that is impossible, but because, for the glory of God, they too must be forced to obey His commandments. Finally, even no God. For even Christ had died only for the elect,[35] for whose benefit God had decreed His martyrdom from eternity. This, the complete elimination of salvation through the Church and the sacraments (which was in Lutheranism by no means developed to its final conclusions), was what formed the absolutely decisive difference from Catholicism.

[...]

For us the decisive problem is: How was this doctrine borne[36] in an age to which the after-life was not only more important, but in many ways also more certain, than all the interests of life in this world?[37] The question, Am I one of the elect? must sooner or later have arisen for every believer and have forced all other interests into the background. And how can I be sure of this state of grace?[38] For Calvin himself this was not a problem. He felt himself to be a chosen agent of the Lord, and was certain of his own salvation. Accordingly, to the question of how the individual can be certain of his own election, he has at bottom only the answer that we should be content with the knowledge that God has chosen and depend further only on that implicit trust in Christ which is the result of true faith. He rejects in principle the assumption that one can learn from the conduct of others whether they are chosen or damned. It is an unjustifiable attempt to force God's secrets. The elect differ externally in this life in no way from the damned;[39] and even all the subjective experiences of the chosen are, as *ludibria spiritus sancti*, possible for the damned with the single exception of that *finaliter* expectant, trusting faith. The elect thus are and remain God's invisible Church.

Quite naturally this attitude was impossible for his followers as early as Beza, and, above all, for the broad mass of ordinary men. For them the *certitudo salutis* in the sense of the recognizability of the state of grace necessarily became of absolutely dominant importance.[40] So, wherever the doctrine of predestination was held, the question could not be suppressed whether there were any infallible criteria by which membership in the *electi* could be known. Not only has this question continually had a central importance in the development of the Pietism which first arose on the basis of the Reformed Church; it has in fact in a certain sense at times been fundamental to it. But when we consider the great political and social importance of the Reformed doctrine and practice of the Communion, we shall see how great a part was played during the whole seventeenth century outside of Pietism by the possibility of ascertaining the state of grace of the individual. On it depended, for instance, his admission to Communion, i.e. to the central religious ceremony which determined the social standing of the participants.

It was impossible, at least so far as the question of a man's own state of grace arose, to be satisfied[41] with Calvin's trust in the testimony of the expectant faith resulting from grace, even though the orthodox doctrine had never formally abandoned that criterion.[42] Above all, practical pastoral work, which had immediately to deal with all the suffering caused by the doctrine, could not be satisfied. It met these difficulties in various ways.[43] So far as predestination was not reinterpreted, toned down, or fundamentally abandoned,[44] two principal, mutually connected, types of pastoral advice appear. On the one hand it is held to be an absolute duty to consider oneself chosen, and to combat all doubts as temptations of the devil,[45] since lack of self-confidence is the result of insufficient faith, hence of imperfect grace. The exhortation of the apostle to make fast one's own call is here interpreted as a duty to attain certainty of one's own election and justification in the daily struggle of life. In the place of the humble sinners to whom Luther promises grace if they trust themselves to God in penitent faith are bred those self-confident saints[46] whom we can rediscover in the hard Puritan merchants of the heroic age of capitalism and in isolated instances down to the present. On the other hand, in order to attain that self-confidence intense worldly activity is recommended as the most suitable means.[47] It and it alone disperses religious doubts and gives the certainty of grace.

[...]

If we now ask further, by what fruits the Calvinist thought himself able to identify true faith? the answer is: by a type of Christian conduct which served to increase the glory of God. Just what does so serve is to be seen in his own will as revealed either directly through the Bible or indirectly through the purposeful order of the world which he has created (lex naturæ).[48] Especially by comparing the condition of one's own soul with that of the elect, for instance the patriarchs, according to the Bible, could the state of one's own grace be known.[49] Only one of the elect really has the *fides efficax*,[50] only he is able by virtue of his rebirth (*regeneratio*) and the resulting sanctification (*sanctificatio*) of

his whole life, to augment the glory of God by real, and not merely apparent, good works. It was through the consciousness that his conduct, at least in its fundamental character and constant ideal (*propositum obœdientiæ*), rested on a power[51] within himself working for the glory of God; that it is not only willed of God but rather done by God[52] that he attained the highest good towards which this religion strove, the certainty of salvation.[53] That it was attainable was proved by 2 Cor. xiii. 5.[54] Thus, however useless good works might be as a means of attaining salvation, for even the elect remain beings of the flesh, and everything they do falls infinitely short of divine standards, nevertheless, they are indispensable as a sign of election.[55] They are the technical means, not of purchasing salvation, but of getting rid of the fear of damnation. In this sense they are occasionally referred to as directly necessary for salvation[56] or the *possessio salutis* is made conditional on them.[57]

In practice this means that God helps those who help themselves.[58] Thus the Calvinist, as it is sometimes put, himself creates[59] his own salvation, or, as would be more correct, the conviction of it. But this creation cannot, as in Catholicism, consist in a gradual accumulation of individual good works to one's credit, but rather in a systematic self-control which at every moment stands before the inexorable alternative, chosen or damned.

ACETICISM AND THE SPIRIT OF CAPITALISM

This worldly Protestant asceticism, as we may recapitulate up to this point, acted powerfully against the spontaneous enjoyment of possessions; it restricted consumption, especially of luxuries. On the other hand, it had the psychological effect of freeing the acquisition of goods from the inhibitions of traditionalistic ethics. It broke the bonds of the impulse of acquisition in that it not only legalized it, but (in the sense discussed) looked upon it as directly willed by God. The campaign against the temptations of the flesh, and the dependence on external things, was, as besides the Puritans the great Quaker apologist Barclay expressly says, not a struggle against the rational acquisition, but against the irrational use of wealth.

But this irrational use was exemplified in the outward forms of luxury which their code condemned as idolatry of the flesh,[60] however natural they had appeared to the feudal mind. On the other hand, they approved the rational and utilitarian uses of wealth which were willed by God for the needs of the individual and the community. They did not wish to impose mortification[61] on the man of wealth, but the use of his means for necessary and practical things. The idea of comfort characteristically limits the extent of ethically permissible expenditures. It is naturally no accident that the development of a manner of living consistent with that idea may be observed earliest and most clearly among the most consistent representatives of this whole attitude toward life. Over against the glitter and ostentation of feudal magnificence which, resting on an unsound economic basis, prefers a sordid elegance to a sober simplicity, they set the clean and solid comfort of the middle-class home as an ideal.[62]

On the side of the production of private wealth, asceticism condemned both dishonesty and impulsive avarice. What was condemned as covetousness, Mammonism, etc., was the pursuit of riches for their own sake. For wealth in itself was a temptation. But here asceticism was the power "which ever seeks the good but ever creates evil";[63] what was evil in its sense was possession and its temptations. For, in conformity with the Old Testament and in analogy to the ethical valuation of good works, asceticism looked upon the pursuit of wealth as an end in itself as highly reprehensible; but the attainment of it as a fruit of labour in a calling was a sign of God's blessing. And even more important: the religious valuation of restless, continuous, systematic work in a worldly calling, as the highest means to asceticism, and at the same time the surest and most evident proof of rebirth and genuine faith, must have been the most powerful conceivable lever for the expansion of that attitude toward life which we have here called the spirit of capitalism.[64]

When the limitation of consumption is combined with this release of acquisitive activity, the inevitable practical result is obvious: accumulation of capital through ascetic compulsion to save.[65] The restraints which were imposed upon the consumption of wealth naturally served to increase it by making possible the productive investment of capital. How strong this influence was is not, unfortunately, susceptible of exact statistical demonstration. In New England the connection is so evident that it did not escape the eye of so discerning a historian as Doyle.[66] But also in Holland, which was really only dominated by strict Calvinism for seven years, the greater simplicity of life in the more seriously religious circles, in combination with great wealth, led to an excessive propensity to accumulation.[67]

[...]

As far as the influence of the Puritan outlook extended, under all circumstances—and this is, of course, much more important than the mere encouragement of capital accumulation—it favoured the development of a rational bourgeois economic life; it was the most important, and above all the only consistent influence in the development of that life. It stood at the cradle of the modern economic man.

To be sure, these Puritanical ideals tended to give way under excessive pressure from the temptations of wealth, as the Puritans themselves knew very well. With great regularity we find the most genuine adherents of Puritanism among the classes which were rising from a lowly status,[68] the small bourgeois and farmers, while the *beati possidentes*, even among Quakers, are often found tending to repudiate the old ideals.[69] It was the same fate which again and again befell the predecessor of this worldly asceticism, the monastic asceticism of the Middle Ages. In the latter case, when rational economic activity had worked out its full effects by strict regulation of conduct and limitation of consumption, the wealth accumulated either succumbed directly to the nobility, as in the time before the Reformation, or monastic discipline threatened to break down, and one of the numerous reformations became necessary.

In fact the whole history of monasticism is in a certain sense the history of a continual struggle with the problem of the secularizing influence of wealth. The same is true on a grand scale of the worldly asceticism of Puritanism. The great revival of Methodism, which preceded the expansion of English industry toward the end of the eighteenth century, may well be compared with such a monastic reform. We may hence quote here a passage[70] from John Wesley himself which might well serve as a motto for everything which has been said above. For it shows that the leaders of these ascetic movements understood the seemingly paradoxical relationships which we have here analysed perfectly well, and in the same sense that we have given them.[71] He wrote:

I fear, wherever riches have increased, the essence of religion has decreased in the same proportion. Therefore I do not see how it is possible, in the nature of things, for any revival of true religion to continue long. For religion must necessarily produce both industry and frugality, and these cannot but produce riches. But as riches increase, so will pride, anger, and love of the world in all its branches. How then is it possible that Methodism, that is, a religion of the heart, though it flourishes now as a green bay tree, should continue in this state? For the Methodists in every place grow diligent and frugal; consequently they increase in goods. Hence they proportionately increase in pride, in anger, in the desire of the flesh, the desire of the eyes, and the pride of life. So, although the form of religion remains, the spirit is swiftly vanishing away. Is there no way to prevent this—this continual decay of pure religion? We ought to prevent people from being diligent and frugal; *we must exhort all Christians to gain all they can, and to save all they can; that is, in effect, to grow rich.*[72]

There follows the advice that those who gain all they can and save all they can should also give all they can, so that they will grow in grace and lay up a treasure in heaven. It is clear that Wesley here expresses, even in detail, just what we have been trying to point out.[73]

As Wesley here says, the full economic effect of those great religious movements, whose significance for economic development lay above all in their ascetic educative influence, generally came only after the peak of the purely religious enthusiasm was past. Then the intensity of the search for the Kingdom of God commenced gradually to pass over into sober economic virtue; the religious roots died out slowly, giving way to utilitarian worldliness. Then, as Dowden puts it, as in *Robinson Crusoe*, the isolated economic man who carries on missionary activities on the side[74] takes the place of the lonely spiritual search for the Kingdom of Heaven of Bunyan's pilgrim, hurrying through the marketplace of Vanity.

When later the principle "to make the most of both worlds" became dominant in the end, as Dowden has remarked, a good conscience simply became one of the means of enjoying a comfortable bourgeois life, as is well expressed in the German proverb about the soft pillow. What the great religious epoch of the seventeenth century bequeathed to its utilitarian successor was, however, above all an amazingly good, we may even say a pharisaically good, conscience in the acquisition of money, so long as it took place legally. Every trace of the *deplacere vix potest* has disappeared.[75]

A specifically bourgeois economic ethic had grown up. With the consciousness of standing in the fullness of God's grace and being visibly blessed by Him, the bourgeois business man, as long as he remained within the bounds of formal correctness, as long as his moral conduct was spotless and the use to which he put his wealth was not objectionable, could follow his pecuniary interests as he would and feel that he was fulfilling a duty in doing so. The power of religious asceticism provided him in addition with sober, conscientious, and unusually industrious workmen, who clung to their work as to a life purpose willed by God.[76]

Finally, it gave him the comforting assurance that the unequal distribution of the goods of this world was a special dispensation of Divine Providence, which in these differences, as in particular grace, pursued secret ends unknown to men.[77] Calvin himself had made the much-quoted statement that only when the people, i.e. the mass of labourers and craftsmen, were poor did they remain obedient to God.[78] In the Netherlands (Pieter de la Court and others), that had been secularized to the effect that the mass of men only labour when necessity forces them to do so. This formulation of a leading idea of capitalistic economy later entered into the current theories of the productivity of low wages. Here also, with the dying out of the religious root, the utilitarian interpretation crept in unnoticed, in the line of development which we have again and again observed.

[...]

Now naturally the whole ascetic literature of almost all denominations is saturated with the idea that faithful labour, even at low wages, on the part of those whom life offers no other opportunities, is highly pleasing to God. In this respect Protestant Asceticism added in itself nothing new. But it not only deepened this idea most powerfully, it also created the force which was alone decisive for its effectiveness: the psychological sanction of it through the conception of this labour as a calling, as the best, often in the last analysis the only means of attaining certainty of grace.[79] And on the other hand it legalized the exploitation of this specific willingness to work, in that it also interpreted the employer's business activity as a calling.[80] It is obvious how powerfully the exclusive search for the Kingdom of God only through the fulfilment of duty in the calling, and the strict asceticism which Church discipline naturally imposed, especially on the propertyless classes, was bound to affect the

productivity of labour in the capitalistic sense of the word. The treatment of labour as a calling became as characteristic of the modern worker as the corresponding attitude toward acquisition of the business man. It was a perception of this situation, new at his time, which caused so able an observer as Sir William Petty to attribute the economic power of Holland in the seventeenth century to the fact that the very numerous dissenters in that country (Calvinists and Baptists) "are for the most part thinking, sober men, and such as believe that Labour and Industry is their duty towards God".[81]

Calvinism opposed organic social organization in the fiscal-monopolistic form which it assumed in Anglicanism under the Stuarts, especially in the conceptions of Laud, this alliance of Church and State with the monopolists on the basis of a Christian-social ethical foundation. Its leaders were universally among the most passionate opponents of this type of politically privileged commercial, putting-out, and colonial capitalism. Over against it they placed the individualistic motives of rational legal acquisition by virtue of one's own ability and initiative. And, while the politically privileged monopoly industries in England all disappeared in short order, this attitude played a large and decisive part in the development of the industries which grew up in spite of and against the authority of the State.[82] The Puritans (Prynne, Parker) repudiated all connection with the large-scale capitalistic courtiers and projectors as an ethically suspicious class. On the other hand, they took pride in their own superior middle-class business morality, which formed the true reason for the persecutions to which they were subjected on the part of those circles. Defoe proposed to win the battle against dissent by boycotting bank credit and withdrawing deposits. The difference of the two types of capitalistic attitude went to a very large extent hand in hand with religious differences. The opponents of the Nonconformists, even in the eighteenth century, again and again ridiculed them for personifying the spirit of shopkeepers, and for having ruined the ideals of old England. Here also lay the difference of the Puritan economic ethic from the Jewish; and contemporaries (Prynne) knew well that the former and not the latter was the bourgeois capitalistic ethic.[83]

One of the fundamental elements of the spirit of modern capitalism, and not only of that but of all modern culture: rational conduct on the basis of the idea of the calling, was born—that is what this discussion has sought to demonstrate—from the spirit of Christian asceticism. One has only to re-read the passage from Franklin, quoted at the beginning of this essay, in order to see that the essential elements of the attitude which was there called the spirit of capitalism are the same as what we have just shown to be the content of the Puritan worldly asceticism,[84] only without the religious basis, which by Franklin's time had died away. The idea that modern labour has an ascetic character is of course not new. Limitation to specialized work, with a renunciation of the Faustian universality of man which it involves, is a condition of any valuable work in the modern world; hence deeds and renunciation inevitably condition each other to-day. This fundamentally ascetic trait of middle-class life, if it attempts to be a way of life at all, and not simply the absence of any, was what Goethe wanted to teach, at the height of his wisdom, in the *Wanderjahren*, and in the end which he gave to the life of his Faust.[85] For him the realization meant a renunciation, a departure from an age of full and beautiful humanity, which can no more be repeated in the course of our cultural development than can the flower of the Athenian culture of antiquity.

The Puritan wanted to work in a calling; we are forced to do so. For when asceticism was carried out of monastic cells into everyday life, and began to dominate worldly morality, it did its part in building the tremendous cosmos of the modern economic order. This order is now bound to the technical and economic conditions of machine production which to-day determine the lives of all the individuals who are born into this mechanism, not only those directly concerned with economic acquisition, with irresistible force. Perhaps it will so determine them until the last ton of fossilized coal is burnt. In Baxter's view the care for external goods should only lie on the shoulders of the "saint like a light cloak, which can be thrown aside at any moment".[86] But fate decreed that the cloak should become an iron cage.

Since asceticism undertook to remodel the world and to work out its ideals in the world, material goods have gained an increasing and finally an inexorable power over the lives of men as at no previous period in history. To-day the spirit of religious asceticism—whether finally, who knows?—has escaped from the cage. But victorious capitalism, since it rests on mechanical foundations, needs its support no longer. The rosy blush of its laughing heir, the Enlightenment, seems also to be irretrievably fading, and the idea of duty in one's calling prowls about in our lives like the ghost of dead religious beliefs. Where the fulfilment of the calling cannot directly be related to the highest spiritual and cultural values, or when, on the other hand, it need not be felt simply as economic compulsion, the individual generally abandons the attempt to justify it at all. In the field of its highest development, in the United States, the pursuit of wealth, stripped of its religious and ethical meaning, tends to become associated with purely mundane passions, which often actually give it the character of sport.[87]

No one knows who will live in this cage in the future, or whether at the end of this tremendous development entirely new prophets will arise, or there will be a great rebirth of old ideas and ideals, or, if neither, mechanized petrification, embellished with a sort of convulsive self-importance. For of the last stage of this cultural development, it might well be truly said: "Specialists without spirit, sensualists without heart; this nullity imagines that it has attained a level of civilization never before achieved."

But this brings us to the world of judgments of value and of faith, with which this purely historical discussion need not be burdened. The next task would be rather to show the significance of ascetic rationalism, which has only been touched in the foregoing sketch, for the content of practical social ethics, thus for the types of organization and the functions of social groups from the conventicle to the State. Then its relations to humanistic rationalism,[88] its ideals of life and cultural influence; further to the development of philosophical and scientific empiricism, to technical development and to spiritual ideals would have to be analysed. Then its historical development from the mediaeval beginnings of worldly asceticism to its dissolution into pure utilitarianism would have to be traced out through all the areas of ascetic religion. Only then could the quantitative cultural significance of ascetic Protestantism in its relation to the other plastic elements of modern culture be estimated.

Here we have only attempted to trace the fact and the direction of its influence to their motives in one, though a very important point. But it would also further be necessary to investigate how Protestant Asceticism was in turn influenced in its development and its character by the totality of social conditions, especially economic.[89] The modern man is in general, even with the best will, unable to give religious ideas a significance for culture and national character which they deserve. But it is, of course, not my aim to substitute for a one-sided materialistic an equally one-sided spiritualistic causal interpretation of culture and of history. Each is equally possible,[90] but each, if it does not serve as the preparation, but as the conclusion of an investigation, accomplishes equally little in the interest of historical truth.[91]

1. The exceptions are explained, not always, but frequently, by the fact that the religious leanings of the labouring force of an industry are naturally, in the first instance, determined by those of the locality in which the industry is situated, or from which its labour is drawn. This circumstance often alters the impression given at first glance by some statistics of religious adherence, for instance in the Rhine provinces. Furthermore, figures can naturally only be conclusive if individual specialized occupations are carefully distinguished in them. Otherwise very large employers may sometimes be grouped together with master craftsmen who work alone, under the category of "proprietors of enterprises". Above all, the fully developed capitalism of the present day, especially so far as the great unskilled lower strata of labour are concerned, has become independent of any influence which religion may have had in the past. I shall return to this point.

2. Compare, for instance, Schell, *Der Katholizismus als Prinzip des Fortschrittes* (Würzburg, 1897), p. 31, and v. Hertling, *Das Prinzip des Katholizismus und die Wissenschaft* (Freiburg, 1899), p. 58.

3. One of my pupils has gone through what is at this time the most complete statistical material we possess on this subject: the religious statistics of Baden. See Martin Offenbacher, "Konfession und soziale Schichtung", *Eine Studie uber die wirtschaftliche Lage der Katholiken und Protestanten in Baden* (Tübingen und Leipzig, 1901), Vol. IV, part v, of the *Volkswirtschaftliche Abhandlungen der badischen Hochschulen*. The facts and figures which are used for illustration below are all drawn from this study.

4. For instance, in 1895 in Baden there was taxable capital available for the tax on returns from capital:

    > Per 1,000 Protestants .... 954,000 marks
    > Per 1,000 Catholics .... 589,000 marks

    It is true that the Jews, with over four millions per 1,000, were far ahead of the rest. (For details see Offenbacher, *op. cit.*, p. 21.)

5. On this point compare the whole discussion in Offenbacher's study.

6. On this point also Offenbacher brings forward more detailed evidence for Baden in his first two chapters.

7. The population of Baden was composed in 1895 as follows: Protestants, 37.0 per cent; Catholics, 61.3 per cent; Jewish, 1.5 per cent. The students of schools beyond the compulsory public school stage were, however, divided as follows (Offenbacher, p. 16):

	PROTESTANT	CATHOLIC	JEWS
	Per Cent	Per Cent	Per Cent
Gymnasien	43	46	9.5
Realgymnasien	69	31	9
Oberrealschulen	52	41	7
Realschulen	49	40	11
Höhere Bürgerschulen	51	37	12
Average	48	42	10

(In the *Gymnasium* the main emphasis is on the classics. In the *Realgymnasium* Greek is dropped and Latin reduced in favour of modern languages, mathematics and science. The *Realschule* and *Oberrealschule* are similar to the latter except that Latin is dropped entirely in favour of modern languages. See G. E. Bolton, *The Secondary School System in Germany*, New York, 1900.—Translator's Note.)

The same thing may be observed in Prussia, Bavaria, Würtemberg, Alsace-Lorraine, and Hungary (see figures in Offenbacher, pp. 16 ff.).

8. See the figures in the preceding note, which show that the Catholic attendance at secondary schools, which is regularly less than the Catholic share of the total population by a third, only exceeds this by a few per cent in the case of the grammar schools (mainly in preparation for theological studies). With reference to the subsequent discussion it may further be noted as characteristic that in Hungary those affiliated with the Reformed Church exceed even the average Protestant record of attendance at secondary schools. (See Offenbacher, p. 19, note.)

9. For the proofs see Offenbacher, p. 54, and the tables at the end of his study.

10. Especially well illustrated by passages in the works of Sir William Petty, to be referred to later.

11. Petty's reference to the case of Ireland is very simply explained by the fact that the Protestants were only involved in the capacity of absentee landlords. If he had meant to maintain more he would have been wrong, as the situation of the Scotch-Irish shows. The typical relationship between Protestantism and capitalism existed in Ireland as well as elsewhere. (On the Scotch-Irish see C. A. Hanna, *The Scotch-Irish*, two vols., Putnam, New York.)

12. This is not of course to deny that the latter facts have exceedingly important consequences. As I shall show later the fact that many protestant sects were small and hence homogeneous minorities, as were all the strict Calvinists outside of Geneva and New England, even where they were in possession of political power, was of fundamental significance for the development of their whole character, including their manner of participation in economic life. The migration of exiles of all the religions of the earth, Indian, Arabian, Chinese, Syrian, Phoenician Greek, Lombard, to other countries as bearers of the commercial lore of highly developed areas, has been of universal occurrence and has nothing to do with our problem. Brentano, in the essay to which I shall often refer, *Die Anfange des modern Kapitalismus*, calls to witness his own family. But bankers of foreign extraction have existed at all times and in all countries as the representatives of commercial experience and connections. They are not peculiar to modern capitalism, and were looked upon with ethical mistrust by the Protestants (see below). The case of the Protestant families, such as the Muralts, Pestalozzi, etc., who migrated to Zurich from Locarno, was different. They very soon became identified with a specifically modern (industrial) type of capitalistic development.

13. These passages represent a very brief summary of some aspects of Weber's methodological views. At about the same time that he wrote this essay he was engaged in a thorough criticism and revaluation of the methods of the Social Sciences, the result of which was a point of view in many ways different from the prevailing one, especially outside of Germany. In order thoroughly to understand the significance of this essay in its wider bearings on Weber's sociological work as a whole it is necessary to know what his methodological aims were. Most of his writings on this subject have been assembled since his death (in 1920) in the volume *Gesammelte Aufsätze zur Wissenschaftslehre*. A shorter exposition of the main position is contained in the opening chapters of *Wirtschaft und Gesellschaft, Grundriss der Sozialökonomik*, III.—Translator's Note.

14. The final passage is from *Necessary Hints to Those That would Be Rich* (written 1736, Works, Sparks edition, II, p. 80), the rest from *Advice to a Young Tradesman* (written 1748, Sparks edition, II, pp. 87 ff.). The italics in the text are Franklin's.

15. *Der Amerikamüde* (Frankfurt, 1835), well known to be an imaginative paraphrase of Lenau's impressions of America. As a work of art the book would to-day be somewhat difficult to enjoy, but it is incomparable as a document of the (now long since blurred-over) differences between the German and the American outlook, one may even say of the type of spiritual life which, in spite of everything, has remained common to all Germans, Catholic and Protestant alike, since the German mysticism of the Middle Ages, as against the Puritan capitalistic valuation of action.

16. Sombart has used this quotation as a motto for his section dealing with the genesis of capitalism (*Der moderne Kapitalismus*, first edition, I, p. 193. See also p. 390).

17. Which quite obviously does not mean either that Jacob Fugger was a morally indifferent or an irreligious man, or that Benjamin Franklin's ethic is completely covered by the above quotations. It scarcely required Brentano's quotations (*Die Anfänge des modernen Kapitalismus*, pp. 150 ff.) to protect this well-known philanthropist from the misunderstanding which Brentano seems to attribute to me. The problem is just the reverse: how could such a philanthropist come to write these particular sentences (the especially characteristic form of which Brentano has neglected to reproduce) in the manner of a moralist?

18. This is the basis of our difference from Sombart in stating the problem. Its very considerable practical significance will become clear later. In anticipation, however, let it be remarked that Sombart has by no means neglected this ethical aspect of the capitalistic entrepreneur. But in his view of the problem it appears as a result of capitalism, whereas for our purposes we must assume the opposite as an hypothesis. A final position can only be taken up at the end of the investigation. For Sombart's view see *op. cit.*, pp. 357, 380, etc. His reasoning here connects with the brilliant analysis given in Simmel's *Philosophie des Geldes* (final chapter). Of the polemics which he has brought forward against me in his *Bourgeois* I shall come to speak later. At this point any thorough discussion must be postponed.

19. "I grew convinced that truth, sincerity, and integrity in dealings between man and man were of the utmost importance to the felicity of life; and I formed written resolutions, which still remain in my journal book to practise them ever while I lived. Revelation had indeed no weight with me as such; but I entertained an opinion that, though certain actions might not be bad because they were forbidden by it, or good because it commanded them, yet probably these actions might be forbidden because they were bad for us, or commanded because they were beneficial to us in their own nature, all the circumstances of things considered." *Autobiography* (ed. F. W. Pine, Henry Holt, New York, 1916), p. 112.

20. "I therefore put myself as much as I could out of sight and started it"—that is the project of a library which he had initiated—"as a scheme of a *number of friends*, who had requested me to go about and propose it to such as they thought lovers of reading. In this way my affair went on smoothly, and I ever after practised it on such occasions; and from my frequent successes, can heartily recommend it. The present little sacrifice of your vanity will afterwards be amply repaid. If it remains awhile uncertain to whom the merit belongs, someone more vain than yourself will be encouraged to claim it, and then even envy will be disposed to do you justice by plucking those assumed feathers and restoring them to their right owner." *Autobiography*, p. 140.

21. Brentano (*op. cit.*, pp. 125, 127, note 1) takes this remark as an occasion to criticize the later discussion of "that rationalization and discipline" to which worldly asceticism* has subjected men. That, he says, is a rationalization toward an irrational mode of life. He is, in fact, quite correct. A thing is never irrational in itself, but only from a particular rational point of view. For the unbeliever every religious way of life is irrational, for the hedonist every ascetic standard, no matter whether, measured with respect to its particular basic values, that opposing asceticism is a rationalization. If this essay makes any contribution at all, may it be to bring out the complexity of the only superficially simple concept of the rational.

    This seemingly paradoxical term has been the best translation I could find for Weber's *innerweltliche Askese*, which means asceticism practised within the world as contrasted with *ausserweltliche Askese*, which withdraws from the world (for instance into a monastery). Their precise meaning will appear in the course of Weber's discussion. It is none of the prime points of his essay that asceticism does not need to flee from the world to be ascetic. I shall consistently employ the terms worldly and otherworldly to denote the contrast between the two kinds of asceticism.—Translator's Note.

22. In reply to Brentano's (*Die Anfänge des modernen Kapitalismus*, pp. 150 ff.) long and somewhat

inaccurate apologia for Franklin, whose ethical qualities I am supposed to have misunderstood, I refer only to this statement, which should, in my opinion, have been sufficient to make that apologia superfluous.

23. The two terms profession and calling I have used in translation of the German *Beruf*, whichever seemed best to fit the particular context. Vocation does not carry the ethical connotation in which Weber is interested. It is especially to be remembered that profession in this sense is not contrasted with business, but it refers to a particular attitude toward one's occupation, no matter what that occupation may be. This should become abundantly clear from the whole of Weber's argument.—Translator's Note.

24. I make use of this opportunity to insert a few anti-critical remarks in advance of the main argument. Sombart (*Bourgeois*) makes the untenable statement that this ethic of Franklin is a word-for-word repetition of some writings of that great and versatile genius of the Renaissance, Leon Battista Alberti, who besides theoretical treatises on Mathematics, Sculpture, Painting, Architecture, and Love (he was personally a woman-hater), wrote a work in four books on household management (*Della Famiglia*). (Unfortunately, I have not at the time of writing been able to procure the edition of Mancini, but only the older one of Bonucci.) The passage from Franklin is printed above word for word. Where then are corresponding passages to be found in Alberti's work, especially the maxim "time is money", which stands at the head, and the exhortations which follow it? The only passage which, so far as I know, bears the slightest resemblance to it is found towards the end of the first book of *Della Famiglia* (ed. Bonucci, II, p. 353), where Alberti speaks in very general terms of money as the *nervus rerum* of the household, which must hence be handled with special care, just as Cato spoke in *De Re Rustica*. To treat Alberti, who was very proud of his descent from one of the most distinguished cavalier families of Florence (*Nobilissimi Cavalieri, op. cit.*, pp. 213, 228, 247, etc.), as a man of mongrel blood who was filled with envy for the noble families because his illegitimate birth, which was not in the least socially disqualifying, excluded him as a bourgeois from association with the nobility, is quite incorrect. It is true that the recommendation of large enterprises as alone worthy of a *nobile è onesta famiglia* and a *libero è nobile animo*, and as costing less labour is characteristic of Alberti

(p. 209; compare *Del governo della Famiglia*, IV, p. 55, as well as p. 116 in the edition for the Pandolfini). Hence the best thing is a putting-out business for wool and silk. Also an ordered and painstaking regulation of his household, i.e. the limiting of expenditure to income. This is the *santa masserizia*, which is thus primarily a principle of maintenance, a given standard of life, and not of acquisition (as no one should have understood better than Sombart). Similarly, in the discussion of the nature of money, his concern is with the management of consumption funds (money or *possessioni*), not with that of capital; all that is clear from the expression of it which is put into the mouth of Gianozzo. He recommends, as protection against the uncertainty of *fortuna*, early habituation to continuous activity, which is also (pp. 73–4) alone healthy in the long run, *in cose magnifiche è ample*, and avoidance of laziness, which always endangers the maintenance of one's position in the world. Hence a careful study of a suitable trade in case of a change of fortune, but every *opera mercenaria* is unsuitable (*op. cit.*, I, p. 209). His idea of *tranquillita dell' animo* and his strong tendency toward the Epicurean λάθε βιώζ (*vivere a sè stesso*, p. 262); especially his dislike of any office (p. 258) as a source of unrest, of making enemies, and of becoming involved in dishonourable dealings; the ideal of life in a country villa; his nourishment of vanity through the thought of his ancestors; and his treatment of the honour of the family (which on that account should keep its fortune together in the Florentine manner and not divide it up) as a decisive standard and ideal—all these things would in the eyes of every Puritan have been sinful idolatry of the flesh, and in those of Benjamin Franklin the expression of incomprehensible aristocratic nonsense. Note, further, the very high opinion of literary things (for the *industria* is applied principally to literary and scientific work), which is really most worthy of a man's efforts. And the expression of the *masserizia*, in the sense of "rational conduct of the household" as the means of living independently of others and avoiding destitution, is in general put only in the mouth of the illiterate Gianozzo as of equal value. Thus the origin of this concept, which comes (see below) from monastic ethics, is traced back to an old priest (p. 249).

Now compare all this with the ethic and manner of life of Benjamin Franklin, and especially of his Puritan ancestors; the works of the Renaissance *littérateur* addressing himself to the humanistic aristocracy, with Franklin's works addressed to the masses of the lower middle class (he especially mentions clerks) and with the tracts and sermons of the Puritans, in order to comprehend the depth of the difference. The economic rationalism of Alberti, everywhere supported by references to ancient authors, is most clearly related to the treatment of economic problems in the works of Xenophon (whom he did not know), of Cato, Varro, and Columella (all of whom he quotes), except that especially in Cato and Varro, *acquisition* as such stands in the foreground in a different way from that to be found in Alberti. Furthermore, the very occasional comments of Alberti on the use of the *fattori*, their division of labour and discipline, on the unreliability of the peasants, etc., really sound as if Cato's homely wisdom were taken from the field of the ancient slave-using household and applied to that of free labour in domestic industry and the metayer system. When Sombart (whose reference to the Stoic ethic is quite misleading) sees economic rationalism as "developed to its farthest conclusions" as early as Cato, he is, with a correct interpretation, not entirely wrong. It is possible to unite the *diligens pater familias* of the Romans with the ideal of the *massajo* of Alberti under the same category. It is above all characteristic for Cato that a landed estate is valued and judged as an object for the investment of consumption funds. The concept of *industria*, on the other hand, is differently coloured on account of Christian influence. And there is just the difference. In the conception of *industria*, which comes from monastic asceticism and which was developed by monastic writers, lies the seed of an *ethos* which was fully developed later in the Protestant worldly asceticism. Hence, as we shall often point out, the relationship of the two, which, however, is less close to the official Church doctrine of St. Thomas than to the Florentine and Siennese mendicant-moralists. In Cato and also in Alberti's own writings this *ethos* is lacking; for both it is a matter of worldly wisdom, not of ethic. In Franklin there is also a utilitarian strain. But the ethical quality of the sermon to young business men is impossible to mistake, and that is the characteristic thing. A lack of care in the handling of money means to him that one so to speak murders capital embryos, and hence it is an ethical defect.

An inner relationship of the two (Alberti and Franklin) exists in fact only in so far as Alberti, whom Sombart calls pious, but who actually, although he took the sacraments and held a Roman benefice, like so many humanists, did not himself (except for two quite colourless passages) in any way make use of religious motives as a justification of the manner of life he recommended, had not yet, Franklin on the other hand no longer, related his recommendation of economy to religious conceptions. Utilitarianism, in Alberti's preference for wool and silk manufacture, also the mercantilist social utilitarianism "that many people should be given employment" (see Alberti, *op. cit.*, p. 292), is in this field at least formally the sole justification for the one as for the other. Alberti's discussions of this subject form an excellent example of the sort of economic rationalism which really existed as a reflection of economic conditions, in the work of authors interested purely in "the thing for its own sake" everywhere and at all times; in the Chinese classicism and in Greece and Rome no less than in the Renaissance and the age of the Enlightenment. There is no doubt that just as in ancient times with Cato, Varro, and Columella, also here with Alberti and others of the same type, especially in the doctrine of *industria*, a sort of economic rationality is highly developed. But how can anyone believe that such a literary *theory* could develop into a revolutionary force at all comparable to the way in which a religious belief was able to set the sanctions of salvation and damnation on the fulfillment of a particular (in this case methodically rationalized) manner of life? What, as compared with it, a really religiously oriented rationalization of conduct looks like, may be seen, outside of the Puritans of all denominations, in the cases of the Jains, the Jews, certain ascetic sects of the Middle Ages, the Bohemian Brothers (an offshoot of the Hussite movement), the Skoptsi and Stundists in Russia, and numerous monastic orders, however much all these may differ from each other.

The essential point of the difference is (to anticipate) that an ethic based on religion places certain psychological sanctions (not of an economic character) on the maintenance of the attitude prescribed by it, sanctions which, so long as the religious belief remains alive, are highly effective, and which mere worldly wisdom like that of Alberti does not have at its disposal. Only in so far as these sanctions work, and, above all, in the direction in which they work, which is often very different from the doctrine of the theologians, does such an ethic gain an independent influence on the conduct of life and thus on the economic order. This is, to speak frankly, the point of this whole essay, which I had not expected to find so completely overlooked.

Later on I shall come to speak of the theological moralists of the late Middle Ages, who were relatively friendly to capital (especially Anthony of Florence and Bernhard of Siena), and whom Sombart has also seriously misinterpreted. In any case Alberti did not belong to that group. Only the concept of *industria* did he take from monastic lines of thought, no matter through what intermediate links. Alberti, Pandolfini, and their kind are representatives of that attitude which, in spite of all its outward obedience, was inwardly already emancipated from the tradition of the Church. With all its resemblance to the current Christian ethic, it was to a large extent of the antique pagan character, which Brentano thinks I have ignored in its significance for the development of modern economic thought (and also modern economic policy). That I do not deal with its influence here is quite true. It would be out of place in a study of the Protestant ethic and the spirit of capitalism. But, as will appear in a different connection, far from denying its significance, I have been and am for good reasons of the opinion that its sphere and direction of influence were entirely different from those of the Protestant ethic (of which the spiritual ancestry, of no small practical importance, lies in the sects and in the ethics of Wyclif and Hus). It was not the mode of life of the rising bourgeoisie which was influenced by this other attitude, but the policy of statesmen and princes; and these two partly, but by no means always, convergent lines of development should for purposes of analysis be kept perfectly distinct. So far as Franklin is concerned, his tracts of advice to business men, at present used for school reading in America, belong in fact to a category of works which have influenced practical life, far more than Alberti's large book, which hardly became known outside of learned circles. But I have expressly denoted him as a man who stood beyond the direct influence of the Puritan view of life, which had paled considerably in the meantime, just as the whole English enlightenment, the relations of which to Puritanism have often been set forth.

25. Unfortunately Brentano (*op. cit.*) has thrown every kind of struggle for gain, whether peaceful or warlike, into one pot, and has then set up as the specific criterion of capitalistic (as contrasted, for instance, with feudal) profit-seeking, its acquisitiveness of *money* (instead of land). Any further differentiation, which alone could lead to a clear conception, he has not only refused to make, but has made against the concept of the spirit of (modern) capitalism which we have formed for our purposes, the (to me) incomprehensible objection that it already includes in its assumptions what is supposed to be proved.

26. Of course we cannot here enter into the question of where these limits lie, nor can we evaluate the familiar theory of the relation between high wages and the high productivity of labour which was first suggested by Brassey, formulated and maintained theoretically by Brentano, and both historically and theoretically by Schulze-Gaevernitz. The discussion was again opened by Hasbach's penetrating studies (*Schmollers Jahrbuch*, 1903, pp. 385–91 and 417 ff.), and is not yet finally settled. For us it is here sufficient to assent to the fact which is not, and cannot be, doubted by anyone, that low wages and high profits, low wages and favourable opportunities for industrial development, are at least not simply identical, that generally speaking training for capitalistic culture, and with it the possibility of capitalism as an economic system, are not brought about simply through mechanical financial operations. All examples are purely illustrative.

27. It must be remembered that this was written twenty-five years ago, when the above statement was by no means the commonplace that it is now, even among economists, to say nothing of business men.— Translator's Note.

28. The establishment even of capitalistic industries has hence often not been possible without large migratory movements from areas of older culture. However correct Sombart's remarks on the difference between the personal skill and trade secrets of the handicraftsman and the scientific, objective modern technique may be, at the time of the rise of capitalism the difference hardly existed. In fact the, so to speak, ethical qualities of the capitalistic workman (and to a certain extent also of the entrepreneur) often had a higher scarcity value than the skill of the craftsman, crystallized in traditions hundreds of years old. And even present-day industry is not yet by any means entirely independent in its choice of location of such qualities of the population, acquired by long-standing tradition and education in intensive labour.

It is congenial to the scientific prejudices of to-day, when such a dependence is observed to ascribe it to congenital racial qualities rather than to tradition and education, in my opinion with very doubtful validity.

29. How a compromise with the prohibition of usury was achieved is shown, for example, in Book 1, chapter 65, of the statutes of the *Arte di Calimala* (at present I have only the Italian edition in Emiliani-Guidici, *Stor. dei Com. Ital.*, III, p. 246), "Procurino i consoli con quelli frate, che parra loro, che perdono si faccia e come fare si possa il meglio per I'amore di ciascuno, del dono, merito o guiderdono, ovvero interesse per I'anno presente e secondo che altra volta fatto fue." It is thus a way for the guild to secure exemption for its members on account of their official positions, without defiance of authority. The suggestions immediately following, as well as the immediately preceding idea to book all interest and profits as gifts, are very characteristic of the amoral attitude towards profits on capital. To the present stock exchange black list against brokers who hold back the difference between top price and actual selling price, often corresponded the outcry against those who pleaded before the ecclesiastical court with the *exceptio usurariæ pravitatis*.

30. Compare on the following: Scheibe, *Calvins Prädestinationslehre* (Halle, 1897). On Calvinistic theology in general, Heppe, *Dogmatik des evangelisch-reformierten Kirche* (Elberfeld, 1861).

31. *Corpus Reformatorum*, LXXVII, pp. 186 ff.

32. The preceding exposition of the Calvinistic doctrine can be found in much the same form as here given, for instance in Hoornbeek's *Theologia practica* (Utrecht, 1663), L. II, c. 1; *de predestinatione*, the section stands characteristically directly under the heading *De Deo*. The Biblical foundation for it is principally the first chapter of the Epistle to the Ephesians. It is unnecessary for us here to analyse the various inconsistent attempts to combine with the predestination and providence of God the responsibility and free will of the individual. They began as early as in Augustine's first attempt to develop the doctrine.

33. "The deepest community (with God) is found not in institutions or corporations or churches, but in the secrets of a solitary heart", as Dowden puts the essential point in his fine book *Puritan and Anglican* (p. 234). This deep spiritual loneliness of the individual applied as well to the Jansenists of Port Royal, who were also predestinationists.

34. "Contra qui huiusmodi cœtum [namely a Church which maintains a pure doctrine, sacraments, and Church discipline] contemnunt … salutis suae certi esse non possunt; et qui in illo contemtu perseverat electus non est." Olevian, *De subst. Fœd.*, p. 222.

35. "It is said that God sent His Son to save the human race, but that was not His purpose. He only wished to help a few out of their degradation—and I say unto you that God dies only for the elect" (sermon held in 1609 at Broek, near Rogge, Wtenbogaert, II, p. 9. Compare Nuyens, *op. cit.*, II, p. 232). The explanation of the role of Christ is also confused in *Hanserd Knolly's Confession*. It is everywhere assumed that God did not need his instrumentality.

36. Hundeshagen (*Beitr. z. Kirchenverfassungsgesch. u. Kirchenpolitik*, 1864, I, p. 37) takes the view, since often repeated, that predestination was a dogma of the theologians, not a popular doctrine. But that is only true if the people is identified with the mass of the uneducated lower classes. Even then it has only limited validity. Köhler (*op. cit.*) found that in the forties of the nineteenth century just those masses (meaning the *petite bourgeoisie* of Holland) were thoroughly imbued with predestination. Anyone who denied the double decree was to them a heretic and a condemned soul. He himself was asked about the time of his rebirth (in the sense of predestination). Da Costa and the separation of de Kock were greatly influenced by it. Not only Cromwell, in whose case Zeller (*Das Theologische System Zwinglis*, p. 17) has already shown the effects of the dogma most effectively, but also his army knew very well what it was about. Moreover, the canons of the synods of Dordrecht and Westminster were national questions of the first importance. Cromwell's tryers and ejectors admitted only believers in predestination, and Baxter (*Life*, I, p. 72), although he was otherwise its opponent, considers its effect on the quality of the clergy to be important. That the Reformed Pietists, the members of the English and Dutch conventicles, should not have understood the doctrine is quite impossible. It was precisely what drove them together to seek the *certitudo salutis*.

What significance the doctrine of predestination does or does not have when it remains a dogma of the theologians is shown by perfectly orthodox Catholicism, to which it was by no means strange as an esoteric doctrine under various forms. What is important is that the idea of the individual's obligation to consider himself of the elect and prove it to himself was always denied. Compare for the

Catholic doctrine, for instance, A. Van Wyck, Tract. *de prædestinatione* (Cologne, 1708). To what extent Pascal's doctrine of predestination was correct, we cannot inquire here.

Hundeshagen, who dislikes the doctrine, evidently gets his impressions primarily from German sources. His antipathy is based on the purely deductive opinion that it necessarily leads to moral fatalism and antinomianism. This opinion has already been refuted by Zeller, *op. cit.* That such a result was possible cannot, of course, be denied. Both Melanchthon and Wesley speak of it. But it is characteristic that in both cases it is combined with an emotional religion of faith. For them, lacking the rational idea of proof, this consequence was in fact not unnatural.

The same consequences appeared in Islam. But why? Because the Mohammedan idea was that of predetermination, not predestination, and was applied to fate in this world, not in the next. In consequence the most important thing, the proof of the believer in predestination, played no part in Islam. Thus only the fearlessness of the warrior (as in the case of moira) could result, but there were no consequences for rationalization of life; there was no religious sanction for them. See the (Heidelberg) theological dissertation of F. Ullrich, *Die Vorherbestimmungslehre im Islam u. Christenheit,* 1900. The modifications of the doctrine which came in practice, for instance Baxter, did not disturb it in essence so long as the idea that the election of God, and its proof, fell upon the concrete individual, was not shaken. Finally, and above all, all the great men of Puritanism (in the broadest sense) took their departure from this doctrine, whose terrible seriousness deeply influenced their youthful development. Milton like, in declining order it is true, Baxter, and, still later, the free-thinker Franklin. Their later emancipation from its strict interpretation is directly parallel to the development which the religious movement as a whole underwent in the same direction. And all the great religious revivals, at least in Holland, and most of those in England, took it up again.

37. As is true in such a striking way of the basic atmosphere of Bunyan's *Pilgrim's Progress*.

38. This question meant less to the later Lutheran, even apart from the doctrine of predestination, than to the Calvinist. Not because he was less interested in the salvation of his soul, but because, in the form which the Lutheran Church had taken, its character

as an institution for salvation (*Heilsanstalt*) came to the fore. The individual thus felt himself to be an object of its care and dependent on it. The problem was first raised within Lutheranism characteristically enough through the Pietist movement. The question of *certitudo salutis* itself has, however, for every non-sacramental religion of salvation, whether Buddhism, Jainism, or anything else, been absolutely fundamental; that must not be forgotten. It has been the origin of all psychological drives of a purely religious character.

39. Thus expressly in the letter to Bucer, *Corp. Ref.* 29, pp. 883 f. Compare with that again Scheibe, *op. cit.*, p. 30.

40. The *Westminster Confession* (XVIII, p. 2) also assures the elect of indubitable certainty of grace, although with all our activity we remain useless servants and the struggle against evil lasts one's whole life long. But even the chosen one often has to struggle long and hard to attain the *certitudo* which the consciousness of having done his duty gives him and of which a true believer will never entirely be deprived.

41. The orthodox Calvinistic doctrine referred to faith and the consciousness of community with God in the sacraments, and mentioned the "other fruits of the Spirit" only incidentally. See the passages in Heppe, *op. cit.*, p. 425. Calvin himself most emphatically denied that works were indications of favour before God, although he, like the Lutherans, considered them the fruits of belief (*Instit. Christ*, III, 2, 37, 38). The actual evolution to the proof of faith through works, which is characteristic of asceticism, is parallel to a gradual modification of the doctrines of Calvin. As with Luther, the true Church was first marked off primarily by purity of doctrine and sacraments, but later the *disciplina* came to be placed on an equal footing with the other two. This evolution may be followed in the passages given by Heppe, *op. cit.*, pp. 194–5, as well as in the manner in which Church members were acquired in the Netherlands by the end of the sixteenth century (express subjection by agreement to Church discipline as the principal prerequisite).

42. For example, Olevian, *De substantia fœderis gratuiti inter Deum et electos* (1585), p. 257; Heidegger, *Corpus Theologiæ*, XXIV, p. 87; and other passages in Heppe, *Dogmatik der ev. ref. Kirche* (1861), p. 425.

43. On this point see the remarks of Schneckenburger, *op. cit.*, p. 48.

44. Thus, for example, in Baxter the distinction between mortal and venial sin reappears in a truly Catholic

sense. The former is a sign of the lack of grace which can only be attained by the conversion of one's whole life. The latter is not incompatible with grace.

45. As held in many different shades by Baxter, Bailey, Sedgwick, Hoornbeek. Further see examples given by Schneckenburger, *op. cit.*, p. 262.

46. The conception of the state of grace as a sort of social estate (somewhat like that of the ascetics of the early Church) is very common. See for instance Schortinghuis, *Het innige Christendom* (1740 proscribed by the States-General)!

47. Thus, as we shall see later, in countless passages, especially the conclusion, of Baxter's *Christian Directory*. This recommendation of worldly activity as a means of overcoming one's own feeling of moral inferiority is reminiscent of Pascal's psychological interpretation of the impulse of acquisition and ascetic activity as means to deceive oneself about one's own moral worthlessness. For him the belief in predestination and the conviction of the original sinfulness of everything pertaining to the flesh resulted only in renunciation of the world and the recommendation of contemplation as the sole means of lightening the burden of sin and attaining certainty of salvation. Of the orthodox Catholic and the Jansenist versions of the idea of calling an acute analysis has been made by Dr. Paul Honigsheim in the dissertation cited above (part of a larger study, which it is hoped will be continued). The Jansenists lacked every trace of a connection between certainty of salvation and worldly activity. Their concept of calling has, even more strongly than the Lutheran or even the orthodox Catholic, the sense of acceptance of the situation in life in which one finds oneself, sanctioned not only, as in Catholicism by the social order, but also by the voice of one's own conscience (Honigsheim, *op. cit.*, pp. 139 ff.).

48. Of the significance of this for the material content of social ethics some hint has been given above. Here we are interested not in the content, but in the motives of moral action.

49. How this idea must have promoted the penetration of Puritanism with the Old Testament Hebrew is evident.

50. Thus the Savoy Declaration says of the members of the *ecclesia pura* that they are "saints by effectual calling, visibly manifested by their profession and walking".

51. "A Principle of Goodness", Charnock in the *Works of the Puritan Divines*, p. 175.

52. Conversion is, as Sedgwick puts it, an "exact copy of the decree of predestination". And whoever is chosen is also called to obedience and made capable of it, teaches Bailey. Only those whom God calls to His faith (which is expressed in their conduct) are true believers, not merely temporary believers, according to the (Baptist) Confession of Hanserd Knolly.

53. Compare, for instance, the conclusion to Baxter's *Christian Directory*.

54. Thus, for instance, Charnock, *Self-Examination*, p. 183, in refutation of the Catholic doctrine of *dubitatio*.

55. This argument recurs again and again in Hoornbeek, *Theologia practica*. For instance, I, p. 160; II, pp. 70, 72, 182.

56. For instance, the *Conf. Helvet*, 16, says "et improprie his [the works] *salus adtribuitur*".

57. With all the above compare Schneckenburger, pp. 80 ff.

58. Augustine is supposed to have said "si non es prædestinatus, fac ut prædestineris".

59. One is reminded of a saying of Goethe with essentially the same meaning: "How can a man know himself? Never by observation, but through action. Try to do your duty and you will know what is in you. And what is your duty? Your daily task."

60. This is, as must continually be emphasized, the final decisive religious motive (along with the purely ascetic desire to mortify the flesh). It is especially clear in the Quakers.

61. Baxter (*Saints' Everlasting Rest*, p. 12) repudiates this with precisely the same reasoning as the Jesuits: the body must have what it needs, otherwise one becomes a slave to it.

62. This ideal is clearly present, especially for Quakerism, in the first period of its development, as has already been shown in important points by Weingarten in his *Englische Revolution-skirchen*. Also Barclay's thorough discussion (*op. cit.*, pp. 519 ff., 533) shows it very clearly. To be avoided are: (1) Worldly vanity; thus all ostentation, frivolity, and use of things having no practical purpose, or which are valuable only for their scarcity (i.e. for vanity's sake). (2) Any unconscientious use of wealth, such as excessive expenditure for not very urgent needs above necessary provision for the real needs of life and for the future. The Quaker was, so to speak, a living law of marginal utility. "Moderate use of the creature" is definitely permissible, but in particular

one might pay attention to the quality and durability of materials so long as it did not lead to vanity. On all this compare *Morgenblatt für gebildete Leser*, 1846, pp. 216 ff. Especially on comfort and solidity among the Quakers, compare Schneckenburger, *Vorlesungen*, pp. 96 f.

63. Adapted by Weber from Faust, Act I. Goethe there depicts Mephistopheles as "Die Kraft, die stets das Böse will, und stets das Gute schafft".—Translator's Note.

64. It has already been remarked that we cannot here enter into the question of the class relations of these religious movements (see the essays on the *Wirtschaftsethik der Weltreligionen*). In order to see, however, that for example Baxter, of whom we make so much use in this study, did not see things solely as a bourgeois of his time, it will suffice to recall that even for him in the order of the religious value of callings, after the learned professions comes the husband-man, and only then mariners, clothiers, booksellers, tailors, etc. Also, under mariners (characteristically enough) he probably thinks at least as often of fishermen as of shipowners. In this regard several things in the *Talmud* are in a different class. Compare, for instance, in Wünsche, *Babyl Talmud*, II, pp. 20, 21, the sayings of Rabbi Eleasar, which though not unchallenged, all contend in effect that business is better than agriculture. In between see II, 2, p. 68, on the wise investment of capital: one-third in land, one-third in merchandise, and one-third in cash.

For those to whom no causal explanation is adequate without an economic (or materialistic as it is unfortunately still called) interpretation, it may be remarked that I consider the influence of economic development on the fate of religious ideas to be very important and shall later attempt to show how in our case the process of mutual adaptation of the two took place. On the other hand, those religious ideas themselves simply cannot be deduced from economic circumstances. They are in themselves, that is beyond doubt, the most powerful plastic elements of national character, and contain a law of development and a compelling force entirely their own. Moreover, the most important differences, so far as non-religious factors play a part, are, as with Lutheranism and Calvinism, the result of political circumstances, not economic.

65. That is what Eduard Bernstein means to express when he says, in the essay referred to above (pp. 625, 681), "Asceticism is a bourgeois virtue." His discussion is the first which has suggested these important relationships. But the connection is a much wider one than he suspected. For not only the accumulation of capital, but the ascetic rationalization of the whole of economic life was involved.

For the American Colonies, the difference between the Puritan North, where, on account of the ascetic compulsion to save, capital in search of investment was always available, from the conditions in the South has already been clearly brought out by Doyle.

66. Doyle, *The English in America*, II, chap. i. The existence of ironworks (1643), weaving for the market (1659), and also the high development of the handicrafts in New England in the first generation after the foundation of the colonies are, from a purely economic view-point, astounding. They are in striking contrast to the conditions in the South, as well as the non-Calvinistic Rhode Island with its complete freedom of conscience. There, in spite of the excellent harbour, the report of the Governor and Council of 1686 said: "The great obstruction concerning trade is the want of merchants and men of considerable estates amongst us" (Arnold, *History of the State of Rhode Island*, p. 490). It can in fact hardly be doubted that the compulsion continually to reinvest savings, which the Puritan curtailment of consumption exercised, played a part. In addition there was the part of Church discipline which cannot be discussed here.

67. That, however, these circles rapidly diminished in the Netherlands is shown by Busken-Huet's discussion (*op. cit.*, II, chaps. iii and iv). Nevertheless, Groen van Prinsterer says (*Handb. der Gesch. van het Vaderland*, third edition, par. 303, note, p. 254), "De Nederlanders verkoopen veel en verbruiken weinig", even of the time after the Peace of Westphalia.

68. This is noted by Petty (*Pol. Arith.*), and all the contemporary sources without exception speak in particular of the Puritan sectarians, Baptists, Quakers, Mennonites, etc., as belonging partly to a propertyless class, partly to one of small capitalists, and contrast them both with the great merchant aristocracy and the financial adventurers. But it was from just this small capitalist class, and not from the great financial magnates, monopolists, Government contractors, great lenders to the King, colonial entrepreneurs, promoters, etc., that there originated what was characteristic of Occidental capitalism: the middle-class organization of industrial labour on

the basis of private property (see Unwin, *Industrial Organization in the Sixteenth and Seventeenth Centuries*, London, 1914, pp. 196 ff.). To see that this difference was fully known even to contemporaries, compare Parker's *Discourse Concerning Puritans* of 1641, where the contrast to promoters and courtiers is also emphasized.

69.   On the way in which this was expressed in the politics of Pennsylvania in the eighteenth century, especially during the War of Independence, see Sharpless, *A Quaker Experiment in Government*, Philadelphia, 1902.

70.   Quoted in Southey, *Life of Wesley*, chap. xxix (second American edition, II, p. 308). For the reference, which I did not know, I am indebted to a letter from Professor Ashley (1913). Ernst Troeltsch, to whom I communicated it for the purpose, has already made use of it.

71.   The reading of this passage may be recommended to all those who consider themselves to-day better informed on these matters than the leaders and contemporaries of the movements themselves. As we see, they knew very well what they were doing and what dangers they faced. It is really inexcusable to contest so lightly, as some of my critics have done, facts which are quite beyond dispute, and have hitherto never been disputed by anyone. All I have done is to investigate their underlying motives somewhat more carefully. No one in the seventeenth century doubted the existence of these relationships (compare Manley, *Usury of 6 per Cent. Examined*, 1669, p. 137). Besides the modern writers already noted, poets like Heine and Keats, as well as historians like Macaulay, Cunningham, Rogers, or an essayist such as Matthew Arnold, have assumed them as obvious. From the most recent literature see Ashley, *Birmingham Industry and Commerce* (1913). He has also expressed his complete agreement with me in correspondence. On the whole problem now compare the study by H. Levy referred to above, note 91.

72.   Weber's italics.

73.   That exactly the same things were obvious to the Puritans of the classical era cannot perhaps be more clearly shown than by the fact that in Bunyan Mr. Money-Love argues that one may become religious in order to get rich, for instance to attract customers. For why one has become religious makes no difference (see p. 114, Tauchnitz edition).

74.   Defoe was a zealous Nonconformist.

75.   Spener also (*Theologische Bedenken*, pp. 426, 429, 432 ff.), although he holds that the merchant's calling is full of temptations and pitfalls, nevertheless declares in answer to a question: "I am glad to see, so far as trade is concerned, that my dear friend knows no scruples, but takes it as an art of life, which it is, in which much good may be done for the human race, and God's will may be carried out through love." This is more fully justified in other passages by mercantilist arguments. Spener, at times in a purely Lutheran strain, designates the desire to become rich as the main pitfall, following 1 Tim. vi, viii, and ix, and referring to Jesus Sirach (see above), and hence rigidly to be condemned. But, on the other hand, he takes some of it back by referring to the prosperous sectarians who yet live righteously (see above, note 39). As the result of industrious work wealth is not objectionable to him either. But on account of the Lutheran influence his standpoint is less consistent than that of Baxter.

76.   Baxter, *op. cit.*, II, p. 16, warns against the employment of "heavy, flegmatic, sluggish, fleshly, slothful persons" as servants, and recommends preference for godly servants, not only because ungodly servants would be mere eye-servants, but above all because "a truly godly servant will do all your service in obedience to God, as if God Himself had bid him do it". Others, on the other hand, are inclined "to make no great matter of conscience of it". However, the criterion of saintliness of the workman is not for him the external confession of faith, but the "conscience to do their duty". It appears here that the interests of God and of the employers are curiously harmonious. Spener also (*Theologische Bedenken*, III, p. 272), who otherwise strongly urges taking time to think of God, assumes it to be obvious that workers must be satisfied with the extreme minimum of leisure time (even on Sundays). English writers have rightly called the Protestant immigrants the pioneers of skilled labour. See also proofs in H. Levy, *Die Grundlagen des ökonomischen Liberalimus in der Geschichte der englischen Volkswirtschaft*, p. 53.

77.   The analogy between the unjust (according to human standards) predestination of only a few and the equally unjust, but equally divinely ordained, distribution of wealth, was too obvious to be escaped. See for example Hoornbeek, *op. cit.*, I, p. 153. Furthermore, as for Baxter, *op. cit.*, I, p. 380, poverty is very often a symptom of sinful slothfulness.

78.   Thomas Adams (*Works of the Puritan Divines*, p. 158) thinks that God probably allows so many people to remain poor because He knows that they would not

be able to withstand the temptations that go with wealth. For wealth all too often draws men away from religion.

79.	Baxter's activity in Kidderminster, a community absolutely debauched when he arrived, which was almost unique in the history of the ministry for its success, is at the same time a typical example of how asceticism educated the masses to labour, or, in Marxian terms, to the production of surplus value, and thereby for the first time made their employment in the capitalistic labour relation (putting-out industry, weaving, etc.) possible at all. That is very generally the causal relationship. From Baxter's own view-point he accepted the employment of his charges in capitalistic production for the sake of his religious and ethical interests. From the standpoint of the development of capitalism these latter were brought into the service of the development of the spirit of capitalism.

80.	Furthermore, one may well doubt to what extent the joy of the mediaeval craftsman in his creation, which is so commonly appealed to, was effective as a psychological motive force. Nevertheless, there is undoubtedly something in that thesis. But in any case asceticism certainly deprived all labour of this worldly attractiveness, to-day for ever destroyed by capitalism, and oriented it to the beyond. Labour in a calling as such is willed by God. The impersonality of present-day labour, what, from the standpoint of the individual, is its joyless lack of meaning, still has a religious justification here. Capitalism at the time of its development needed labourers who were available for economic exploitation for conscience' sake. To-day it is in the saddle, and hence able to force people to labour without transcendental sanctions.

81.	Petty, *Political Arithmetick, Works*, edited by Hull, I, p. 262.

82.	On these conflicts and developments see H. Levy in the book cited above. The very powerful hostility of public opinion to monopolies, which is characteristic of England, originated historically in a combination of the political struggle for power against the Crown—the Long Parliament excluded monopolists from its membership—with the ethical motives of Puritanism; and the economic interests of the small bourgeois and moderate-scale capitalists against the financial magnates in the seventeenth century. The Declaration of the Army of August 2, 1652, as well the Petition of the Levellers of January 28, 1653, demand, besides the abolition of excises, tariffs, and

indirect taxes, and the introduction of a single tax on estates, above all free trade, i.e. the abolition of the monopolistic barriers to trade at home and abroad, as a violation of the natural rights of man.

83.	Compare H. Levy, *Die Grundlagen des ökonomischen Liberalismus in des Geschichte des englischen Volkswirtschaft*, pp. 51 f.

84.	That those other elements, which have here not yet been traced to their religious roots, especially the idea that honesty is the best policy (Franklin's discussion of credit), are also of Puritan origin, must be proved in a somewhat different connection (see the following essay [not translated here]). Here I shall limit myself to repeating the following remark of J. A. Rowntree (*Quakerism, Past and Present*, pp. 95–6), to which E. Bernstein has called my attention: "Is it merely a coincidence, or is it a consequence, that the lofty profession of spirituality made by the Friends has gone hand in hand with shrewdness and tact in the transaction of mundane affairs? Real piety favours the success of a trader by insuring his integrity and fostering habits of prudence and forethought, important items in obtaining that standing and credit in the commercial world, which are requisites for the steady accumulation of wealth" (see the following essay). "Honest as a Huguenot" was as proverbial in the seventeenth century as the respect for law of the Dutch which Sir W. Temple admired, and, a century later, that of the English as compared with those Continental peoples that had not been through this ethical schooling.

85.	Well analysed in Bielschowsky's *Goethe*, II, chap. xviii. For the development of the scientific cosmos Windelband, at the end of his *Blütezeit der deutschen Philosophie* (Vol. II of the *Gesch. d. Neueren Philosophie*), has expressed a similar idea.

86.	*Saints' Everlasting Rest*, chap. xii.

87.	"Couldn't the old man be satisfied with his $75,000 a year and rest? No! The frontage of the store must be widened to 400 feet. Why? That beats everything, he says. In the evening when his wife and daughter read together, he wants to go to bed. Sundays he looks at the clock every five minutes to see when the day will be over—what a futile life!" In these terms the son-in-law (who had emigrated from Germany) of the leading dry-goods man of an Ohio city expressed his judgment of the latter, a judgment which would undoubtedly have seemed simply incomprehensible to the old man. A symptom of German lack of energy.

88. This remark alone (unchanged since his criticism) might have shown Brentano (*op. cit.*) that I have never doubted its independent significance. That humanism was also not pure rationalism has lately again been strongly emphasized by Borinski in the *Abhandl. der Münchener Akad. der Wiss.*, 1919.

89. The academic oration of v. Below, *Die Ursachen der Reformation* (Freiburg, 1916), is not concerned with this problem, but with that of the Reformation in general, especially Luther. For the question dealt with here, especially the controversies which have grown out of this study, I may refer finally to the work of Hermelink, *Reformation und Gegenreformation*, which, however, is also primarily concerned with other problems.

90. For the above sketch has deliberately taken up only the relations in which an influence of religious ideas on the material culture is really beyond doubt. It would have been easy to proceed beyond that to a regular construction which logically deduced everything characteristic of modern culture from Protestant rationalism. But that sort of thing may be left to the type of dilettante who believes in the unity of the group mind and its reducibility to a single formula. Let it be remarked only that the period of capitalistic development lying before that which we have studied was everywhere in part determined by religious influences, both hindering and helping. Of what sort these were belongs in another chapter. Furthermore, whether, of the broader problems sketched above, one or another can be dealt with in the limits of this Journal [the essay first appeared in the *Archiv für Sozialwissenschaft und Sozialpolitik*— Translator's Note] is not certain in view of the problems to which it is devoted. On the other hand, to write heavy tomes, as thick as they would have to be in this case, and dependent on the work of others (theologians and historians), I have no great inclination (I have left these sentences unchanged).

For the tension between ideals and reality in early capitalistic times before the Reformation, see now Strieder, *Studien zur Geschichte der kapit. Organizationsformen*, 1914, Book II. (Also as against the work of Keller, cited above, which was utilized by Sombart.)

91. I should have thought that this sentence and the remarks and notes immediately preceding it would have sufficed to prevent any misunderstanding of what this study was meant to accomplish, and I find no occasion for adding anything. Instead of following up with an immediate continuation in terms of the above programme, I have, partly for fortuitous reasons, especially the appearance of Troeltsch's *Die Soziallehren der christlichen Kirchen und Gruppen*, which disposed of many things I should have had to investigate in a way in which I, not being a theologian, could not have done it; but partly also in order to correct the isolation of this study and to place it in relation to the whole of cultural development, determined, first, to write down some comparative studies of the general historical relationship of religion and society. These follow. Before them is placed only a short essay in order to clear up the concept of sect used above, and at the same time to show the significance of the Puritan conception of the Church for the capitalistic spirit of modern times.

1. Go online to Write Out Loud about your own examples of the disenchantment that Weber suggests has overcome the capitalist spirit.

2. Log on to Weber's Profile Page for a biography of his life and work.

3. Check out the Interactive Reading and watch psychologist Barry Schwartz discuss how the "iron cage" of bureaucracy has lead to a breakdown of everyday wisdom in modern society.

19

Basic Sociological Terms

Max Weber

THE DEFINITION OF SOCIOLOGY AND OF SOCIAL ACTION

Sociology (in the sense in which this highly ambiguous word is used here) is a science concerning itself with the interpretive understanding of social action and thereby with a causal explanation of its course and consequences. We shall speak of "action" insofar as the acting individual attaches a subjective meaning to his behavior—be it overt or covert, omission or acquiescence. Action is "social" insofar as its subjective meaning takes account of the behavior of others and is thereby oriented in its course.[1]

Methodological foundations[2]

1. "Meaning" may be of two kinds. The term may refer first to the actual existing meaning in the given concrete case of a particular actor, or to the average or approximate meaning attributable to a given plurality of actors; or secondly to the theoretically conceived *pure type*[3] of subjective meaning attributed to the hypothetical actor or actors in a given type of action. In no case does it refer to an objectively "correct" meaning or one which is "true" in some metaphysical sense. It is this which distinguishes the empirical sciences of action, such as sociology and history, from the dogmatic disciplines in that area, such as jurisprudence, logic, ethics, and esthetics, which seek to ascertain the "true" and "valid" meanings associated with the objects of their investigation.

2. The line between meaningful action and merely reactive behavior to which no subjective meaning is attached, cannot be sharply drawn empirically. A very considerable part of all sociologically relevant behavior, especially purely traditional behavior, is marginal between the two. In the case of some psychophysical processes, meaningful, i.e., subjectively understandable, action is not to be found at all; in others it is discernible only by the psychologist. Many mystical experiences which cannot be adequately communicated in words are, for a person who is not susceptible to such experiences, not fully understandable. At the same time the ability to perform a similar action is not a necessary prerequisite to understanding; "one need not have been Caesar in order to understand Caesar." "Recapturing an experience" is important for accurate understanding, but not an absolute precondition for its interpretation. Understandable and non-understandable components of a process are often intermingled and bound up together.

3. All interpretation of meaning, like all scientific observations, strives for clarity and verifiable accuracy of insight and comprehension (*Evidenz*).[4] The basis for certainty in understanding can be either rational, which can be further subdivided into logical and mathematical, or

it can be of an emotionally empathic or artistically appreciative quality. Action is rationally evident chiefly when we attain a completely clear intellectual grasp of the action-elements in their intended context of meaning. Empathic or appreciative accuracy is attained when, through sympathetic participation, we can adequately grasp the emotional context in which the action took place. The highest degree of rational understanding is attained in cases involving the meanings of logically or mathematically related propositions; their meaning may be immediately and unambiguously intelligible. We have a perfectly clear understanding of what it means when somebody employs the proposition $2 \times 2 = 4$ or the Pythagorean theorem in reasoning or argument, or when someone correctly carries out a logical train of reasoning according to our accepted modes of thinking. In the same way we also understand what a person is doing when he tries to achieve certain ends by choosing appropriate means on the basis of the facts of the situation, as experience has accustomed us to interpret them. The interpretation of such rationally purposeful action possesses, for the understanding of the choice of means, the highest degree of verifiable certainty. With a lower degree of certainty, which is, however, adequate for most purposes of explanation, we are able to understand errors, including confusion of problems of the sort that we ourselves are liable to, or the origin of which we can detect by sympathetic self-analysis.

On the other hand, many ultimate ends or values toward which experience shows that human action may be oriented, often cannot be understood completely, though sometimes we are able to grasp them intellectually. The more radically they differ from our own ultimate values, however, the more difficult it is for us to understand them empathically. Depending upon the circumstances of the particular case we must be content either with a purely intellec-

tual understanding of such values or when even that fails, sometimes we must simply accept them as given data. Then we can try to understand the action motivated by them on the basis of whatever opportunities for approximate emotional and intellectual interpretation seem to be available at different points in its course. These difficulties confront, for instance, people not susceptible to unusual acts of religious and charitable zeal, or persons who abhor extreme rationalist fanaticism (such as the fanatic advocacy of the "rights of man").

The more we ourselves are susceptible to such emotional reactions as anxiety, anger, ambition, envy, jealousy, love, enthusiasm, pride, vengefulness, loyalty, devotion, and appetites of all sorts, and to the "irrational" conduct which grows out of them, the more readily can we empathize with them. Even when such emotions are found in a degree of intensity of which the observer himself is completely incapable, he can still have a significant degree of emotional understanding of their meaning and can interpret intellectually their influence on the course of action and the selection of means.

For the purposes of a typological scientific analysis it is convenient to treat all irrational, affectually determined elements of behavior as factors of deviation from a conceptually pure type of rational action. For example a panic on the stock exchange can be most conveniently analysed by attempting to determine first what the course of action would have been if it had not been influenced by irrational affects; it is then possible to introduce the irrational components as accounting for the observed deviations from this hypothetical course. Similarly, in analysing a political or military campaign it is convenient to determine in the first place what would have been a rational course, given the ends of the participants and adequate knowledge of all the circumstances. Only in this way is it possible to assess the causal significance of irrational factors as accounting for the deviations from this type. The construction of a purely rational course of action in such cases serves the sociologist as a type (ideal type) which has the merit of clear understandability and lack of ambiguity. By comparison with this it is possible to understand the ways in which actual action is influenced by irrational factors of all sorts, such as affects and errors, in that they account for the deviation from the line of conduct which would be expected on the hypothesis that the action were purely rational.

Only in this respect and for these reasons of methodological convenience is the method of sociology "rationalistic." It is naturally not legitimate to interpret this procedure as involving a rationalistic bias of sociology, but only as a methodological device. It certainly does not involve a belief in the actual predominance of rational elements in human life, for on the question of how far this predominance does or does not exist, nothing whatever has been said. That there is, however, a danger of rationalistic interpretations where they are out of place cannot be denied. All experience unfortunately confirms the existence of this danger.

4. In all the sciences of human action, account must be taken of processes and phenomena which are devoid of subjective meaning, in the role of stimuli, results, favoring or hindering circumstances. To be devoid of meaning is not identical with being lifeless or non-human; every artifact, such as for example a machine, can be understood only in terms of the meaning which its production and use have had or were intended to have; a meaning which may derive from a relation to exceedingly various purposes. Without reference to this meaning such an object remains wholly unintelligible. That which is intelligible or understandable about it is thus its relation to human action in the role either of means or of end; a relation of which the actor or actors can be said to have

been aware and to which their action has been oriented. Only in terms of such categories is it possible to "understand" objects of this kind. On the other hand processes or conditions, whether they are animate or inanimate, human or non-human, are in the present sense devoid of meaning in so far as they cannot be related to an intended purpose. That is to say they are devoid of meaning if they cannot be related to action in the role of means or ends but constitute only the stimulus, the favoring or hindering circumstances. It may be that the flooding of the Dollart [at the mouth of the Ems river near the Dutch–German border] in 1277 had historical significance as a stimulus to the beginning of certain migrations of considerable importance. Human mortality, indeed the organic life cycle from the helplessness of infancy to that of old age, is naturally of the very greatest sociological importance through the various ways in which human action has been oriented to these facts. To still another category of facts devoid of meaning belong certain psychic or psychophysical phenomena such as fatigue, habituation, memory, etc.; also certain typical states of euphoria under some conditions of ascetic mortification; finally, typical variations in the reactions of individuals according to reaction-time, precision, and other modes. But in the last analysis the same principle applies to these as to other phenomena which are devoid of meaning. Both the actor and the sociologist must accept them as data to be taken into account.

It is possible that future research may be able to discover non-interpretable uniformities underlying what has appeared to be specifically meaningful action, though little has been accomplished in this direction thus far. Thus, for example, differences in hereditary biological constitution, as of "races," would have to be treated by sociology as given data in the same way as the physiological facts of the need of nutrition or the effect of senescence on action. This would be the case if, and insofar as, we had statistically conclusive proof of their influence on sociologically relevant behavior. The recognition of the causal significance of such factors would not in the least alter the specific task of sociological analysis or of that of the other sciences of action, which is the interpretation of action in terms of its subjective meaning. The effect would be only to introduce certain non-interpretable data of the same order as others which are already present, into the complex of subjectively understandable motivation at certain points. (Thus it may come to be known that there are typical relations between the frequency of certain types of teleological orientation of action or of the degree of certain kinds of rationality and the cephalic index or skin color or any other biologically inherited characteristic.)

5. Understanding may be of two kinds: the first is the direct observational understanding[5] of the subjective meaning of a given act as such, including verbal utterances. We thus understand by direct observation, in this case, the meaning of the proposition $2 \times 2 = 4$ when we hear or read it. This is a case of the direct rational understanding of ideas. We also understand an outbreak of anger as manifested by facial expression, exclamations or irrational movements. This is direct observational understanding of irrational emotional reactions. We can understand in a similar observational way the action of a woodcutter or of somebody who reaches for the knob to shut a door or who aims a gun at an animal. This is rational observational understanding of actions.

Understanding may, however, be of another sort, namely explanatory understanding. Thus we understand in terms of *motive* the meaning an actor attaches to the proposition twice two equals four, when he states it or writes it down, in that we understand what makes him do this

at precisely this moment and in these circumstances. Understanding in this sense is attained if we know that he is engaged in balancing a ledger or in making a scientific demonstration, or is engaged in some other task of which this particular act would be an appropriate part. This is rational understanding of motivation, which consists in placing the act in an intelligible and more inclusive context of meaning.[6] Thus we understand the chopping of wood or aiming of a gun in terms of motive in addition to direct observation if we know that the woodchopper is working for a wage or is chopping a supply of firewood for his own use or possibly is doing it for recreation. But he might also be working off a fit of rage, an irrational case. Similarly we understand the motive of a person aiming a gun if we know that he has been commanded to shoot as a member of a firing squad, that he is fighting against an enemy, or that he is doing it for revenge. The last is affectually determined and thus in a certain sense irrational. Finally we have a motivational understanding of the outburst of anger if we know that it has been provoked by jealousy, injured pride, or an insult. The last examples are all affectually determined and hence derived from irrational motives. In all the above cases the particular act has been placed in an understandable sequence of motivation, the understanding of which can be treated as an explanation of the actual course of behavior. Thus for a science which is concerned with the subjective meaning of action, explanation requires a grasp of the complex of meaning in which an actual course of understandable action thus interpreted belongs. In all such cases, even where the processes are largely affectual, the subjective meaning of the action, including that also of the relevant meaning complexes, will be called the intended meaning.[7] (This involves a departure from ordinary usage, which speaks of intention in this sense only in the case of rationally purposive action.)

6. In all these cases understanding involves the interpretive grasp of the meaning present in one of the following contexts: (a) as in the historical approach, the actually intended meaning for concrete individual action; or (b) as in cases of sociological mass phenomena, the average of, or an approximation to, the actually intended meaning; or (c) the meaning appropriate to a scientifically formulated pure type (an ideal type) of a common phenomenon. The concepts and "laws" of pure economic theory are examples of this kind of ideal type. They state what course a given type of human action would take if it were strictly rational, unaffected by errors or emotional factors and if, furthermore, it were completely and unequivocally directed to a single end, the maximization of economic advantage. In reality, action takes exactly this course only in unusual cases, as sometimes on the stock exchange; and even then there is usually only an approximation to the ideal type. (On the purpose of such constructions, see my essay in *AfS*, 19 [cf. n. 5] and point 11 below.)

Every interpretation attempts to attain clarity and certainty, but no matter how clear an interpretation as such appears to be from the point of view of meaning, it cannot on this account claim to be the causally valid interpretation. On this level it must remain only a peculiarly plausible hypothesis. In the first place the "conscious motives" may well, even to the actor himself, conceal the various "motives" and "repressions" which constitute the real driving force of his action. Thus in such cases even subjectively honest self-analysis has only a relative value. Then it is the task of the sociologist to be aware of this motivational situation and to describe and analyse it, even though it has not actually been concretely part of the conscious intention of the actor; possibly not at all, at least not fully. This is a borderline case of the interpretation of meaning. Secondly, processes of action which seem to an observer to be the same or similar may fit into exceedingly various complexes of motive in the case of the actual actor. Then even though the situations appear superficially to be very similar we must actually understand them or interpret them as very different, perhaps, in terms of meaning, directly opposed. (Simmel, in his *Probleme der Geschichtsphilosophie,* gives a number of examples.) Third, the actors in any given situation are often subject to opposing and conflicting impulses, all of which we are able to understand. In a large number of cases we know from experience it is not possible to arrive at even an approximate estimate of the relative strength of conflicting motives and very often we cannot be certain of our interpretation. Only the actual outcome of the conflict gives a solid basis of judgment.

More generally, verification of subjective interpretation by comparison with the concrete course of events is, as in the case of all hypotheses, indispensable. Unfortunately this type of verification is feasible with relative accuracy only in the few very special cases susceptible of psychological experimentation. In very different degrees of approximation, such verification is also feasible in the limited number of cases of mass phenomena which can be statistically described and unambiguously interpreted. For the rest there remains only the possibility of comparing the largest possible number of historical or contemporary processes which, while otherwise similar, differ in the one decisive point of their relation to the particular motive or factor the role of which is being investigated. This is a fundamental task of comparative sociology. Often, unfortunately, there is available only the uncertain procedure of the "imaginary experiment" which consists in thinking away certain elements of a chain of motivation and working out the course of action which would then probably ensue, thus arriving at a causal judgment.[8]

For example, the generalization called Gresham's Law is a rationally clear interpretation of human action under certain conditions and under the assumption that it will follow a purely rational course. How far any actual course of action corresponds to this can be verified only by the available statistical evidence for the actual disappearance of under-valued monetary units from circulation. In this case our information serves to demonstrate a high degree of accuracy. The facts of experience were known before the generalization, which was formulated afterwards; but without this successful interpretation our need for causal understanding would evidently be left unsatisfied. On the other hand, without the demonstration that what can here be assumed to be a theoretically adequate interpretation also is in some degree relevant to an actual course of action, a "law," no matter how fully demonstrated theoretically, would be worthless for the understanding of action in the real world. In this case the correspondence between the theoretical interpretation of motivation and its empirical verification is entirely satisfactory and the cases are numerous enough so that verification can be considered established. But to take another example, Eduard Meyer has advanced an ingenious theory of the causal significance of the battles of Marathon, Salamis, and Platea for the development of the cultural peculiarities of Greek, and hence, more generally, Western, civilization.[9] This is derived from a meaningful interpretation of certain symptomatic facts having to do with the attitudes of the Greek oracles and prophets towards the Persians. It can only be directly verified by reference to the examples of the conduct of the Persians in cases where they were victorious, as in Jerusalem, Egypt, and Asia Minor, and even this verification must necessarily remain unsatisfactory in certain respects. The striking rational plausibility of the hypothesis must here necessarily be relied on as a support. In very many cases of historical interpretation which seem highly plausible, however, there is not even a possibility of the order of verification which was feasible in this case. Where this is true the interpretation must necessarily remain a hypothesis.

7. A motive is a complex of subjective meaning which seems to the actor himself or to the observer an adequate ground for the conduct in question. The interpretation of a coherent course of conduct is "subjectively adequate" (or "adequate on the level of meaning"), insofar as, according to our habitual modes of thought and feeling, its component parts taken in their mutual relation are recognized to constitute a "typical" complex of meaning.[10] It is more common to say "correct." The interpretation of a sequence of events will on the other hand be called *causally* adequate insofar as, according to established generalizations from experience, there is a probability that it will always actually occur in the same way. An example of adequacy on the level of meaning in this sense is what is, according to our current norms of calculation or thinking, the correct solution of an arithmetical problem. On the other hand, a causally adequate interpretation of the same phenomenon would concern the statistical probability that, according to verified generalizations from experience, there would be a correct or an erroneous solution of the same problem. This also refers to currently accepted norms but includes taking account of typical errors or of typical confusions. Thus causal explanation depends on being able to determine that there is a probability, which in the rare ideal case can be numerically stated, but is always in some sense calculable, that a given observable event (overt or subjective) will be followed or accompanied by another event.

A correct causal interpretation of a concrete course of action is arrived at when the overt action and the motives have both been correctly apprehended and at the same time their relation has become meaningfully comprehensible. A correct causal interpretation of typical action means that the process which is claimed to be typical is shown to be both adequately grasped on the level of meaning and at the same time the interpretation is to some degree causally adequate. If adequacy in respect to meaning is lacking, then no matter how high the degree of uniformity and how precisely its probability can be numerically determined, it is still an incomprehensible statistical probability, whether we deal with overt or subjective processes. On the other hand, even the most perfect adequacy on the level of meaning has causal significance from a sociological point of view only insofar as there is some kind of proof for the existence of a probability[11] that action in fact normally takes the course which has been held to be meaningful. For this there must be some degree of determinable frequency of approximation to an average or a pure type.

Statistical uniformities constitute understandable types of action, and thus constitute sociological generalizations, only when they can be regarded as manifestations of the understandable subjective meaning of a course of social action. Conversely, formulations of a rational course of subjectively understandable action constitute sociological types of empirical process only when they can be empirically observed with a significant degree of approximation. By no means is the actual likelihood of the occurrence of a given course of overt action always directly proportional to the clarity of subjective interpretation. Only actual experience can prove whether this is so in a given case. There are statistics of processes devoid of subjective meaning, such as death rates, phenomena of fatigue, the production rate of machines, the amount of rainfall, in exactly the same sense as there are statistics of meaningful phenomena. But only when the phenomena are meaningful do we speak of sociological statistics. Examples are such cases as crime rates, occupational distributions, price statistics, and statistics of crop acreage. Naturally there are many cases where both components are involved, as in crop statistics.

[…]

Social action

1. Social action, which includes both failure to act and passive acquiescence, may be oriented to the past, present, or expected future behavior of others. Thus it may be motivated by revenge for a past attack, defence against present, or measures of defence against future aggression. The "others" may be individual persons, and may be known to the actor as such, or may constitute an indefinite plurality and may be entirely unknown as individuals. (Thus, money is a means of exchange which the actor accepts in payment because he orients his action to the expectation that a large but unknown number of individuals he is personally unacquainted with will be ready to accept it in exchange on some future occasion.)

2. Not every kind of action, even of overt action, is "social" in the sense of the present discussion. Overt action is non-social if it is oriented solely to the behavior of inanimate objects. Subjective attitudes constitute social action only so far as they are oriented to the behavior of others. For example, religious behavior is not social if it is simply a matter of contemplation or of solitary prayer. The economic activity of an individual is social only if it takes account of the behavior of someone else. Thus very generally it becomes social insofar as the actor assumes that others will respect his actual control over economic goods. Concretely it is social, for instance, if in relation to the actor's own consumption the future wants of others are taken into account and this becomes one consideration affecting the actor's own saving. Or, in another

connexion, production may be oriented to the future wants of other people.

3. Not every type of contact of human beings has a social character; this is rather confined to cases where the actor's behavior is meaningfully oriented to that of others. For example, a mere collision of two cyclists may be compared to a natural event. On the other hand, their attempt to avoid hitting each other, or whatever insults, blows, or friendly discussion might follow the collision, would constitute "social action."

4. Social action is not identical either with the similar actions of many persons or with every action influenced by other persons. Thus, if at the beginning of a shower a number of people on the street put up their umbrellas at the same time, this would not ordinarily be a case of action mutually oriented to that of each other, but rather of all reacting in the same way to the like need of protection from the rain. It is well known that the actions of the individual are strongly influenced by the mere fact that he is a member of a crowd confined within a limited space. Thus, the subject matter of studies of "crowd psychology," such as those of Le Bon, will be called "action conditioned by crowds." It is also possible for large numbers, though dispersed, to be influenced simultaneously or successively by a source of influence operating similarly on all the individuals, as by means of the press. Here also the behavior of an individual is influenced by his membership in a "mass" and by the fact that he is aware of being a member. Some types of reaction are only made possible by the mere fact that the individual acts as part of a crowd. Others become more difficult under these conditions. Hence it is possible that a particular event or mode of human behavior can give rise to the most diverse kinds of feeling—gaiety, anger, enthusiasm, despair, and passions of all sorts—in a crowd situation which would not occur

at all or not nearly so readily if the individual were alone. But for this to happen there need not, at least in many cases, be any meaningful relation between the behavior of the individual and the fact that he is a member of a crowd. It is not proposed in the present sense to call action "social" when it is merely a result of the effect on the individual of the existence of a crowd as such and the action is not oriented to that fact on the level of meaning. At the same time the borderline is naturally highly indefinite. In such cases as that of the influence of the demagogue, there may be a wide variation in the extent to which his mass clientele is affected by a meaningful reaction to the fact of its large numbers; and whatever this relation may be, it is open to varying interpretations.

But furthermore, mere "imitation" of the action of others, such as that on which Tarde has rightly laid emphasis, will not be considered a case of specifically social action if it is purely reactive so that there is no meaningful orientation to the actor imitated. The borderline is, however, so indefinite that it is often hardly possible to discriminate. The mere fact that a person is found to employ some apparently useful procedure which he learned from someone else does not, however, constitute, in the present sense, social action. Action such as this is not oriented to the action of the other person, but the actor has, through observing the other, become acquainted with certain objective facts; and it is these to which his action is oriented. His action is then *causally* determined by the action of others, but not meaningfully. On the other hand, if the action of others is imitated because it is fashionable or traditional or exemplary, or lends social distinction, or on similar grounds, it is meaningfully oriented either to the behavior of the source of imitation or of third persons or of both. There are of course all manner of transitional cases between the two types of imitation. Both the phenomena discussed above, the behavior of crowds and imitation, stand on the indefinite borderline of social action. The same is true, as will often appear, of traditionalism and charisma. The reason for the indefiniteness of the line in these and other cases lies in the fact that both the orientation to the behavior of others and the meaning which can be imputed by the actor himself, are by no means always capable of clear determination and are often altogether unconscious and seldom fully self-conscious. Mere "influence" and meaningful orientation cannot therefore always be clearly differentiated on the empirical level. But conceptually it is essential to distinguish them, even though merely reactive imitation may well have a degree of sociological importance at least equal to that of the type which can be called social action in the strict sense. Sociology, it goes without saying, is by no means confined to the study of social action; this is only, at least for the kind of sociology being developed here, its central subject matter, that which may be said to be decisive for its status as a science. But this does not imply any judgment on the comparative importance of this and other factors.

TYPES OF SOCIAL ACTION

Social action, like all action, may be oriented in four ways. It may be

(1) *instrumentally rational* (*zweckrational*), that is, determined by expectations as to the behavior of objects in the environment and of other human beings; these expectations are used as "conditions" or "means" for the attainment of the actor's own rationally pursued and calculated ends;

(2) *value-rational* (*wertrational*), that is, determined by a conscious belief in the value for its own

sake of some ethical, aesthetic, religious, or other form of behavior, independently of its prospects of success;

(3) *affectual* (especially emotional), that is, determined by the actor's specific affects and feeling states;

(4) *traditional*, that is, determined by ingrained habituation.

1. Strictly traditional behavior, like the reactive type of imitation discussed above, lies very close to the borderline of what can justifiably be called meaningfully oriented action, and indeed often on the other side. For it is very often a matter of almost automatic reaction to habitual stimuli which guide behavior in a course which has been repeatedly followed. The great bulk of all everyday action to which people have become habitually accustomed approaches this type. Hence, its place in a systematic classification is not merely that of a limiting case because, as will be shown later, attachment to habitual forms can be up-held with varying degrees of self-consciousness and in a variety of senses. In this case the type may shade over into value rationality (*Wertrationalität*).

2. Purely affectual behavior also stands on the borderline of what can be considered "meaningfully" oriented, and often it, too, goes over the line. It may, for instance, consist in an uncontrolled reaction to some exceptional stimulus. It is a case of sublimation when affectually determined action occurs in the form of conscious release of emotional tension. When this happens it is usually well on the road to rationalization in one or the other or both of the above senses.

3. The orientation of value-rational action is distinguished from the affectual type by its clearly self-conscious formulation of the

ultimate values governing the action and the consistently planned orientation of its detailed course to these values. At the same time the two types have a common element, namely that the meaning of the action does not lie in the achievement of a result ulterior to it, but in carrying out the specific type of action for its own sake. Action is affectual if it satisfies a need for revenge, sensual gratification, devotion, contemplative bliss, or for working off emotional tensions (irrespective of the level of sublimation).

Examples of pure value-rational orientation would be the actions of persons who, regardless of possible cost to themselves, act to put into practice their convictions of what seems to them to be required by duty, honor, the pursuit of beauty, a religious call, personal loyalty, or the importance of some "cause" no matter in what it consists. In our terminology, value-rational action always involves "commands" or "demands" which, in the actor's opinion, are binding on him. It is only in cases where human action is motivated by the fulfillment of such unconditional demands that it will be called value-rational. This is the case in widely varying degrees, but for the most part only to a relatively slight extent. Nevertheless, it will be shown that the occurrence of this mode of action is important enough to justify its formulation as a distinct type; though it may be remarked that there is no intention here of attempting to formulate in any sense an exhaustive classification of types of action.

4. Action is instrumentally rational (*zweckrational*) when the end, the means, and the secondary results are all rationally taken into account and weighed. This involves rational consideration of alternative means

to the end, of the relations of the end to the secondary consequences, and finally of the relative importance of different possible ends. Determination of action either in affectual or in traditional terms is thus incompatible with this type. Choice between alternative and conflicting ends and results may well be determined in a value-rational manner. In that case, action is instrumentally rational only in respect to the choice of means. On the other hand, the actor may, instead of deciding between alternative and conflicting ends in terms of a rational orientation to a system of values, simply take them as given subjective wants and arrange them in a scale of consciously assessed relative urgency. He may then orient his action to this scale in such a way that they are satisfied as far as possible in order of urgency, as formulated in the principle of "marginal utility." Value-rational action may thus have various different relations to the instrumentally rational action. From the latter point of view, however, value-rationality is always irrational. Indeed, the more the value to which action is oriented is elevated to the status of an absolute value, the more "irrational" in this sense the corresponding action is. For, the more unconditionally the actor devotes himself to this value for its own sake, to pure sentiment or beauty, to absolute goodness or devotion to duty, the less is he influenced by considerations of the consequences of his action. The orientation of action wholly to the rational achievement of ends without relation to fundamental values is, to be sure, essentially only a limiting case.

5. It would be very unusual to find concrete cases of action, especially of social action, which were oriented *only* in one or another of these ways. Furthermore, this

classification of the modes of orientation of action is in no sense meant to exhaust the possibilities of the field, but only to formulate in conceptually pure form certain sociologically important types to which actual action is more or less closely approximated or, in much the more common case, which constitute its elements. The usefulness of the classification for the purposes of this investigation can only be judged in terms of its results.

NOTES

Unless otherwise noted, all notes in this chapter are by Talcott Parsons. For Parsons' exposition and critique of Weber's methodology, see his introduction to *The Theory of Social and Economic Organization* and his *Structure of Social Action*.

1. In this series of definitions Weber employs several important terms which need discussion. In addition to *Verstehen,* which has already been commented upon, there are four important ones: *Deuten, Sinn, Handeln,* and *Verhalten. Deuten* has generally been translated as "interpret." As used by Weber in this context it refers to the interpretation of subjective states of mind and the meanings which can be imputed as intended by an actor. Any other meaning of the word "interpretation" is irrelevant to Weber's discussion. The term *Sinn* has generally been translated as "meaning"; and its variations, particularly the corresponding adjectives, *sinnhaft, sinnvoll, sinnfremd,* have been dealt with by appropriately modifying the term *meaning.* The reference here again is always to features of the content of subjective states of mind or of symbolic systems which are ultimately referable to such states of mind.

    The terms *Handeln* and *Verhalten* are directly related. *Verhalten* is the broader term referring to any mode of behavior of human individuals, regardless of the frame of reference in terms of which it is analysed. "Behavior" has seemed to be the most appropriate English equivalent. *Handeln,* on the other hand, refers to the concrete phenomenon of human behavior only insofar as it is capable of "under-

standing," in Weber's technical sense, in terms of subjective categories. The most appropriate English equivalent has seemed to be "action." This corresponds to [Parsons'] usage in *The Structure of Social Action* and would seem to be fairly well established. "Conduct" is also similar and has sometimes been used. *Deuten, Verstehen,* and *Sinn* are thus applicable to human behavior only insofar as it constitutes action or conduct in this specific sense.

2. Weber's text in Part One is organized in a manner frequently found in the German academic literature of his day, in that he first lays down certain fundamental definitions and then proceeds to comment on them. These comments, which apparently were not intended to be "read" in the ordinary sense, but rather serve as reference material for the clarification and systematization of the theoretical concepts and their implications, are in the German edition printed in a smaller type, a convention which we have followed in the rest of Part One. However, while in most cases the comments are relatively brief, under the definitions of "sociology" and "social action" Weber wrote what are essentially methodological essays (sec. 1: A–B), which because of their length we have printed in the ordinary type. (R)

3. Weber means by "pure type" what he himself generally called and what has come to be known in the literature about his methodology as the "ideal type." The reader may be referred for general orientation to Weber's own essay (to which he himself refers below), "Die 'Objektivität' sozialwissenschaftlicher Erkenntnis" ("'Objectivity' in Social Science and Social Policy," in *Max Weber: The Methodology of the Social Sciences.* Edward Shils and Henry Finch, trans. and eds. (Glencoe: The Free Press, 1949), 50–113; originally published in *AfS,* vol. 19, 1904, reprinted in *GAzW,* 146–214); to two works of Alexander von Schelting, "Die logische Theorie der historischen Kulturwissenschaften von Max Weber," *AfS,* vol. 49, 1922, 623ff and *Max Webers Wissenschaftslehre,* 1934; Talcott Parsons, *The Structure of Social Action* (New York: McGraw-Hill, 1937), ch. 16; Theodore Abel, *Systematic Sociology in Germany* (New York: Columbia University Press, 1929). [See now also Raymond Aron, *German Sociology,* trans. by M. and T. Bottomore (New York: The Free Press of Glencoe, 1964), based on 2nd French ed. of 1950.]

4. This is an imperfect rendering of the German term *Evidenz,* for which, unfortunately, there is no good English equivalent. It has hence been rendered in a

number of different ways, varying with the particular context in which it occurs. The primary meaning refers to the basis on which a scientist or thinker becomes satisfied of the certainty or acceptability of a proposition. As Weber himself points out, there are two primary aspects of this. On the one hand a conclusion can be "seen" to follow from given premises by virtue of logical, mathematical, or possibly other modes of meaningful relation. In this sense one "sees" the solution of an arithmetical problem or the correctness of the proof of a geometrical theorem. The other aspect is concerned with empirical observation. If an act of observation is competently performed, in a similar sense one "sees" the truth of the relevant descriptive proposition. The term *Evidenz* does not refer to the process of observing, but to the quality of its result, by virtue of which the observer feels justified in affirming a given statement. Hence "certainty" has seemed a suitable translation in some contexts, "clarity" in others, "accuracy" in still others. The term "intuition" is not usable because it refers to the process rather than to the result.

5. Weber here uses the term *aktuelles Verstehen*, which he contrasts with *erklärendes Verstehen*. The latter he also refers to as *motivationsmässig*. "Aktuell" in this context has been translated as "observational." It is clear from Weber's discussion that the primary criterion is the possibility of deriving the meaning of an act or symbolic expression from immediate observation without reference to any broader context. In *erklärendes Verstehen*, on the other hand, the particular act must be placed in a broader context of meaning involving facts which cannot be derived from immediate observation of a particular act or expression.

6. The German term is *Sinnzusammenhang*. It refers to a plurality of elements which form a coherent whole on the level of meaning. There are several possible modes of meaningful relation between such elements, such as logical consistency, the esthetic harmony of a style, or the appropriateness of means to an end. In any case, however, a *Sinnzusammenhang* must be distinguished from a system of elements which are causally interdependent. There seems to be no single English term or phrase which is always adequate. According to variations in context, "context of meaning," "complex of meaning," and sometimes "meaningful system" have been employed.

7. The German is *gemeinter Sinn*. Weber departs from ordinary usage not only in broadening the mean-

ing of this conception. As he states at the end of the present methodological discussion, he does not restrict the use of this concept to cases where a clear self-conscious awareness of such meaning can be reasonably attributed to every individual actor. Essentially, what Weber is doing is to formulate an operational concept. The question is not whether in a sense obvious to the ordinary person such an intended meaning "really exists," but whether the concept is capable of providing a logical framework within which scientifically important observations can be made. The test of validity of the observations is not whether their object is immediately clear to common sense, but whether the results of these technical observations can be satisfactorily organized and related to those of others in a systematic body of knowledge.

8. The above passage is an exceedingly compact statement of Weber's theory of the logical conditions of proof of causal relationship. He developed this most fully in his essay on "'Objectivity' in Social Science . . .," *op. cit.* It is also discussed in other parts of *GAzW*. The best and fullest secondary discussion is to be found in Schelting's book, *Max Webers Wissenschaftslehre*. There is a briefer discussion in Parsons' *Structure of Social Action*, ch. 16.

9. See Eduard Meyer, *Geschichte des Altertums*, 1901, vol. III, 420, 444ff, and Weber's essay on "Critical Studies in the Logic of the Cultural Sciences," in Shils and Finch, eds., *op. cit.*, 113–188; also in *GAzW*, 215–90. (R)

10. The expression *sinnhafte Adäquanz* is one of the most difficult of Weber's technical terms to translate. In most places the cumbrous phrase "adequacy on the level of meaning" has had to be employed. It should be clear from the progress of the discussion that what Weber refers to is a satisfying level of knowledge for the particular purposes of the subjective state of mind of the actor or actors. He is, however, careful to point out that *causal* adequacy involves in addition to this a satisfactory correspondence between the results of observations from the subjective point of view and from the objective; that is, observations of the overt course of action which can be described without reference to the state of mind of the actor. For a discussion of the methodological problem involved here, see *Structure of Social Action*, chaps. II and V.

11. This is the first occurrence in Weber's text of the term *Chance* which he uses very frequently. It is here

translated by "probability," because he uses it as interchangeable with *Wahrscheinlichkeit*. As the term "probability" is used in a technical mathematical and statistical sense, however, it implies the possibility of numerical statement. In most of the cases where Weber uses *Chance* this is out of the question. It is, however, possible to speak in terms of higher and lower degrees of probability. To avoid confusion with the technical mathematical concept, the term "likelihood" will often be used in the translation. It is by means of this concept that Weber, in a highly ingenious way, has bridged the gap between the interpretation of meaning and the inevitably more complex facts of overt action.

COMPANION WEBSITE

1. Go online to Write Out Loud about Weber's idea of *verstehen*—the interpretive understanding of social action.
2. For more on *verstehen* and ideal-types, log on to Weber's Profile Page.
3. Check out the Supplementary Sources for *Pathway to Meltdown* for more classic writings from Weber, including the full text of his famous "Science as a Vocation" essay, courtesy of Routledge.

20

The Types of Legitimate Domination

Max Weber

DOMINATION AND LEGITIMACY

Domination was defined above (ch. I:16) as the probability that certain specific commands (or all commands) will be obeyed by a given group of persons. It thus does not include every mode of exercising "power" or "influence" over other persons. Domination ("authority")[1] in this sense may be based on the most diverse motives of compliance: all the way from simple habituation to the most purely rational calculation of advantage. Hence every genuine form of domination implies a minimum of voluntary compliance, that is, an *interest* (based on ulterior motives or genuine acceptance) in obedience.

Not every case of domination makes use of economic means; still less does it always have economic objectives. However, normally the rule over a considerable number of persons requires a staff (cf. ch. I:12), that is, a *special* group which can normally be trusted to execute the general policy as well as the specific commands. The members of the administrative staff may be bound to obedience to their superior (or superiors) by custom, by affectual ties, by a purely material complex of interests, or by ideal (*wertrationale*) motives. The quality of these motives largely determines the type of domination. *Purely* material interests and calculations of advantages as the basis of solidarity between the chief and his administrative staff result, in this as in other con-nexions, in a relatively unstable situation. Normally other elements, affectual and ideal, supplement such interests. In certain exceptional cases the former alone may be decisive. In everyday life these relationships, like others, are governed by custom and material calculation of advantage. But custom, personal advantage, purely affectual or ideal motives of solidarity, do not form a sufficiently reliable basis for a given domination. In addition there is normally a further element, the belief in *legitimacy*.

Experience shows that in no instance does domination voluntarily limit itself to the appeal to material or affectual or ideal motives as a basis for its continuance. In addition every such system attempts to establish and to cultivate the belief in its legitimacy. But according to the kind of legitimacy which is claimed, the type of obedience, the kind of administrative staff developed to guarantee it, and the mode of exercising authority, will all differ fundamentally. Equally fundamental is the variation in effect. Hence, it is useful to classify the types of domination according to the kind of claim to legitimacy typically made by each. In doing this, it is best to start from modern and therefore more familiar examples.

1. The choice of this rather than some other basis of classification can only be justified by its results. The fact that certain other typical criteria of variation are thereby neglected for the time being and can only be introduced

at a later stage is not a decisive difficulty. The legitimacy of a system of control has far more than a merely "ideal" significance, if only because it has very definite relations to the legitimacy of property.

2. Not every claim which is protected by custom or law should be spoken of as involving a relation of authority. Otherwise the worker, in his claim for fulfilment of the wage contract, would be exercising authority over his employer because his claim can, on occasion, be enforced by order of a court. Actually his formal status is that of party to a contractual relationship with his employer, in which he has certain "rights" to receive payments. At the same time the concept of an authority relationship (*Herrschaftsverhältnis*) naturally does not exclude the possibility that it has originated in a formally free contract. This is true of the *authority* of the employer over the worker as manifested in the former's rules and instructions regarding the work process; and also of the *authority* of a feudal lord over a vassal who has freely entered into the relation of fealty. That subjection to military discipline is formally "involuntary" while that to the discipline of the factory is voluntary does not alter the fact that the latter is also a case of subjection to *authority*. The position of a bureaucratic official is also entered into by contract and can be freely resigned, and even the status of "subject" can often be freely entered into and (in certain circumstances) freely repudiated. Only in the limiting case of the slave is formal subjection to authority absolutely involuntary.

On the other hand, we shall not speak of formal domination if a monopolistic position permits a person to exert economic power, that is, to dictate the terms of exchange to contractual partners. Taken by itself, this does not constitute authority any more than any other kind of influence which is derived from some kind of superiority, as by virtue of erotic attractiveness, skill in sport or in discussion. Even if a big bank is in a position to force other banks into a cartel arrangement, this will not alone be sufficient to justify calling it an authority. But if there is an immediate relation of command and obedience such that the management of the first bank can give orders to the others with the claim that they shall, and the probability that they will, be obeyed regardless of particular content, and if their carrying out is supervised, it is another matter. Naturally, here as everywhere the transitions are gradual; there are all sorts of intermediate steps between mere indebtedness and debt slavery. Even the position of a "salon" can come very close to the borderline of authoritarian domination and yet not necessarily constitute "authority." Sharp differentiation in concrete fact is often impossible, but this makes clarity in the analytical distinctions all the more important.

3. Naturally, the legitimacy of a system of domination may be treated sociologically only as the probability that to a relevant degree the appropriate attitudes will exist, and the corresponding practical conduct ensue. It is by no means true that every case of submissiveness to persons in positions of power is primarily (or even at all) oriented to this belief. Loyalty may be hypocritically simulated by individuals or by whole groups on purely opportunistic grounds, or carried out in practice for reasons of material self-interest. Or people may submit from individual weakness and helplessness because there is no acceptable alternative. But these considerations are not decisive for the classification of types of domination. What is important is the fact that in a given case the particular claim to legitimacy is to a significant degree and according to its type treated as "valid"; that this fact confirms the position of the persons claiming authority and that it helps to determine the choice of means of its exercise.

Furthermore, a system of domination may—as often occurs in practice—be so completely protected, on the one hand by the obvious community of interests between the chief and his administrative staff (bodyguards, Pretorians, "red" or "white" guards) as opposed to the subjects, on the other hand by the helplessness of the latter, that it can afford to drop even the pretense of a claim to legitimacy. But even then the mode of legitimation of the relation between chief and his staff may vary widely according to the type of basis of the relation of the authority between them, and, as will be shown, this variation is highly significant for the structure of domination.

4. "Obedience" will be taken to mean that the action of the person obeying follows in essentials such a course that the content of the command may be taken to have become the basis of action for its own sake. Furthermore, the fact that it is so taken is referable only to the formal obligation, without regard to the actor's own attitude to the value or lack of value of the content of the command as such.

5. Subjectively, the causal sequence may vary, especially as between "intuition" and "sympathetic agreement." This distinction is not, however, significant for the present classification of types of authority.

6. The scope of determination of social relationships and cultural phenomena by virtue of domination is considerably broader than appears at first sight. For instance, the authority exercised in the schools has much to do with the determination of the forms of speech and of written language which are regarded as orthodox. Dialects used as the "chancellery language" of autocephalous political units, hence of their rulers, have often become orthodox forms of speech and writing and have even led to the formation of separate "nations" (for instance, the separation of Holland from Germany). The rule by parents and the school, however, extends far beyond the determination of such cultural patterns, which are perhaps only apparently formal, to the formation of the young, and hence of human beings generally.

7. The fact that the chief and his administrative staff often appear formally as servants or agents of those they rule, naturally does nothing whatever to disprove the quality of dominance. There will be occasion later to speak of the substantive features of so-called "democracy." But a certain minimum of assured power to issue commands, thus of domination, must be provided for in nearly every conceivable case.

THE THREE PURE TYPES OF AUTHORITY (DOMINATION)

There are three pure types of legitimate domination. The validity of the claims to legitimacy may be based on:

1. Rational grounds—resting on a belief in the legality of enacted rules and the right of those elevated to authority under such rules to issue commands (legal authority).
2. Traditional grounds—resting on an established belief in the sanctity of immemorial traditions and the legitimacy of those exercising authority under them (traditional authority); or finally,
3. Charismatic grounds—resting on devotion to the exceptional sanctity, heroism or exemplary character of an individual person, and of the normative patterns or order revealed or ordained by him (charismatic authority).

In the case of legal authority, obedience is owed to the legally established impersonal order. It extends to the persons exercising the authority of office under it by virtue of the formal legality of their commands and only within the scope of authority of the office. In the case of traditional authority, obedience is owed to the *person* of the chief who occupies the traditionally sanctioned position of authority and who is (within its sphere) bound by tradition. But here the obligation of obedience is a matter of personal loyalty within the area of accustomed obligations. In the case of charismatic authority, it is the charismatically qualified leader as such who is obeyed by virtue of personal trust in his revelation, his heroism or his exemplary qualities so far as they fall within the scope of the individual's belief in his charisma.

1. The usefulness of the above classification can only be judged by its results in promoting systematic analysis. The concept of "charisma" ("the gift of grace") is taken from the vocabulary of early Christianity. For the Christian hierocracy Rudolf Sohm, in his *Kirchenrecht*, was the first to clarify the substance of the concept, even though he did not use the same terminology. Others (for instance, Holl in *Enthusiasmus und Bussgewalt*) have clarified certain important consequences of it. It is thus nothing new.

2. The fact that none of these three ideal types, the elucidation of which will occupy the following pages, is usually to be found in historical cases in "pure" form, is naturally not a valid objection to attempting their conceptual formulation in the sharpest possible form. In this respect the present case is no different from many others. Later on (sec. II ff.) the transformation of pure charisma by the process of routinization will be discussed and thereby the relevance of the concept to the understanding of empirical systems of authority considerably increased. But even so it may be said of every historical phenomenon of authority that it is not likely to be "as an open book." Analysis in terms of sociological types has, after all, as compared with purely empirical historical investigation, certain advantages which should not be minimized. That is, it can in the particular case of a concrete form of authority determine what conforms to or approximates such types as "charisma," "hereditary charisma," "the charisma of office," "patriarchy," "bureaucracy," the authority of status groups, and in doing so it can work with relatively unambiguous concepts. But the idea that the whole of concrete historical reality can be exhausted in the conceptual scheme about to be developed is as far from the author's thoughts as anything could be.

[...]

LEGAL AUTHORITY: THE PURE TYPE

Legal authority rests on the acceptance of the validity of the following mutually inter-dependent ideas.

1. That any given legal norm may be established by agreement or by imposition, on grounds of expediency or value-rationality or both, with a claim to obedience at least on the part of the members of the organization. This is, however, usually extended to include all persons within the sphere of power in question—which in the case of territorial bodies is the territorial area—who stand in certain social relationships or carry out forms of social action which in the order governing the organization have been declared to be relevant.

2. That every body of law consists essentially in a consistent system of abstract rules which have normally been intentionally established. Furthermore, administration of law is held to consist in the application of these rules to particular cases; the administrative process in the rational pursuit of the interests which are specified in the order governing the organization within the limits laid down by legal precepts and following principles which are capable of generalized formulation and are approved in the order governing the group, or at least not disapproved in it.

3. That thus the typical person in authority, the "superior," is himself subject to an impersonal order by orienting his actions to it in his own dispositions and commands. (This is true not only for persons exercising legal authority who are in the usual sense "officials," but, for instance, for the elected president of a state.)

4. That the person who obeys authority does so, as it is usually stated, only in his capacity as a "member" of the organization and what he obeys is only "the law." (He may in this connection be the member of an association, of a community, of a church, or a citizen of a state.)

5. In conformity with point 3, it is held that the members of the organization, insofar as they obey a person in authority, do not owe this obedience to him as an individual, but to the impersonal order. Hence, it follows that there is an obligation to obedience only within the sphere of the rationally delimited jurisdiction which, in terms of the order, has been given to him.

The following may thus be said to be the fundamental categories of rational legal authority:

(1) A continuous rule-bound conduct of official business.

(2) A specified sphere of competence (jurisdiction). This involves: (a) A sphere of obligations to perform functions which has been marked off as part of a systematic division of labor. (b) The provision of the incumbent with the necessary powers. (c) That the necessary means of compulsion are clearly defined and their use is subject to definite conditions. A unit exercising authority which is organized in this way will be called an "administrative organ" or "agency" (*Behörde*).

There are administrative organs in this sense in large-scale private enterprises, in parties and armies, as well as in the state and the church. An elected president, a cabinet of ministers, or a body of elected "People's Representatives" also in this sense constitute administrative organs. This is not, however, the place to discuss these concepts. Not every administrative organ is provided with compulsory powers. But this distinction is not important for present purposes.

(3) The organization of offices follows the principle of hierarchy; that is, each lower office is under the control and supervision of a higher one. There is a right of appeal and of statement of grievances from the lower to the higher. Hierarchies differ in respect to whether and in what cases complaints can lead to a "correct" ruling from a higher authority itself, or whether the responsibility for such changes is left to the lower office, the conduct of which was the subject of the complaint.

(4) The rules which regulate the conduct of an office may be technical rules or norms.[2] In both cases, if their application is to be fully rational, specialized training is necessary. It is thus normally true that only a person who has demonstrated an adequate technical training is qualified to be a member of the administrative staff of such an organized group, and hence only such persons are eligible for appointment to official positions. The administrative staff of a rational organization thus typically consists of "officials," whether the organization be devoted to political, hierocratic, economic—in particular, capitalistic—or other ends.

(5) In the rational type it is a matter of principle that the members of the administrative staff should be completely separated from ownership of the means of production or administration. Officials, employees, and workers attached to the administrative staff do not themselves own the non-human means of production and administration. These are rather provided for their use, in kind or in money, and the official is obligated to render an accounting of their use. There exists, furthermore, in principle complete separation of the organization's property (respectively, capital), and the personal property (household) of the

official. There is a corresponding separation of the place in which official functions are carried out—the "office" in the sense of premises—from the living quarters.

(6) In the rational type case, there is also a complete absence of appropriation of his official position by the incumbent. Where "rights" to an office exist, as in the case of judges, and recently of an increasing proportion of officials and even of workers, they do not normally serve the purpose of appropriation by the official, but of securing the purely objective and independent character of the conduct of the office so that it is oriented only to the relevant norms.

(7) Administrative acts, decisions, and rules are formulated and recorded in writing, even in cases where oral discussion is the rule or is even mandatory. This applies at least to preliminary discussions and proposals, to final decisions, and to all sorts of orders and rules. The combination of written documents and a continuous operation by officials constitutes the "office" (*Bureau*)[3] which is the central focus of all types of modern organized action.

(8) Legal authority can be exercised in a wide variety of different forms which will be distinguished and discussed later. The following ideal-typical analysis will be deliberately confined for the time being to the administrative staff that is most unambiguously a structure of domination: "officialdom" or "bureaucracy."

In the above outline no mention has been made of the kind of head appropriate to a system of legal authority. This is a consequence of certain considerations which can only be made entirely understandable at a later stage in the analysis. There are very important types of rational domination which, with respect to the ultimate source of authority, belong to other categories. This is true of the hereditary charismatic type, as illustrated by hereditary monarchy, and of the pure charismatic type of a president chosen by a plebiscite. Other cases involve rational elements at important points, but are made up of a combination of bureaucratic and charismatic components, as is true of the cabinet form of government. Still others are subject to the authority of the chiefs of other organizations, whether their character be charismatic or bureaucratic; thus the formal head of a government department under a parliamentary regime may be a minister who occupies his position because of his authority in a party. The type of rational, legal administrative staff is capable of application in all kinds of situations and contexts. It is the most important mechanism for the administration of everyday affairs. For in that sphere, the exercise of authority consists precisely in administration.

LEGAL AUTHORITY: THE PURE TYPE (CONTINUED)

The purest type of exercise of legal authority is that which employs a bureaucratic administrative staff. Only the supreme chief of the organization occupies his position of dominance (*Herrenstellung*) by virtue of appropriation, of election, or of having been designated for the succession. But even *his* authority consists in a sphere of legal "competence." The whole administrative staff under the supreme authority then consists, in the purest type, of individual officials (constituting a "monocracy" as opposed to the "collegial" type, which will be discussed below) who are appointed and function according to the following criteria:

(1) They are personally free and subject to authority only with respect to their impersonal official obligations.

(2) They are organized in a clearly defined hierarchy of offices.

(3) Each office has a clearly defined sphere of competence in the legal sense.

(4) The office is filled by a free contractual relationship. Thus, in principle, there is free selection.

(5) Candidates are selected on the basis of technical qualifications. In the most rational case, this is tested by examination or guaranteed by diplomas certifying technical training, or both. They are *appointed*, not elected.

(6) They are remunerated by fixed salaries in money, for the most part with a right to pensions. Only under certain circumstances does the employing authority, especially in private organizations, have a right to terminate the appointment, but the official is always free to resign. The salary scale is graded according to rank in the hierarchy; but in addition to this criterion, the responsibility of the position and the requirements of the incumbent's social status may be taken into account (cf. ch. IV).

(7) The office is treated as the sole, or at least the primary, occupation of the incumbent.

(8) It constitutes a career. There is a system of "promotion" according to seniority or to achievement, or both. Promotion is dependent on the judgment of superiors.

(9) The official works entirely separated from ownership of the means of administration and without appropriation of his position.

(10) He is subject to strict and systematic discipline and control in the conduct of the office.

[...]

Bureaucratic administration means fundamentally domination through knowledge. This is the feature of it which makes it specifically rational. This consists on the one hand in technical knowledge which, by itself, is sufficient to ensure it a position of extraordinary power. But in addition to this, bureaucratic organizations, or the holders of power who make use of them, have the tendency to increase their power still further by the knowledge growing out of experience in the service. For they acquire through the conduct of office a special knowledge of facts and have available a store of documentary material peculiar to themselves. While not peculiar to bureaucratic organizations, the concept of "official secrets" is certainly typical of them. It stands in relation to technical knowledge in somewhat the same position as commercial secrets do to technological training. It is a product of the striving for power.

Superior to bureaucracy in the knowledge of techniques and facts is only the capitalist entrepreneur, within his own sphere of interest. He is the only type who has been able to maintain at least relative immunity from subjection to the control of rational bureaucratic knowledge. In large-scale organizations, all others are inevitably subject to bureaucratic control, just as they have fallen under the dominance of precision machinery in the mass production of goods.

In general, bureaucratic domination has the following social consequences:

(1) The tendency to "levelling" in the interest of the broadest possible basis of recruitment in terms of technical competence.

(2) The tendency to plutocracy growing out of the interest in the greatest possible length of technical training. Today this often lasts up to the age of thirty.

(3) The dominance of a spirit of formalistic impersonality: *"Sine ira et studio,"* without hatred or passion, and hence without affection or enthusiasm. The dominant norms are concepts of straightforward duty without regard to personal considerations. Everyone is subject to formal equality of treatment; that is, everyone in the same empirical situation. This is

the spirit in which the ideal official conducts his office.

The development of bureaucracy greatly favors the leveling of status, and this can be shown historically to be the normal tendency. Conversely, every process of social levelling creates a favorable situation for the development of bureaucracy by eliminating the office-holder who rules by virtue of status privileges and the appropriation of the means and powers of administration; in the interests of "equality," it also eliminates those who can hold office on an honorary basis or as an avocation by virtue of their wealth. Everywhere bureaucratization foreshadows mass democracy, which will be discussed in another connection.

The "spirit" of rational bureaucracy has normally the following general characteristics:

(1) Formalism, which is promoted by all the interests which are concerned with the security of their own personal situation, whatever this may consist in. Otherwise the door would be open to arbitrariness and hence formalism is the line of least resistance.

(2) There is another tendency, which is apparently, and in part genuinely, in contradiction to the above. It is the tendency of officials to treat their official function from what is substantively a utilitarian point of view in the interest of the welfare of those under their authority. But this utilitarian tendency is generally expressed in the enactment of corresponding regulatory measures which themselves have a formal character and tend to be treated in a formalistic spirit. (This will be further discussed in the Sociology of Law). This tendency to substantive rationality is supported by all those subject to authority who are not included in the group mentioned above as interested in the protection of advantages already secured. The problems which open up at this point belong in the theory of "democracy."

TRADITIONAL AUTHORITY: THE PURE TYPE

Authority will be called traditional if legitimacy is claimed for it and believed in by virtue of the sanctity of age-old rules and powers. The masters are designated according to traditional rules and are obeyed because of their traditional status (*Eigenwürde*). This type of organized rule is, in the simplest case, primarily based on personal loyalty which results from common upbringing. The person exercising authority is not a "superior," but a personal master, his administrative staff does not consist mainly of officials but of personal retainers, and the ruled are not "members" of an association but are either his traditional "comrades" (sec. 7a) or his "subjects." Personal loyalty, not the official's impersonal duty, determines the relations of the administrative staff to the master.

Obedience is owed not to enacted rules but to the person who occupies a position of authority by tradition or who has been chosen for it by the traditional master. The commands of such a person are legitimized in one of two ways:

a) partly in terms of traditions which themselves directly determine the content of the command and are believed to be valid within certain limits that cannot be overstepped without endangering the master's traditional status;

b) partly in terms of the master's discretion in that sphere which tradition leaves open to him; this traditional prerogative rests primarily on the fact that the obligations of personal obedience tend to be essentially unlimited.

Thus there is a double sphere:

a) that of action which is bound to specific traditions;

b) that of action which is free of specific rules.

In the latter sphere, the master is free to do good turns on the basis of his personal pleasure and likes, particularly in return for gifts—the historical sources of dues (*Gebühren*). So far as his action follows principles at all, these are governed by considerations of ethical common sense, of equity or of utilitarian expediency. They are not formal principles, as in the case of legal authority. The exercise of power is oriented toward the consideration of how far master and staff can go in view of the subjects' traditional compliance without arousing their resistance. When resistance occurs, it is directed against the master or his servant personally, the accusation being that he failed to observe the traditional limits of his power. Opposition is not directed against the system as such—it is a case of "traditionalist revolution."

In the pure type of traditional authority it is impossible for law or administrative rule to be deliberately created by legislation. Rules which in fact are innovations can be legitimized only by the claim that they have been "valid of yore," but have only now been recognized by means of "Wisdom" [the *Weistum* of ancient Germanic law]. Legal decisions as "finding of the law" (*Rechtsfindung*) can refer only to documents of tradition, namely to precedents and earlier decisions.

[…]

CHARISMATIC AUTHORITY AND CHARISMATIC COMMUNITY

The term "charisma" will be applied to a certain quality of an individual personality by virtue of which he is considered extraordinary and treated as endowed with supernatural, superhuman, or at least specifically exceptional powers or qualities. These are such as are not accessible to the ordinary person, but are regarded as of divine origin or as exemplary, and on the basis of them the individual concerned is treated as a "leader." In primitive circumstances this peculiar kind of quality is thought of as resting on magical powers, whether of prophets, persons with a reputation for therapeutic or legal wisdom, leaders in the hunt, or heroes in war. How the quality in question would be ultimately judged from any ethical, aesthetic, or other such point of view is naturally entirely indifferent for purposes of definition. What is alone important is how the individual is actually regarded by those subject to charismatic authority, by his "followers" or "disciples."

> For present purposes it will be necessary to treat a variety of different types as being endowed with charisma in this sense. It includes the state of a "berserk" whose spells of maniac passion have, apparently wrongly, sometimes been attributed to the use of drugs. In medieval Byzantium a group of these men endowed with the charisma of fighting frenzy was maintained as a kind of weapon. It includes the "shaman," the magician who in the pure type has to be subject to epileptoid seizures as a means of falling into trances. Another type is represented by Joseph Smith, the founder of Mormonism, who may have been a very sophisticated swindler (although this cannot be definitely established). Finally it includes the type of *littérateur*, such as Kurt Eisner,[4] who is overwhelmed by his own demagogic success. Value-free sociological analysis will treat all these on the same level as it does the charisma of men who are the "greatest" heroes, prophets, and saviors according to conventional judgements.

I. It is recognition on the part of those subject to authority which is decisive for the validity of charisma. This recognition is freely given and guaranteed by what is held to be a proof, originally always a miracle, and consists in devotion to the corresponding revelation, hero worship, or absolute trust in the leader. But where charisma is genuine, it is not this which is the basis of the claim to legitimacy. This basis lies rather in the conception that it is the duty of those subject to charismatic authority to recognize its genuineness and to act accordingly. Psychologically this recognition is a matter of complete personal devotion to the possessor of the quality, arising out of enthusiasm, or of despair and hope.

No prophet has ever regarded his quality as dependent on the attitudes of the masses toward him. No elective king or military leader has ever treated those who have resisted him or tried to ignore him otherwise than as delinquent in duty. Failure to take part in a military expedition under such leader, even though the recruitment is formally voluntary, has universally met with disdain.

II. If proof and success elude the leader for long, if he appears deserted by his god or his magical or heroic powers, above all, if his leadership fails to benefit his followers, it is likely that his charismatic authority will disappear. This is the genuine meaning of the divine right of kings (*Gottesgnadentum*).

Even the old Germanic kings were sometimes rejected with scorn. Similar phenomena are very common among so-called primitive peoples. In China the charismatic quality of the monarch, which was transmitted unchanged by heredity, was upheld so rigidly that any misfortune whatever, not only defeats in war, but drought, floods, or astronomical phenomena which were considered unlucky, forced him to do public penance and might even force his abdication. If such things occurred, it was a sign that he did not possess the requisite charismatic virtue and was thus not a legitimate "Son of Heaven."

III. An organized group subject to charismatic authority will be called a charismatic community (*Gemeinde*). It is based on an emotional form of communal relationship (*Vergemeinschaftung*). The administrative staff of a charismatic leader does not consist of "officials"; least of all are its members technically trained. It is not chosen on the basis of social privilege nor from the point of view of domestic or personal dependency. It is rather chosen in terms of the charismatic qualities of its members. The prophet has his disciples; the warlord his bodyguard; the leader, generally, his agents (*Vertrauensmänner*). There is no such thing as appointment or dismissal, no career, no promotion. There is only a call at the instance of the leader on the basis of the charismatic qualification of those he summons. There is no hierarchy; the leader merely intervenes in general or in individual cases when he considers the members of his staff lacking in charismatic qualification for a given task. There is no such thing as a bailiwick or definite sphere of competence, and no appropriation of official powers on the basis of social privileges. There may, however, be territorial or functional limits to charismatic powers and to the individual's mission. There is no such thing as a salary or a benefice.

Disciples or followers tend to live primarily in a communistic relationship with their leader on means which have been provided by voluntary gift. There are no established administrative organs. In their place are agents who have been provided with charismatic authority by their chief or who possess charisma of their own. There is no system of formal rules, of abstract legal principles, and hence no process of rational judicial decision oriented to them. But equally there is no legal wisdom oriented to judicial precedent. Formally concrete judgments are newly created from case to case and are originally regarded as divine judgments and revelations. From a substantive point of view, every charismatic authority would have to subscribe to the proposition, "It is written … but I say unto you …" The genuine prophet, like the genuine military leader and every true leader in this sense, preaches, creates, or demands *new* obligations—most typically, by virtue of revelation, oracle, inspiration, or of his own will, which are recognized by the members of the religious, military, or party group because they come from such a source. Recognition is a duty. When such an authority comes into conflict with the competing authority of another who also claims charismatic sanction, the only recourse is to some kind of a contest, by magical means or an actual physical battle of the leaders. In principle, only one side can be right in such a conflict; the other must be guilty of a wrong which has to be expiated.

Since it is "extra-ordinary," charismatic authority is sharply opposed to rational, and particularly bureaucratic, authority, and to traditional authority, whether in its patriarchal, patrimonial, or estate variants, all of which are everyday forms of domination; while the charismatic type is the direct antithesis of this. Bureaucratic authority is specifically rational in the sense of being bound to intellectually analysable rules; while charismatic authority is specifically irrational in the sense of being foreign to all rules. Traditional authority is bound to the precedents handed down from the past and to this extent is also oriented to rules. Within the sphere of its claims, charismatic authority repudiates the past, and is in this sense a specifically revolutionary force. It recognizes no appropriation of positions of power by virtue of the possession of property, either on the part of a chief or of socially privileged groups. The only basis of legitimacy for it is personal charisma so long as it is proved; that is, as long as it receives recognition and as long as the followers and disciples prove their usefulness charismatically.

> The above is scarcely in need of further discussion. What has been said applies to purely plebiscitary rulers (Napoleon's "rule of genius" elevated people of humble origin to thrones and high military commands) just as much as it applies to religious prophets or war heroes.

IV. Pure charisma is specifically foreign to economic considerations. Wherever it appears, it constitutes a "call" in the most emphatic sense of the word, a "mission" or a "spiritual duty." In the pure type, it disdains and repudiates economic exploitation of the gifts of grace as a source of income, though, to be sure, this often remains more an ideal than a fact. It is not that charisma always demands a renunciation of property or even of acquisition, as under certain circumstances prophets and their disciples do. The heroic warrior and his followers actively seek booty; the elective ruler or the charismatic party leader requires the material means of power. The former in addition requires a brilliant display of his authority to bolster his prestige. What is despised, so long as the genuinely charismatic type is adhered to, is traditional or rational everyday economizing, the attainment of a regular income by continuous economic activity devoted to this end. Support by gifts, either on a grand scale involving donation, endowment, bribery and honoraria, or by begging, constitute the voluntary type of support. On the other hand, "booty" and extortion, whether by force or by other means, is the typical form of charismatic provision for needs. From the point of view of rational economic activity, charismatic want satisfaction is a typical anti-economic force. It repudiates any sort of involvement in the everyday routine world. It can only tolerate, with an attitude of complete emotional indifference, irregular, unsystematic acquisitive acts. In that it relieves the recipient of economic concerns, dependence on property income can be the economic basis of a charismatic mode of life for some groups; but that is unusual for the normal charismatic "revolutionary."

> The fact that incumbency of church office has been forbidden to the Jesuits is a rationalized application of this principle of discipleship. The fact that all the "virtuosi" of asceticism, the mendicant orders, and fighters for a faith belong in this category, is quite clear. Almost all prophets have been supported by voluntary gifts. The well-known saying of St. Paul, "If a man does not work, neither shall he eat," was directed against the parasitic swarm of charismatic missionaries. It obviously has nothing to do with a positive valuation of economic activity for its own sake, but only lays it down as a duty of each individual somehow to provide for his own support. This because he realized that the purely charismatic parable of the lilies of the field was not capable of literal application, but at best "taking no thought for the morrow" could be hoped for. On the other hand, in a case of a primarily artistic type of charismatic discipleship it is conceivable that insulation from economic struggle should mean limitation of those really eligible to the "economically independent"; that is, to persons

living on income from property. This has been true of the circle of Stefan George, at least in its primary intentions.

V. In traditionalist periods, charisma is *the* great revolutionary force. The likewise revolutionary force of "reason" works from *without:* by altering the situations of life and hence its problems, finally in this way changing men's attitudes toward them; or it intellectualizes the individual. Charisma, on the other hand, *may* effect a subjective or *internal* reorientation born out of suffering, conflicts, or enthusiasm. It may then result in a radical alteration of the central attitudes and directions of action with a completely new orientation of all attitudes toward the different problems of the "world."[5] In prerationalistic periods, tradition and charisma between them have almost exhausted the whole of the orientation of action.

[...]

THE RISE OF THE CHARISMATIC COMMUNITY AND THE PROBLEM OF SUCCESSION

In its pure form charismatic authority has a character specifically foreign to everyday routine structures. The social relationships directly involved are strictly personal, based on the validity and practice of charismatic personal qualities. If this is not to remain a purely transitory phenomenon, but to take on the character of a permanent relationship, a "community" of disciples or followers or a party organization or any sort of political or hierocratic organization, it is necessary for the character of charismatic authority to become radically changed. Indeed, in its pure form charismatic authority may be said to exist only *in statu nascendi*. It cannot remain stable, but becomes either traditionalized or rationalized, or a combination of both.

The following are the principal motives underlying this transformation: (a) The ideal and also the material interests of the followers in the continuation and the continual reactivation of the community, (b) the still stronger ideal and also stronger material interests of the members of the administrative staff, the disciples, the party workers, or others in continuing their relationship. Not only this, but they have an interest in continuing it in such a way that both from an ideal and a material point of view, their own position is put on a stable everyday basis. This means, above all, making it possible to participate in normal family relationships or at least to enjoy a secure social position in place of the kind of discipleship which is cut off from ordinary worldly connections, notably in the family and in economic relationships.

These interests generally become conspicuously evident with the disappearance of the personal charismatic leader and with the problem of *succession*. The way in which this problem is met—if it is met at all and the charismatic community continues to exist or now begins to emerge—is of crucial importance for the character of the subsequent social relationships. The following are the principal possible types of solution:—

(a) The *search* for a new charismatic leader on the basis of criteria of the qualities which will fit him for the position of authority.

This is to be found in a relatively pure type in the process of choice of a new Dalai Lama. It consists in the search for a child with characteristics which are interpreted to mean that he is a reincarnation of the Buddha. This is very similar to the choice of the new Bull of Apis.

In this case the legitimacy of the new charismatic leader is bound to certain distinguishing characteristics; thus, to rules with respect to which a tradition arises. The result is a process of traditionalization in favor of which the purely personal character of leadership is reduced.

(b) *Revelation* manifested in oracles, lots, divine judgments, or other techniques of selection. In this case the legitimacy of the new leader is dependent on the legitimacy of the *technique* of his selection. This involves a form of legalization.

It is said that at times the *Shofetim* [Judges] of Israel had this character. Saul is said to have been chosen by the old war oracle.

(c) Designation on the part of the original charismatic leader of his own successor and his recognition on the part of the followers.

> This is a very common form. Originally, the Roman magistracies were filled entirely in this way. The system survived most clearly into later times in the appointment of the dictator and in the institution of the *interrex*.[6]

In this case legitimacy is *acquired* through the act of designation.

(d) Designation of a successor by the charismatically qualified administrative staff and his recognition by the community. In its typical form this process should quite definitely not be interpreted as "election" or "nomination" or anything of the sort. It is not a matter of free selection, but of one which is strictly bound to objective duty. It is not to be determined merely by majority vote, but is a question of arriving at the correct designation, the designation of the right person who is truly endowed with charisma. It is quite possible that the minority and not the majority should be right in such a case. Unanimity is often required. It is obligatory to acknowledge a mistake and persistence in error is a serious offense. Making a wrong choice is a genuine wrong requiring expiation. Originally it was a magical offence.

Nevertheless, in such a case it is easy for legitimacy to take on the character of an acquired right which is justified by standards of the correctness of the process by which the position was acquired, for the most part, by its having been acquired in accordance with certain formalities such as coronation.

> This was the original meaning of the coronation of bishops and kings in the Western world by the clergy or the high nobility with the "consent" of the community. There are numerous analogous phenomena all over the world. The fact that this is the origin of the modern conception of "election" raises problems which will have to be gone into later.[7]

(e) The conception that charisma is a quality transmitted by heredity; thus that it is participated in by the kinsmen of its bearer, particularly by his closest relatives. This is the case of *hereditary charisma*. The order of hereditary succession in such a case need not be the same as that which is in force for appropriated rights, but may differ from it. It is also sometimes necessary to select the proper heir within the kinship group by some of the methods just spoken of.

> Thus in certain African states brothers have had to fight for the succession. In China, succession had to take place in such a way that the relation of the living group to the ancestral spirits was not disturbed. The rule either of seniority or of designation by the followers has been very common in the Orient. Hence, in the House of Osman, it used to be obligatory to kill off all other possible aspirants.

Only in Medieval Europe and in Japan, elsewhere sporadically, has the principle of primogeniture, as governing the inheritance of authority, become clearly established. This has greatly facilitated the consolidation of political groups in that it has eliminated struggle between a plurality of candidates from the same charismatic family.

In the case of hereditary charisma, recognition is no longer paid to the charismatic qualities of the individual, but to the legitimacy of the position he has acquired by hereditary succession. This may lead in the direction either of traditionalization or of legalization. The concept of divine right is fundamentally altered and now comes to mean authority by virtue of a personal right which is not dependent on the recognition of those subject to authority. Personal charisma may be totally absent.

Hereditary monarchy is a conspicuous illustration. In Asia there have been very numerous hereditary priesthoods; also, frequently, the hereditary charisma of kinship groups has been treated as a criterion of social rank and of eligibility for fiefs and benefices.

(f) The concept that charisma may be transmitted by ritual means from one bearer to another or may be created in a new person. The concept was originally magical. It involves a dissociation of charisma from a particular individual, making it an objective, transferable entity. In particular, it may become the *charisma of office*. In this case the belief in legitimacy is no longer directed to the individual, but to the acquired qualities and to the effectiveness of the ritual acts.

> The most important example is the transmission of priestly charisma by anointing, consecration, or the laying on of hands; and of royal authority, by anointing and by coronation. The *character in-delebilis* thus acquired means that the charismatic qualities and powers of the office are emancipated from the personal qualities of the priest. For precisely this reason, this has, from the Donatist and the Montanist heresies down to the Puritan revolution, been the subject of continual conflicts. The "hireling" of the Quakers is the preacher endowed with the charisma of office.

TYPES OF APPROPRIATION BY THE CHARISMATIC STAFF

Concomitant with the routinization of charisma with a view to insuring adequate succession, go the interests in its routinization on the part of the administrative staff. It is only in the initial stages and so long as the charismatic leader acts in a way which is completely outside everyday social organization, that it is possible for his followers to live communistically in a community of faith and enthusiasm, on gifts, booty, or sporadic acquisition. Only the members of the small group of enthusiastic disciples and followers are prepared to devote their lives purely idealistically to their call. The great majority of disciples and followers will in the long run "make their living" out of their "calling" in a material sense as well. Indeed, this must be the case if the movement is not to disintegrate.

Hence, the routinization of charisma also takes the form of the appropriation of powers and of economic advantages by the followers or disciples, and of regulating recruitment. This process of traditionalization or of legalization, according to whether rational legislation is involved or not, may take any one of a number of typical forms.

1. The original basis of recruitment is personal charisma. However, with routinization, the followers or disciples may set up norms for recruitment, in particular involving training or tests of eligibility. Charisma can only be "awakened" and "tested"; it cannot be "learned" or "taught." All types of magical asceticism, as practiced by magicians and heroes, and all novitiates, belong in this category. These are means of closing the administrative staff. (On the charismatic type of education, see ch. IV below [unfinished].)

Only the proved novice is allowed to exercise authority. A genuine charismatic leader is in a position to oppose this type of prerequisite for membership; his successor is not free to do so, at least if he is chosen by the administrative staff.

> This type is illustrated by the magical and warrior asceticism of the "men's house" with initiation ceremonies and age groups. An individual who has not successfully gone through the initiation, remains a "woman"; that is, he is excluded from the charismatic group.

2. It is easy for charismatic norms to be transformed into those defining a traditional social status (on a hereditary charismatic basis). If the leader is chosen on a hereditary basis, the same is likely to happen in the selection and deployment of the staff and even the followers. The term "clan state" (*Geschlechterstaat*) will be applied when a political

body is organized strictly and completely in terms of this principle of hereditary charisma. In such a case, all appropriation of governing powers, of fiefs, benefices, and all sorts of economic advantages follow the same pattern. The result is that all powers and advantages of all sorts become traditionalized. The heads of families, who are traditional gerontocrats or patriarchs without personal charismatic legitimacy, regulate the exercise of these powers which cannot be taken away from their family. It is not the type of position he occupies which determines the rank of a man or of his family, but rather the hereditary charismatic rank of his family determines the position he will occupy.

> Japan, before the development of bureaucracy, was organized in this way. The same was undoubtedly true of China as well where, before the rationalization which took place in the territorial states, authority was in the hands of the "old families." Other types of examples are furnished by the caste system in India, and by Russia before the mestnichestvo was introduced. Indeed, all hereditary social classes with established privileges belong in the same category.

3. The administrative staff may seek and achieve the creation and appropriation of *individual* positions and the corresponding economic advantages for its members. In that case, according to whether the tendency is to traditionalization or legalization, there will develop (a) benefices, (b) offices, or (c) fiefs. In the first case a prebendal organization will result; in the second, patrimonialism or bureaucracy; in the third, feudalism. These revenue sources become appropriated and replace provision from gifts or booty without settled relation to the everyday economic structure.

Case (a), benefices, may consist in rights to the proceeds of begging, to payments in kind, or to the proceeds of money taxes, or finally, to the proceeds of fees. The latter may result from the former through the regulation of the original provision by free gifts or by "booty" in terms of a rational organization or finance.

> Regularized begging is found in Buddhism; benefices in kind, in the Chinese and Japanese "rice rents"; support by money taxation has been the rule in all the rationalized conquest states. The last case is common everywhere, especially on the part of priests and judges and, in India, even the military authorities.

Case (b), the transformation of the charismatic mission into an office, may have more of a patrimonial or more of a bureaucratic character. The former is much the more common; the latter is found principally in Antiquity and in the modern Western world. Elsewhere it is exceptional.

In case (c), only land may be appropriated as a fief, whereas the position as such retains its originally charismatic character, or powers and authority may be fully appropriated as fiefs. It is difficult to distinguish the two cases. However, orientation to the charismatic character of the position was slow to disappear, also in the Middle Ages.

STATUS HONOR AND THE LEGITIMATION OF AUTHORITY

For charisma to be transformed into an everyday phenomenon, it is necessary that its anti-economic character should be altered. It must be adapted to some form of fiscal organization to provide for the needs of the group and hence to the economic conditions necessary for raising taxes and contributions. When a charismatic movement develops in the direction of prebendal provision, the "laity" becomes differentiated from the "clergy"—derived from κλῆρος, meaning a "share"—, that is, the participating members of the charismatic administrative staff which has now become routinized. These are the priests of the developing "church." Correspondingly, in a developing political body—the "state" in the rational case—vassals, benefice-holders, officials or appointed party officials (instead of voluntary party workers and functionaries) are differentiated from the "tax payers."

> This process is very conspicuous in Buddhism and in the Hindu sects—see the Sociology of Religion below. The same is true in all conquest states which have become rationalized to form permanent structures; also of parties and other originally charismatic structures.

It follows that, in the course of routinization, the charismatically ruled organization is largely transformed into one of the everyday authorities, the patrimonial form, especially in its estate-type or bureaucratic variant. Its original peculiarities are apt to be retained in the charismatic status honor acquired by heredity or office-holding. This applies to all who participate in the appropriation, the chief himself and the members of his staff. It is thus a matter of the type of prestige enjoyed by ruling groups. A hereditary monarch by "divine right" is not a simple patrimonial chief, patriarch, or sheik; a vassal is not a mere household retainer or official. Further details must be deferred to the analysis of status groups.

As a rule, routinization is not free of conflict. In the early stages personal claims on the charisma of the chief are not easily forgotten and the conflict between the charisma of the office or of hereditary status with personal charisma is a typical process in many historical situations.

1. The power of absolution—that is, the power to absolve from mortal sins—was held originally only by personal charismatic martyrs or ascetics, but became transformed into a power of the office of bishop or priest. This process was much slower in the Orient than in the Occident because in the latter is was influenced by the Roman conception of office. Revolutions under a charismatic leader, directed against hereditary charismatic powers or the powers of office, are to be found in all types of organizations, from states to trade unions. (This last is particularly conspicuous at the present time [1918/20].) The more highly developed the interdependence of different economic units in a monetary economy, the greater the pressure of the everyday needs of the followers of the charismatic movement becomes. The effect of this is to strengthen the tendency to routinization, which is everywhere operative, and as a rule has rapidly won out. Charisma is a phenomenon typical of prophetic movements or of expansive political movements in their early stages. But as soon as domination is well established, and above all as soon as control over large masses of people exists, it gives way to the forces of everyday routine.

2. One of the decisive motives underlying all cases of the routinization of charisma is naturally the striving for security. This means legitimization, on the one hand, of positions of authority and social prestige, on the other hand, of the economic advantages enjoyed by the followers and sympathizers of the leader. Another important motive, however, lies in the objective necessity of adapting the order and the staff organization to the normal, everyday needs and conditions of carrying on administration. In this connection, in particular, there are always points at which traditions of administrative practice and of judicial decision can take hold as these are needed by the normal administrative staff and those subject to its authority. It is further necessary that there should be some definite order introduced into the organization of the administrative staff itself. Finally, as will be discussed in detail below, it is necessary for the administrative staff and all its administrative practices to be adapted to everyday economic conditions. It is not possible for the costs of permanent, routine administration to be met by "booty," contributions, gifts, and hospitality, as is typical of the pure type of military and prophetic charisma.

NOTES

Unless otherwise indicated, all notes are by Parsons.

1. Weber put *Autorität* in quotation marks and parentheses behind *Herrschaft*, referring to an alternative colloquial term, but the sentence makes it clear that this does not yet specify the basis of compliance. However, the chapter is devoted to a typology of legitimate domination, which will alternatively be translated as authority. The chapter begins with a reformulation of ch. X in Part Two, and then presents a concise classification of the more descriptive exposition in chs. XI–XVI. (R)

2. Weber does not explain this distinction. By a "technical rule" he probably means a prescribed course of action which is dictated primarily on grounds touching efficiency of the performance of the immediate functions, while by "norms" he probably means rules which limit conduct on grounds other than those of efficiency. Of course, in one sense all rules are norms in that they are prescriptions for conduct, conformity with which is problematical.

3. It has seemed necessary to use the English word "office" in three different meanings, which are distinguished in Weber's discussion by at least two terms. The first is *Amt*, which means "office" in the sense of the institutionally defined status of a person. The second is the "work premises," as in the expression "he spent the afternoon in his office." For this Weber uses *Bureau* as also for the third meaning which he has just defined, the "organized work process of a group." In this last sense an office is a particular type of "enterprise," or *Betrieb* in Weber's sense. This use is established in English in such expressions as "the District Attorney's Office has such and such functions." Which of the three meanings is involved in a given case will generally be clear from the context.

4. Kurt Eisner, a brilliant Social Democratic (not Communist) intellectual proclaimed the Bavarian Republic in Nov. 1918. He was murdered on Feb. 21, 1919. When the death sentence of the murderer, Count Arco, was commuted to a life sentence in Jan. 1920, Weber announced at the beginning of one of his lectures that he favored Arco's execution on substantive and pragmatic grounds. In the next lecture this resulted in a packed audience and noisy right-wing demonstration, which prevented Weber from lecturing. See now the account of two eyewitnesses in René König and Johannes Winckelmann, eds., *Max Weber zum Gedächtnis*. Special issue 7 of the *Kölner Zeitschrift für Soziologie*, 1963, 24–29. On this period, cf. also the references in ch. II, n. 20. (R)

5. Weber here uses *Welt* in quotation marks, indicating that it refers to its meaning in what is primarily a religious context. It is the sphere of "worldly" things and interests as distinguished from transcendental religious interests.

6. Cf. Theodor Mommsen, *Abriss des römischen Staatsrechts*. First ed. 1893, sec. ed., 1907, 102ff, 162f. (W)

7. Cf. Fritz Rörig, *Geblütsrecht und freie Wahl in ihrer Auswirkung auf die deutsche Geschichte* (Abhandlungen der Berliner Akademie, 1945/6, Philosophische Historische Klasse Nr. 6). (W)

COMPANION WEBSITE

1. Go online to Write Out Loud about your own examples of charismatic leaders who fell victim to the power of routine and rationalization.

2. For a look into the darker side of authority, check out the film *Quiet Rage* in the *Pathway to Meltdown* Supplementary Sources.

3. For a list of films illustrating the legitimate types of domination, including a funny clip from *Monty Python and the Holy Grail*, go to the Supplementary Sources.

21

Bureaucracy

Max Weber

CHARACTERISTICS OF MODERN BUREAUCRACY

Modern officialdom functions in the following manner:

I. There is the principle of official *jurisdictional areas*, which are generally ordered by rules, that is, by laws or administrative regulations. This means:

   (1) The regular activities required for the purposes of the bureaucratically governed structure are assigned as official duties.

   (2) The authority to give the commands required for the discharge of these duties is distributed in a stable way and is strictly delimited by rules concerning the coercive means, physical, sacerdotal, or otherwise, which may be placed at the disposal of officials.

   (3) Methodical provision is made for the regular and continuous fulfillment of these duties and for the exercise of the corresponding rights; only persons who qualify under general rules are employed.

   In the sphere of the state these three elements constitute a bureaucratic *agency*, in the sphere of the private economy they constitute a bureaucratic *enterprise*. Bureaucracy, thus understood, is fully developed in political and ecclesiastical communities only in the modern state, and in the private economy only in the most advanced institutions of capitalism. Permanent agencies, with fixed jurisdiction, are not the historical rule but rather the exception. This is even true of large political structures such as those of the ancient Orient, the Germanic and Mongolian empires of conquest, and of many feudal states. In all these cases, the ruler executes the most important measures through personal trustees, table-companions, or court-servants. Their commissions and powers are not precisely delimited and are temporarily called into being for each case.

II. The principles of *office hierarchy* and of channels of appeal (*Instanzenzug*) stipulate a clearly established system of super- and subordination in which there is a supervision of the lower offices by the higher ones. Such a system offers the governed the possibility of appealing, in a precisely regulated manner, the decision of a lower office to the corresponding superior authority. With the full development of the bureaucratic type, the office hierarchy is *monocratically* organized. The principle of hierarchical office authority is found in all bureaucratic structures: in state and ecclesiastical structures as well as in large party organizations and private enterprises. It does not matter for the character of bureaucracy whether its authority is called "private" or "public."

When the principle of jurisdictional "competency" is fully carried through, hierarchical subordination—at least in public office—does not mean that the "higher" authority is authorized simply to take over the business of the "lower." Indeed, the opposite is the rule; once an office has been set up, a new incumbent will always be appointed if a vacancy occurs.

III. The management of the modern office is based upon written documents (the "files"), which are preserved in their original or draft form, and upon a staff of subaltern officials and scribes of all sorts. The body of officials working in an agency along with the respective apparatus of material implements and the files makes up a *bureau* (in private enterprises often called the "counting house," *Kontor*).

In principle, the modern organization of the civil service separates the bureau from the private domicile of the official and, in general, segregates official activity from the sphere of private life. Public monies and equipment are divorced from the private property of the official. This condition is everywhere the product of a long development. Nowadays, it is found in public as well as in private enterprises; in the latter, the principle extends even to the entrepreneur at the top. In principle, the Kontor (office) is separated from the household, business from private correspondence, and business assets from private wealth. The more consistently the modern type of business management has been carried through, the more are these separations the case. The beginnings of this process are to be found as early as the Middle Ages.

It is the peculiarity of the modern entrepreneur that he conducts himself as the "first official" of his enterprise, in the very same way in which the ruler of a specifically modern bureaucratic state [Frederick II of Prussia] spoke of himself as "the first servant" of the state.

The idea that the bureau activities of the state are intrinsically different in character from the management of private offices is a continental European notion and, by way of contrast, is totally foreign to the American way.

IV. Office management, at least all specialized office management—and such management is distinctly modern—usually presupposes thorough training in a field of specialization. This, too, holds increasingly for the modern executive and employee of a private enterprise, just as it does for the state officials.

V. When the office is fully developed, official activity demands the *full working capacity* of the official, irrespective of the fact that the length of his obligatory working hours in the bureau may be limited. In the normal case, this too is only the product of a long development, in the public as well as in the private office. Formerly the normal state of affairs was the reverse: Official business was discharged as a secondary activity.

VI. The management of the office follows *general rules*, which are more or less stable, more or less exhaustive, and which can be learned. Knowledge of these rules represents a special technical expertise which the officials possess. It involves jurisprudence, administrative or business management.

The reduction of modern office management to rules is deeply embedded in its very nature. The theory of modern public administration, for instance, assumes that the authority to order certain matters by decree—which has been legally granted to an agency—does not entitle the agency to regulate the matter by individual commands given for each case, but only to regulate the matter abstractly. This stands in extreme contrast to the regulation of all relationships through individual privileges and bestowals of favor, which, as we shall see, is absolutely dominant in patrimonialism, at least in so far as such relationships are not fixed by sacred tradition.

THE POSITION OF THE OFFICIAL WITHIN AND OUTSIDE OF BUREAUCRACY

All this results in the following for the internal and external position of the official:

Office holding as a vocation

That the office is a "vocation" (*Beruf*) finds expression, first, in the requirement of a prescribed course of training, which demands the entire working capacity for a long period of time, and in generally prescribed special examinations as prerequisites of employment. Furthermore, it finds expression in that the position of the official is in the nature of a "duty" (*Pflicht*). This determines the character of his relations in the following manner: Legally and actually, office holding is not considered ownership of a source of income, to be exploited for rents or emoluments in exchange for the rendering of certain services, as was normally the case during the Middle Ages and frequently up to the threshold of recent times, nor is office holding considered a common exchange of services, as in the case of free employment contracts. Rather, entrance into an office, including one in the private economy, is considered an acceptance of a specific duty of fealty to the purpose of the office (*Amtstreue*) in return for the grant of a secure existence. It is decisive for the modern loyalty to an office that, in the pure type, it does not establish a relationship to a *person*, like the vassal's or disciple's faith under feudal or patrimonial authority, but rather is devoted to *impersonal* and *functional* purposes. These purposes, of course, frequently gain an ideological halo from cultural values, such as state, church, community, party or enterprise, which appear as surrogates for a this-worldly or other-worldly personal master and which are embodied by a given group.

The political official—at least in the fully developed modern state—is not considered the personal servant of a ruler. Likewise, the bishop, the priest and the preacher are in fact no longer, as in early Christian times, carriers of a purely personal charisma, which offers other-worldly sacred values under the personal mandate of a master, and in principle responsible only to him, to everybody who appears worthy of them and asks for them. In spite of the partial survival of the old theory, they have become officials in the service of a functional purpose, a purpose which in the present-day "church" appears at once impersonalized and ideologically sanctified.

The social position of the official

Social esteem and status convention. Whether he is in a private office or a public bureau, the modern official, too, always strives for and usually attains a distinctly elevated *social esteem* vis-à-vis the governed. His social position is protected by prescription about rank order and, for the political official, by special prohibitions of the criminal code against "insults to the office" and "contempt" of state and church authorities.

The social position of the official is normally highest where, as in old civilized countries, the following conditions prevail: a strong demand for administration by trained experts; a strong and stable social differentiation, where the official predominantly comes from socially and economically privileged strata because of the social distribution of power or the costliness of the required training and of status conventions. The possession of educational certificates or patents—discussed below (sec. 13 A)—is usually linked with qualification for office; naturally, this enhances the "status element" in the social position of the official. Sometimes the status factor is explicitly acknowledged; for example, in the prescription that the acceptance of an aspirant to an office career depends upon the consent ("election") by the members of the official body. This is the case in the officer corps of the German army. Similar phenomena, which promote a guild-like closure of officialdom, are typically found in the patrimonial and, particularly, in prebendal official-dom of the past. The desire to resurrect such policies in changed forms is by no means infrequent among modern bureaucrats; it played a role, for instance, in the demands of the largely proletarianized [*zem-stvo-*] officials (the *tretii element*) during the Russian revolution [of 1905].

Usually the social esteem of the officials is especially low where the demand for expert administration and the hold of status conventions are weak. This is often the case in new settlements by virtue of the great economic opportunities and the great instability of their social stratification: witness the United States.

Appointment versus election: consequences for expertise. Typically, the bureaucratic official is appointed by a superior authority. An official elected by the governed is no longer a purely bureaucratic figure. Of course, a formal election may hide an appointment—in politics especially by party bosses. This does not depend upon legal statutes, but upon the way in which the party mechanism functions. Once firmly organized, the parties can turn a formally free election into the mere acclamation of a candidate designated by the party chief, or at least into a contest, conducted according to certain rules, for the election of one of two designated candidates.

In all circumstances, the designation of officials by means of an election modifies the rigidity of hierarchical subordination. In principle, an official who is elected has an autonomous position vis-à-vis his superiors, for he does not derive his position "from above" but "from below," or at least not from a superior authority of the official hierarchy but from powerful party men ("bosses"), who also determine his further career. The career of the elected official is not primarily dependent upon his chief in the administration. The official who is not elected, but appointed by a master, normally functions, from a technical point of view, more accurately because it is more likely that purely functional points of consideration and qualities will determine his selection and career. As laymen, the governed can evaluate the expert qualifications of a candidate for office only in terms of experience, and hence only after his service. Moreover, if political parties are involved in any sort of selection of officials by election, they quite naturally tend to give decisive weight not to technical competence but to the services a follower renders to the party boss. This holds for the designation of otherwise freely elected officials by party bosses when they determine the slate of candidates as well as for the free appointment of officials by a chief who has himself been elected. The contrast, however, is relative: substantially similar conditions hold where legitimate monarchs and their subordinates appoint officials, except that partisan influences are then less controllable.

Where the demand for administration by trained experts is considerable, and the party faithful have to take into account an intellectually developed, educated, and free "public opinion," the use of unqualified officials redounds upon the party in power at the next election. Naturally, this is more likely to happen when the officials are appointed by the chief. The demand for a trained administration now exists in the United States, but wherever, as in the large cities, immigrant votes are "corralled," there is, of course, no effective public opinion. Therefore, popular election not only of the administrative chief but also of his subordinate officials usually endangers, at least in very large administrative bodies which are difficult to supervise, the expert qualification of the officials as well as the precise functioning of the bureaucratic mechanism, besides weakening the dependence of the officials upon the hierarchy. The superior qualification and integrity of Federal judges appointed by the president, as over and against elected judges, in the United States is well known, although both types of officials are selected primarily in terms of party considerations. The great changes in American metropolitan administrations demanded by reformers have been effected essentially by elected mayors working with an apparatus of officials who were appointed by them. These reforms have thus come about in a "caesarist" fashion. Viewed technically, as an organized form of domination, the efficiency of "caesarism," which often grows out of democracy, rests in general upon the position of the "caesar" as a free trustee of the masses (of the army or of the citizenry), who is unfettered by tradition. The "caesar" is thus the unrestrained master of a body of highly qualified military officers and officials whom he selects freely and personally without regard to tradition or to any other impediments. Such "rule of the personal genius," however, stands in conflict with the formally "democratic" principle of a generally elected officialdom.

[...]

THE LEVELING OF SOCIAL DIFFERENCES

In spite of its indubitable technical superiority, bureaucracy has everywhere been a relatively late development. A number of obstacles have contributed to this, and only under certain social and political conditions have they definitely receded into the background.

Administrative democratization

Bureaucratic organization has usually come into power on the basis of a leveling of economic and social differences. This leveling has been at least relative, and has concerned the significance of social and economic differences for the assumption of administrative functions.

Bureaucracy inevitably accompanies modern *mass democracy*, in contrast to the democratic self-government of small homogeneous units. This results from its characteristic principle: the abstract regularity of the exercise of authority, which is a result of the demand for "equality before the law" in the personal and functional sense—hence, of the horror of "privilege," and the principled rejection of doing business "from case to case." Such regularity

also follows from the social preconditions of its origin. Any non-bureaucratic administration of a large social structure rests in some way upon the fact that existing social, material, or honorific preferences and ranks are connected with administrative functions and duties. This usually means that an economic or a social exploitation of position, which every sort of administrative activity provides to its bearers, is the compensation for the assumption of administrative functions.

Bureaucratization and democratization within the administration of the state therefore signify an increase of the cash expenditures of the public treasury, in spite of the fact that bureaucratic administration is usually more "economical" in character than other forms. Until recent times—at least from the point of view of the treasury—the cheapest way of satisfying the need for administration was to leave almost the entire local administration and lower judicature to the landlords of Eastern Prussia. The same is true of the administration by justices of the peace in England. Mass democracy which makes a clean sweep of the feudal, patrimonial, and—at least in intent—the plutocratic privileges in administration unavoidably has to put paid professional labor in place of the historically inherited "avocational" administration by notables.

Mass parties and the bureaucratic consequences of democratization

This applies not only to the state. For it is no accident that in their own organizations the democratic mass parties have completely broken with traditional rule by notables based upon personal relationships and personal esteem. Such personal structures still persist among many old conservative as well as old liberal parties, but democratic mass parties are bureaucratically organized under the leadership of party officials, professional party and trade union secretaries, etc. In Germany, for instance, this has happened in the Social Democratic party and in the agrarian mass-movement; in England earliest in the caucus democracy of Gladstone and Chamberlain which spread from Birmingham in the 1870s. In the United States, both parties since Jackson's administration have developed bureaucratically. In France, however, attempts to organize disciplined political parties on the basis of an election system that would compel bureaucratic organization have repeatedly failed. The resistance of local circles of notables against the otherwise unavoidable bureaucratization of the parties, which would encompass the entire country and break their influence, could not be overcome. Every advance of simple election techniques based on numbers alone as, for instance, the system of proportional representation, means a strict and inter-local bureaucratic organization of the parties and therewith an increasing domination of party bureaucracy and discipline, as well as the elimination of the local circles of notables—at least this holds for large states.

The progress of bureaucratization within the state administration itself is a phenomenon paralleling the development of democracy, as is quite obvious in France, North America, and now in England. Of course, one must always remember that the term "democratization" can be misleading. The *demos* itself, in the sense of a shapeless mass, never "governs" larger associations, but rather is governed. What changes is only the way in which the executive leaders are selected and the measure of influence which the *demos*, or better, which social circles from its midst are able to exert upon the content and the direction of administrative activities by means of "public opinion." "Democratization," in the sense here intended, does not necessarily mean an increasingly active share of the subjects in government. This may be a result of democratization, but it is not necessarily the case.

We must expressly recall at this point that the political concept of democracy, deduced from the "equal rights" of the governed, includes these further postulates: (1) prevention of the development of a closed status group of officials in the interest of a universal accessibility of office, and (2) minimization of the authority of officialdom in the interest of expanding the sphere of influence of "public opinion" as far as practicable. Hence, wherever possible, political democracy strives to shorten the term of office through election and recall, and to be relieved from a limitation to candidates with special expert qualifications. Thereby democracy inevitably comes into conflict with the bureaucratic tendencies which have been produced by its very fight against the notables. The loose term "democratization" cannot be used here, in so far as it is understood to mean the minimization of the civil servants' power in favor of the greatest possible "direct" rule of the *demos*, which in practice means the respective party leaders of the *demos*. The decisive aspect here—indeed it is rather exclusively so—is the *leveling of the governed* in face of the governing and bureaucratically articulated group, which in its turn may occupy a quite autocratic position, both in fact and in form.

COMPANION WEBSITE

1. Go online to Write Out Loud about what Weber means when he writes that bureaucracy came about through a "leveling of social and economic differences."
2. Log on to Weber's Profile Page to learn more about the endless red tape associated with bureaucracy.
3. Check out the *Pathway to Meltdown* Supplementary Sources for a list of films illustrating the absurdity of modern bureaucracies.

22

Class, Status, Party

Max Weber

THE DISTRIBUTION OF POWER WITHIN THE POLITICAL COMMUNITY: CLASS, STATUS, PARTY[1]

Economically determined power and the status order

The structure of every legal order directly influences the distribution of power, economic or otherwise, within its respective community. This is true of all legal orders and not only that of the state. In general, we understand by "power" the chance of a man or a number of men to realize their own will in a social action even against the resistance of others who are participating in the action.

"Economically conditioned" power is not, of course, identical with "power" as such. On the contrary, the emergence of economic power may be the consequence of power existing on other grounds. Man does not strive for power only in order to enrich himself economically. Power, including economic power, may be valued for its own sake. Very frequently the striving for power is also conditioned by the social honor it entails. Not all power, however, entails social honor: The typical American Boss, as well as the typical big speculator, deliberately relinquishes social honor. Quite generally, "mere economic" power, and especially "naked" money power, is by no means a recognized basis of social honor. Nor is power the only basis of social honor. Indeed, social honor, or prestige, may even be the basis of economic power, and very frequently has been. Power, as well as honor, may be guaranteed by the legal order, but, at least normally, it is not their primary source. The legal order is rather an additional factor that enhances the chance to hold power or honor; but it can not always secure them.

The way in which social honor is distributed in a community between typical groups participating in this distribution we call the "status order." The social order and the economic order are related in a similar manner to the legal order. However, the economic order merely defines the way in which economic goods and services are distributed and used. Of course, the status order is strongly influenced by it, and in turn reacts upon it.

Now: "classes," "status groups," and "parties" are phenomena of the distribution of power within a community.

Determination of class situation by market situation

In our terminology, "classes" are not communities; they merely represent possible, and frequent, bases for social action. We may speak of a "class" when (1) a number of people have in common a specific causal component of their life chances, insofar as (2) this component is represented exclusively by economic interests in the possession of goods and opportunities for income, and (3) is represented under the conditions of the commodity or labor markets. This is "class situation."

It is the most elemental economic fact that the way in which the disposition over material property is distributed among a plurality of people, meeting competitively in the market for the purpose of exchange, in itself creates specific life chances. The mode of distribution, in accord with the law of marginal utility, excludes the non-wealthy from competing for highly valued goods; it favors the owners and, in fact, gives to them a monopoly to acquire such goods. Other things being equal, the mode of distribution monopolizes the opportunities for profitable deals for all those who, provided with goods, do not necessarily have to exchange them. It increases, at least generally, their power in the price struggle with those who, being propertyless, have nothing to offer but their labor or the resulting products, and who are compelled to get rid of these products in order to subsist at all. The mode of distribution gives to the propertied a monopoly on the possibility of transferring property from the sphere of use as "wealth" to the sphere of "capital," that is, it gives them the entrepreneurial function and all chances to share directly or indirectly in returns on capital. All this holds true within the area in which pure market conditions prevail. "Property" and "lack of property" are, therefore, the basic categories of all class situations. It does not matter whether these two categories become effective in the competitive struggles of the consumers or of the producers.

Within these categories, however, class situations are further differentiated: on the one hand, according to the kind of property that is usable for returns; and, on the other hand, according to the kind of services that can be offered in the market. Ownership of dwellings; workshops; warehouses; stores; agriculturally usable land in large or small holdings—a quantitative difference with possibly qualitative consequences; ownership of mines; cattle; men (slaves); disposition over mobile instruments of production, or capital goods of all sorts, especially money or objects that can easily be exchanged for money; disposition over products of one's own labor or of others' labor differing according to their various distances from consumability; disposition over transferable monopolies of any kind—all these distinctions differentiate the class situations of the propertied just as does the "meaning" which they can give to the use of property, especially to property which has money equivalence. Accordingly, the propertied, for instance, may belong to the class of rentiers or to the class of entrepreneurs.

Those who have no property but who offer services are differentiated just as much according to their kinds of services as according to the way in which they make use of these services, in a continuous or discontinuous relation to a recipient. But always this is the generic connotation of the concept of class: that the kind of chance in the *market* is the decisive moment which presents a common condition for the individual's fate. Class situation is, in this sense, ultimately market situation. The effect of naked possession *per se*, which among cattle breeders gives the non-owning slave or serf into the power of the cattle owner, is only a forerunner of real "class" formation. However, in the cattle loan and in the naked severity of the law of debts in such communities for the first time mere "possession" as such emerges as decisive for the fate of the individual; this is much in contrast to crop-raising communities, which are based on labor. The creditor-debtor relation becomes the basis of "class situations" first in the cities, where a "credit market," however primitive, with rates of interest increasing according to the extent of dearth and factual monopolization of lending in the hands of a plutocracy could develop. Therewith "class struggles" begin.

Those men whose fate is not determined by the chance of using goods or services for themselves on the market, e.g., slaves, are not, however, a class in the technical sense of the term. They are, rather, a status group.

Social action flowing from class interest

According to our terminology, the factor that creates "class" is unambiguously economic interest, and indeed, only those interests involved in the existence of the market. Nevertheless, the concept of class-interest is an ambiguous one: even as an empirical concept it is ambiguous as soon as one understands by it something other than the factual direction of interests following with a certain probability from the class situation for a certain average of those people subjected to the class situation. The class situation and other circumstances remaining the same, the direction in which the individual worker, for instance, is likely to pursue his interests may vary widely, according to whether he is constitutionally qualified for the task at hand to a high, to an average, or to a low degree. In the same way, the direction of interests may vary according to whether or not social action of a larger or smaller portion of those commonly affected by the class situation, or even an association among them, e.g., a trade union, has grown out of the class situation, from which the individual may expect promising results for himself. The emergence of an association or even of mere social action from a common class situation is by no means a universal phenomenon.

The class situation may be restricted in its efforts to the generation of essentially *similar* reactions, that is to say, within our terminology, of "mass behavior." However, it may not even have this result. Furthermore, often merely amorphous social action emerges. For example, the "grumbling" of workers known in ancient Oriental ethics: The moral disapproval of the work-master's conduct, which in its practical significance was probably equivalent to an increasingly typical phenomenon of precisely the latest industrial development, namely, the slowdown of laborers by virtue of tacit agreement. The degree in which "social action" and possibly associations emerge from the mass behavior of the members of a class is linked to general cultural conditions, especially to those of an intellectual sort. It is also linked to the extent of the contrasts that have already evolved, and is especially linked to the transparency of the connections between the causes and the consequences of the class situation. For however different life chances may be, this fact in itself, according to all experience, by no means gives birth to "class action" (social action by the members of a class). For that, the real conditions and the results of the class situation must be distinctly recognizable. For only then the contrast of life chances can be felt not as an absolutely given fact to be accepted, but as a resultant from either (1) the given distribution of property, or (2) the structure of the concrete economic order. It is only then that people may react against the class structure not only through acts of intermittent and irrational protest, but in the form of rational association. There have been "class situations" of the first category (1), of a specifically naked and transparent sort, in the urban centers of Antiquity and during the Middle Ages; especially then when great fortunes were accumulated by factually monopolized trading in local industrial products or in foodstuffs; furthermore, under certain conditions, in the rural economy of the most diverse periods, when agriculture was increasingly exploited in a profit-making manner. The most important historical example of the second category (2) is the class situation of the modern proletariat.

Types of class struggle

Thus every class may be the carrier of any one of the innumerable possible forms of class action, but this is not necessarily so. In any case, a class does not in itself constitute a group (*Gemeinschaft*). To treat "class" conceptually as being equivalent to "group" leads to distortion. That men in the same class situation regularly react in mass actions to such tangible situations as economic ones in the direction of those interests that are most adequate to their average number is an important and after all simple fact for the understanding of historical events. However, this fact must not lead to that kind of pseudo-scientific operation with the concepts of class and class interests which is so frequent these days and which has found its most classic expression in the statement of a talented author, that the individual may be in error concerning his interests but that the class is infallible about its interests.

If classes as such are not groups, nevertheless class situations emerge only on the basis of social action. However, social action that brings forth class situations is not basically action among members of the identical class; it is an action among members of different classes. Social actions that directly determine the class situation of the worker and the entrepreneur are: the labor market, the commodities market, and the capitalistic enterprise. But, in its turn, the existence of a capitalistic enterprise presupposes that a very specific kind of social action exists to protect the possession of goods *per se*, and especially the power of individuals to dispose, in principle freely, over the means of production: a certain kind of legal order. Each kind of class situation, and above all when it rests upon the power of property *per se*, will become most clearly efficacious when all other determinants of reciprocal relations are, as far as possible, eliminated in their significance. It is in this way that the use of the power of property in the market obtains its most sovereign importance.

Now status groups hinder the strict carrying through of the sheer market principle. In the present context they are of interest only from this one point of view. Before we briefly consider them, note that not much of a general nature can be said about the more specific kinds of antagonism between classes (in our meaning of the term). The great shift, which has been going on continuously in the past, and up to our times, may be summarized, although at a cost of some precision: the struggle in which class situations are effective has progressively shifted from consumption credit toward, first, competitive struggles in the commodity market and then toward wage disputes on the labor market. The class struggles of Antiquity—to the extent that they were genuine class struggles and not struggles between status groups—were initially carried on by peasants and perhaps also artisans threatened by debt bondage and struggling against urban creditors. For debt bondage is the normal result of the differentiation of wealth in commercial cities, especially in seaport cities. A similar situation has existed among cattle breeders. Debt relationships as such produced class action up to the days of Catilina. Along with this, and with an increase in provision of grain for the city by transporting it from the outside, the struggle over the means of sustenance emerged. It centered in the first place around the provision of bread and determination of the price of bread. It lasted throughout Antiquity and the entire Middle Ages. The propertyless flocked together against those who actually and supposedly were interested in the dearth of bread. This fight spread until it involved all those commodities essential to the way of life and to handicraft production. There were only incipient discussions of wage disputes in Antiquity and in the Middle Ages. But they have been slowly increasing up into modern times. In the earlier periods they were completely secondary to slave rebellions as well as to conflicts in the commodity market.

The propertyless of Antiquity and of the Middle Ages protested against monopolies, pre-emption, forestalling, and the withholding of goods from the market in order to raise prices. Today the central issue is the determination of the price of labor. The transition is represented by the fight for access to the market and for the determination of the price of products. Such fights went on between merchants and workers in the putting-out system of domestic handicraft during the transition to modern times. Since it is quite a general phenomenon we must mention here that the class antagonisms that are conditioned through the market situations are usually most bitter between those who actually and directly participate as opponents in price wars. It is not the rentier, the share-holder, and the banker who suffer the ill will of the worker, but almost exclusively the manufacturer and the business executives who are the direct opponents of workers in wage conflicts. This is so in spite of the fact that it is precisely the cash boxes of the rentier, the shareholder, and the banker into which the more or less unearned gains flow, rather than into the pockets of the manufacturers or of the business executives. This simple state of affairs has very frequently been decisive for the role the class situation has played in the formation of political parties. For example, it has made possible the varieties of patriarchal socialism and the frequent attempts—formerly, at least—of threatened status groups to form alliances with the proletariat against the bourgeoisie.

Status honor

In contrast to classes, *Stände* (*status groups*) are normally groups. They are, however, often of an amorphous kind. In contrast to the purely economically determined "class situation," we wish to designate as *status situation* every typical component of the life of men that is determined by a specific, positive or negative, social estimation of *honor*. This honor may be connected with any quality shared by a plurality, and, of course, it can be knit to a class situation: class distinctions are linked in the most varied ways with status distinctions. Property as such is not always recognized as a status qualification, but in the long run it is, and with extraordinary regularity. In the subsistence economy of neighborhood associations, it is often simply the richest who is the "chieftain." However, this often is only an honorific preference. For example, in the so-called pure modern democracy, that is, one devoid of any expressly ordered status privileges for individuals, it may be that only the families coming under approximately the same tax class dance with one another. This example is reported of certain smaller Swiss cities.

But status honor need not necessarily be linked with a class situation. On the contrary, it normally stands in sharp opposition to the pretensions of sheer property.

Both propertied and propertyless people can belong to the same status group, and frequently they do with very tangible consequences. This equality of social esteem may, however, in the long run become quite precarious. The equality of status among American gentlemen, for instance, is expressed by the fact that outside the subordination determined by the different functions of business, it would be considered strictly repugnant—wherever the old tradition still prevails—if even the richest boss, while playing billiards or cards in his club would not treat his clerk as in every sense fully his equal in birthright, but would bestow upon him the condescending status-conscious "benevolence" which the German boss can never dissever from his attitude. This is one of the most important reasons why in America the German clubs have never been able to attain the attraction that the American clubs have.

In content, status honor is normally expressed by the fact that above all else a specific *style of life* is expected from all those who wish to belong to the circle. Linked with this expectation are restrictions on social intercourse (that is, intercourse which is not subservient to economic or any other purposes). These restrictions may confine normal marriages to within the status circle and may lead to complete endogamous closure. Whenever this is not a mere individual and socially irrelevant imitation of another style of life, but consensual action of this closing character, the status development is under way.

In its characteristic form, stratification by status groups on the basis of conventional styles of life evolves at the present time in the United States out of the traditional democracy. For example, only the resident of a certain street ("the Street") is considered as belonging to "society," is qualified for social intercourse, and is visited and invited. Above all, this differentiation evolves in such a way as to make for strict submission to the fashion that is dominant at a given time in society. This submission to fashion also exists among men in America to a degree unknown in Germany; it appears as an indication of the fact that a given man puts forward a *claim* to qualify as a gentleman. This submission decides, at least *prima facie*, that he will be treated as such. And this recognition becomes just as important for his employment chances in swank establishments, and above all, for social intercourse and marriage with "esteemed" families, as the qualification for dueling among Germans. As for the rest, status honor is usurped by certain families resident for a long time, and, of course, correspondingly wealthy (e.g. F.F.V., the First Families of Virginia), or by the actual or alleged descendants of the "Indian Princess" Pocahontas, of the Pilgrim fathers, or of the Knickerbockers, the members of almost inaccessible sects and all sorts of circles setting themselves apart by means of any other characteristics and badges. In this case stratification is purely conventional and rests largely on usurpation (as does almost all status honor in its beginning). But the road to legal privilege, positive or negative, is easily traveled as soon as a certain stratification of the social order has in fact been "lived in" and has achieved stability by virtue of a stable distribution of economic power.

Ethnic segregation and caste

Where the consequences have been realized to their full extent, the status group evolves into a closed caste. Status distinctions are then guaranteed not merely by conventions and laws, but also by religious sanctions. This occurs in such a way that every physical contact with a member of any caste that is considered to be lower by the members of a higher caste is considered as making for a ritualistic impurity and a stigma which must be expiated by a religious act. In addition, individual castes develop quite distinct cults and gods.

In general, however, the status structure reaches such extreme consequences only where there are underlying differences which are held to be "ethnic." The caste is, indeed, the normal form in which ethnic communities that believe in blood relationship and exclude exogamous marriage and social intercourse usually associate with one another. As mentioned before [ch. VI:*vi*:6], such a caste situation is part of the phenomenon of pariah peoples and is found all over the world. These people form communities, acquire specific occupational traditions of handicrafts or of other arts, and cultivate a belief in their ethnic community. They live in a diaspora strictly segregated from all personal intercourse, except that of an unavoidable sort, and their situation is legally precarious. Yet, by virtue of their economic indispensability, they are tolerated, indeed frequently privileged, and they live interspersed in the political communities. The Jews are the most impressive historical example.

A status segregation grown into a caste differs in its structure from a mere ethnic segregation: the caste structure transforms the horizontal and unconnected coexistences of ethnically segregated groups into a vertical social system of super- and subordination. Correctly formulated: a comprehensive association integrates the ethnically divided communities into one political unit. They differ precisely in this way: ethnic co-existence, based on mutual repulsion and disdain, allows each ethnic community to consider its own honor as the highest one; the caste structure brings about a social subordination and an acknowledgement of "more honor" in favor of the privileged caste and status groups. This is due to the fact that in the caste structure ethnic distinctions as such have become "functional" distinctions within the political association (warriors, priests, artisans that are politically important for war and for building, and so on). But even pariah peoples who are most despised (for example, the Jews) are usually apt to continue cultivating the belief in their own specific "honor," a belief that is equally peculiar to ethnic and to status groups.

However, with the negatively privileged status groups the sense of dignity takes a specific deviation. A sense of dignity is the precipitation in individuals of social honor and of conventional demands which a positively privileged status group raises for the deportment of its members. The sense of dignity that characterizes positively privileged status groups is naturally related to their "being" which does not transcend itself, that is, it is related to their "beauty and excellence" (καλοκἀγαοία). Their kingdom is "of this world." They live for the present and by exploiting their great past. The sense of dignity of the negatively privileged strata naturally refers to a future lying beyond the present, whether it is of this life or of another. In other words, it must be nurtured by the belief in a providential mission and by a belief in a specific honor before God. The chosen people's dignity is nurtured by a belief either that in the beyond "the last will be the first," or that in this life a Messiah will appear to bring forth into the light of the world which has cast them out the hidden honor of the pariah people. This simple state of affairs, and not the resentment which is so strongly emphasized in Nietzsche's much-admired construction in the *Genealogy of Morals*, is the source of the religiosity cultivated by pariah status groups (see above, ch. VI:*vi*:5); moreover, resentment applies only to a limited extent; for one of Nietzsche's main examples, Buddhism, it is not at all applicable.

For the rest, the development of status groups from ethnic segregations is by no means the normal phenomenon. On the contrary. Since objective "racial differences" are by no means behind every subjective sentiment of an ethnic community, the question of an ultimately racial foundation of status structure is rightly a question of the concrete individual case. Very frequently a status group is instrumental in the production of a thoroughbred anthropological type. Certainly status groups are to a high degree effective in producing extreme types, for they select personally qualified individuals (e.g. the knighthood selects those who are fit for warfare, physically and psychically). But individual selection is far from being the only, or the predominant, way in which status groups are formed: political membership or class situation has at all times been at least as frequently decisive. And today the class situation is by far the predominant factor. After all, the possibility of a style of life expected for members of a status group is usually conditioned economically.

Status privileges

For all practical purposes, stratification by status goes hand in hand with a monopolization of ideal and material goods or opportunities, in a manner we have come to know as typical. Besides the specific status honor, which always rests upon distance and exclusiveness, honorific preferences may consist of the privilege of wearing special costumes, of eating special dishes taboo to others, of carrying arms—which is most obvious in its consequences—, the right to be a dilettante, for example, to play certain musical instruments. However, material monopolies provide the most effective motives for the exclusiveness of a status group; although, in themselves, they are rarely sufficient, almost always they come into play to some extent. Within a status circle there is the question of intermarriage: the interest of the families in the monopolization of potential bridegrooms is at least of equal importance and is parallel to the interest in the monopolization of daughters. The daughters of the members must be provided for. With an increased closure of the status group, the conventional preferential opportunities for special employment grow into a legal monopoly of special offices for the members. Certain goods become objects for monopolization by status groups, typically, entailed estates, and frequently also the possession of serfs or bondsmen and, finally, special trades. This monopolization occurs positively when the status group is exclusively entitled to own and to manage them; and negatively when, in order to maintain its specific way of life, the status group must *not* own and manage them. For the decisive role of a style of life in status honor means that status groups are the specific bearers of all conventions. In whatever way it may be manifest, all stylization of life either originates in status groups or is at least conserved by them. Even if the principles of status conventions differ greatly, they reveal certain typical traits, especially among the most privileged strata. Quite generally, among privileged status groups there is a status disqualification that operates against the performance of common physical labor. This disqualification is now "setting in" in America against the old tradition of esteem for labor. Very frequently every rational economic pursuit, and especially entrepreneurial activity, is looked upon as a disqualification of status. Artistic and literary activity is also considered degrading work as soon as it is exploited for income, or at least when it is connected with hard physical exertion. An example is the sculptor working like a mason in his dusty smock as over against the painter in his salon-like studio and those forms of musical practice that are acceptable to the status group.

Economic conditions and effects of status stratification

The frequent disqualification of the gainfully employed as such is a direct result of the principle of status stratification, and of course, of this principle's opposition to a distribution of power which is regulated exclusively through the market. These two factors operate along with various individual ones, which will be touched upon below.

We have seen above that the market and its processes knows no personal distinctions: "functional" interests dominate it. It knows nothing of honor. The status order means precisely the reverse: stratification in terms of honor and styles of life peculiar to status groups as such. The status order would be threatened at its very root if mere economic acquisition and naked economic power still bearing the stigma of its extra-status origin could bestow upon anyone who has won them the same or even greater

honor as the vested interests claim for themselves. After all, given equality of status honor, property *per se* represents an addition even if it is not overtly acknowledged to be such. Therefore all groups having interest in the status order react with special sharpness precisely against the pretensions of purely economic acquisition. In most cases they react the more vigorously the more they feel themselves threatened. Calderon's respectful treatment of the peasant, for instance, as opposed to Shakespeare's simultaneous ostensible disdain of the *canaille* illustrates the different way in which a firmly structured status order reacts as compared with a status order that has become economically precarious. This is an example of a state of affairs that recurs everywhere. Precisely because of the rigorous reactions against the claims of property *per se*, the "parvenu" is never accepted, personally and without reservation, by the privileged status groups, no matter how completely his style of life has been adjusted to theirs. They will only accept his descendants who have been educated in the conventions of their status group and who have never besmirched its honor by their own economic labor.

As to the general *effect* of the status order, only one consequence can be stated, but it is a very important one: the hindrance of the free development of the market. This occurs first for those goods that status groups directly withhold from free exchange by monopolization, which may be effected either legally or conventionally. For example, in many Hellenic cities during the "status era" and also originally in Rome, the inherited estate (as shown by the old formula for placing spendthrifts under a guardian)[2] was monopolized, as were the estates of knights, peasants, priests, and especially the clientele of the craft and merchant guilds. The market is restricted, and the power of naked property *per se*, which gives its stamp to class formation, is pushed into the background. The results of this process can be most varied. Of course, they do not necessarily weaken the contrasts in the economic situation. Frequently they strengthen these contrasts, and in any case, where stratification by status permeates a community as strongly as was the case in all political communities of Antiquity and of the Middle Ages, one can never speak of a genuinely free market competition as we understand it today. There are wider effects than this direct exclusion of special goods from the market. From the conflict between the status order and the purely economic order mentioned above, it follows that in most instances the notion of honor peculiar to status absolutely abhors that which is essential to the market: hard bargaining. Honor abhors hard bargaining among peers and occasionally it taboos it for the members of a status group in general. Therefore, everywhere some status groups, and usually the most influential, consider almost any kind of overt participation in economic acquisition as absolutely stigmatizing.

With some over-simplification, one might thus say that classes are stratified according to their relations to the production and acquisition of goods; whereas status groups are stratified according to the principles of their *consumption* of goods as represented by special styles of life.

An "occupational status group," too, is a status group proper. For normally, it successfully claims social honor only by virtue of the special style of life which may be determined by it. The differences between classes and status groups frequently overlap. It is precisely those status communities most strictly segregated in terms of honor (viz. the Indian castes) who today show, although within very rigid limits, a relatively high degree of indifference to pecuniary income. However, the Brahmins seek such income in many different ways.

As to the general economic conditions making for the predominance of stratification by status, only the following can be said. When the bases of the acquisition and distribution of goods are relatively stable, stratification by status is favored. Every technological repercussion and economic transformation threatens stratification by status and pushes the class situation into the foreground. Epochs and countries in which the naked class situation is of predominant significance are regularly the periods of technical and economic transformations. And every slowing down of the change in economic stratification leads, in due course, to the growth of status structures and makes for a resuscitation of the important role of social honor.

Parties

Whereas the genuine place of classes is within the economic order, the place of status groups is within the social order, that is, within the sphere of the distribution of honor. From within these spheres, classes and status groups influence one another and the legal order and are in turn influenced by it. *"Parties"* reside in the sphere of power. Their action is oriented toward the acquisition of social power, that is to say, toward influencing social action no matter what its content may be. In principle, parties may exist in a social club as well as in a state. As over against the actions of classes and status groups, for which this is not necessarily the case, party-oriented social action always involves association. For it is always directed toward a goal which is striven for in a planned manner. This goal may be a cause (the party may aim at realizing a program for ideal or material purposes), or the goal may be personal (sinecures, power, and from these, honor for the leader and the followers of the party). Usually the party aims at all these simultaneously. Parties are, therefore, only possible within groups that have an associational character, that is, some rational order and a staff of persons available who are ready to enforce it. For parties aim precisely at influencing this staff, and if possible, to recruit from it party members.

In any individual case, parties may represent interests determined through class situation or status situation, and they may recruit their following respectively from one or the other. But they need be neither purely class nor purely status parties; in fact, they are more likely to be mixed types, and sometimes they are neither. They may represent ephemeral or enduring structures. Their means of attaining power may be quite varied, ranging from naked violence of any sort to canvassing for votes with coarse or subtle means: money, social influence, the force of speech, suggestion, clumsy hoax, and so on to the rougher or more artful tactics of obstruction in parliamentary bodies.

The sociological structure of parties differs in a basic way according to the kind of social action which they struggle to influence; that means, they differ according to whether or not the community is stratified by status or by classes. Above all else, they vary according to the structure of domination. For their leaders normally deal with its conquest. In our general terminology, parties are not only products of modern forms of domination. We shall also designate as parties the ancient and medieval ones, despite the fact that they differ basically from modern parties. Since a party always struggles for political control (*Herrschaft*), its organization too is frequently strict and "authoritarian." Because of these variations between the forms of domination, it is impossible to say anything about the structure of parties without discussing them first. Therefore, we shall now turn to this central phenomenon of all social organization.

Before we do this, we should add one more general observation about classes, status groups and parties: The fact that they presuppose a larger association, especially the framework of a polity, does not mean that they are confined to it. On the contrary, at all times it has been the order of the day that such association (even when it aims at the use of military force in common) reaches beyond the state boundaries. This can be seen in the [interlocal] solidarity of interests of oligarchs and democrats in Hellas, of Guelphs and Ghibellines in the Middle Ages, and within the Calvinist party during the age of religious struggles; and all the way up to the solidarity of landlords (International Congresses of Agriculture), princes (Holy Alliance, Karlsbad Decrees [of 1819]), socialist workers, conservatives (the longing of Prussian conservatives for Russian intervention in 1850). But their aim is not necessarily the establishment of a new territorial dominion. In the main they aim to influence the existing polity.

NOTES

1. All subheadings by Gerth and Mills. The major terminological change in this section is the elimination of the dichotomy of "communal" versus "societal" action and the substitution of "group" for "community." (R)
2. On the *bona paterna avitaque* of the Roman disemancipation formula, cf. also *infra*, ch. XVI:*v*, at n. 33. (Wi)

COMPANION WEBSITE

1. Go online to Write Out Loud about your own thoughts on how class is different than status, and why people sharing the same status honor can act as a group.
2. Log on to Weber's Profile Page to learn more about how his views on class are different than Marx's thoughts on the subject.

23

One-Dimensional Man

Herbert Marcuse

A COMFORTABLE, SMOOTH, reasonable, demo-cratic unfreedom prevails in advanced indus-trial civilization, a token of technical progress. Indeed, what could be more rational than the sup-pression of individuality in the mechanization of socially necessary but painful performances; the concentration of individual enterprises in more effective, more productive corporations; the regula-tion of free competition among unequally equipped economic subjects; the curtailment of preroga-tives and national sovereignties which impede the international organization of resources. That this technological order also involves a political and intellectual coordination may be a regrettable and yet promising development.

The rights and liberties which were such vital factors in the origins and earlier stages of industrial society yield to a higher stage of this society: they are losing their traditional rationale and content. Freedom of thought, speech, and conscience were—just as free enterprise, which they served to promote and protect—essentially *critical* ideas, designed to replace an obsolescent material and intellectual culture by a more productive and rational one. Once institutionalized, these rights and liberties shared the fate of the society of which they had become an integral part. The achievement cancels the premises.

To the degree to which freedom from want, the concrete substance of all freedom, is becoming a real possibility, the liberties which pertain to a state of lower productivity are losing their former con-tent. Independence of thought, autonomy, and the right to political opposition are being deprived of their basic critical function in a society which seems increasingly capable of satisfying the needs of the individuals through the way in which it is organ-ized. Such a society may justly demand accept-ance of its principles and institutions, and reduce the opposition to the discussion and promotion of alternative policies *within* the status quo. In this respect, it seems to make little difference whether the increasing satisfaction of needs is accomplished by an authoritarian or a non-authoritarian system. Under the conditions of a rising standard of living, non-conformity with the system itself appears to be socially useless, and the more so when it entails tangible economic and political disadvantages and threatens the smooth operation of the whole. Indeed, at least in so far as the necessities of life are involved, there seems to be no reason why the production and distribution of goods and services should proceed through the competitive concur-rence of individual liberties.

Freedom of enterprise was from the beginning not altogether a blessing. As the liberty to work or to starve, it spelled toil, insecurity, and fear for the vast majority of the population. If the indi-vidual were no longer compelled to prove himself on the market, as a free economic subject, the disappearance of this kind of freedom would be one of the greatest achievements of civilization. The technological processes of mechanization and standardization might release individual energy into a yet uncharted realm of freedom beyond necessity. The very structure of human existence would be altered; the individual would be liberated from the work world's imposing upon him alien needs and alien possibilities. The individual would be free to exert autonomy over a life that would be his own. If the productive apparatus could be organized and directed toward the satisfaction of the vital needs, its control might well be centralized; such control would not prevent individual autonomy, but render it possible.

This is a goal within the capabilities of advanced industrial civilization, the "end" of technological rationality. In actual fact, however, the contrary trend operates: the apparatus imposes its economic and political requirements for defense and expansion on labor time and free time, on the material and intellectual culture. By virtue of the way it has organized its technological base, contemporary industrial society tends to be totalitarian. For "totalitarian" is not only a terroristic political coordination of society, but also a non-terroristic economic-technical coordination which operates through the manipulation of needs by vested interests. It thus precludes the emergence of an effective opposition against the whole. Not only a specific form of government or party rule makes for totalitarianism, but also a specific system of production and distribution which may well be compatible with a "pluralism" of parties, newspapers, "countervailing powers," etc.[1]

Today political power asserts itself through its power over the machine process and over the technical organization of the apparatus. The government of advanced and advancing industrial societies can maintain and secure itself only when it succeeds in mobilizing, organizing, and exploiting the technical, scientific, and mechanical productivity available to industrial civilization. And this productivity mobilizes society as a whole, above and beyond any particular individual or group interests. The brute fact that the machine's physical (only physical?)

power surpasses that of the individual, and of any particular group of individuals, makes the machine the most effective political instrument in any society whose basic organization is that of the machine process. But the political trend may be reversed; essentially the power of the machine is only the stored-up and projected power of man. To the extent to which the work world is conceived of as a machine and mechanized accordingly, it becomes the *potential* basis of a new freedom for man.

Contemporary industrial civilization demonstrates that it has reached the stage at which "the free society" can no longer be adequately defined in the traditional terms of economic, political, and intellectual liberties, not because these liberties have become insignificant, but because they are too significant to be confined within the traditional forms. New modes of realization are needed, corresponding to the new capabilities of society.

Such new modes can be indicated only in negative terms because they would amount to the negation of the prevailing modes. Thus economic freedom would mean freedom *from* the economy—from being controlled by economic forces and relationships; freedom from the daily struggle for existence, from earning a living. Political freedom would mean liberation of the individuals *from* politics over which they have no effective control. Similarly, intellectual freedom would mean the restoration of individual thought now absorbed by mass communication and indoctrination, abolition of "public opinion" together with its makers. The unrealistic sound of these propositions is indicative, not of their utopian character, but of the strength of the forces which prevent their realization. The most effective and enduring form of warfare against liberation is the implanting of material and intellectual needs that perpetuate obsolete forms of the struggle for existence.

The intensity, the satisfaction and even the character of human needs, beyond the biological level, have always been preconditioned. Whether or not the possibility of doing or leaving, enjoying or destroying, possessing or rejecting something is seized as a *need* depends on whether or not it can be seen as desirable and necessary for the prevailing societal institutions and interests. In this sense, human needs are historical needs and, to the extent to which the society demands the repressive development of the individual, his needs themselves and their claim for satisfaction are subject to overriding critical standards.

We may distinguish both true and false needs. "False" are those which are superimposed upon the individual by particular social interests in his repression: the needs which perpetuate toil, aggressiveness, misery, and injustice. Their satisfaction might be most gratifying to the individual, but this happiness is not a condition which has to be maintained and protected if it serves to arrest the development of the ability (his own and others) to recognize the disease of the whole and grasp the chances of curing the disease. The result then is euphoria in unhappiness. Most of the prevailing needs to relax, to have fun, to behave and consume in accordance with the advertisements, to love and hate what others love and hate, belong to this category of false needs.

Such needs have a societal content and function which are determined by external powers over which the individual has no control; the development and satisfaction of these needs is heteronomous. No matter how much such needs may have become the individual's own, reproduced and fortified by the conditions of his existence; no matter how much he identifies himself with them and finds himself in their satisfaction, they continue to be what they were from the beginning—products of a society whose dominant interest demands repression.

The prevalence of repressive needs is an accomplished fact, accepted in ignorance and defeat, but a fact that must be undone in the interest of the happy individual as well as all those whose misery is the price of his satisfaction. The only needs that have an unqualified claim for satisfaction are the vital ones—nourishment, clothing, lodging at the attainable level of culture. The satisfaction of these needs is the prerequisite for the realization of *all* needs, of the unsublimated as well as the sublimated ones.

For any consciousness and conscience, for any experience which does not accept the prevailing societal interest as the supreme law of thought and behavior, the established universe of needs and satisfactions is a fact to be questioned—questioned in terms of truth and falsehood. These terms are historical throughout, and their objectivity is historical. The judgment of needs and their satisfaction, under the given conditions, involves standards of *priority*—standards which refer to the optimal development of the individual, of all individuals, under the optimal utilization of the material and intellectual resources available to man. The resources are calculable. "Truth" and "falsehood" of needs designate objective conditions to the extent to which the universal satisfaction of vital needs and, beyond it, the progressive alleviation of toil and poverty, are universally valid standards. But as historical standards, they do not only vary according to area and stage of development, they also can be defined only in (greater or lesser) *contradiction* to the prevailing ones. What tribunal can possibly claim the authority of decision?

In the last analysis, the question of what are true and false needs must be answered by the individuals themselves, but only in the last analysis; that is, if and when they are free to give their own answer. As long as they are kept incapable of being autonomous, as long as they are indoctrinated and manipulated (down to their very instincts), their answer to this question cannot be taken as their own. By the same token, however, no tribunal can justly arrogate to itself the right to decide which needs should be developed and satisfied. Any such tribunal is reprehensible, although our revulsion does not do away with the question: how can the people who have been the object of effective and productive domination by themselves create the conditions of freedom?[2]

The more rational, productive, technical, and total the repressive administration of society becomes, the more unimaginable the means and ways by which the administered individuals might break their servitude and seize their own liberation. To be sure, to impose Reason upon an entire society is a paradoxical and scandalous idea—although one might dispute the righteousness of a society which ridicules this idea while making its own population into objects of total administration. All liberation depends on the consciousness of servitude, and the emergence of this consciousness is always hampered by the predominance of needs and satisfactions which, to a great extent, have become the individual's own. The process always replaces one system of preconditioning by another; the optimal goal is the replacement of false needs by true ones, the abandonment of repressive satisfaction.

The distinguishing feature of advanced industrial society is its effective suffocation of those needs which demand liberation—liberation also from that which is tolerable and rewarding and comfortable—while it sustains and absolves the destructive power and repressive function of the affluent society. Here, the social controls exact the overwhelming need for the production and consumption of waste; the need for stupefying work where it is no longer a real necessity; the need for modes of relaxation which soothe and prolong this stupefication; the need for maintaining such deceptive liberties as free competition at administered prices, a free press which censors itself, free choice between brands and gadgets.

Under the rule of a repressive whole, liberty can be made into a powerful instrument of domination. The range of choice open to the individual is not the decisive factor in determining the degree of human freedom, but *what* can be chosen and what *is* chosen by the individual. The criterion for free choice can never be an absolute one, but neither is it entirely relative. Free election of masters does not abolish the masters or the slaves. Free choice among a wide variety of goods and services does not

signify freedom if these goods and services sustain social controls over a life of toil and fear—that is, if they sustain alienation. And the spontaneous reproduction of superimposed needs by the individual does not establish autonomy; it only testifies to the efficacy of the controls.

Our insistence on the depth and efficacy of these controls is open to the objection that we overrate greatly the indoctrinating power of the "media," and that by themselves the people would feel and satisfy the needs which are now imposed upon them. The objection misses the point. The preconditioning does not start with the mass production of radio and television and with the centralization of their control. The people enter this stage as preconditioned receptacles of long standing; the decisive difference is in the flattening out of the contrast (or conflict) between the given and the possible, between the satisfied and the unsatisfied needs. Here, the so-called equalization of class distinctions reveals its ideological function. If the worker and his boss enjoy the same television program and visit the same resort places, if the typist is as attractively made up as the daughter of her employer, if the Negro owns a Cadillac, if they all read the same newspaper, then this assimilation indicates not the disappearance of classes, but the extent to which the needs and satisfactions that serve the preservation of the Establishment are shared by the underlying population.

Indeed, in the most highly developed areas of contemporary society, the transplantation of social into individual needs is so effective that the difference between them seems to be purely theoretical. Can one really distinguish between the mass media as instruments of information and entertainment, and as agents of manipulation and indoctrination? Between the automobile as nuisance and as convenience? Between the horrors and the comforts of functional architecture? Between the work for national defense and the work for corporate gain? Between the private pleasure and the commercial and political utility involved in increasing the birth rate?

We are again confronted with one of the most vexing aspects of advanced industrial civilization: the rational character of its irrationality. Its productivity and efficiency, its capacity to increase and spread comforts, to turn waste into need, and destruction into construction, the extent to which this civilization transforms the object world into an extension of man's mind and body makes the very notion of alienation questionable. The people recognize themselves in their commodities; they find their soul in their automobile, hi-fi set, split-level home, kitchen equipment. The very mechanism which ties the individual to his society has changed, and social control is anchored in the new needs which it has produced.

The prevailing forms of social control are technological in a new sense. To be sure, the technical structure and efficacy of the productive and destructive apparatus has been a major instrumentality for subjecting the population to the established social division of labor throughout the modern period. Moreover, such integration has always been accompanied by more obvious forms of compulsion: loss of livelihood, the administration of justice, the police, the armed forces. It still is. But in the contemporary period, the technological controls appear to be the very embodiment of Reason for the benefit of all social groups and interests— to such an extent that all contradiction seems irrational and all counteraction impossible.

No wonder then that, in the most advanced areas of this civilization, the social controls have been introjected to the point where even individual protest is affected at its roots. The intellectual and emotional refusal "to go along" appears neurotic and impotent. This is the socio-psychological aspect of the political event that marks the contemporary period: the passing of the historical forces which, at the preceding stage of industrial society, seemed to represent the possibility of new forms of existence.

But the term "introjection" perhaps no longer describes the way in which the individual by himself reproduces and perpetuates the external controls exercised by his society. Introjection suggests a variety of relatively spontaneous processes by which a Self (Ego) transposes the "outer" into the "inner." Thus introjection implies the existence of an inner dimension distinguished from and even antagonistic to the external exigencies—an individual consciousness and an individual unconscious *apart from* public opinion and behavior.[3] The idea of "inner freedom" here has its reality: it designates the private space in which man may become and remain "himself."

Today this private space has been invaded and whittled down by technological reality. Mass production and mass distribution claim the *entire* individual, and industrial psychology has long since ceased to be confined to the factory. The manifold processes of introjection seem to be ossified in almost mechanical reactions. The result is, not adjustment but *mimesis:* an immediate identification of the individual with *his* society and, through it, with the society as a whole.

This immediate, automatic identification (which may have been characteristic of primitive forms of association) reappears in high industrial civilization; its new "immediacy," however, is the product of a sophisticated, scientific management and organization. In this process, the "inner" dimension of the mind in which opposition to the status quo can take root is whittled down. The loss of this dimension, in which the power of negative thinking—the critical power of Reason—is at home, is the ideological counterpart to the very material process in which advanced industrial society silences and reconciles the opposition. The impact of progress turns Reason into submission to the facts of life, and to the dynamic capability of producing more and bigger facts of the same sort of life. The efficiency of the system blunts the individuals' recognition that it contains no facts which do not communicate the repressive power of the whole. If the individuals find themselves in the things which shape their life, they do so, not by giving, but by accepting the law of things—not the law of physics but the law of their society.

I have just suggested that the concept of alienation seems to become questionable when the individuals identify themselves with the existence which is imposed upon them and have in it their own development and satisfaction. This identification is not illusion but reality. However, the reality constitutes a more progressive stage of alienation. The latter has become entirely objective; the subject which is alienated is swallowed up by its alienated existence. There is only one dimension, and it is everywhere and in all forms. The achievements of progress defy ideological indictment as well as justification; before their tribunal, the "false consciousness" of their rationality becomes the true consciousness.

This absorption of ideology into reality does not, however, signify the "end of ideology." On the contrary, in a specific sense advanced industrial culture is *more* ideological than its predecessor, inasmuch as today the ideology is in the process of production itself.[4] In a provocative form, this proposition reveals the political aspects of the prevailing technological rationality. The productive apparatus and the goods and services which it produces "sell" or impose the social system as a whole. The means of mass transportation and communication, the commodities of lodging, food, and clothing, the irresistible output of the entertainment and information industry carry with them prescribed attitudes and habits, certain intellectual and emotional reactions which bind the consumers more or less pleasantly to the producers and, through the latter, to the whole. The products indoctrinate and manipulate; they promote a false consciousness which is immune against its falsehood. And as these beneficial products become available to more individuals in more social classes, the indoctrination they carry ceases to be publicity; it becomes a way of life. It is a good way of life—much better than before—and as a good way of life, it militates against qualitative change. Thus emerges a pattern of *one-dimensional thought and behavior* in which ideas, aspirations, and objectives that, by their content, transcend the established universe of discourse and action are either repelled or reduced to terms of this universe. They are redefined by the rationality of the given system and of its quantitative extension.

The trend may be related to a development in scientific method: operationalism in the physical, behaviorism in the social sciences. The common feature is a total empiricism in the treatment of concepts; their meaning is restricted to the representation of particular operations and behavior. The operational point of view is well illustrated by P. W. Bridgman's analysis of the concept of length:[5]

> We evidently know what we mean by length if we can tell what the length of any and every object is, and for the physicist nothing more is required. To find the length of an object, we have to perform certain physical operations. The concept of length is therefore fixed when the operations by which length is measured are fixed: that is, the concept of length involves as much and nothing more than the set of operations by which length is determined. In general, we mean by any concept nothing more than a set of operations; *the concept is synonymous with the corresponding set of operations.*

Bridgman has seen the wide implications of this mode of thought for the society at large:[6]

> To adopt the operational point of view involves much more than a mere restriction of the sense in which we understand 'concept,' but means a far-reaching change in all our habits of thought, in that we shall no longer permit ourselves to use as tools in our thinking concepts of which we cannot give an adequate account in terms of operations.

Bridgman's prediction has come true. The new mode of thought is today the predominant tendency in philosophy, psychology, sociology, and other fields.

Many of the most seriously troublesome concepts are being "eliminated" by showing that no adequate account of them in terms of operations or behavior can be given. The radical empiricist onslaught (I shall subsequently, in chapters VII and VIII, examine its claim to be empiricist) thus provides the methodological justification for the debunking of the mind by the intellectuals—a positivism which, in its denial of the transcending elements of Reason, forms the academic counterpart of the socially required behavior.

Outside the academic establishment, the "far-reaching change in all our habits of thought" is more serious. It serves to coordinate ideas and goals with those exacted by the prevailing system, to enclose them in the system, and to repel those which are irreconcilable with the system. The reign of such a one-dimensional reality does not mean that materialism rules, and that the spiritual, metaphysical, and bohemian occupations are petering out. On the contrary, there is a great deal of "Worship together this week," "Why not try God," Zen, existentialism, and beat ways of life, etc. But such modes of protest and transcendence are no longer contradictory to the status quo and no longer negative. They are rather the ceremonial part of practical behaviorism, its harmless negation, and are quickly digested by the status quo as part of its healthy diet.

One-dimensional thought is systematically promoted by the makers of politics and their purveyors of mass information. Their universe of discourse is populated by self-validating hypotheses which, incessantly and monopolistically repeated, become hypnotic definitions or dictations. For example, "free" are the institutions which operate (and are operated on) in the countries of the Free World; other transcending modes of freedom are by definition either anarchism, communism, or propaganda. "Socialistic" are all encroachments on private enterprises not undertaken by private enterprise itself (or by government contracts), such as universal and comprehensive health insurance, or the protection of nature from all too sweeping commercialization, or the establishment of public services which may hurt private profit. This totalitarian logic of accomplished facts has its Eastern counterpart. There, freedom is the way of life instituted by a communist regime, and all other transcending modes of freedom are either capitalistic, or revisionist, or leftist sectarianism. In both camps, non-operational ideas are non-behavioral and subversive. The movement of thought is stopped at barriers which appear as the limits of Reason itself.

Such limitation of thought is certainly not new. Ascending modern rationalism, in its speculative as well as empirical form, shows a striking contrast between extreme critical radicalism in scientific and philosophic method on the one hand, and an uncritical quietism in the attitude toward established and functioning social institutions. Thus Descartes' *ego cogitans* was to leave the "great public bodies" untouched, and Hobbes held that "the present ought always to be preferred, maintained, and accounted best." Kant agreed with Locke in justifying revolution *if and when* it has succeeded in organizing the whole and in preventing subversion.

However, these accommodating concepts of Reason were always contradicted by the evident misery and injustice of the "great public bodies" and the effective, more or less conscious rebellion against them. Societal conditions existed which provoked and permitted real dissociation from the established state of affairs; a private as well as political dimension was present in which dissociation could develop into effective opposition, testing its strength and the validity of its objectives.

With the gradual closing of this dimension by the society, the self-limitation of thought assumes a larger significance. The interrelation between scientific-philosophical and societal processes, between theoretical and practical Reason, asserts itself "behind the back" of the scientists and philosophers. The society bars a whole type of oppositional operations and behavior; consequently, the concepts pertaining to them are rendered illusory or meaningless. Historical transcendence appears as metaphysical transcendence, not acceptable to science and scientific thought. The operational and behavioral point of view, practiced as a "habit of thought" at large, becomes the view of the established universe of discourse and action, needs and aspirations. The "cunning of Reason" works, as it so often did, in the interest of the powers that be. The insistence on operational and behavioral concepts turns against the efforts to free thought and behavior *from* the given reality and *for* the suppressed alternatives. Theoretical and practical Reason, academic and social behaviorism meet on common ground: that of an advanced society which makes scientific and technical progress into an instrument of domination.

"Progress" is not a neutral term; it moves toward specific ends, and these ends are defined by the possibilities of ameliorating the human condition. Advanced industrial society is approaching the stage where continued progress would demand the radical subversion of the prevailing direction and organization of progress. This stage would be reached when material production (including the necessary services) becomes automated to the extent that all vital needs can be satisfied while necessary labor time is reduced to marginal time. From this point on, technical progress would transcend the realm of necessity, where it served as the instrument of domination and exploitation which thereby limited its rationality; technology would become subject to the free play of faculties in the struggle for the pacification of nature and of society.

Such a state is envisioned in Marx's notion of the "abolition of labor." The term "pacification of existence" seems better suited to designate the historical alternative of a world which—through an international conflict which transforms and suspends the contradictions within the established societies—advances on the brink of a global war. "Pacification of existence" means the development of man's struggle with man and with nature, under conditions where the competing needs, desires, and aspirations are no longer organized by vested interests in domination and scarcity—an organization which perpetuates the destructive forms of this struggle.

Today's fight against this historical alternative finds a firm mass basis in the underlying population, and finds its ideology in the rigid orientation of thought and behavior to the given universe of facts. Validated by the accomplishments of science and technology, justified by its growing productivity, the status quo defies all transcendence. Faced with the possibility of pacification on the grounds of its technical and intellectual achievements, the mature industrial society closes itself against this alternative. Operationalism, in theory and practice, becomes the theory and practice of *containment*. Underneath its obvious dynamics, this society is a thoroughly static system of life: self-propelling in its oppressive productivity and in its beneficial coordination. Containment of technical progress goes hand in hand with its growth in the established direction. In spite of the political fetters imposed by the status quo, the more technology appears capable of creating the conditions for pacification, the more are the minds and bodies of man organized against this alternative.

The most advanced areas of industrial society exhibit throughout these two features: a trend toward consummation of technological rationality, and intensive efforts to contain this trend within the established institutions. Here is the internal contradiction of this civilization: the irrational element in its rationality. It is the token of its achievements. The industrial society which makes technology and science its own is organized for the ever-more-effective domination of man and nature, for the ever-more-effective utilization of its resources. It becomes irrational when the success of these efforts opens new dimensions of human realization. Organization for peace is different from organization for war; the institutions which served the struggle for existence cannot serve the pacification of existence. Life as an end is qualitatively different from life as a means.

Such a qualitatively new mode of existence can never be envisaged as the mere by-product of economic and political changes, as the more or less spontaneous effect of the new institutions which constitute the necessary prerequisite. Qualitative change also involves a change in the *technical* basis on which this society rests—one which sustains the economic and political institutions through which the "second nature" of man as an aggressive object of administration is stabilized. The techniques of industrialization are political techniques; as such, they prejudge the possibilities of Reason and Freedom.

To be sure, labor must precede the reduction of labor, and industrialization must precede the development of human needs and satisfactions. But as all freedom depends on the conquest of alien necessity, the realization of freedom depends on the *techniques* of this conquest. The highest productivity of labor can be used for the perpetuation of labor, and the most efficient industrialization can serve the restriction and manipulation of needs.

When this point is reached, domination—in the guise of affluence and liberty—extends to all spheres of private and public existence, integrates all authentic opposition, absorbs all alternatives.

Technological rationality reveals its political character as it becomes the great vehicle of better domination, creating a truly totalitarian universe in which society and nature, mind and body are kept in a state of permanent mobilization for the defense of this universe.

NOTES

1. See p. 50.
2. See p. 40.
3. The change in the function of the family here plays a decisive role: its "socializing" functions are increasingly taken over by outside groups and media. See my *Eros and Civilization* (Boston: Beacon Press, 1955), p. 96 ff.
4. Theodor W. Adorno, *Prismen. Kulturkritik und Gesellschaft.* (Frankfurt: Suhrkamp, 1955), p. 24 f.
5. P. W. Bridgman, *The Logic of Modern Physics* (New York: Macmillan, 1928), p. 5. The operational doctrine has since been refined and qualified. Bridgman himself has extended the concept of "operation" to include the "paper-and-pencil" operations of the theorist (in Philipp J. Frank, *The Validation of Scientific Theories* [Boston: Beacon Press, 1954], Chap. II). The main impetus remains the same: it is "desirable" that the paper-and-pencil operations "be capable of eventual contact, although perhaps indirectly, with instrumental operations."
6. P. W. Bridgman, *The Logic of Modern Physics,* loc. cit., p. 31.

COMPANION WEBSITE

1. Go online to Write Out Loud about some contemporary examples of consumerist culture that Marcuse argued have made society "one-dimensional."
2. Log on to the *Pathway to Meltdown* Supplementary Sources Page to watch *Generation Like*, a PBS documentary that compellingly argues how marketing encourages today's teens to be increasingly one-dimensional.
3. Also check out the Supplementary Sources Page for more readings from the Frankfurt School, including Theodor Adorno's "How to Look at Television."

24

Toward a Rational Society

Jurgen Habermas

WHEN C. P. SNOW PUBLISHED *The Two Cultures* in 1959, he initiated a discussion of the relation of science and literature which has been going on in other countries as well as in England. Science in this connection has meant the strictly empirical sciences, while literature has been taken more broadly to include methods of interpretation in the cultural sciences. The treatise with which Aldous Huxley entered the controversy, however, *Literature and Science*, does limit itself to confronting the natural sciences with the belles-lettres.

Huxley distinguishes the two cultures primarily according to the specific experiences with which they deal: literature makes statements mainly about private experiences, the sciences about intersubjectively accessible experiences. The latter can be expressed in a formalized language, which can be made universally valid by means of general definitions. In contrast, the language of literature must verbalize what is in principle unrepeatable and must generate an intersubjectivity of mutual understanding in each concrete case. But this distinction between private and public experience allows only a first approximation to the problem. The element of ineffability that literary expression must overcome derives less from a private experience encased in subjectivity than from the constitution of these experiences within the horizon of a life-historical environment. The events whose connection is the object of the law-like hypotheses of the sciences can be described in a spatio-temporal coordinate system, but they do not make up a world:

> The world with which literature deals is the world in which human beings are born and live and finally die; the world in which they love and hate, in which they experience triumph and humiliation, hope and despair; the world of sufferings and enjoyments, of madness and common sense, of silliness, cunning and wisdom; the world of social pressures and individual impulses, of reason against passion, of instincts and conventions, of shared language and unsharable feelings and sensations ...[1]

In contrast, science does not concern itself with the contents of a life-world of this sort, which is culture-bound, ego-centered, and pre-interpreted in the ordinary language of social groups and socialized individuals:

> ... As a professional chemist, say, a professional physicist or physiologist, [the scientist] is the inhabitant of a radically different universe—not the universe of given appearances, but the world of inferred fine structures, not the experienced world of unique events and diverse qualities, but the world of quantified regularities.[2]

Huxley juxtaposes the *social life-world* and the *worldless universe of facts*. He also sees precisely the way in which the sciences transpose their information about this worldless universe into the life-world of social groups:

Knowledge is power and, by a seeming paradox, it is through their knowledge of what happens in this unexperienced world of abstractions and inferences that scientists have acquired their enormous and growing power to control, direct, and modify the world of manifold appearances in which human beings are privileged and condemned to live.[3]

But Huxley does not take up the question of the relation of the two cultures at this juncture, where the sciences enter the social life-world through the technical exploitation of their information. Instead he postulates an immediate relation. Literature should assimilate scientific statements as such, so that science can take on "flesh and blood."

… Until some great artist comes along and tells us what to do, we shall not know how the muddled words of the tribe and the too precise words of the textbooks should be poetically purified, so as to make them capable of harmonizing our private and unsharable experiences with the scientific hypotheses in terms of which they are explained.[4]

This postulate is based, I think, on a misunderstanding. Information provided by the strictly empirical sciences can be incorporated in the social life-world only through its technical utilization, as technological knowledge, serving the expansion of our power of technical control. Thus, such information is not on the same level as the action-orienting self-understanding of social groups. Hence, without mediation, the information content of the sciences cannot be relevant to that part of practical knowledge which gains expression in literature. It can only attain significance through the detour marked by the practical results of technical progress. Taken for itself, knowledge of atomic physics remains without consequence for the interpretation of our life-world, and to this extent the cleavage between the two cultures is inevitable. Only when with the aid of physical theories we can carry out nuclear fission, only when information is exploited for the development of productive or destructive forces,

can its revolutionary practical results penetrate the literary consciousness of the life-world: poems arise from consideration of Hiroshima and not from the elaboration of hypotheses about the transformation of mass into energy.

The idea of an atomic poetry that would elaborate on hypotheses follows from false premises. In fact, the problematic relation of literature and science is only one segment of a much broader problem: *How is it possible to translate technically exploitable knowledge into the practical consciousness of a social life-world?* This question obviously sets a new task, not only or even primarily for literature. The skewed relation of the two cultures is so disquieting only because, in the seeming conflict between the two competing cultural traditions, a true life-problem of scientific civilization becomes apparent: namely, how can the relation between technical progress and the social life-world, which today is still clothed in a primitive, traditional, and unchosen form, be reflected upon and brought under the control of rational discussion?

To a certain extent practical questions of government, strategy, and administration had to be dealt with through the application of technical knowledge even at an earlier period. Yet today's problem of transposing technical knowledge into practical consciousness has changed not merely its order of magnitude. The mass of technical knowledge is no longer restricted to pragmatically acquired techniques of the classical crafts. It has taken, the form of scientific information that can be exploited for technology. On the other hand, behavior-controlling traditions no longer naively define the self-understanding of modern societies. Historicism has broken the natural-traditional validity of action-orienting value systems. Today, the self-understanding of social groups and their worldview as articulated in ordinary language is mediated by the hermeneutic appropriation of traditions as traditions. In this situation questions of life conduct demand a rational discussion that is not focused exclusively either on technical means or on the application of traditional behavioral norms. The reflection that is required extends beyond the production of technical knowledge and the hermeneutical clarification of traditions to the employment of technical means in historical situations whose objective conditions (potentials, institutions, interests) have to be interpreted anew each time in the framework of a self-understanding determined by tradition.

This problem-complex has only entered consciousness within the last two or three generations. In the nineteenth century one could still maintain that the sciences entered the conduct of life through two separate channels: through the technical exploitation of scientific information and through the processes of individual education and culture during academic study. Indeed, in the German university system, which goes back to Humboldt's reform, we still maintain the fiction that the sciences develop their action-orienting power through educational processes within the life history of the individual student. I should like to show that the intention designated by Fichte as a "transformation of knowledge into works" can no longer be carried out in the private sphere of education, but rather can be realized only on the politically relevant level at which technically exploitable knowledge is translatable into the context of our life-world. Though literature participates in this, it is primarily a problem of the sciences themselves.

At the beginning of the nineteenth century, in Humboldt's time, it was still impossible, looking at Germany, to conceive of the scientific transformation of social life. Thus, the university reformers did not have to break seriously with the tradition of practical philosophy. Despite the profound ramifications of revolutions in the political order, the structures of the preindustrial work world persisted, permitting for the last time, as it were, the classical view of the relation of theory to practice. In this tradition, the technical capabilities employed in the sphere of social labor are not capable of immediate direction by theory. They must be pragmatically practiced according to traditional patterns of skill. Theory, which is concerned with the immutable essence of things beyond the mutable region of human affairs, can obtain practical validity only by molding the manner of life of men engaged in theory. Understanding the cosmos as a whole yields norms of individual human behavior, and it is through the actions of the philosophically educated that theory assumes a positive form. This was the only relation of theory to practice incorporated in the traditional idea of university education. Even where Schelling attempts to provide the physician's practice with a scientific basis in natural philosophy, the medical *craft* is unexpectedly transformed into a medical *praxiology*. The physician must orient himself to Ideas derived from natural philosophy in the same way that the subject of moral action orients itself through the Ideas of practical reason.

Since then it has become common knowledge that the scientific transformation of medicine succeeds only to the extent that the pragmatic doctrine of the medical art can be transformed into the control of isolated natural processes, checked by scientific method. The same holds for other areas of social labor. Whether it is a matter of rationalizing the production of goods, management and administration, construction of machine tools, roads, or airplanes, or the manipulation of electoral, consumer, or leisure-time behavior, the professional practice in question will always have to assume the form of technical control of objectified processes.

In the early nineteenth century, the maxim that scientific knowledge is a source of culture required a strict separation between the university and the technical school because the preindustrial forms of professional practice were impervious to theoretical guidance. Today, research processes are coupled with technical conversion and economic exploitation, and production and administration in the industrial system of labor generate feedback for science. The application of science in technology and the feedback of technical progress to research have become the substance of the world of work. In these circumstances, unyielding opposition to the decomposition of the university into specialized schools can no longer invoke the old argument. Today, the reason given for delimiting study on the university model from the professional sphere is not that the latter is still foreign to science, but conversely, that science—to the very extent that it has penetrated professional practice—has estranged itself from humanistic culture. The philosophical conviction of German idealism that scientific knowledge is a source of culture no longer holds for the strictly empirical scientist. It was once possible for theory, via humanistic culture, to become a practical force. Today, theories can become technical power while remaining unpractical, that is, without being expressly oriented to the interaction of a community of human beings. Of course, the sciences now transmit a specific capacity: but the capacity for control, which they teach, is not the same capacity for life and action that was to be expected of the scientifically educated and cultivated.

The cultured possessed orientation in action. Their culture was universal only in the sense of the universality of a culture-bound horizon of a world in which scientific experiences could be interpreted and turned into practical abilities, namely, into a reflected consciousness of the practically necessary. The only type of experience which is admitted as scientific today according to positivistic criteria is not capable of this transposition into practice. The capacity for *control* made possible by the empirical sciences is not to be confused with the capacity for *enlightened action*. But is science, therefore, completely discharged of this task of action-orientation, or does the question of academic education in the framework of a civilization transformed by scientific means arise again today as a problem of the sciences themselves?

First, production processes were revolutionized by scientific methods. Then expectations of technically correct functioning were also transferred to those areas of society that had become independent in the course of the industrialization of labor and thus supported planned organization. The power of technical control over nature made possible by science is extended today directly to society: for every isolatable social system, for every cultural area that has become a separate, closed system whose relations can be analyzed immanently in terms of presupposed system goals, a new discipline emerges in the social sciences. In the same measure, however, the problems of technical control solved by science are transformed into life problems. For the scientific control of natural and social processes—in a word, technology—does not release men from action. Just as before, conflicts must be decided, interests realized, interpretations found—through both action and transaction structured by ordinary language. Today, however, these practical problems are themselves in large measure determined by the system of our technical achievements.

But if technology proceeds from science, and I mean the technique of influencing human behavior no less than that of dominating nature, then the assimilation of this technology into the practical life-world, bringing the technical control of particular areas within the reaches of the communication of acting men, really requires scientific reflection. The prescientific horizon of experience becomes infantile when it naively incorporates contact with the products of the most intensive rationality.

Culture and education can then no longer indeed be restricted to the ethical dimension of personal attitude. Instead, in the political dimension at issue, the theoretical guidance of action must proceed from a scientifically explicated understanding of the world.

The relation of technical progress and social life-world and the translation of scientific information into practical consciousness is not an affair of private cultivation.

I should like to reformulate this problem with reference to political decision-making. In what follows we shall understand "technology" to mean scientifically rationalized control of objectified processes. It refers to the system in which research and technology are coupled with feedback from the economy and administration. We shall understand "democracy" to mean the institutionally secured forms of general and public communication that deal with the practical question of how men can and want to live under the objective conditions of their ever-expanding power of control. Our problem can then be stated as one of the relation of technology and democracy: how can the power of technical control be brought within the range of the consensus of acting and transacting citizens?

I should like first to discuss two antithetical answers. The first, stated in rough outline, is that of Marxian theory. Marx criticizes the system of capitalist production as a power that has taken on its own life in opposition to the interests of productive freedom, of the producers. Through the private form of appropriating socially produced goods, the technical process of producing use values falls under the alien law of an economic process that produces exchange values. Once we trace this self-regulating character of the accumulation of capital back to its origins in private property in the means of production, it becomes possible for mankind to comprehend economic compulsion as an alienated result of its own free productive activity and then abolish it. Finally, the reproduction of social life can be rationally planned as a process of producing use values; society places this process under its technical control. The latter is exercised democratically in accordance with the will and insight of the associated individuals. Here Marx equates the practical insight of a political public with successful technical control. Meanwhile we have learned that even a well-functioning planning bureaucracy with scientific control of the production of goods and services is not a sufficient condition for realizing the associated material and intellectual productive forces in the interest of the enjoyment and freedom of an emancipated society. For Marx did not reckon

with the possible emergence at every level of a discrepancy between scientific control of the material conditions of life and a democratic decision-making process. This is the philosophical reason why socialists never anticipated the authoritarian welfare state, where social wealth is relatively guaranteed while political freedom is excluded.

Even if technical control of physical and social conditions for preserving life and making it less burdensome had attained the level that Marx expected would characterize a communist stage of development, it does not follow that they would be linked automatically with social emancipation of the sort intended by the thinkers of the Enlightenment in the eighteenth century and the Young Hegelians in the nineteenth. For the techniques with which the development of a highly industrialized society could be brought under control can no longer be interpreted according to an instrumental model, as though appropriate means were being organized for the realization of goals that are either presupposed without discussion or clarified through communication.

Hans Freyer and Helmut Schelsky have outlined a counter-model which recognizes technology as an independent force. In contrast to the primitive state of technical development, the relation of the organization of means to given or pre-established goals today seems to have been reversed. The process of research and technology—which obeys immanent laws—precipitates in an unplanned fashion new methods for which we then have to find purposeful application. Through progress that has become automatic, Freyer argues, abstract potential continually accrues to us in renewed thrusts. Subsequently, both life interests and fantasy that generates meaning have to take this potential in hand and expend it on concrete goals. Schelsky refines and simplifies this thesis to the point of asserting that technical progress produces not only unforeseen methods but the unplanned goals and applications themselves: technical potentialities command their own practical realization. In particular, he puts forth this thesis with regard to the highly complicated objective exigencies that in political situations allegedly prescribe solutions without alternatives.

> Political norms and laws are replaced by objective exigencies of scientific-technical civilization, which are not posited as political decisions and cannot be understood as norms of conviction or weltanschauung. Hence, the idea of democracy loses its classical substance, so to speak. In place of the political will of the people emerges an objective exigency, which man himself produces as science and labor.

In the face of research, technology, the economy, and administration—integrated as a system that has become autonomous—the question prompted by the neohumanistic ideal of culture, namely, how can society possibly exercise sovereignty over the technical conditions of life and integrate them into the practice of the life-world, seems hopelessly obsolete. In the technical state such ideas are suited at best for "the manipulation of motives to help bring about what must happen anyway from the point of view of objective necessity."

It is clear that this thesis of the autonomous character of technical development is not correct. The pace and *direction* of technical development today depend to a great extent on public investments: in the United States the defense and space administrations are the largest sources of research contracts. I suspect that the situation is similar in the Soviet Union. The assertion that politically consequential decisions are reduced to carrying out the immanent exigencies of disposable techniques and that therefore they can no longer be made the theme of practical considerations, serves in the end merely to conceal pre-existing, unreflected social interests and prescientific decisions. As little as we can accept the optimistic convergence of technology and democracy, the pessimistic assertion that technology excludes democracy is just as untenable.

These two answers to the question of how the force of technical control can be made subject to the consensus of acting and transacting citizens are inadequate. Neither of them can deal appropriately with the problem with which we are objectively confronted in the West and East, namely, how we can actually bring under control the preexisting, unplanned relations of technical progress and the social life-world. The tensions between productive forces and social intentions that Marx diagnosed and whose explosive character has intensified in an unforeseen manner in the age of thermonuclear weapons are the consequence of an ironic relation of theory to practice. The direction of technical progress is still largely determined today by social interests that arise autochthonously out of the compulsion of the reproduction of social life without being reflected upon and confronted with the declared political self-understanding of social groups. In consequence, new technical capacities erupt without preparation into existing forms of life-activity and conduct. New potentials for expanded power of technical control make obvious the disproportion between the results of the most organized rationality and unreflected goals, rigidified value systems, and obsolete ideologies.

Today, in the industrially most advanced systems, an energetic attempt must be made consciously to take in hand the mediation between technical progress and the conduct of life in the major industrial societies, a mediation that has previously taken place without direction, as a mere continuation of natural history. This is not the place to discuss the social, economic, and political conditions on which a long-term central research policy would have to depend. It is not enough for a social system to fulfill the conditions of technical rationality. Even if the cybernetic dream of a virtually instinctive self-stabilization could be realized, the value system would have contracted in the meantime to a set of rules for the maximization of power and comfort; it would be equivalent to the biological base value of survival at any cost, that is, ultrastability. Through the unplanned sociocultural consequences of technological progress, the human species has challenged itself to learn not merely to affect its social destiny, but to control it. This challenge of technology cannot be met with technology alone. It is rather a question of setting into motion a politically effective discussion that rationally brings the social potential constituted by technical knowledge and ability into a defined and controlled relation to our practical knowledge and will. On the one hand, such discussion could enlighten those who act politically about the tradition-bound self-understanding of their interests in relation to what is technically possible and feasible. On the other hand, they would be able to judge practically, in the light of their now articulated and newly interpreted needs, the direction and the extent to which they want to develop technical knowledge for the future.

This *dialectic of potential and will* takes place today without reflection in accordance with interests for which public justification is neither demanded nor permitted. Only if we could elaborate this dialectic with political consciousness could we succeed in directing the mediation of technical progress and the conduct of social life, which until now has occurred as an extension of natural history; its conditions being left outside the framework of discussion and planning. The fact that this is a matter for reflection means that it does not belong to the professional competence of specialists. The substance of domination is not dissolved by the power of technical control. To the contrary, the former can simply hide behind the latter. The irrationality of domination, which today has become a collective peril to life, could be mastered only by the development of a political decision-making process tied to the principle of general discussion free from domination. Our only hope for the rationalization of the power structure lies in conditions that favor political power for thought developing through dialogue. The redeeming power of reflection cannot be supplanted by the extension of technically exploitable knowledge.

NOTES

1. Aldous Huxley, *Literature and Science* (New York, 1963), p. 8.
2. *Ibid*.
3. *Ibid*., p. 9.
4. *Ibid*., p. 107.

COMPANION WEBSITE

1. Go online to Write Out Loud about whether you agree with Habermas's point that technology on its own cannot improve society.
2. Browse the *Pathway to Meltdown* Supplementary Sources for an interview with Thomas Wheatland, author of *The Frankfurt School in Exile*.
3. Log on to the Frankfurt School's Profile Page to learn more about Habermas and the other provocative theorists of critical social theory.

25

Discipline and Punish

Michel Foucault

ON 2 MARCH 1757 DAMIENS THE regicide was condemned to make the *amende honorable* before the main door of the Church of Paris', where he was to be 'taken and conveyed in a cart, wearing nothing but a shirt, holding a torch of burning wax weighing two pounds'; then, 'in the said cart, to the Place de Grève, where, on a scaffold that will be erected there, the flesh will be torn from his breasts, arms, thighs and calves with red-hot pincers, his right hand, holding the knife with which he committed the said parricide, burnt with sulphur, and, on those places where the flesh will be torn away, poured molten lead, boiling oil, burning resin, wax and sulphur melted together and then his body drawn and quartered by four horses and his limbs and body consumed by fire, reduced to ashes and his ashes thrown to the winds' (*Pièces originales* ..., 372–4).

'Finally, he was quartered,' recounts the *Gazette d'Amsterdam* of 1 April 1757. 'This last operation was very long, because the horses used were not accustomed to drawing; consequently, instead of four, six were needed; and when that did not suffice, they were forced, in order to cut off the wretch's thighs, to sever the sinews and hack at the joints...

'It is said that, though he was always a great swearer, no blasphemy escaped his lips; but the excessive pain made him utter horrible cries, and he often repeated: "My God, have pity on me! Jesus, help me!" The spectators were all edified by the solicitude of the parish priest of St Paul's who despite his great age did not spare himself in offering consolation to the patient.'

Bouton, an officer of the watch, left us his account: 'The sulphur was lit, but the flame was so poor that only the top skin of the hand was burnt, and that only slightly. Then the executioner, his sleeves rolled up, took the steel pincers, which had been especially made for the occasion, and which were about a foot and a half long, and pulled first at the calf of the right leg, then at the thigh, and from there at the two fleshy parts of the right arm; then at the breasts. Though a strong, sturdy fellow, this executioner found it so difficult to tear away the pieces of flesh that he set about the same spot two or three times, twisting the pincers as he did so, and what he took away formed at each part a wound about the size of a six-pound crown piece.

'After these tearings with the pincers, Damiens, who cried out profusely, though without swearing, raised his head and looked at himself; the same executioner dipped an iron spoon in the pot containing the boiling potion, which he poured liberally over each wound. Then the ropes that were to be harnessed to the horses were attached with cords to the patient's body; the horses were then harnessed and placed alongside the arms and legs, one at each limb.

'Monsieur Le Breton, the clerk of the court, went up to the patient several times and asked him if he had anything to say. He said he had not; at each torment, he cried out, as the damned in hell are supposed to cry out, "Pardon, my God! Pardon, Lord." Despite all this pain, he raised his head from time to time and looked at himself boldly. The cords had been tied so tightly by the men who pulled the ends that they caused him indescribable pain. Monsieur Le Breton went up to him again and asked him if he had anything to say; he said no. Several confessors went up to him and spoke to him at length; he willingly kissed the crucifix that was held out to him; he opened his lips and repeated: "Pardon, Lord."

'The horses tugged hard, each pulling straight on a limb, each horse held by an executioner. After a quarter of an hour, the same ceremony was repeated and finally, after several attempts, the direction of the horses had to be changed, thus: those at the arms were made to pull towards the head, those at the thighs towards the arms, which broke the arms at the joints. This was repeated several times without success. He raised his head and looked at himself. Two more horses had to be added to those harnessed to the thighs, which made six horses in all. Without success.

'Finally, the executioner, Samson, said to Monsieur Le Breton that there was no way or hope of succeeding, and told him to ask their Lordships if they wished him to have the prisoner cut into pieces. Monsieur Le Breton, who had come down from the town, ordered that renewed efforts be made, and this was done; but the horses gave up and one of those harnessed to the thighs fell to the ground. The confessors returned and spoke to him again. He said to them (I heard him): "Kiss me, gentlemen." The parish priest of St Paul's did not dare to, so Monsieur de Marsilly slipped under the rope holding the left arm and kissed him on the forehead. The executioners gathered round and Damiens told them not to swear, to carry out their task and that he did not think ill of them; he begged them to pray to God for him, and asked the parish priest of St Paul's to pray for him at the first mass.

'After two or three attempts, the executioner Samson and he who had used the pincers each drew out a knife from his pocket and cut the body at the thighs instead of severing the legs at the joints; the four horses gave a tug and carried off the two thighs after them, namely, that of the right side first, the other following; then the same was done to the arms, the shoulders, the arm-pits and the four limbs; the flesh had to be cut almost to the bone, the horses pulling hard carried off the right arm first and the other afterwards.

'When the four limbs had been pulled away, the confessors came to speak to him; but his executioner told them that he was dead, though the truth was that I saw the man move, his lower jaw moving from side to side as if he were talking. One of the executioners even said shortly afterwards that when they had lifted the trunk to throw it on the stake, he was still alive. The four limbs were untied from the ropes and thrown on the stake set up in the enclosure in line with the scaffold, then the trunk and the rest were covered with logs and faggots, and fire was put to the straw mixed with this wood.

'… In accordance with the decree, the whole was reduced to ashes. The last piece to be found in the embers was still burning at half-past ten in the evening. The pieces of flesh and the trunk had taken about four hours to burn. The officers of whom I was one, as also was my son, and a detachment of archers remained in the square until nearly eleven o'clock.

'There were those who made something of the fact that a dog had lain the day before on the grass where the fire had been, had been chased away several times, and had always returned. But it is not difficult to understand that an animal found this place warmer than elsewhere' (quoted in Zevaes, 201–14).

Eighty years later, Léon Faucher drew up his rules 'for the House of young prisoners in Paris':

'Art. 17. The prisoners' day will begin at six in the morning in winter and at five in summer. They will work for nine hours a day throughout the year.

Two hours a day will be devoted to instruction. Work and the day will end at nine o'clock in winter and at eight in summer.

Art. 18. *Rising*. At the first drum-roll, the prisoners must rise and dress in silence, as the supervisor opens the cell doors. At the second drum-roll, they must be dressed and make their beds. At the third, they must line up and proceed to the chapel for morning prayer. There is a five-minute interval between each drum-roll.

Art. 19. The prayers are conducted by the chaplain and followed by a moral or religious reading. This exercise must not last more than half an hour.

Art. 20. *Work*. At a quarter to six in the summer, a quarter to seven in winter, the prisoners go down into the courtyard where they must wash their hands and faces, and receive their first ration of bread. Immediately afterwards, they form into work-teams and go off to work, which must begin at six in summer and seven in winter.

Art. 21. *Meal*. At ten o'clock the prisoners leave their work and go to the refectory; they wash their hands in their courtyards and assemble in divisions. After the dinner, there is recreation until twenty minutes to eleven.

Art. 22. *School*. At twenty minutes to eleven, at the drum-roll, the prisoners form into ranks, and proceed in divisions to the school. The class lasts two hours and consists alternately of reading, writing, drawing and arithmetic.

Art. 23. At twenty minutes to one, the prisoners leave the school, in divisions, and return to their courtyards for recreation. At five minutes to one, at the drum-roll, they form into work-teams.

Art. 24. At one o'clock they must be back in the workshops: they work until four o'clock.

Art. 25. At four o'clock the prisoners leave their workshops and go into the courtyards where they wash their hands and form into divisions for the refectory.

Art. 26. Supper and the recreation that follows it last until five o'clock: the prisoners then return to the workshops.

Art. 27. At seven o'clock in the summer, at eight in winter, work stops; bread is distributed for the last time in the workshops. For a quarter of an hour one of the prisoners or supervisors reads a passage from some instructive or uplifting work. This is followed by evening prayer.

Art. 28. At half-past seven in summer, half-past eight in winter, the prisoners must be back in their cells after the washing of hands and the inspection of clothes in the courtyard; at the first drum-roll, they must undress, and at the second get into bed. The cell doors are closed and the supervisors go the rounds in the corridors, to ensure order and silence' (Faucher, 274–82).

We have, then, a public execution and a time-table. They do not punish the same crimes or the same type of delinquent. But they each define a certain penal style. Less than a century separates them. It was a time when, in Europe and in the United States, the entire economy of punishment was redistributed. It was a time of great 'scandals' for traditional justice, a time of innumerable projects for reform. It saw a new theory of law and crime, a new moral or political justification of the right to punish; old laws were abolished, old customs died out. 'Modern' codes were planned or drawn up: Russia, 1769; Prussia, 1780; Pennsylvania and Tuscany, 1786; Austria, 1788; France, 1791, Year IV, 1808 and 1810. It was a new age for penal justice.

Among so many changes, I shall consider one: the disappearance of torture as a public spectacle. Today we are rather inclined to ignore it; perhaps, in its time, it gave rise to too much inflated rhetoric; perhaps it has been attributed too readily and too emphatically to a process of 'humanization', thus dispensing with the need for further analysis. And, in any case, how important is such a change, when compared with the great institutional transformations, the formulation of explicit, general codes and unified rules of procedure; with the almost universal adoption of the jury system, the definition of the essentially corrective character of the penalty and the tendency, which has become increasingly marked since the nineteenth century, to adapt punishment to the individual offender? Punishment of a less immediately physical kind, a certain discretion in the art of inflicting pain, a combination of more subtle, more subdued sufferings, deprived of their visible display, should not all this be treated as a special case, an incidental effect of deeper changes? And yet the fact remains that a few decades saw the disappearance of the tortured, dismembered, amputated body, symbolically branded on face or shoulder, exposed alive or dead to public view. The body as the major target of penal repression disappeared.

PANOPTICISM

Bentham's *Panopticon* is the architectural figure of this composition. We know the principle on which it was based: at the periphery, an annular building; at the centre, a tower; this tower is pierced with wide windows that open onto the inner side of the ring; the peripheric building is divided into cells, each of which extends the whole width of the building; they have two windows, one on the inside, corresponding to the windows of the tower; the other, on the outside, allows the light to cross the cell from one end to the other. All that is needed, then, is to place a supervisor in a central tower and to shut up in each cell a madman, a patient, a condemned man, a worker or a schoolboy. By the effect of backlighting, one can observe from the tower, standing out precisely against the light, the small captive shadows in the cells of the periphery. They are like so many cages, so many small theatres, in which each actor is alone, perfectly individualized and constantly visible. The panoptic mechanism arranges spatial unities that make it possible to see constantly and to recognize immediately. In short, it reverses the principle of the dungeon; or rather of its three functions—to enclose, to deprive of light and to hide—it preserves only the first and

eliminates the other two. Full lighting and the eye of a supervisor capture better than darkness, which ultimately protected. Visibility is a trap.

To begin with, this made it possible—as a negative effect—to avoid those compact, swarming, howling masses that were to be found in places of confinement, those painted by Goya or described by Howard. Each individual, in his place, is securely confined to a cell from which he is seen from the front by the supervisor; but the side walls prevent him from coming into contact with his companions. He is seen, but he does not see; he is the object of information, never a subject in communication. The arrangement of his room, opposite the central tower, imposes on him an axial visibility; but the divisions of the ring, those separated cells, imply a lateral invisibility. And this invisibility is a guarantee of order. If the inmates are convicts, there is no danger of a plot, an attempt at collective escape, the planning of new crimes for the future, bad reciprocal influences; if they are patients, there is no danger of contagion; if they are madmen there is no risk of their committing violence upon one another; if they are schoolchildren, there is no copying, no noise, no chatter, no waste of time; if they are workers, there are no disorders, no theft, no coalitions, none of those distractions that slow down the rate of work, make it less perfect or cause accidents. The crowd, a compact mass, a locus of multiple exchanges, individualities merging together, a collective effect, is abolished and replaced by a collection of separated individualities. From the point of view of the guardian, it is replaced by a multiplicity that can be numbered and supervised; from the point of view of the inmates, by a sequestered and observed solitude (Bentham, 60–64).

Hence the major effect of the Panopticon: to induce in the inmate a state of conscious and permanent visibility that assures the automatic functioning of power. So to arrange things that the surveillance is permanent in its effects, even if it is discontinuous in its action; that the perfection of power should tend to render its actual exercise unnecessary; that this architectural apparatus should be a machine for creating and sustaining a power relation independent of the person who exercises it; in short, that the inmates should be caught up in a power situation of which they are themselves the bearers. To achieve this, it is at once too much and too little that the prisoner should be constantly observed by an inspector: too little, for what matters is that he knows himself to be observed; too much, because he has no need in fact of being so. In view of this, Bentham laid down the principle that power should be visible and unverifiable. Visible: the inmate will constantly have before his eyes the tall outline of the central tower from which he is spied upon. Unverifiable: the inmate must never know whether he is being looked at at any one moment; but he must be sure that he may always be so. In order to make the presence or absence of the inspector unverifiable, so that the prisoners, in their cells, cannot even see a shadow, Bentham envisaged not only venetian blinds on the windows of the central observation hall, but, on the inside, partitions that intersected the hall at right angles and, in order to pass from one quarter to the other, not doors but zig-zag openings; for the slightest noise, a gleam of light, a brightness in a half-opened door would betray the presence of the guardian.[1] The Panopticon is a machine for dissociating the see/being seen dyad: in the peripheric ring, one is totally seen, without ever seeing; in the central tower, one sees everything without ever being seen.[2]

It is an important mechanism, for it automatizes and disindividualizes power. Power has its principle not so much in a person as in a certain concerted distribution of bodies, surfaces, lights, gazes; in an arrangement whose internal mechanisms produce the relation in which individuals are caught up. The ceremonies, the rituals, the marks by which the sovereign's surplus power was manifested are useless. There is a machinery that assures dissymmetry, disequilibrium, difference. Consequently, it does not matter who exercises power. Any individual, taken almost at random, can operate the machine: in the absence of the director, his family, his friends, his visitors, even his servants (Bentham, 45). Similarly, it does not matter what motive animates him: the curiosity of the indiscreet, the malice of a child, the thirst for knowledge of a philosopher who wishes to visit this museum of human nature, or the perversity of those who take pleasure in spying and punishing. The more numerous those anonymous and temporary observers are, the greater the risk for the inmate of being surprised and the greater his anxious awareness of being observed. The Panopticon is a marvellous machine which, whatever use one may wish to put it to, produces homogeneous effects of power.

A real subjection is born mechanically from a fictitious relation. So it is not necessary to use force to constrain the convict to good behaviour, the madman to calm, the worker to work, the schoolboy to application, the patient to the observation of the regulations. Bentham was surprised that panoptic institutions could be so light: there were no more bars, no more chains, no more heavy locks; all that was needed was that the separations should be clear and the openings well arranged. The heaviness of the old 'houses of security', with their fortress-like architecture, could be replaced by the simple, economic geometry of a 'house of certainty'. The efficiency of power, its constraining force have, in a sense, passed over to the other side—to the side of its surface of application. He who is subjected to a field of visibility, and who knows it, assumes responsibility for the constraints of power; he makes them play spontaneously upon himself; he inscribes in himself the power relation in which he simultaneously plays both roles; he becomes the principle of his own subjection. By this very fact, the external power may throw off its physical weight; it tends to the non-corporal; and, the more it approaches this limit, the more constant, profound and permanent are its effects: it is a perpetual victory that avoids any physical confrontation and which is always decided in advance.

[...]

'Discipline' may be identified neither with an institution nor with an apparatus; it is a type of power, a modality for its exercise, comprising a whole set of instruments, techniques, procedures, levels of application, targets; it is a 'physics' or an 'anatomy' of power, a technology. And it may be taken over either by 'specialized' institutions (the penitentiaries or 'houses of correction' of the nineteenth century), or by institutions that use it as an essential instrument for a particular end (schools, hospitals), or by pre-existing authorities that find in it a means of reinforcing or reorganizing their internal mechanisms of power (one day we should show how intra-familial relations, essentially in the parents–children cell, have become 'disciplined', absorbing since the classical age external schemata, first educational and military, then medical, psychiatric, psychological, which have made the family the privileged locus of emergence for the disciplinary question of the normal and the abnormal); or by apparatuses that have made discipline their principle of internal functioning (the disciplinarization of the administrative apparatus from the Napoleonic period), or finally by state apparatuses whose major, if not exclusive, function is to assure that discipline reigns over society as a whole (the police).

On the whole, therefore, one can speak of the formation of a disciplinary society in this movement that stretches from the enclosed disciplines, a sort of social 'quarantine', to an indefinitely generalizable mechanism of 'panopticism'. Not because the disciplinary modality of power has replaced all the others; but because it has infiltrated the others, sometimes undermining them, but serving as an intermediary between them, linking them together, extending them and above all making it possible to bring the effects of power to the most minute and distant elements. It assures an infinitesimal distribution of the power relations.

A few years after Bentham, Julius gave this society its birth certificate (Julius, 384–6). Speaking of the panoptic principle, he said that there was much more there than architectural ingenuity: it was an event in the 'history of the human mind'. In appearance, it is merely the solution of a technical problem; but, through it, a whole type of society emerges. Antiquity had been a civilization of spectacle. 'To render accessible to a multitude of men the inspection of a small number of objects': this was the problem to which the architecture of temples, theatres and circuses responded. With spectacle, there was a predominance of public life, the intensity of festivals, sensual proximity. In these rituals in which blood flowed, society found new vigour and formed for a moment a single great body. The modern age poses the opposite problem: 'To procure for a small number, or even for a single individual, the instantaneous view of a great multitude.' In a society in which the principal elements are no longer the community and public life, but, on the one hand, private individuals and, on the other, the state, relations can be regulated only in a form that is the exact reverse of the spectacle: 'It was to the modern age, to the ever-growing influence of the state, to its ever more profound intervention in all the details and all the relations of social life, that was reserved the task of increasing and perfecting its guarantees, by using and directing towards that great aim the building and distribution of buildings intended to observe a great multitude of men at the same time.'

Julius saw as a fulfilled historical process that which Bentham had described as a technical programme. Our society is one not of spectacle, but of surveillance; under the surface of images, one invests bodies in depth; behind the great abstraction of exchange, there continues the meticulous, concrete training of useful forces; the circuits of communication are the supports of an accumulation and a centralization of knowledge; the play of signs defines the anchorages of power; it is not that the beautiful totality of the individual is amputated, repressed, altered by our social order, it is rather that the individual is carefully fabricated in it, according to a whole technique of forces and bodies. We are much less Greeks than we believe. We are neither in the amphitheatre, nor on the stage, but in the panoptic machine, invested by its effects of power, which we bring to ourselves since we are part of its mechanism. The importance, in historical mythology, of the Napoleonic character probably derives from the fact that it is at the point of junction of the monarchical, ritual exercise of sovereignty and the hierarchical, permanent exercise of indefinite discipline. He is the individual who looms over everything with a single gaze which no detail, however minute, can escape: 'You may consider that no part of the Empire is without surveillance, no crime, no offence, no contravention that remains unpunished, and that the eye of the genius who can enlighten all embraces the whole of this vast machine, without, however, the slightest detail escaping his attention' (Treilhard, 14). At the moment of its full blossoming, the disciplinary society still assumes with the Emperor the old aspect of the power of spectacle. As a monarch who is at one and the same time a usurper of the ancient throne and the organizer of the new state, he combined into a single symbolic, ultimate figure the whole of the long process by which the pomp of sovereignty, the necessarily spectacular manifestations of power, were extinguished one by one in the daily exercise of surveillance, in a panopticism in which the vigilance of intersecting gazes was soon to render useless both the eagle and the sun.

The formation of the disciplinary society is connected with a number of broad historical processes—economic, juridico-political and, lastly, scientific—of which it forms part.

1. Generally speaking, it might be said that the disciplines are techniques for assuring the ordering of human multiplicities. It is true that there is nothing exceptional or even characteristic in this: every system of power is presented with the same prob-

lem. But the peculiarity of the disciplines is that they try to define in relation to the multiplicities a tactics of power that fulfils three criteria: firstly, to obtain the exercise of power at the lowest possible cost (economically, by the low expenditure it involves; politically, by its discretion, its low exteriorization, its relative invisibility, the little resistance it arouses); secondly, to bring the effects of this social power to their maximum intensity and to extend them as far as possible, without either failure or interval; thirdly, to link this 'economic' growth of power with the output of the apparatuses (educational, military, industrial or medical) within which it is exercised; in short, to increase both the docility and the utility of all the elements of the system. This triple objective of the disciplines corresponds to a well-known historical conjuncture. One aspect of this conjuncture was the large demographic thrust of the eighteenth century; an increase in the floating population (one of the primary objects of discipline is to fix; it is an anti-nomadic technique); a change of quantitative scale in the groups to be supervised or manipulated (from the beginning of the seventeenth century to the eve of the French Revolution, the school population had been increasing rapidly, as had no doubt the hospital population; by the end of the eighteenth century, the peace-time army exceeded 200,000 men). The other aspect of the conjuncture was the growth in the apparatus of production, which was becoming more and more extended and complex; it was also becoming more costly and its profitability had to be increased. The development of the disciplinary methods corresponded to these two processes, or rather, no doubt, to the new need to adjust their correlation. Neither the residual forms of feudal power nor the structures of the administrative monarchy, nor the local mechanisms of supervision, nor the unstable, tangled mass they all formed together could carry out this role: they were hindered from doing so by the irregular and inadequate extension of their network, by their often conflicting functioning, but above all by the 'costly' nature of the power that was exercised in them. It was costly in several senses: because directly it cost a great deal to the Treasury; because the system of corrupt offices and farmed-out taxes weighed indirectly, but very heavily, on the population; because the resistance it encountered forced it into a cycle of perpetual reinforcement; because it proceeded essentially by levying (levying on money or products by royal, seigniorial, ecclesiastical taxation; levying on men or time by *corvées* of press-ganging, by locking up or banishing vagabonds). The development of the disciplines marks the appearance of elementary techniques belonging to a quite different economy: mechanisms of power which, instead of proceeding by deduction, are integrated into the productive efficiency of the apparatuses from within, into the growth of this efficiency and into the use of what it produces. For the old principle of 'levying-violence', which governed the economy of power, the disciplines substitute the principle of 'mildness-production-profit'. These are the techniques that make it possible to adjust the multiplicity of men and the multiplication of the apparatuses of production (and this means not only 'production' in the strict sense, but also the production of knowledge and skills in the school, the production of health in the hospitals, the production of destructive force in the army).

In this task of adjustment, discipline had to solve a number of problems for which the old economy of power was not sufficiently equipped. It could reduce the inefficiency of mass phenomena: reduce what, in a multiplicity, makes it much less manageable than a unity; reduce what is opposed to the use of each of its elements and of their sum; reduce everything that may counter the advantages of number. That is why discipline fixes; it arrests or regulates movements; it clears up confusion; it dissipates compact groupings of individuals wandering about the country in unpredictable ways; it establishes calculated distributions. It must also master all the forces that are formed from the very constitution of an organized multiplicity; it must neutralize the

effects of counter-power that spring from them and which form a resistance to the power that wishes to dominate it: agitations, revolts, spontaneous organizations, coalitions—anything that may establish horizontal conjunctions. Hence the fact that the disciplines use procedures of partitioning and verticality, that they introduce, between the different elements at the same level, as solid separations as possible, that they define compact hierarchical networks, in short, that they oppose to the intrinsic, adverse force of multiplicity the technique of the continuous, individualizing pyramid. They must also increase the particular utility of each element of the multiplicity, but by means that are the most rapid and the least costly, that is to say, by using the multiplicity itself as an instrument of this growth. Hence, in order to extract from bodies the maximum time and force, the use of those overall methods known as time-tables, collective training, exercises, total and detailed surveillance. Furthermore, the disciplines must increase the effect of utility proper to the multiplicities, so that each is made more useful than the simple sum of its elements: it is in order to increase the utilizable effects of the multiple that the disciplines define tactics of distribution, reciprocal adjustment of bodies, gestures and rhythms, differentiation of capacities, reciprocal coordination in relation to apparatuses or tasks. Lastly, the disciplines have to bring into play the power relations, not above but inside the very texture of the multiplicity, as discreetly as possible, as well articulated on the other functions of these multiplicities and also in the least expensive way possible: to this correspond anonymous instruments of power, coextensive with the multiplicity that they regiment, such as hierarchical surveillance, continuous registration, perpetual assessment and classification. In short, to substitute for a power that is manifested through the brilliance of those who exercise it, a power that insidiously objectifies those on whom it is applied; to form a body of knowledge about these individuals, rather than to deploy the ostentatious signs of sovereignty. In a word, the disciplines are the ensemble of minute technical inventions that made it possible to increase the useful size of multiplicities by decreasing the inconveniences of the power which, in order to make them useful, must control them. A multiplicity, whether in a workshop or a nation, an army or a school, reaches the threshold of a discipline when the relation of the one to the other becomes favourable.

If the economic take-off of the West began with the techniques that made possible the accumulation of capital, it might perhaps be said that the methods for administering the accumulation of men made possible a political take-off in relation to the traditional, ritual, costly, violent forms of power, which soon fell into disuse and were superseded by a subtle, calculated technology of subjection. In fact, the two processes—the accumulation of men and the accumulation of capital—cannot be separated; it would not have been possible to solve the problem of the accumulation of men without the growth of an apparatus of production capable of both sustaining them and using them; conversely, the techniques that made the cumulative multiplicity of men useful accelerated the accumulation of capital. At a less general level, the technological mutations of the apparatus of production, the division of labour and the elaboration of the disciplinary techniques sustained an ensemble of very close relations (cf. Marx, *Capital*, vol. 1, chapter XIII and the very interesting analysis in Guerry and Deleule). Each makes the other possible and necessary; each provides a model for the other. The disciplinary pyramid constituted the small cell of power within which the separation, coordination and supervision of tasks was imposed and made efficient; and analytical partitioning of time, gestures and bodily forces constituted an operational schema that could easily be transferred from the groups to be subjected to the mechanisms of production; the massive projection of military methods onto industrial organization was an example of this modelling of the division of labour following the model laid down by the schemata of power. But, on the other hand, the

technical analysis of the process of production, its 'mechanical' breaking-down, were projected onto the labour force whose task it was to implement it: the constitution of those disciplinary machines in which the individual forces that they bring together are composed into a whole and therefore increased is the effect of this projection. Let us say that discipline is the unitary technique by which the body is reduced as a 'political' force at the least cost and maximized as a useful force. The growth of a capitalist economy gave rise to the specific modality of disciplinary power, whose general formulas, techniques of submitting forces and bodies, in short, 'political anatomy', could be operated in the most diverse political régimes, apparatuses or institutions.

2. The panoptic modality of power—at the elementary, technical, merely physical level at which it is situated—is not under the immediate dependence or a direct extension of the great juridico-political structures of a society; it is nonetheless not absolutely independent. Historically, the process by which the bourgeoisie became in the course of the eighteenth century the politically dominant class was masked by the establishment of an explicit, coded and formally egalitarian juridical framework, made possible by the organization of a parliamentary, representative régime. But the development and generalization of disciplinary mechanisms constituted the other, dark side of these processes. The general juridical form that guaranteed a system of rights that were egalitarian in principle was supported by these tiny, everyday, physical mechanisms, by all those systems of micro-power that are essentially non-egalitarian and asymmetrical that we call the disciplines. And although, in a formal way, the representative régime makes it possible, directly or indirectly, with or without relays, for the will of all to form the fundamental authority of sovereignty, the disciplines provide, at the base, a guarantee of the submission of forces and bodies. The real, corporal disciplines constituted the foundation of the formal, juridical liberties. The contract may have been regarded as the ideal foundation of

law and political power; panopticism constituted the technique, universally widespread, of coercion. It continued to work in depth on the juridical structures of society, in order to make the effective mechanisms of power function in opposition to the formal framework that it had acquired. The 'Enlightenment', which discovered the liberties, also invented the disciplines.

In appearance, the disciplines constitute nothing more than an infra-law. They seem to extend the general forms defined by law to the infinitesimal level of individual lives; or they appear as methods of training that enable individuals to become integrated into these general demands. They seem to constitute the same type of law on a different scale, thereby making it more meticulous and more indulgent. The disciplines should be regarded as a sort of counter-law. They have the precise role of introducing insuperable asymmetries and excluding reciprocities. First, because discipline creates between individuals a 'private' link, which is a relation of constraints entirely different from contractual obligation; the acceptance of a discipline may be underwritten by contract; the way in which it is imposed, the mechanisms it brings into play, the non-reversible subordination of one group of people by another, the 'surplus' power that is always fixed on the same side, the inequality of position of the different 'partners' in relation to the common regulation, all these distinguish the disciplinary link from the contractual link, and make it possible to distort the contractual link systematically from the moment it has as its content a mechanism of discipline. We know, for example, how many real procedures undermine the legal fiction of the work contract: workshop discipline is not the least important. Moreover, whereas the juridical systems define juridical subjects according to universal norms, the disciplines characterize, classify, specialize; they distribute along a scale, around a norm, hierarchize individuals in relation to one another and, if necessary, disqualify and invalidate. In any case, in the space and during the time in which they exercise their control and bring into play the asymmetries of their power, they effect a suspension of the law that is never total, but is never annulled either. Regular and institutional as it may be, the discipline, in its mechanism, is a 'counter-law'. And, although the universal juridicism of modern society seems to fix limits on the exercise of power, its universally widespread panopticism enables it to operate, on the underside of the law, a machinery that is both immense and minute, which supports, reinforces, multiplies the asymmetry of power and undermines the limits that are traced around the law. The minute disciplines, the panopticisms of every day may well be below the level of emergence of the great apparatuses and the great political struggles. But, in the genealogy of modern society, they have been, with the class domination that traverses it, the political counterpart of the juridical norms according to which power was redistributed. Hence, no doubt, the importance that has been given for so long to the small techniques of discipline, to those apparently insignificant tricks that it has invented, and even to those 'sciences' that give it a respectable face; hence the fear of abandoning them if one cannot find any substitute; hence the affirmation that they are at the very foundation of society, and an element in its equilibrium, whereas they are a series of mechanisms for unbalancing power relations definitively and everywhere; hence the persistence in regarding them as the humble, but concrete form of every morality, whereas they are a set of physico-political techniques.

To return to the problem of legal punishments, the prison with all the corrective technology at its disposal is to be resituated at the point where the codified power to punish turns into a disciplinary power to observe; at the point where the universal punishments of the law are applied selectively to certain individuals and always the same ones; at the point where the redefinition of the juridical subject by the penalty becomes a useful training of the criminal; at the point where the law is inverted and passes outside itself, and where the counter-law becomes the effective and institutionalized content of the juridical forms. What generalizes the power to punish, then, is not the universal consciousness of the law in each juridical subject; it is the regular extension, the infinitely minute web of panoptic techniques.

3. Taken one by one, most of these techniques have a long history behind them. But what was new, in the eighteenth century, was that, by being combined and generalized, they attained a level at which the formation of knowledge and the increase of power regularly reinforce one another in a circular process. At this point, the disciplines crossed the 'technological' threshold. First the hospital, then the school, then, later, the workshop were not simply 'reordered' by the disciplines; they became, thanks to them, apparatuses such that any mechanism of objectification could be used in them as an instrument of subjection, and any growth of power could give rise in them to possible branches of knowledge; it was this link, proper to the technological systems, that made possible within the disciplinary element the formation of clinical medicine, psychiatry, child psychology, educational psychology, the rationalization of labour. It is a double process, then: an epistemological 'thaw' through a refinement of power relations; a multiplication of the effects of power through the formation and accumulation of new forms of knowledge.

NOTES

1. In the *Postscript to the Panopticon*, 1791, Bentham adds dark inspection galleries painted in black around the inspector's lodge, each making it possible to observe two storeys of cells.
2. In his first version of the *Panopticon*, Bentham had also imagined an acoustic surveillance, operated by means of pipes leading from the cells to the central tower. In the *Postscript* he abandoned the idea, perhaps because he could not introduce into it the principle of dissymmetry and prevent the prisoners from hearing the inspector as well as the inspector hearing them. Julius tried to develop a system of dissymmetrical listening (Julius, 18).

COMPANION WEBSITE

1. Go online to Write Out Loud about the new kinds of knowledge that online surveillance sites like Facebook might produce.
2. And check out the *Pathway to Meltdown* Supplementary Sources for more web content, films, and readings about the ubiquity of surveillance technologies in modern societies.
3. Log on to Foucault's Profile Page to learn more about the life and thought of one of contemporary social theory's most influential scholars.

26

Modernity and the Holocaust

Zygmunt Bauman

'WOULDN'T YOU BE HAPPIER IF I HAD been able to show you that all the perpetrators were crazy?' asks the great historian of the Holocaust, Raul Hilberg. Yet this is precisely what he is *unable* to show. The truth he does show brings no comfort. It is unlikely to make anybody happy. 'They were educated men of their time. That is the crux of the question whenever we ponder the meaning of Western Civilization after Auschwitz. Our evolution has outpaced our understanding; we can no longer assume that we have a full grasp of the workings of our social institutions, bureaucratic structures, or technology.'[1]

This is certainly bad news for philosophers, sociologists, theologians and all the other learned men and women who are professionally concerned with understanding and explaining. Hilberg's conclusions mean that they have not done their job well; they cannot explain what has happened and why, and they cannot help us to understand it. This charge is bad enough as far as the scientists go (it is bound to make the scholars restless, and may even send them, as they say, back to the drawing board), but in itself it is not a cause for public alarm. There have been, after all, many other important events in the past that we feel we do not fully understand. Sometimes this makes us angry; most of the time, however, we do not feel particularly perturbed. After all – so we console ourselves – these past events are matters of *academic interest*.

But are they? It is not the Holocaust which we find difficult to grasp in all its monstrosity. *It is our Western Civilization which the occurrence of the Holocaust has made all but incomprehensible* – and this at a time when we thought we had come to terms with it and seen through its innermost drives and even through its prospects, and at a time of its worldwide, unprecedented cultural expansion. If Hilberg is right, and our most crucial social institutions elude our mental and practical grasp, then it is not just the professional academics who ought to be worried. True, the Holocaust occurred almost half a century ago. True, its immediate results are fast receding into the past. The generation that experienced it at first hand has almost died out. But – and this is an awesome, sinister 'but' – these once-familiar features of our civilization, which the Holocaust had made mysterious again, are still very much part of our life. They have not gone away. Neither has, therefore, the *possibility* of the Holocaust.

We shrug off such a possibility. We pooh-pooh the few obsessed people riled by our balance of mind. We have a special, derisive name for them – 'prophets of doom'. It comes easy to dismiss their anguished warnings. Are we not vigilant already? Do we not condemn violence, immorality, cruelty? Do we not muster all our ingenuity and considerable, constantly growing resources to fight them? And besides, is there anything at all in our life that points to the sheer possibility of a catastrophe? Life is getting better and more comfortable. On the whole, our institutions seem to cope. Against the enemy, we are well protected, and our friends surely won't do anything nasty. Granted, we hear from time to time of atrocities that some not particularly civilized, and for this reason spiritually far-away people, visit upon their equally barbaric neighbours. Ewe massacre a million Ibos, having first called them vermin, criminals, money-grabbers and subhumans without culture;[2] Iraqis poison-gas their Kurdish citizens without even bothering to call them names; Tamils massacre Singhalese; Ethiopians exterminate Eritreans; Ugandans exterminate themselves (or was it the other way round?). It is all sad, of course, but what can it possibly have to do with us? If it proves anything at all, it certainly proves how bad it is to be unlike us, and how good it is to be safe and sound behind the shield of our superior civilization.

Just how untoward our complacency may prove in the end becomes apparent once we recall that still in 1941 the Holocaust was not expected; that, given the extant knowledge of the 'facts of the case', it was not expectable; and that, when it finally came to pass one year later, it met with universal incredulity. People refused to believe the facts they stared at. Not that they were obtuse or ill-willed. It was just that nothing they had known before had prepared them to believe. For all they had known and believed, the mass murder for which they did not even have a name yet was, purely and simply, unimaginable. In 1988, it is unimaginable again. In 1988, however, we know what we did not know in 1941; that also *the unimaginable ought to be imagined.*

THE PROBLEM

There are two reasons for which the Holocaust, unlike many other topics of academic study, cannot be seen as a matter of solely academic interest; and for which the problem of the Holocaust cannot be reduced to the subject-matter of historical research and philosophical contemplation.

The first reason is that the Holocaust, even if it is plausible that, 'as a central historical event – not unlike the French Revolution, the discovery of America, or the discovery of the wheel – it has changed the course of subsequent history,'[3] has most certainly changed little, if anything, in the course of the subsequent history of our collective consciousness and self-understanding. It made little visible impact on our image of the meaning and historical tendency of modern civilization. It left the social sciences in general, and sociology in particular, virtually unmoved and intact, except for the still marginal regions of specialist research, and some dark and ominous warnings of the morbid proclivities of modernity. Both exceptions are consistently kept at a distance from the canon of sociological practice. For these reasons, our understanding of the factors and mechanisms that once made the Holocaust possible has not significantly advanced. And with the understanding not much improved over that of half a century ago, we could be once more unprepared to notice and decode the warning signs – were they now, as they had been then, blatantly displayed all around.

The second reason is that whatever happened to the 'course of history', nothing much happened to those products of history which in all probability contained the potentiality of the Holocaust – or at least we cannot be sure that it did. For all we know (or, rather, for all we do not know) they may still be with us, waiting for their chance. We can only suspect that the conditions that once before gave birth to the Holocaust have not been radically transformed. If there was something in our social order which made the Holocaust possible in 1941, we cannot be sure that it has been eliminated since then. A growing number of renowned and respected scholars warns us that we had better not be complacent:

> The ideology and system which gave rise to [Auschwitz] remains intact. This means that the nation-state itself is out of control and capable of triggering acts of social cannibalism on an undreamed-of scale. If not checked, it can consume an entire civilization in fire. It cannot carry a

humanitarian mission; its trespasses cannot be checked by legal and moral codes, it has no conscience. (Henry L. Feingold)[4]

Many features of contemporary 'civilized' society encourage the easy resort to genocidal holocausts …

The sovereign territorial state claims, as an integral part of its sovereignty, the right to commit genocide, or engage in genocidal massacres, against people under its rule, and … the UN, for all practical purposes, defends this right. (Leo Kuper)[5]

Within certain limits set by political and military power considerations, the modern state may do anything it wishes to those under its control. There is no moral-ethical limit which the state cannot transcend if it wishes to do so, because there is no moral-ethical power higher than the state. In matters of ethics and morality, the situation of the individual in the modern state is in principle roughly equivalent to the situation of the prisoner in Auschwitz: either act in accord with the prevailing standards of conduct enforced by those in authority, or risk whatever consequences they may wish to impose …

Existence now is more and more recognizably in accord with the principles that governed life and death in Auschwitz. (George M. Kren and Leon Rappoport)[6]

Overwhelmed by the emotions which even a perfunctory reading of the Holocaust records cannot but arouse, some of the quoted authors are prone to exaggerate. Some of their statements sound incredible – and certainly unduly alarmist. They may be even counterproductive; if everything we know is like Auschwitz, then one can live with Auschwitz, and in many a case live reasonably well. If the principles that ruled over life and death of Auschwitz inmates were like these that rule our own, then what has all this outcry and lamentation been about? Truly, one would be well advised to avoid the temptation to deploy the inhuman imagery of the Holocaust in the service of a partisan stance towards larger or smaller, but on the whole, routine

and daily human conflicts. Mass destruction was the extreme form of antagonism and oppression, yet not all cases of oppression, communal hatred and injustice are 'like' the Holocaust. Overt, and hence superficial similarity is a poor guide to causal analysis. Contrary to what Kren and Rappoport suggest, having to choose between conformity and bearing the consequences of disobedience does not necessarily mean living in Auschwitz, and the principles preached and practised by most contemporary states do not suffice to make their citizens into Holocaust victims.

The real cause for concern, one that cannot be easily argued away, nor dismissed as a natural yet misleading outcome of post-Holocaust trauma, lies elsewhere. It can be gleaned from two related facts.

First, ideational processes that by their own inner logic may lead to genocidal projects, and the technical resources that permit implementation of such projects, not only have been proved fully compatible with modern civilization, but have been conditioned, created and supplied by it. The Holocaust did not just, mysteriously, avoid clash with the social norms and institutions of modernity. It was these norms and institutions that made the Holocaust feasible. Without modern civilization and its most central essential achievements, there would be no Holocaust.

Second, all those intricate networks of checks and balances, barriers and hurdles which the civilizing process has erected and which, as we hope and trust, would defend us from violence and constrain all over ambitious and unscrupulous powers, have been proven ineffective. When it came to mass murder, the victims found themselves alone. Not only had they been fooled by an apparently peaceful and humane, legalistic and orderly society – their sense of security became a most powerful factor of their downfall.

To put it bluntly, there are reasons to be worried because we know now that *we live in a type of society that made the Holocaust possible, and that contained nothing which could stop the Holocaust from happening.*

For these reasons alone it is necessary to study the lessons of the Holocaust. Much more is involved in such a study than the tribute to the memory of murdered millions, settling the account with the murderers and healing the still-festering moral wounds of the passive and silent witnesses.

Obviously, the study itself, even a most diligent study, is not a sufficient guarantee against the return of mass murderers and numb bystanders. Yet without such a study, we would not even know how likely or improbable such a return may be.

GENOCIDE EXTRAORDINARY

Mass murder is not a modern invention. History is fraught with communal and sectarian enmities, always mutually damaging and potentially destructive, often erupting into overt violence, sometimes leading to massacre, and in some cases resulting in extermination of whole populations and cultures. On the face of it, this fact denies the uniqueness of the Holocaust. In particular, it seems to deny the intimate link between the Holocaust and modernity, the 'elective affinity' between the Holocaust and modern civilization. It suggests instead that murderous communal hatred has always been with us and will probably never go away; and that the only significance of modernity in this respect is that, contrary to its promise and to the widespread expectations, it did not file smooth the admittedly rough edges of human coexistence and thus has not put a definite end to man's inhumanity to man. Modernity has not delivered on its promise. Modernity has failed. But modernity bears no responsibility for the episode of the Holocaust – as genocide accompanied human history from the start.

This is not, however, the lesson contained in the experience of the Holocaust. No doubt the Holocaust was another episode in the long series of attempted mass murders and the not much shorter series of accomplished ones. It also bore features that it did not share with any of the past cases of genocide. It is these features which deserve special attention. They had a distinct modern flavour. Their presence suggests that modernity contributed to the Holocaust more directly than through its own weakness and ineptitude. It suggests that the role of modern civilization in the incidence and the perpetration of the Holocaust was active, not passive. It suggests that the Holocaust was as much a product, as it was a failure, of modern civilization. Like everything else done in the modern – rational, planned, scientifically informed, expert, efficiently managed, co-ordinated – way, the Holocaust left behind and put to shame all its alleged pre-modern equivalents, exposing them as primitive, wasteful and ineffective by comparison. Like everything else in our modern society, the Holocaust was an accomplishment in every respect superior, if measured by the standards that this society has preached and institutionalized. It towers high above the past genocidal episodes in the same way as the modern industrial plant towers above the craftsman's cottage workshop, or the modern industrial farm, with its tractors, combines and pesticides, towers above the peasant farmstead with its horse, hoe and hand-weeding.

On 9 November 1938 an event took place in Germany which went down in history under the name of *Kristallnacht*. Jewish businesses, seats of worship, and homes were attacked by an unruly, though officially encouraged and surreptitiously controlled, mob; they were broken down, set on fire, vandalized. About one hundred persons lost their lives. *Kristallnacht* was the only large-scale pogrom that occurred on the streets of German towns throughout the duration of the Holocaust. It was also the one episode of the Holocaust that followed the established, centuries-old tradition of anti-Jewish mob violence. It did not differ much from past pogroms; it hardly stood out from the long line of crowd violence stretching from ancient time, through the Middle Ages and up to the almost contemporary, but still largely pre-modern, Russia,

Poland or Rumania. Were the Nazis' treatment of the Jews composed only of *Kristallnächte* and suchlike events, it would hardly add anything but an extra paragraph, a chapter at best, to the multi-volume chronicle of emotions running amok, of lynching mobs, of soldier looting and raping their way through the conquered towns. This was not, however, to be.

This was not to be for a simple reason: one could neither conceive of, nor make, mass murder on the Holocaust scale of no matter how many *Kristallnächte*.

Consider the numbers. The German state annihilated approximately six million Jews. At the rate of 100 per day this would have required nearly 200 years. Mob violence rests on the wrong psychological basis, on violent emotion. People can be manipulated into fury, but fury cannot be maintained for 200 years. Emotions, and their biological basis, have a natural time course; lust, even blood lust, is eventually sated. Further, emotions are notoriously fickle, can be turned. A lynch mob is unreliable, it can sometimes be moved by sympathy – say by a child's suffering. To eradicate a 'race' it is essential to kill the children.

Thorough, comprehensive, exhaustive murder required the replacement of the mob with a bureaucracy, the replacement of shared rage with obedience to authority. The requisite bureaucracy would be effective whether manned by extreme or tepid anti-Semites, considerably broadening the pool of potential recruits; it would govern the actions of its members not by arousing passions but by organizing routines; it would only make distinctions it was designed to make, not those its members might be moved to make, say, between children and adults, scholar and thief, innocent and guilty; it would be responsive to the will of the ultimate authority through a hierarchy of responsibility – whatever that will might be.[7]

Rage and fury are pitiably primitive and inefficient as tools of mass annihilation. They normally peter out before the job is done. One cannot build grand designs on them. Certainly not such designs as reach beyond momentary effects like a wave of terror, the breakdown of an old order, clearing the ground for a new rule. Genghis Khan and Peter the Hermit did not need modern technology and modern, scientific methods of management and co-ordination. Stalin or Hitler did. It is the adventurers and dilettantes like Genghis Khan and Peter the Hermit that our modern, rational society has discredited and, arguably, put paid to. It is the practitioners of cool, thorough and systematic genocide like Stalin and Hitler for whom the modern, rational society paved the way.

Most conspicuously, the modern cases of genocide stand out for their sheer scale. On no other occasion but during Hitler's and Stalin's rule were so many people murdered in such a short time. This is not, however, the only novelty, perhaps not even a primary one – merely a by-product of other, more seminal features. Contemporary mass murder is distinguished by a virtual absence of all spontaneity on the one hand, and the prominence of rational, carefully calculated design on the other. It is marked by an almost complete elimination of contingency and chance, and independence from group emotions and personal motives. It is set apart by merely sham or marginal – disguising or decorative – role of ideological mobilization. But first and foremost, it stands out by its purpose.

Murderous motives in general, and motives for mass murder in particular, have been many and varied. They range from pure, cold-blooded calculation of competitive gain, to equally pure, disinterested hatred or heterophobia. Most communal strifes and genocidal campaigns against aborigines lie comfortably within this range. If accompanied by an ideology, the latter does not go much further than a simple 'us or them' vision of the world, and a precept: 'There is no room for both of us', or 'The only good injun is a dead injun'. The adversary is expected to follow mirror-image principles only if allowed to. Most genocidal ideologies rest on a devious symmetry of assumed intentions and actions.

Truly modern genocide is different. *Modern genocide is genocide with a purpose.* Getting rid of the adversary is not an end in itself. It is a means to an end: a necessity that stems from the ultimate objective, a step that one has to take if one wants ever to reach the end of the road. *The end itself is a grand vision of a better, and radically different, society.* Modern genocide is an element of social engineering, meant to bring about a social order conforming to the design of the perfect society.

To the initiators and the managers of modern genocide, society is a subject of planning and conscious design. One can and should do more about the society than change one or several of its many details, improve it here or there, cure some of its troublesome ailments. One can and should set oneself goals more ambitious and radical: one can and should remake the society, force it to conform to an overall, scientifically conceived plan. One can create a society that is objectively better than the one 'merely existing' – that is, existing without conscious intervention. Invariably, there is an aesthetic dimension to the design: the ideal world about to be built conforms to the standards of superior beauty. Once built, it will be richly satisfying, like a perfect work of art; it will be a world which, in Alberti's immortal words, no adding, diminishing or altering could improve.

This is a gardener's vision, projected upon a world-size screen. The thoughts, feelings, dreams and drives of the designers of the perfect world are familiar to every gardener worth his name, though perhaps on a somewhat smaller scale. Some gardeners hate the weeds that spoil their design – that ugliness in the midst of beauty, litter in the midst of serene order. Some others are quite unemotional about them: just a problem to be solved, an extra job to be done. Not that it makes a difference to the weeds; both gardeners exterminate them. If asked or given a chance to pause and ponder, both would agree: weeds must die, not so much because of what they are, as because of what the beautiful, orderly garden ought to be.

Modern culture is a garden culture. It defines itself as the design for an ideal life and a perfect arrangement of human conditions. It constructs its own identity out of distrust of nature. In fact, it defines itself and nature, and the distinction between them, through its endemic distrust of spontaneity and its longing for a better, and necessarily artificial, order. Apart from the overall plan, the artificial *order* of the garden needs tools and raw materials. It also needs defence – against the unrelenting danger of what is, obviously, a disorder. The order, first conceived of as a design, determines what is a tool, what is a raw material, what is useless, what is irrelevant, what is harmful, what is a weed or a pest. It classifies all elements of the universe by their relation to itself. This relation is the only meaning it grants them and tolerates – and the only justification of the gardener's actions, as differentiated as the relations themselves. From the point of view of the design all actions are instrumental, while all the objects of action are either facilities or hindrances.

Modern genocide, like modern culture in general, is a gardener's job. It is just one of the many chores that people who treat society as a garden need to undertake. If garden design defines its weeds, there are weeds wherever there is a garden. And weeds are to be exterminated. Weeding out is a creative, not a destructive activity. It does not differ in kind from other activities which combine in the construction and sustenance of the perfect garden. All visions of society-as-garden define parts of the social habitat as human weeds. Like all other weeds, they must be segregated, contained, prevented from spreading, removed and kept outside the society boundaries; if all these means prove insufficient, they must be killed.

Stalin's and Hitler's victims were not killed in order to capture and colonize the territory they occupied. Often they were killed in a dull, mechanical fashion with no human emotions – hatred included – to enliven it. They were killed because they did not fit, for one reason or another, the scheme of a perfect society. Their killing was not the work of destruction, but creation. They were eliminated, so that an objectively better human world – more efficient, more moral, more beautiful – could be established. A Communist world. Or a racially pure, Aryan world. In both cases, a harmonious world, conflict-free, docile in the hands of their rulers, orderly, controlled. People tainted with ineradicable blight of their past or origin could not be fitted into such an unblemished, healthy and shining world. Like weeds, their nature could not be changed. They could not be improved or re-educated. They had to be eliminated for reasons of genetic or ideational heredity – of a natural mechanism, resilient and immune to cultural processing.

The two most notorious and extreme cases of modern genocide did not betray the spirit of modernity. They did not deviously depart from the main track of the civilizing process. They were the most consistent, uninhibited expressions of that spirit. They attempted to reach the most ambitious aims of the civilizing process most other processes stop short of, not necessarily for the lack of good will. They showed what the rationalizing, designing, controlling dreams and efforts of modern civilization are able to accomplish if not mitigated, curbed or counteracted.

These dreams and efforts have been with us for a long time. They spawned the vast and powerful arsenal of technology and managerial skills. They gave birth to institutions which serve the sole purpose of instrumentalizing human behaviour to such an extent that any aim may be pursued with efficiency and vigour, with or without ideological dedication or moral approval on the part of the pursuers. They legitimize the rulers' monopoly on ends and the confinement of the ruled to the role of means. They define most actions as means, and means as subordination – to the ultimate end, to those who set it, to supreme will, to supra-individual knowledge.

Emphatically, this does not mean that we all live daily according to Auschwitz principles. From the fact that the Holocaust is modern, it does not follow that modernity is a Holocaust. The Holocaust is a by-product of the modern drive to a fully designed, fully controlled world, once the drive is getting out of control and running wild. Most of the time, modernity is prevented from doing so. Its ambitions clash with the pluralism of the human world; they stop short of their fulfilment for the lack of an absolute power absolute enough and a monopolistic agency monopolistic enough to be able to disregard, shrug off, or overwhelm all autonomous, and thus countervailing and mitigating, forces.

PECULIARITY OF MODERN GENOCIDE

When the modernist dream is embraced by an absolute power able to monopolize modern vehicles of rational action, and when that power attains freedom from effective social control, genocide follows. A modern genocide – like the Holocaust. The short circuit (one almost wishes to say: a chance encounter) between an ideologically obsessed power elite and the tremendous facilities of rational, systemic action developed by modern society, may happen relatively seldom. Once it does happen, however, certain aspects of modernity are revealed which under different circumstances are less visible and hence may be easily 'theorized away'.

Modern Holocaust is unique in a double sense. *It is unique among other historic cases of genocide because it is modern. And it stands unique against the quotidianity of modern society because it brings together some ordinary factors of modernity which normally are kept apart.* In this second sense of its uniqueness, only the combination of factors in unusual and rare, not the factors that are combined. Separately, each factor is common and normal. And the knowledge of saltpetre, sulphur or charcoal is not complete unless one knows and remembers that, if mixed, they turn into gunpowder.

The simultaneous uniqueness and normality of the Holocaust has found excellent expression in the summary of Sarah Gordon's findings:

> systematic extermination, as opposed to sporadic pogroms, could be carried out only by extremely powerful government, and probably could have succeeded only under the cover of wartime conditions. It was only the advent of Hitler and his radical anti-Semitic followers and their subsequent centralization of power that made the extermination of European Jewry possible ... the process of organized exclusion and murder required cooperation by huge sections of the military and bureaucracy, as well as acquiescence among the German people, whether or not they approved of Nazi persecution and extermination.[8]

Gordon names several factors which had to come together to produce the Holocaust: radical (and, as we remember from the last chapter, modern: racist and exterminatory) antisemitism of the Nazi type; transformation of that antisemitism into the practical policy of a powerful, centralized state; that state being in command of a huge, efficient bureaucratic apparatus; 'state of emergency' – an extraordinary, wartime condition, which allowed that government and the bureaucracy it controlled to get away with things which could, possibly, face more serious obstacles in time of peace; and the non-interference, the passive acceptance of those things by the population at large. Two among those factors (one can argue that the two can be reduced to one: with Nazis in power, war was virtually inevitable) could be seen as coincidental – not necessary attributes of a modern society, though always its possibility. The remaining factors, however, are fully 'normal'. They are constantly present in every modern society, and their presence has been made both possible and inescapable by those processes which are properly associated with the rise and entrenchment of modern civilization.

In the preceding chapter I have tried to unravel the connection between radical, exterminatory antisemitism, and the socio-political and cultural transformations usually referred to as the development of modern society. In the last chapter of the book I shall attempt to analyse those social mechanisms, also set in motion under contemporary conditions, that silence or neutralize moral inhibitions and, more generally, make people refrain from resistance against evil. Here I intend to focus on one only, yet arguably the most crucial among the constituent factors of the Holocaust: the typically modern, technological-bureaucratic patterns of action and the mentality they institutionalize, generate, sustain and reproduce.

There are two antithetical ways in which one can approach the explanation of the Holocaust. One can consider the horrors of mass murder as evidence of the fragility of civilization, or one can see them as evidence of its awesome potential. One can argue that, with criminals in control, civilized rules of behaviour may be suspended, and thus the eternal beast always hiding just beneath the skin of the socially drilled being may break free. Alternatively, one can argue that, once armed with the sophisticated technical and conceptual products of modern civilization, men can do things their nature would otherwise prevent them from doing. To put it differently; one can, following the Hobbesian tradition, conclude that the inhuman pre-social state has not yet been fully eradicated, all civilizing efforts notwithstanding. Or one can, on the contrary, insist that the civilizing process has succeeded in substituting artificial and flexible patterns of human conduct for natural drives, and hence made possible a scale of inhumanity and destruction which had remained inconceivable as long as natural predispositions guided human action. I propose to opt for the second approach, and substantiate it in the following discussion.

The fact that most people (including many a social theorist) instinctively choose the first, rather than the second, approach, is a testimony to the remarkable success of the etiological myth which, in one variant or another, Western civilization has deployed over the years to legitimize its spatial hegemony by projecting it as temporal superiority. Western civilization has articulated its struggle for domination in terms of the holy battle of humanity against barbarism, reason against ignorance, objectivity against prejudice, progress against degeneration, truth against superstition, science against magic, rationality against passion. It has interpreted the history of its ascendance as the gradual yet relentless substitution of human mastery over nature for the mastery of nature over man. It has presented its own accomplishment as, first and foremost, a decisive advance in human freedom of action, creative potential and security. It has identified freedom and security with its own type of social order: Western, modern society is defined as *civilized* society, and a civilized society in turn is understood as a state from which most of the natural ugliness and morbidity, as well as most of the immanent human propensity to cruelty and violence, have been eliminated or at least suppressed. The popular image of civilized society is, more than anything else, that of the absence of violence; of a gentle, polite, soft society.

Perhaps the most salient symbolic expression of this master-image of civilization is the sanctity of the human body: the care which is taken not to invade that most private of spaces, to avoid bodily contact, to abide by the culturally prescribed bodily distance; and the trained disgust and repulsion we feel whenever we see or hear of that sacred space being trespassed on. Modern civilization can afford the fiction of the sanctity and autonomy of the human body thanks to the efficient mechanisms of self-control it has developed, and on the whole successfully reproduced in the process of individual education. Once effective, the reproduced mechanisms of self-control dispose of the need of subsequent external interference with the body. On the other hand, privacy of the body underlines personal responsibility for its behaviour, and thus adds powerful sanctions to the bodily drill. (In recent years the severity of sanctions, keenly exploited by the consumer market, have finally produced the tendency to interiorize demand for the drill; development of individual self-control tends to be itself self-controlled, and pursued in a DIY fashion.) Cultural prohibition against coming into too close a contact with another body serves therefore as an effective safeguard against diffuse, contingent influences which may, if allowed, counteract the centrally administered pattern of social order. Non-violence of the daily and diffuse human intercourse is an indispensable condition, and a constant output, of the centralization of coercion.

All in all, the overall non-violent character of modern civilization is an illusion. More exactly, it is an integral part of its self-apology and self-apotheosis; in short, of its legitimizing myth. It is not true that our civilization exterminates violence due to the inhuman, degrading or immoral character of the latter. If modernity

> is indeed antithetical to the wild passions of barbarism, it is not at all antithetical to efficient, dispassionate destruction, slaughter, and torture … As the quality of thinking grows more rational, the quantity of destruction increases. In our time, for example, terrorism and torture are no longer instruments of passions; they have become instruments of political rationality.[9]

What in fact has happened in the course of the civilizing process, is the redeployment of violence, and the re-distribution of access to violence. Like so many other things which we have been trained to abhor and detest, violence has been taken out of sight, rather than forced out of existence. It has become invisible, that is, from the vantage point of narrowly circumscribed and privatized personal experience. It has been enclosed instead in segregated and isolated territories, on the whole inaccessible to ordinary members of society; or evicted to the 'twilight areas', off-limits for a large majority (and the majority which counts) of society's members; or exported to distant places which on the whole are irrelevant for the life-business of civilized humans (one can always cancel holiday bookings).

The ultimate consequence of all this is the concentration of violence. Once centralized and free from competition, means of coercion would be capable of reaching unheard of results even if not technically perfected. Their concentration, however, triggers and boosts the escalation of technical improvements, and thus the effects of concentration are further magnified. As Anthony Giddens repeatedly emphasized (see, above all, his *Contemporary Critique of Historical Materialism* (1981), and *The Constitution of Society* (1984)), the removal of violence from the daily life of civilized societies has always been intimately associated with a thoroughgoing militarization of inter-societal exchange and inner-societal production of order; standing armies and police forces brought together technically superior weapons and superior technology of bureaucratic management. For the last two centuries, the number of people who have suffered violent death as the result of such militarization has been steadily growing to reach a volume unheard of before.

The Holocaust absorbed an enormous volume of means of coercion. Having harnessed them in the service of a single purpose, it also added stimulus to their further specialization and technical perfection. More, however, than the sheer quantity of tools of destruction, and even their technical quality, what mattered was the way in which they were deployed. Their formidable effectiveness, relied mostly on the subjection of their use to purely bureaucratic, technical considerations (which made their use all but totally immune to the countervailing pressures, such as they might have been submitted to if the means of violence were controlled by dispersed and unco-ordinated agents and deployed in a diffuse way). Violence has been turned into a technique. Like all techniques, it is free from emotions and purely rational. 'It is, in fact, entirely reasonable, if "reason" means instrumental reason, to apply American military force, B-52's, napalm, and all the rest to "communist-dominated" Viet-Nam (clearly an "undesirable object"), as the "operator" to transform it into a "desirable object".'[10]

EFFECTS OF THE HIERARCHICAL AND FUNCTIONAL DIVISIONS OF LABOUR

Use of violence is most efficient and cost-effective when the means are subjected to solely instrumental-rational criteria, and thus dissociated from moral evaluation of the ends. As I pointed out in the first chapter, such dissociation is an operation all bureaucracies are good at. One may even say that it provides the essence of bureaucratic structure and process, and with it the secret of that tremendous growth of mobilizing and co-ordinating potential, and of the rationality and efficiency of action, which modern civilization has achieved thanks to the development of bureaucratic administration. The dissociation is by and large an outcome of two parallel processes, which are both central to the bureaucratic model of action. The first is the *meticulous functional division of labour* (as additional to, and distinct in its consequences, from linear graduation of power and subordination); the second is the *substitution of technical for a moral responsibility*.

All division of labour (also such division as results from the mere hierarchy of command) creates a distance between most of the contributors to the final outcome of collective activity, and the outcome itself. Before the last links in the bureaucratic chain of power (the direct executors) confront their task, most of the preparatory operations which brought about that confrontation have been already performed by persons who had no personal experience, and sometimes not the knowledge either, of the task in question. Unlike in a pre-modern unit of work, in which all steps of the hierarchy share in the same occupational skills, and the practical knowledge of working operations actually grows towards the top of the ladder (the master knows the same as his journeyman or apprentice, only more and better), persons occupying successive rungs of modern bureaucracy differ sharply in the kind of expertise and professional training their jobs require. They may be able to put themselves imaginatively into their subordinates' position; this may even help in maintaining 'good human relations' inside the office – but it is not the condition of proper performance of the task, nor of the effectiveness of the bureaucracy as a whole. In fact, most bureaucracies do not treat seriously the romantic recipe that requires every bureaucrat, and particularly those who occupy the top, to 'start from the bottom' so that on the way to the summit they should acquire, and memorize, the experience of the entire slope. Mindful of the multiplicity of skills which the managerial jobs of various magnitudes demand, most bureaucracies practise instead separate avenues of recruitment for different levels of the hierarchy. Perhaps it is true that each soldier carries a marshal's baton in his knapsack, but few marshals, and few colonels or captains for that matter, keep soldiers' bayonets in their briefcases.

What such practical and mental distance from the final product means is that most functionaries of the bureaucratic hierarchy may give commands without full knowledge of their effects. In many cases they would find it difficult to visualize those effects. Usually, they only have an abstract, detached awareness of them; the kind of knowledge which is best expressed in statistics, which measure the results without passing any judgement, and certainly not moral ones. In their files and their minds the results are at best diagramatically represented as curves or sectors of a circle; ideally, they would appear as a column of numbers. Graphically or numerically represented, the final outcomes of their commands are devoid of substance. The graphs measure the *progress* of work, they say nothing about the nature of the operation or its objects. The graphs make tasks of widely different character mutually exchangeable; only the quantifiable success or failure matter, and seen from that point of view, the tasks do not differ.

All these effects of distance created by the hierarchical division of labour are radically magnified once the division becomes functional. Now it is not just the lack of direct, personal experience of the actual execution of the task to which successive command contribute their share, but also the lack of similarity between the task at hand and the task of the office as a whole (one is not a miniature version, or an icon, of the other), which distances the contributor from the job performed by the bureaucracy of which he is a part. The psychological impact of such distantiation is profound and far-reaching. It is one thing to give a command to load bombs on the plane, but quite different to take care of regular steel supply in a bomb factory. In the first case, the command-giver may have no vivid, visual impression of the devastation the bomb is about to cause. In the second case, however, the supply manager does not, if he chooses to, have to think about the use to which bombs are put at all. Even in abstract, purely notional knowledge of the final outcome is redundant, and certainly irrelevant as far as the success of his own part of the operation goes. In a functional division of labour, everything one does is in principle *multifinal*; that is, it can be combined and integrated into more than one meaning-determining totality. By itself, the function is devoid of meaning, and the meaning which will be eventually bestowed on it is in no way pre-empted by the actions of its perpetrators. It will be 'the others' (in most cases anonymous and out of reach) who will some time, somewhere, decide that meaning. 'Would workers in the chemical plants that produced napalm accept responsibility for burned babies?' ask Kren and Rappoport. 'Would such workers even be aware that others might reasonably think they were responsible?'[11] Of course they wouldn't. And there is no bureaucratic reason why they should. The splitting of the baby-burning process in minute functional tasks and then separating the tasks from each other have made such awareness irrelevant – and exceedingly difficult to achieve. Remember as well that it is chemical plants that produce napalm, not any of their individual workers ...

The second process responsible for distantiation is closely related to the first. The substitution of technical for moral responsibility would not be conceivable without the meticulous functional dissection and separation of tasks. At least it would not be conceivable to the same extent. The substitution takes place, to a degree, already within the purely linear graduation of control. Each person within the hierarchy of command is accountable to his immediate superior, and thus is naturally interested in his opinion and his approval of the work. However much this approval matters to him, he is still, though only theoretically, aware of what the ultimate outcome of his work is bound to be. And so there is at least an abstract chance of one awareness being measured against the other; benevolence of superiors being confronted with repulsiveness of the effects. And whenever comparison is feasible, so is the choice. Within a purely linear division of command, technical responsibility remains, at least in theory, vulnerable. It may still be called to justify itself in moral terms and to compete with moral conscience. A functionary may, for instance, decide that by giving a particular command his superior overstepped his terms of reference, as he moved from the domain of purely technical interest to that charged with ethical significance (shooting soldiers is OK; shooting babies is a different matter); and that the duty to obey an authoritative command does not extend so far as to justify what the functionary considers as morally unacceptable deeds. All these theoretical possibilities disappear, however, or are considerably weakened, once the linear hierarchy of command is supplemented, or replaced, by functional division and separation of tasks. The triumph of technical responsibility is then complete, unconditional, and for all practical purposes, unassailable.

Technical responsibility differs from moral responsibility in that it forgets that the action is a means to something other than itself. As outer connections of action are effectively removed from the field of vision, the bureaucrat's own act becomes an end in itself. It can be judged only by its intrinsic criteria of propriety and success. Hand-in-hand with the vaunted relative autonomy of the official conditioned by his functional specialization, comes his remoteness from the overall effects of divided yet co-ordinated labour of the organization as a whole. Once isolated from their distant consequences, most functionally specialized acts either pass moral test easily, or are morally indifferent. When unencumbered by moral worries, the act can be judged on unambiguously rational grounds. What matters then is whether the act has been performed according to the best available technological know-how, and whether its output has been cost-effective. Criteria are clear-cut and easy to operate.

For our topic, two effects of such context of bureaucratic action are most important. First is the fact that the skills, expert knowledge, inventiveness and dedication of actors, complete with their personal motives that prompted them to deploy these qualities in full, can be fully mobilized and put to the service of the overall bureaucratic purpose even if (or perhaps because) the actors retain relative functional autonomy towards this purpose and even if this purpose does not agree with the actors' own moral philosophy. To put it bluntly, *the result is the irrelevance of moral standards for the technical success of the bureaucratic operation.* The instinct of workmanship, which according to Thorstein Veblen is present in every actor, focuses fully on proper performance of the job in hand. The practical devotion to the task may be further enhanced by the actor's craven character and severity of his superiors, or by the actor's interest in promotion, the actor's ambition or disinterested curiosity, or by many other personal circumstances, motives, or character features – but, on the whole, workmanship will suffice even in their absence. By and large, the actors want to excel; whatever they do, they want to do well. Once, thanks to the complex functional differentiation within bureaucracy, they have been distantiated from the ultimate outcomes of the operation to which they contribute, their moral concerns can concentrate fully on the good performance of the job at hand. Morality boils down to the commandment to be a good, efficient and diligent expert and worker.

DEHUMANIZATION OF BUREAUCRATIC OBJECTS

Another, equally important effect of bureaucratic context of action is *dehumanization of the objects of bureaucratic operation*; the possibility to express these objects in purely technical, ethically neutral terms.

We associate dehumanization with horrifying pictures of the inmates of concentration camps – humiliated by reducing their action to the most basic level of primitive survival, by preventing them from deploying cultural (both bodily and behavioural) symbols of human dignity, by depriving them even of recognizably human likeness. As Peter Marsh put it, 'Standing by the fence of Auschwitz, looking at these emaciated skeletons with shrunken skin and hollowed eyes – who could believe that these were really people?'[12] These pictures, however, represent only an extreme manifestation of a tendency which may be discovered in all bureaucracies, however benign and innocuous the tasks in which they are currently engaged. I suggest that the discussion of the dehumanizing tendency, rather than being focused on its most sensational and vile, but fortunately uncommon, manifestations, ought to concentrate on the more universal, and for this reason potentially more dangerous, manifestations.

Dehumanization starts at the point when, thanks to the distantiation, the objects at which the bureaucratic operation is aimed can, and are, reduced to a set of quantitative measures. For railway managers, the only meaningful articulation of their object is in terms of tonnes per kilometre. They do not deal with humans, sheep, or barbed wire; they only deal with the cargo, and this means an entity consisting entirely of measurements and devoid of quality. For most bureaucrats, even such a category as cargo would mean too strict a quality-bound restriction. They deal only with the financial effects of their actions. Their object is money. Money is the sole object that appears on both input and output ends, *and pecunia,* as the ancients shrewdly observed, definitely *non olet*. As they grow, bureaucratic companies seldom allow themselves to be confined to one qualitatively distinct area of activity. They spread sideways, guided in their movements by a sort of *lucrotropism* – a sort of gravitational pulling force of the highest returns on their capital. As we remember, the whole operation of the Holocaust was managed by the Economic Administration Section of the *Reichsicherheithauptamt*. We know that this one assignment, exceptionally, was not intended as a stratagem or a camouflage.

Reduced, like all other objects of bureaucratic management, to pure, quality-free measurements, human objects lose their distinctiveness. They are already dehumanized – in the sense that the language in which things that happen to them (or are done *to* them) are narrated, safeguards its referents from ethical evaluation. In fact, this language is unfit for normative-moral statements. It is only humans that may be objects of ethical propositions. (True, moral statements do extend sometimes to other, non-human living beings; but they may do so only by expanding from their original anthropomorphic foothold.) Humans lose this capacity once they are reduced to ciphers.

Dehumanization is inextricably related to the most essential, rationalizing tendency of modern bureaucracy. As all bureaucracies affect in some measure some human objects, the adverse impact of dehumanization is much more common than the habit to identify it almost totally with its genocidal effects would suggest. Soldiers are told to shoot *targets,* which *fall* when they are *hit*. Employees of big companies are encouraged to destroy *competition*. Officers of welfare agencies operate *discretionary awards* at one time, *personal credits* at another. Their objects are *supplementary benefit recipients*. It is difficult to perceive and remember the humans behind all such technical terms. The point is that as far as the bureaucratic goals go, they are better not perceived and not remembered.

Once effectively dehumanized, and hence cancelled as potential subjects of moral demands, human objects of bureaucratic task-performance are viewed with ethical indifference, which soon turns into disapprobation and censure when their resistance, or lack of co-operation, slows down the smooth flow of bureaucratic routine. Dehumanized objects cannot possibly possess a 'cause', much less a 'just' one; they have no 'interests' to be considered, indeed no claim to subjectivity. Human objects become therefore a 'nuisance factor'. Their obstreperousness further strengthens the self-esteem and the bonds of comradeship that unite the functionaries. The latter see themselves now as companions in a difficult struggle, calling for courage, self-sacrifice and selfless dedication to the cause. It is not the objects of bureaucratic action, but its subjects who suffer and deserve compassion and moral praise. They may justly derive pride and assurance of their own dignity from crushing the recalcitrance of their victims – much as they are proud of overriding any other obstacle. Dehumanization of the objects and positive moral self-evaluation reinforce each other. The functionaries may faithfully serve any goal while their moral conscience remains unimpaired.

The overall conclusion is that the bureaucratic mode of action, as it has been developed in the course of the modernizing process, contains all the technical elements which proved necessary in the execution of genocidal tasks. This mode can be put to the service of a genocidal objective without major revision of its structure, mechanisms and behavioural norms.

Moreover, contrary to widespread opinion, bureaucracy is not merely a tool, which can be used with equal facility at one time for cruel and morally contemptible, at another for deeply humane purposes. Even if it does move in any direction in which it is pushed, bureaucracy is more like a loaded dice. It has a logic and a momentum of its own. It renders some solutions more, and other solutions less, probable. Given an initial push (being confronted with a purpose), it will – like the brooms of the sorcerer's apprentice – easily move

beyond all thresholds at which many of those who gave it the push would have stopped, were they still in control of the process they triggered. Bureaucracy is programmed to seek the optimal solution. It is programmed to measure the optimum in such terms as would not distinguish between one human object and another, or between human and inhuman objects. What matters is the efficiency and lowering of costs of their processing.

THE ROLE OF BUREAUCRACY IN THE HOLOCAUST

It so happened in Germany half a century ago that bureaucracy was given the task of making Germany *judenrein* – clean of Jews. Bureaucracy started from what bureaucracies start with: the formulation of a precise definition of the object, then registering those who fitted the definition and opening a file for each. It proceeded to segregate those in the files from the rest of the population, to which the received brief did not apply. Finally, it moved to evicting the segregated category from the land of the Aryans which was to be cleansed – by nudging it to emigrate first, and deporting it to non-German territories once such territories found themselves under German control. By that time bureaucracy developed wonderful cleansing skills, not to be wasted and left to rust. *Bureaucracy which acquitted itself so well of the task of cleansing Germany made more ambitious tasks feasible, and their choice well-nigh natural.* With such a superb cleaning facility, why stop at the *Heimat* of the Aryans? Why refrain from cleaning the whole of their empire? True, as the empire was now ecumenical, it had no 'outside' left where the dumping ground for the Jewish litter could be disposed of. Only one direction of deportation remained; upward, in smoke.

For many years now historians of the Holocaust have been split into the 'intentionalist' and the 'functionalist' camps. The first insist that killing the Jews was from the start Hitler's firm decision, waiting only for opportune conditions to emerge. The second credit Hitler with only a general idea of 'finding a solution' to the 'Jewish problem': clear only as far as the vision of 'clean Germany' goes, but vague and muddled as to the practical steps to be taken to bring that vision closer. Historical scholarship ever more convincingly supports the functionalist view. Whatever the ultimate outcome of the debate, however, there is hardly any doubt that the space extending between the idea and its execution was filled wall-to-wall with bureaucratic action. Neither is there any doubt that however vivid was Hitler's imagination, it would have accomplished little if it had not been taken over, and translated into routine process of problem-solving, by a huge and rational bureaucratic apparatus. Finally, and perhaps most importantly, the bureaucratic mode of action left its indelible impression of the Holocaust process. Its fingerprints are all over the Holocaust history, for everyone to see. True, bureaucracy did not hatch the fear of racial contamination and the obsession with racial hygiene. For that it needed visionaries, as bureaucracy picks up where visionaries stop. But bureaucracy made the Holocaust. And it made it in its own image.

Hilberg has suggested that the moment the first German official had written the first rule of Jewish exclusion, the fate of the European Jews was sealed. There is a most profound and terrifying truth in this comment. What bureaucracy needed was the definition of its task. Rational and efficient as it was, it could be trusted to see the task to its end.

Bureaucracy contributed to the perpetuation of the Holocaust not only through its inherent capacities and skills, but also through its immanent ailments. The tendency of all bureaucracies to lose sight of the original goal and to concentrate on the means instead – the means which turn into the ends – has been widely noted, analysed and described. The Nazi bureaucracy did not escape its impact. Once set in motion, the machinery of murder developed its own impetus: the more it excelled in cleansing the territories it controlled of the Jews, the more actively it sought new lands where it could exercise its newly acquired skills. With the approaching military defeat of Germany, the original purpose of the *Endlösung* was becoming increasingly unreal. What kept the murdering machine going then was solely its own routine and impetus. The skills of mass murder had to be used simply because they were there. The experts created the objects for their own expertise. We remember the experts of Jewish Desks in Berlin introducing every new petty restriction on German Jews who had long before all but disappeared from German soil; we remember the SS commanders who forbade the *Wehrmacht* generals from keeping alive the Jewish craftsmen they badly needed for military operations. But nowhere was the morbid tendency of substituting the means for the ends more visible than in the uncanny and macabre episode of the murder of Romanian and Hungarian Jews, perpetrated with the Eastern Front just a few miles away, and at an enormous cost to the war effort: priceless rail carriages and engines, troops and administrative resources were diverted from military tasks in order to cleanse distant parts of Europe for the German habitat which was never to be.

Bureaucracy is intrinsically *capable* of genocidal action. To *engage* in such an action, it needs an encounter with another invention of modernity: a bold design of a better, more reasonable and rational social order – say a racially uniform, or a classless society – and above all the capacity of drawing such designs and determination to make them efficacious. Genocide follows when two common and abundant inventions of modern times meet. It is only their meeting which has been, thus far, uncommon and rare.

BANKRUPTCY OF MODERN SAFEGUARDS

Physical violence and its threat

is no longer a perpetual insecurity that it brings into the life of the individual, but a peculiar form of security ... a continuous, uniform pressure is exerted on individual life by the physical violence stored behind the scenes of everyday life, a pressure totally familiar and hardly perceived, conduct and drive economy having been adjusted from earliest youth to this social structure.[13]

In these words, Norbert Elias restated the familiar self-definition of civilized society. Elimination of violence from daily life is the main assertion around which that definition revolves. As we have seen, the apparent elimination is in fact merely an eviction, leading to the reassembly of resources and disposition of centres of violence in new locations within the social system. According to Elias, the two developments are closely interdependent. The area of daily life is comparatively free from violence precisely because somewhere in the wings physical violence is stored – in quantities that put it effectively out of the control of ordinary members of society and endow it with irresistible power to suppress unauthorized outbursts of violence. Daily manners mellowed mainly because people are now threatened with violence in case they are violent – with violence they cannot match or reasonably hope to repel. The disappearance of violence from the horizon of daily life is thus one more manifestation of the centralizing and monopolizing tendencies of modern power; violence is absent from individual intercourse because it is now controlled by forces definitely outside the individual reach. But the forces are not outside *everybody's* reach. Thus the much vaunted mellowing of manners (which Elias, following the etiological myth of the West, celebrates with such a relish), and the cosy security of daily life that follows have their price. A price which we, dwellers in the house of modernity, may be called to pay at any time. Or made to pay, without being called first.

Pacification of daily life means at the same time its defencelessness. By agreeing, or being forced to renounce the use of physical force in their reciprocal relations, members of modern society disarm themselves in front of the unknown and normally invisible, yet potentially sinister and always formidable managers of coercion. Their weakness is worrying not so much because of the high probability that the managers of coercion will indeed take advantage of it and hurry to turn the means of violence they control against the disarmed society, as for the simple fact that whether such advantage will or will not be taken, does not in principle depend on what ordinary men and women do. By themselves, the members of modern society cannot prevent the use of massive coercion from happening. Mellowing of manners goes hand-in-hand with a radical shift in control over violence.

Awareness of the constant threat which the characteristically modern imbalance of power contains would make life unbearable, were it not for our trust in safeguards which we believe have been built into the fabric of modern, civilized society. Most of the time we have no reason to think that the trust is misguided. Only on a few dramatic occasions a doubt is cast on the reliability of the safeguards. Perhaps the main significance of the Holocaust lies in its having been one of the most redoubtable of such occasions to date. *In the years leading to the Final Solution the most trusted of the safeguards had been put to a test. They all failed – one by one, and all together.*

Perhaps the most spectacular was the failure of science – as a body of ideas, and as a network of institutions of enlightenment and training. The deadly potential of the most revered principles and accomplishments of modern science has been exposed. The emancipation of reason from emotions, of rationality from normative pressures, of effectiveness from ethics have been the battle-cries of science since its inception. Once implemented, however, they made science, and the formidable technological applications it spawned, into docile instruments in the hands of unscrupulous power. The dark and ignoble role which science played in the perpetuation of the Holocaust was both direct and indirect.

Indirectly (though centrally to its general social function), science cleared the way to genocide through sapping the authority, and questioning the binding force, of all normative thinking, particularly that of religion and ethics. Science looks back at its history as the long and victorious struggle of reason over superstition and irrationality. In as far as religion and ethics could not rationally legitimize the demands they made on human behaviour, they stood condemned and found their authority denied. As values and norms had been proclaimed immanently and irreparably subjective, instrumentality was left as the only field where the search for excellence was feasible. Science wanted to be value-free and took pride in being such. By institutional pressure and by ridicule, it silenced the preachers of morality. In the process, it made itself morally blind and speechless. It dismantled all the barriers that could stop it from co-operating, with enthusiasm and abandon, in designing the most effective and rapid methods of mass sterilization or mass killing; or from conceiving of the concentration camps' slavery as a unique and wonderful opportunity to conduct medical research for the advancement of scholarship and – of course – of mankind.

Science (or this time, rather the scientists) helped the Holocaust perpetrators directly as well. Modern science is a gigantic and complex institution. Research costs dear, as it requires huge buildings, expensive equipment and large teams of highly paid experts. Thus science depends on a constant flow of money and non-monetary resources, which only equally large institutions are able to offer and to guarantee. Science is not, however, mercantile, nor are the scientists avaricious. Science is about truth, and scientists are about pursuing it. Scientists are overwhelmed with curiosity and excited by the unknown. If measured by all other earthly concerns, including monetary, curiosity is disinterested. It is only the value of knowledge and truth which scientists preach and search. It is just a coincidence, and preferably a minor irritant, that curiosity cannot be sated, and the truth found, without ever-growing funds, ever-more costly laboratories, ever-larger

salary bills. What scientists want is merely to be allowed to go where their thirst for knowledge prompts them.

A government who stretches its helpful hand and offers just that can count on the scientists' gratitude and co-operation. Most scientists would be prepared in exchange to surrender quite a long list of lesser precepts. They would be prepared, for instance, to make do with the sudden disappearance of some of their colleagues with the wrong shape of nose or biographical entry. If they object at all, it will be that taking all these colleagues away in one swoop may put the research schedule in jeopardy. (This is not a slur nor a squib; this is what the protests of German academics, medics and engineers, if recorded at all, boiled down to. Less still was heard from their Soviet equivalents during the purges.) With relish, German scientists boarded the train drawn by the Nazi locomotive towards the brave, new, racially purified and German-dominated world. Research projects grew more ambitious by the day, and research institutes grew more populous and resourceful by the hour. Little else mattered.

In his fascinating new study of the contribution of biology and medical science to the designing and implementing of Nazi racial policy Robert Proctor puts paid to the popular myth of science under Nazism as, first and foremost, the victim of persecution and an object of intense indoctrination from above (a myth dating at least from Joseph Needham's influential *The Nazi Attack on International Science*, published in 1941). In the light of Proctor's meticulous research, the widespread opinion sorely underestimates the degree to which political initiatives (indeed, some of the most gruesome among them) were generated by the scientific community itself, rather than imposed from outside on reluctant yet craven boffins, and the extent to which racial policy itself was initiated and managed by the recognized scientists with academically impeccable credentials. If there was coercion, 'it often took the form of one part of the scientific community coercing another'. On the whole, 'many of the social and intellectual foundations [for racial programmes] were laid down long before the rise of Hitler to power', and biomedical scientists 'played an active, even leading role in the initiation, administration, and execution of the Nazi racial programmes'.[14] That the biomedical scientists in question were by no standards a lunatic or fanatical fringe of the profession is shown by Proctor's painstaking study of the composition of the editorial boards of 147 medical journals published in Nazi Germany. After Hitler's rise to power, the boards remained either unchanged or they replaced only a small minority of their members (in all probability, the change is accounted for by the removal of Jewish scholars).[15]

At best, the cult of rationality, institutionalized as modern science, proved impotent to prevent the state from turning into organized crime; at worst, it proved instrumental in bringing the transformation about. Its rivals, however, did not earn a higher score either. In their silence German academics had plenty of companions. Most conspicuously, they were joined by the Churches – all of them. Silence in the face of the organized inhumanity was the only item on which the Churches, so often at loggerheads, found themselves in agreement. None of them attempted to reclaim its flouted authority. None of the Churches (as distinct from single, and mostly isolated churchmen) acknowledged its responsibility for deeds perpetrated in a country it claimed as its domain, and by people in its pastoral charge. (Hitler never left the Catholic Church; neither was he excommunicated.) None upheld its right to pass moral judgements on its flock and impose penitence on the wayward.

Most pertinently, the culturally trained revulsion against violence proved a poor safeguard against organized coercion; while civilized manners showed an astounding ability to cohabit, peacefully and harmoniously, with mass murder. The protracted, and often painful, civilizing process failed to erect a single foolproof barrier against the genocide. Those mechanisms needed the civilized code of behaviour to co-ordinate criminal actions in such a way that

they seldom clashed with the self-righteousness of the perpetrators. Among the bystanders, the civilized disgust of inhumanity did not prove strong enough to encourage an active resistance to it. Most bystanders reacted as civilized norms advise and prompt us to react to things unsightly and barbaric; they turned their eyes the other way. The few who stood up against cruelty did not have norms or social sanctions to support them and reassure. They were loners, who in justification of their fight against evil could only quote one of their distinguished ancestors: 'Ich kann nicht anders.'

In the face of an unscrupulous team saddling the powerful machine of the modern state with its monopoly of physical violence and coercion, the most vaunted accomplishments of modern civilization failed as safeguards against barbarism. *Civilization proved incapable of guaranteeing moral use of the awesome powers it brought into being.*

CONCLUSIONS

If we ask now what the original sin was which allowed this to happen, the collapse (or non-emergence) of democracy seems to be the most convincing answer. In the absence of traditional authority, the only checks and balances capable of keeping the body politic away from extremities can be supplied by political democracy. The latter is not, however, quick to arrive, and it is slower still to take root once the hold of the old authority and system of control had been broken – particularly if the breaking was done in a hurry. Such situations of interregnum and instability tend to occur during and after deep-reaching revolutions, which succeed in paralysing old seats of social power without as yet replacing them with new ones – and create for this reason a state of affairs in *which political and military forces are neither counterbalanced nor restrained by resourceful and influential social ones.*

Such situations emerged, arguably, in pre-modern times as well – in the wake of bloody conquests or protracted internecine strifes which led on occasion to well-nigh complete self-annihilation of established elites. The expectable consequences of such situations were, however, different. A general collapse of the larger social order normally followed. War destruction seldom reached as low as the grass-root, communal networks of social control; communally regulated local islands of social order were now exposed to erratic acts of violence and pillage, but they had themselves to fall back upon once the social organization above the local level disintegrated. In most cases, even the most profound blows to traditional authorities in pre-modern societies differed from modern upheavals in two crucial aspects; first, they left the primeval, communal controls of order intact or at least still viable; and second, they weakened, rather than strengthened the possibility of organized action on a supra-communal level, as the social organization of the higher order fell apart and whatever exchange was left between localities was once again subjected to a free play of unco-ordinated forces.

Under modern conditions, on the contrary, upheavals of a similar kind occur, on the whole, after communal mechanisms of social regulation have all but disappeared and local communities ceased to be self-sufficient and self-reliant. Instead of an instinctive reflex of 'falling back' upon one's own resources, the void tends to be filled by new, but again supra-communal, forces, which seek to deploy the state monopoly of coercion to impose a new order on the societal scale. Instead of collapsing, political power becomes therefore virtually the only force behind the emerging order. In its drive it is neither stopped nor restrained by economic and social forces, seriously undermined by the destruction or paralysis of old authorities.

This is, of course, a theoretical model, seldom implemented in full in historical practice. Its use consists however in drawing attention to those social dislocations that seem to make the surfacing of genocidal tendencies more likely. Dislocations may differ in form and intensity, but they are united by the general effect of *the pronounced supremacy of political over economic and social power, of the state over the society.* They went perhaps deepest and farthest in the case of the Russian Revolution and the subsequent prolonged monopoly of the state as the only factor of social integration and order-reproduction. Yet also in Germany they went farther and deeper than it is popularly believed. Arriving after the brief Weimar interlude, the Nazi rule undertook and completed the revolution that the Weimar Republic – that uneasy interplay of old and new (but immature) elites which only at the surface resembled political democracy – was, for various reasons, incapable of administering. Old elites were considerably weakened or pushed aside. One by one, the forms of articulation of economic and social forces were dissembled and replaced with new, centrally supervised forms emanating from, and legitimized by, the state. All classes were profoundly affected, but the most radical blow was delivered to the classes that can carry non-political power only collectively, i.e. to the non-proprietary classes, and to the working class above all. Etatization or disbanding of all autonomous labour institutions coupled with the subjection of local government to almost total central control, left the popular masses virtually powerless and, for all practical purposes, excluded from the political process. Resistance of social forces was prevented additionally by the surrounding of state activity with an impenetrable wall of secrecy – indeed, the state conspiracy of silence against the very population it ruled. The overall and ultimate effect was the replacement of traditional authorities not by the new vibrant forces of self-governing citizenship, but by an almost total monopoly of the political state, with social powers prevented from self-articulation, and thus from forming a structural foundation of political democracy.

Modern conditions made possible the emergence of a resourceful state, capable of replacing the whole network of social and economic controls by political command and administration. More importantly still, modern conditions provide substance for that command and administration. Modernity, as we remember, is an age of artificial order and of grand societal designs, the era of planners, visionaries, and – more generally – 'gardeners' who treat society as a virgin plot of land to be expertly designed and then cultivated and doctored to keep to the designed form.

There is no limit to ambition and self-confidence. Indeed, through the spectacles of modern power 'mankind' seems so omnipotent and its individual members so 'incomplete', inept and submissive, and so much in need of improvement, that treating people as plants to be trimmed (if necessary, uprooted) or cattle to be bred does not look fanciful or morally odious. One of the earliest and principal ideologists of German National Socialism, R. W. Darré, took the practices of animal husbandry as the pattern of 'population policy' to be implemented by the future *volkish* government:

> He who leaves the plants in a garden to themselves will soon find to his surprise that the garden is overgrown by weeds and that even the basic character of the plants has changed. If therefore the garden is to remain the breeding ground for the plants, if, in other words, it is to lift itself above the harsh rule of natural forces, then the forming will of a gardener is necessary, a gardener who, by providing suitable conditions for growing, or by keeping harmful influences away, or by both together, carefully tends what needs tending, and ruthlessly eliminates the weeds which would deprive the better plants of nutrition, air, light, and sun ... Thus we are facing the realization that questions of breeding are not trivial for political thought, but that they have to be at the centre of all considerations, and that their answers must follow from the spiritual, from the ideological attitude of a people. We must even assert that a people can only reach spiritual and moral equilibrium if a well-conceived breeding plan stands at the very *centre* of its culture ...[16]

Darré spelled out in unambiguous and radical terms the 'reality-improving' ambitions which form the essence of the modern stance and which only the resources of modern power allow us to entertain seriously.

Periods of deep social dislocations are times when this most remarkable feature of modernity comes into its own. Indeed, at no other time does society seem to be so formless – 'unfinished', indefinite and pliable – literally waiting for a vision and a skilful and resourceful designer to give it a form. At no other time does society seem so devoid of forces and tendencies of its own, and hence incapable of resisting the hand of the gardener, and ready to be squeezed into any form he chooses. *The combination of malleability and helplessness constitutes an attraction which few self-confident adventurous visionaries could resist. It also constitutes a situation in which they cannot be resisted.*

The carriers of the grand design at the helm of modern state bureaucracy, emancipated from the constraints of non-political (economic, social, cultural) powers; this is the recipe for genocide. Genocide arrives as an integral part of the process through which the grand design is implemented. *The design gives it the legitimation; state bureaucracy gives it the vehicle; and the paralysis of society gives it the 'road clear' sign.*

The conditions propitious to the perpetration of genocide are thus special, yet not at all exceptional. Rare, but not unique. Not being an immanent attribute of modern society, they are not an alien phenomenon either. As far as modernity goes, genocide is neither abnormal nor a case of malfunction. It demonstrates what the rationalizing, engineering tendency of modernity is capable of if not checked and mitigated, if the pluralism of social powers is indeed eroded – as the modern ideal of purposefully designed, fully controlled, conflict-free, orderly and harmonious society would have it. Any impoverishment of grass-root ability to articulate interests and self-govern, every assault on social and cultural pluralism and the opportunities of its political expression, every attempt to fence off the untrammelled freedom of the state by a wall of political secrecy, each step towards the weakening of the social foundations of political democracy make a social disaster on a Holocaust scale just a little bit more feasible. Criminal designs need social vehicles to be effective. But so does the vigilance of those who want to prevent their implementation.

Thus far the vehicles for vigilance seem in short supply, while there is no shortage of institutions that seem capable of serving criminal designs or – worse still – incapable of preventing an, ordinary task-oriented activity from acquiring a criminal dimension. Joseph Weizenbaum, one of the most acute observers and analysts of the social impact of information technology (admittedly a recent development, not available at the time of the Nazi Holocaust), suggests that the capacity for genocidal action has been, if anything, increased:

> Germany implemented the 'final solution' of its 'Jewish Problem' as a textbook exercise in instrumental reasoning. Humanity briefly shuddered when it could no longer avert its gaze from what had happened, when the photographs taken by the killers themselves began to circulate, and when the pitiful survivors re-emerged into the light. But in the end, it made no difference. The same logic, the same cold and ruthless application of calculating reason, slaughtered at least as many people during the next twenty years as had fallen victim to the technicians of the thousand-year Reich. We have learned nothing. Civilization is as imperilled today as it was then.[17]

And the reasons why instrumental rationality, and the human networks developed to serve it, remain morally blind now as they were then, are virtually unchanged. In 1966, more than twenty years after the gruesome discovery of the Nazi crime, a group of distinguished scholars designed the scientifically elegant and exemplary rational project of the *electronic battlefield* for the use of the generals of the Vietnam war. 'These men were able to give the counsel they gave because they were operating at an enormous psychological distance from the people who would be maimed and killed by the weapons systems that would result from the idea they communicated to their sponsors.'[18]

Thanks to rapidly advancing new information technology, which more than any technology that preceded it has succeeded in obliterating the humanity of its human objects ('People, things, events are "programmed", one speaks of "inputs" and "outputs", of feedback loops, variables, percentages, processes, and so on, until eventually all contact with concrete situations is abstracted away. Then only graphs, data sets, printouts are left'[19]) – the psychological distance grows unstoppably and on an unprecedented pace. So does the autonomy of purely technological progress from any deliberately chosen and discursively agreed human purposes. Today more than at any other time, available technological means undermine their own applications and subordinate the evaluation of the latter to their own criteria of efficiency and effectiveness. By the same token, the authority of political and moral evaluation of action has been reduced to a minor consideration – if not discredited and rendered irrelevant. Action can hardly need any other justification than the recognition that the available technology has made it feasible. Jacques Ellul has warned that, having emancipated itself from the constraint of discursively-set social tasks, technology

> never advances toward anything but *because* it is pushed from behind. The technician does not know why he is working, and generally he does not care. He works *because* he has instruments allowing him to perform a certain task, to succeed in a new operation … There is no call towards a goal; there is constraint by an engine placed in the back and not tolerating any halt to the machine.[20]

There seems to be less hope than before that the civilized guarantees against inhumanity can be relied upon to control the application of human instrumental-rational potential, once the calculation of efficiency has been awarded supreme authority in deciding political purposes.

NOTES

1. Raul Hilberg, 'Significance of the Holocaust', in *The Holocaust: Ideology, Bureaucracy, and Genocide,* ed. Henry Friedlander & Sybil Milton (Millwood, NY: Kraus International Publications, 1980), pp. 101–2.
2. Cf. Colin Legum in *The Observer,* 12 October 1966.
3. Henry L. Feingold, 'How Unique is the Holocaust?' in *Genocide: Critical Issues of the Holocaust,* ed. Alex Grobman & David Landes (Los Angeles: Simon Wiesenthal Centre, 1983), p. 397.
4. Feingold, 'How Unique is the Holocaust?', p. 401.
5. Leo Kuper, *Genocide: Its Political Use in the Twentieth Century* (New Haven: Yale University Press, 1981), pp. 137, 161. Kuper's forebodings found a most sinister confirmation in the words of the Iraqi ambassador in London. Interviewed on Channel 4 on 2 September 1988 about the continuing genocide of Iraqi Kurds, the ambassador indignantly replied to the charges that the Kurds, their well-being, and their fate were Iraq's internal affairs and that no one had the right to interfere with the actions undertaken by a sovereign state inside its borders.
6. George A. Kren & Leon Rappoport, *The Holocaust and the Crisis of Human Behaviour* (New York: Holmes & Meier, 1980), pp. 130, 143.
7. John P. Sabini & Mary Silver, 'Destroying the Innocent with a Clear Conscience: A Sociopsychology of the Holocaust', in *Survivors, Victims, and Perpetrators: Essays in the Nazi Holocaust,* ed. Joel E. Dinsdale (Washington: Hemisphere Publishing Corporation, 1980), pp. 329–30.
8. Sarah Gordon, *Hitler, Germans, and the 'Jewish Question'* (Princeton: Princeton University Press, 1984), pp. 48–9.
9. Kren & Rappoport, *The Holocaust and the Crisis,* p. 140.
10. Joseph Weizenbaum, *Computer Power and Human Reason: From Judgment to Calculation* (San Francisco: W. H. Freeman, 1976), p. 252.
11. Kren & Rappoport, *The Holocaust and the Crisis,* p. 141.
12. Peter Marsh, *Aggro: The Illusion of Violence* (London: J. M. Dent & Sons, 1978), p. 120.
13. Norbert Elias, *The Civilising Process: State Formation and Civilization,* trans. Edmund Jephcott (Oxford: Basil Blackwell, 1982), pp. 238–9.
14. Robert Proctor, *Racial Hygiene: Medicine under the Nazis* (Cambridge Mass.: Harvard University Press, 1988), p. 4, 6.
15. Proctor, *Racial Hygiene,* pp. 315–24.
16. R. W. Darré, 'Marriage Laws and the Principles of Breeding' (1930), in: *Nazi Ideology before 1933: A Documentation,* trans. Barbara Hiller and Leila J. Gupp (Manchester: Manchester University Press, 1978), p. 115.
17. Weizenbaum, *Computer Power,* p. 256.
18. Weizenbaum, *Computer Power,* p. 275.
19. Weizenbaum, *Computer Power,* p. 253.
20. Jacques Ellul, *Technological System,* trans. Joachim Neugroschel (New York: Continuum, 1980), pp. 272, 273.

COMPANION WEBSITE

1. Go online to Write Out Loud about your own thoughts about social norms, institutions of modernity, and how they relate to the Holocaust.
2. Browse the *Pathway to Meltdown* Supplementary Sources for more takes on Bauman, including Michael Mann's *The Dark Side of Democracy.*
3. Check out the Interactive Reading to learn more about how modernity can actually help to facilitate genocidal projects, such as the Holocaust.

Shifting the Paradigm

Excluded Voices, Alternative Knowledges

Introductory Essay:
Webs of Knowledge in the Digital Divide

The commercially available Internet of the early 1990s carried with it a promise that technological barriers would no longer impede the flow of information. Citizens could get the information they needed to make effective democratic choices, get better jobs, and improve their overall well-being. This is to say, the Internet shifted the paradigm for how we think about media, technology, and knowledge itself, offering instantaneous access to real-time events from almost every perspective imaginable. Indeed, it didn't merely open new doors to information—it tore the old ones from their hinges, set them ablaze, and scattered the ashes into the great expanse of the worldwide web. Or so we thought.

Not long after the Internet was introduced, scholars and policymakers grew concerned about the truth of its great egalitarian promise. Early evidence of a so-called "digital divide" meant that although the Internet offered a faster, flashier vehicle of communication, not everyone would be able to take the ride.

According to research conducted in the later 1990s by the National Telecommunications and Information Administration, early Internet users in the United States tended to be younger, more educated, and wealthier than non-users. Internet use also varied a lot by race, with Asian Americans and non-Hispanic whites going online more often than other groups. Many of these gaps remain today, even as connectivity continues to spread. A 2009 report by the Pew Research Center's Internet and American Life Project, for instance, found that 65 percent of white Americans had broadband access at home in 2009, compared to only 46 percent of African Americans. And, like the Internet itself, the digital divide has gone global—the International Telecommunications Union and the United Nations report there were more than 8 times as many Internet users in the United States as on the entire continent of Africa in 2004.

But the digital divide is more than just a gap in access to knowledge found on the Internet—maybe even more importantly, the divide affects how that knowledge gets produced in the first place. Sociologists Eszter Hargittai and Gina Walejko have found that a "participation gap" lurks within the cracks and crevices of the digital divide. They argue that the creative content produced and uploaded to the Internet by young people is determined more by their socioeconomic status than the new opportunities that the Internet provides. Rather than leveling the playing field, the Internet might simply reproduce it.

Findings like this have interesting, and troublesome, implications for the flow of information online. The Internet provides access to seemingly endless amounts of knowledge, but what would that knowledge look like if everyone had a hand in its creation?

Think back for a moment to Durkheim's definition of a social fact. Social facts are social constructions that confront us as if they are an external reality separate from any sort of origin. What we know about that external reality is what we might call an ontological understanding—knowledge of *what is* in the social world. But, if we delve into *how* that understanding of "what is" is constructed, or, more simply, *how we know what we know* about social reality, then we are looking at knowledge from the standpoint of epistemology. When we look at a social fact from an epistemological perspective, then our ontology—the "what is"—of what we know gets challenged. A bit disarmingly, by examining how we know what we know, we can begin to question everything we knew in the first place.

The theorists in this section grapple with this issue from perspectives that were excluded when the canon of social theory was being constructed. Incorporating race and gender into social theory is more than simply getting a perspective on society that is attuned to difference. Rather, it is about questioning whether a theory of society is legitimate at all if the categories used to construct it exclude particular times, places, and standpoints.

Like the Internet, social theory is a vast intellectual landscape in which conventional wisdom often gets spun like a top. Yet, also like the Internet, it has historically been an uneven landscape—the top gets spun in some directions but not others. If the map of social theory is incomplete because some voices were excluded when it was drafted, then perhaps it's time to draft a new one.

Classical Connections: W.E.B. Du Bois and Simone de Beauvoir

The term "paradigm shift" was coined by Thomas Kuhn to capture the moment when mysteries that cannot be explained by one scientific worldview lead to the revolutionary creation of a new one. It is a bit misleading to say that the theorists in this section shifted the paradigm of social theory, though, because each of them questioned whether a paradigm should exist in the first place. In fact, each of these theorists found themselves stuck between a paradigm consisting of concepts, theories, and taken-for-granted abstractions, and a lived experience that did not fit within that paradigm, a lived experience shaped by oppression, subjugation, and exclusion.

This feeling of being stuck in the middle is vividly expressed in the work of W.E.B. Du Bois, a profound social theorist and public intellectual who has only recently received recognition on the level of the other classical theorists in this volume. In *The Souls of Black Folk*, Du Bois draws from history, sociology, literature, and black spirituals to capture what it was like to live as a black person in early twentieth-century America. Perhaps what is most striking in his writing is how he brings himself front and center, turning his own experience into a microcosm of a bigger social process. In this way, Du Bois artfully conveys how the social structures of racism interact with its intersubjective and psychological dimensions.

Like Weber, Du Bois was struck by the paradoxical conundrums of modernity, particularly the persistence of segregation in American society despite the freeing of slaves decades earlier. According to Du Bois, segregation persisted into the twentieth century not just through institutions like housing, education, or labor, but also through cultural legacy—that is, the stereotypes and assumptions about skin color that seeped deep into the public imagination and shaped the everyday lives of people of color. Put simply, segregation was an objective, structural condition of American society as well as an experiential, subjective one.

Du Bois makes this connection between larger social forces and individual lived experiences through his metaphor of the veil. In his book *The New Politics of Race*, Howard Winant describes how this metaphor is meant to capture both the conflict of racism at the societal level (i.e. the color line) and knowledge of "the other" held at the interpersonal level. Through the veil, what Du Bois called "double-consciousness," emerges the psychological and social experience of seeing the world through the lens of both a black person and an American—two disconnected lenses that hinder a more unified sense of self.

Du Bois' concept of double-consciousness is similar to Simmel's concept of "the stranger," which is discussed in the next section of this book. You can learn more about both theorists and their ideas on each of their Profile Pages.

Although we present the first two chapters from *The Souls of Black Folk* in chronological order, each was written as a stand-alone essay, so you may find it useful to read them in reverse order. In "Of the Dawn of Freedom," Du Bois traces the history of the Freedmen's Bureau, an organization charged with assisting former slaves in acquiring education and fair employment. He shows how social institutions, such as civil courts in the South, prevented the Bureau from achieving many of its goals, thus leading to the persistence of segregation. In "Of Our Spiritual Strivings," Du Bois uses his quintessential precision and eloquence to introduce us to his concepts of the veil and double-consciousness. When read together (in whatever order you choose), these selections capture how race operates as both a social construct and a lived experience.

If Du Bois laid the foundation for how to think about the color line, then French philosopher Simone de Beauvoir set the standard for thinking about the boundaries of gender. Beauvoir is a more philosophical writer than many of the theorists in this volume, but recent re-readings of *The Second Sex* by feminist scholars have highlighted its more phenomenological tones. You might recall from Berger and Luckmann's *Social Construction of Reality* reading that phenomenology is the study of lived experience and meaning; Beauvoir is interested in how meaning gets attributed to gender and how such meaning leads to the oppression of women.

Let's step back for a moment to think about something a bit less philosophical and maybe sort of childish: the playground teeter-totter. As two kids on a seesaw shift their weight and kick their legs, the teeter-totter tips and, well, teeters. The seesaw's inherent relational properties allow it to do this—for one end to go up, the other end must go down.

A teeter-totter, then, is sort of like a dialectical relationship of opposing forces, which Beauvoir uses to illustrate the relationship between men and women as social constructs. According to Beauvoir, the meaning of "woman," which she describes as the inferior and inessential Other, has historically only been defined through its relationship to "man," the superior and essential Subject. And, since how we attribute meaning to a category like gender shapes how we then act out or embody it, Beauvoir, in the introduction to *The Second Sex* included here, is able to logically examine why women identify themselves by gender in ways that men do not.

Beauvoir's argument that the meaning attached to women is defined by their relationship to men is similar to Du Bois' thoughts on race. For both theorists, marginalized populations identify themselves through the eyes of a more powerful group (a metaphor that we will see again in the next set of readings). Each thinker was expressing concern over the paradoxical and constraining nature of binary categories—which hold tremendous significance for the people who occupy them—in a multifaceted and complex society.

The Second Sex remains a pivotal text of the feminist movement and for feminist theory today. We have included the introduction to the book here because it serves as a useful starting point for Beauvoir's take on gender as a social construction and lived reality, but we suggest interested readers pick up the whole book. Most notably, Beauvoir's assertion that one is not born, but becomes, a woman inspired much of contemporary theorist Judith Butler's work, which we will discuss in our last section.

Beauvoir draws upon Hegel's master/slave dialectic here. To read more about Hegel's dialectic, log on to Marx's Profile Page.

Contemporary Extensions: Paradigm Shift Re-Wired

In *Souls of Black Folk*, Du Bois recounts a childhood story about a young girl who refused a card he had offered her. It was because of his race. Stories like this help show the complex and often overlooked ways in which race operates in our social and political lives. Similarly, in *Racial Formation in the United States*, Michael Omi and Howard Winant tell the story of Susie Phipps, the descendent of a white plantation owner and a black slave in the seventeenth century who tried to change her racial classification from black to white in the 1980s. That Phipps' racial classification could *not* be changed illustrates how large-scale social and political institutions, such as the media, education system, and public policy, determine the meaning of racial categories. And, it is through those same institutions that meanings are contested, negotiated, and transformed. In the excerpt included here, Omi and Winant offer their definition of race as a fluid social construct, and their theory of racial formation at the individual and collective levels. Much like Du Bois, Omi and Winant make the case that race is central to the American social and political experience.

The next set of theorists look at race and ethnicity from a different vantage point. Postcolonial theory emerged after the African and Caribbean independence movements of the 1960s and 1970s, as scholars and activists came to grips with the long-lasting cultural and psychological effects of colonial rule. Some of the most vivid accounts of colonial domination are felt in the work of Frantz Fanon, a French-trained psychiatrist from Martinique who is best known for his role as an anti-colonial revolutionary and author. In *Black Skin, White Masks*, Fanon grapples with the role language plays in what we know about ourselves. Under colonial rule, subjects are expected to adopt the colonizer's language, whether it is Belgian, French, or English. The most sinister part of this so-called "white mask," according to Fanon, is that the colonized person is unable to recognize herself as fully human, because the very language she speaks is the language of those who subjugate her. Still, to resist the language of the colonizer means risking the loss of the only language she has ever known—that is, losing her voice.

Fanon is one of the most fervent postcolonial theorists, but Edward W. Said is perhaps the best known. Though his research interests and sociological contributions were broad, we focus here on a selection from *Orientalism*. In it, Said argues that Europe and, later, the United States were able to define themselves culturally and socially through "imaginative geography," or the social construction of other regions as less advanced than or more inferior to the regions doing the imagining. Said is particularly concerned with how Asian and Arab countries—known then as "the Orient" in Europe in the United States —were understood in this way.

The PBS series, *Race: The Power of an Illusion*, and its companion website provide a boatload of useful information on race as a social, political, and economic construct. Go to the Supplementary Sources for more information.

A vivid example of how the "white mask" operates can be found in Gillo Pontecorvo's powerful film, *Battle of Algiers*, summarized in the Supplementary Sources.

Go to the Supplementary Sources for books and films that explore colonialism and its social and psychological consequences.

According to Said, the re-imagining of the Orient that made it seem more distant and more inferior typically occurred through the use of images and texts. As colonial officers returned from abroad, universities in England and the United States began establishing Oriental studies programs. These academic programs turned the Orient into a peculiar puzzle that needed to be picked apart and solved. Similarly, images of Arabs and Muslims in early twentieth-century novels and films depicted them as docile, exotic, and backwards. This is a process of discursive domination, much like the type Fanon and Beauvoir described, which depends on subjugation through stereotypes and language. It is a process that continues today as stereotypical images from the Middle East and central Asia continue to make the front pages of newspapers and websites.

We began this section with the importance of lived experiences in shaping social theory and will end on a similar note. The importance of lived experiences in producing knowledge is at the core of standpoint theory, a method associated with feminist scholar Dorothy Smith, which suggests our knowledge about the social world depends on our particular locations within it. In *The Conceptual Practices of Power*, Smith shows how sociology has long been based on the experiences of men, and so, social theory has largely focused on male-dominated spheres, like politics, law, and the economy. Smith calls for social theory to redirect itself to the lived experiences of women and the oppression they have experienced. Like Du Bois, Smith argues that women have historically experienced the social world through two lenses— one provided through social science that tells women the way the world supposedly works, and another, subjective one based on lived experience of oppression that does not jibe with social scientific "facts." And this is the heart of standpoint theory—there is no such thing as a purely objective standpoint. No view is not located—somehow unaffected or "unbiased" by social location. For Smith, and the "standpoint theorists" she inspired, the most accurate knowledge of the social world necessarily stems from the lived experience of those who are located in it. If you want to theorize about the social reality of women, according to Smith, you'd better begin with women's experiences and knowledge.

Patricia Hill Collins extends—as well as complicates—Smith's observations by suggesting that gender is only one category that shapes lived experiences and structures social inequality. Collins adds that race interacts with gender to produce unique epistemologies, or ways of knowing. She adds that epistemologies are always political, meaning they can serve as sites of resistance against systems of oppression and inequality. So, Black feminist epistemology is Collins's theoretical approach, but it is also a call to action for Black women intellectuals, and the broader social science community to deconstruct the dominant assumptions that knowledge can be purely objective and universal. In Black feminist epistemologies and others, knowledge is based on lived

For more from Dorothy Smith, take a look at her essay, "K is Mentally Ill," available in full to instructors in the "Additional Readings" section of the *Social Theory Re-Wired* website.

experiences of oppression and shared through narratives about the lived experiences of others.

Collins's work challenges us to rethink objectivity—the idea that all things can be known through one, dominant way of knowing. Alternative epistemologies, in addition to being a standpoint from which to interpret and make sense of oppression, are also sites for resisting oppression. First, though, those alternative epistemologies must be known; we must recognize that all standpoints can contain valuable sources of knowledge. This doesn't mean the same thing, however, as saying that all standpoints are equally true or valid. Rather, it means that what people know about the world is always illumined and distorted by their positions within it. For Collins, as well as many other critical race and feminist scholars, social theory has been distorted because it has largely refused to take into account the particular insights that women of color have to offer. Such insights challenge the white, male-centered categories historically used to construct social theory. Despite the many insights such theories offer, too often these binaries—whether West versus non-West, male versus female, objective versus subjective—constrain us from generating new, more accurate, inventive, and ethically sound social theory. The theorists in this section demonstrate that the way forward may require a new set of categories—and a new set of voices—altogether.

Collins is perhaps best known for her idea of intersectionality. For more on intersectionality, visit the Feminist Theory Profile Page on the *Social Theory Re-Wired* website.

Want more Patricia Hill Collins? Instructors can download and assign full-text excerpts from her latest book, *Black Sexual Politics,* available in "Additional Readings."

Plug In

Social theory is like the Internet: It expands our understanding of the social world, but access to its creation has always been limited. And, if everyone fails to have access to its construction, then the knowledge that gets created is incomplete, even distorted. If Marx, Weber, and Durkheim opened the doors to new understandings of society to some, W.E.B Du Bois, Simone de Beauvoir, and the other "excluded voices" in this section have worked to make sure new doors are unlocked—and remain open—for those who have long been barred entry. These scholars recognize that the potential of social theory is immense, but its greatest promises remain unfulfilled.

Classical Connections: W.E.B. Du Bois and Simone de B

SHIFT

362

from th
decid'
in'

The Souls of

W.E.B. Du Bois

O water, voice of my heart, crying in the sand,
All night long crying with a mournful cry,
As I lie and listen, and cannot understand
The voice of my heart in my side or the voice of the sea,
O water, crying for rest, is it I, is it I?
All night long the water is crying to me.

Unresting water, there shall never be rest
Till the last moon droop and the last tide fail,
And the fire of the end begin to burn in the west;
And the heart shall be weary and wonder and cry
  like the sea,
All life long crying without avail,
As the water all night long is crying to me.

ARTHUR SYMONS.[1]

BETWEEN ME AND THE OTHER world there is ever an unasked question: unasked by some through feelings of delicacy; by others through the difficulty of rightly framing it. All, nevertheless, flutter round it. They approach me in a half-hesitant sort of way, eye me curiously or compassionately, and then, instead of saying directly, How does it feel to be a problem? they say, I know an excellent colored man in my town; or, I fought at Mechanicsville;[2] or, Do not these Southern outrages make your blood boil? At these I smile, or am interested, or reduce the boiling to a simmer, as the occasion may require. To the real question, How does it feel to be a problem? I answer seldom a word.

And yet, being a problem is a strange experience,—peculiar even for one who has never been anything else, save perhaps in babyhood and in Europe. It is in the early days of rollicking boyhood that the revelation first bursts upon one, all in a day, as it were. I remember well when the shadow swept across me. I was a little thing, away up in the hills of New England, where the dark Housatonic winds between Hoosac and Taghkanic to the sea. In a wee wooden school-house, something put it into the boys' and girls' heads to buy gorgeous visiting-cards—ten cents a package—and exchange. The exchange was merry, till one girl, a tall newcomer, refused my card,—refused it peremptorily, with a glance. Then it dawned upon me with a certain suddenness that I was different from the others; or like, mayhap, in heart and life and longing, but shut out from their world by a vast veil. I had thereafter no desire to tear down that veil, to creep through; I held all beyond it in common contempt, and lived above it in a region of blue sky and great wandering shadows. That sky was bluest when I could beat my mates at examination-time, or beat them at a foot-race, or even beat their stringy heads. Alas, with the years all this fine contempt began to fade; for the worlds I longed for, and all their dazzling opportunities, were theirs, not mine. But they should not keep these prizes, I said; some, all, I would wrest

m. Just how I would do it I could never by reading law, by healing the sick, by telling the wonderful tales that swam in my head,— some way. With other black boys the strife was not so fiercely sunny: their youth shrunk into tasteless sycophancy, or into silent hatred of the pale world about them and mocking distrust of everything white; or wasted itself in a bitter cry, Why did God make me an outcast and a stranger in mine own house? The shades of the prison-house closed round about us all: walls strait and stubborn to the whitest, but relentlessly narrow, tall, and unscalable to sons of night who must plod darkly on in resignation, or beat unavailing palms against the stone, or steadily, half hopelessly, watch the streak of blue above.

After the Egyptian and Indian, the Greek and Roman, the Teuton and Mongolian, the Negro is a sort of seventh son, born with a veil, and gifted with second-sight[3] in this American world,—a world which yields him no true self-consciousness, but only lets him see himself through the revelation of the other world. It is a peculiar sensation, this double-consciousness, this sense of always looking at one's self through the eyes of others, of measuring one's soul by the tape of a world that looks on in amused contempt and pity. One ever feels his two-ness,—an American, a Negro; two souls, two thoughts, two unreconciled strivings; two warring ideals in one dark body, whose dogged strength alone keeps it from being torn asunder.

The history of the American Negro is the history of this strife,— this longing to attain self-conscious manhood, to merge his double self into a better and truer self. In this merging he wishes neither of the older selves to be lost. He would not Africanize America, for America has too much to teach the world and Africa. He would not bleach his Negro soul in a flood of white Americanism, for he knows that Negro blood has a message for the world. He simply wishes to make it possible for a man to be both a Negro and an American, without being cursed and spit upon by his fellows, without having the doors of Opportunity closed roughly in his face.

This, then, is the end of his striving: to be a co-worker in the kingdom of culture, to escape both death and isolation, to husband and use his best powers and his latent genius. These powers of body and mind have in the past been strangely wasted, dispersed, or forgotten. The shadow of a mighty Negro past flits through the tale of Ethiopia the Shadowy and of Egypt the Sphinx. Throughout history, the powers of single black men flash here and there like falling stars, and die sometimes before the world has rightly gauged their brightness. Here in America, in the few days since Emancipation, the black man's turning hither and thither in hesitant and doubtful striving has often made his very strength to lose effectiveness, to seem like absence of power, like weakness. And yet it is not weakness,— it is the contradiction of double aims. The double-aimed struggle of the black artisan—on the one hand to escape white contempt for a nation of mere hewers of wood and drawers of water, and on the other hand to plough and nail and dig for a poverty-stricken horde—could only result in making him a poor craftsman, for he had but half a heart in either cause. By the poverty and ignorance of his people, the Negro minister or doctor was tempted toward quackery and demagogy; and by the criticism of the other world, toward ideals that made him ashamed of his lowly tasks. The would-be black *savant* was confronted by the paradox that the knowledge his people needed was a twice-told tale to his white neighbors, while the knowledge which would teach the white world was Greek to his own flesh and blood. The innate love of harmony and beauty that set the ruder souls of his people a-dancing and a-singing raised but confusion and doubt in the soul of the black artist; for the beauty revealed to him was the soul-beauty of a race which his larger audience despised, and he could not articulate the message of another people. This waste of double aims, this seeking to satisfy two unreconciled ideals, has wrought sad havoc with the courage and faith and deeds of ten thousand thousand people,—has sent them often wooing false gods and invoking false means of salvation, and at times has even seemed about to make them ashamed of themselves.

Away back in the days of bondage they thought to see in one divine event the end of all doubt and disappointment; few men ever worshipped Freedom with half such unquestioning faith as did the American Negro for two centuries. To him, so far as he thought and dreamed, slavery was indeed the sum of all villainies, the cause of all sorrow, the root of all prejudice; Emancipation was the key to a promised land of sweeter beauty than ever stretched before the eyes of wearied Israelites. In song and exhortation swelled one refrain—Liberty; in his tears and curses the God he implored had Freedom in his right hand. At last it came,—suddenly, fearfully, like a dream. With one wild carnival of blood and passion came the message in his own plaintive cadences:—

> "Shout, O children!
> Shout, you're free!
> For God has bought your liberty!"[4]

Years have passed away since then,—ten, twenty, forty; forty years of national life, forty years of renewal and development, and yet the swarthy spectre sits in its accustomed seat at the Nation's feast. In vain do we cry to this our vastest social problem:—

> "Take any shape but that, and my firm nerves
> Shall never tremble!"[5]

The Nation has not yet found peace from its sins; the freedman has not yet found in freedom his promised land. Whatever of good may have come in these years of change, the shadow of a deep disappointment rests upon the Negro people,—a disappointment all the more bitter because the unattained ideal was unbounded save by the simple ignorance of a lowly people.

The first decade was merely a prolongation of the vain search for freedom, the boon that seemed ever barely to elude their grasp,—like a tantalizing will-o'-the-wisp, maddening and misleading the headless host. The holocaust of war, the terrors of the Ku-Klux Klan, the lies of carpet-baggers, the disorganization of industry, and the contradictory advice of friends and foes, left the bewildered serf with no new watchword beyond the old cry for freedom. As the time flew, however, he began to grasp a new idea. The ideal of liberty demanded for its attainment powerful means, and these the Fifteenth Amendment gave him. The ballot, which before he had looked upon as a visible sign of freedom, he now regarded as the chief means of gaining and perfecting the liberty with which war had partially endowed him. And why not? Had not votes made war and emancipated millions? Had not votes enfranchised the freedmen? Was anything impossible to a power that had done all this? A million black men started with renewed zeal to vote themselves into the kingdom. So the decade flew away, the revolution of 1876[6] came, and left the half-free serf weary, wondering, but still inspired. Slowly but steadily, in the following years, a new vision began gradually to replace the dream of political power,—a powerful movement, the rise of another ideal to guide the unguided, another pillar of fire by night after a clouded day. It was the ideal of "book-learning"; the curiosity, born of compulsory ignorance, to know and test the power of the cabalistic letters of the white man, the longing to know. Here at last seemed to have been discovered the mountain path to Canaan; longer than the highway of Emancipation and law, steep and rugged, but straight, leading to heights high enough to overlook life.

Up the new path the advance guard toiled, slowly, heavily, doggedly; only those who have watched and guided the faltering feet, the misty minds, the dull understandings, of the dark pupils of these schools know how faithfully, how piteously, this people strove to learn. It was weary work. The cold statistician wrote down the inches of progress here and there, noted also where here and there a foot had slipped or some one had fallen. To the tired climbers, the horizon was ever dark, the mists were often cold, the Canaan was always dim and far away. If, however, the vistas disclosed as yet no goal, no resting-place, little but flattery and criticism, the journey at least gave leisure for reflection and self-examination; it changed the child of Emancipation to the youth with dawning self-consciousness, self-realization, self-respect. In those sombre forests of his striving his own soul rose before him, and he saw himself,—darkly as through a veil; and yet he saw in himself some faint revelation of his power, of his mission. He began to have a dim feeling that, to attain his place in the world, he must be himself, and not another. For the first time he sought to analyze the burden he bore upon his back, that dead-weight of social degradation partially masked behind a half-named Negro problem. He felt his poverty; without a cent, without a home, without land, tools, or savings, he had entered into competition with rich, landed, skilled neighbors. To be a poor man is hard, but to be a poor race in a land of dollars is the very bottom of hardships. He felt the weight of his ignorance,—not simply of letters, but of life, of business, of the humanities; the accumulated sloth and shirking and awkwardness of decades and centuries shackled his hands and feet. Nor was his burden all poverty and ignorance. The red stain of bastardy, which two centuries of systematic legal defilement of Negro women had stamped upon his race, meant not only the loss of ancient African chastity, but also the hereditary weight of a mass of corruption from white adulterers, threatening almost the obliteration of the Negro home.

A people thus handicapped ought not to be asked to race with the world, but rather allowed to give all its time and thought to its own social problems. But alas! while sociologists gleefully count his bastards and his prostitutes, the very soul of the toiling, sweating black man is darkened by the shadow of a vast despair. Men call the shadow prejudice, and learnedly explain it as the natural defence of culture against barbarism, learning against ignorance, purity against crime, the "higher" against the "lower" races. To which the Negro cries Amen! and swears that to so much of this strange prejudice as is founded on just homage to civilization, culture, righteousness, and progress, he humbly bows and meekly does obeisance. But before that nameless prejudice that leaps beyond all this he stands helpless, dismayed, and well-nigh speechless; before that personal disrespect and mockery, the ridicule and systematic humiliation, the distortion of fact and wanton license of fancy, the cynical ignoring of the better and the boisterous welcoming of the worse, the all-pervading desire to inculcate disdain for everything black, from Toussaint[7] to the devil,—before this there rises a sickening despair that would disarm and discourage any nation save that black host to whom "discouragement" is an unwritten word.

But the facing of so vast a prejudice could not but bring the inevitable self-questioning, self-disparagement, and lowering of ideals which ever accompany repression and breed in an atmosphere of contempt and hate. Whisperings and portents came borne upon the four winds: Lo! we are diseased and dying, cried the dark hosts; we cannot write, our voting is vain; what need of education, since we must always cook and serve? And the Nation echoed and enforced this self-criticism, saying: Be content to be servants, and nothing more; what need of higher culture for half-men? Away with the black man's ballot, by force or fraud,—and behold the suicide of a race! Nevertheless, out of the evil came something of good,—the more careful adjustment of education to real life, the clearer perception of the Negroes' social responsibilities, and the sobering realization of the meaning of progress.

So dawned the time of *Sturm und Drang*: storm and stress to-day rocks our little boat on the mad waters of the world-sea; there is within and without the sound of conflict, the burning of body and rending of soul; inspiration strives with doubt, and faith with vain questionings. The bright ideals of the past,—physical freedom, political power, the training of brains and the training of hands,—all these in turn have waxed and waned, until even the last grows dim and overcast. Are they all wrong,—all false? No, not that, but each alone was over-simple and incomplete,—the dreams of a credulous race-childhood, or the fond imaginings of the other world which does not know and does not want to know our power. To be really true, all these ideals must be melted and welded into one. The training of the schools we need to-day more than ever,—the training of deft hands, quick eyes and ears, and above all the broader, deeper, higher culture of gifted minds and pure hearts. The power of the ballot we need in sheer self-defence,—else what shall save us from a second slavery? Freedom, too, the long-sought, we still seek,—the freedom of life and limb, the freedom to work and think, the freedom to love and aspire. Work, culture, liberty,—all these we need, not singly but together, not successively but together, each growing and aiding each, and all striving toward that vaster ideal that swims before the Negro people, the ideal of human brotherhood, gained through the unifying ideal of Race; the ideal of fostering and developing the traits and talents of the Negro, not in opposition to or contempt for other races, but rather in large conformity to the greater ideals of the American Republic, in order that some day on American soil two world-races may give each to each those characteristics both so sadly lack. We the darker ones come even now not altogether empty-handed: there are to-day no truer exponents of the pure human spirit of the Declaration of Independence than the American Negroes; there is no true American music but the wild sweet melodies of the Negro slave; the American fairy tales and folklore are Indian and African; and, all in all, we black men seem the sole oasis of simple faith and reverence in a dusty desert of dollars and smartness. Will America be poorer if she replace her brutal dyspeptic blundering with light-hearted but

determined Negro humility? wit with loving jovial good- music with the soul of the So

Merely a concrete test principles of the great republic and the spiritual striving of t the travail of souls whose burden is almost beyond the measure of their strength, but who bear it in the name of an historic race, in the name of this the land of their fathers' fathers, and in the name of human opportunity.

***

And now what I have briefly sketched in large outline let me on coming pages tell again in many ways, with loving emphasis and deeper detail, that men may listen to the striving in the souls of black folk.

NOTES

1. *Arthur Symons*: the epigraph is drawn from *The Crying of Waters* (1903) by Arthur Symons. The music which follows is an excerpt of the traditional Negro spiritual, 'Nobody Knows the Trouble I've Seen'. The scholar Eric Sundquist has pointed out that Du Bois, in choosing the musical selections that precede each chapter, made use of transcriptions (sometimes with slight variations) from two important nineteenth-century collections of spirituals: J.B.T. Marsh, *The Story of the Jubilee Singers with their Songs* (Boston: Houghton Mifflin, 1872); M.F. Armstrong and Helen W. Ludlow, *Hampton and its Students*, arranged by Thomas P. Fenner (New York: G.P. Putnam's Sons, 1874). See Sundquist, 'Swing Low: *The Souls of Black Folk*', in *To Wake the Nations: Race in the Making of American Literature* (Cambridge, Mass.: Harvard University Press, 1993), 457–539.

2. *Mechanicsville*: the location in Virginia of a crucial Civil War battle (also known as the battle of Beaver Dam Creek) of June 1862.

3. *born with a veil … second-sight*: in African American folk culture, it is believed that children born with a caul (a membrane from the placenta covering the infant's face at birth) are gifted with prophetic and psychic abilities.

out, O children! … liberty!': the refrain of the Negro spiritual 'Shout, O Children!'

'Take any shape … tremble!': from Shakespeare, *Macbeth*, III. iv. 102–3.

6. *revolution of 1876*: the results of the presidential elections of 1876 were contested by three states, Louisiana, Florida, and South Carolina, which supported the Democrat Samuel J. Tilden over the Republican Rutherford B. Hayes. Some Southern Democrats threatened to secede from the Union. The Hayes-Tilden compromise resolved the dispute: Hayes was named the president, and the North agreed not to interfere further in the status of the freedmen, effectively ending the period of Reconstruction.

7. *Toussaint*: Toussaint L'Ouverture (1746–1803), the leader of the Haitian Revolution, in which the slave population overthrew French rule and defeated the army of Napoleon.

COMPANION WEBSITE

1. Go online to Write Out Loud about how Du Bois's idea of "double-consciousness" resembles Simmel's idea of "the stranger."

2. Browse the Supplementary Sources for *Shifting the Paradigm* for a link to the W.E.B. Du Bois Institute at Harvard University's website.

3. Check out the Interactive Reading and watch critical race scholar Patricia Williams discuss how double-consciousness is still experienced today.

The Second Sex

Simone de Beauvoir

I HESITATED A LONG TIME BEFORE writing a book on woman. The subject is irritating, especially for women; and it is not new. Enough ink has flowed over the quarrel about feminism; it is now almost over: let's not talk about it anymore. Yet it is still being talked about. And the volumes of idiocies churned out over this past century do not seem to have clarified the problem. Besides, is there a problem? And what is it? Are there even women? True, the theory of the eternal feminine still has its followers; they whisper, "Even in Russia, *women* are still very much women"; but other well-informed people—and also at times those same ones—lament, "Woman is losing herself, woman is lost." It is hard to know any longer if women still exist, if they will always exist, if there should be women at all, what place they hold in this world, what place they should hold. "Where are the women?" asked a short-lived magazine recently.[1] But first, what is a woman? "*Tota mulier in utero:* she is a womb," some say. Yet speaking of certain women, the experts proclaim, "They are not women," even though they have a uterus like the others. Everyone agrees there are females in the human species; today, as in the past, they make up about half of humanity; and yet we are told that "femininity is in jeopardy"; we are urged, "Be women, stay women, become women." So not every female human being is necessarily a woman; she must take part in this mysterious and endangered reality known as femininity. Is femininity secreted by the ovaries? Is it enshrined in a Platonic heaven? Is a frilly petticoat enough to bring it down to earth? Although some women zealously strive to embody it, the model has never been patented. It is typically described in vague and shimmering terms borrowed from a clairvoyant's vocabulary. In Saint Thomas's time it was an essence defined with as much certainty as the sedative quality of a poppy. But conceptualism has lost ground: biological and social sciences no longer believe there are immutably determined entities that define given characteristics like those of the woman, the Jew, or the black; science considers characteristics as secondary reactions to a *situation*. If there is no such thing today as femininity, it is because there never was. Does the word "woman," then, have no content? It is what advocates of Enlightenment philosophy, rationalism, or nominalism vigorously assert: women are, among human beings, merely those who are arbitrarily designated by the word "woman"; American women in particular are inclined to think that woman as such no longer exists. If some backward individual still takes herself for a woman, her friends advise her to undergo psychoanalysis to get rid of this obsession. Referring to a book—a very irritating one at that—*Modern Woman: The Lost Sex*, Dorothy Parker wrote: "I cannot be fair about books that treat women as women. My idea is that all of us, men as well as women, whoever we are, should be considered as human beings." But nominalism is a doctrine that falls a bit short; and it is easy for antifeminists to show that women *are* not men. Certainly woman like man is a human being; but such an assertion is abstract; the fact is that every concrete human being is always uniquely situated. To reject the notions of the eternal feminine, the black soul, or the Jewish character is not to deny that there are today Jews, blacks, or women: this denial is not a liberation for those concerned but an inauthentic flight. Clearly, no woman can claim without bad faith to be situated beyond her sex. A few years ago, a well-known woman writer refused to have her portrait appear in a series of photographs devoted specifically to women writers. She wanted to be included in the men's category; but to get this privilege, she used her husband's influence. Women who assert they are men still claim masculine consideration and respect. I also remember a young Trotskyite standing on a platform during a stormy meeting, about to come to blows in spite of her obvious fragility. She was denying her feminine frailty; but it was for the love of a militant man she wanted to be equal to. The defiant position that American women occupy proves they are haunted by the feeling of their own femininity. And the truth is that anyone can clearly see that humanity is split into two categories of individuals with manifestly different clothes, faces, bodies, smiles, movements, interests, and occupations; these differences are perhaps superficial; perhaps they are destined to disappear. What is certain is that for the moment they exist in a strikingly obvious way.

If the female function is not enough to define woman, and if we also reject the explanation of the "eternal feminine," but if we accept, even temporarily, that there are women on the earth, we then have to ask: What is a woman?

Merely stating the problem suggests an immediate answer to me. It is significant that I pose it. It would never occur to a man to write a book on the singular situation of males in humanity.[2] If I want to define myself, I first have to say, "I am a woman"; all other assertions will arise from this basic truth. A man never begins by positing himself

as an individual of a certain sex: that he is a man is obvious. The categories masculine and feminine appear as symmetrical in a formal way on town hall records or identification papers. The relation of the two sexes is not that of two electrical poles: the man represents both the positive and the neuter to such an extent that in French *hommes* designates human beings, the particular meaning of the word *vir* being assimilated into the general meaning of the word "homo." Woman is the negative, to such a point that any determination is imputed to her as a limitation, without reciprocity. I used to get annoyed in abstract discussions to hear men tell me: "You think such and such a thing because you're a woman." But I know my only defense is to answer, "I think it because it is true," thereby eliminating my subjectivity; it was out of the question to answer, "And you think the contrary because you are a man," because it is understood that being a man is not a particularity; a man is in his right by virtue of being man; it is the woman who is in the wrong. In fact, just as for the ancients there was an absolute vertical that defined the oblique, there is an absolute human type that is masculine. Woman has ovaries and a uterus; such are the particular conditions that lock her in her subjectivity; some even say she thinks with her hormones. Man vainly forgets that his anatomy also includes hormones and testicles. He grasps his body as a direct and normal link with the world that he believes he apprehends in all objectivity, whereas he considers woman's body an obstacle, a prison, burdened by everything that particularizes it. "The female is female by virtue of a certain *lack* of qualities," Aristotle said. "We should regard women's nature as suffering from natural defectiveness." And Saint Thomas in his turn decreed that woman was an "incomplete man," an "incidental" being. This is what the Genesis story symbolizes, where Eve appears as if drawn from Adam's "supernumerary" bone, in Bossuet's words. Humanity is male, and man defines woman, not in herself, but in relation to himself; she is not considered an autonomous being. "Woman, the relative being," writes

Michelet. Thus Monsieur Benda declares in *Le rapport d'Uriel* (Uriel's Report): "A man's body has meaning by itself, disregarding the body of the woman, whereas the woman's body seems devoid of meaning without reference to the male. Man thinks himself without woman. Woman does not think herself without man." And she is nothing other than what man decides; she is thus called "the sex," meaning that the male sees her essentially as a sexed being; for him she is sex, so she is it in the absolute. She is determined and differentiated in relation to man, while he is not in relation to her; she is the inessential in front of the essential. He is the Subject; he is the Absolute. She is the Other.[3]

The category of *Other* is as original as consciousness itself. The duality between Self and Other can be found in the most primitive societies, in the most ancient mythologies; this division did not always fall into the category of the division of the sexes, it was not based on any empirical given: this comes out in works like Granet's on Chinese thought, and Dumézil's on India and Rome. In couples such as Varuna–Mitra, Uranus–Zeus, Sun–Moon, Day–Night, no feminine element is involved at the outset; neither in Good–Evil, auspicious and inauspicious, left and right, God and Lucifer; alterity is the fundamental category of human thought. No group ever defines itself as One without immediately setting up the Other opposite itself. It only takes three travelers brought together by chance in the same train compartment for the rest of the travelers to become vaguely hostile "others." Village people view anyone not belonging to the village as suspicious "others." For the native of a country inhabitants of other countries are viewed as "foreigners"; Jews are the "others" for anti-Semites, blacks for racist Americans, indigenous people for colonists, proletarians for the propertied classes. After studying the diverse forms of primitive society in depth, Lévi-Strauss could conclude: "The passage from the state of Nature to the state of Culture is defined by man's ability to think biological relations as systems of oppositions; duality, alternation, opposition,

and symmetry, whether occurring in defined or less clear form, are not so much phenomena to explain as fundamental and immediate givens of social reality."[4] These phenomena could not be understood if human reality were solely a *Mitsein*[5] based on solidarity and friendship. On the contrary, they become clear if, following Hegel, a fundamental hostility to any other consciousness is found in consciousness itself; the subject posits itself only in opposition; it asserts itself as the essential and sets up the other as inessential, as the object.

But the other consciousness has an opposing reciprocal claim: traveling, a local is shocked to realize that in neighboring countries locals view him as a foreigner; between villages, clans, nations, and classes there are wars, potlatches, agreements, treaties, and struggles that remove the absolute meaning from the idea of the *Other* and bring out its relativity; whether one likes it or not, individuals and groups have no choice but to recognize the reciprocity of their relation. How is it, then, that between the sexes this reciprocity has not been put forward, that one of the terms has been asserted as the only essential one, denying any relativity in regard to its correlative, defining the latter as pure alterity? Why do women not contest male sovereignty? No subject posits itself spontaneously and at once as the inessential from the outset; it is not the Other who, defining itself as Other, defines the One; the Other is posited as Other by the One positing itself as One. But in order for the Other not to turn into the One, the Other has to submit to this foreign point of view. Where does this submission in woman come from?

There are other cases where, for a shorter or longer time, one category has managed to dominate another absolutely. It is often numerical inequality that confers this privilege: the majority imposes its law on or persecutes the minority. But women are not a minority like American blacks, or like Jews: there are as many women as men on the earth. Often, the two opposing groups concerned were once independent of each other; either they were not aware of each other in the past, or they accepted each other's autonomy; and some historical event subordinated the weaker to the stronger: the Jewish Diaspora, slavery in America, and the colonial conquests are facts with dates. In these cases, for the oppressed there was a *before:* they share a past, a tradition, sometimes a religion, or a culture. In this sense, the parallel Bebel draws between women and the proletariat would be the best founded: proletarians are not a numerical minority either, and yet they have never formed a separate group. However, not *one* event but a whole historical development explains their existence as a class and accounts for the distribution of *these* individuals in this class. There have not always been proletarians: there have always been women; they are women by their physiological structure; as far back as history can be traced, they have always been subordinate to men; their dependence is not the consequence of an event or a becoming, it did not *happen.* Alterity here appears to be an absolute, partly because it falls outside the accidental nature of historical fact. A situation created over time can come undone at another time—blacks in Haiti for one are a good example; on the contrary, a natural condition seems to defy change. In truth, nature is no more an immutable given than is historical reality. If woman discovers herself as the inessential and never turns into the essential, it is because she does not bring about this transformation herself. Proletarians say "we." So do blacks. Positing themselves as subjects, they thus transform the bourgeois or whites into "others." Women—except in certain abstract gatherings such as conferences—do not use "we"; men say "women," and women adopt this word to refer to themselves; but they do not posit themselves authentically as Subjects. The proletarians made the revolution in Russia, the blacks in Haiti, the Indo-Chinese are fighting in Indochina. Women's actions have never been more than symbolic agitation; they have won only what men have been willing to concede to them; they

have taken nothing; they have received.[6] It is that they lack the concrete means to organize themselves into a unit that could posit itself in opposition. They have no past, no history, no religion of their own; and unlike the proletariat, they have no solidarity of labor or interests; they even lack their own space that makes communities of American blacks, the Jews in ghettos, or the workers in Saint-Denis or Renault factories. They live dispersed among men, tied by homes, work, economic interests, and social conditions to certain men—fathers or husbands— more closely than to other women. As bourgeois women, they are in solidarity with bourgeois men and not with women proletarians; as white women, they are in solidarity with white men and not with black women. The proletariat could plan to massacre the whole ruling class; a fanatic Jew or black could dream of seizing the secret of the atomic bomb and turning all of humanity entirely Jewish or entirely black: but a woman could not even dream of exterminating males. The tie that binds her to her oppressors is unlike any other. The division of the sexes is a biological given, not a moment in human history. Their opposition took shape within an original *Mitsein*, and she has not broken it. The couple is a fundamental unit with the two halves riveted to each other: cleavage of society by sex is not possible. This is the fundamental characteristic of woman: she is the Other at the heart of a whole whose two components are necessary to each other.

One might think that this reciprocity would have facilitated her liberation; when Hercules spins wool at Omphale's feet, his desire enchains him. Why was Omphale unable to acquire long-lasting power? Medea, in revenge against Jason, kills her children: this brutal legend suggests that the bond attaching the woman to her child could have given her a formidable upper hand. In *Lysistrata*, Aristophanes lightheartedly imagined a group of women who, uniting together for the social good, tried to take advantage of men's need for them: but it is only a comedy. The legend that claims that the ravished Sabine women resisted their ravishers with obstinate sterility also recounts that by whipping them with leather straps, the men magically won them over into submission. Biological need—sexual desire and desire for posterity—which makes the male dependent on the female, has not liberated women socially. Master and slave are also linked by a reciprocal economic need that does not free the slave. That is, in the master–slave relation, the master does not *posit* the need he has for the other; he holds the power to satisfy this need and does not mediate it; the slave, on the other hand, out of dependence, hope, or fear, internalizes his need for the master; however equally compelling the need may be to them both, it always plays in favor of the oppressor over the oppressed: this explains the slow pace of working-class liberation, for example. Now, woman has always been, if not man's slave, at least his vassal; the two sexes have never divided the world up equally; and still today, even though her condition is changing, woman is heavily handicapped. In no country is her legal status identical to man's, and often it puts her at a considerable disadvantage. Even when her rights are recognized abstractly, long-standing habit keeps them from being concretely manifested in customs. Economically, men and women almost form two castes; all things being equal, the former have better jobs, higher wages, and greater chances to succeed than their new female competitors; they occupy many more places in industry, in politics, and so forth, and they hold the most important positions. In addition to their concrete power, they are invested with a prestige whose tradition is reinforced by the child's whole education: the present incorporates the past, and in the past all history was made by males. At the moment that women are beginning to share in the making of the world, this world still belongs to men: men have no doubt about this, and women barely doubt it. Refusing to be the Other, refusing complicity with man, would mean renouncing all the advantages an alliance with the superior caste confers on them. Lord-man will materially protect liege-woman and will be in charge of justifying her existence: along with the economic risk, she eludes the metaphysical risk of a freedom that must invent its goals without help. Indeed, beside every individual's claim to assert himself as subject—an ethical claim—lies the temptation to flee freedom and to make himself into a thing: it is a pernicious path because the individual, passive, alienated, and lost, is prey to a foreign will, cut off from his transcendence, robbed of all worth. But it is an easy path: the anguish and stress of authentically assumed existence are thus avoided. The man who sets the woman up as an *Other* will thus find in her a deep complicity. Hence woman makes no claim for herself as subject because she lacks the concrete means, because she senses the necessary link connecting her to man without positing its reciprocity, and because she often derives satisfaction from her role as *Other*.

But a question immediately arises: How did this whole story begin? It is understandable that the duality of the sexes, like all duality, be expressed in conflict. It is understandable that if one of the two succeeded in imposing its superiority, it had to establish itself as absolute. It remains to be explained how it was that man won at the outset. It seems possible that women might have carried off the victory, or that the battle might never be resolved. Why is it that this world has always belonged to men and that only today things are beginning to change? Is this change a good thing? Will it bring about an equal sharing of the world between men and women or not?

These questions are far from new; they have already had many answers; but the very fact that woman is *Other* challenges all the justifications that men have ever given: these were only too clearly dictated by their own interest. "Everything that men have written about women should be viewed with suspicion, because they are both judge and party," wrote Poulain de la Barre, a little-known seventeenth-century feminist. Males have always and everywhere paraded their satisfaction of feeling they are kings of creation. "Blessed be the Lord our God, and the Lord of all worlds that has not made me a woman," Jews say in their morning prayers; meanwhile, their wives resignedly murmur: "Blessed be the Lord for creating me according to his will." Among the blessings Plato thanked the gods for was, first, being born free and not a slave and, second, a man and not a woman. But males could not have enjoyed this privilege so fully had they not considered it as founded in the absolute and in eternity: they sought to make the fact of their supremacy a right. "Those who made and compiled the laws, being men, favored their own sex, and the jurisconsults have turned the laws into principles," Poulain de la Barre continues. Lawmakers, priests, philosophers, writers, and scholars have gone to great lengths to prove that women's subordinate condition was willed in heaven and profitable on earth. Religions forged by men reflect this will for domination: they found ammunition in the legends of Eve and Pandora. They have put philosophy and theology in their service, as seen in the previously cited words of Aristotle and Saint Thomas. Since ancient times, satirists and moralists have delighted in depicting women's weaknesses. The violent indictments brought against them all through French literature are well-known: Montherlant, with less verve, picks up the tradition from Jean de Meung. This hostility seems sometimes founded but is often gratuitous; in truth, it covers up a more or less skillfully camouflaged will to self-justification. "It is much easier to accuse one sex than to excuse the other," says Montaigne. In certain cases, the process is transparent. It is striking, for example, that the Roman code limiting a wife's rights invokes "the imbecility and fragility of the sex" just when a weakening family structure makes her a threat to male heirs. It is striking that in the sixteenth century, to keep a married woman under wardship, the authority of Saint Augustine affirming "the wife is

an animal neither reliable nor stable" is called on, whereas the unmarried woman is recognized as capable of managing her own affairs. Montaigne well understood the arbitrariness and injustice of the lot assigned to women: "Women are not wrong at all when they reject the rules of life that have been introduced into the world, inasmuch as it is the men who have made these without them. There is a natural plotting and scheming between them and us." But he does not go so far as to champion their cause. It is only in the eighteenth century that deeply democratic men begin to consider the issue objectively. Diderot, for one, tries to prove that, like man, woman is a human being. A bit later, John Stuart Mill ardently defends women. But these philosophers are exceptional in their impartiality. In the nineteenth century the feminist quarrel once again becomes a partisan quarrel; one of the consequences of the Industrial Revolution is that women enter the labor force: at that point, women's demands leave the realm of the theoretical and find economic grounds; their adversaries become all the more aggressive; even though landed property is partially discredited, the bourgeoisie clings to the old values where family solidity guarantees private property: it insists all the more fiercely that woman's place be in the home as her emancipation becomes a real threat; even within the working class, men tried to thwart women's liberation because women were becoming dangerous competitors— especially as women were used to working for low salaries.[7] To prove women's inferiority, antifeminists began to draw not only, as before, on religion, philosophy, and theology but also on science: biology, experimental psychology, and so forth. At most they were willing to grant "separate but equal status" to the *other* sex.[8] That winning formula is most significant: it is exactly that formula the Jim Crow laws put into practice with regard to black Americans; this so-called egalitarian segregation served only to introduce the most extreme forms of discrimination. This convergence is in no way pure chance:

whether it is race, caste, class, or sex reduced to an inferior condition, the justification process is the same. "The eternal feminine" corresponds to "the black soul" or "the Jewish character." However, the Jewish problem on the whole is very different from the two others: for the anti-Semite, the Jew is more an enemy than an inferior, and no place on this earth is recognized as his own; it would be preferable to see him annihilated. But there are deep analogies between the situations of women and blacks: both are liberated today from the same paternalism, and the former master caste wants to keep them "in their place," that is, the place chosen for them; in both cases, they praise, more or less sincerely, the virtues of the "good black," the carefree, childlike, merry soul of the resigned black, and the woman who is a "true woman"—frivolous, infantile, irresponsible, the woman subjugated to man. In both cases, the ruling caste bases its argument on the state of affairs it created itself. The familiar line from George Bernard Shaw sums it up: The white American relegates the black to the rank of shoe-shine boy, and then concludes that blacks are only good for shining shoes. The same vicious circle can be found in all analogous circumstances: when an individual or a group of individuals is kept in a situation of inferiority, the fact is that he or they *are* inferior. But the scope of the verb *to be* must be understood; bad faith means giving it a substantive value, when in fact it has the sense of the Hegelian dynamic: *to be* is to have become, to have been made as one manifests oneself. Yes, women in general *are* today inferior to men; that is, their situation provides them with fewer possibilities: the question is whether this state of affairs must be perpetuated.

Many men wish it would be: not all men have yet laid down their arms. The conservative bourgeoisie continues to view women's liberation as a danger threatening their morality and their interests. Some men feel threatened by women's competition. In *Hebdo-Latin* the other day, a student declared: "Every woman student who takes a posi-

tion as a doctor or lawyer is *stealing* a place from us." That student never questioned his rights over this world. Economic interests are not the only ones in play. One of the benefits that oppression secures for the oppressor is that the humblest among them feels *superior:* in the United States a "poor white" from the South can console himself for not being a "dirty nigger"; and more prosperous whites cleverly exploit this pride. Likewise, the most mediocre of males believes himself a demigod next to women. It was easier for M. de Montherlant to think himself a hero in front of women (handpicked, by the way) than to act the man among men, a role that many women assumed better than he did. Thus, in one of his articles in *Le Figaro Littéraire* in September 1948, M. Claude Mauriac—whom everyone admires for his powerful originality—could[9] write about women: "*We* listen in a tone [*sic!*] of polite indifference … to the most brilliant one among them, knowing that her intelligence, in a more or less dazzling way, reflects ideas that come from *us.*" Clearly his female interlocutor does not reflect M. Mauriac's own ideas, since he is known not to have any; that she reflects ideas originating with men is possible: among males themselves, more than one of them takes as his own opinions he did not invent; one might wonder if it would not be in M. Claude Mauriac's interest to converse with a good reflection of Descartes, Marx, or Gide rather than with himself; what is remarkable is that with the ambiguous "*we,*" he identifies with Saint Paul, Hegel, Lenin, and Nietzsche, and from their heights he looks down on the herd of women who dare to speak to him on an equal footing; frankly, I know of more than one woman who would not put up with M. Mauriac's "tone of polite indifference."

I have stressed this example because of its disarming masculine naïveté. Men profit in many other more subtle ways from woman's alterity. For all those suffering from an inferiority complex, this is a miraculous liniment; no one is more arrogant toward women, more aggressive or more disdainful, than a man anxious about his own virility. Those who are not threatened by their fellow men are far more likely to recognize woman as a counterpart; but even for them the myth of the Woman, of the Other, remains precious for many reasons;[10] they can hardly be blamed for not wanting to lightheartedly sacrifice all the benefits they derive from the myth: they know what they lose by relinquishing the woman of their dreams, but they do not know what the woman of tomorrow will bring them. It takes great abnegation to refuse to posit oneself as unique and absolute Subject. Besides, the vast majority of men do not explicitly make this position their own. They do not *posit* woman as inferior: they are too imbued today with the democratic ideal not to recognize all human beings as equals. Within the family, the male child and then the young man sees the woman as having the same social dignity as the adult male; afterward, he experiences in desire and love the resistance and independence of the desired and loved woman; married, he respects in his wife the spouse and the mother, and in the concrete experience of married life she affirms herself opposite him as a freedom. He can thus convince himself that there is no longer a social hierarchy between the sexes and that on the whole, in spite of their differences, woman is an equal. As he nevertheless recognizes some points of inferiority—professional incapacity being the predominant one—he attributes them to nature. When he has an attitude of benevolence and partnership toward a woman, he applies the principle of abstract equality; and he does not *posit* the concrete inequality he recognizes. But as soon as he clashes with her, the situation is reversed. He will apply the concrete inequality theme and will even allow himself to disavow abstract equality.[11] This is how many men affirm, with quasi good faith, that women *are* equal to men and have no demands to make, and *at the same time* that women will never be equal to men and that their demands are in vain. It is difficult for men to measure the enormous extent of social discrimination that seems insignificant from the outside and whose moral and intellectual repercussions are so deep in woman that they appear to spring from an original nature.[12] The man most sympathetic to women never knows her concrete situation fully. So there is no good reason to believe men when they try to defend privileges whose scope they cannot even fathom. We will not let ourselves be intimidated by the number and violence of attacks against women; nor be fooled by the self-serving praise showered on the "real woman"; nor be won over by men's enthusiasm for her destiny, a destiny they would not for the world want to share.

We must not, however, be any less mistrustful of feminists' arguments: very often their attempt to polemicize robs them of all value. If the "question of women" is so trivial, it is because masculine arrogance turned it into a "quarrel"; when people quarrel, they no longer reason well. What people have endlessly sought to prove is that woman is superior, inferior, or equal to man: created after Adam, she is obviously a secondary being, some say; on the contrary, say others, Adam was only a rough draft, and God perfected the human being when he created Eve; her brain is smaller, but relatively bigger; Christ was made man, but perhaps out of humility. Every argument has its opposite, and both are often misleading. To see clearly, one needs to get out of these ruts; these vague notions of superiority, inferiority, and equality that have distorted all discussions must be discarded in order to start anew.

But how, then, will we ask the question? And in the first place, who are we to ask it? Men are judge and party: so are women. Can an angel be found? In fact, an angel would be ill qualified to speak, would not understand all the givens of the problem; as for the hermaphrodite, it is a case of its own: it is not both a man and a woman, but neither man nor woman. I think certain women are still best suited to elucidate the situation of women. It is a sophism to claim that Epimenides should be enclosed within the concept of Cretan and all Cretans within the concept of liar: it is not a mysterious essence that dictates good or bad faith to men and women; it is their situation that disposes them to seek the truth to a greater or lesser extent. Many women today, fortunate to have had all the privileges of the human being restored to them, can afford the luxury of impartiality: we even feel the necessity of it. We are no longer like our militant predecessors; we have more or less won the game; in the latest discussions on women's status, the UN has not ceased to imperiously demand equality of the sexes, and indeed many of us have never felt our femaleness to be a difficulty or an obstacle; many other problems seem more essential than those that concern us uniquely: this very detachment makes it possible to hope our attitude will be objective. Yet we know the feminine world more intimately than men do because our roots are in it; we grasp more immediately what the fact of being female means for a human being, and we care more about knowing it. I said that there are more essential problems; but this one still has a certain importance from our point of view: How will the fact of being women have affected our lives? What precise opportunities have been given us, and which ones have been denied? What destiny awaits our younger sisters, and in which direction should we point them? It is striking that most feminine literature is driven today by an attempt at lucidity more than by a will to make demands; coming out of an era of muddled controversy, this book is one attempt among others to take stock of the current state.

But it is no doubt impossible to approach any human problem without partiality: even the way of asking the questions, of adopting perspectives, presupposes hierarchies of interests; all characteristics comprise values; every so-called objective description is set against an ethical background. Instead of trying to conceal those principles that are more or less explicitly implied, we would be better off stating them from the start; then it would not be necessary to specify on each page the meaning given to the words "superior," "inferior," "better," "worse," "progress," "regression," and so on. If we examine some of the books on women, we see that one of the most frequently held points of view is that of public good or general interest: in reality, this is taken to mean the interest of society as each one wishes to maintain or establish it. In our opinion, there is no public good other than one that assures the citizens' private good; we judge institutions from the point of view of the concrete opportunities they give to individuals. But neither do we confuse the idea of private interest with happiness: that is another frequently encountered point of view; are women in a harem not happier than a woman voter? Is a housewife not happier than a woman worker? We cannot really know what the word "happiness" means, and still less what authentic values it covers; there is no way to measure the happiness of others, and it is always easy to call a situation that one would like to impose on others happy: in particular, we declare happy those condemned to stagnation, under the pretext that happiness is immobility. This is a notion, then, we will not refer to. The perspective we have adopted is one of existentialist morality. Every subject posits itself as a transcendence concretely, through projects; it accomplishes its freedom only by perpetual surpassing toward other freedoms; there is no other justification for present existence than its expansion toward an indefinitely open future. Every time transcendence lapses into immanence, there is degradation of existence into "in-itself," of freedom into facticity; this fall is a moral fault if the subject consents to it; if this fall is inflicted on the subject, it takes the form of frustration and oppression; in both cases it is an absolute evil. Every individual concerned with justifying his existence experiences his existence as an indefinite need to transcend himself. But what singularly defines the situation of woman is that being, like all humans, an autonomous freedom, she discovers and chooses herself in a world where men force her to assume herself as Other: an attempt is made to freeze her as an object and doom her to immanence, since her transcendence will be forever transcended by another essential and sovereign consciousness. Woman's drama lies in this conflict between the fundamental claim of every subject, which always posits itself as essential, and the demands of a situation that constitutes her as inessential. How, in the feminine condition, can a human being accomplish herself? What paths are open to her? Which ones lead to dead ends? How can she find independence within dependence? What circumstances limit women's freedom and can she overcome them? These are the fundamental questions we would like to elucidate. This means that in focusing on the individual's possibilities, we will define these possibilities not in terms of happiness but in terms of freedom.

Clearly this problem would have no meaning if we thought that a physiological, psychological, or economic destiny weighed on woman. So we will begin by discussing woman from a biological, psychoanalytical, and historical materialist point of view. We will then attempt to positively demonstrate how "feminine reality" has been constituted, why woman has been defined as Other, and what the consequences have been from men's point of view. Then we will describe the world from the woman's point of view such as it is offered to her,[13] and we will see the difficulties women are up against just when, trying to escape the sphere they have been assigned until now, they seek to be part of the human *Mitsein*.

NOTES

1. Out of print today, titled *Franchise*.
2. The Kinsey Report, for example, confines itself to defining the sexual characteristics of the American man, which is completely different.
3. This idea has been expressed in its most explicit form by E. Levinas in his essay *Le temps et l'autre* (*Time and the Other*). He expresses it like this: "Is there not a situation where alterity would be borne by a being in a positive sense, as essence? What is the alterity that does not purely and simply enter into the opposition of two species of the same genus? I think that the absolutely contrary contrary, whose contrariety is in no way affected by the relationship that can be

established between it and its correlative, the contrariety that permits its terms to remain absolutely other, is the feminine. Sex is not some specific difference … Neither is the difference between the sexes a contradiction … Neither is the difference between the sexes the duality of two complementary terms, for two complementary terms presuppose a preexisting whole … [A]lterity is accomplished in the feminine. The term is on the same level as, but in meaning opposed to, consciousness." I suppose Mr. Levinas is not forgetting that woman also is consciousness for herself. But it is striking that he deliberately adopts a man's point of view, disregarding the reciprocity of the subject and the object. When he writes that woman is mystery, he assumes that she is mystery for man. So this apparently objective description is in fact an affirmation of masculine privilege.

4. See Claude Levi-Strauss, *Les structures élémentaires de la parenté* (*The Elementary Structures of Kinship*). I thank Claude Lévi-Strauss for sharing the proofs of his thesis, which I drew on heavily, particularly in the second part, pp. 76–89.

5. *Mitsein* can be translated as "being with." The French term *réalité humaine* (human reality) has been problematically used to translate Heidegger's *Dasein*.—Trans.

6. See second part, page 126.

7. See Part Two, pp. 135–136.

8. *"L'égalité dans la différence"* in the French text. Literal translation: "different but equal."—Trans.

9. At least he thought he could.

10. The article by Michel Carrouges on this theme in *Cahiers du Sud*, no. 292, is significant. He writes with indignation: "If only there were no feminine myth but only bands of cooks, matrons, prostitutes, and bluestockings with functions of pleasure or utility!" So, according to him, woman has no existence for herself; he only takes into account her *function* in the male world. Her finality is in man; in fact, it is possible to prefer her poetic "function" to all others. The exact question is why she should be defined in relation to the man.

11. For example, man declares that he does not find his wife in any way diminished just because she does not have a profession: work in the home is just as noble and so on. Yet at the first argument he remonstrates, "You wouldn't be able to earn a living without me."

12. Describing this very process will be the object of Volume II of this study.

13. This will be the subject of a second volume.

COMPANION WEBSITE

1. Go online to Write Out Loud about how being a female and being a woman are not necessarily the same thing.
2. Log on to the Feminist Theory Profile Page to read more on Simone de Beauvoir and the history of feminist thought and politics.
3. Browse the *Shifting the Paradigm* Supplementary Sources for a link to the Feministing blog, an online resource for anyone interested in feminist analyses of popular culture and politics.

Racial Formation in the United States

Michael Omi and Howard Winant

IN 1982–83, SUSIE GUILLORY PHIPPS unsuccessfully sued the Louisiana Bureau of Vital Records to change her racial classification from black to white. The descendant of an 18th-century white planter and a black slave, Phipps was designated "black" in her birth certificate in accordance with a 1970 state law which declared anyone with at least 1/32nd "Negro blood" to be black.

The Phipps case raised intriguing questions about the concept of race, its meaning in contemporary society, and its use (and abuse) in public policy. Assistant Attorney General Ron Davis defended the law by pointing out that some type of racial classification was necessary to comply with federal record-keeping requirements and to facilitate programs for the prevention of genetic diseases. Phipps's attorney, Brian Begue, argued that the assignment of racial categories on birth certificates was unconstitutional and that the 1/32nd designation was inaccurate. He called on a retired Tulane University professor who cited research indicating that most Louisiana whites have at least 1/20th "Negro" ancestry.

In the end, Phipps lost. The court upheld the state's right to classify and quantify racial identity.[1]

Phipps's problematic racial identity, and her effort to resolve it through state action, is in many ways a parable of America's unsolved racial dilemma. It illustrates the difficulties of defining race and assigning individuals or groups to racial categories. It shows how the racial legacies of the past—slavery and bigotry—continue to shape the present. It

reveals both the deep involvement of the state in the organization and interpretation of race, and the inadequacy of state institutions to carry out these functions. It demonstrates how deeply Americans both as individuals and as a civilization are shaped, and indeed haunted, by race.

Having lived her whole life thinking that she was white, Phipps suddenly discovers that by legal definition she is not. In U.S. society, such an event is indeed catastrophic.[2] But if she is not white, of what race is she? The *state* claims that she is black, based on its rules of classification,[3] and another state agency, the court, upholds this judgment. But despite these classificatory standards which have imposed an either-or logic on racial identity, Phipps will not in fact "change color." Unlike what would have happened during slavery times if one's claim to whiteness was successfully challenged, we can assume that despite the outcome of her legal challenge, Phipps will remain in most of the social relationships she had occupied before the trial. Her socialization, her familial and friendship networks, her cultural orientation, will not change. She will simply have to wrestle with her newly acquired "hybridized" condition. She will have to confront the "Other" within.

The designation of racial categories and the determination of racial identity is no simple task. For centuries, this question has precipitated intense debates and conflicts, particularly in the U.S.—disputes over natural and legal rights, over the distribution of resources, and indeed, over who shall live and who shall die.

A crucial dimension of the Phipps case is that it illustrates the inadequacy of claims that race is a mere matter of variations in human physiognomy, that it is simply a matter of skin color. But if race cannot be understood in this manner, how *can* it be understood? We cannot fully hope to address this topic—no less than the meaning of race, its role in society, and the forces which shape it—in one chapter, nor indeed in one book. Our goal in this chapter, however, is far from modest: we wish to offer at least the outlines of a theory of race and racism.

WHAT IS RACE?

There is a continuous temptation to think of race as an *essence*, as something fixed, concrete, and objective. And there is also an opposite temptation: to imagine race as a mere *illusion*, a purely ideological construct which some ideal non-racist social order would eliminate. It is necessary to challenge both these positions, to disrupt and reframe the rigid and bipolar manner in which they are posed and debated, and to transcend the presumably irreconcilable relationship between them.

The effort must be made to understand race as an unstable and "decentered" complex of social meanings constantly being transformed by political struggle. With this in mind, let us propose a definition: *race is a concept which signifies and symbolizes social conflicts and interests by referring to different types of human bodies*. Although the concept of race invokes biologically based human characteristics (so-called "phenotypes"), selection of these particular human features for purposes of racial signification is always and necessarily a social and historical process. In contrast to the other major distinction of this type, that of gender, there is no biological basis for distinguishing among human groups along the lines of race.[4] Indeed, the categories employed to differentiate among human groups along racial

lines reveal themselves, upon serious examination, to be at best imprecise, and at worst completely arbitrary.

If the concept of race is so nebulous, can we not dispense with it? Can we not "do without" race, at least in the "enlightened" present? This question has been posed often, and with greater frequency in recent years.[5] An affirmative answer would of course present obvious practical difficulties: it is rather difficult to jettison widely held beliefs, beliefs which moreover are central to everyone's identity and understanding of the social world. So the attempt to banish the concept as an archaism is at best counterintuitive. But a deeper difficulty, we believe, is inherent in the very formulation of this schema, in its way of posing race as a *problem*, a misconception left over from the past, and suitable now only for the dustbin of history.

A more effective starting point is the recognition that despite its uncertainties and contradictions, the concept of race continues to play a fundamental role in structuring and representing the social world. The task for theory is to explain this situation. It is to avoid both the utopian framework which sees race as an illusion we can somehow "get beyond," and also the essentialist formulation which sees race as something objective and fixed, a biological datum.[6] Thus we should think of race as an element of social structure rather than as an irregularity within it; we should see race as a dimension of human representation rather than an illusion. These perspectives inform the theoretical approach we call racial formation.

RACIAL FORMATION

We define *racial formation* as the sociohistorical process by which racial categories are created, inhabited, transformed, and destroyed. Our attempt to elaborate a theory of racial formation will proceed in two steps. First, we argue that racial formation is a process of historically situated *projects* in which human bodies and social structures are represented and organized. Next we link racial formation to the evolution of hegemony, the way in which society is organized and ruled. Such an approach, we believe, can facilitate understanding of a whole range of contemporary controversies and dilemmas involving race, including the nature of racism, the relationship of race to other forms of differences, inequalities, and oppression such as sexism and nationalism, and the dilemmas of racial identity today.

From a racial formation perspective, race is a matter of both social structure and cultural representation. Too often, the attempt is made to understand race simply or primarily in terms of only one of these two analytical dimensions.[7] For example, efforts to explain racial inequality as a purely social structural phenomenon are unable to account for the origins, patterning, and transformation of racial difference.

Conversely, many examinations of racial difference—understood as a matter of cultural attributes *à la* ethnicity theory, or as a society-wide signification system, *à la* some poststructuralist accounts—cannot comprehend such structural phenomena as racial stratification in the labor market or patterns of residential segregation.

An alternative approach is to think of racial formation processes as occurring through a linkage between structure and representation. Racial *projects* do the ideological "work" of making these links. *A racial project is simultaneously an interpretation, representation, or explanation of racial dynamics, and an effort to reorganize and redistribute resources along particular racial lines.* Racial projects connect what race *means* in a particular discursive practice and the ways in which both social structures and everyday experiences are racially *organized*, based upon that meaning. Let us consider this proposition, first in terms of large-scale or macro-level social processes, and then in terms of other dimensions of the racial formation process.

Racial formation as a macro-level social process

To *interpret the meaning of race is to frame it social structurally*. Consider for example, this statement by Charles Murray on welfare reform:

> My proposal for dealing with the racial issue in social welfare is to repeal every bit of legislation and reverse every court decision that in any way requires, recommends, or awards differential treatment according to race, and thereby put us back onto the track that we left in 1965. We may argue about the appropriate limits of government intervention in trying to enforce the ideal, but at least it should be possible to identify the ideal: Race is not a morally admissible reason for treating one person differently from another. Period.[8]

Here there is a partial but significant analysis of the meaning of race: it is not a morally valid basis upon which to treat people "differently from one another." We may notice someone's race, but we cannot act upon that awareness. We must act in a "color-blind" fashion. This analysis of the meaning of race is immediately linked to a specific conception of the role of race in the social structure: it can play no part in government action, save in "the enforcement of the ideal." No state policy can legitimately require, recommend, or award different status according to race. This example can be classified as a particular type of racial project in the present-day U.S.—a "neoconservative" one.

Conversely, *to recognize the racial dimension in social structure is to interpret the meaning of race.* Consider the following statement by the late Supreme Court Justice Thurgood Marshall on minority "set-aside" programs:

> A profound difference separates governmental actions that themselves are racist, and governmental actions that seek to remedy the effects of prior racism or to prevent neutral government activity from perpetuating the effects of such racism.[9]

Here the focus is on the racial dimensions of *social structure*—in this case of state activity and policy. The argument is that state actions in the past and present have treated people in very different ways according to their race, and thus the government cannot retreat from its policy responsibilities in this area. It cannot suddenly declare itself "colorblind" without in fact perpetuating the same type of differential, racist treatment.[10] Thus, race continues to signify difference and structure inequality. Here, racialized social structure is immediately linked to an interpretation of the meaning of race. This example too can be classified as a particular type of racial project in the present-day U.S.—a "liberal" one.

To be sure, such political labels as "neoconservative" or "liberal" cannot fully capture the complexity of racial projects, for these are always multiply determined, politically contested, and deeply shaped by their historical context. Thus, encapsulated within the neoconservative example cited here are certain egalitarian commitments which derive from a previous historical context in which they played a very different role, and which are rearticulated in neoconservative racial discourse precisely to oppose a more open-ended, more capacious conception of the meaning of equality. Similarly, in the liberal example, Justice Marshall recognizes that the contemporary state, which was formerly the architect of segregation and the chief enforcer of racial difference, has a tendency to reproduce those patterns of inequality in a new guise. Thus he admonishes it (in dissent, significantly) to fulfill its responsibilities to uphold a robust conception of equality. These particular instances, then, demonstrate how racial projects are always concretely framed, and thus are always contested and unstable. The social structures they uphold or attack, and the representations of race they articulate, are never invented out of the air, but exist in a definite historical context, having descended from previous conflicts. This contestation appears to be permanent in respect to race.

These two examples of contemporary racial projects are drawn from mainstream political debate; they may be characterized as center-right and center-left expressions of contemporary racial politics.[11] We can, however, expand the discussion of racial formation processes far beyond these familiar examples. In fact, we can identify racial projects in at least three other analytical dimensions: first, the political spectrum can be broadened to include radical projects, on both the left and right, as well as along other political axes. Second, analysis of racial projects can take place not only at the macro-level of racial policy-making, state activity, and collective action, but also at the micro-level of everyday experience. Third, the concept of racial projects can be applied across historical time, to identify racial formation dynamics in the past. We shall now offer examples of each of these types of racial projects.

The political spectrum of racial formation

We have encountered examples of a neoconservative racial project, in which the significance of race is denied, leading to a "color-blind" racial politics and "hands off" policy orientation; and of a "liberal" racial project, in which the significance of race is affirmed, leading to an egalitarian and "activist" state policy. But these by no means exhaust the political possibilities. Other racial projects can be readily identified on the contemporary U.S. scene. For example, "far right" projects, which uphold biologistic and racist views of difference, explicitly argue for white supremacist policies. "New right" projects overtly claim to hold "color-blind" views, but covertly manipulate racial fears in order to achieve political gains.[12] On the left, "radical democratic" projects invoke notions of racial "difference" in combination with egalitarian politics and policy.

Further variations can also be noted. For example, "nationalist" projects, both conservative and radical, stress the incompatibility of racially defined group identity with the legacy of white supremacy, and therefore advocate a social structural solution of separation, either complete or partial.[13] As we saw in Chapter 3, nationalist currents represent a profound legacy of the centuries of racial absolutism that initially defined the meaning of race in the U.S. Nationalist concerns continue to influence racial debate in the form of Afrocentrism and other expressions of identity politics.

Taking the range of politically organized racial projects as a whole, we can "map" the current pattern of racial formation at the level of the public sphere, the "macro-level" in which public debate and mobilization takes place.[14] But important as this is, the terrain on which racial formation occurs is broader yet.

Racial formation as everyday experience

At the micro-social level, racial projects also link signification and structure, not so much as efforts to shape policy or define large-scale meaning, but as the applications of "common sense." To see racial projects operating at the level of everyday life, we have only to examine the many ways in which, often unconsciously, we "notice" race.

One of the first things we notice about people when we meet them (along with their sex) is their race. We utilize race to provide clues about *who* a person is. This fact is made painfully obvious when we encounter someone whom we cannot conveniently racially categorize—someone who is, for example, racially "mixed" or of an ethnic/racial group we are not familiar with. Such an encounter becomes a source of discomfort and momentarily a crisis of racial meaning.

Our ability to interpret racial meanings depends on preconceived notions of a racialized social structure. Comments such as, "Funny, you don't look black," betray an underlying image of what black should be. We expect people to act out their apparent racial identities; indeed we become disoriented when they do not. The black banker harassed by police while walking in casual clothes through his own well-off neighborhood, the Latino or white kid rapping in perfect Afro patois, the unending *faux pas* committed by whites who assume that the non-whites they encounter are servants or tradespeople, the belief that non-white colleagues are less qualified persons hired to fulfill affirmative action guidelines, indeed the whole gamut of racial stereotypes—that "white men can't jump," that Asians can't dance, etc., etc.—all testify to the way a racialized social structure shapes racial experience and conditions meaning. Analysis of such stereotypes reveals the always present, already active link between our view of the social structure—its demography, its laws, its customs, its threats—and our conception of what race means.

Conversely, our ongoing interpretation of our experience in racial terms shapes our relations to the institutions and organizations through which we are imbedded in social structure. Thus we expect differences in skin color, or other racially coded characteristics, to explain social differences. Temperament, sexuality, intelligence, athletic ability, aesthetic preferences, and so on are presumed to be fixed and discernible from the palpable mark of race. Such diverse questions as our confidence and trust in others (for example, clerks or salespeople, media figures, neighbors), our sexual preferences and romantic images, our tastes in music, films, dance, or sports, and our very ways of talking, walking, eating, and dreaming become racially coded simply because we live in a society where racial awareness is so pervasive. Thus in ways too comprehensive even to monitor consciously, and despite periodic calls—neoconservative and otherwise—for us to ignore race and adopt "color-blind" racial attitudes, skin color "differences" continue to rationalize distinct treatment of racially identified individuals and groups.

To summarize the argument so far: the theory of racial formation suggests that society is suffused with racial projects, large and small, to which all are subjected. This racial "subjection" is quint-essentially ideological. Everybody learns some combination, some version, of the rules of racial classification, and of her own racial identity, often without obvious teaching or conscious inculcation. Thus are we inserted in a comprehensively racialized social structure. Race becomes "common sense"—a way of comprehending, explaining, and acting in the world. A vast web of racial projects mediates between the discursive or representational means in which race is identified and signified on the one hand, and the institutional and organizational forms in which it is routinized and standardized on the other. These projects are the heart of the racial formation process.

Under such circumstances, it is not possible to represent race discursively without simultaneously locating it, explicitly or implicitly, in a social structural (and historical) context. Nor is it possible to organize, maintain, or transform social structures without simultaneously engaging, once more either explicitly or implicitly, in racial signification. Racial formation, therefore, is a kind of synthesis, an outcome, of the interaction of racial projects on a society-wide level. These projects are, of course, vastly different in scope and effect. They include large-scale public action, state activities, and interpretations of racial conditions in artistic, journalistic, or academic fora,[15] as well as the seemingly infinite number of racial judgments and practices we carry out at the level of individual experience.

Since racial formation is always historically situated, our understanding of the significance of race, and of the way race structures society, has changed enormously over time. The processes of racial formation we encounter today, the racial projects large and small which structure U.S. society in so many ways, are merely the present-day outcomes of a complex historical evolution. The contemporary racial order remains transient. By knowing something of how it evolved, we can perhaps better discern where it is heading. We therefore turn next to a historical survey of the racial formation process, and the conflicts and debates it has engendered.

THE EVOLUTION OF MODERN RACIAL AWARENESS

The identification of distinctive human groups, and their association with differences in physical appearance, goes back to prehistory, and can be found in the earliest documents—in the Bible, for example, or in Herodotus. But the emergence of a modern conception of race does not occur until the rise of Europe and the arrival of Europeans in the Americas. Even the hostility and suspicion with which Christian Europe viewed its two significant non-Christian "Others"—the Muslims and the Jews—cannot be viewed as more than a rehearsal for racial formation, since these antagonisms, for all their bloodletting and chauvinism, were always and everywhere religiously interpreted.[16]

It was only when European explorers reached the Western Hemisphere, when the oceanic seal separating the "old" and the "new" worlds was breached, that the distinctions and categorizations fundamental to a racialized social structure, and to a discourse of race, began to appear. The European explorers were the advance guard of merchant capitalism, which sought new openings for trade. What they found exceeded their wildest dreams, for never before and never again in human history has an opportunity for the appropriation of wealth remotely approached that presented by the "discovery."[17]

But the Europeans also "discovered" people, people who looked and acted differently. These "natives" challenged their "discoverers'" pre-existing conceptions of the origins and possibilities of the human species.[18] The representation and interpretation of the meaning of the indigenous peoples' existence became a crucial matter, one which would affect the outcome of the enterprise of conquest.

For the "discovery" raised disturbing questions as to whether *all* could be considered part of the same "family of man," and more practically, the extent to which native peoples could be exploited and enslaved. Thus religious debates flared over the attempt to reconcile the various Christian metaphysics with the existence of peoples who were more "different" than any whom Europe had previously known.[19]

In practice, of course, the seizure of territories and goods, the introduction of slavery through the *encomienda* and other forms of coerced native labor, and then through the organization of the African slave trade—not to mention the practice of outright extermination—all presupposed a worldview which distinguished Europeans, as children of God, full-fledged human beings, etc., from "Others." Given the dimensions and the ineluctability of the European onslaught, given the conquerors' determination to appropriate both labor and goods, and given the presence of an axiomatic and unquestioned Christianity among them, the ferocious division of society into Europeans and "Others" soon coalesced. This was true despite the famous 16th-century theological and philosophical debates about the identity of indigenous peoples.[20]

Indeed debates about the nature of the "Others" reached their practical limits with a certain dispatch. Plainly they would never touch the essential: nothing, after all, would induce the Europeans to pack up and go home. We cannot examine here the early controversies over the status of American souls. We simply wish to emphasize that the "discovery" signalled a break from the previous proto-racial awareness by which Europe contemplated its "Others" in a relatively disorganized fashion. In other words, the "conquest of America" was not simply an epochal historical event—however unparalleled in its importance. It was also the advent of a consolidated social structure of exploitation, appropriation, domination. Its representation, first in religious terms, but soon enough in scientific and political ones, initiated modern racial awareness.

The conquest, therefore, was the first—and given the dramatic nature of the case, perhaps the greatest—racial formation project. Its significance was by no means limited to the Western Hemisphere, for it began the work of constituting Europe as the metropole, the center, of a group of empires which could take, as Marx would later write, "the globe for a theater."[21] It represented this new imperial structure as a struggle between civilization and barbarism, and implicated in this representation all the great European philosophies, literary traditions, and social theories of the modern age.[22] In short, just as the noise of the "big bang" still resonates through the universe, so the overdetermined construction of world "civilization" as a product of the rise of Europe and the subjugation of the rest of us, still defines the race concept.

FROM RELIGION TO SCIENCE

After the initial depredations of conquest, religious justifications for racial difference gradually gave way to scientific ones. By the time of the Enlightenment, a general awareness of race was pervasive, and most of the great philosophers of Europe, such as Hegel, Kant, Hume, and Locke, had issued virulently racist opinions.

The problem posed by race during the late 18th century was markedly different than it had been in the age of "discovery," expropriation, and slaughter. The social structures in which race operated were no longer primarily those of military conquest and plunder, nor of the establishment of thin beachheads of colonization on the edge of what had once seemed a limitless wilderness. Now the issues were much more complicated: nation-building, establishment of national economies in the world trading system, resistance to the arbitrary authority of monarchs, and the assertion of the "natural rights" of "man," including the right of revolution.[23] In such a situation, racially organized exploitation, in the form of slavery, the expansion of colonies, and the continuing expulsion of native peoples, was both necessary and newly difficult to justify.

The invocation of scientific criteria to demonstrate the "natural" basis of racial hierarchy was both a logical consequence of the rise of this form of knowledge, and an attempt to provide a more subtle and nuanced account of human complexity in the new, "enlightened" age. Spurred on by the classificatory scheme of living organisms devised by Linnaeus in *Systema Naturae* (1735), many scholars in the 18th and 19th centuries dedicated themselves to the identification and ranking of variations in humankind. Race was conceived as a *biological* concept, a matter of species. Voltaire wrote that "the negro race is a species of men (sic) as different from ours ... as the breed of spaniels is from that of greyhounds," and in a formulation echoing down from his century to our own, declared that

> If their understanding is not of a different nature from ours ..., it is at least greatly inferior. They are not capable of any great application or association of ideas, and seem formed neither for the advantages nor the abuses of philosophy.[24]

Jefferson, the preeminent exponent of the Enlightenment doctrine of "the rights of man" on North American shores, echoed these sentiments:

> In general their existence appears to participate more of sensation than reflection... . [I]n memory they are equal to whites, in reason much inferior ... [and] in imagination they are dull, tasteless, and anomalous... . I advance it therefore ... that the blacks, whether originally a different race, or made distinct by time and circumstances, are inferior to the whites... . Will not a lover of natural history, then, one who views the gradations in all the animals with the eye of philosophy, excuse an effort to keep those in the department of Man (sic) as distinct as nature has formed them?[25]

Such claims of species distinctiveness among humans justified the inequitable allocation of political and social rights, while still upholding the doctrine of "the rights of man." The quest to obtain a precise scientific definition of race sustained debates which continue to rage today. Yet despite efforts ranging from Dr. Samuel Morton's studies of cranial capacity[26] to contemporary attempts to base racial classification on shared gene pools,[27] the concept of race has defied biological definition.

In the 19th century, Count Joseph Arthur de Gobineau drew upon the most respected scientific studies of his day to compose his four-volume *Essay on the Inequality of Races* (1853–1855).[28] He not only greatly influenced the racial thinking of the period, but his themes would be echoed in the racist ideologies of the next one hundred years: beliefs that superior races produced superior cultures and that racial intermixtures resulted in the degradation of the superior racial stock. These ideas found expression, for instance, in the eugenics movement launched by Darwin's cousin, Francis Galton, which had an immense impact on scientific and sociopolitical thought in Europe and the U.S.[29] In the wake of civil war and emancipation, and with immigration from southern and Eastern Europe as well as East Asia running high, the U.S. was particularly fertile ground for notions such as social darwinism and eugenics.

Attempts to discern the *scientific meaning* of race continue to the present day. For instance, an essay by Arthur Jensen which argued that hereditary factors shape intelligence not only revived the "nature or nurture" controversy, but also raised highly volatile questions about racial equality itself.[30] All such attempts seek to remove the concept of race from the historical context in which it arose and developed. They employ an *essentialist* approach which suggests instead that the truth of race is a matter of innate characteristics, of which skin color and other physical attributes provide only the most obvious, and in some respects most superficial, indicators.

FROM SCIENCE TO POLITICS

It has taken scholars more than a century to reject biologistic notions of race in favor of an approach which regards race as a *social* concept. This trend has been slow and uneven, and even today remains somewhat embattled, but its overall direction seems clear. At the turn of the century Max Weber discounted biological explanations for racial conflict and instead highlighted the social and political factors which engendered such conflict.[31] W. E. B. Du Bois argued for a sociopolitical definition of race by identifying "the color line" as "the problem of the 20th century."[32] Pioneering cultural anthropologist Franz Boas rejected attempts to link racial identifications and cultural traits, labelling as pseudoscientific any assumption of a continuum of "higher" and "lower" cultural groups.[33] Other early exponents of social, as opposed to biological, views of race included Robert E. Park, founder of the "Chicago school" of sociology, and Alain Leroy Locke, philosopher and theorist of the Harlem Renaissance.[34]

Perhaps more important than these and subsequent intellectual efforts, however, were the political struggles of racially defined groups themselves. Waged all around the globe under a variety of banners such as anticolonialism and civil rights, these battles to challenge various structural and cultural racisms have been a major feature of 20th-century politics. The racial horrors of the 20th century—colonial slaughter and apartheid, the genocide of the holocaust, and the massive bloodlettings required to end these evils—have also indelibly marked the theme of race as a political issue *par excellence*.

As a result of prior efforts and struggles, we have now reached the point of fairly general agreement that race is not a biologically given but rather a socially constructed way of differentiating human beings. While a tremendous achievement, the transcendence of biologistic conceptions of race does not provide any reprieve from the dilemmas of racial injustice and conflict, nor from controversies over the significance of race in the present. Views of race as socially constructed simply recognize the fact that these conflicts and controversies are now more properly framed on the terrain of politics. By privileging politics in the analysis which follows we do not mean to suggest that race has been displaced as a concern of scientific inquiry, or that struggles over cultural representation are no longer important. We do argue, however, that race is now a preeminently political phenomenon. Such an assertion invites examination of the evolving role of racial politics in the U.S. This is the subject to which we now turn.

DICTATORSHIP, DEMOCRACY, HEGEMONY

For most of its existence both as European colony and as an independent nation, the U.S. was a *racial dictatorship*. From 1607 to 1865—258 years—most non-whites were firmly eliminated from the sphere of politics.[35] After the Civil War there was the brief egalitarian experiment of Reconstruction which terminated ignominiously in 1877. In its wake followed almost a century of legally sanctioned segregation and denial of the vote, nearly absolute in the South and much of the Southwest, less effective in the North and far West, but formidable in any case.[36] These barriers fell only in the mid-1960s, a mere quarter-century ago. Nor did the successes of the black movement and its allies mean that all obstacles to their political participation had now been abolished. Patterns of racial inequality have proven, unfortunately, to be quite stubborn and persistent.

It is important, therefore, to recognize that in many respects, racial dictatorship is the norm against which all U.S. politics must be measured. The centuries of racial dictatorship have had three very large consequences: first, they defined "American" identity as white, as the negation of racialized "otherness"—at first largely African and indigenous, later Latin American and Asian as well.[37] This negation took shape in both law and custom, in public institutions and in forms of cultural representation. It became the archetype of hegemonic rule in the U.S. It was the successor to the conquest as the "master" racial project.

Second, racial dictatorship organized (albeit sometimes in an incoherent and contradictory fashion) the "color line" rendering it the fundamental division in U.S. society. The dictatorship elaborated, articulated, and drove racial divisions not only through institutions, but also through psyches, extending up to our own time the racial obsessions of the conquest and slavery periods.

Third, racial dictatorship consolidated the oppositional racial consciousness and organization originally framed by marronage[38] and slave revolts, by indigenous resistance, and by nationalisms of various sorts. Just as the conquest created the "native" where once there had been Pequot, Iroquois, or Tutelo, so too it created the "black" where once there had been Asante or Ovimbundu, Yoruba or Bakongo.

The transition from a racial dictatorship to a racial democracy has been a slow, painful, and contentious one; it remains far from complete. A recognition of the abiding presence of racial dictatorship, we contend, is crucial for the development of a theory of racial formation in the U.S. It is also crucial to the task of relating racial formation to the broader context of political practice, organization, and change.

In this context, a key question arises: in what way is racial formation related to politics as a whole? How, for example, does race articulate with other axes of oppression and difference—most importantly class and gender—along which politics is organized today?

The answer, we believe, lies in the concept of *hegemony*. Antonio Gramsci—the Italian communist who placed this concept at the center of his life's work—understood it as the conditions neces-

sary, in a given society, for the achievement and consolidation of rule. He argued that hegemony was always constituted by a combination of coercion and consent. Although rule can be obtained by force, it cannot be secured and maintained, especially in modern society, without the element of consent. Gramsci conceived of consent as far more than merely the legitimation of authority. In his view, consent extended to the incorporation by the ruling group of many of the key interests of subordinated groups, often to the explicit disadvantage of the rulers themselves.[39] Gramsci's treatment of hegemony went even farther: he argued that in order to consolidate their hegemony, ruling groups must elaborate and maintain a popular system of ideas and practices—through education, the media, religion, folk wisdom, etc.—which he called "common sense." It is through its production and its adherence to this "common sense," this ideology (in the broadest sense of the term), that a society gives its consent to the way in which it is ruled.[40]

These provocative concepts can be extended and applied to an understanding of racial rule. In the Americas, the conquest represented the violent introduction of a new form of rule whose relationship with those it subjugated was almost entirely coercive. In the U.S., the origins of racial division, and of racial signification and identity formation, lie in a system of rule which was extremely dictatorial. The mass murders and expulsions of indigenous people, and the enslavement of Africans, surely evoked and inspired little consent in their founding moments.

Over time, however, the balance of coercion and consent began to change. It is possible to locate the origins of hegemony right within the heart of racial dictatorship, for the effort to possess the oppressor's tools—religion and philosophy in this case—was crucial to emancipation (the effort to possess oneself). As Ralph Ellison reminds us, "The slaves often took the essence of the aristocratic ideal (as they took Christianity) with far more seriousness than their masters."[41] In their language, in their religion with its focus on the Exodus theme and on Jesus's tribulations, in their music with its figuring of suffering, resistance, perseverance, and transcendence, in their interrogation of a political philosophy which sought perpetually to rationalize their bondage in a supposedly "free" society, the slaves incorporated elements of racial rule into their thought and practice, turning them against their original bearers.

Racial rule can be understood as a slow and uneven historical process which has moved from dictatorship to democracy, from domination to hegemony. In this transition, hegemonic forms of racial rule—those based on consent—eventually came to supplant those based on coercion. Of course, before this assertion can be accepted, it must be qualified in important ways. By no means has the U.S. established racial democracy at the end of the century, and by no means is coercion a thing of the past. But the sheer complexity of the racial questions U.S. society confronts today, the welter of competing racial projects and contradictory racial experiences which Americans undergo, suggests that hegemony is a useful and appropriate term with which to characterize contemporary racial rule.

Our key theoretical notion of racial projects helps to extend and broaden the question of rule. Projects are the building blocks not just of racial formation, but of hegemony in general. Hegemony operates by simultaneously structuring and signifying. As in the case of racial opposition, gender or class-based conflict today links structural inequity and injustice on the one hand, and identifies and represents its subjects on the other. The success of modern-day feminism, for example, has depended on its ability to reinterpret gender as a matter of both injustice and identity/difference.

Today, political opposition necessarily takes shape on the terrain of hegemony. Far from ruling principally through exclusion and coercion (though again, these are hardly absent) hegemony operates by including its subjects, incorporating its

opposition. *Pace* both Marxists and liberals, there is no longer any universal or privileged region of political action or discourse.[42] Race, class, and gender all represent potential antagonisms whose significance is no longer given, if it ever was.

Thus race, class, and gender (as well as sexual orientation) constitute "regions" of hegemony, areas in which certain political projects can take shape. They share certain obvious attributes in that they are all "socially constructed," and they all consist of a field of projects whose common feature is their linkage of social structure and signification.

Going beyond this, it is crucial to emphasize that race, class, and gender, are not fixed and discrete categories, and that such "regions" are by no means autonomous. They overlap, intersect, and fuse with each other in countless ways. Such mutual determinations have been illustrated by Patricia Hill Collins's survey and theoretical synthesis of the themes and issues of black feminist thought.[43] They are also evident in Evelyn Nakano Glenn's work on the historical and contemporary racialization of domestic and service work.[44] In many respects, race is gendered and gender is racialized. In institutional and everyday life, any clear demarcation of specific forms of oppression and difference is constantly being disrupted.

There are no clear boundaries between these "regions" of hegemony, so political conflicts will often invoke some or all these themes simultaneously. Hegemony is tentative, incomplete, and "messy." For example, the 1991 Hill-Thomas hearings, with their intertwined themes of race and gender inequality, and their frequent genuflections before the altar of hard work and upward mobility, managed to synthesize various race, gender, and class projects in a particularly explosive combination.[45]

What distinguishes political opposition today—racial or otherwise—is its insistence on identifying itself and speaking for itself, its determined demand for the transformation of the social structure, its refusal of the "common sense" understandings which the hegemonic order imposes. Nowhere is this refusal of "common sense" more needed, or more imperilled, than in our understanding of racism.

WHAT IS RACISM?

Since the ambiguous triumph of the civil rights movement in the mid-1960s, clarity about what racism means has been eroding. The concept entered the lexicon of "common sense" only in the 1960s. Before that, although the term had surfaced occasionally,[46] the problem of racial injustice and inequality was generally understood in a more limited fashion, as a matter of prejudiced attitudes or bigotry on the one hand,[47] and discriminatory practices on the other.[48] Solutions, it was believed, would therefore involve the overcoming of such attitudes, the achievement of tolerance, the acceptance of "brotherhood," etc., and the passage of laws which prohibited discrimination with respect to access to public accommodations, jobs, education, etc. The early civil rights movement explicitly reflected such views. In its espousal of integration and its quest for a "beloved community" it sought to overcome racial prejudice. In its litigation activities and agitation for civil rights legislation it sought to challenge discriminatory practices.

The later 1960s, however, signalled a sharp break with this vision. The emergence of the slogan "black power" (and soon after, of "brown power," "red power," and "yellow power"), the wave of riots that swept the urban ghettos from 1964 to 1968, and the founding of radical movement organizations of nationalist and Marxist orientation, coincided with the recognition that racial inequality and injustice had much deeper roots. They were not simply the product of prejudice, nor was discrimination only a matter of intentionally informed action. Rather, prejudice was an almost unavoidable outcome of patterns of socialization which were "bred in the bone," affecting not only whites but even minorities themselves.[49] Discrimination, far from manifesting itself only (or even principally) through individual actions or conscious policies, was a structural feature of U.S. society, the product of centuries of systematic exclusion, exploitation, and disregard of racially defined minorities.[50] It was this combination of relationships—prejudice, discrimination, and institutional inequality—which defined the concept of racism at the end of the 1960s.

NOTES

1. *San Francisco Chronicle*, 14 September 1982, 19 May 1983. Ironically, the 1970 Louisiana law was enacted to supersede an old Jim Crow statute which relied on the idea of "common report" in determining an infant's race. Following Phipps's unsuccessful attempt to change her classification and have the law declared unconstitutional, a legislative effort arose which culminated in the repeal of the law. See *San Francisco Chronicle*, 23 June 1983.

2. Compare the Phipps case to Andrew Hacker's well-known "parable" in which a white person is informed by a mysterious official that "the organization he represents has made a mistake" and that "… [a]ccording to their records …, you were to have been born black to another set of parents, far from where you were raised." How much compensation, Hacker's official asks, would "you" require to undo the damage of this unfortunate error? See Hacker, *Two Nations: Black and White, Separate, Hostile, Unequal* (New York: Charles Scribner's Sons, 1992) pp. 31–32.

3. On the evolution of Louisiana's racial classification system, see Virginia Dominguez, *White By Definition: Social Classification in Creole Louisiana* (New Brunswick: Rutgers University Press, 1986).

4. This is not to suggest that gender is a biological category while race is not. Gender, like race, is a social construct. However, the biological division of humans into sexes—two at least, and possibly intermediate ones as well—is not in dispute. This provides a basis for argument over gender divisions—how "natural," etc.—which does not exist with regard to race. To ground an argument for the "natural" existence of race, one must resort to philosophical anthropology.

5. "The truth is that there are no races, there is nothing in the world that can do all we ask race to do for us … The evil that is done is done by the concept, and by easy—yet impossible—assumptions as to its application." (Kwame Anthony Appiah, *In My Father's House: Africa in the Philosophy of Culture* [New York: Oxford University Press, 1992].) Appiah's eloquent and learned book fails, in our view, to dispense with the race concept, despite its anguished attempt to do so; this indeed is the source of its author's anguish. We agree with him as to the non-objective character of race, but fail to see how this recognition justifies its abandonment. This argument is developed below.

6. We understand essentialism as *belief in real, true human, essences, existing outside or impervious to social and historical context.* We draw this definition, with some small modifications, from Diana Fuss, *Essentially Speaking: Feminism, Nature, & Difference* (New York: Routledge, 1989) p. xi.

7. Michael Omi and Howard Winant, "On the Theoretical Status of the Concept of Race" in Warren Crichlow and Cameron McCarthy, eds., *Race, Identity, and Representation in Education* (New York: Routledge, 1993).

8. Charles Murray, *Losing Ground: American Social Policy, 1950–1980* (New York: Basic Books, 1984), p. 223.

9. Justice Thurgood Marshall, dissenting in *City of Richmond v. J. A. Croson Co.*, 488 U.S. 469 (1989).

10. See, for example, Derrick Bell, "Remembrances of Racism Past: Getting Past the Civil Rights Decline." in Herbert Hill and James E. Jones, Jr., eds., *Race in America: The Struggle for Equality* (Madison: The University of Wisconsin Press, 1993) pp. 75–76; Gertrude Ezorsky, *Racism and Justice: The Case for Affirmative Action* (Ithaca: Cornell University Press, 1991) pp. 109–111; David Kairys, *With Liberty and Justice for Some: A Critique of the Conservative Supreme Court* (New York: The New Press, 1993) pp. 138–41.

11. Howard Winant has developed a tentative "map" of the system of racial hegemony in the U.S. circa 1990, which focuses on the spectrum of racial projects running from the political right to the political left. See Winant, "Where Culture Meets Structure: Race in the 1990s," in idem, *Racial Conditions: Politics, Theory, Comparisons* (Minneapolis: University of Minnesota Press, 1994).

12. A familiar example is use of racial "code words." Recall George Bush's manipulations of racial fear in the 1988 "Willie Horton" ads, or Jesse Helms's use of the coded term "quota" in his 1990 campaign against Harvey Gantt.

13. From this perspective, far right racial projects can also be interpreted as "nationalist." See Ronald Walters, "White Racial Nationalism in the United States," *Without Prejudice* Vol. 1, no. 1 (Fall 1987).

14. To be sure, any effort to divide racial formation patterns according to social structural location—"macro" vs. "micro," for example—is necessarily an analytic device. In the concrete, there is no such dividing line. See Winant, "Where Culture Meets Structure."

15. We are not unaware, for example, that publishing this work is in itself a racial project.

16. Antisemitism only began to be racialized in the 18th century, as George L. Mosse clearly shows in his important *Toward the Final Solution: A History of European Racism* (New York: Howard Fertig, 1978).

17. As Marx put it:

> The discovery of gold and silver in America, the extirpation, enslavement, and entombment in mines of the aboriginal population, the beginning of the conquest and looting of the East Indies, the turning of Africa into a warren for the commercial hunting of blackskins, signalized the rosy dawn of the era of capitalist production. These idyllic proceedings are the chief momenta of primitive accumulation. (Karl Marx, *Capital*, Vol. I (New York: International Publishers, 1967) p. 751.)

> David E. Stannard argues that the wholesale slaughter perpetrated upon the native peoples of the Western hemisphere is unequalled in history, even in our own bloody century. See his *American Holocaust: Columbus and the Conquest of the New World* (New York: Oxford University Press, 1992).

18. Winthrop Jordan provides a detailed account of the sources of European attitudes about color and race in *White Over Black: American Attitudes Toward the Negro, 1550–1812* (New York: Norton, 1977 [1968]) pp. 3–43.

19. In a famous instance, a 1550 debate in Valladolid pitted the philosopher and translator of Aristotle, Gines de Sepulveda, against the Dominican Bishop of the Mexican state of Chiapas, Bartolome de Las Casas. Discussing the native peoples, Sepulveda argued that:

> In wisdom, skill, virtue and humanity, these people are as inferior to the Spaniards as children are to adults and women to men; there is as great a difference between them as there is between

savagery and forbearance, between violence and moderation, almost—I am inclined to say, as between monkeys and men (Sepúlveda, *Democrates Alter*, quoted in Tsvetan Todorov, *The Conquest of America: The Question of the Other* (New York: Harper and Row, 1984), p. 153).

In contrast, Las Casas defended the humanity and equality of the native peoples, both in terms of their way of life—which he idealized as one of innocence, gentleness, and generosity—and in terms of their readiness for conversion to Catholicism, which for him as for Sepulveda was the true and universal religion (Las Casas, "Letter to the Council of the Indies," quoted ibid, p. 163). William E. Connolly interrogates the linkages proposed by Todorov between early Spanish colonialism and contemporary conceptions of identity and difference in *Identity/Difference: Democratic Negotiations of Political Paradox* (Ithaca: Cornell University Press, 1991) pp. 40–48.

20. In Virginia, for example, it took about two decades after the establishment of European colonies to extirpate the indigenous people of the greater vicinity; fifty years after the establishment of the first colonies, the elaboration of slave codes establishing race as *prima facie* evidence for enslaved status was well under way. See Jordan, *White Over Black*.

21. Marx, *Capital*, p. 751.

22. Edward W. Said, *Culture and Imperialism* (New York: Alfred A. Knopf, 1993).

23. David Brion Davis, *The Problem of Slavery in The Age of Revolution* (Ithaca: Cornell University Press, 1975).

24. Quoted in Thomas F. Gossett, *Race: The History of an Idea in America* (New York: Schocken Books, 1965) p. 45.

25. Thomas *Jefferson, Notes on Virginia* [1787], in Merrill D. Peterson, *Writings of Thomas Jefferson* (New York: The Library of America, 1984) pp. 264–66, 270. Thanks to Kimberly Benston for drawing our attention to this passage.

26. Proslavery physician Samuel George Morton (1799–1851) compiled a collection of 800 crania from all parts of the world which formed the sample for his studies of race. Assuming that the larger the size of the cranium translated into greater intelligence, Morton established a relationship between race and skull capacity. Gossett reports that "In 1849, one of his studies included the following results: the English skulls in his collection proved to be the largest, with an average cranial capacity of 96 cubic inches. The Americans and Germans were rather poor seconds, both with cranial capacities of 90 cubic inches. At the bottom of the list were the Negroes with 83 cubic inches, the Chinese with 82, and the Indians with 79." Gossett, *Race*, p. 74. More recently, Steven Jay Gould has reexamined Morton's data, and shown that his research data were deeply, though unconsciously, manipulated to agree with his "a priori conviction about racial ranking." (Gould, *The Mismeasure of Man* (New York: W. W. Norton, 1981) pp. 50-69).

27. Definitions of race founded upon a common pool of genes have not held up when confronted by scientific research which suggests that the differences *within* a given human population are every bit as great as those *between* populations. See L. L. Cavalli-Sforza, "The Genetics of Human Populations," *Scientific American* (September 1974) pp. 81–89.

28. A fascinating summary critique of Gobineau is provided in Tsvetan Todorov, *On Human Diversity: Nationalism, Racism, and Exoticism in French Thought*, trans. Catherine Porter (Cambridge, MA: Harvard University Press, 1993), esp. pp. 129–40.

29. Two recent histories of eugenics are Allen Chase, *The Legacy of Malthus* (New York: Knopf, 1977); Daniel J. Kevles, *In the Name of Eugenics: Genetics and the Uses of Human Heredity* (New York: Knopf, 1985).

30. Arthur Jensen, "How Much Can We Boost IQ and Scholastic Achievement?" *Harvard Educational Review* 39 (1969) pp. 1–123.

31. See Weber, *Economy and Society*, Vol. I (Berkeley: University of California Press, 1978), pp. 385–87; Ernst Moritz Manasse, "Max Weber on Race," *Social Research*, Vol. 14 (1947) pp. 191–221.

32. Du Bois, *The Souls of Black Folk* (New York: Penguin, 1989 [1903]), p. 13. Du Bois himself wrestled heavily with the conflict between a fully sociohistorical conception of race, and the more essentialized and deterministic vision he encountered as a student in Berlin. In "The Conservation of Races" (1897) we can see his first mature effort to resolve this conflict in a vision which combined racial solidarity and a commitment to social equality. See Du Bois, "The Conservation of Races," in Dan S. Green and Edwin D. Driver, eds., *W. E. B. Du Bois On Sociology and the Black Community* (Chicago: University of Chicago Press, 1978) pp. 238–49; Manning Marable, *W. E. B. Du Bois: Black Radical Democrat* (Boston: Twayne, 1986) pp. 35–38. For a contrary, and we believe incorrect reading, see Appiah, *In My Father's House*, pp. 28–46.

33. A good collection of Boas's work is George W. Stocking, ed., *The Shaping of American Anthropology, 1883–1911: A Franz Boas Reader* (Chicago: University of Chicago Press, 1974).

34. Robert E. Park's *Race and Culture* (Glencoe, IL: Free Press, 1950) can still provide insight; see also Stanford H. Lyman, *Militarism, Imperialism, and Racial Accommodation: An Analysis and Interpretation of the Early Writings of Robert E. Park* (Fayetteville: University of Arkansas Press, 1992); Locke's views are concisely expressed in Alain Leroy Locke, *Race Contacts and Interracial Relations*, ed. Jeffrey C. Stewart (Washington, DC: Howard University Press, 1992), originally a series of lectures given at Howard University.

35. Japanese, for example, could not become naturalized citizens until passage of the 1952 McCarran-Walter Act. It took over 160 years, since the passage of the Law of 1790, to allow all "races" to be eligible for naturalization.

36. Especially when we recall that until around 1960, the majority of blacks, the largest racially defined minority group, lived in the South.

37. Toni Morrison, *Playing in the Dark: Whiteness and the Literary Imagination* (Cambridge, MA: Harvard University Press, 1992); Richard Drinnon, *Facing West: The Metaphysics of Indian-Hating and Empire-Building* (Minneapolis: University of Minnesota Press, 1980); Michael Paul Rogin, *Fathers and Children: Andrew Jackson and the Subjugation of the American Indian* (New York: Knopf, 1975).

38. This term refers to the practice, widespread throughout the Americas, whereby runaway slaves formed communities in remote areas, such as swamps, mountains, or forests, often in alliance with dispossessed indigenous peoples.

39. Antonio Gramsci, *Selections from the Prison Notebooks*, edited and translated by Quintin Hoare and Geoffrey Nowell Smith (New York: International Publishers, 1971) p. 182.

40. Anne Showstack Sassoon, *Gramsci's Politics*, 2nd ed. (London: Hutchinson, 1987); Sue Golding, *Gramsci's Democratic Theory: Contributions to Post-Liberal Democracy* (Toronto: University of Toronto Press, 1992).

41. Ralph Ellison, *Shadow and Act* (New York: New American Library, 1966) p. xiv.

42. Chantal Mouffe makes a related argument in "Radical Democracy: Modern or Postmodern?" in Andrew Ross, ed., *Universal Abandon: The Politics of Postmodernism* (Minneapolis: University of Minnesota Press, 1988).

43. Patricia Hill Collins, *Black Feminist Thought: Knowledge, Consciousness, and the Politics of Empowerment* (New York and London: Routledge, 1991).

44. Evelyn Nakano Glenn, "From Servitude to Service Work: Historical Continuities in the Racial Division of Paid Reproductive Labor," *Signs: Journal of Women in Culture & Society*, Vol. 18, no. 1 (Autumn 1992).

45. Toni Morrison, ed., *Race-ing Justice, En-gendering Power: Essays on Anita Hill, Clarence Thomas, and the Construction of Social Reality* (New York: Pantheon, 1992).

46. For example, in Magnus Hirschfeld's prescient book, *Racism* (London: Victor Gollancz, 1938).

47. This was the framework, employed in the crucial study of Myrdal and his associates; see Gunnar Myrdal, *An American Dilemma: The Negro Problem and Modern Democracy*, 20th Anniversary Edition (New York: Harper and Row, 1962 [1944]). See also the articles by Thomas F. Pettigrew and George Fredrickson in Pettigrew et al., *Prejudice: Selections from The Harvard Encyclopedia of American Ethnic Groups* (Cambridge, MA: The Belknap Press of Harvard University, 1982).

48. On discrimination, see Frederickson in ibid. In an early essay which explicitly sought to modify the framework of the Myrdal study, Robert K. Merton recognized that prejudice and discrimination need not coincide, and indeed could combine in a variety of ways. See Merton, "Discrimination and the American Creed," in R. M. McIver, ed., *Discrimination and National Welfare* (New York: Harper and Row, 1949).

49. Gordon W. Allport, *The Nature of Prejudice* (Cambridge, MA: Addison-Wesley, 1954) remains a classic work in the field; see also Philomena Essed, *Understanding Everyday Racism: An Interdisciplinary Theory* (Newbury Park, CA: Sage, 1991). A good overview of black attitudes toward black identities is provided in William E. Cross, Jr., *Shades of Black: Diversity in African-American Identity* (Philadelphia: Temple University Press, 1991).

50. Stokely Carmichael and Charles V. Hamilton first popularized the notion of "institutional" forms of discrimination in *Black Power: The Politics of Liberation in America* (New York: Vintage, 1967), although the basic concept certainly predated that work. Indeed, President Lyndon Johnson made a similar argument in his 1965 speech at Howard University:

But freedom is not enough. You do not wipe away the scars of centuries by saying: Now you are free to go where you want, do as you desire, and choose the leaders you please.

You do not take a person who, for years, has been hobbled by chains and liberate him (sic), bring him up to the starting line of a race and then say, "You are free to compete with all the others," and still justly believe that you have been completely fair.

Thus it is not enough just to open the gates of opportunity. All our citizens must have the opportunity to walk through those gates.

This is the next and more profound stage of the battle for civil rights. We seek not just freedom but opportunity—not just legal equity but human ability—not just equality as a right but equality as a fact and as a result. (Lyndon B. Johnson, "To Fulfill These Rights," reprinted in Lee Rainwater and William L. Yancey, *The Moynihan Report and the Politics of Controversy* [Cambridge, MA: MIT Press, 1967, p. 125].)

This speech, delivered at Howard University on June 4, 1965, was written in part by Daniel Patrick Moynihan. A more systematic treatment of the institutional racism approach is David T. Wellman, *Portraits of White Racism* (New York: Cambridge University Press, 1977).

COMPANION WEBSITE

1. Go online to Write Out Loud about how racial formations are both a structural condition and an everyday experience.
2. Check out the Supplementary Sources for *Shifting the Paradigm* for links to great documentaries about racial formation in the U.S., including PBS's stellar *Race: The Power of an Illusion.*
3. Log on to the Critical Race and Postcolonial Theory Profile Page to learn more about the theoretical traditions Omi and Winant are building on.

30

Black Skin, White Masks

Frantz Fanon

I ASCRIBE A BASIC IMPORTANCE to the phenomenon of language. That is why I find it necessary to begin with this subject, which should provide us with one of the elements in the colored man's comprehension of the dimension of *the other*. For it is implicit that to speak is to exist absolutely for the other.

The black man has two dimensions. One with his fellows, the other with the white man. A Negro behaves differently with a white man and with another Negro. That this self-division is a direct result of colonialist subjugation is beyond question. … No one would dream of doubting that its major artery is fed from the heart of those various theories that have tried to prove that the Negro is a stage in the slow evolution of monkey into man. Here is objective evidence that expresses reality.

But when one has taken cognizance of this situation, when one has understood it, one considers the job completed. How can one then be deaf to that voice rolling down the stages of history: "What matters is not to know the world but to change it."

This matters appallingly in our lifetime.

To speak means to be in a position to use a certain syntax, to grasp the morphology of this or that language, but it means above all to assume a culture, to support the weight of a civilization. Since the situation is not one-way only, the statement of it should reflect the fact. Here the reader is asked to concede certain points that, however unacceptable they may seem in the beginning, will find the measure of their validity in the facts.

The problem that we confront in this chapter is this: The Negro of the Antilles will be proportionately whiter—that is, he will come closer to being a real human being—in direct ratio to his mastery of the French language. I am not unaware that this is one of man's attitudes face to face with Being. A man who has a language consequently possesses the world expressed and implied by that language. What we are getting at becomes plain: Mastery of language affords remarkable power. Paul Valery knew this, for he called language "the god gone astray in the flesh."[1]

In a work now in preparation I propose to investigate this phenomenon.[2] For the moment I want to show why the Negro of the Antilles, whoever he is, has always to face the problem of language. Furthermore, I will broaden the field of this description and through the Negro of the Antilles include every colonized man.

Every colonized people—in other words, every people in whose soul an inferiority complex has been created by the death and burial of its local cultural originality—finds itself face to face with the language of the civilizing nation; that is, with the culture of the mother country. The colonized is elevated above his jungle status in proportion to his adoption of the mother country's cultural standards. He becomes whiter as he renounces his blackness, his jungle. In the French colonial army, and particularly in the Senegalese regiments, the black officers serve first of all as interpreters. They are used to convey the master's orders to their fellows, and they too enjoy a certain position of honor.

There is the city, there is the country. There is the capital, there is the province. Apparently the problem in the mother country is the same. Let us take a Lyonnais in Paris: He boasts of the quiet of his city, the intoxicating beauty of the quays of the Rhône, the splendor of the plane trees, and all those other things that fascinate people who have nothing to do. If you meet him again when he has returned from Paris, and especially if you do not know the capital, he will never run out of its praises: Paris-city-of-light, the Seine, the little garden restaurants, know Paris and die. ...

The process repeats itself with the man of Martinique. First of all on his island: Basse-Pointe, Marigot, Gros-Morne, and, opposite, the imposing Fort-de-France. Then, and this is the important point, beyond his island. The Negro who knows the mother country is a demigod. In this connection I offer a fact that must have struck my compatriots. Many of them, after stays of varying length in metropolitan France, go home to be deified. The most eloquent form of ambivalence is adopted toward them by the native, the-one-who-never-crawled-out-of-his-hole, the *bitaco*. The black man who has lived in France for a length of time returns radically changed. To express it in genetic terms, his phenotype undergoes a definitive, an absolute mutation.[3] Even before he had gone away, one could tell from the almost aerial manner of his carriage that new forces had been set in motion. When he met a friend or an acquaintance, his greeting was no longer the wide sweep of the arm: With great reserve our "new man" bowed slightly. The habitually raucous voice hinted at a gentle inner stirring as of rustling breezes. For the Negro knows that over there in France there is a stereotype of him that will fasten on to him at the pier in Le Havre or Marseille: "Ah come fom Mahtinique, it's the fuhst time Ah've eveh come

to Fance." He knows that what the poets call the *divine gurgling* (listen to Creole) is only a halfway house between pidgin-nigger and French. The middle class in the Antilles never speak Creole except to their servants. In school the children of Martinique are taught to scorn the dialect. One avoids *Creolisms*. Some families completely forbid the use of Creole, and mothers ridicule their children for speaking it.

> My mother wanting a son to keep in mind
> if you do not know your history lesson
> you will not go to mass on Sunday in
> your Sunday clothes
> that child will be a disgrace to the family
> that child will be our curse
> shut up I told you you must speak French
> the French of France
> the Frenchman's French
> French French[4]

Yes, I must take great pains with my speech, because I shall be more or less judged by it. With great contempt they will say of me, "He doesn't even know how to speak French."

In any group of young men in the Antilles, the one who expresses himself well, who has mastered the language, is inordinately feared; keep an eye on that one, he is almost white. In France one says, "He talks like a book." In Martinique, "He talks like a white man."

THE FACT OF BLACKNESS

"Dirty nigger!" Or simply, "Look, a Negro!"

I came into the world imbued with the will to find a meaning in things, my spirit filled with the desire to attain to the source of the world, and then I found that I was an object in the midst of other objects.

Sealed into that crushing objecthood, I turned beseechingly to others. Their attention was a liberation, running over my body suddenly abraded into nonbeing, endowing me once more with an agility that I had thought lost, and by taking me out of the world, restoring me to it. But just as I reached the other side, I stumbled, and the movements, the attitudes, the glances of the other fixed me there, in the sense in which a chemical solution is fixed by a dye. I was indignant; I demanded an explanation. Nothing happened. I burst apart. Now the fragments have been put together again by another self.

As long as the black man is among his own, he will have no occasion, except in minor internal conflicts, to experience his being through others. There is of course the moment of "being for others," of which Hegel speaks, but every ontology is made unattainable in a colonized and civilized society. It would seem that this fact has not been given sufficient attention by those who have discussed the question. In the *Weltanschauung* of a colonized people there is an impurity, a flaw that outlaws any ontological explanation. Someone may object that this is the case with every individual, but such an objection merely conceals a basic problem. Ontology—once it is finally admitted as leaving existence by the wayside—does not permit us to understand the being of the black man. For not only must the black man be black; he must be black in relation to the white man. Some critics will take it on themselves to remind us that this proposition has a converse. I say that this is false. The black man has no ontological resistance in the eyes of the white man. Over-night the Negro has been given two frames of reference within which he has had to place himself. His metaphysics, or, less pretentiously, his customs and the sources on which they were based, were wiped out because they were in conflict with a civilization that he did not know and that imposed itself on him.

The black man among his own in the twentieth century does not know at what moment his inferiority comes into being through the other. Of course I have talked about the black problem with friends, or, more rarely, with American Negroes. Together we protested, we asserted the equality of all men in the world. In the Antilles there was also that little gulf that exists among the almost-white, the mulatto, and the nigger. But I was satisfied with an intellectual understanding of these differences. It was not really dramatic. And then. …

And then the occasion arose when I had to meet the white man's eyes. An unfamiliar weight burdened me. The real world challenged my claims. In the white world the man of color encounters difficulties in the development of his bodily schema. Consciousness of the body is solely a negating activity. It is a third-person consciousness. The body is surrounded by an atmosphere of certain uncertainty. I know that if I want to smoke, I shall have to reach out my right arm and take the pack of cigarettes lying at the other end of the table. The matches, however, are in the drawer on the left, and I shall have to lean back slightly. And all these movements are made not out of habit but out of implicit knowledge. A slow composition of my *self* as a body in the middle of a spatial and temporal world—such seems to be the schema. It does not impose itself on me; it is, rather, a definitive structuring of the self and of the world—definitive because it creates a real dialectic between my body and the world.

For several years certain laboratories have been trying to produce a serum for "denegrification"; with all the earnestness in the world, laboratories have sterilized their test tubes, checked their scales, and embarked on researches that might make it possible for the miserable Negro to whiten himself and thus to throw off the burden of that corporeal malediction. Below the corporeal schema I had sketched a historico-racial schema. The elements that I used had been provided for me not by "residual sensations and perceptions primarily of a tactile, vestibular, kinesthetic, and visual character,"[5] but by the other, the white man, who had woven me out of a thousand details, anecdotes, stories. I thought that what I had in hand was to construct a physiological self, to balance space, to localize sensations, and here I was called on for more.

"Look, a Negro!" It was an external stimulus that flicked over me as I passed by. I made a tight smile.

"Look, a Negro!" It was true. It amused me.

"Look, a Negro!" The circle was drawing a bit tighter. I made no secret of my amusement.

"Mama, see the Negro! I'm frightened!" Frightened! Frightened! Now they were beginning to be afraid of me. I made up my mind to laugh myself to tears, but laughter had become impossible.

I could no longer laugh, because I already knew that there were legends, stories, history, and above all *historicity*, which I had learned about from Jaspers. Then, assailed at various points, the corporeal schema crumbled, its place taken by a racial epidermal schema. In the train it was no longer a question of being aware of my body in the third person but in a triple person. In the train I was given not one but two, three places. I had already stopped being amused. It was not that I was finding febrile coordinates in the world. I existed triply: I occupied space. I moved toward the other … and the evanescent other, hostile but not opaque, transparent, not there, disappeared. Nausea… .

I was responsible at the same time for my body, for my race, for my ancestors. I subjected myself to an objective examination, I discovered my blackness, my ethnic characteristics; and I was battered down by tom-toms, cannibalism, intellectual deficiency, fetishism, racial defects, slave-ships, and above all else, above all: "Sho' good eatin'."

On that day, completely dislocated, unable to be abroad with the other, the white man, who unmercifully imprisoned me, I took myself far off from my own presence, far indeed, and made myself an object. What else could it be for me but an amputation, an excision, a hemorrhage that spattered my whole body with black blood? But I did not want this revision, this thematization. All I wanted was to be a man among other men. I wanted to come lithe and young into a world that was ours and to help to build it together.

But I rejected all immunization of the emotions. I wanted to be a man, nothing but a man. Some identified me with ancestors of mine who had been enslaved or lynched: I decided to accept this. It was on the universal level of the intellect that I understood this inner kinship—I was the grandson of slaves in exactly the same way in which President Lebrun was the grandson of tax-paying, hard-working peasants. In the main, the panic soon vanished.

In America, Negroes are segregated. In South America, Negroes are whipped in the streets, and Negro strikers are cut down by machine-guns. In West Africa, the Negro is an animal. And there beside me, my neighbor in the university, who was born in Algeria, told me: "As long as the Arab is treated like a man, no solution is possible."

"Understand, my dear boy, color prejudice is something I find utterly foreign. … But of course, come in, sir, there is no color prejudice among us. … Quite, the Negro is a man like ourselves. … It is not because he is black that he is less intelligent than we are. … I had a Senegalese buddy in the army who was really clever. …"

Where am I to be classified? Or, if you prefer, tucked away?

"A Martinican, a native of 'our' old colonies."

Where shall I hide?

"Look at the nigger! … Mama, a Negro! … Hell, he's getting mad. … Take no notice, sir, he does not know that you are as civilized as we. …"

My body was given back to me sprawled out, distorted, recolored, clad in mourning in that white winter day. The Negro is an animal, the Negro is bad, the Negro is mean, the Negro is ugly; look, a nigger, it's cold, the nigger is shivering, the nigger is shivering because he is cold, the little boy is trembling because he is afraid of the nigger, the nigger is shivering with cold, that cold that goes through your bones, the handsome little boy is trembling because he thinks that the nigger is quivering with rage, the little white boy throws himself into his mother's arms: Mama, the nigger's going to eat me up.

All round me the white man, above the sky tears at its navel, the earth rasps under my feet, and there is a white song, a white song. All this whiteness that burns me. …

I sit down at the fire and I become aware of my uniform. I had not seen it. It is indeed ugly. I stop there, for who can tell me what beauty is?

Where shall I find shelter from now on? I felt an easily identifiable flood mounting out of the countless facets of my being. I was about to be angry. The fire was long since out, and once more the nigger was trembling.

"Look how handsome that Negro is! …"

"Kiss the handsome Negro's ass, madame!"

Shame flooded her face. At last I was set free from my rumination. At the same time I accomplished two things: I identified my enemies and I made a scene. A grand slam. Now one would be able to laugh.

The field of battle having been marked out, I entered the lists.

What? While I was forgetting, forgiving, and wanting only to love, my message was flung back in my face like a slap. The white world, the only honorable one, barred me from all participation. A man was expected to behave like a man. I was expected to behave like a black man—or at least like a nigger. I shouted a greeting to the world and the world slashed away my joy. I was told to stay within bounds, to go back where I belonged.

They would see, then! I had warned them, anyway. Slavery? It was no longer even mentioned, that unpleasant memory. My supposed inferiority? A hoax that it was better to laugh at. I forgot it all, but only on condition that the world not protect itself against me any longer. I had incisors to test. I was sure they were strong. And besides. …

What! When it was I who had every reason to hate, to despise, I was rejected? When I should have been begged, implored, I was denied the slightest recognition? I resolved, since it was impossible for me to get away from an *inborn complex*, to assert myself as a BLACK MAN. Since the other hesitated to recognize me, there remained only one solution: to make myself known.

THE NEGRO AND HEGEL

Self-consciousness exists in itself *and* for itself, *in that and by the fact that it exists for another self-consciousness; that is to say, it is only by being acknowledged or recognized.*

–Hegel, The Phenomenology of Mind

Man is human only to the extent to which he tries to impose his existence on another man in order to be recognized by him. As long as he has not been effectively recognized by the other, that other will remain the theme of his actions. It is on that other being, on recognition by that other being, that his own human worth and reality depend. It is that other being in whom the meaning of his life is condensed.

There is not an open conflict between white and black. One day the White Master, *without conflict*, recognized the Negro slave.

But the former slave wants to *make himself recognized*.

At the foundation of Hegelian dialectic there is an absolute reciprocity which must be emphasized. It is in the degree to which I go beyond my own immediate being that I apprehend the existence of the other as a natural and more than natural reality. If I close the circuit, if I prevent the accomplishment of movement in two directions, I keep the other within himself. Ultimately, I deprive him even of this being-for-itself.

The only means of breaking this vicious circle that throws me back on myself is to restore to the other, through mediation and recognition, his human reality, which is different from natural reality. The other has to perform the same operation. "Action from one side only would be useless, because what is to happen can only be brought about by means of both. …"; "*they recognize themselves as mutually recognizing each other.*"[6]

In its immediacy, consciousness of self is simple being-for-itself. In order to win the certainty of oneself, the incorporation of the concept of recognition is essential. Similarly, the other is waiting for recognition by us, in order to burgeon into the universal consciousness of self. Each consciousness of self is in quest of absoluteness. It wants to be recognized as a primal value without reference to life, as a transformation of subjective certainty (*Gewissheit*) into objective truth (*Wahrheit*).

When it encounters resistance from the other, self-consciousness undergoes the experience of *desire*—the first milestone on the road that leads to the dignity of the spirit. Self-consciousness accepts the risk of its life, and consequently it threatens the other in his physical being. "It is solely by risking life that freedom is obtained; only thus is it tried and proved that the essential nature of self-consciousness is not *bare existence*, is not the merely immediate form in which it at first makes its appearance, is not its mere absorption in the expanse of life."[7]

Thus human reality in-itself-for-itself can be achieved only through conflict and through the risk that conflict implies. This risk means that I go beyond life toward a supreme good that is the transformation of subjective certainty of my own worth into a universally valid objective truth.

As soon as I *desire* I am asking to be considered. I am not merely here-and-now, sealed into thingness. I am for somewhere else and for something else. I demand that notice be taken of my negating activity insofar as I pursue something other than life; insofar as I do battle for the creation of a human world—that is, of a world of reciprocal recognitions.

He who is reluctant to recognize me opposes me. In a savage struggle I am willing to accept convulsions of death, invincible dissolution, but also the possibility of the impossible.[8]

The other, however, can recognize me without struggle: "The individual, who has not staked his life, may, no doubt, be recognized as a *person*, but he has not attained the truth of this recognition as an independent self-consciousness."[9]

Historically, the Negro steeped in the inessentiality of servitude was set free by his master. He did not fight for his freedom.

Out of slavery the Negro burst into the lists where his masters stood. Like those servants who are allowed once every year to dance in the drawing room, the Negro is looking for a prop. The Negro has not become a master. When there are no longer slaves, there are no longer masters.

The Negro is a slave who has been allowed to assume the attitude of a master.

The white man is a master who has allowed his slaves to eat at his table.

One day a good white master who had influence said to his friends, "Let's be nice to the niggers. ..."

The other masters argued, for after all it was not an easy thing, but then they decided to promote the machine-animal-men to the supreme rank of *men*.

Slavery shall no longer exist on French soil.

The upheaval reached the Negroes from without. The black man was acted upon. Values that had not been created by his actions, values that had not been born of the systolic tide of his blood, danced in a hued whirl round him. The upheaval did not make a difference in the Negro. He went from one way of life to another, but not from one life to another. Just as when one tells a much improved patient that in a few days he will be discharged from the hospital, he thereupon suffers a relapse, so the announcement of the liberation of the black slaves produced psychoses and sudden deaths.

It is not an announcement that one hears twice in a lifetime. The black man contented himself with thanking the white man, and the most forceful proof of the fact is the impressive number of statues erected all over France and the colonies to show white France stroking the kinky hair of this nice Negro whose chains had just been broken.

"Say thank you to the nice man," the mother tells her little boy ... but we know that often the little boy is dying to scream some other, more resounding expression. ...

The white man, in the capacity of master,[10] said to the Negro, "From now on you are free."

But the Negro knows nothing of the cost of freedom, for he has not fought for it. From time to time he has fought for Liberty and Justice, but these were always white liberty and white justice; that is, values secreted by his masters. The former slave, who can find in his memory no trace of the struggle for liberty or of that anguish of liberty of which Kierkegaard speaks, sits unmoved before the young white man singing and dancing on the tightrope of existence.

When it does happen that the Negro looks fiercely at the white man, the white man tells him: "Brother, there is no difference between us." And yet the Negro *knows* that there is a difference. He *wants* it. He wants the white man to turn on him and shout: "Damn nigger." Then he would have that unique chance—to "show them... ."

But most often there is nothing—nothing but indifference, or a paternalistic curiosity.

The former slave needs a challenge to his humanity, he wants a conflict, a riot. But it is too late: The French Negro is doomed to bite himself and just to bite. I say "the French Negro," for the American Negro is cast in a different play. In the United States, the Negro battles and is battled. There are laws that, little by little, are invalidated under the Constitution. There are other laws that forbid certain forms of discrimination. And we can be sure that nothing is going to be given free.

There is war, there are defeats, truces, victories.

"The twelve million black voices"[11] howled against the curtain of the sky. Torn from end to end, marked with the gashes of teeth biting into the belly of interdiction, the curtain fell like a burst balloon.

On the field of battle, its four corners marked by the scores of Negroes hanged by their testicles, a monument is slowly being built that promises to be majestic.

And, at the top of this monument, I can already see a white man and a black man *hand in hand*.

For the French Negro the situation is unbearable. Unable ever to be sure whether the white man considers him consciousness in-itself-for-itself, he must forever absorb himself in uncovering resistance, opposition, challenge.

This is what emerges from some of the passages of the book that Mounier has devoted to Africa.[12] The young Negroes whom he knew there sought to maintain their alterity. Alterity of rupture, of conflict, of battle.

The self takes its place by opposing itself, Fichte said. Yes and no.

I said in my introduction that man is a *yes*. I will never stop reiterating that.

Yes to life. *Yes* to love. *Yes* to generosity.

But man is also a *no*. *No* to scorn of man. *No* to degradation of man. *No* to exploitation of man. *No* to the butchery of what is most human in man: freedom.

Man's behavior is not only reactional. And there is always resentment in a *reaction*. Nietzsche had already pointed that out in *The Will to Power*.

To educate man to be *actional*, preserving in all his relations his respect for the basic values that constitute a human world, is the prime task of him who, having taken thought, prepares to act.

NOTES

1. *Charmes* (Paris, Gallimard, 1952).
2. *Le langage et l'agressivité.*
3. By that I mean that Negroes who return to their original environments convey the impression that they have completed a cycle, that they have added to themselves something that was lacking. They return literally full of themselves.
4. Léon-G. Damas, "Hoquet," in *Pigments*, in Leopold S.-Senghor, ed., *Anthologie de la nouvelle poésie nègre et malgache* (Paris, Presses Universitaires de France, 1948), pp. 15–17.

5. Jean Lhermitte, *L'Image de notre corps* (Paris, Nouvelle Revue critique, 1939), p. 17.
6. G. W. F. Hegel, *The Phenomenology of Mind*, trans. by J. B. Baillie, 2nd rev. ed. (London, Allen & Unwin, 1949), pp. 230, 231.
7. *Ibid.*, p. 233.
8. When I began this book, I wanted to devote one section to a study of the death wish among Negroes. I believed it necessary because people are forever saying that Negroes never commit suicide.

    M. Achille did not hesitate to maintain this in a lecture, and Richard Wright, in one of his stories, has a white character say, "If I were a Negro I'd kill myself … ," in the sense that only a Negro could submit to such treatment without feeling drawn to suicide.

    Since then, M. Deshaies has taken the question of suicide as the subject of his thesis. He demonstrates that the studies by Jaensch, who contrasted the disintegrated-personality "type" (blue eyes, white skin) to the integrated-personality "type" (brown eyes and skin), are predominantly specious.

    According to Durkheim, Jews never committed suicide. Now it is the Negroes. Very well: "The Detroit municipal hospital found that 16.6% of its suicide cases were Negroes, although the proportion of Negroes in the total population is only 7.6%. In Cincinnati, the number of Negro suicides is more than double that of whites; this may result in part from the amazing sexual disparity among Negro suicides: 358 women against 76 men." (Gabriel Deshaies, *Psychologie du suicide*, note 23.)
9. Hegel, *op. cit.*, p. 233.
10. I hope I have shown that here the master differs basically from the master described by Hegel. For Hegel there is reciprocity; here the master laughs at the consciousness of the slave. What he wants from the slave is not recognition but work.

    In the same way, the slave here is in no way identifiable with the slave who loses himself in the object and finds in his work the source of his liberation.

    The Negro wants to be like the master.

    Therefore he is less independent than the Hegelian slave.

    In Hegel the slave turns away from the master and turns toward the object.

    Here the slave turns toward the master and abandons the object.
11. In English in the original. (Translator's note.)
12. Emmanuel Mounier, *L'éveil de l'Afrique noire* (Paris, Éditions du Seuil, 1948).

COMPANION WEBSITE

1. Go online to Write Out Loud about what Fanon means when he writes that speaking is to take on "the weight of a civilization."
2. Browse the *Shifting the Paradigm* Supplementary Sources for a list of films that vividly portray colonial rule, politics and struggle, including the classic *The Battle of Algiers*.
3. Also check out the Supplementary Sources to watch full episodes of *Black in Latin America*, a series that explores the impact of colonialism on racial identity in Latin America.

31

Orientalism

Edward W. Said

I

On a visit to Beirut during the terrible civil war of 1975–1976 a French journalist wrote regretfully of the gutted downtown area that "it had once seemed to belong to … the Orient of Chateaubriand and Nerval."[1] He was right about the place, of course, especially so far as a European was concerned. The Orient was almost a European invention, and had been since antiquity a place of romance, exotic beings, haunting memories and landscapes, remarkable experiences. Now it was disappearing; in a sense it had happened, its time was over. Perhaps it seemed irrelevant that Orientals themselves had something at stake in the process, that even in the time of Chateaubriand and Nerval Orientals had lived there, and that now it was they who were suffering; the main thing for the European visitor was a European representation of the Orient and its contemporary fate, both of which had a privileged communal significance for the journalist and his French readers.

Americans will not feel quite the same about the Orient, which for them is much more likely to be associated very differently with the Far East (China and Japan, mainly). Unlike the Americans, the French and the British—less so the Germans, Russians, Spanish, Portuguese, Italians, and Swiss— have had a long tradition of what I shall be calling *Orientalism*, a way of coming to terms with the Orient that is based on the Orient's special place in European Western experience. The Orient is not only adjacent to Europe; it is also the place of Europe's greatest and richest and oldest colonies, the source of its civilizations and languages, its cultural contestant, and one of its deepest and most recurring images of the Other. In addition, the Orient has helped to define Europe (or the West) as its contrasting image, idea, personality, experience. Yet none of this Orient is merely imaginative. The Orient is an integral part of European *material* civilization and culture. Orientalism expresses and represents that part culturally and even ideologically as a mode of discourse with supporting institutions, vocabulary, scholarship, imagery, doctrines, even colonial bureaucracies and colonial styles. In contrast, the American understanding of the Orient will seem considerably less dense, although our recent Japanese, Korean, and Indochinese adventures ought now to be creating a more sober, more realistic "Oriental" awareness. Moreover, the vastly expanded American political and economic role in the Near East (the Middle East) makes great claims on our understanding of that Orient.

It will be clear to the reader (and will become clearer still throughout the many pages that follow) that by Orientalism I mean several things, all of them, in my opinion, interdependent. The most readily accepted designation for Orientalism is an academic one, and indeed the label still serves in a number of academic institutions. Anyone who teaches, writes about, or researches the Orient—and this applies whether the person is an anthropologist, sociologist, historian, or philologist—either in its specific or its general aspects, is an Orientalist, and what he or she does is Orientalism. Compared with *Oriental studies* or *area studies*, it is true that the term *Orientalism* is less preferred by specialists today, both because it is too vague and general and because it connotes the high-handed executive attitude of nineteenth-century and early-twentieth-century European colonialism. Nevertheless books are written and congresses held with "the Orient" as their main focus, with the Orientalist in his new or old guise as their main authority. The point is that even if it does not survive as it once did, Orientalism lives on academically through its doctrines and theses about the Orient and the Oriental.

Related to this academic tradition, whose fortunes, transmigrations, specializations, and transmissions are in part the subject of this study, is a more general meaning for Orientalism. Orientalism is a style of thought based upon an ontological and epistemological distinction made between "the Orient" and (most of the time) "the Occident." Thus a very large mass of writers, among whom are poets, novelists, philosophers, political theorists, economists, and imperial administrators, have accepted the basic distinction between East and West as the starting point for elaborate theories, epics, novels, social descriptions, and political accounts concerning the Orient, its people, customs, "mind," destiny, and so on. *This* Orientalism can accommodate Aeschylus, say, and Victor Hugo, Dante and Karl Marx. A little later in this introduction I shall deal with the methodological problems one encounters in so broadly construed a "field" as this.

The interchange between the academic and the more or less imaginative meanings of Orientalism is a constant one, and since the late eighteenth century there has been a considerable, quite disciplined—perhaps even regulated—traffic between the two. Here I come to the third meaning of Orientalism, which is something more historically and materially defined than either of the other two. Taking the late eighteenth century as a very roughly defined starting point Orientalism can be discussed and analyzed as the corporate institution for dealing with the Orient—dealing with it by making statements about it, authorizing views of it, describing it, by teaching it, settling it, ruling over it: in short, Orientalism as a Western style for dominating, restructuring, and having authority over the Orient. I have found it useful here to employ Michel Foucault's notion of a discourse, as described by him in *The Archaeology of Knowledge* and in *Discipline and Punish*, to identify Orientalism. My contention is that without examining Orientalism as a discourse one cannot possibly understand the enormously systematic discipline by which European culture was able to manage—and even produce—the Orient politically, sociologically, militarily, ideologically, scientifically, and imaginatively during the post-Enlightenment period. Moreover, so authoritative a position did Orientalism have that I believe no one writing, thinking, or acting on the Orient could do so without taking account of the limitations on thought and action imposed by Orientalism. In brief, because of Orientalism the Orient was not (and is not) a free subject of thought or action. This is not to say that Orientalism unilaterally determines what can be said about the Orient, but that it is the whole network of interests inevitably brought to bear on (and therefore always involved in) any occasion when that peculiar entity "the Orient" is in question. How this happens is what this book tries to demonstrate. It also tries to show that European culture gained in strength and identity by setting itself off against the Orient as a sort of surrogate and even underground self.

Historically and culturally there is a quantitative as well as a qualitative difference between the Franco-British involvement in the Orient and—until the period of American ascendancy after World War

II—the involvement of every other European and Atlantic power. To speak of Orientalism therefore is to speak mainly, although not exclusively, of a British and French cultural enterprise, a project whose dimensions take in such disparate realms as the imagination itself, the whole of India and the Levant, the Biblical texts and the Biblical lands, the spice trade, colonial armies and a long tradition of colonial administrators, a formidable scholarly corpus, innumerable Oriental "experts" and "hands," an Oriental professorate, a complex array of "Oriental" ideas (Oriental despotism, Oriental splendor, cruelty, sensuality), many Eastern sects, philosophies, and wisdoms domesticated for local European use—the list can be extended more or less indefinitely. My point is that Orientalism derives from a particular closeness experienced between Britain and France and the Orient, which until the early nineteenth century had really meant only India and the Bible lands. From the beginning of the nineteenth century until the end of World War II France and Britain dominated the Orient and Orientalism; since World War II America has dominated the Orient, and approaches it as France and Britain once did. Out of that closeness, whose dynamic is enormously productive even if it always demonstrates the comparatively greater strength of the Occident (British, French, or American), comes the large body of texts I call Orientalist.

It should be said at once that even with the generous number of books and authors that I examine, there is a much larger number that I simply have had to leave out. My argument, however, depends neither upon an exhaustive catalogue of texts, dealing with the Orient nor upon a clearly delimited set of texts, authors, and ideas that together make up the Orientalist canon. I have depended instead upon a different methodological alternative—whose backbone in a sense is the set of historical generalizations I have so far been making in this Introduction—and it is these I want now to discuss in more analytical detail.

II

I have begun with the assumption that the Orient is not an inert fact of nature. It is not merely *there*, just as the Occident itself is not just *there* either. We must take seriously Vico's great observation that men make their own history, that what they can know is what they have made, and extend it to geography: as both geographical and cultural entities—to say nothing of historical entities—such locales, regions, geographical sectors as "Orient" and "Occident" are man-made. Therefore as much as the West itself, the Orient is an idea that has a history and a tradition of thought, imagery, and vocabulary that have given it reality and presence in and for the West. The two geographical entities thus support and to an extent reflect each other.

Having said that, one must go on to state a number of reasonable qualifications. In the first place, it would be wrong to conclude that the Orient was *essentially* an idea, or a creation with no corresponding reality. When Disraeli said in his novel *Tancred* that the East was a career, he meant that to be interested in the East was something bright young Westerners would find to be an all-consuming passion; he should not be interpreted as saying that the East was *only* a career for Westerners. There were—and are—cultures and nations whose location is in the East, and their lives, histories, and customs have a brute reality obviously greater than anything that could be said about them in the West. About that fact this study of Orientalism has very little to contribute, except to acknowledge it tacitly. But the phenomenon of Orientalism as I study it here deals principally, not with a correspondence between Orientalism and Orient, but with the internal consistency of Orientalism and its ideas about the Orient (the East as career) despite or beyond any correspondence, or lack thereof, with a "real" Orient. My point is that Disraeli's statement about the East refers mainly to that created consistency, that regular constellation of ideas as the pre-eminent thing about the Orient, and not to its mere being, as Wallace Stevens's phrase has it.

A second qualification is that ideas, cultures, and histories cannot seriously be understood or studied without their force, or more precisely their configurations of power, also being studied. To believe that the Orient was created—or, as I call it, "Orientalized"—and to believe that such things happen simply as a necessity of the imagination, is to be disingenuous. The relationship between Occident and Orient is a relationship of power, of domination, of varying degrees of a complex hegemony, and is quite accurately indicated in the title of K. M. Panikkar's classic *Asia and Western Dominance*.[2] The Orient was Orientalized not only because it was discovered to be "Oriental" in all those ways considered common-place by an average nineteenth-century European, but also because it *could be*—that is, submitted to being—*made* Oriental. There is very little consent to be found, for example, in the fact that Flaubert's encounter with an Egyptian courtesan produced a widely influential model of the Oriental woman; she never spoke of herself, she never represented her emotions, presence, or history. *He* spoke for and represented her. He was foreign, comparatively wealthy, male, and these were historical facts of domination that allowed him not only to possess Kuchuk Hanem physically but to speak for her and tell his readers in what way she was "typically Oriental." My argument is that Flaubert's situation of strength in relation to Kuchuk Hanem was not an isolated instance. It fairly stands for the pattern of relative strength between East and West, and the discourse about the Orient that it enabled.

This brings us to a third qualification. One ought never to assume that the structure of Orientalism is nothing more than a structure of lies or of myths which, were the truth about them to be told, would simply blow away. I myself believe that Orientalism is more particularly valuable as a sign of European-Atlantic power over the Orient than it is as a veridic discourse about the Orient (which is what, in its academic or scholarly form, it claims to be). Nevertheless, what we must respect and try to grasp is the sheer knitted-together strength of Orientalist discourse, its very close ties to the enabling socio-economic and political institutions, and its redoubtable durability. After all, any system of ideas that can remain unchanged as teachable wisdom (in academies, books, congresses, universities, foreign-service institutes) from the period of Ernest Renan in the late 1840s until the present in the United States must be something more formidable than a mere collection of lies. Orientalism, therefore, is not an airy European fantasy about the Orient, but a created body of theory and practice in which, for many generations, there has been a considerable material investment. Continued investment made Orientalism, as a system of knowledge about the Orient, an accepted grid for filtering through the Orient into Western consciousness, just as that same investment multiplied—indeed, made truly productive—the statements proliferating out from Orientalism into the general culture.

Gramsci has made the useful analytic distinction between civil and political society in which the former is made up of voluntary (or at least rational and noncoercive) affiliations like schools, families, and unions, the latter of state institutions (the army, the police, the central bureaucracy) whose role in the polity is direct domination. Culture, of course, is to be found operating within civil society, where the influence of ideas, of institutions, and of other persons works not through domination but by what Gramsci calls consent. In any society not totalitarian, then, certain cultural forms predominate over others, just as certain ideas are more influential than others; the form of this cultural leadership is what Gramsci has identified as *hegemony*, an indispensable concept for any understanding of cultural life in the industrial West. It is hegemony, or rather the result of cultural hegemony at work, that gives Orientalism the durability and the strength I have been speaking about so far. Orientalism is never far from what Denys Hay has called the idea of Europe,[3] a collective notion identifying "us" Europeans as against all "those" non-Europeans, and indeed it can be argued that the major component in European culture is precisely what made that culture hegemonic both in and outside Europe: the idea of European identity as a superior one in comparison with all the non-European peoples and cultures. There is in addition the hegemony of European ideas about the Orient, themselves reiterating European superiority over Oriental backwardness, usually overriding the possibility that a more independent, or more skeptical, thinker might have had different views on the matter.

In a quite constant way, Orientalism depends for its strategy on this flexible *positional* superiority, which puts the Westerner in a whole series of possible relationships with the Orient without ever losing him the relative upper hand. And why should it have been otherwise, especially during the period of extraordinary European ascendancy from the late Renaissance to the present? The scientist, the scholar, the missionary, the trader, or the soldier was in, or thought about, the Orient because he *could be there*, or could think about it, with very little resistance on the Orient's part. Under the general heading of knowledge of the Orient, and within the umbrella of Western hegemony over the Orient during the period from the end of the eighteenth century, there emerged a complex Orient suitable for study in the academy, for display in the museum, for reconstruction in the colonial office, for theoretical illustration in anthropological, biological, linguistic, racial, and historical theses about mankind and the universe, for instances of economic and sociological theories of development, revolution, cultural personality, national or religious character. Additionally, the imaginative examination of things Oriental was based more or less exclusively upon a sovereign Western consciousness out of whose unchallenged centrality an Oriental world emerged, first according to

general ideas about who or what was an Oriental, then according to a detailed logic governed not simply by empirical reality but by a battery of desires, repressions, investments, and projections. If we can point to great Orientalist works of genuine scholarship like Silvestre de Sacy's *Chrestomathie arabe* or Edward William Lane's *Account of the Manners and Customs of the Modern Egyptians*, we need also to note that Renan's and Gobineau's racial ideas came out of the same impulse, as did a great many Victorian pornographic novels (see the analysis by Steven Marcus of "The Lustful Turk"[4]).

And yet, one must repeatedly ask oneself whether what matters in Orientalism is the general group of ideas overriding the mass of material—about which who could deny that they were shot through with doctrines of European superiority, various kinds of racism, imperialism, and the like, dogmatic views of "the Oriental" as a kind of ideal and unchanging abstraction?—or the much more varied work produced by almost uncountable individual writers, whom one would take up as individual instances of authors dealing with the Orient. In a sense the two alternatives, general and particular, are really two perspectives on the same material: in both instances one would have to deal with pioneers in the field like William Jones, with great artists like Nerval or Flaubert. And why would it not be possible to employ both perspectives together, or one after the other? Isn't there an obvious danger of distortion (of precisely the kind that academic Orientalism has always been prone to) if either too general or too specific a level of description is maintained systematically?

My two fears are distortion and inaccuracy, or rather the kind of inaccuracy produced by too dogmatic a generality and too positivistic a localized focus. In trying to deal with these problems I have tried to deal with three main aspects of my own contemporary reality that seem to me to point the way out of the methodological or perspectival difficulties I have been discussing, difficulties that might force one, in the first instance, into writing a coarse polemic on so unacceptably general a level of description as not to be worth the effort, or in the second instance, into writing so detailed and atomistic a series of analyses as to lose all track of the general lines of force informing the field, giving it its special cogency. How then to recognize individuality and to reconcile it with its intelligent, and by no means passive or merely dictatorial, general and hegemonic context?

IMAGINATIVE GEOGRAPHY AND ITS REPRESENTATIONS

Orientalizing the Oriental. Strictly speaking, Orientalism is a field of learned study. In the Christian West, Orientalism is considered to have commenced its formal existence with the decision of the Church Council of Vienne in 1312 to establish a series of chairs in "Arabic, Greek, Hebrew, and Syriac at Paris, Oxford, Bologna, Avignon, and Salamanca."[5] Yet any account of Orientalism would have to consider not only the professional Orientalist and his work but also the very notion of a field of study based on a geographical, cultural, linguistic, and ethnic unit called the Orient. Fields, of course, are made. They acquire coherence and integrity in time because scholars devote themselves in different ways to what seems to be a commonly agreed-upon subject matter. Yet it goes without saying that a field of study is rarely as simply defined as even its most committed partisans—usually scholars, professors, experts, and the like—claim it is. Besides, a field can change so entirely, in even the most traditional disciplines like philology, history, or theology, as to make an all-purpose definition of subject matter almost impossible. This is certainly true of Orientalism, for some interesting reasons.

To speak of scholarly specialization as a geographical "field" is, in the case of Orientalism, fairly revealing since no one is likely to imagine a field

symmetrical to it called Occidentalism. Already the special, perhaps even eccentric attitude of Orientalism becomes apparent. For although many learned disciplines imply a position taken towards, say, *human* material (a historian deals with the human past from a special vantage point in the present), there is no real analogy for taking a fixed, more or less total geographical position towards a wide variety of social, linguistic, political, and historical realities. A classicist, a Romance specialist, even an Americanist focuses on a relatively modest portion of the world, not on a full half of it. But Orientalism is a field with considerable geographical ambition. And since Orientalists have traditionally occupied themselves with things Oriental (a specialist in Islamic law, no less than an expert in Chinese dialects or in Indian religions, is considered an Orientalist by people who call themselves Orientalists), we must learn to accept enormous, indiscriminate size plus an almost infinite capacity for subdivision as one of the chief characteristics of Orientalism—one that is evidenced in its confusing amalgam of imperial vagueness and precise detail.

All of this describes Orientalism as an academic discipline. The "ism" in Orientalism serves to insist on the distinction of this discipline from every other kind. The rule in its historical development as an academic discipline has been its increasing scope, not its greater selectiveness.

[...]

Such eclecticism as this had its blind spots, nevertheless. Academic Orientalists for the most part were interested in the classical period of whatever language or society it was that they studied. Not until quite late in the century, with the single major exception of Napoleon's Institut d'Égypte, was much attention given to the academic study of the modern, or actual, Orient. Moreover, the Orient studied was a textual universe by and large; the impact of the Orient was made through books and manuscripts, not, as in the impress of Greece on the Renaissance, through mimetic artifacts like sculpture and pottery. Even the rapport between an Orientalist and the Orient was textual, so much so that it is reported of some of the early-nineteenth-century German Orientalists that their first view of an eight-armed Indian statue cured them completely of their Orientalist taste.[6] When a learned Orientalist traveled in the country of his specialization, it was always with unshakable abstract maxims about the "civilization" he had studied; rarely were Orientalists interested in anything except proving the validity of these musty "truths" by applying them, without great success, to uncomprehending, hence degenerate, natives. Finally, the very power and scope of Orientalism produced not only a fair amount of exact positive knowledge about the Orient but also a kind of second-order knowledge—lurking in such places as the "Oriental" tale, the mythology of the mysterious East, notions of Asian inscrutability—with a life of its own, what V. G. Kiernan has aptly called "Europe's collective day-dream of the Orient."[7] One happy result of this is that an estimable number of important writers during the nineteenth century were Oriental enthusiasts: It is perfectly correct, I think, to speak of a genre of Orientalist writing as exemplified in the works of Hugo, Goethe, Nerval, Flaubert, Fitzgerald, and the like. What inevitably goes with such work, however, is a kind of free-floating mythology of the Orient, an Orient that derives not only from contemporary attitudes and popular prejudices but also from what Vico called the conceit of nations and of scholars. I have already alluded to the political uses of such material as it has turned up in the twentieth century.

Today an Orientalist is less likely to call himself an Orientalist than he was almost any time up to World War II. Yet the designation is still useful, as when universities maintain programs or departments in Oriental languages or Oriental civilizations. There is an Oriental "faculty" at Oxford, and a department of Oriental studies at Princeton. As recently as 1959, the British government empow-ered a commission "to review developments in the Universities in the fields of Oriental, Slavonic, East European and African studies ... and to consider, and advise on, proposals for future development."[8] The Hayter Report, as it was called when it appeared in 1961, seemed untroubled by the broad designation of the word *Oriental*, which it found serviceably employed in American universities as well. For even the greatest name in modern Anglo-American Islamic studies, H. A. R. Gibb, preferred to call himself an Orientalist rather than an Arabist. Gibb himself, classicist that he was, could use the ugly neologism "area study" for Orientalism as a way of showing that area studies and Orientalism after all were interchangeable geographical titles.[9] But this, I think, ingenuously belies a much more interesting relationship between knowledge and geography. I should like to consider that relationship briefly.

Despite the distraction of a great many vague desires, impulses, and images, the mind seems persistently to formulate what Claude Lévi-Strauss has called a science of the concrete.[10] A primitive tribe, for example, assigns a definite place, function, and significance to every leafy species in its immediate environment. Many of these grasses and flowers have no practical use; but the point Lévi-Strauss makes is that mind requires order, and order is achieved by discriminating and taking note of everything, placing everything of which the mind is aware in a secure, refindable place, therefore giving things some role to play in the economy of objects and identities that make up an environment. This kind of rudimentary classification has a logic to it, but the rules of the logic by which a green fern in one society is a symbol of grace and in another is considered maleficent are neither predictably rational nor universal. There is always a measure of the purely arbitrary in the way the distinctions between things are seen. And with these distinctions go values whose history, if one could unearth it completely, would probably show the same measure of arbitrariness. This is evident enough in the case of fashion. Why do wigs, lace collars, and high buckled shoes appear, then disappear, over a period of decades? Some of the answer has to do with utility and some with the inherent beauty of the fashion. But if we agree that all things in history, like history itself, are made by men, then we will appreciate how possible it is for many objects or places or times to be assigned roles and given meanings that acquire objective validity only *after* the assignments are made. This is especially true of relatively uncommon things, like foreigners, mutants, or "abnormal" behavior.

It is perfectly possible to argue that some distinctive objects are made by the mind, and that these objects, while appearing to exist objectively, have only a fictional reality. A group of people living on a few acres of land will set up boundaries between their land and its immediate surroundings and the territory beyond, which they call "the land of the barbarians." In other words, this universal practice of designating in one's mind a familiar space which is "ours" and an unfamiliar space beyond "ours" which is "theirs" is a way of making geographical distinctions that *can be* entirely arbitrary. I use the word "arbitrary" here because imaginative geography of the "our land–barbarian land" variety does not require that the barbarians acknowledge the distinction. It is enough for "us" to set up these boundaries in our own minds; "they" become "they" accordingly, and both their territory and their mentality are designated as different from "ours." To a certain extent modern and primitive societies seem thus to derive a sense of their identities negatively. A fifth-century Athenian was very likely to feel himself to be nonbarbarian as much as he positively felt himself to be Athenian. The geographic boundaries accompany the social, ethnic, and cultural ones in expected ways. Yet often the sense in which someone feels himself to be not-foreign is based on a very unrigorous idea of what is "out there," beyond one's own territory. All kinds of suppositions, associations, and fictions appear to crowd the unfamiliar space outside one's own.

The French philosopher Gaston Bachelard once wrote an analysis of what he called the poetics of space.[11] The inside of a house, he said, acquires a sense of intimacy, secrecy, security, real or imagined, because of the experiences that come to seem appropriate for it. The objective space of a house—its corners, corridors, cellar, rooms—is far less important than what poetically it is endowed with, which is usually a quality with an imaginative or figurative value we can name and feel: thus a house may be haunted, or homelike, or prisonlike, or magical. So space acquires emotional and even rational sense by a kind of poetic process, whereby the vacant or anonymous reaches of distance are converted into meaning for us here. The same process occurs when we deal with time. Much of what we associate with or even know about such periods as "long ago" or "the beginning" or "at the end of time" is poetic— made up. For a historian of Middle Kingdom Egypt, "long ago" will have a very clear sort of meaning, but even this meaning does not totally dissipate the imaginative, quasi-fictional quality one senses lurking in a time very different and distant from our own. For there is no doubt that imaginative geography and history help the mind to intensify its own sense of itself by dramatizing the distance and difference between what is close to it and what is far away. This is no less true of the feelings we often have that we would have been more "at home" in the sixteenth century or in Tahiti.

Yet there is no use in pretending that all we know about time and space, or rather history and geography, is more than anything else imaginative. There are such things as positive history and positive geography which in Europe and the United States have impressive achievements to point to. Scholars now do know more about the world, its past and present, than they did, for example, in Gibbon's time. Yet this is not to say that they know all there is to know, nor, more important, is it to say that what they know has effectively dispelled the imaginative geographical and historical knowledge I have been considering. We need not decide here whether this kind of imaginative knowledge infuses history and geography, or whether in some way it overrides them. Let us just say for the time being that it is there as something *more* than what appears to be merely positive knowledge.

Almost from earliest times in Europe the Orient was something more than what was empirically known about it. At least until the early eighteenth century, as R. W. Southern has so elegantly shown, European understanding of one kind of Oriental culture, the Islamic, was ignorant but complex.[12] For certain associations with the East—not quite ignorant, not quite informed—always seem to have gathered around the notion of an Orient. Consider first the demarcation between Orient and West. It already seems bold by the time of the *Iliad*. Two of the most profoundly influential qualities associated with the East appear in Aeschylus' *The Persians*, the earliest Athenian play extant, and in *The Bacchae* of Euripides, the very last one extant. Aeschylus portrays the sense of disaster overcoming the Persians when they learn that their armies, led by King Xerxes, have been destroyed by the Greeks. The chorus sings the following ode:

> Now all Asia's land
> Moans in emptiness.
> Xerxes led forth, oh oh!
> Xerxes destroyed, woe woe!
> Xerxes' plans have all miscarried
> In ships of the sea.
> Why did Darius then
> Bring no harm to his men
> When he led them into battle,
> That beloved leader of men from Susa?[13]

What matters here is that Asia speaks through and by virtue of the European imagination, which is depicted as victorious over Asia, that hostile "other" world beyond the seas. To Asia are given the feelings of emptiness, loss, and disaster that seem thereafter to reward Oriental challenges to the West; and also, the lament that in some glorious past Asia fared better, was itself victorious over Europe.

In *The Bacchae*, perhaps the most Asiatic of all the Attic dramas, Dionysus is explicitly connected with his Asian origins and with the strangely threatening excesses of Oriental mysteries. Pentheus, king of Thebes, is destroyed by his mother, Agave, and her fellow bacchantes. Having defied Dionysus by not recognizing either his power or his divinity, Pentheus is thus horribly punished, and the play ends with a general recognition of the eccentric god's terrible power. Modern commentators on *The Bacchae* have not failed to note the play's extraordinary range of intellectual and aesthetic effects; but there has been no escaping the additional historical detail that Euripides "was surely affected by the new aspect that the Dionysiac cults must have assumed in the light of the foreign ecstatic religions of Bendis, Cybele, Sabazius, Adonis, and Isis, which were introduced from Asia Minor and the Levant and swept through Piraeus and Athens during the frustrating and increasingly irrational years of the Peloponnesian War."[14]

The two aspects of the Orient that set it off from the West in this pair of plays will remain essential motifs of European imaginative geography. A line is drawn between two continents. Europe is powerful and articulate; Asia is defeated and distant. Aeschylus *represents* Asia, makes her speak in the person of the aged Persian queen, Xerxes' mother. It is Europe that articulates the Orient; this articulation is the prerogative, not of a puppet master, but of a genuine creator, whose life-giving power represents, animates, constitutes the otherwise silent and dangerous space beyond familiar boundaries. There is an analogy between Aeschylus's orchestra, which contains the Asiatic world as the playwright conceives it, and the learned envelope of Orientalist scholarship, which also will hold in the vast, amorphous Asiatic sprawl for sometimes sympathetic but always dominating scrutiny. Secondly, there is the motif of the Orient as insinuating danger. Rationality is undermined by Eastern excesses, those mysteriously attractive opposites to what seem to be normal values. The difference separating East from West is symbolized by the sternness with which, at first, Pentheus rejects the hysterical bacchantes. When later he himself becomes a bacchant, he is destroyed not so much for having given in to Dionysus as for having incorrectly assessed Dionysus's menace in the first place. The lesson that Euripides intends is dramatized by the presence in the play of Cadmus and Tiresias, knowledgeable older men who realize that "sovereignty" alone does not rule men;[15] there is such a thing as judgment, they say, which means sizing up correctly the force of alien powers and expertly coming to terms with them. Hereafter Oriental mysteries will be taken seriously, not least because they challenge the rational Western mind to new exercises of its enduring ambition and power.

But one big division, as between West and Orient, leads to other smaller ones, especially as the normal enterprises of civilization provoke such outgoing activities as travel, conquest, new experiences. In classical Greece and Rome geographers, historians, public figures like Caesar, orators, and poets added to the fund of taxonomic lore separating races, regions, nations, and minds from each other; much of that was self-serving, and existed to prove that Romans and Greeks were superior to other kinds of people. But concern with the Orient had its own tradition of classification and hierarchy. From at least the second century BC on, it was lost on no traveler or eastward-looking and ambitious Western potentate that Herodotus—historian, traveler, inexhaustibly curious chronicler—and Alexander—king warrior, scientific conqueror—had been in the Orient before. The Orient was therefore subdivided into realms previously known, visited, conquered, by Herodotus and Alexander as well as their epigones, and those realms not previously known, visited, conquered. Christianity completed the setting up of main intra-Oriental spheres: there was a Near Orient and a Far Orient, a familiar Orient, which René Grousset calls "L'empire du Levant,"[16] and a

novel Orient. The Orient therefore alternated in the mind's geography between being an Old World to which one returned, as to Eden or Paradise, there to set up a new version of the old, and being a wholly new place to which one came as Columbus came to America, in order to set up a New World (although, ironically, Columbus himself thought that he discovered a new part of the Old World). Certainly neither of these Orients was purely one thing or the other: it is their vacillations, their tempting suggestiveness, their capacity for entertaining and confusing the mind, that are interesting.

Consider how the Orient, and in particular the Near Orient, became known in the West as its great complementary opposite since antiquity. There were the Bible and the rise of Christianity; there were travelers like Marco Polo who charted the trade routes and patterned a regulated system of commercial exchange, and after him Lodovico di Varthema and Pietro della Valle; there were fabulists like Mandeville; there were the redoubtable conquering Eastern movements, principally Islam, of course; there were the militant pilgrims, chiefly the Crusaders. Altogether an internally structured archive is built up from the literature that belongs to these experiences. Out of this comes a restricted number of typical encapsulations: the journey, the history, the fable, the stereotype, the polemical confrontation. These are the lenses through which the Orient is experienced, and they shape the language, perception, and form of the encounter between East and West. What gives the immense number of encounters some unity, however, is the vacillation I was speaking about earlier. Something patently foreign and distant acquires, for one reason or another, a status more rather than less familiar. One tends to stop judging things either as completely novel or as completely well known; a new median category emerges, a category that allows one to see new things, things seen for the first time, as versions of a previously known thing. In essence such a category is not so much a way of receiving new information as it is a method of controlling what seems to be a threat to some established view of things. If the mind must suddenly deal with what it takes to be a radically new form of life—as Islam appeared to Europe in the early Middle Ages—the response on the whole is conservative and defensive. Islam is judged to be a fraudulent new version of some previous experience, in this case Christianity. The threat is muted, familiar values impose themselves, and in the end the mind reduces the pressure upon it by accommodating things to itself as either "original" or "repetitious." Islam thereafter is "handled": its novelty and its suggestiveness are brought under control so that relatively nuanced discriminations are now made that would have been impossible had the raw novelty of Islam been left unattended. The Orient at large, therefore, vacillates between the West's contempt for what is familiar and its shivers of delight in—or fear of—novelty.

Yet where Islam was concerned, European fear, if not always respect, was in order. After Mohammed's death in 632, the military and later the cultural and religious hegemony of Islam grew enormously. First Persia, Syria, and Egypt, then Turkey, then North Africa fell to the Muslim armies; in the eighth and ninth centuries Spain, Sicily, and parts of France were conquered. By the thirteenth and fourteenth centuries Islam ruled as far east as India, Indonesia, and China. And to this extraordinary assault Europe could respond with very little except fear and a kind of awe. Christian authors witnessing the Islamic conquests had scant interest in the learning, high culture, and frequent magnificence of the Muslims, who were, as Gibbon said, "coeval with the darkest and most slothful period of European annals." (But with some satisfaction he added, "since the sum of science has risen in the West, it should seem that the Oriental studies have languished and declined."[17]) What Christians typically felt about the Eastern armies was that they had "all the appearance of a swarm of bees, but with a heavy hand ... they

devastated everything": so wrote Erchembert, a cleric in Monte Cassino in the eleventh century.[18]

Not for nothing did Islam come to symbolize terror, devastation, the demonic, hordes of hated barbarians. For Europe, Islam was a lasting trauma. Until the end of the seventeenth century the "Ottoman peril" lurked alongside Europe to represent for the whole of Christian civilization a constant danger, and in time European civilization incorporated that peril and its lore, its great events, figures, virtues, and vices, as something woven into the fabric of life. In Renaissance England alone, as Samuel Chew recounts in his classic study *The Crescent and the Rose*, "a man of average education and intelligence" had at his fingertips, and could watch on the London stage, a relatively large number of detailed events in the history of Ottoman Islam and its encroachments upon Christian Europe.[19] The point is that what remained current about Islam was some necessarily diminished version of those great dangerous forces that it symbolized for Europe. Like Walter Scott's Saracens, the European representation of the Muslim, Ottoman, or Arab was always a way of controlling the redoubtable Orient, and to a certain extent the same is true of the methods of contemporary learned Orientalists, whose subject is not so much the East itself as the East made known, and therefore less fearsome, to the Western reading public.

There is nothing especially controversial or reprehensible about such domestications of the exotic; they take place between all cultures, certainly, and between all men. My point, however, is to emphasize the truth that the Orientalist, as much as anyone in the European West who thought about or experienced the Orient, performed this kind of mental operation. But what is more important still is the limited vocabulary and imagery that impose themselves as a consequence. The reception of Islam in the West is a perfect case in point, and has been admirably studied by Norman Daniel. One constraint acting upon Christian thinkers who tried to understand Islam was an analogical one; since Christ is the basis of Christian faith, it was assumed—quite incorrectly—that Mohammed was to Islam as Christ was to Christianity. Hence the polemic name "Mohammedanism" given to Islam, and the automatic epithet "imposter" applied to Mohammed.[20] Out of such and many other misconceptions "there formed a circle which was never broken by imaginative exteriorisation. ... The Christian concept of Islam was integral and self-sufficient."[21] Islam became an image—the word is Daniel's but it seems to me to have remarkable implications for Orientalism in general—whose function was not so much to represent Islam in itself as to represent it for the medieval Christian.

> The invariable tendency to neglect what the Qur'an meant, or what Muslims thought it meant, or what Muslims thought or did in any given circumstances, necessarily implies that Qur'anic and other Islamic doctrine was presented in a form that would convince Christians; and more and more extravagant forms would stand a chance of acceptance as the distance of the writers and public from the Islamic border increased. It was with very great reluctance that what Muslims said Muslims believed was accepted as what they did believe. There was a Christian picture in which the details (even under the pressure of facts) were abandoned as little as possible, and in which the general outline was never abandoned. There were shades of difference, but only with a common framework. All the corrections that were made in the interests of an increasing accuracy were only a defence of what had newly been realised to be vulnerable, a shoring up of a weakened structure. Christian opinion was an erection which could not be demolished, even to be rebuilt.[22]

This rigorous Christian picture of Islam was intensified in innumerable ways, including—during the Middle Ages and early Renaissance—a large variety of poetry, learned controversy, and popular superstition.[23] By this time the Near Orient had been all but incorporated in the common world-picture of Latin Christianity—as in the *Chanson de Roland* the worship of Saracens is portrayed as embracing Mahomet *and* Apollo. By the middle of the fifteenth century, as R. W. Southern has brilliantly shown, it became apparent to serious European thinkers "that something would have to be done about Islam," which had turned the situation around somewhat by itself arriving militarily in Eastern Europe. Southern recounts a dramatic episode between 1450 and 1460 when four learned men, John of Segovia, Nicholas of Cusa, Jean Germain, and Aeneas Silvius (Pius II), attempted to deal with Islam through *contraferentia*, or "conference." The idea was John of Segovia's: it was to have been a staged conference with Islam in which Christians attempted the wholesale conversion of Muslims. "He saw the conference as an instrument with a political as well as a strictly religious function, and in words which will strike a chord in modern breasts he exclaimed that even if it were to last ten years it would be less expensive and less damaging than war." There was no agreement between the four men, but the episode is crucial for having been a fairly sophisticated attempt—part of a general European attempt from Bede to Luther—to put a representative Orient in front of Europe, to *stage* the Orient and Europe together in some coherent way, the idea being for Christians to make it clear to Muslims that Islam was just a misguided version of Christianity. Southern's conclusion follows:

> Most conspicuous to us is the inability of any of these systems of thought [European Christian] to provide a fully satisfying explanation of the phenomenon they had set out to explain [Islam]—still less to influence the course of practical events in a decisive way. At a practical level, events never turned out either so well or so ill as the most intelligent observers predicted; and it is perhaps worth noticing that they never turned out better than when the best judges confidently expected a happy ending. Was there any progress [in Christian knowledge of Islam]? I must express my conviction

that there was. Even if the solution of the problem remained obstinately hidden from sight, the statement of the problem became more complex, more rational, and more related to experience. ... The scholars who labored at the problem of Islam in the Middle Ages failed to find the solution they sought and desired; but they developed habits of mind and powers of comprehension which, in other men and in other fields, may yet deserve success.[24]

The best part of Southern's analysis, here and elsewhere in his brief history of Western views of Islam, is his demonstration that it is finally Western ignorance which becomes more refined and complex, not some body of positive Western knowledge which increases in size and accuracy. For fictions have their own logic and their own dialectic of growth or decline. Onto the character of Mohammed in the Middle Ages was heaped a bundle of attributes that corresponded to the "character of the [twelfth-century] prophets of the 'Free Spirit' who did actually arise in Europe, and claim credence and collect followers." Similarly, since Mohammed was viewed as the disseminator of a false Revelation, he became as well the epitome of lechery, debauchery, sodomy, and a whole battery of assorted treacheries, all of which derived "logically" from his doctrinal impostures.[25] Thus the Orient acquired representatives, so to speak, and representations, each one more concrete, more internally congruent with some Western exigency, than the ones that preceded it. It is as if, having once settled on the Orient as a locale suitable for incarnating the infinite in a finite shape, Europe could not stop the practice; the Orient and the Oriental, Arab, Islamic, Indian, Chinese, or whatever, become repetitious pseudo-incarnations of some great original (Christ, Europe, the West) they were supposed to have been imitating. Only the source of these rather narcissistic Western ideas about the Orient changed in time, not their character. Thus we will find it commonly believed in the twelfth and thirteenth centuries that Arabia was "on the fringe of the Christian world,

a natural asylum for heretical outlaws,"[26] and that Mohammed was a cunning apostate, whereas in the twentieth century an Orientalist scholar, an erudite specialist, will be the one to point out how Islam is really no more than second-order Arian heresy.[27]

Our initial description of Orientalism as a learned field now acquires a new concreteness. A field is often an enclosed space. The idea of representation is a theatrical one: the Orient is the stage on which the whole East is confined. On this stage will appear figures whose role it is to represent the larger whole from which they emanate. The Orient then seems to be, not an unlimited extension beyond the familiar European world, but rather a closed field, a theatrical stage affixed to Europe. An Orientalist is but the particular specialist in knowledge for which Europe at large is responsible, in the way that an audience is historically and culturally responsible for (and responsive to) dramas technically put together by the dramatist. In the depths of this Oriental stage stands a prodigious cultural repertoire whose individual items evoke a fabulously rich world: the Sphinx, Cleopatra, Eden, Troy, Sodom and Gomorrah, Astarte, Isis and Osiris, Sheba, Babylon, the Genii, the Magi, Nineveh, Prester John, Mahomet, and dozens more; settings, in some cases names only, half-imagined, half-known; monsters, devils, heroes; terrors, pleasures, desires.

[...]

This whole didactic process is neither difficult to understand nor difficult to explain. One ought again to remember that all cultures impose corrections upon raw reality, changing it from free-floating objects into units of knowledge. The problem is not that conversion takes place. It is perfectly natural for the human mind to resist the assault on it of untreated strangeness; therefore cultures have always been inclined to impose complete transformations on other cultures, receiving these other cultures not as they are but as, for the benefit of the receiver, they ought to be. To the Westerner, however, the Oriental was always *like* some aspect of the West; to some of the German Romantics, for example, Indian religion was essentially an Oriental version of Germano-Christian pantheism. Yet the Orientalist makes it his work to be always converting the Orient from something into something else: he does this for himself, for the sake of his culture, in some cases for what he believes is the sake of the Oriental. This process of conversion is a disciplined one: it is taught, it has its own societies, periodicals, traditions, vocabulary, rhetoric, all in basic ways connected to and supplied by the prevailing cultural and political norms of the West. And, as I shall demonstrate, it tends to become more rather than less total in what it tries to do, so much so that as one surveys Orientalism in the nineteenth and twentieth centuries the overriding impression is of Orientalism's insensitive schematization of the entire Orient.

[...]

Imaginative geography, from the vivid portraits to be found in the *Inferno* to the prosaic niches of d'Herbelot's *Bibliothèque orientale*, legitimates a vocabulary, a universe of representative discourse peculiar to the discussion and understanding of Islam and of the Orient. What this discourse considers to be a fact—that Mohammed is an imposter, for example—is a component of the discourse, a statement the discourse compels one to make whenever the name Mohammed occurs. Underlying all the different units of Orientalist discourse—by which I mean simply the vocabulary employed whenever the Orient is spoken or written about—is a set of representative figures, or tropes. These figures are to the actual Orient—or Islam, which is my main concern here—as stylized costumes are to characters in a play; they are like, for example, the cross that Everyman will carry, or the particolored costume worn by Harlequin in a *commedia dell'arte* play. In other words, we need not look for correspondence between the language used to depict the Orient and the Orient itself, not so much because the language is inaccurate but because it is not even trying to be accurate. What it is trying to do, as Dante tried to do in the *Inferno*, is at one and the same time to characterize the Orient as alien and to incorporate it schematically on a theatrical stage whose audience, manager, and actors are *for* Europe, and only for Europe. Hence the vacillation between the familiar and the alien; Mohammed is always the imposter (familiar, because he pretends to be like the Jesus we know) and always the Oriental (alien, because although he is in some ways "like" Jesus, he is after all not like him).

Rather than listing all the figures of speech associated with the Orient—its strangeness, its difference, its exotic sensuousness, and so forth—we can generalize about them as they were handed down through the Renaissance. They are all declarative and self-evident; the tense they employ is the timeless eternal; they convey an impression of repetition and strength; they are always symmetrical to, and yet diametrically inferior to, a European equivalent, which is sometimes specified, sometimes not. For all these functions it is frequently enough to use the simple copula *is*. Thus, Mohammed *is* an imposter, the very phrase canonized in d'Herbelot's *Bibliothèque* and dramatized in a sense by Dante. No background need be given; the evidence necessary to convict Mohammed is contained in the "is." One does not qualify the phrase, neither does it seem necessary to say that Mohammed *was* an imposter, nor need one consider for a moment that it may not be necessary to repeat the statement. It *is* repeated, he *is* an imposter, and each time one says it, he becomes more of an imposter and the author of the statement gains a little more authority in having declared it. Thus Humphrey Prideaux's famous seventeenth-century biography of Mohammed is subtitled *The True Nature of Imposture*. Finally, of course, such categories as imposter (or Oriental, for that matter) imply, indeed require, an opposite that is neither fraudulently something else nor endlessly in need of explicit identification. And that opposite is "Occidental," or in Mohammed's case, Jesus.

Philosophically, then, the kind of language, thought, and vision that I have been calling Orientalism very generally is a form of radical realism; anyone employing Orientalism, which is the habit for dealing with questions, objects, qualities, and regions deemed Oriental, will designate, name, point to, fix what he is talking or thinking about with a word or phrase, which then is considered either to have acquired, or more simply to be, reality. Rhetorically speaking, Orientalism is absolutely anatomical and enumerative: to use its vocabulary is to engage in the particularizing and dividing of things Oriental into manageable parts. Psychologically, Orientalism is a form of paranoia, knowledge of another kind, say, from ordinary historical knowledge. These are a few of the results, I think, of imaginative geography and of the dramatic boundaries it draws. There are some specifically modern transmutations of these Orientalized results, however, to which I must now turn.

NOTES

1. Thierry Desjardins, *Le Martyre du Liban* (Paris: Plon, 1976), p. 14.
2. K. M. Panikkar, *Asia and Western Dominance* (London: George Allen & Unwin, 1959).
3. Denys Hay, *Europe: The Emergence of an Idea*, 2nd ed. (Edinburgh: Edinburgh University Press, 1968).
4. Steven Marcus, *The Other Victorians: A Study of Sexuality and Pornography in Mid-Nineteenth Century England* (1966; reprint ed., New York: Bantam Books, 1967), pp. 200–19.
5. R. W. Southern, *Western Views of Islam in the Middle Ages* (Cambridge, Mass.: Harvard University Press, 1962), p. 72. See also Francis Dvornik, *The Ecumenical Councils* (New York: Hawthorn Books, 1961), pp. 65–6: "Of special interest is the eleventh canon directing that chairs for teaching Hebrew, Greek, Arabic and Chaldean should be created at the main universities.

The suggestion was Raymond Lull's, who advocated learning Arabic as the best means for the conversion of the Arabs. Although the canon remained almost without effect as there were few teachers of Oriental languages, its acceptance indicates the growth of the missionary idea in the West. Gregory X had already hoped for the conversion of the Mongols, and Franciscan friars had penetrated into the depths of Asia in their missionary zeal. Although these hopes were not fulfilled, the missionary spirit continued to develop." See also Johann W. Fück, *Die Arabischen Studien in Europa bis in den Anfang des 20. Jahrhunderts* (Leipzig: Otto Harrassowitz, 1955).
6. See René Gérard, *L'Orient et la pensée romantique allemande* (Paris: Didier, 1963), p. 112.
7. Kiernan, *Lords of Human Kind*, p. 131.
8. University Grants Committee, *Report of the Sub-Committee on Oriental, Slavonic, East European and African Studies* (London: Her Majesty's Stationery Office, 1961).
9. H. A. R. Gibb, *Area Studies Reconsidered* (London: School of Oriental and African Studies, 1964).
10. See Claude Lévi-Strauss, *The Savage Mind* (Chicago: University of Chicago Press, 1967), chaps. 1–7.
11. Gaston Bachelard, *The Poetics of Space*, trans. Maria Jolas (New York: Orion Press, 1964).
12. Southern, *Western Views of Islam*, p. 14.
13. Aeschylus, *The Persians*, trans. Anthony J. Podleck (Englewood Cliffs, N. J.: Prentice-Hall, 1970), pp. 73–4.
14. Euripides, *The Bacchae*, trans. Geoffrey S. Kirk (Englewood Cliffs, N. J.: Prentice-Hall, 1970), p. 3. For further discussion of the Europe-Orient distinction see Santo Mazzarino, *Fra oriente e occidente: Ricerche di storia greca arcaica* (Florence: La Nuova Italia, 1947), and Denys Hay, *Europe: The Emergence of an Idea* (Edinburgh: Edinburgh University Press, 1968).
15. Euripides, *Bacchae*, p. 52.
16. René Grousset, *L'Empire du Levant: Histoire de la question d'Orient* (Paris: Payot, 1946).
17. Edward Gibbon, *The History of the Decline and Fall of the Roman Empire* (Boston: Little, Brown & Co., 1855), 6: 399.
18. Norman Daniel, *The Arabs and Medieval Europe* (London: Longmans, Green & Co., 1975), p. 56.
19. Samuel C. Chew, *The Crescent and the Rose: Islam and England During the Renaissance* (New York: Oxford University Press, 1937), p. 103.
20. Norman Daniel, *Islam and the West: The Making of an Image* (Edinburgh: University Press, 1960), p. 33.

See also James Kritzeck, *Peter the Venerable and Islam* (Princeton, N. J.: Princeton University Press, 1964).

21. Daniel, *Islam and the West*, p. 252.
22. Ibid., pp. 259–60.
23. See for example William Wistar Comfort, "The Literary Rôle of the Saracens in the French Epic," *PMLA* 55 (1940): 628–59.
24. Southern, *Western Views of Islam*, pp. 91–2, 108–9.
25. Daniel, *Islam and the West*, pp. 246, 96, and passim.
26. Ibid., p. 84.
27. Duncan Black Macdonald, "Whither Islam?" *Muslim World* 23 (January 1933): 2.

COMPANION WEBSITE

1. Go online to Write Out Loud about imaginative geographies and what Said means when he writes that the Orient is constantly converted "from something into something else."
2. Check out the *Shifting the Paradigm* Supplementary Sources for great companion materials to Said's *Orientalism*, including Andrea Elliott's Pulitzer Prize-winning *New York Times* series on Muslims in America.
3. And also browse the Supplementary Sources for great documentaries and feature films that give a more complex portrayal of Muslims and the Middle East, including *New Muslim Cool* and *Persepolis*.

32

The Conceptual Practices of Power

Dorothy Smith

IT IS NOT ENOUGH TO SUPPLEMENT an established sociology by addressing ourselves to what has been left out or overlooked, or by making women's issues into sociological issues. That does not change the standpoint built into existing sociological procedures, but merely makes the sociology of women an addendum to the body of objectified knowledge.

The first difficulty is that how sociology is thought—its methods, conceptual schemes, and theories—has been based on and built up within the male social universe, even when women have participated in its doing. This sociology has taken for granted not only an itemized inventory of issues or subject matters (industrial sociology, political sociology, social stratification, and so forth) but the fundamental social and political structures under which these become relevant and are ordered. There is thus a disjunction between how women experience the world and the concepts and theoretical schemes by which society's self-consciousness is inscribed. My early explorations of these issues included a graduate seminar in which we discussed the possibility of a women's sociology. Two students expressed their sense that theories of the emergence of leadership in small groups just did not apply to what had happened in an experimental group situation they had participated in. They could not find the correlates of the theory in their experiences.

A second difficulty is that the worlds opened up by speaking from the standpoint of women have not been and are not on a basis of equality with the objectified bodies of knowledge that have constituted and expressed the standpoint of men. The worlds of men have had, and still have, an authority over the worlds that are traditionally women's and still are predominantly women's—the worlds of household, children, and neighborhood. And though women do not inhabit only these worlds, for the vast majority of women they are the primary ground of our lives, shaping the course of our lives and our participation in other relations. Furthermore, objectified knowledges are part of the world from which our kind of society is governed. The domestic world stands in a dependent relation to that other, and its whole character is subordinate to it.

The two difficulties are related to each other in a special way. The effect of the second interacting with the first is to compel women to think their world in the concepts and terms in which men think theirs. Hence the established social forms of consciousness alienate women from their own experience.

The profession of sociology has been predicated on a universe grounded in men's experience and relationships and still largely appropriated by men as their "territory." Sociology is part of the practice by which we are all governed; that practice establishes its relevances. Thus the institutions that lock sociology into the structures occupied by men are the same institutions that lock women into the situations in which we have found ourselves oppressed. To unlock the latter leads logically to an unlocking of the former. What follows, then, or rather what then becomes possible—for it is of course by no means inevitable—is less a shift in the subject matter than a different conception of how sociology might become a means of understanding our experience and the conditions of our experience (both women's and men's) in contemporary capitalist society.

RELATIONS OF RULING AND OBJECTIFIED KNOWLEDGE

When I speak here of governing or ruling I mean something more general than the notion of government as political organization. I refer rather to that total complex of activities, differentiated into many spheres, by which our kind of society is ruled, managed, and administered. It includes what the business world calls *management*, it includes the professions, it includes government and the activities of those who are selecting, training, and indoctrinating those who will be its governors. The last includes those who provide and elaborate the procedures by which it is governed and develop methods for accounting for how it is done—namely, the business schools, the sociologists, the economists. These are the institutions through which we are ruled and through which we, and I emphasize this *we*, participate in ruling.

Sociology, then, I conceive as much more than a gloss on the enterprise that justifies and rationalizes it, and at the same time as much less than "science." The governing of our kind of society is done in abstract concepts and symbols, and sociology helps create them by transposing the actualities of people's lives and experience into the conceptual currency with which they can be governed.

Thus the relevances of sociology are organized in terms of a perspective on the world, a view from the top that takes for granted the pragmatic procedures of governing as those that frame and identify its subject matter. Issues are formulated because they are administratively relevant, not because they are significant first in the experience of those who live them. The kinds of facts and events that matter to sociologists have already been shaped and given their character and substance by the methods and practice of governing. Mental illness, crimes, riots, violence, work satisfaction, neighbors and neighborhoods, motivation, and so on—these are the constructs of the practice of government. Many of these constructs, such as mental illness, crimes, or neighborhoods, are constituted as discrete phenomena in the institutional contexts of ruling; others arise as problems in relation to the actual practice of government or management (for example, concepts of violence, motivation, or work satisfaction).

The governing processes of our society are organized as social entities external to those persons who participate in and perform them. Sociologists study these entities under the heading of formal organization. They are objectified structures with goals, activities, obligations, and so on, separate from those of the persons who work for them. The academic professions are similarly constituted. Members of a discipline accumulate knowledge that is then appropriated by the discipline as its own. The work of members aims at contributing to that body of knowledge.

As graduate students learning to become sociologists, we learn to think sociology as it is thought and to practice it as it is practiced. We learn that some topics are relevant and others are not. We learn to discard our personal experience as a source of reliable information about the character of the world and to confine and focus our insights within the conceptual frameworks and relevances of the discipline. Should we think other kinds of thoughts or experience the world in a different way or with horizons that pass beyond the conceptual, we must discard them or find some way to sneak them in. We learn a way of thinking about the world that is recognizable to its practitioners as the sociological way of thinking.

We learn to practice the sociological subsumption of the actualities of ourselves and of other people. We find out how to treat the world as instances of a sociological body of knowledge. The procedure operates as a sort of conceptual imperialism. When we write a thesis or a paper, we learn that the first thing to do is to latch it on to the discipline at some point. This may be by showing how it is a problem within an existing theoretical and conceptual framework. The boundaries of inquiry are thus set within the framework of what is already established. Even when this becomes, as it happily often does, a ceremonial authorization of a project that has little to do with the theory used to authorize it, we still work within the vocabularies and within the conceptual boundaries of "the sociological perspective."

An important set of procedures that serve to separate the discipline's body of knowledge from its practitioners is known as *objectivity*. The ethic of objectivity and the methods used in its practice are concerned primarily with the separation of knowers from what they know and in particular with the separation of what is known from knowers' interests, "biases," and so forth, that are not authorized by the discipline. In the social sciences the pursuit of objectivity makes it possible for people to be paid to pursue a knowledge to which they are otherwise indifferent. What they feel and think about society can be kept out of what they are professionally or academically interested in. Correlatively, if they are interested in exploring a topic sociologically, they must find ways of converting their private interest into an objectified, unbiased form.

WOMEN'S EXCLUSION FROM THE GOVERNING CONCEPTUAL MODE

The suppression of the local and particular as a site of knowledge has been and remains gender organized. The domestic sites of women's work, traditionally identified with women, are outside and subservient to this structure. Men have functioned as subjects in the mode of governing; women have been anchored in the local and particular phase of the bifurcated world. It has been a condition of a man's being able

to enter and become absorbed in the conceptual mode, and to forget the dependence of his being in that mode upon his bodily existence, that he does not have to focus his activities and interests upon his bodily existence. Full participation in the abstract mode of action requires liberation from attending to needs in the concrete and particular. The organization of work in managerial and professional circles depends upon the alienation of subjects from their bodily and local existence. The structure of work and the structure of career take for granted that these matters have been provided for in such a way that they will not interfere with a man's action and participation in that world. Under the traditional gender regime, providing for a man's liberation from Bierstedt's Aristotelian categories is a woman who keeps house for him, bears and cares for his children, washes his clothes, looks after him when he is sick, and generally provides for the logistics of his bodily existence.

Women's work in and around professional and managerial settings performs analogous functions. Women's work mediates between the abstracted and conceptual and the material form in which it must travel to communicate. Women do the clerical work, the word processing, the interviewing for the survey; they take messages, handle the mail, make appointments, and care for patients. At almost every point women mediate for men at work the relationship between the conceptual mode of action and the actual concrete forms in which it is and must be realized, and the actual material conditions upon which it depends.

Marx's concept of alienation is applicable here in a modified form. The simplest formulation of alienation posits a relation between the work individuals do and an external order oppressing them in which their work contributes to the strength of the order that oppresses them. This is the situation of women in this relation. The more successful women are in mediating the world of concrete particulars so that men do not have to become engaged with (and therefore conscious of) that world as a condition to their abstract activities, the more complete men's absorption in it and the more effective its authority. The dichotomy between the two worlds organized on the basis of gender separates the dual forms of consciousness; the governing consciousness dominates the primary world of a locally situated consciousness but cannot cancel it; the latter is a subordinated, suppressed, absent, but absolutely essential ground of the governing consciousness. The gendered organization of subjectivity dichotomizes the two worlds, estranges them, and silences the locally situated consciousness by silencing women.

KNOWING A SOCIETY FROM WITHIN: A WOMAN'S PERSPECTIVE

An alternative sociological approach must somehow transcend this contradiction without reentering Bierstedt's "transcendental realm." Women's standpoint, as I am analyzing it here, discredits sociology's claim to constitute an objective knowledge independent of the sociologist's situation. Sociology's conceptual procedures, methods, and relevances organize its subject matter from a determinate position in society. This critical disclosure is the basis of an alternative way of thinking sociology. If sociology cannot avoid being situated, then it should take that as its beginning and build it into its methodological and theoretical strategies. As it is now, these strategies separate a sociologically constructed world from that of direct experience; it is precisely that separation that must be undone.

I am not proposing an immediate and radical transformation of the subject matter and methods of the discipline nor the junking of everything that has gone before. What I am suggesting is more in the nature of a reorganization of the relationship of sociologists to the object of our knowledge and of our problematic. This reorganization involves first placing sociologists where we are actually situated, namely, at the beginning of those acts by which we know or will come to know, and second, making

our direct embodied experience of the everyday world the primary ground of our knowledge.

A sociology worked on in this way would not have as its objective a body of knowledge subsisting in and of itself; inquiry would not be justified by its contribution to the heaping up of such a body. We would reject a sociology aimed primarily at itself. We would not be interested in contributing to a body of knowledge whose uses are articulated to relations of ruling in which women participate only marginally, if at all. The professional sociologist is trained to think in the objectified modes of sociological discourse, to think sociology as it has been and is thought; that training and practice has to be discarded. Rather, as sociologists we would be constrained by the actualities of how things come about in people's direct experience, including our own. A sociology for women would offer a knowledge of the social organization and determinations of the properties and events of our directly experienced world.[1] Its analyses would become part of our ordinary interpretations of the experienced world, just as our experience of the sun's sinking below the horizon is transformed by our knowledge that the world turns away from a sun that seems to sink.

The only way of knowing a socially constructed world is knowing it from within. We can never stand outside it. A relation in which sociological phenomena are objectified and presented as external to and independent of the observer is itself a special social practice also known from within. The relation of observer and object of observation, of sociologist to "subject," is a specialized social relationship. Even to be a stranger is to enter a world constituted from within as strange. The strangeness itself is the mode in which it is experienced.

When Jean Briggs[2] made her ethnographic study of the ways in which an Eskimo people structure and express emotion, what she learned emerged for her in the context of the actual developing relations between her and the family with whom she lived and other members of the group. Her account situates her knowledge in the context of those relationships and in the actual sites in which the work of family subsistence was done. Affections, tensions, and quarrels, in some of which she was implicated, were the living texture in which she learned what she describes. She makes it clear how this context structured her learning and how what she learned and can speak of became observable to her.

Briggs tells us what is normally discarded in the anthropological or sociological telling. Although sociological inquiry is necessarily a social relation, we have learned to dissociate our own part in it. We recover only the object of our knowledge as if it stood all by itself. Sociology does not provide for seeing that there are always two terms to this relation. An alternative sociology must preserve in it the presence, concerns, and experience of the sociologist as knower and discoverer.

To begin from direct experience and to return to it as a constraint or "test" of the adequacy of a systematic knowledge is to begin from where we are located bodily. The actualities of our everyday world are already socially organized. Settings, equipment, environment, schedules, occasions, and so forth, as well as our enterprises and routines, are socially produced and concretely and symbolically organized prior to the moment at which we enter and at which inquiry begins. By taking up a standpoint in our original and immediate knowledge of the world, sociologists can make their discipline's socially organized properties first observable and then problematic.

When I speak of *experience* I do not use the term as a synonym for *perspective*. Nor in proposing a sociology grounded in the sociologist's actual experience am I recommending the self-indulgence of inner exploration or any other enterprise with self as sole focus and object. Such subjectivist interpretations of *experience* are themselves an aspect of that organization of consciousness that suppresses the locally situated side of the bifurcated consciousness and transports us straight into mind country, stashing away the concrete conditions and practices upon which it depends. We can never escape the circles of our own heads if we accept that as our territory. Rather, sociologists' investigation of our

directly experienced world as a problem is a mode of discovering or rediscovering the society from within. We begin from our own original but tacit knowledge and from within the acts by which we bring it into our grasp in making it observable and in understanding how it works. We aim not at a reiteration of what we already (tacitly) know, but at an exploration of what passes beyond that knowledge and is deeply implicated in how it is.

SOCIOLOGY AS STRUCTURING RELATIONS BETWEEN SUBJECT AND OBJECT

Our knowledge of the world is given to us in the modes by which we enter into relations with the object of knowledge. But in this case the object of our knowledge is or originates in the co-ordering of activities among "subjects." The constitution of an objective sociology as an authoritative version of how things are is done from a position in and as part of the practices of ruling in our kind of society. Our training as sociologists teaches us to ignore the uneasiness at the junctures where multiple and diverse experiences are transformed into objectified forms. That juncture shows in the ordinary problems respondents have of fitting their experience of the world to the questions in the interview schedule. The sociologist who is a woman finds it hard to preserve this exclusion, for she discovers, if she will, precisely that uneasiness in her relation to her discipline as a whole. The persistence of the privileged sociological version (or versions) relies upon a substructure that has already discredited and deprived of authority to speak the voices of those who know the society differently. The objectivity of a sociological version depends upon a special relationship with others that makes it easy for sociologists to remain outside the others' experience and does not require them to recognize that experience as a valid contention.

Riding a train not long ago in Ontario I saw a family of Indians—woman, man, and three children—standing together on a spur above a river watching the train go by. I realized that I could tell this incident—the train, those five people seen on the other side of the glass—as it was, but that my description was built on my position and my interpretations. I have called them "Indians" and a family; I have said they were watching the train. My understanding has already subsumed theirs. Everything may have been quite different for them. My description is privileged to stand as what actually happened because theirs is not heard in the contexts in which I may speak. If we begin from the world as we actually experience it, it is at least possible to see that we are indeed located and that what we know of the other is conditional upon that location. There are and must be different experiences of the world and different bases of experience. We must not do away with them by taking advantage of our privileged speaking to construct a sociological version that we then impose upon them as their reality. We may not rewrite the other's world or impose upon it a conceptual framework that extracts from it what fits with ours. Their reality, their varieties of experience, must be an unconditional datum. It is the place from which inquiry begins.

A BIFURCATION OF CONSCIOUSNESS

My experience in the train epitomizes a sociological relation. I am already separated from the world as it is experienced by those I observe. That separation is fundamental to the character of that experience. Once I become aware of how my world is put together as a practical everyday matter and of how my relations are shaped by its concrete conditions (even in so simple a matter as that I am sitting in the train and it travels, but those people standing on the spur do not), I am led into the discovery that I cannot understand the nature of my experienced world by staying within its ordinary boundaries of assumption and knowledge. To account for that moment on the train and for the relation between the two experiences (or more) and the two positions from which those experiences begin I must posit a larger socioeconomic order in back of that moment.

The coming together that makes the observation possible as well as how we were separated and drawn apart as well as how I now make use of that here—these properties are determined elsewhere than in that relation itself.

Furthermore, how our knowledge of the world is mediated to us becomes a problem of knowing how that world is organized for us prior to our participation in it. As intellectuals we ordinarily receive it as a media world, a world of texts, images, journals, books, talk, and other symbolic modes. We discard as an essential focus of our practice other ways of knowing. Accounting for that mode of knowing and the social organization that sets it up for us again leads us back into an analysis of the total socioeconomic order of which it is part. Inquiry remaining within the circumscriptions of the directly experienced cannot explore and explicate the relations organizing the everyday matrices of direct experience.

If we address the problem of the conditions as well as the perceived forms and organization of immediate experience, we should include in it the events as they actually happen and the ordinary material world we encounter as a matter of fact: the urban renewal project that uproots four hundred families; how it is to live on welfare as an ordinary daily practice; cities as the actual physical structures in which we move; the organization of academic occasions such as that in which this chapter originated. When we examine them, we find that there are many aspects of how these things come about of which we, as sociologists, have little to say. We have a sense that the events entering our experience originate somewhere in a human intention, but we are unable to track back to find it and to find out how it got from there to here.

Or take this room in which I work or that room in which you are reading and treat that as a problem. If we think about the conditions of our activity here, we can trace how these chairs, this table, the walls, our clothing, our presence come to be here; how these places (yours and mine) are cleaned and maintained; and so forth. There are human activities, intentions, and relations that are not apparent as such in the actual material conditions of our work. The social organization of the setting is not wholly available to us in its appearance. We bypass in the immediacy of the specific practical activity a complex division of labor that is an essential precondition to it. Such preconditions are fundamentally mysterious to us and present us with problems in grasping social relations with which sociology is ill equipped to deal. We experience the world as largely incomprehensible beyond the limits of what we know in a common sense. No amount of observation of face-to-face relations, no amount of commonsense knowledge of everyday life, will take us beyond our essential ignorance of how it is put together. Our direct experience of it makes it (if we will) a problem, but it does not offer any answers. We experience a world of "appearances," the determinations of which lie beyond it.

We might think of the appearances of our direct experience as a multiplicity of surfaces, the properties and relations among which are generated by social organizations not observable in their effects. The relations underlying and generating the characteristics of our own directly experienced world bring us into unseen relations with others. Their experience is necessarily different from ours. If we would begin from our experienced world and attempt to analyze and account for how it is, we must posit others whose experience is not the same as ours.

Women's situation in sociology discloses to us a typical bifurcate structure with the abstracted, conceptual practices on the one hand and the concrete realizations, the maintenance routines, and so forth, on the other. Taking each for granted depends upon being fully situated in one or the other so that the other does not appear in contradiction to it. Women's direct experience places us a step back, where we can recognize the uneasiness that comes from sociology's claim to be about the world we live in, and, at the same time, its failure to account for or even describe the actual features we experience. Yet we cannot find the inner principle of our own activity through exploring what is directly experienced. We do not see how it is put together because it is determined elsewhere. The very organization of the world that has been assigned to us as the primary locus of our being, shaping other projects and desires, is determined by and subordinate to the relations of society founded in a capitalist mode of production. The aim of an alternative sociology would be to explore and unfold the relations beyond our direct experience that shape and determine it. An alternative sociology would be a means to anyone of understanding how the world comes about for us and how it is organized so that it happens to us as it does in our experience. An alternative sociology, from the standpoint of women, makes the everyday world its problematic.

NOTES

1. Dorothy E. Smith, *The everyday world as problematic: A feminist sociology* (Boston: Northeastern University Press, 1987).
2. Jean Briggs, *Never in anger* (Cambridge: Harvard University Press, 1970).

COMPANION WEBSITE

1. Go online to Write Out Loud about what Smith might say about some of the classical concepts discussed earlier in *Social Theory Re-Wired*.
2. Log on to the Feminist Theory Profile Page to learn more about Dorothy Smith's contributions to sociology, including her work in *institutional ethnography*.
3. Check out the *Shifting the Paradigm* Supplementary Sources for an additional reading from Smith, "K is Mentally Ill."

33

Black Feminist Thought

Patricia Hill Collins

WHY U.S. BLACK FEMINIST THOUGHT?

Black feminism remains important because U.S. Black women constitute an oppressed group. As a collectivity, U.S. Black women participate in a *dialectical* relationship linking African-American women's oppression and activism. Dialectical relationships of this sort mean that two parties are opposed and opposite. As long as Black women's subordination within intersecting oppressions of race, class, gender, sexuality, and nation persists, Black feminism as an activist response to that oppression will remain needed.

In a similar fashion, the overarching purpose of U.S. Black feminist thought is also to resist oppression, both its practices and the ideas that justify it. If intersecting oppressions did not exist, Black feminist thought and similar oppositional knowledges would be unnecessary. As a critical social theory, Black feminist thought aims to empower African-American women within the context of social injustice sustained by intersecting oppressions. Since Black women cannot be fully empowered unless intersecting oppressions themselves are eliminated, Black feminist thought supports broad principles of social justice that transcend U.S. Black women's particular needs.

Because so much of U.S. Black feminism has been filtered through the prism of the U.S. context, its contours have been greatly affected by the specificity of American multiculturalism (Takaki 1993). In particular, U.S. Black feminist thought and practice respond to a fundamental contradiction of U.S. society. On the one hand, democratic promises of individual freedom, equality under the law, and social justice are made to all American citizens. Yet on the other hand, the reality of differential group treatment based on race, class, gender, sexuality, and citizenship status persists. Groups organized around race, class, and gender in and of themselves are not inherently a problem. However, when African-Americans, poor people, women, and other groups discriminated against see little hope for group-based advancement, this situation constitutes social injustice.

Within this overarching contradiction, U.S. Black women encounter a distinctive set of social practices that accompany our particular history within a unique matrix of domination characterized by intersecting oppressions. Race is far from being the only significant marker of group difference— class, gender, sexuality, religion, and citizenship status all matter greatly in the United States (Andersen and Collins 1998). Yet for African-American women, the effects of institutionalized racism remain visible and palpable. Moreover, the institutionalized racism that African-American women encounter relies heavily on racial segregation and accompanying discriminatory practices designed to deny U.S. Blacks equitable treatment. Despite important strides to desegregate U.S. society since 1970, racial segregation remains deeply entrenched in housing, school-ing, and employment (Massey and Denton 1993). For many African-American women, racism is not something that exists in the distance. We encoun-ter racism in everyday situations in work-places, stores, schools, housing, and daily social interac-tion (St. Jean and Feagin 1998). Most Black women do not have the opportunity to befriend White women and men as neighbors, nor do their chil-dren attend school with White children. Racial seg-regation remains a fundamental feature of the U.S. social landscape, leaving many African-Americans with the belief that "the more things change, the more they stay the same" (Collins 1998a, 11–43). Overlaying these persisting inequalities is a rhetoric of color blindness designed to render these social inequalities invisible. In a context where many believe that to talk of race fosters racism, equality allegedly lies in treating everyone the same. Yet as Kimberle Crenshaw (1997) points out, "it is fairly obvious that treating different things the same can generate as much inequality as treating the same things differently" (p. 285).

Although racial segregation is now organized differently than in prior eras (Collins 1998a, 11–43), being Black and female in the United States continues to expose African-American women to certain common experiences. U.S. Black women's similar work and family experiences as well as our participation in diverse expressions of African-American culture mean that, overall, U.S. Black women as a group live in a different world from that of people who are not Black and female. For individual women, the particular experiences that accrue to living as a Black woman in the United States can stimulate a distinctive consciousness concerning our own experiences and society overall. Many African-American women grasp this connection between what one does and how one thinks. Hannah Nelson, an elderly Black domestic worker, discusses how work shapes the perspectives of African-American and White women: "Since I have to work, I don't really have to worry about most of the things that most of the white women I have worked for are worrying about. And if these women did their own work, they would think just like I do—about this, anyway" (Gwaltney 1980, 4). Ruth Shays, a Black inner-city resident, points out how variations in men's and women's experiences lead to differences in perspective. "The mind of the man and the mind of the woman is the same" she notes, "but this business of living makes women use their minds in ways that men don't even have to think about" (Gwaltney 1980, 33).

A recognition of this connection between expe-rience and consciousness that shapes the everyday lives of individual African-American women often pervades the works of Black women activists and scholars. In her autobiography, Ida B. Wells-Barnett describes how the lynching of her friends had such an impact on her worldview that she subsequently devoted much of her life to the anti-lynching cause (Duster 1970). Sociologist Joyce Ladner's discom-fort with the disparity between the teachings of mainstream scholarship and her experiences as a young Black woman in the South led her to write *Tomorrow's Tomorrow* (1972), a groundbreaking study of Black female adolescence. Similarly, the transformed consciousness experienced by Janie, the light-skinned heroine of Zora Neale Hurston's (1937) classic *Their Eyes Were Watching God*, from obedient granddaughter and wife to a self-defined African-American woman, can be directly traced to her experiences with each of her three husbands. In one scene Janie's second husband, angry because she served him a dinner of scorched rice, underdone fish, and soggy bread, hits her. That incident stimu-lates Janie to stand "where he left her for unmea-sured time" and think. And in her thinking "her image of Jody tumbled down and shattered ... [S]he had an inside and an outside now and suddenly she knew how not to mix them" (p. 63).

Overall, these ties between what one does and what one thinks illustrated by *individual* Black women can also characterize Black women's expe-riences and ideas as a *group*. Historically, racial segregation in housing, education, and employment fostered group commonalities that encouraged the formation of a group-based, collective standpoint.[1] For example, the heavy concentration of U.S. Black women in domestic work coupled with racial segregation in housing and schools meant that U.S. Black women had common organizational networks that enabled them to share experiences and construct a collective body of wisdom. This collective wisdom on how to survive as U.S. Black women constituted a distinctive Black women's standpoint on gender-specific patterns of racial segregation and its accompanying economic penalties.

The presence of Black women's collective wisdom challenges two prevailing interpretations of the consciousness of oppressed groups. One approach claims that subordinate groups identify with the powerful and have no valid independent interpretation of their own oppression. The second assumes the oppressed are less human than their rulers, and are therefore less capable of interpreting their own experiences (Rollins 1985; Scott 1985). Both approaches see any independent consciousness expressed by African-American women and other oppressed groups as being either not of our own making or inferior to that of dominant groups. More importantly, both explanations suggest that the alleged lack of political activism on the part of oppressed groups stems from our flawed consciousness of our own subordination.[2]

Historically, Black women's group location in intersecting oppressions produced commonalities among individual African-American women. At the same time, while common experiences may predispose Black women to develop a distinctive group consciousness, they guarantee neither that such a consciousness will develop among all women nor that it will be articulated as such by the group. As historical conditions change, so do the links among the types of experiences Black women will have and any ensuing group consciousness concerning those experiences. Because group standpoints are situated in, reflect, and help shape unjust power relations, standpoints are not static (Collins 1998a, 201–28). Thus, common challenges may foster similar angles of vision leading to a group knowledge or standpoint among African-American women. Or they may not.

U.S. BLACK FEMINISM IN TRANSNATIONAL CONTEXT

Black women scholars and professionals cannot afford to ignore the straits of our sisters who are acquainted with the immediacy of oppression in a way many of us are not. The process of empowerment cannot be simplistically defined in accordance with our own particular class interests. We must learn to lift as we climb.

ANGELA DAVIS 1989, 9

Within U.S. Black feminism, race, class, gender, and sexuality constitute mutually constructing systems of oppression (Davis 1981; Smith 1983; Lorde 1984; Crenshaw 1991). Intersectional paradigms make two important contributions to understanding the connections between knowledge and empowerment. For one, they stimulate new interpretations of African-American women's experiences. Much of the work on U.S. Black women reported in earlier chapters relies on intersectional paradigms of some sort. For example, African-American women's confinement to domestic work revealed how race and gender influenced Black women's social class experiences. Similarly, the sexual politics of Black womanhood that shaped Black women's experiences with pornography, prostitution, and rape relied upon racist, sexist, and heterosexist ideologies to construct Black women's sexualities as deviant. Not only do intersectional paradigms prove useful in explaining U.S. Black women's experiences, such paradigms suggest that intersecting oppressions also shape the experiences of other groups as well. Puerto Ricans, U.S. White men, Asian American gays and lesbians, U.S. White women, and other historically identifiable groups all have distinctive histories that reflect their unique placement in intersecting oppressions (Andersen and Collins 1998).

Intersectional paradigms make a second important contribution to untangling the relationships between knowledge and empowerment—they shed new light on how domination is organized. The term *matrix of domination* describes this overall social organization within which intersecting oppressions originate, develop, and are contained. In the United States, such domination has occurred through schools, housing, employment, government, and other social institutions that regulate the actual patterns of intersecting oppressions that Black women encounter. Just as intersecting oppressions take on historically specific forms that change in response to human actions—racial segregation persists, but not in the forms that it took in prior historical eras—so the shape of domination itself changes.

As the particular form assumed by intersecting oppressions in one social location, any matrix of domination can be seen as an historically specific organization of power in which social groups are embedded and which they aim to influence. When Maria Stewart asked, "How long shall the fair daughters of Africa be compelled to bury their minds and talents beneath a load of iron pots and kettles?" (Richardson 1987), her query focused on the dialectical relationship linking oppression and activism for one period of time, the early 1800s, and in one social location, the United States. When Angela Davis counsels that privileged Black women not "ignore the straits of our sisters who are acquainted with the immediacy of oppression in a way many of us are not," she stresses the need for new ways of conceptualizing oppression and activism that take class differences of a global matrix of domination into account. All contexts of domination incorporate some combination of intersecting oppressions, and considerable variability exists from one matrix of domination to the next as to how oppression and activism will be organized. For example, as Senegalese feminists (Imam et al. 1997), Black

American feminists (Guy-Sheftall 1995b), and Black British feminists (Mirza 1997) all point out, social institutions in Senegal, the United States, and the United Kingdom reflect intersecting oppressions of race, class, gender, and sexuality. Yet social relations within these three nation-states differ: Domination is structured differently in Senegal, the United States, and the United Kingdom. Thus, regardless of how any given matrix is actually organized either across time or from society to society, the concept of a matrix of domination encapsulates the universality of intersecting oppressions as organized through diverse local realities.

Placing U.S. Black women's experiences in the center of analysis without privileging those experiences shows how intersectional paradigms can be especially important for rethinking the particular matrix of domination that characterizes U.S. society. Claims that systems of race, social class, gender, and sexuality form mutually constructing features of social organization foster a basic rethinking of U.S. social institutions. For example, using intersecting paradigms to investigate U.S. Black women's experiences challenges deeply held beliefs that work and family constitute separate spheres of social organization. Since U.S. Black women's experiences have never fit the logic of work in the public sphere juxtaposed to family obligations in the private sphere, these categories lose meaning. As the persistent racial discrimination in schooling, housing, jobs, and public services indicates, Black women's experiences certainly challenge U.S. class ideologies claiming that individual merit is all that matters in determining social rewards. The sexual politics of Black womanhood reveals the fallacy of assuming that gender affects all women in the same way—race and class matter greatly. U.S. Black women's activism, especially its dual commitment to struggles for group survival and to institutional transformation, suggests that understandings of the political should be rethought. Thus, by using intersectional paradigms to explain both the U.S. matrix of domination and Black women's individual and collective agency within it, Black feminist thought helps reconceptualize social relations of domination and resistance.

NATION AND NATIONALISM

Despite these contributions, U.S. Black feminist thought must continue to develop even more complex analyses of intersecting oppressions—how such oppressions are organized, their effect on group composition and history, their influence on individual consciousness, and, most importantly, collective strategies of resistance. Moving from race, class, and gender to generate analyses that include heterosexism as a system of oppression certainly constitutes a step in the right direction. But U.S. Black feminism will remain hindered in its goal of fostering Black women's empowerment in a context of social justice unless it incorporates more comprehensive analyses of how nation can constitute another form of oppression (Anthias and Yuval-Davis 1992; Yuval-Davis 1997).

Race, class, gender, and sexuality all remain closely intertwined with nation. In exploring these connections, it is important to distinguish among the terms nation, nation-state, and nationalism. These terms are often used interchangeably, but they refer to different things. A *nation* consists of a collection of people who have come to believe that they have been shaped by a common past and are destined to share a common future. That belief is usually nurtured by common cultural characteristics, such as language and customs; a well-defined geographic territory; the belief in a common history or origin; the belief that closer ties exist among members of the nation than with outsiders; a sense of difference from groups around them; and a shared hostility toward outsider groups. *Nationalism* is a political ideology that is expressed by any group that self-defines as a distinctive people or nation. Nationalist ideologies strive to foster beliefs and practices which permit a people or nation to control

its own destiny. When any one group acquires sufficient state power that allows it to realize its goals, it controls a *nation-state*.

In the United States, because affluent White men control government and industry, public policies usually benefit this group. In other words, despite the U.S. Constitution's stated commitment to equality of all American citizens, historically, the differential treatment of U.S. Blacks, women, the working class, and other subordinated groups meant that the United States operated as a nation-state that disproportionately benefited affluent White men. Because this group controls schools, the news media, and other social institutions that legitimate what counts as truth, it possesses the authority to obscure its own power and to redefine its own special interests as being national interests. In response to this situation, U.S. Blacks, Chicanos, Puerto Ricans, Native Americans, and other similar groups have often themselves embraced nationalist ideologies. Because such ideologies stress solidarity and resistance, such ideologies have effectively been used in challenging U.S. state policies.

Women are important within nationalist philosophies, whether the nationalism is forwarded by dominant groups who wield nation-state power, or by subordinated groups who use nationalist ideologies to challenge their oppression. Groups on both sides of state power view the women in their group in particular ways. Because women are capable of becoming mothers, women are central to three elements in nationalist thinking, namely, issues of sexuality and fertility, of motherhood, and of being symbols of the nation (Yuval-Davis 1997). In the United States, all women experience the peculiar situation of being responsible for reproducing the nation-state's population, passing on an American national culture, and accepting the role of being inscribed with that same national culture. But within the U.S. matrix of domination, this entire process is racialized, is organized in class-specific ways, and has varying impact on women of diverse sexualities. Women are differentially evaluated based on their perceived value to give birth to the right kind of children, pass on appropriate American family values, and become worthy symbols of the nation. Black women, White women, Latinas, Native American women, and Asian American women all occupy different positions within gender, class, race, and nation as intersecting systems of power.

Because American citizenship is so often taken for granted among U.S. Black women, we often have difficulty seeing not only how deeply nationalistic U.S. society actually is, but how its nationalisms affect us. African-American women encounter differential treatment based on our perceived value as giving birth to the wrong race of children, as unable to socialize them properly because we bring them into bad family structures, and as unworthy symbols for U.S. patriotism. This treatment is based, in part, on ideologies that view U.S. Black women as the Other, the mammies, matriarchs, welfare mothers, and jezebels who mark the boundaries of normality for American women overall. African-American women and many others typically have difficulty seeing the assumptions that underlie this situation because American nation-state policies obscure how American national interests in actuality are special interests. These same assumptions also limit understanding of how U.S. nationalism operates globally. In this context, working exclusively within prevailing nationalistic assumptions fosters views of the U.S. matrix of domination where the effects of nationalism become difficult to see, let alone resist, because they seem so everyday and taken for granted.

One important assumption that affects African-American women is how ideas about family influence understandings of American national identity. Just as ideas about sexuality permeate multiple systems of oppression (see Chapter 6), ideas about family perform a similar function (Collins 1998b).

Similarly, ideas about motherhood become especially important to American national identity. Whereas all women are assigned the duty of reproducing the national group's population, and of passing on a national culture while simultaneously being inscribed with that same national culture, in the United States, these ideas about race, class, motherhood, and citizenship influence public policies. For example, U.S. population policies broadly defined aim to discourage Black women from having children, claiming that Black women make poor mothers and that their children end up receiving handouts from the state (Roberts 1997). In contrast, middle-class White women are encouraged to increase their fertility, and are assisted by a dazzling array of new reproductive technologies in the quest for the healthy White baby (Hartouni 1997). Working-class White women are encouraged to deliver healthy White babies, but place them for adoption with more worthy middle-class families (Collins 1999a). The fertility of undocumented women of color is seen as a threat to the nation-state, especially if such women's children gain citizenship and apply for public services (Chang 1994). Women thus emerge as being much more important to U.S. nation-state policies than is popularly believed.

Despite the contributions of incorporating ideas about motherhood and nation within U.S. Black feminist thought, the emphasis remains on U.S. *domestic* policies. U.S. Black feminist thought contains considerable work that assesses how U.S. educational, employment, taxation, and social welfare policies affect African-American women's lives. This is important scholarship, yet in the absence of studies that examine U.S. Black women in a global context, such work can foster the assumption that U.S. *foreign* policy is not important for African-American women. Stopping analysis at the U.S. border thus functions to contain U.S. Black feminist thought to Black women's interactions with groups that are already in the United States—Black men, White women, other racial/ethnic populations—groups that already hold American citizenship or that aspire to attain it.

Shifting to a global analysis not only reveals new dimensions of U.S. Black women's experiences in the particular matrix of domination that characterizes U.S. society, but it also illuminates how a transnational matrix of domination presents certain challenges for women of African descent. Intersecting oppressions do not stop at U.S. borders. Intersecting oppressions of race, class, gender, sexuality, and nation constitute global phenomena that have a particular organization in the United States. Nested within this U.S. version are distinctive group histories characterized by a unique combination of factors. U.S. Black women's experiences constitute one such group history that can be seen in the context of the particular social movements within the United States, the domestic policies of varying levels of U.S. government, and a global matrix of domination affecting women of African descent in general. Black women in Nigeria, Trinidad and Tobago, the United Kingdom, Botswana, Brazil, and other nation-states are similarly located. They encounter the contours of local social movements, the policies of their nation-states, and the same global matrix of domination in which U.S. Black women are situated. All of these groups of women thus are positioned with situations of domination that are characterized by intersecting oppressions, yet their angle of vision on domination will vary greatly.

Shifting to a transnational context also brings women's rights activities to the forefront of discussion (Lindsay 1980). In a transnational context, women in African, Latin American, and Asian nations have not sat idly by, waiting for middle-class, White women from North American and Western European nation-states to tell them what to do. Instead, using the United Nations as a vehicle, women from quite diverse backgrounds have identified gender oppression as a major theme affecting women transnationally (see, e.g., *Rights of Women* 1998). These women are not just "theorizing" about oppression; their theory emerges from within the practical terrain of activism.

Within this broad transnational context, women of African descent have a distinctive, shared legacy that in turn is part of a global women's movement. At the same time, due to the peculiar combination of the legacy of African cultures, a history of racial oppressions organized via slavery, colonialism, and imperialism, and an emerging global racism that, assisted by modern technology, moves across national borders with dizzying speed, women of African descent encounter particular issues. For example, just as African-American women constitute one of the poorest groups within the United States, so do Black women in Brazil. Similarly, in the context of global women's poverty, women in Africa remain among the poorest. In this sense, women of African descent share much with women's rights struggles globally, but do so through particular Black diasporic experiences characterized by substantial heterogeneity.

Despite the national barriers that separate women of African descent, Black women's experiences demonstrate marked similarities that "illustrate how the persistence of the legacy of colonialism with its racial/ethnic, sexist and class biases has resulted in a system of 'global gendered apartheid'—a global economic system characterized by the exploitation of the labour of women of colour everywhere" (Antrobus 1995, 55). In this context, as social theorist Obioma Nnaemeka points out, "as people of African descent, our attention should not be solely on how blacks in Africa and those in the African Diaspora are *related with* each another, but also on how they *relate to* each other" (1998b, 377). One task, then, lies in stimulating dialogue across the very real limitations of national boundaries, to develop new ways of relating to one another, in order to unpack the interconnectedness of Black women's experiences.

BLACK WOMEN IN TRANSNATIONAL CONTEXT

In 1981, U.S. Black feminist theorist Barbara Smith identified her definition of what it meant to be radical: "What I really feel is radical is trying to make coalitions with people who are different from you.

I feel it is radical to be dealing with race and sex and class and sexual identity all at one time. I think *that* is really radical because it has never been done before" (Smith and Smith 1981, 126). Whereas U.S. Black feminism has traveled some distance toward Smith's vision of radicalism, coalitions among U.S. Black women and among women of African descent differentially placed in "global gendered apartheid" face some tough questions. Such coalitions must attend not only to different histories, they must be aware of the varying strengths and limitations that groups bring to social justice efforts. Women of African descent thus remain differentially placed within an overarching matrix of "global gendered apartheid" organized via a plethora of distinct nation-state politics. As a result, dialogues among Black women across national boundaries remain difficult. But they are necessary because they promise to shed light on current issues within U.S. Black feminism that now appear to be "American" yet may be better understood in transnational context.

Placing African-American women's experiences in a transnational context simultaneously provides a new angle of vision on U.S. Black feminism as a social justice project and decenters the White/Black binary that has long plagued U.S. feminism. Within the U.S. White/Black framework, U.S. Black feminism can be seen only as a derivative movement. African-American women who self-define as Black feminists can be accused of being "White" identified, as if no independent Black feminist consciousness is possible.

BLACK FEMINIST EPISTEMOLOGY

A small girl and her mother passed a statue depicting a European man who had barehandedly subdued a ferocious lion. The little girl stopped, looked puzzled and asked, "Mama, something's wrong with that statue. Everybody knows that a man can't whip a lion." "But darling," her mother replied, "you must remember that the man made the statue."

AS TOLD BY KATIE G. CANNON

As critical social theory, U.S. Black feminist thought reflects the interests and standpoint of its creators. Tracing the origin and diffusion of Black feminist thought or any comparable body of specialized knowledge reveals its affinity to the power of the group that created it (Mannheim 1936). Because elite White men control Western structures of knowledge validation, their interests pervade the themes, paradigms, and epistemologies of traditional scholarship. As a result, U.S. Black women's experiences as well as those of women of African descent transnationally have been routinely distorted within or excluded from what counts as knowledge.

U.S. Black feminist thought as specialized thought reflects the distinctive themes of African-American women's experiences. Black feminist thought's core themes of work, family, sexual politics, motherhood, and political activism rely on paradigms that emphasize the importance of intersecting oppressions in shaping the U.S. matrix of domination. But expressing these themes and paradigms has not been easy because Black women have had to struggle against White male interpretations of the world.

In this context, Black feminist thought can best be viewed as subjugated knowledge. Traditionally, the suppression of Black women's ideas within White-male-controlled social institutions led African-American women to use music, literature, daily conversations, and everyday behavior as important locations for constructing a Black feminist consciousness. More recently, higher education and the news media have emerged as increasingly important sites for Black feminist intellectual activity. Within these new social locations, Black feminist thought has often become highly visible, yet curiously, despite this visibility, it has become differently subjugated (Collins 1998a, 32–43).

Investigating the subjugated knowledge of subordinate groups—in this case a Black women's standpoint and Black feminist thought—requires more ingenuity than that needed to examine the standpoints and thought of dominant groups. I found my training as a social scientist inadequate to the task of studying the subjugated knowledge of a Black women's standpoint. This is because subordinate groups have long had to use alternative ways to create independent self-definitions and self-valuations and to rearticulate them through our own specialists. Like other subordinate groups, African-American women not only have developed a distinctive Black women's standpoint, but have done so by using alternative ways of producing and validating knowledge.

Epistemology constitutes an overarching theory of knowledge (Harding 1987). It investigates the standards used to assess knowledge or *why* we believe what we believe to be true. Far from being the apolitical study of truth, epistemology points to the ways in which power relations shape who is believed and why. For example, various descendants of Sally Hemmings, a Black woman owned by Thomas Jefferson, claimed repeatedly that Jefferson fathered her children. These accounts forwarded by Jefferson's African-American descendants were ignored in favor of accounts advanced by his White progeny. Hemmings's descendants were routinely disbelieved until their knowledge claims were validated by DNA testing.

Distinguishing among epistemologies, paradigms, and methodologies can prove to be useful in understanding the significance of competing epistemologies (Harding 1987). In contrast to epistemologies, *paradigms* encompass interpretive frameworks such as intersectionality that are used to explain social phenomena.[3] *Methodology* refers to the broad principles of how to conduct research and how interpretive paradigms are to be applied.[4] The level of epistemology is important because it determines which questions merit investigation, which interpretive frameworks will be used to analyze findings, and to what use any ensuing knowledge will be put.

In producing the specialized knowledge of U.S. Black feminist thought, Black women intellectuals often encounter two distinct epistemologies: one representing elite White male interests and the other expressing Black feminist concerns. Whereas many variations of these epistemologies exist, it is possible to distill some of their distinguishing features that transcend differences among the paradigms within them. Epistemological choices about whom to trust, what to believe, and why something is true are not benign academic issues. Instead, these concerns tap the fundamental question of which versions of truth will prevail.

EUROCENTRIC KNOWLEDGE VALIDATION PROCESSES AND U.S. POWER RELATIONS

In the United States, the social institutions that legitimate knowledge as well as the Western or Eurocentric epistemologies that they uphold constitute two interrelated parts of the dominant knowledge validation processes. In general, scholars, publishers, and other experts represent specific interests and credentialing processes, and their knowledge claims must satisfy the political and epistemological criteria of the contexts in which they reside (Kuhn 1962; Mulkay 1979). Because this enterprise is controlled by elite White men, knowledge validation processes reflect this group's interests.[5] Although designed to represent and protect the interests of powerful White men, neither schools, government, the media and other social institutions that house these processes nor the actual epistemologies that they promote need be managed by White men themselves. White women, African-American men and women, and other people of color may be enlisted to enforce these connections between power relations and what counts as truth. Moreover, not all White men accept these power relations that privilege Eurocentrism. Some have revolted and subverted social institutions and the ideas they promote.

Two political criteria influence knowledge validation processes. First, knowledge claims are evaluated by a group of experts whose members bring with them a host of sedimented experiences that reflect their group location in intersecting oppressions. No scholar can avoid cultural ideas and his or her placement in intersecting oppressions of race, gender, class, sexuality, and nation. In the United States, this means that a scholar making a knowledge claim typically must convince a scholarly community controlled by elite White avowedly heterosexual men holding U.S. citizenship that a given claim is justified. Second, each community of experts must maintain its credibility as defined by the larger population in which it is situated and from which it draws its basic, taken-for-granted knowledge. This means that scholarly communities that challenge basic beliefs held in U.S. culture at large will be deemed less credible than those that support popular ideas. For example, if scholarly communities stray too far from widely held beliefs about Black womanhood, they run the risk of being discredited.

When elite White men or any other overly homogeneous group dominates knowledge validation processes, both of these political criteria can work to suppress Black feminist thought. Given that the general U.S. culture shaping the taken-for-granted knowledge of the community of experts is permeated by widespread notions of Black female inferiority, new knowledge claims that seem to violate this fundamental assumption are likely to be viewed as anomalies (Kuhn 1962). Moreover, specialized thought challenging notions of Black female inferiority is unlikely to be generated from within White-male-controlled academic settings because both the kinds of questions asked and the answers to them would necessarily reflect a basic lack of familiarity with Black women's realities. Even those who think they are familiar can reproduce stereotypes. Believing that they are already knowledgeable, many scholars staunchly defend controlling images of U.S. Black women as mammies, matriarchs, and jezebels, and allow these commonsense beliefs to permeate their scholarship.

The experiences of African-American women scholars illustrate how individuals who wish to rearticulate a Black women's standpoint through Black feminist thought can be suppressed by prevailing knowledge validation processes. Exclusion from basic literacy, quality educational experiences, and faculty and administrative positions has limited U.S. Black women's access to influential academic positions (Zinn et al. 1986; Moses 1989). Black women have long produced knowledge claims that contested those advanced by elite White men. But because Black women have been denied positions of authority, they often relied on alternative knowledge validation processes to generate competing knowledge claims. As a consequence, academic disciplines typically rejected such claims. Moreover, any credentials controlled by White male academicians could then be denied to Black women who used alternative standards on the grounds that Black women's work did not constitute credible research.

Black women with academic credentials who seek to exert the authority that our status grants us to propose new knowledge claims about African-American women face pressures to use our authority to help legitimate a system that devalues and excludes the majority of Black women. When an outsider group—in this case, African-American women—recognizes that the insider group—namely, elite White men—requires special privileges from the larger society, those in power must find ways of keeping the outsiders out and at the same time having them acknowledge the legitimacy of this procedure. Accepting a few "safe" outsiders addresses this legitimation problem (Berger and Luckmann 1966). One way of excluding the majority of Black women from the knowledge validation process is to permit a few Black women to acquire positions of authority in institutions that legitimate knowledge, and to encourage us to work within the taken-for-granted assumptions of Black female inferiority shared by the scholarly community and the culture at large. Those Black women who accept these assumptions are likely to be rewarded by their institutions. Those challenging the assumptions can be placed under surveillance and run the risk of being ostracized.

African-American women academicians who persist in trying to rearticulate a Black women's standpoint also face potential rejection of our knowledge claims on epistemological grounds. Just as the material realities of powerful and dominated groups produce separate standpoints, these groups may also deploy distinctive epistemologies or theories of knowledge. Black women scholars may know that something is true—at least, by standards widely accepted among African-American women—but be unwilling or unable to legitimate our claims using prevailing scholarly norms. For any discourse, new knowledge claims must be consistent with an existing body of knowledge that the group controlling the interpretive context accepts as true. Take, for example, the differences between how U.S. Black women interpret their experiences as single mothers and how prevailing social science research analyzes the same reality. Whereas Black women stress their struggles with job discrimination, inadequate child support, inferior housing, and street violence, far too much social science research seems mesmerized by images of lazy "welfare queens" content to stay on the dole. The methods used to validate knowledge claims must also be acceptable to the group controlling the knowledge validation process. Individual African-American women's narratives about being single mothers are often rendered invisible in quantitative research methodologies that erase individuality in favor of proving patterns of welfare abuse. Thus, one important issue facing Black women intellectuals is the question of what constitutes adequate justification that a given knowledge claim, such as a fact or theory, is true. Just as Hemmings's descendants were routinely disbelieved, so are many Black women not seen as credible witnesses for our own experiences. In this climate, Black women academics who choose to believe other Black women can become suspect.

Criteria for methodological adequacy associated with positivism illustrate the standards that Black women scholars, especially those in the social sciences, would have to satisfy in legitimating Black feminist thought. Though I describe Western or Eurocentric epistemologies as a single cluster, many interpretive frameworks or paradigms are subsumed under this category. Moreover, my focus on positivism should be interpreted neither to mean that all dimensions of positivism are inherently problematic for Black women nor that nonpositivist frameworks are better.

Positivist approaches aim to create scientific descriptions of reality by producing objective generalizations. Because researchers have widely differing values, experiences, and emotions, genuine science is thought to be unattainable unless all human characteristics except rationality are eliminated from the research process. By following strict methodological rules, scientists aim to distance themselves from the values, vested interests, and emotions generated by their class, race, sex, or unique situation. By decontextualizing themselves, they allegedly become detached observers and manipulators of nature (Jaggar 1983; Harding 1986).

Several requirements typify positivist methodological approaches. First, research methods generally require a distancing of the researcher from her or his "object" of study by defining the researcher as a "subject" with full human subjectivity and by objectifying the "object" of study (Keller 1985; Asante 1987). A second requirement is the absence of emotions from the research process (Jaggar 1983). Third, ethics and values are deemed inappropriate in the research process, either as the reason for scientific inquiry or as part of the research process itself (Richards 1980). Finally, adversarial debates, whether written or oral, become the preferred method of ascertaining truth: The arguments that can withstand the greatest assault and survive intact become the strongest truths (Moulton 1983).

Such criteria ask African-American women to objectify ourselves, devalue our emotional life, displace our motivations for furthering knowledge about Black women, and confront in an adversarial relationship those with more social, economic, and professional power. On the one hand, it seems unlikely that Black women would rely exclusively on positivist paradigms in rearticulating a Black women's standpoint. For example, Black women's experiences in sociology illustrate diverse responses to encountering an entrenched positivism. Given Black women's long-standing exclusion from sociology prior to 1970, the sociological knowledge about race and gender produced during their absence, and the symbolic importance of Black women's absence to sociological self-definitions as a science, African-American women acting as agents of knowledge faced a complex situation. In order to refute the history of Black women's unsuitability for science, they had to invoke the tools of sociology by using positivistic frameworks to demonstrate their capability as scientists. However, they simultaneously needed to challenge the same structure that granted them legitimacy. Their responses to this dilemma reflect the strategic use of the tools of positivism when needed, coupled with overt challenges to positivism when that seemed feasible (Collins 1998a, 95–123).

On the other hand, many Black women have had access to another epistemology that encompasses standards for assessing truth that are widely accepted among African-American women. An experiential, material base underlies a Black feminist epistemology, namely, collective experiences and accompanying worldviews that U.S. Black women sustained based on our particular history. The historical conditions of Black women's work, both in Black civil society and in paid employment, fostered a series of experiences that when shared and passed on become the collective wisdom of a Black women's standpoint. Moreover, a set of principles for assessing knowledge claims may be available to those having these shared experiences. These principles pass into a more general Black women's wisdom and, further, into what I call here a Black feminist epistemology.

This alternative epistemology uses different standards that are consistent with Black women's criteria for substantiated knowledge and with our criteria for methodological adequacy. Certainly this alternative Black feminist epistemology has been devalued by dominant knowledge validation processes and may not be claimed by many African-American women. But if such an epistemology exists, what are its contours? Moreover, what are its actual and potential contributions to Black feminist thought?

[…]

BLACK WOMEN AS AGENTS OF KNOWLEDGE

Social movements of the 1950s, 1960s, and 1970s stimulated a greatly changed intellectual and political climate in the United States. Compared to the past, many more U.S. Black women became legitimated agents of knowledge. No longer passive objects of knowledge manipulated within prevailing knowledge validation processes, African-American women aimed to speak for ourselves.

African-American women in the academy and other positions of authority who aim to advance Black feminist thought now encounter the often conflicting epistemological standards of three key groups. First, Black feminist thought must be validated by ordinary African-American women who, in the words of Hannah Nelson, grow to womanhood "in a world where the saner you are, the madder you are made to appear" (Gwaltney 1980, 7). To be credible in the eyes of this group, Black feminist intellectuals must be personal advocates for their material, be accountable for the consequences of their work, have lived or experienced their material in some fashion, and be willing to engage in dialogues about their findings with ordinary, everyday people.

Historically, living life as an African-American woman facilitated this endeavor because knowledge validation processes controlled in part or in full by Black women occurred in particular organizational settings. When Black women were in charge of our own self-definitions, these four dimensions of Black feminist epistemology—lived experience as a criterion of meaning, the use of dialogue, the ethic of personal accountability, and the ethic of caring—came to the forefront. When the core themes and interpretive frameworks of Black women's knowledge were informed by Black feminist epistemology, a rich tradition of Black feminist thought ensued.

Traditionally women engaged in this overarching intellectual and political project were blues singers, poets, autobiographers, storytellers, and orators. They became Black feminist intellectuals both by doing intellectual work and by being validated as such by everyday Black women. Black women in academia could not openly join their ranks without incurring a serious penalty. In racially segregated environments that routinely excluded the majority of African-American women, only a select few were able to defy prevailing norms and explicitly embrace Black feminist epistemology. Zora Neale Hurston was one such figure. Consider Alice Walker's description of Hurston:

> In my mind, Zora Neale Hurston, Billie Holiday, and Bessie Smith form a sort of unholy trinity. Zora *belongs* in the tradition of black women singers, rather than among "the literati." … Like Billie and Bessie she followed her own road, believed in her own gods, pursued her own dreams, and refused to separate herself from "common" people.

(Walker 1977, xvii–xviii)

For her time, Zora Neale Hurston remains an exception, for prior to 1950, few African-American women earned advanced degrees, and most of those who did complied with prevailing knowledge validation processes.

The community of Black women scholars constitutes a second constituency whose epistemological standards must be met. As the number of Black women academics grows, this heterogeneous collectivity shares a similar social location in higher education, yet finds a new challenge in building group solidarities across differences. African-American women scholars place varying amounts of importance on furthering Black feminist scholarship. However, despite this newfound diversity, since more African-American women earn advanced degrees, the range of Black feminist scholarship has expanded. Historically, African-American women may have brought sensibilities gained from Black feminist epistemology to their scholarship. But gaining legitimacy often came with the cost of rejecting such an epistemology. Studying Black women's lives at all placed many careers at risk. More recently, increasing numbers of African-American women scholars have chosen to study Black women's experiences, and to do so by relying on elements of Black feminist epistemology in framing their work. For example, Valerie Lee's (1996) study of African-American midwives in the South deploys an innovative merger of Black women's fiction, ethnographic method, and personal narrative, to good effect.

A third group whose epistemological standards must be met consists of dominant groups who still control schools, graduate programs, tenure processes, publication outlets, and other mechanisms that legitimate knowledge. African-American women academics who aim to advance Black feminist thought typically must use dominant Eurocentric epistemologies for this group. The difficulties these Black women now face lie less in demonstrating that they could master White male epistemologies than in resisting the hegemonic nature of these patterns of thought in order to see, value, and use existing alternative Black feminist ways of knowing. For Black women who are agents of knowledge within academia, the marginality that accompanies outsider-within status can be the source of both frustration and creativity. In an attempt to minimize the differences between the cultural context of African-American communities and the expectations of mainstream social institutions, some women dichotomize their behaviour and become two different people. Over time, the strain of doing this can be enormous. Others reject Black women's accumulated wisdom and work against their own best interests by enforcing the dominant group's specialized thought. Still others manage to inhabit both contexts but do so critically, using perspectives gained from their outsider-within social locations as a source of insights and ideas. But while such women can make substantial contributions as agents of knowledge, they rarely do so without substantial personal cost. "Eventually it comes to you," observes Lorraine Hansberry, "the thing that makes you exceptional, if you are at all, is inevitably that which must also make you lonely" (1969, 148).

Just as migrating between Black and White families raised special issues for Black women domestic workers, moving among different and competing interpretive communities raises similar epistemological concerns for Black feminist thinkers. The dilemma facing Black women scholars, in particular, engaged in creating Black feminist thought illustrates difficulties that can accompany grappling with multiple interpretive communities. A knowledge claim that meets the criteria of adequacy for one group and thus is judged to be acceptable may not be translatable into the terms of a different group. Using the example of Black English, June Jordan illustrates the difficulty of moving among epistemologies:

> You cannot "translate" instances of Standard English preoccupied with abstraction or with nothing/nobody evidently alive into Black English. That would warp the language into uses antithetical to the guiding perspective of its community of users. Rather you must first change those Standard English sentences, themselves, into ideas consistent with the person-centered assumptions of Black English.
>
> (Jordan 1985, 130)

Although both worldviews share a common vocabulary, the ideas themselves defy direct translation.

Once Black women scholars face the notion that on certain dimensions of a Black women's standpoint, it may be fruitless to try to translate into other frameworks truths validated by Black feminist epistemology, then other choices emerge. Rather than trying to uncover universal knowledge claims that can withstand the translation from one epistemology to another (initially, at least), Black women intellectuals might find efforts to rearticulate a Black women's standpoint especially fruitful. Rearticulating a Black women's standpoint refashions the particular and reveals the more universal human dimensions of Black women's everyday lives. "I date all my work," notes Nikki Giovanni, "because I think poetry, or any writing, is but a reflection of the moment. The universal comes from the particular" (1988, 57). Lorraine Hansberry expresses a similar idea: "I believe that one of the most sound ideas in dramatic writing is that in order to create the universal, you must pay very great attention to the specific. Universality, I think, emerges from the truthful identity of what is" (1969, 128).

TOWARD TRUTH

The existence of Black feminist thought suggests another path to the universal truths that might accompany the "truthful identity of what is." In this volume I place Black women's subjectivity in the center of analysis and examine the interdependence of the everyday, taken-for-granted knowledge shared by African-American women as a group, the more specialized knowledge produced by Black women intellectuals, and the social conditions shaping both types of thought. This approach allows me to describe the creative tension linking how social conditions influenced a Black women's standpoint and how the power of the ideas themselves gave many African-American women the strength to shape those same social conditions. I approach Black feminist thought as situated in a context of domination and not as a system of ideas divorced from political and economic reality. Moreover, I present Black feminist thought as subjugated knowledge in that African-American women have long struggled to find alternative locations and epistemologies for validating our own self-definitions. In brief, I examined the situated, subjugated standpoint of African-American women in order to understand Black feminist thought as a partial perspective on domination.

Because U.S. Black women have access to the experiences that accrue to being both Black and female, an alternative epistemology used to rearticulate a Black women's standpoint should reflect the convergence of both sets of experiences. Race and gender may be analytically distinct, but in Black women's everyday lives, they work together. The search for the distinguishing features of an alternative epistemology used by African-American women reveals that some ideas that Africanist scholars identify as characteristically "Black" often bear remarkable resemblance to similar ideas claimed by feminist scholars as characteristically "female." This similarity suggests that the actual contours of intersecting oppressions can vary dramatically and yet generate some uniformity in the epistemologies used by subordinate groups. Just as U.S. Black women and African women encountered diverse patterns of intersecting oppressions yet generated similar agendas concerning what mattered in their feminisms, a similar process may be at work regarding the epistemologies of oppressed groups. Thus the significance of a Black feminist epistemology may lie in its ability to enrich our understanding of how subordinate groups create knowledge that fosters both their empowerment and social justice.

This approach to Black feminist thought allows African-American women to explore the epistemological implications of transversal politics. Eventually this approach may get us to a point at which, claims Elsa Barkley Brown, "all people can learn to center in another experience, validate it, and judge it by its own standards without need of comparison or need to adopt that framework as their own" (1989, 922). In such politics, "one has no need to 'decenter' anyone in order to center someone else; one has only to constantly, appropriately, 'pivot the center' " (p. 922).

Rather than emphasizing how a Black women's standpoint and its accompanying epistemology differ from those of White women, Black men, and other collectivities, Black women's experiences serve as one specific social location for examining points of connection among multiple epistemologies. Viewing Black feminist epistemology in this way challenges additive analyses of oppression claiming that Black women have a more accurate view of oppression than do other groups. Such approaches suggest that oppression can be quantified and compared and that adding layers of oppression produces a potentially clearer standpoint (Spelman 1988). One implication of some uses of standpoint theory is that the more subordinated the group, the purer the vision available to them. This is an outcome of the origins of standpoint approaches in Marxist social theory, itself reflecting the binary thinking of its Western origins. Ironically, by quantifying and ranking human oppressions, standpoint theorists invoke criteria for methodological adequacy that resemble those of positivism. Although it is tempting to claim that Black women are more oppressed than everyone else and therefore have the best standpoint from which to understand the mechanisms, processes, and effects of oppression, this is not the case.

Instead, those ideas that are validated as true by African-American women, African-American men, Latina lesbians, Asian-American women, Puerto Rican men, and other groups with distinctive standpoints, with each group using the epistemological approaches growing from its unique standpoint, become the most "objective" truths. Each group speaks from its own standpoint and shares its own partial, situated knowledge. But because each group perceives its own truth as partial, its knowledge is unfinished. Each group becomes better able to consider other groups' standpoints without relinquishing the uniqueness of its own standpoint or suppressing other groups' partial perspectives. "What is always needed in the appreciation of art, of life," maintains Alice Walker, "is the larger perspective. Connections made, or at least attempted, where none existed before, the straining to encompass in one's glance at the varied world the common thread, the unifying theme through immense diversity" (1983, 5). Partiality, and not universality, is the condition of being heard; individuals and groups forwarding knowledge claims without owning their position are deemed less credible than those who do.

Alternative knowledge claims in and of themselves are rarely threatening to conventional knowledge. Such claims are routinely ignored, discredited, or simply absorbed and marginalized in existing paradigms. Much more threatening is the challenge that alternative epistemologies offer to the basic process used by the powerful to legitimate knowledge claims that in turn justify their right to rule. If the epistemology used to validate knowledge comes into question, then all prior knowledge claims validated under the dominant model become suspect. Alternative epistemologies challenge all certified knowledge and open up the question of whether what has been taken to be true can stand the test of alternative ways of validating truth. The existence of a self-defined Black women's standpoint using Black feminist epistemology calls into question the content of what currently passes as truth and simultaneously challenges the process of arriving at that truth.

[...]

THE POLITICS OF EMPOWERMENT

Rethinking Black feminism as a social justice project involves developing a complex notion of empowerment. Shifting the analysis to investigating how the matrix of domination is structured along certain axes—race, gender, class, sexuality, and nation—as well as how it operates through interconnected domains of power—structural, interpersonal, disciplinary, and hegemonic—reveals that the dialectical relationship linking oppression and activism is far more complex than simple models of oppressors and oppressed would suggest. This inclusive perspective enables African-American women to avoid labeling one form of oppression as more important than others, or one expression of activism as more radical than another. It also creates conceptual space to identify some new linkages. Just as oppression is complex, so must resistance aimed at fostering empowerment demonstrate a similar complexity.

When it comes to power, the challenges raised by the synergistic relationship among domains of power generate new opportunities and constraints for African-American women who now desegregate schools and workplaces, as well as those who do not. On the one hand, entering places that denied access to our mothers provides new opportunities for fostering social justice. Depending on the setting, using the insights gained via outsider-within status can be a stimulus to creativity that helps both African-American women and our new organizational homes. On the other hand, the commodification of outsider-within status whereby African-American women's value to an organization lies solely in our ability to market a seemingly permanent marginal status can suppress Black women's empowerment. Being a permanent outsider within can never lead to power because the category, by definition, requires marginality. Each individual must find her own way, recognizing that her personal biography, while unique, is never as unique as she thinks.

When it comes to knowledge, Black women's empowerment involves rejecting the dimensions of knowledge that perpetuate objectification, commodification, and exploitation. African-American women and others like us become empowered when we understand and use those dimensions of our individual, group, and formal educational ways of knowing that foster our humanity. When Black women value our self-definitions, participate in Black women's domestic and transnational activist traditions, view the skills gained in schools as part of a focused education for Black community development, and invoke Black feminist epistemologies as central to our worldviews, we empower ourselves. C. Wright Mills's (1959) concept of the "sociological imagination" identifies its task and its promise as a way of knowing that enables individuals to grasp the relations between history and biography within society. Resembling the holistic epistemology required by Black feminism, using one's point of view to engage the sociological imagination can empower the individual. "My fullest concentration of energy is available to me," Audre Lorde maintains, "only when I integrate all the parts of who I am, openly, allowing power from particular sources of my living to flow back and forth freely through all my different selves, without the restriction of externally imposed definition" (1984, 120–21). Developing a Black women's standpoint to engage a collective Black feminist imagination can empower the group.

Black women's empowerment involves revitalizing U.S. Black feminism as a social justice project organized around the dual goals of empowering African-American women and fostering social justice in a transnational context. Black feminist thought's emphasis on the ongoing interplay between Black women's oppression and Black women's activism presents the matrix of domination and its interrelated domains of power as responsive to human agency. Such thought views the world as a dynamic place where the goal is not merely to survive or to fit in or to cope; rather, it becomes a place where we feel ownership and accountability. The existence of Black feminist thought suggests that there is always choice, and power to act, no matter how bleak the situation may appear to be. Viewing the world as one in the making raises the issue of individual responsibility for bringing about change. It also shows that while individual empowerment is key, only collective action can effectively generate the lasting institutional transformation required for social justice.

In 1831 Maria Stewart asked, "How long shall the fair daughters of Africa be compelled to bury their minds and talents beneath a load of iron pots and kettles?" (Richardson 1987, 38). Stewart's response speaks eloquently to the connections between knowledge, consciousness, and the politics of empowerment:

> Until union, knowledge and love begin to flow among us. How long shall a mean set of men flatter us with their smiles, and enrich themselves with our hard earnings; their wives' fingers sparkling with rings, and they themselves laughing at our folly? Until we begin to promote and patronize each other. … Do you ask, what can we do? Unite and build a store of your own. … Do you ask where is the money? We have spent more than enough for nonsense, to do what building we should want. (Richardson 1987, 38)

NOTES

1. For discussions of the concept of standpoint, see Hartsock (1983a, 1983b), Jaggar (1983), and Smith (1987). Even though I use standpoint epistemologies as an organizing concept in this volume, they remain controversial. For a helpful critique of standpoint epistemologies, see Harding (1986). See my extended discussion of standpoint theory (Collins 1998a, 201–28). Canadian sociologist Dorothy Smith (1987) also views women's lived, everyday world as stimulating theory. But the everyday she examines is individual, a situation reflecting in part the isolation of White, middle-class women. In contrast, I contend that the collective values in U.S. Black neighborhoods, when

combined with the working-class experiences of the majority of Black women, historically provided collective as well as individual everyday worlds. Thus, U.S. Black culture continually created via lived Black experience with racial segregation provided a social context for the emergence of a Black women's standpoint. Whereas the contexts in which this collective standpoint developed are changing, the purpose or need for it has not.

2.   Scott (1985) defines consciousness as the symbols, norms, and ideological forms people create to give meaning to their acts. For de Lauretis (1986), consciousness is a process, a "particular configuration of subjectivity ... produced at the intersection of meaning with experience.... Consciousness is grounded in personal history, and self and identity are understood within particular cultural contexts. Consciousness ... is never fixed, never attained once and for all, because discursive boundaries change with historical conditions" (p. 8). It is important to distinguish between individual and group consciousness.

3.   Many scholars view positivism and postmodernism, for example, as competing epistemologies, each with their own theories of what counts as truth and why. In contrast, I view positivism and postmodernism as yet another binary whose opposition to each other unifies them within an overarching Western epistemology (Collins 1998a, 126–37). The prior discussion of intersecting oppressions of race, class, gender, sexuality, and nation aims to sketch out an alternative paradigm that, as I discuss later in this chapter, may constitute an important part of Black feminist epistemology.

4.   For example, qualitative and quantitative methodologies represent two important methodological approaches that are often associated with Western humanities and the sciences respectively. A particular methodology may become identified with an epistemological approach and its interpretive frameworks. Whereas methodology refers to a broader theory of how to do research, nothing in a research methodology is inherently White or Black, male or female. Certain methodologies can become coded as "white" and/or "male" and thus work to disadvantage Black women (Collins 1998a, 101–105). Particular techniques used in the course of research, for example, interviewing and survey analysis, constitute research *methods* or specific tools that need not be attached to any particular group's interests. Whereas patterns of using specific techniques may vary among groups—White men may work with large-scale data sets whereas Black women may rely more on one-on-one interviewing—methods can be used for a variety of purposes.

5.   Sandra Harding provides a useful definition of Eurocentrism that parallels my use here (Harding 1998, 12–15). Western or Eurocentric social and political thought contains three interrelated approaches to ascertaining "truth" that are routinely portrayed as competing epistemologies. The first, reflected in positivist science, has long claimed that absolute truths exist and that the task of scholarship is to develop objective, unbiased tools of science to measure these truths. But many social theories have challenged the concepts and epistemology of this version of science as representing the vested interests of elite White men and therefore as being less valid when applied to experiences of other groups and, more recently, to White male recounting of their own exploits. The second approach, earlier versions of standpoint theories that were themselves rooted in a Marxist positivism, essentially reversed positivist science's assumptions concerning whose truth would prevail. These approaches suggest that the oppressed allegedly have a clearer view of "truth" than their oppressors because they lack the blinders created by the dominant group's ideology. But this version of standpoint theory basically duplicates the positivist belief in one "true" interpretation of reality and, like positivist science, comes with its own set of problems. Postmodernism, the third approach, has been forwarded as the antithesis of and inevitable outcome of rejecting a positivist science. Within postmodern logic, groups themselves become suspect as well as any specialized thought. In extreme postmodern discourse, each group's thought is equally valid. No group can claim to have a better interpretation of the "truth" than another. In a sense, postmodernism represents the opposite of scientific ideologies of objectivity (Collins 1998a, 124–54).

REFERENCES

Anderson, Margaret L. and Patricia Hill Collins, eds. 1998. *Race, Class, and Gender: An Anthology, Third Edition*. Belmont, CA: Wadsworth Press.

Anthias, Floya, and Nira Yuval-Davis. 1992. *Racialized Boundaries: Race, Nation, Gender, Colour and Class in the Anti-Racist Struggle*. New York: Routledge.

Antrobus, Peggy. 1995. "Women in the Caribbean: The Quadruple Burden of Gender, Race, Class and Imperialism." In *Connecting Across Cultures and Continents: Black Women Speak Out on Identity, Race and Development*, ed. Achola O. Pala, 53–60. New York: United Nations Development Fund for Women.

Asante, Molefi Kete. 1987. *The Afrocentric Idea*. Philadelphia: Temple University Press.

Berger, Peter L, and Thomas Luckmann. 1966. *The Social Construction of Reality*. New York: Doubleday.

Brown, Elsa Barkley. 1989. "African-American Women's Quilting: A Framework for Conceptualizing and Teaching African-American Women's History." *Signs* 14 (4): 921–29.

Cannon, Katie G. 1985. "The Emergence of a Black Feminist Consciousness." In *Feminist Interpretations of the Bible*, ed. Letty M. Russell, 30–40. Philadelphia: Westminster Press.

Chang, Grace. 1994. "Undocumented Latinas: The New 'Employable Mothers.'" In *Mothering: Ideology, Experience, and Agency*, ed. Evelyn Nakano Glenn, Grace Chang, and Linda Rennie Forcey, 259–86. New York: Routledge.

Collins, Patricia Hill. 1998a. *Fighting Words: Black Women and the Search for Justice*. Minneapolis: University of Minnesota Press.

———. 1998b. "It's All in the Family Intersections of Gender, Race, and Nation." *Hypatia* 13 (3): 62–82.

———. 1999. "Producing the Mothers of the Nation: Race, Class and Contemporary U.S. Population Policies." Forthcoming in *Women, Citizenship and Difference*, ed. Nira Yuval-Davis. London: Zed Books.

Crenshaw, Kimberle Williams. 1991. "Mapping the Margins: Intersectionality, Identity Politics, and Violence Against Women of Color." *Stanford Law Review* 43 (6): 1241–99.

———. 1997. "Color Blindness, History, and the Law." In *The House That Race Built*, ed. Wahneema Lubiano, 280–88. New York: Pantheon.

Davis, Angela Y. 1981. *Women, Race and Class*. New York: Random House.

———. 1989. *Women, Culture, and Politics*. New York: Random House.

de Lauretis, Teresa. 1986. "Feminist Studies/Critical Studies: Issues, Terms, and Contexts." In *Feminist Studies/Critical Studies*, ed. Teresa de Lauretis, 1–19. Bloomington: Indiana University Press.

Duster, Alfreda M., ed. 1970. *Crusade for Justice: The Autobiography of Ida B. Wells*. Chicago: University of Chicago Press.

Giovanni, Nikki. 1988. *Sacred Cows … and Other Edibles*. New York: Quill/William Morrow.

Guy-Sheftall, Beverly. ed. 1995b. *Words of Fire: An Anthology of African American Feminist Thought*. New York: New Press.

Gwaltney, John Langston. 1980. *Drylongso, A Self-Portrait of Black America*. New York: Vintage.

Hansberry, Lorraine. 1969. *To Be Young, Gifted and Black*. New York: Signet.

Harding, Sandra. 1986. *The Science Question in Feminism*. Ithaca, NY: Cornell University Press.

———. 1987. "Introduction: Is There a Feminist Method?" In *Feminism and Methodology*, ed. Sandra Harding, 1–14. Bloomington: Indiana University Press.

———. 1998. *Is Science Multicultural? Postcolonialisms, Feminisms, and Epistemologies*. Bloomington: Indiana University Press.

Hartouni, Valerie. 1997. "Breached Birth: Anna Johnson and the Reproduction of Raced Bodies." In *Cultural Conceptions: On Reproductive Technologies and the Remaking of Life*, 85–98. Minneapolis: University of Minnesota Press.

Hartsock, Nancy M. 1983a. "The Feminist Standpoint: Developing the Ground for a Specifically Feminist Historical Materialism." In *Discovering Reality*, ed. Sandra Harding and Merrill B. Hintikka, 283–310. Boston: D. Reidel.

———. 1983b. *Money, Sex and Power*. Boston: Northeastern University Press.

Hurston, Zora Neale. [1937] 1969. *Their Eyes Were Watching God*. Greenwich, CT: Fawcett.

Imam, Ayesha, Amina Mama, and Fatou Sow, eds. 1997. *Engendering African Social Sciences*. Dakar, Senegal: Council for the Development of Economic and Social Research.

Jaggar, Alison M. 1983. *Feminist Politics and Human Nature*. Totawa, NJ: Rowman & Allanheld.

Jordan, June. 1985. *On Call*. Boston: South End Press.

Keller, Evelyn Fox. 1985. *Reflections on Gender and Science*. New Haven, CT: Yale University Press.

Kuhn, Thomas. 1962. *The Structure of Scientific Revolutions*, 2nd ed. Chicago: University of Chicago Press.

Ladner, Joyce. 1972. *Tomorrow's Tomorrow*. Garden City, NY: Doubleday.

Lee, Valerie. 1996. *Granny Midwives and Black Women Writers: Double-Dutched Readings*. New York: Routledge.

Lindsay, Beverly, ed. 1980. *Comparative Perspectives of Third World Women: The Impact of Race, Sex, and Class*. New York: Praeger.

Lorde, Audre. 1984. *Sister Outsider*. Trumansberg, NY: Crossing Press.

Mannheim, Karl. 1936. *Ideology and Utopia*. New York: Harcourt, Brace & World.

Massey, Douglas S., and Nancy A. Denton. 1993. *American Apartheid: Segregation and the Making of the Underclass*. Cambridge, MA: Harvard University Press.

Mills, C. Wright. 1959. *The Sociological Imagination*. New York: Oxford University Press.

Mirza, Heidi Safia, ed. 1997. *Black British Feminism: A Reader*. New York: Routledge.

Moses, Yolanda T. 1989. *Black Women in Academe: Issues and Strategies*. Project on the Status and Education of Women. Washington, D.C.: American Association of American Colleges.

Moulton, Janice. 1983. "A Paradigm of Philosophy: The Adversary Method." In *Discovering Reality*, ed. Sandra Harding and Merrill B. Hintikka, 149–64. Boston: D. Reidel.

Mulkay, Michael. 1979. *Science and the Sociology of Knowledge*. Boston: Unwin Hyman.

Nnaemeka, Obioma. 1998b. "This Women's Studies Business: Beyond Politics and History." In *Sisterhood, Feminisms, and Power: From Africa to the Diaspora*, ed. Obioma Nnaemeka, 351–86. Trenton, NJ: Africa World Press.

Richards, Dona. 1980. "European Mythology: The Ideology of 'Progress.' " In *Contemporary Black Thought*, ed. Molefi Kete Asante and Abdulai S. Vandi, 59–79. Beverly Hills, CA: Sage.

Richardson, Marilyn, ed. 1987. *Maria W. Stewart, America's First Black Woman Political Writer*. Bloomington: Indiana University Press.

Rights of Women: A Guide to the Most Important United Nations Treaties on Women's Human Rights. 1998. New York: International Women's Tribune Centre.

Roberts, Dorothy. 1997. *Killing the Black Body: Race, Reproduction, and the Meaning of Liberty*. New York: Pantheon.

Rollins, Judith. 1985. *Between Women, Domestics and Their Employers*. Philadelphia: Temple University Press.

St. Jean, Yanick and Joe R. Feagin. 1998. *Double Burden: Black Women and Everyday Racism*. Armonk, NY: M.E. Sharpe.

Scott, James C. 1985. *Weapons of the Weak: Everyday Forms of Peasant Resistance*. New Haven, CT: Yale University Press.

Smith, Barbara and Beverly Smith. 1981. "Across the Kitchen Table: A Sister-to-Sister Dialogue." In *This Bridge Called My Back: Writings by Radical Women of Color*, ed. Cherrie Moraga and Gloria Anzaldua, 113–27. Watertown, MA: Persephone Press.

Smith, Beverly. 1983. "The Wedding." In *Home Girls: A Black Feminist Anthology*, ed. Barbara Smith, 171–76. New York: Kitchen Table Press.

Smith, Dorothy. 1987. *The Everyday World as Problematic*. Boston: Northeastern University Press.

Spelman, Elizabeth V. 1988. *Inessential Woman: Problems of Exclusion in Feminist Thought*. Boston: Beacon.

Takaki, Ronald. 1993. *A Different Mirror: A History of Multicultural America*. Boston: Little, Brown.

Walker, Alice. 1977. "Zora Neale Hurston: A Cautionary Tale and a Partisan View." Foreword to *Zora Neale Hurston: A Literary Biography*, by Robert Hemenway, xi–xviii. Urbana: University of Illinois Press.

———. 1983. *In Search of Our Mother's Gardens*. New York: Harcourt Brace Jovanovich.

Yuval-Davis, Nira. 1997. *Gender and Nation*. Thousand Oaks, CA: Sage.

Zinn, Maxine Baca, Lynn Weber Cannon, Elizabeth Higginbotham, and Bonnie Thornton Dill. 1986. "The Costs of Exclusionary Practices in Women's Studies." *Signs* 11 (2): 290–303.

COMPANION WEBSITE

1. Go online to Write Out Loud about how the criteria of positivism are particularly problematic for alternative epistemologies.
2. Check out the Interactive Reading to deconstruct popular images from mass media from an intersectional perspective.
3. Go to the Supplementary Sources for *Shifting the Paradigm* for an additional reading from one of Collins's latest books, *Black Sexual Politics*.

Rise of the Avatar

Connecting Self and Society

Introductory Essay:
Through the Looking Glass of Facebook

You don't need a social theory book to tell you that we're living in the age of social networking. Websites like Instagram, Twitter, and Facebook are immensely popular and allow people to connect with friends and family, share information, and relate personal experiences to others at the click of a mouse. Online profiles also let us create virtual identities, or avatars, cyber-extensions of ourselves that are, in many cases, seen by more people a day than our physical beings. Who we are is increasingly shaped by these virtual expansions of ourselves into cyberspace. And while virtual social environments create all sorts of new possibilities (like making friends with someone from across the globe), they also present new problems, like having your online account hacked, your identity stolen, or your profile page filled with embarrassing and humiliating comments.

For an intriguing article from The New Yorker on how we stylize our identities for online dating sites, see the Supplementary Sources.

Despite the relative newness of these social networking sites (remember, Facebook just launched in 2004!), the basic point that our individual lives are enmeshed in these larger webs of connection and communication is as old as social theory itself. Social theorists in general and sociologists in particular have often been stereotyped as emphasizing the social *instead of* the individual, but the readings that follow show otherwise. A variety of social theorists, both classical and contemporary, have written insightful theories of what it means to be an individual in an inescapably social world—it's not only that we are always embedded in a larger social environment, but, even more profoundly, we can only become who we are by virtue of our connections to a larger collective. As the classical sociologist Charles Horton Cooley argued, the human self is like a "looking glass" or mirror. We can only develop a sense of self by having our identities reflected back to us by the members of our social communities. Without social networks (online or offline), we would lose our sense of what it means to be an individual.

If this argument that we are only an individual self through immersion in collective experience seems too abstract, imagine that one day you logged onto your Facebook account and found your profile page completely devoid of comments. No matter what you did, no matter how many hilarious YouTube videos you linked to or how many updates about your cat you posted, no one, not even your own mother, responded with a comment, or even a "like." Imagine this happened for weeks on end. What sorts of questions would you begin to ask?

"Why don't people like me?"

"Does anyone even know I'm here?"

"Since when did my mom get a freaking Facebook account!?"

Even online, our identities need community. Without it, our sense of individuality becomes compromised.

In the following pages, you'll be reading some of the most influential theories on the social foundations of identity. You'll connect to George H. Mead's comprehensive theory of the social genesis of the self, Georg Simmel's vivid analyses of the social psychology of the modern city, Michel Foucault's provocative history of sexual identity, and more. By the end of this section, you just might find out that you're not exactly who you thought you were. In fact, you *should* learn that who you are individually is inextricably connected to a vast web of relations, for better and for worse.

Classical Connections: George Herbert Mead and Georg Simmel

Though the telephone was still the latest in social networking technology when they wrote, George Herbert Mead and Georg Simmel remain two of the foundational theorists of the social origins of human identity. Mead and Simmel crafted some of the most insightful work on how the individual originates in the collective and how our psychological lives become intimately intertwined with larger social forces.

We begin this section on identity with the classic work of American sociologist, psychologist, and philosopher George Herbert Mead. In his appropriately titled opening salvo, "Self," Mead has us ponder how, because we are self-conscious creatures, humans can take ourselves as objects of experience. In other words, unlike most other animals, we not only experience objects in our surrounding environment (things like sounds, smells, and physical obstacles), we also experience our own personalities and identities in an object-like fashion. We understand ourselves *as selves*—as identifiable persons with distinct qualities, characteristics, feelings, thoughts, and biographies.

In many ways, the fact that we each have a "self" is one of the most basic facts of human experience—without it, something like a Facebook profile wouldn't even make sense, the authors of this book wouldn't even know to write about social theorists, let alone think to put their names on the cover. Yet, even though it is so fundamental to who we are, *how* we end up with a sense of self is one of the most difficult questions in the history of human thought. Countless theologians have argued that self-consciousness is a gift from God, while many philosophers have said it is an outgrowth of the progress of Reason, neuroscientists have plumbed the recesses of the brain, and psychoanalysts have, well, they've generally blamed your mother. Mead, for his part, looked to the social world for an answer.

For Mead, the fact that we are a self-conscious species springs from the equally important fact that we are a social and communicative species. Well before Facebook and Twitter, Mead recognized that human beings were all about finding ways to gab to each other about one another. He saw our chatty nature not only as expressing a penchant for gossip (true enough), but, more importantly, as the very foundation of the self.

A sense of self, Mead writes, arises as we enter into the "conversation of gestures" that make up our lives with other human beings. This "conversation" encompasses all of our symbolic communication, from the nuanced wink of an eye to a treatise on social theory, from ancient rock paintings to those seven "likes" you just posted on your friend's profile page. Only through these many acts of conversing with and taking the perspectives of others, Mead says, can we begin to see something of ourselves. And it's when we can internalize these perspectives as our own viewpoint (as a "Me"), that we begin to understand what it means to be an "I," an Ellen, Joe, Kathy, or Duane. In short, we can only know ourselves through others, through the people, groups, and institutions with which we create and share our experiences. Without this social experience, there would be no experience of an individual self. And definitely no Facebook (sorry, Mark Zuckerberg).

While Mead will provide you with the most general and comprehensive theory of the self, the great German sociologist and philosopher Georg Simmel will connect you, through two of his classic works, to how the transition to our characteristically modern forms of collective life have deeply affected our individual hearts and minds. In his "The Metropolis and Mental Life," Simmel notes that the modern individual often inhabits social environments where she is confronted with a historically unprecedented array of cultural options, and nowhere is this more evident than in the modern city. Want something to eat? Well, you can have Indian high cuisine, Chinese takeout, or hit up the tamale stand over on 68th Street. Want to check out the art scene? Well, there's the contemporary art museum, the Institute for Russian Art, that place downtown where they sell folk art, the neo-beatnik coffee shop down the block, and on and on.

Simmel is quick to point out that the plethora of opportunities available in the modern city gives us a great deal of individual freedom. Yet, it can also

For a strikingly similar take on the origins of self-consciousness from the standpoint of current evolutionary theory, see the references to Michael Tomasello's *The Cultural Origins of Human Cognition* in the Supplementary Sources.

overwhelm us. Presented with more options than one person can possibly ever hope to experience in a lifetime, the modern individual runs the risk of stunting her psychological growth. We become mere cultural dabblers, people who get to experience and know a bit of everything but never the depths of any one cultural phenomenon. In many ways, what Simmel was saying about the physical metropolis a hundred years ago resonates with worries that the massive amounts of information available in our digital age actually overwhelm us more than make us smarter. At a time when there is a cable news station or website that caters to every political viewpoint and a reality show for seemingly anyone willing to allow a camera into their personal lives, we become unable to distinguish between fact and fiction, "real news" and tabloid fodder, entertainment and true life. Like Simmel before them, insightful social commentators today see the modern individual as increasingly free, but also, perhaps, increasingly shallow. How the city embodied this paradox and struggle of the modern self–society relationship was what so intrigued Simmel.

For a more recent take on Simmel's idea that all of these choices can overwhelm us, check out Barry Schwartz's *The Paradox of Choice* in the Supplementary Sources.

Simmel was also fascinated by the proliferation of certain social roles. In the second reading from his work, you'll plug in to his views on how, in contemporary times, many people—including ourselves—occupy the identity of "The Stranger." By "the stranger," Simmel is not talking about a totally unknown person, someone who shows up today but is gone tomorrow. Rather, in his own words, the stranger is "the person who comes today and stays tomorrow."

For Simmel, what is strange about the stranger is that he is an "outsider within," embedded in the community but not wholly belonging to it, both near to and distant from people at the same time. In Simmel's sense of the term, strangers are like all of those "friends" you have on Facebook who aren't really your friends, people you "know of" because of some general similarities or acquaintances but don't truly know in a closer sense. The stranger is also your mail carrier, the corner grocery store clerk, your sociology professor, and all of those other people who are, on the one hand, in contact with you on a regular basis but, on the other, could (and possibly will) leave your life tomorrow without causing you much worry or confusion. And the stranger is also you, whenever you are fulfilling your near-but-distant role toward other people in your job, volunteer work, or online.

The stranger, then, is only connected to the broader social community by the most general (and generic) commonalities. Yet, by virtue of his simultaneous nearness and distance from others, Simmel recognizes that the stranger is also an important part of social life. The stranger, because he is detached from many aspects of the community, is often valued for his objectivity, for being able to take a distanced and dispassionate view of events and relationships. The stranger is also someone we turn to, paradoxically, as a close confidant. Because of the stranger's detachment from the intimacies of our everyday lives, we feel he will not judge us in a biased or harsh manner.

People's relationships with their therapists are some of the best examples of the importance of the stranger's confidant role, but we could also look to reality television and daytime talk shows as a larger cultural movement encouraging us to tell our deepest personal secrets to strangers. Simmel, meet Oprah.

It's a strange world indeed.

Contemporary Extensions: Identity Re-Wired

The insights provided by classical accounts of identity like those of Mead and Simmel have been taken up and re-wired by some of contemporary theory's most prominent thinkers. The readings in this contemporary section look for both the social origins and consequences of our senses of self. And no contemporary theorist analyzed the everyday, often unnoticed trials and tribulations of the self quite like Erving Goffman.

Heavily influenced by Mead's ideas about the social and symbolic nature of the self, Goffman turned his keen (and sometimes mischievous) intellectual attention to the most mundane scenes of everyday life—to business meetings, parties, chance meetings between strangers, interactions between employers and employees or doctors and patients (and, make no mistake, if he were alive today, Goffman would be taking field notes on every social networking site he could get his hands on). In each of these settings, Goffman was interested in how we craft, manage, and maintain a particular sense of self.

In this excerpt from his most influential book, *The Presentation of Self in Everyday Life*, you'll connect with Goffman's "dramaturgical perspective." For Goffman, the everyday management of identity was best analyzed as one would study a play or theatrical drama. In the boring humdrum of normal life, Goffman, like Jacque in Shakespeare's *As You Like It*, saw all the world as a stage, replete with props, cues, stage directions, and a cast of characters all trying to play their parts. In the reading, you'll be introduced to a great deal of Goffman's unique theoretical terminology, but at the core of his theoretical perspective on the self are his ideas about "impression management."

Much of what makes social life resemble a play, Goffman believes, is the fact that we understand—and other people perceive—our actions as reflecting something about ourselves. Goffman recognized that almost everything we do—from what we eat to what kind of music we like creates in our minds (and others') an impression of our character as a person. More importantly, we spend a great deal of time and effort *managing* these impressions, highlighting some things about ourselves for particular audiences while hiding others.

For example, if you've ever pondered changing that profile picture of your rowdy weekend in Las Vegas because you can't decide if it a) makes you look like a laid-back, fun-loving person to your friends or b) makes you look like a

Take a look in the Supplementary Sources for a list of documentaries exploring issues of the self in contemporary society.

booze-guzzling heathen to your boss and parents—congratulations! You were managing your impressions. Or, if you've ever said to a group of people "I don't really care what other people think about me" because you really care that those people think you don't care what they think—well, now you're really deep into Goffman's social universe.

For Goffman, we may be sincere or cynical about the way we present our identities to others, but the fundamental fact of the matter is that we always do perform our parts on the big stage of the social. And while we may be tempted to think that who we are is a private phenomenon that we then choose to share with others, Goffman makes a strong case that it's actually the other way around. We *are* the parts we play, the masks we don as we perform with others.

While Goffman's work plugs us into the interactional dramas of everyday life, the next two theorists ask us to explore the social foundations of what we normally think of as the most private and individual parts of our beings—our sexualities and genders. In the reading from *The History of Sexuality*, Michel Foucault provocatively questions why we have come to think about sex and sexuality as expressing something deeply authentic or "true" about who we are. While the idea that sex expresses something core to our identities seems self-evident to many of us today, Foucault observes that this was not so in all times and places. In fact, Foucault argues that the very idea of having "a sexuality" is a modern invention, a reality constructed through specific social procedures and discourses that didn't appear in the West until around the seventeenth century.

Chief among these procedures for "producing the truth about sex," according to Foucault, was the confession. Originating in the practices of the Church, but then spreading to the courts, clinics, schools, to today's television talk shows and Internet communities, the confession is one of our most significant and widespread cultural practices. We live in, Foucault argues, "a singularly confessing society," and "Western man has become a confessing animal."

Many may see the confession as expressing and possibly even liberating some deeply hidden truths about ourselves. But Foucault provocatively argues that the confession actually constructs or produces these so-called truths. Through confession, he states, Western societies have created a science of sex and made one's "sexuality" foundational to who we are as individuals. While many may see being more "open" about our sexualities as a liberating step forward, Foucault argues this openness to confession is the primary pathway through which sex—and now sexuality—is socially organized, monitored, and controlled by a variety of institutions. Foucault might say, "let's *not* talk about sex, baby."

In the next reading from *Gender Trouble*, leading contemporary social and feminist theorist Judith Butler takes up and reworks some of Foucault's

See sociologist Joshua Gamson's book, *Freaks Talk Back*, for an intriguing (and often funny) analysis of sex and television talk shows (Supplementary Sources).

Log on to the Feminist Theory Profile Page to learn more about Judith Butler, one of contemporary feminism's most influential social theorists.

critiques of "the truth" about sex and applies them to gender. Perhaps the most influential theorization of gender identity since Beauvoir, Butler's *Gender Trouble* challenges previous feminist scholarship that assumed there was a stable pre-existing identity called "woman" that could be at the natural foundation of feminist politics and thought. Instead, much like Foucault, Butler argues that what we call "woman" (or "man" for that matter) is produced through social procedures and discourses. In Butler's view, feminist discourses (as well as other discourses about gender) do not simply represent but help construct "woman."

Of course, this presents a sticky problem for feminism. Without the category "woman," who is feminism about and for? Butler tackles this issue through an analysis that seeks not only to decouple gender from sex, challenging the so-called "naturalness" of each, but also presents a radically relational perspective on gender identity. More specifically, Butler thinks that one's identity as a woman is not something one essentially is, but rather something one momentarily *becomes* within social relations among other identity categories (especially those of other gender categories such as "man" and sexual categories such as "straight," "gay," "bisexual," etc.). Akin to Foucault, Butler argues that even our seemingly most fundamental identity attributes are, in reality, constantly performed, produced, and policed.

After reading Butler, check out biologist Anne Fausto-Sterling's take on the many varieties of human sex and sexual identity in the Supplementary Sources.

The final reading in our section on identity is from one of sociology's most influential living theorists, Anthony Giddens. Renowned for his ability to provide theoretical insights on a vast array of important sociological topics, the excerpt from Giddens' book *Modernity and Self-Identity* showcases his thoughts on the trials and tribulations of maintaining a coherent sense of self in the modern world. In the opening paragraphs of the reading, Giddens explains his understanding that the self is, above all, about biography. More precisely, our identities depend on our ability to maintain a story of our lives. Out of the multitudes of experience we undergo over the course of our lives, we humans attempt to create a coherent and understandable account of where we have been, where we are, and where we are going. It is only by crafting, maintaining, and revising this story of our individual selves that we come to have personal identities at all.

But modernity, Giddens writes, makes maintaining a coherent biography complicated. In fact, the modern self is faced with a number of paradoxes or tensions, as Giddens sees it. For example, Giddens states that there is a characteristically modern tension between the fragmentation versus unification of the self. On one hand, the complexity and diversity characteristic of modern social life puts our sense of self under the constant threat of splitting into a million pieces. At work you are expected to be one kind of person, at home with your family another, with your friends someone else entirely, and on and on. Giddens argues that the necessity to be constantly performing a different version of the self for each new situation can make maintaining a cohesive sense of who you are feel pretty exhausting, if not downright impossible. But, on the other hand, it's also the case that the diversity of social possibilities creates room for crafting a truly unique biography. In outlining several of these key dilemmas of modern self-identity, Giddens shows that the dynamic relationship between self and society is fraught with both peril and possibility in our increasingly complex, modern world.

Plug In

Who the hell do you think you are?

Maybe not at all what you thought after reading the theorists in this section. If there is one lesson to take from these thinkers, it is probably this: Who we are as individuals is fundamentally connected to our lives in the collective. Whether we're in the classroom or on the Web, in church or at the therapist's office, we can only truly understand what is "on the inside" by looking outward, toward the social.

34

Self

George Herbert Mead

THE SELF AND THE ORGANISM

In our statement of the development of intelligence we have already suggested that the language process is essential for the development of the self. The self has a character which is different from that of the physiological organism proper. The self is something which has a development; it is not initially there, at birth, but arises in the process of social experience and activity, that is, develops in the given individual as a result of his relations to that process as a whole and to other individuals within that process. The intelligence of the lower forms of animal life, like a great deal of human intelligence, does not involve a self. In our habitual actions, for example, in our moving about in a world that is simply there and to which we are so adjusted that no thinking is involved, there is a certain amount of sensuous experience such as persons have when they are just waking up, a bare thereness of the world. Such characters about us may exist in experience without taking their place in relationship to the self. One must, of course, under those conditions, distinguish between the experience that immediately takes place and our own organization of it into the experience of the self. One says upon analysis that a certain item had its place in his experience, in the experience of his self. We do inevitably tend at a certain level of sophistication to organize all experience into that of a self. We do so intimately identify our experiences, especially our affective experiences, with the self that it takes a moment's abstraction to realize that pain and pleasure can be there without being the experience of the self. Similarly, we normally organize our memories upon the string of our self. If we date things we always date them from the point of view of our past experiences. We frequently have memories that we cannot date, that we cannot place. A picture comes before us suddenly and we are at a loss to explain when that experience originally took place. We remember perfectly distinctly the picture, but we do not have it definitely placed, and until we can place it in terms of our past experience we are not satisfied. Nevertheless, I think it is obvious when one comes to consider it that the self is not necessarily involved in the life of the organism, nor involved in what we term our sensuous experience, that is, experience in a world about us for which we have habitual reactions.

We can distinguish very definitely between the self and the body. The body can be there and can operate in a very intelligent fashion without there being a self involved in the experience. The self has the characteristic that it is an object to itself, and that characteristic distinguishes it from other objects and from the body. It is perfectly true that the eye can see the foot, but it does not see the body as a whole. We cannot see our backs; we can feel certain portions of them, if we are agile, but we cannot get an experience of our whole body. There are, of course, experiences which are somewhat vague and difficult of location, but the bodily experiences are for us organized about a self. The foot and hand belong to the self. We can see our feet, especially if we look at them from the wrong end of an opera glass, as strange things which we have difficulty in recognizing as our own. The parts of the body are quite distinguishable from the self. We can lose parts of the body without any serious invasion of the self. The mere ability to experience different parts of the body is not different from the experience of a table. The table presents a different feel from what the hand does when one hand feels another, but it is an experience of something with which we come definitely into contact. The body does not experience itself as a whole, in the sense in which the self in some way enters into the experience of the self.

It is the characteristic of the self as an object to itself that I want to bring out. This characteristic is represented in the word "self," which is a reflexive, and indicates that which can be both subject and object. This type of object is essentially different from other objects, and in the past it has been distinguished as conscious, a term which indicates an experience with, an experience of, one's self. It was assumed that consciousness in some way carried this capacity of being an object to itself. In giving a behavioristic statement of consciousness we have to look for some sort of experience in which the physical organism can become an object to itself.[1]

When one is running to get away from someone who is chasing him, he is entirely occupied in this action, and his experience may be swallowed up in the objects about him, so that he has, at the time being, no consciousness of self at all. We must be, of course, very completely occupied to have that take place, but we can, I think, recognize that sort of a possible experience in which the self does not enter. We can, perhaps, get some light on that situation through those experiences in which in very intense action there appear in the experience of the individual, back of this intense action, memories and anticipations. Tolstoi as an officer in the war gives an account of having pictures of his past experience in the midst of his most intense action. There are also the pictures that flash into a person's mind when he is drowning. In such instances there is a contrast between an experience that is absolutely wound up in outside activity in which the self as an object does not enter, and an activity of memory and imagination in which the self is the principal object. The self is then entirely distinguishable from an organism that is surrounded by things and acts with reference to things, including parts of its own body. These latter may be objects like other objects, but they are just objects out there in the field, and they do not involve a self that is an object to the organism. This is, I think, frequently overlooked. It is that fact which makes our anthropomorphic reconstructions of animal life so fallacious. How can an individual get outside himself (experientially) in such a way as to become an object to himself? This is the essential psychological problem of selfhood or of self-consciousness; and its solution is to be found by referring to the process of social conduct or activity in which the given person or individual is implicated. The apparatus of reason would not be complete unless it swept itself into its own analysis of the field of experience; or unless the individual brought himself into the same experiential field as that of the other individual selves in relation to whom he acts in any given social situation. Reason cannot become impersonal unless it takes an objective, non-affective attitude toward itself; otherwise we have just consciousness, not *self*-consciousness. And it is necessary to rational conduct that the individual should thus take an objective, impersonal attitude toward himself, that he should become an object to himself. For the individual organism is obviously an essential and important fact or constituent element of the empirical situation in which it acts; and without taking objective account of itself as such, it cannot act intelligently, or rationally.

The individual experiences himself as such, not directly, but only indirectly, from the particular standpoints of other individual members of the same social group, or from the generalized standpoint of the social group as a whole to which he belongs. For he enters his own experience as a self or individual, not directly or immediately, not by becoming a subject to himself, but only in so far as he first becomes an object to himself just as other individuals are objects to him or in his experience; and he becomes an object to himself only by taking the attitudes of other individuals toward himself within a social environment or context of experience and behavior in which both he and they are involved.

The importance of what we term "communication" lies in the fact that it provides a form of behavior in which the organism or the individual may become an object to himself. It is that sort of communication which we have been discussing— not communication in the sense of the cluck of the hen to the chickens, or the bark of a wolf to the pack, or the lowing of a cow, but communication in the sense of significant symbols, communication which is directed not only to others but also to the individual himself. So far as that type of communication is a part of behavior it at least introduces a self. Of course, one may hear without listening; one may see things that he does not realize; do things that he is not really aware of. But it is where one does respond to that which he addresses to another and where that response of his own becomes a part of his conduct, where he not only hears himself but responds to himself, talks and replies to himself as truly as the other person replies to him, that we have behavior in which the individuals become objects to themselves.

Such a self is not, I would say, primarily the physiological organism. The physiological organism is essential to it,[2] but we are at least able to think of a self without it. Persons who believe in immortality, or believe in ghosts, or in the possibility of the self leaving the body, assume a self which is quite distinguishable from the body. How successfully they can hold these conceptions is an open question, but we do, as a fact, separate the self and the organism. It is fair to say that the beginning of the self as an object, so far as we can see, is to be found in the experiences of people that lead to the conception of a "double." Primitive people assume that there is a double, located presumably in the diaphragm, that leaves the body temporarily in sleep and completely in death. It can be enticed out of the body of one's enemy and perhaps killed. It is represented in infancy by the imaginary playmates which children set up, and through which they come to control their experiences in their play.

The self, as that which can be an object to itself, is essentially a social structure, and it arises in social experience. After a self has arisen, it in a certain sense provides for itself its social experiences, and so we can conceive of an absolutely solitary self. But it is impossible to conceive of a self arising outside of social experience. When it has arisen we can think of a person in solitary confinement for the rest of his life, but who still has himself as a companion, and is able to think and to converse with himself as he had communicated with others. That process to which I have just referred, of responding to one's self as another responds to it, taking part in one's own conversation with others, being aware of what one is saying and using that awareness of what one is saying to determine what one is going to say thereafter—that is a process with which we are all familiar. We are continually following up our own address to other persons by an understanding of what we are saying, and using that understanding in the direction of our continued speech. We are finding out what we are going to say, what we are going to do, by saying and doing, and in the process we are continually controlling the process itself. In the conversation of gestures what we say calls out a certain response in another and that in turn changes our own action, so that we shift from what we started to do because of the reply the other makes. The conversation of gestures is the beginning of communication. The individual comes to carry on a conversation of gestures with himself. He says something, and that calls out a certain reply in himself which makes him change what he was going to say. One starts to say something, we will presume an unpleasant something, but when he starts to say it he realizes it is cruel. The effect on himself of what he is saying checks him; there is here a conversation of gestures between the individual and himself. We mean by significant speech that the action is one that affects the individual himself, and that the effect upon the individual himself is part of the intelligent carrying-out of the conversation with others. Now we, so to speak, amputate that social phase and dispense with it for the time being, so that one is talking to one's self as one would talk to another person.[3]

This process of abstraction cannot be carried on indefinitely. One inevitably seeks an audience, has to pour himself out to somebody. In reflective intelligence one thinks to act, and to act solely so that this action remains a part of a social process. Thinking becomes preparatory to social action. The very process of thinking is, of course, simply an inner conversation that goes on, but it is a conversation of gestures which in its completion implies the expression of that which one thinks to an audience. One separates the significance of what he is saying to others from the actual speech and gets it ready before saying it. He thinks it out, and perhaps writes it in the form of a book; but it is still a part of social intercourse in which one is addressing other persons and at the same time addressing one's self, and in which one controls the address to other persons by the response made to one's own gesture. That the person should be responding to himself is necessary to the self, and it is this sort of social conduct which provides behavior within which that self appears. I know of no other form of behavior than the linguistic in which the individual is an object to himself, and, so far as I can see, the individual is not a self in the reflexive sense unless he is an object to himself. It is this fact that gives a critical importance to communication, since this is a type of behavior in which the individual does so respond to himself.

We realize in everyday conduct and experience that an individual does not mean a great deal of what he is doing and saying. We frequently say that such an individual is not himself. We come away from an interview with a realization that we have left out important things, that there are parts of the self that did not get into what was said. What determines the amount of the self that gets into communication is the social experience itself. Of course, a good deal of the self does not need to get expression. We carry on a whole series of different relationships to different people. We are one thing to one man and another thing to another. There are parts of the self which exist only for the self in relationship to itself. We divide ourselves up in all sorts of different selves with reference to our acquaintances. We discuss politics with one and religion with another. There are all sorts of different selves answering to all sorts of different social reactions. It is the social process itself that is responsible for the appearance of the self; it is not there as a self apart from this type of experience.

[...]

THE BACKGROUND OF THE GENESIS OF THE SELF

The problem now presents itself as to how, in detail, a self arises. We have to note something of the background of its genesis. First of all there is the conversation of gestures between animals involving some sort of co-operative activity. There the beginning of the act of one is a stimulus to the other to respond in a certain way, while the beginning of this response becomes again a stimulus to the first to adjust his action to the oncoming response. Such is the preparation for the completed act, and ultimately it leads up to the conduct which is the outcome of this preparation. The conversation of gestures, however, does not carry with it the reference of the individual, the animal, the organism, to itself. It is not acting in a fashion which calls for a response from the form itself, although it is conduct with reference to the conduct of others. We have seen, however, that there are certain gestures that do affect the organism as they affect other organisms and may, therefore, arouse in the organism responses of the same character as aroused in the other. Here, then, we have a situation in which the individual may at least arouse responses in himself and reply to these responses, the condition being that the social stimuli have an effect on the individual which is like that which they have on the other. That, for example, is what is implied in language; otherwise language as significant symbol would disappear, since the individual would not get the meaning of that which he says.

The peculiar character possessed by our human social environment belongs to it by virtue of the peculiar character of human social activity; and that character, as we have seen, is to be found in the process of communication, and more particularly in the triadic relation on which the existence of meaning is based: the relation of the gesture of one organism to the adjustive response made to it by another organism, in its indicative capacity as pointing to the completion or resultant of the act it initiates (the meaning of the gesture being thus the response of the second organism to it as such, or as a gesture). What, as it were, takes the gesture out of the social act and isolates it as such—what makes it something more than just an early phase of an individual act—is the response of another organism, or of other organisms, to it. Such a response is its meaning, or gives it its meaning. The social situation and process of behavior are here presupposed by the acts of the individual organisms implicated therein. The gesture arises as a separable element in the social act, by virtue of the fact that it is selected out

by the sensitivities of other organisms to it; it does not exist as a gesture merely in the experience of the single individual. The meaning of a gesture by one organism, to repeat, is found in the response of another organism to what would be the completion of the act of the first organism which that gesture initiates and indicates.

We sometimes speak as if a person could build up an entire argument in his mind, and then put it into words to convey it to someone else. Actually, our thinking always takes place by means of some sort of symbols. It is possible that one could have the meaning of "chair" in his experience without there being a symbol, but we would not be thinking about it in that case. We may sit down in a chair without thinking about what we are doing, that is, the approach to the chair is presumably already aroused in our experience, so that the meaning is there. But if one is thinking about the chair he must have some sort of a symbol for it. It may be the form of the chair, it may be the attitude that somebody else takes in sitting down, but it is more apt to be some language symbol that arouses this response. In a thought process there has to be some sort of a symbol that can refer to this meaning, that is, tend to call out this response, and also serve this purpose for other persons as well. It would not be a thought process if that were not the case.

Our symbols are all universal.[4] You cannot say anything that is absolutely particular; anything you say that has any meaning at all is universal. You are saying something that calls out a specific response in anybody else provided that the symbol exists for him in his experience as it does for you. There is the language of speech and the language of hands, and there may be the language of the expression of the countenance. One can register grief or joy and call out certain responses. There are primitive people who can carry on elaborate conversations just by expressions of the countenance. Even in these cases the person who communicates is affected by that expression just as he expects somebody else to be affected. Thinking always implies a symbol which will call out the same response in another that it calls out in the thinker. Such a symbol is a universal of discourse; it is universal in its character. We always assume that the symbol we use is one which will call out in the other person the same response, provided it is a part of his mechanism of conduct. A person who is saying something is saying to himself what he says to others; otherwise he does not know what he is talking about.

[...]

What is essential to communication is that the symbol should arouse in one's self what it arouses in the other individual. It must have that sort of universality to any person who finds himself in the same situation. There is a possibility of language whenever a stimulus can affect the individual as it affects the other. With a blind person such as Helen Keller, it is a contact experience that could be given to another as it is given to herself. It is out of that sort of language that the mind of Helen Keller was built up. As she has recognized, it was not until she could get into communication with other persons through symbols which could arouse in herself the responses they arouse in other people that she could get what we term a mental content, or a self.

Another set of background factors in the genesis of the self is represented in the activities of play and the game.

Among primitive people, as I have said, the necessity of distinguishing the self and the organism was recognized in what we term the "double": the individual has a thing-like self that is affected by the individual as it affects other people and which is distinguished from the immediate organism in that it can leave the body and come back to it. This is the basis for the concept of the soul as a separate entity.

We find in children something that answers to this double, namely, the invisible, imaginary companions which a good many children produce in their own experience. They organize in this way the responses which they call out in other persons and

call out also in themselves. Of course, this playing with an imaginary companion is only a peculiarly interesting phase of ordinary play. Play in this sense, especially the stage which precedes the organized games, is a play at something. A child plays at being a mother, at being a teacher, at being a policeman; that is, it is taking different rôles, as we say. We have something that suggests this in what we call the play of animals: a cat will play with her kittens, and dogs play with each other. Two dogs playing with each other will attack and defend, in a process which if carried through would amount to an actual fight. There is a combination of responses which checks the depth of the bite. But we do not have in such a situation the dogs taking a definite rôle in the sense that a child deliberately takes the rôle of another. This tendency on the part of the children is what we are working with in the kindergarten where the rôles which the children assume are made the basis for training. When a child does assume a rôle he has in himself the stimuli which call out that particular response or group of responses. He may, of course, run away when he is chased, as the dog does, or he may turn around and strike back just as the dog does in his play. But that is not the same as playing at something. Children get together to "play Indian." This means that the child has a certain set of stimuli which call out in itself the responses that they would call out in others, and which answer to an Indian. In the play period the child utilizes his own responses to these stimuli which he makes use of in building a self. The response which he has a tendency to make to these stimuli organizes them. He plays that he is, for instance, offering himself something, and he buys it; he gives a letter to himself and takes it away; he addresses himself as a parent, as a teacher; he arrests himself as a policeman. He has a set of stimuli which call out in himself the sort of responses they call out in others. He takes this group of responses and organizes them into a certain whole. Such is the simplest form of being another to one's self. It involves a temporal situation. The child says something in one charac-ter and responds in another character, and then his responding in another character is a stimulus to him-self in the first character, and so the conversation goes on. A certain organized structure arises in him and in his other which replies to it, and these carry on the conversation of gestures between themselves.

If we contrast play with the situation in an organized game, we note the essential difference that the child who plays in a game must be ready to take the attitude of everyone else involved in that game, and that these different rôles must have a definite relationship to each other. Taking a very simple game such as hide-and-seek, everyone with the exception of the one who is hiding is a person who is hunting. A child does not require more than the person who is hunted and the one who is hunting. If a child is playing in the first sense he just goes on playing, but there is no basic organization gained. In that early stage he passes from one rôle to another just as a whim takes him. But in a game where a number of individuals are involved, then the child taking one rôle must be ready to take the rôle of everyone else. If he gets in a ball nine he must have the responses of each position involved in his own position. He must know what everyone else is going to do in order to carry out his own play. He has to take all of these rôles. They do not all have to be present in consciousness at the same time, but at some moments he has to have three or four individuals present in his own attitude, such as the one who is going to throw the ball, the one who is going to catch it, and so on. These responses must be, in some degree, present in his own make-up. In the game, then, there is a set of responses of such others so organized that the attitude of one calls out the appropriate attitudes of the other.

This organization is put in the form of the rules of the game. Children take a great interest in rules. They make rules on the spot in order to help themselves out of difficulties. Part of the enjoyment of the game is to get these rules. Now, the rules are the set of responses which a particular attitude calls out. You can demand a certain response in others if you take a certain attitude. These responses are all in yourself as well. There you get an organized set of such responses as that to which I have referred, which is something more elaborate than the rôles found in play. Here there is just a set of responses that follow on each other indefinitely. At such a stage we speak of a child as not yet having a fully developed self. The child responds in a fairly intelligent fashion to the immediate stimuli that come to him, but they are not organized. He does not organize his life as we would like to have him do, namely, as a whole. There is just a set of responses of the type of play. The child reacts to a certain stimulus, and the reaction is in himself that is called out in others, but he is not a whole self. In his game he has to have an organization of these rôles; otherwise he cannot play the game. The game represents the passage in the life of the child from taking the rôle of others in play to the organized part that is essential to self-consciousness in the full sense of the term.

PLAY, THE GAME, AND THE GENERALIZED OTHER

We were speaking of the social conditions under which the self arises as an object. In addition to language we found two illustrations, one in play and the other in the game, and I wish to summarize and expand my account on these points. I have spoken of these from the point of view of children. We can, of course, refer also to the attitudes of more primitive people out of which our civilization has arisen. A striking illustration of play as distinct from the game is found in the myths and various of the plays which primitive people carry out, especially in religious pageants. The pure play attitude which we find in the case of little children may not be found here, since the participants are adults, and undoubtedly the relationship of these play processes to that which they interpret is more or less in the minds of even the most primitive people. In the process of interpretation of such rituals, there is an organization of play which perhaps might be compared to that which is taking place in the kindergarten in dealing with the plays of little children, where these are made into a set that will have a definite structure or relationship. At least something of the same sort is found in the play of primitive people. This type of activity belongs, of course, not to the everyday life of the people in their dealing with the objects about them—there we have a more or less definitely developed self-consciousness—but in their attitudes toward the forces about them, the nature upon which they depend; in their attitude toward this nature which is vague and uncertain, there we have a much more primitive response; and that response finds its expression in taking the rôle of the other, playing at the expression of their gods and their heroes, going through certain rites which are the representation of what these individuals are supposed to be doing. The process is one which develops, to be sure, into a more or less definite technique and is controlled; and yet we can say that it has arisen out of situations similar to those in which little children play at being a parent, at being a teacher—vague personalities that are about them and which affect them and on which they depend. These are personalities which they take, rôles they play, and in so far control the development of their own personality. This outcome is just what the kindergarten works toward. It takes the characters of these various vague beings and gets them into such an organized social relationship to each other that they build up the character of the little child.[5] The very introduction of organization from outside supposes a lack of organization at this period in the child's experience. Over against such a situation of the little child and primitive people, we have the game as such.

The fundamental difference between the game and play is that in the latter the child must have the attitude of all the others involved in that game. The attitudes of the other players which the participant assumes organize into a sort of unit, and it is that organization which controls the response of the individual. The illustration used was of a person playing base ball. Each one of his own acts is determined by his assumption of the action of the others who are playing the game. What he does is controlled by his being everyone else on that team, at least in so far as those attitudes affect his own particular response. We get then an "other" which is an organization of the attitudes of those involved in the same process.

The organized community or social group which gives to the individual his unity of self may be called "the generalized other." The attitude of the generalized other is the attitude of the whole community.[6] Thus, for example, in the case of such a social group as a ball team, the team is the generalized other in so far as it enters—as an organized process or social activity—into the experience of any one of the individual members of it.

If the given human individual is to develop a self in the fullest sense, it is not sufficient for him merely to take the attitudes of other human individuals toward himself and toward one another within the human social process, and to bring that social process as a whole into his individual experience merely in these terms: he must also, in the same way that he takes the attitudes of other individuals toward himself and toward one another, take their attitudes toward the various phases or aspects of the common social activity or set of social undertakings in which, as members of an organized society or social group, they are all engaged; and he must then, by generalizing these individual attitudes of that organized society or social group itself, as a whole, act toward different social projects which at any given time it is carrying out, or toward the various larger phases of the general social process which constitutes its life and of which these projects are specific manifestations. This getting of the broad activities of any given social whole or organized society as such within the experiential field of any one of the individuals involved or included in that whole is, in other words, the essential basis and prerequisite of the fullest development of that individual's self: only in so far as he takes the attitudes of the organized social group to which he belongs toward the organized, co-operative social activity or set of such activities in which that group as such is engaged, does he develop a complete self or possess the sort of complete self he has developed. And on the other hand, the complex co-operative processes and activities and institutional functionings of organized human society are also possible only in so far as every individual involved in them or belonging to that society can take the general attitudes of all other such individuals with reference to these processes and activities and institutional functionings, and to the organized social whole of experiential relations and interactions thereby constituted—and can direct his own behavior accordingly.

It is in the form of the generalized other that the social process influences the behavior of the individuals involved in it and carrying it on, i.e., that the community exercises control over the conduct of its individual members; for it is in this form that the social process or community enters as a determining factor into the individual's thinking. In abstract thought the individual takes the attitude of the generalized other[7] toward himself, without reference to its expression in any particular other individuals; and in concrete thought he takes that attitude in so far as it is expressed in the attitudes toward his behavior of those other individuals with whom he is involved in the given social situation or act. But only by taking the attitude of the generalized other toward himself, in one or another of these ways, can he think at all; for only thus can thinking—or the internalized conversation of gestures which constitutes thinking—occur. And only through the taking by individuals of the attitude or attitudes of the generalized other toward themselves is the existence of a universe of discourse, as that system of common

or social meanings which thinking presupposes at its context, rendered possible.

[...]

I have pointed out, then, that there are two general stages in the full development of the self. At the first of these stages, the individual's self is constituted simply by an organization of the particular attitudes of other individuals toward himself and toward one another in the specific social acts in which he participates with them. But at the second stage in the full development of the individual's self that self is constituted not only by an organization of these particular individual attitudes, but also by an organization of the social attitudes of the generalized other or the social group as a whole to which he belongs. These social or group attitudes are brought within the individual's field of direct experience, and are included as elements in the structure or constitution of his self, in the same way that the attitudes of particular other individuals are; and the individual arrives at them, or succeeds in taking them, by means of further organizing, and then generalizing, the attitudes of particular other individuals in terms of their organized social bearings and implications. So the self reaches its full development by organizing these individual attitudes of others into the organized social or group attitudes, and by thus becoming an individual reflection of the general systematic pattern of social or group behavior in which it and the others are all involved—a pattern which enters as a whole into the individual's experience in terms of these organized group attitudes which, through the mechanism of his central nervous system, he takes toward himself, just as he takes the individual attitudes of others.

The game has a logic, so that such an organization of the self is rendered possible: there is a definite end to be obtained; the actions of the different individuals are all related to each other with reference to that end so that they do not conflict; one is not in conflict with himself in the attitude of another man on the team. If one has the attitude of the person throwing the ball he can also have the response of catching the ball. The two are related so that they further the purpose of the game itself. They are interrelated in a unitary, organic fashion. There is a definite unity, then, which is introduced into the organization of other selves when we reach such a stage as that of the game, as over against the situation of play where there is a simple succession of one rôle after another, a situation which is, of course, characteristic of the child's own personality. The child is one thing at one time and another at another, and what he is at one moment does not determine what he is at another. That is both the charm of childhood as well as its inadequacy. You cannot count on the child; you cannot assume that all the things he does are going to determine what he will do at any moment. He is not organized into a whole. The child has no definite character, no definite personality.

The game is then an illustration of the situation out of which an organized personality arises. In so far as the child does take the attitude of the other and allows that attitude of the other to determine the thing he is going to do with reference to a common end, he is becoming an organic member of society. He is taking over the morale of that society and is becoming an essential member of it. He belongs to it in so far as he does allow the attitude of the other that he takes to control his own immediate expression. What is involved here is some sort of an organized process. That which is expressed in terms of the game is, of course, being continually expressed in the social life of the child, but this wider process goes beyond the immediate experience of the child himself. The importance of the game is that it lies entirely inside of the child's own experience, and the importance of our modern type of education is that it is brought as far as possible within this realm. The different attitudes that a child assumes are so organized that they exercise a definite control over his response, as the attitudes in a game control his own immediate response. In the game we get an organized other, a generalized other, which is found in the nature of the child itself, and finds its expression in the immediate experience of the child. And it is that organized activity in the child's own nature controlling the particular response which gives unity, and which builds up his own self.

What goes on in the game goes on in the life of the child all the time. He is continually taking the attitudes of those about him, especially the rôles of those who in some sense control him and on whom he depends. He gets the function of the process in an abstract sort of a way at first. It goes over from the play into the game in a real sense. He has to play the game. The morale of the game takes hold of the child more than the larger morale of the whole community. The child passes into the game and the game expresses a social situation in which he can completely enter; its morale may have a greater hold on him than that of the family to which he belongs or the community in which he lives. There are all sorts of social organizations, some of which are fairly lasting, some temporary, into which the child is entering, and he is playing a sort of social game in them. It is a period in which he likes "to belong," and he gets into organizations which come into existence and pass out of existence. He becomes a something which can function in the organized whole, and thus tends to determine himself in his relationship with the group to which he belongs. That process is one which is a striking stage in the development of the child's morale. It constitutes him a self-conscious member of the community to which he belongs.

Such is the process by which a personality arises. I have spoken of this as a process in which a child takes the rôle of the other, and said that it takes place essentially through the use of language. Language is predominantly based on the vocal gesture by means of which co-operative activities in a community are carried out. Language in its significant sense is that vocal gesture which tends to arouse in the individual the attitude which it arouses in others, and it is this perfecting of the self by the gesture which mediates the social activities that gives rise to the process of taking the rôle of the other. The latter phrase is a little unfortunate because it suggests an actor's attitude which is actually more sophisticated than that which is involved in our own experience. To this degree it does not correctly describe that which I have in mind. We see the process most definitely in a primitive form in those situations where the child's play takes different rôles. Here the very fact that he is ready to pay out money, for instance, arouses the attitude of the person who receives money; the very process is calling out in him the corresponding activities of the other person involved. The individual stimulates himself to the response which he is calling out in the other person, and then acts in some degree in response to that situation. In play the child does definitely act out the rôle which he himself has aroused in himself. It is that which gives, as I have said, a definite content in the individual which answers to the stimulus that affects him as it affects somebody else. The content of the other that enters into one personality is the response in the individual which his gesture calls out in the other.

[...]

What goes to make up the organized self is the organization of the attitudes which are common to the group. A person is a personality because he belongs to a community, because he takes over the institutions of that community into his own conduct. He takes its language as a medium by which he gets his personality, and then through a process of taking the different rôles that all the others furnish he comes to get the attitude of the members of the community. Such, in a certain sense, is the structure of a man's personality. There are certain common responses which each individual has toward certain common things, and in so far as those common responses are awakened in the individual when he is affecting other persons he arouses his own self. The structure, then, on which the self is built is this response which is common to all, for one has to be a member of a community to be a self. Such responses are abstract attitudes, but they constitute just what we term a man's character. They give him what we term his principles, the acknowledged attitudes of all members of the community toward what are the values of that community. He is putting himself in the place of the generalized other, which represents the organized responses of all the members of the group. It is that which guides conduct controlled by principles, and a person who has such an organized group of responses is a man whom we say has character, in the moral sense.

It is a structure of attitudes, then, which goes to make up a self, as distinct from a group of habits. We all of us have, for example, certain groups of habits, such as the particular intonations which a person uses in his speech. This is a set of habits of vocal expression which one has but which one does not know about. The sets of habits which we have of that sort mean nothing to us; we do not hear the intonations of our speech that others hear unless we are paying particular attention to them. The habits of emotional expression which belong to our speech are of the same sort. We may know that we have expressed ourselves in a joyous fashion but the detailed process is one which does not come back to our conscious selves. There are whole bundles of such habits which do not enter into a conscious self, but which help to make up what is termed the unconscious self.

After all, what we mean by self-consciousness is an awakening in ourselves of the group of attitudes which we are arousing in others, especially when it is an important set of responses which go to make up the members of the community. It is unfortunate to fuse or mix up consciousness, as we ordinarily use that term, and self-consciousness. Consciousness, as frequently used, simply has reference to the field of experience, but self-consciousness refers to the ability to call out in ourselves a set of definite responses which belong to the others of the group. Consciousness and self-consciousness are not on the same level. A man alone has, fortunately or unfortunately, access to his own toothache, but that is not what we mean by self-consciousness.

I have so far emphasized what I have called the structures upon which the self is constructed, the framework of the self, as it were. Of course we are not only what is common to all: each one of the selves is different from everyone else; but there has to be such a common structure as I have sketched in order that we may be members of a community at all. We cannot be ourselves unless we are also members in whom there is a community of attitudes which control the attitudes of all. We cannot have rights unless we have common attitudes. That which we have acquired as self-conscious persons makes us such members of society and gives us selves. Selves can only exist in definite relationships to other selves. No hard-and-fast line can be drawn between our own selves and the selves of others, since our own selves exist and enter as such into our experience only in so far as the selves of others exist and enter as such into our experience also. The individual possesses a self only in relation to the selves of the other members of his social group; and the structure of his self expresses or reflects the general behavior pattern of this social group to which he belongs, just as does the structure of the self of every other individual belonging to this social group.

[...]

THE "I" AND THE "ME"

We have discussed at length the social foundations of the self, and hinted that the self does not consist simply in the bare organization of social attitudes. We may now explicitly raise the question as to the nature of the "I" which is aware of the social "me." I do not mean to raise the metaphysical question of how a person can be both "I" and "me," but to ask for the significance of this distinction from the point of view of conduct itself. Where in conduct does the "I" come in as over against the "me"? If one

determines what his position is in society and feels himself as having a certain function and privilege, these are all defined with reference to an "I," but the "I" is not a "me" and cannot become a "me." We may have a better self and a worse self, but that again is not the "I" as over against the "me," because they are both selves. We approve of one and disapprove of the other, but when we bring up one or the other they are there for such approval as "me's." The "I" does not get into the limelight; we talk to ourselves, but do not see ourselves. The "I" reacts to the self which arises through the taking of the attitudes of others. Through taking those attitudes we have introduced the "me" and we react to it as an "I."

The simplest way of handling the problem would be in terms of memory. I talk to myself, and I remember what I said and perhaps the emotional content that went with it. The "I" of this moment is present in the "me" of the next moment. There again I cannot turn around quick enough to catch myself. I become a "me" in so far as I remember what I said. The "I" can be given, however, this functional relationship. It is because of the "I" that we say that we are never fully aware of what we are, that we surprise ourselves by our own action. It is as we act that we are aware of ourselves. It is in memory that the "I" is constantly present in experience. We can go back directly a few moments in our experience, and then we are dependent upon memory images for the rest. So that the "I" in memory is there as the spokesman of the self of the second, or minute, or day ago. As given, it is a "me," but it is a "me" which was the "I" at the earlier time. If you ask, then, where directly in your own experience the "I" comes in, the answer is that it comes in as a historical figure. It is what you were a second ago that is the "I" of the "me." It is another "me" that has to take that rôle. You cannot get the immediate response of the "I" in the process.[8] The "I" is in a certain sense that with which we do identify ourselves. The getting of it into experience constitutes one of the problems of most of our conscious experience; it is not directly given in experience.

The "I" is the response of the organism to the attitudes of the others;[9] the "me" is the organized set of attitudes of others which one himself assumes. The attitudes of the others constitute the organized "me," and then one reacts toward that as an "I." I now wish to examine these concepts in greater detail.

There is neither "I" nor "me" in the conversation of gestures; the whole act is not yet carried out, but the preparation takes place in this field of gesture. Now, in so far as the individual arouses in himself the attitudes of the others, there arises an organized group of responses. And it is due to the individual's ability to take the attitudes of these others in so far as they can be organized that he gets self-consciousness. The taking of all of those organized sets of attitudes gives him his "me"; that is the self he is aware of. He can throw the ball to some other member because of the demand made upon him from other members of the team. That is the self that immediately exists for him in his consciousness. He has their attitudes, knows what they want and what the consequence of any act of his will be, and he has assumed responsibility for the situation. Now, it is the presence of those organized sets of attitudes that constitutes that "me" to which he as an "I" is responding. But what that response will be he does not know and nobody else knows. Perhaps he will make a brilliant play or an error. The response to that situation as it appears in his immediate experience is uncertain, and it is that which constitutes the "I."

The "I" is his action over against that social situation within his own conduct, and it gets into his experience only after he has carried out the act. Then he is aware of it. He had to do such a thing and he did it. He fulfils his duty and he may look with pride at the throw which he made. The "me" arises to do that duty—that is the way in which it arises in his experience. He had in him all the attitudes of others, calling for a certain response; that was the "me" of that situation, and his response is the "I."

I want to call attention particularly to the fact that this response of the "I" is something that is more or less uncertain. The attitudes of others which one assumes as affecting his own conduct constitute the "me," and that is something that is there, but the response to it is as yet not given. When one sits down to think anything out, he has certain data that are there. Suppose that it is a social situation which he has to straighten out. He sees himself from the point of view of one individual or another in the group. These individuals, related all together, give him a certain self. Well, what is he going to do? He does not know and nobody else knows. He can get the situation into his experience because he can assume the attitudes of the various individuals involved in it. He knows how they feel about it by the assumption of their attitudes. He says, in effect, "I have done certain things that seem to commit me to a certain course of conduct." Perhaps if he does so act it will place him in a false position with another group. The "I" as a response to this situation, in contrast to the "me" which is involved in the attitudes which he takes, is uncertain. And when the response takes place, then it appears in the field of experience largely as a memory image.

Our specious present as such is very short. We do, however, experience passing events; part of the process of the passage of events is directly there in our experience, including some of the past and some of the future. We see a ball falling as it passes, and as it does pass part of the ball is covered and part is being uncovered. We remember where the ball was a moment ago and we anticipate where it will be beyond what is given in our experience. So of ourselves; we are doing something, but to look back and see what we are doing involves getting memory images. So the "I" really appears experientially as a part of a "me." But on the basis of this experience we distinguish that individual who is doing something from the "me" who puts the problem up to him. The response enters into his experience only when it takes place. If he says he knows what he is going to do, even there he may be mistaken. He starts out to do something and something happens to interfere. The resulting action is always a little different from anything which he could anticipate. This is true even if he is simply carrying out the process of walking. The very taking of his expected steps puts him in a certain situation which has a slightly different aspect from what is expected, which is in a certain sense novel. That movement into the future is the step, so to speak, of the ego, of the "I." It is something that is not given in the "me."

Take the situation of a scientist solving a problem, where he has certain data which call for certain responses. Some of this set of data call for his applying such and such a law, while others call for another law. Data are there with their implications. He knows what such and such coloration means, and when he has these data before him they stand for certain responses on his part; but now they are in conflict with each other. If he makes one response he cannot make another. What he is going to do he does not know, nor does anybody else. The action of the self is in response to these conflicting sets of data in the form of a problem, with conflicting demands upon him as a scientist. He has to look at it in different ways. That action of the "I" is something the nature of which we cannot tell in advance.

The "I," then, in this relation of the "I" and the "me," is something that is, so to speak, responding to a social situation which is within the experience of the individual. It is the answer which the individual makes to the attitude which others take toward him when he assumes an attitude toward them. Now, the attitudes he is taking toward them are present in his own experience, but his response to them will contain a novel element. The "I" gives the sense of freedom, of initiative. The situation is there for us to act in a self-conscious fashion. We are aware of ourselves, and of what the situation is, but exactly how we will act never gets into experience until after the action takes place.

Such is the basis for the fact that the "I" does not appear in the same sense in experience as does the "me." The "me" represents a definite organization of the community there in our own attitudes, and

calling for a response, but the response that takes place is something that just happens. There is no certainty in regard to it. There is a moral necessity but no mechanical necessity for the act. When it does take place then we find what has been done. The above account gives us, I think, the relative position of the "I" and "me" in the situation, and the grounds for the separation of the two in behavior. The two are separated in the process but they belong together in the sense of being parts of a whole. They are separated and yet they belong together. The separation of the "I" and the "me" is not fictitious. They are not identical, for, as I have said, the "I" is something that is never entirely calculable. The "me" does call for a certain sort of an "I" in so far as we meet the obligations that are given in conduct itself, but the "I" is always something different from what the situation itself calls for. So there is always that distinction, if you like, between the "I" and the "me." The "I" both calls out the "me" and responds to it. Taken together they constitute a personality as it appears in social experience. The self is essentially a social process going on with these two distinguishable phases. If it did not have these two phases there could not be conscious responsibility, and there would be nothing novel in experience.

NOTES

1. Man's behavior is such in his social group that he is able to become an object to himself, a fact which constitutes him a more advanced product of evolutionary development than are the lower animals. Fundamentally it is this social fact—and not his alleged possession of a soul or mind with which he, as an individual, has been mysteriously and supernaturally endowed, and with which the lower animals have not been endowed—that differentiates him from them.

2. *a)* All social interrelations and interactions are rooted in a certain common socio-physiological endowment of every individual involved in them. These physiological bases of social

behavior—which have their ultimate seat or locus in the lower part of the individual's central nervous system—are the bases of such behavior, precisely because they in themselves are also social; that is, because they consist in drives or instincts or behavior tendencies, on the part of the given individual, which he cannot carry out or give overt expression and satisfaction to without the co-operative aid of one or more other individuals. The physiological processes of behavior of which they are the mechanisms are processes which necessarily involve more than one individual, processes in which other individuals besides the given individual are perforce implicated. Examples of the fundamental social relations to which these physiological bases of social behavior give rise are those between the sexes (expressing the reproductive instinct), between parent and child (expressing the parental instinct), and between neighbors (expressing the gregarious instinct). These relatively simple and rudimentary physiological mechanisms or tendencies of individual human behavior, besides constituting the physiological bases of all human social behavior, are also the fundamental biological materials of human nature; so that when we refer to human nature, we are referring to something which is essentially social.

b) Sexually and parentally, as well as in its attacks and defenses, the activities of the physiological organism are social in that the acts begun within the organism require their completion in the actions of others. . . . But while the pattern of the individual act may be said to be in these cases social, it is only so in so far as the organism seeks for the stimuli in the attitudes and characters of other forms for the completion of its own responses, and by its behavior tends to maintain the other as a part of its own environment. The actual behavior of the other or the others is not initiated in the individual form as a part of its own pattern of behavior (MS).

3. It is generally recognized that the specifically social expressions of intelligence, or the exercise of what is often called "social intelligence," depend upon the given individual's ability to take the rôles of, or "put himself in the place of," the other individuals implicated with him in given social situations; and upon his consequent sensitivity to their attitudes toward himself and toward one another. These

specifically social expressions of intelligence, of course, acquire unique significance in terms of our view that the whole nature of intelligence is social to the very core—that this putting of one's self in the places of others, this taking by one's self of their rôles or attitudes, is not merely one of the various aspects or expressions of intelligence or of intelligent behavior, but is the very essence of its character. Spearman's "X factor" in intelligence—the unknown factor which, according to him, intelligence contains—is simply (if our social theory of intelligence is correct) this ability of the intelligent individual to take the attitude of the other, or the attitudes of others, thus realizing the significations or grasping the meanings of the symbols or gestures in terms of which thinking proceeds; and thus being able to carry on with himself the internal conversation with these symbols or gestures which thinking involves.

4. Thinking proceeds in terms of or by means of universals. A universal may be interpreted behavioristically as simply the social act as a whole, involving the organization and interrelation of the attitudes of all the individuals implicated in the act, as controlling their overt responses. This organization of the different individual attitudes and interactions in a given social act, with reference to their interrelations as realized by the individuals themselves, is what we mean by a universal; and it determines what the actual overt responses of the individuals involved in the given social act will be, whether that act be concerned with a concrete project of some sort (such as the relation of physical and social means to ends desired) or with some purely abstract discussion, say the theory of relativity or the Platonic ideas.

5. ["The Relation of Play to Education," *University of Chicago Record*, I (1896–97), 140 ff.]

6. It is possible for inanimate objects, no less than for other human organisms, to form parts of the generalized and organized—the completely socialized—other for any given human individual, in so far as he responds to such objects socially or in a social fashion (by means of the mechanism of thought, the internalized conversation of gestures). Any thing—any object or set of objects, whether animate or inanimate, human or animal, or merely physical—toward which he acts, or to which he responds, socially, is an element in what for him is the generalized other; by taking the attitudes of which toward himself he becomes conscious of himself as an object or individual, and thus develops a self or personality. Thus,

for example, the cult, in its primitive form, is merely the social embodiment of the relation between the given social group or community and its physical environment—an organized social means, adopted by the individual members of that group or community, of entering into social relations with that environment, or (in a sense) of carrying on conversations with it; and in this way that environment becomes part of the total generalized other for each of the individual members of the given social group or community.

7. We have said that the internal conversation of the individual with himself in terms of words or significant gestures—the conversation which constitutes the process or activity of thinking—is carried on by the individual from the standpoint of the "generalized other." And the more abstract that conversation is, the more abstract thinking happens to be, the further removed is the generalized other from any connection with particular individuals. It is especially in abstract thinking, that is to say, that the conversation involved is carried on by the individual with the generalized other, rather than with any particular individuals. Thus it is, for example, that abstract concepts are concepts stated in terms of the attitudes of the entire social group or community; they are stated on the basis of the individual's consciousness of the attitudes of the generalized other toward them, as a result of his taking these attitudes of the generalized other and then responding to them. And thus it is also that abstract propositions are stated in a form which anyone—any other intelligent individual—will accept.

8. The sensitivity of the organism brings parts of itself into the environment. It does not, however, bring the life-process itself into the environment, and the complete imaginative presentation of the organism is unable to present the living of the organism. It can conceivably present the conditions under which living takes place but not the unitary life-process. The physical organism in the environment always remains a thing (MS).

9. [For the "I" viewed as the biologic individual, see Supplementary Essays II, III.]

COMPANION WEBSITE

1. Go online to Write Out Loud about the role the mass media might play in the development of the self.
2. Log on to Mead's Profile Page to read more about one of America's most important social theorists.
3. Check out the Interactive Reading for funny but nonetheless instructive videos of how "conversations of gestures" play out in the real world.

35

The Metropolis and Mental Life

Georg Simmel

THE DEEPEST PROBLEMS OF MODERN life flow from the attempt of the individual to maintain the independence and individuality of his existence against the sovereign powers of society, against the weight of the historical heritage and the external culture and technique of life. This antagonism represents the most modern form of the conflict which primitive man must carry on with nature for his own bodily existence. The eighteenth century may have called for liberation from all the ties which grew up historically in politics, in religion, in morality and in economics in order to permit the original natural virtue of man, which is equal in everyone, to develop without inhibition; the nineteenth century may have sought to promote, in addition to man's freedom, his individuality (which is connected with the division of labor) and his achievements which make him unique and indispensable but which at the same time make him so much the more dependent on the complementary activity of others; Nietzsche may have seen the relentless struggle of the individual as the prerequisite for his full development, while Socialism found the same thing in the suppression of all competition—but in each of these the same fundamental motive was at work, namely the resistance of the individual to being levelled, swallowed up in the social-technological mechanism. When one inquires about the products of the specifically modern aspects of contemporary life with reference to their inner meaning—when, so to speak, one examines the body of culture with reference to the soul, as I am to do concerning the metropolis today—the answer will require the investigation of the relationship which such a social structure promotes between the individual aspects of life and those which transcend the existence of single individuals. It will require the investigation of the adaptations made by the personality in its adjustment to the forces that lie outside of it.

The psychological foundation, upon which the metropolitan individuality is erected, is the intensification of emotional life due to the swift and continuous shift of external and internal stimuli. Man is a creature whose existence is dependent on differences, i.e., his mind is stimulated by the difference between present impressions and those which have preceded. Lasting impressions, the slightness in their differences, the habituated regularity of their course and contrasts between them, consume, so to speak, less mental energy than the rapid telescoping of changing images, pronounced differences within what is grasped at a single glance, and the unexpectedness of violent stimuli. To the extent that the metropolis creates these psychological conditions—with every crossing of the street, with the tempo and multiplicity of economic, occupational and social life—it creates in the sensory foundations of mental life, and in the degree of awareness necessitated by our organization as creatures dependent on differences, a deep contrast with the slower, more habitual, more smoothly flowing rhythm of the sensory-mental phase of small town and rural existence. Thereby the essentially intellectualistic character of the mental life of the metropolis becomes intelligible as over against that of the small town which rests more on feelings and emotional relationships. These latter are rooted in the unconscious levels of the mind and develop most readily in the steady equilibrium of unbroken customs. The locus of reason, on the other hand, is in the lucid, conscious upper strata of the mind and it is the most adaptable of our inner forces. In order to adjust itself to the shifts and contradictions in events, it does not require the disturbances and inner upheavals which are the only means whereby more conservative personalities are able to adapt themselves to the same rhythm of events. Thus the metropolitan type—which naturally takes on a thousand individual modifications—creates a protective organ for itself against the profound disruption with which the fluctuations and discontinuities of the external milieu threaten it. Instead of reacting emotionally, the metropolitan type reacts primarily in a rational manner, thus creating a mental predominance through the intensification of consciousness, which in turn is caused by it. Thus the reaction of the metropolitan person to those events is moved to a sphere of mental activity which is least sensitive and which is furthest removed from the depths of the personality.

This intellectualistic quality which is thus recognized as a protection of the inner life against the domination of the metropolis, becomes ramified into numerous specific phenomena. The metropolis has always been the seat of money economy because the many-sidedness and concentration of commercial activity have given the medium of exchange an importance which it could not have acquired in the commercial aspects of rural life. But money economy and the domination of the intellect stand in the closest relationship to one another. They have in common a purely matter-of-fact attitude in the treatment of persons and things in which a formal justice is often combined with an unrelenting hardness. The purely intellectualistic person is indifferent to all things personal because, out of them, relationships and reactions develop which are not to be completely understood by purely rational methods—just as the unique element in events never enters into the principle of money. Money is concerned only with what is common to all, i.e., with the exchange value which reduces all quality and individuality to a purely quantitative level. All emotional relationships between persons rest on their individuality, whereas intellectual relationships deal with persons as with numbers, that is, as with elements which, in themselves, are indifferent, but which are of interest only insofar as they offer something objectively perceivable. It is in this very manner that the inhabitant of the metropolis reckons with his merchant, his customer, and with his servant, and frequently with the persons with whom he is thrown into obligatory association. These relationships stand in distinct contrast with the nature of the smaller circle in which the inevitable knowledge of individual characteristics produces, with an equal inevitability, an emotional tone in conduct, a sphere which is beyond the mere objective weighting of tasks performed and payments made. What is essential here as regards the economic-psychological aspect of the problem is that in less advanced cultures production was for the customer who ordered the product so that the producer and the purchaser knew one another. The modern city, however, is supplied almost exclusively by production for the market, that is, for entirely unknown purchasers who never appear in the actual field of vision of the producers themselves. Thereby, the interests of each party acquire a relentless matter-of-factness, and its rationally calculated economic egoism need not fear any divergence from its set path because of the imponderability of personal relationships. This is all the more the case in the money economy which dominates the metropolis in which the last remnants of domestic production and direct barter of goods have been eradicated and in which the amount of production on direct personal order is reduced daily. Furthermore, this psychological intellectualistic attitude and the money economy are in such close integration that no one is able to say whether it was the former that effected the latter or *vice versa*. What is certain is only that the form of life in the metropolis is the soil which nourishes this interaction most fruitfully, a point which I shall attempt to demonstrate only with the statement of the most outstanding English constitutional historian to the effect that through the entire course of English history London has never acted as the heart of England but often as its intellect and always as its money bag.

In certain apparently insignificant characters or traits of the most external aspects of life are to be found a number of characteristic mental tendencies. The modern mind has become more and more a calculating one. The calculating exactness of practical life which has resulted from a money economy corresponds to the ideal of natural science, namely that of transforming the world into an arithmetical problem and of fixing every one of its parts in a mathematical formula. It has been money economy which has thus filled the daily life of so many people with weighing, calculating, enumerating and the reduction of qualitative values to quantitative terms. Because of the character of calculability which money has there has come into the relationships of the elements of life a precision and a degree of certainty in the definition of the equalities and inequalities and an unambiguousness in agreements and arrangements, just as externally this precision has been brought about through the general diffusion of pocket watches. It is, however, the conditions of the metropolis which are cause as well as effect for this essential characteristic. The relationships and concerns of the typical metropolitan resident are so manifold and complex that, especially as a result of the agglomeration of so many persons with such differentiated interests, their relationships and activities intertwine with one another into a many-membered organism. In view

of this fact, the lack of the most exact punctuality in promises and performances would cause the whole to break down into an inextricable chaos. If all the watches in Berlin suddenly went wrong in different ways even only as much as an hour, its entire economic and commercial life would be derailed for some time. Even though this may seem more superficial in its significance, it transpires that the magnitude of distances results in making all waiting and the breaking of appointments an ill-afforded waste of time. For this reason the technique of metropolitan life in general is not conceivable without all of its activities and reciprocal relationships being organized and coordinated in the most punctual way into a firmly fixed framework of time which transcends all subjective elements. But here too there emerge those conclusions which are in general the whole task of this discussion, namely, that every event, however restricted to this superficial level it may appear, comes immediately into contact with the depths of the soul, and that the most banal externalities are, in the last analysis, bound up with the final decisions concerning the meaning and the style of life. Punctuality, calculability, and exactness, which are required by the complications and extensiveness of metropolitan life are not only most intimately connected with its capitalistic and intellectualistic character but also color the content of life and are conducive to the exclusion of those irrational, instinctive, sovereign human traits and impulses which originally seek to determine the form of life from within instead of receiving it from the outside in a general, schematically precise form. Even though those lives which are autonomous and characterized by these vital impulses are not entirely impossible in the city, they are, none the less, opposed to it *in abstracto*. It is in the light of this that we can explain the passionate hatred of personalities like Ruskin and Nietzsche for the metropolis—personalities who found the value of life only in unschematized individual expressions which cannot be reduced to exact equivalents and in whom, on that account, there flowed from the same source as did that hatred, the hatred of the money economy and of the intellectualism of existence.

The same factors which, in the exactness and the minute precision of the form of life, have coalesced into a structure of the highest impersonality, have, on the other hand, an influence in a highly personal direction. There is perhaps no psychic phenomenon which is so unconditionally reserved to the city as the blasé outlook. It is at first the consequence of those rapidly shifting stimulations of the nerves which are thrown together in all their contrasts and from which it seems to us the intensification of metropolitan intellectuality seems to be derived. On that account it is not likely that stupid persons who have been hitherto intellectually dead will be blasé. Just as an immoderately sensuous life makes one blasé because it stimulates the nerves to their utmost reactivity until they finally can no longer produce any reaction at all, so, less harmful stimuli, through the rapidity and the contradictoriness of their shifts, force the nerves to make such violent responses, tear them about so brutally that they exhaust their last reserves of strength and, remaining in the same milieu, do not have time for new reserves to form. This incapacity to react to new stimulations with the required amount of energy constitutes in fact that blasé attitude which every child of a large city evinces when compared with the products of the more peaceful and more stable milieu.

Combined with this physiological source of the blasé metropolitan attitude there is another which derives from a money economy. The essence of the blasé attitude is an indifference toward the distinctions between things. Not in the sense that they are not perceived, as is the case of mental dullness, but rather that the meaning and the value of the distinctions between things, and therewith of the things themselves, are experienced as meaningless. They appear to the blasé person in a homogeneous, flat and gray color with no one of them worthy of being preferred to another. This psychic mood is the correct subjective reflection of a complete money economy to the extent that money takes the place of all the manifoldness of things and expresses all qualitative distinctions between them in the distinction of "how much." To the extent that money, with its colorlessness and its indifferent quality, can become a common denominator of all values it becomes the frightful leveler—it hollows out the core of things, their peculiarities, their specific values and their uniqueness and incomparability in a way which is beyond repair. They all float with the same specific gravity in the constantly moving stream of money. They all rest on the same level and are distinguished only by their amounts. In individual cases this coloring, or rather this de-coloring of things, through their equation with money, may be imperceptibly small. In the relationship, however, which the wealthy person has to objects which can be bought for money, perhaps indeed in the total character which, for this reason, public opinion now recognizes in these objects, it takes on very considerable proportions. This is why the metropolis is the seat of commerce and it is in it that the purchasability of things appears in quite a different aspect than in simpler economies. It is also the peculiar seat of the blasé attitude. In it is brought to a peak, in a certain way, that achievement in the concentration of purchasable things which stimulates the individual to the highest degree of nervous energy. Through the mere quantitative intensification of the same conditions this achievement is transformed into its opposite, into this peculiar adaptive phenomenon—the blasé attitude—in which the nerves reveal their final possibility of adjusting themselves to the content and the form of metropolitan life by renouncing the response to them. We see that the self-preservation of certain types of personalities is obtained at the cost of devaluing the entire objective world, ending inevitably in dragging the personality downward into a feeling of its own valuelessness.

Whereas the subject of this form of existence must come to terms with it for himself, his self-preservation in the face of the great city requires of him a no less negative type of social conduct. The mental attitude of the people of the metropolis to one another may be designated formally as one of reserve. If the unceasing external contact of numbers of persons in the city should be met by the same number of inner reactions as in the small town, in which one knows almost every person he meets and to each of whom he has a positive relationship, one would be completely atomized internally and would fall into an unthinkable mental condition. Partly this psychological circumstance and partly the privilege of suspicion which we have in the face of the elements of metropolitan life (which are constantly touching one another in fleeting contact) necessitates in us that reserve, in consequence of which we do not know by sight neighbors of years standing and which permits us to appear to small-town folk so often as cold and uncongenial. Indeed, if I am not mistaken, the inner side of this external reserve is not only indifference but more frequently than we believe, it is a slight aversion, a mutual strangeness and repulsion which, in a close contact which has arisen any way whatever, can break out into hatred and conflict. The entire inner organization of such a type of extended commercial life rests on an extremely varied structure of sympathies, indifferences and aversions of the briefest as well as of the most enduring sort. This sphere of indifference is, for this reason, not as great as it seems superficially. Our minds respond, with some definite feeling, to almost every impression emanating from another person. The unconsciousness, the transitoriness and the shift of these feelings seem to raise them only into indifference. Actually this latter would be as unnatural to us as immersion into a chaos of unwished-for suggestions would be unbearable. From these two typical dangers of metropolitan life we are saved by antipathy which is the latent adumbration of actual antagonism since it brings about the sort of distanciation and deflection without which this type of life could not be carried on at all. Its extent and its mixture, the rhythm of its emergence and disappearance, the forms in which it is adequate—these constitute, with the simplified

motives (in the narrower sense) an inseparable totality of the form of metropolitan life. What appears here directly as dissociation is in reality only one of the elementary forms of socialization.

This reserve with its overtone of concealed aversion appears once more, however, as the form or the wrappings of a much more general psychic trait of the metropolis. It assures the individual of a type and degree of personal freedom to which there is no analogy in other circumstances. It has its roots in one of the great developmental tendencies of social life as a whole; in one of the few for which an approximately exhaustive formula can be discovered. The most elementary stage of social organization which is to be found historically, as well as in the present, is this: a relatively small circle almost entirely closed against neighboring foreign or otherwise antagonistic groups but which has however within itself such a narrow cohesion that the individual member has only a very slight area for the development of his own qualities and for free activity for which he himself is responsible. Political and familial groups began in this way as do political and religious communities; the self-preservation of very young associations requires a rigorous setting of boundaries and a centripetal unity and for that reason it cannot give room to freedom and the peculiarities of inner and external development of the individual. From this stage social evolution proceeds simultaneously in two divergent but none the less corresponding directions. In the measure that the group grows numerically, spatially, and in the meaningful content of life, its immediate inner unity and the definiteness of its original demarcation against others are weakened and rendered mild by reciprocal interactions and interconnections. And at the same time the individual gains a freedom of movement far beyond the first jealous delimitation, and gains also a peculiarity and individuality to which the division of labor in groups, which have become larger, gives both occasion and necessity. However much the particular conditions and forces of the individual situation might modify the general scheme, the state and Christianity, guilds and political parties and innumerable other groups have developed in accord with this formula. This tendency seems, to me, however to be quite clearly recognizable also in the development of individuality within the framework of city life. Small town life in antiquity as well as in the Middle Ages imposed such limits upon the movements of the individual in his relationships with the outside world and on his inner independence and differentiation that the modern person could not even breathe under such conditions. Even today the city dweller who is placed in a small town feels a type of narrowness which is very similar. The smaller the circle which forms our environment and the more limited the relationships which have the possibility of transcending the boundaries, the more anxiously the narrow community watches over the deeds, the conduct of life and the attitudes of the individual and the more will a quantitative and qualitative individuality tend to pass beyond the boundaries of such a community.

The ancient *polis* seems in this regard to have had a character of a small town. The incessant threat against its existence by enemies from near and far brought about that stern cohesion in political and military matters, that supervision of the citizen by other citizens, and that jealousy of the whole toward the individual whose own private life was repressed to such an extent that he could compensate himself only by acting as a despot in his own household. The tremendous agitation and excitement, and the unique colorfulness of Athenian life is perhaps explained by the fact that a people of incomparably individualized personalities were in constant struggle against the incessant inner and external oppression of a de-individualizing small town. This created an atmosphere of tension in which the weaker were held down and the stronger were impelled to the most passionate type of self-protection. And with this there blossomed in Athens, what, without being able to define it exactly, must be designated as "the general human character" in the intellectual development of our species. For the correlation, the factual as well as the historical validity of which we are

here maintaining, is that the broadest and the most general contents and forms of life are intimately bound up with the most individual ones. Both have a common prehistory and also common enemies in the narrow formations and groupings, whose striving for self-preservation set them in conflict with the broad and general on the outside, as well as the freely mobile and individual on the inside. Just as in feudal times the "free" man was he who stood under the law of the land, that is, under the law of the largest social unit, but he was unfree who derived his legal rights only from the narrow circle of a feudal community—so today in an intellectualized and refined sense the citizen of the metropolis is "free" in contrast with the trivialities and prejudices which bind the small town person. The mutual reserve and indifference, and the intellectual conditions of life in large social units are never more sharply appreciated in their significance for the independence of the individual than in the dense crowds of the metropolis because the bodily closeness and lack of space make intellectual distance really perceivable for the first time. It is obviously only the obverse of this freedom that, under certain circumstances, one never feels as lonely and as deserted as in this metropolitan crush of persons. For here, as elsewhere, it is by no means necessary that the freedom of man reflect itself in his emotional life only as a pleasant experience.

It is not only the immediate size of the area and population which, on the basis of world-historical correlation between the increase in the size of the social unit and the degree of personal inner and outer freedom, makes the metropolis the locus of this condition. It is rather in transcending this purely tangible extensiveness that the metropolis also becomes the seat of cosmopolitanism. Comparable with the form of the development of wealth—(beyond a certain point property increases in ever more rapid progression as out of its own inner being)—the individual's horizon is enlarged. In the same way, economic, personal and intellectual relations in the city (which are its ideal reflection), grow in a geometrical progression as soon as, for the first time, a certain limit has been passed. Every dynamic extension becomes a preparation not only for a similar extension but rather for a larger one and from every thread which is spun out of it there continue, growing as out of themselves, an endless number of others. This may be illustrated by the fact that within the city the "unearned increment" of ground rent, through a mere increase in traffic, brings to the owner profits which are self-generating. At this point the quantitative aspects of life are transformed qualitatively. The sphere of life of the small town is, in the main, enclosed within itself. For the metropolis it is decisive that its inner life is extended in a wave-like motion over a broader national or international area. Weimar was no exception because its significance was dependent upon individual personalities and died with them, whereas the metropolis is characterized by its essential independence even of the most significant individual personalities; this is rather its antithesis and it is the price of independence which the individual living in it enjoys. The most significant aspect of the metropolis lies in this functional magnitude beyond its actual physical boundaries and this effectiveness reacts upon the latter and gives to it life, weight, importance and responsibility. A person does not end with limits of his physical body or with the area to which his physical activity is immediately confined but embraces, rather, the totality of meaningful effects which emanates from him temporally and spatially. In the same way the city exists only in the totality of the effects which transcend their immediate sphere. These really are the actual extent in which their existence is expressed. This is already expressed in the fact that individual freedom, which is the logical historical complement of such extension, is not only to be understood in the negative sense as mere freedom of movement and emancipation from prejudices and philistinism. Its essential characteristic is rather to be found in the fact that the particularity and incomparability which ultimately every person possesses in some way is actually expressed, giving form to life. That we follow the laws of our inner nature—and this is

what freedom is—becomes perceptible and convincing to us and to others only when the expressions of this nature distinguish themselves from others; it is our irreplaceability by others which shows that our mode of existence is not imposed upon us from the outside.

Cities are above all the seat of the most advanced economic division of labor. They produce such extreme phenomena as the lucrative vocation of the *quatorzieme* in Paris. These are persons who may be recognized by shields on their houses and who hold themselves ready at the dinner hour in appropriate costumes so they can be called upon on short notice in case thirteen persons find themselves at the table. Exactly in the measure of its extension the city offers to an increasing degree the determining conditions for the division of labor. It is a unit which, because of its large size, is receptive to a highly diversified plurality of achievements while at the same time the agglomeration of individuals and their struggle for the customer forces the individual to a type of specialized accomplishment in which he cannot be so easily exterminated by the other. The decisive fact here is that in the life of a city, struggle with nature for the means of life is transformed into a conflict with human beings and the gain which is fought for is granted, not by nature, but by man. For here we find not only the previously mentioned source of specialization but rather the deeper one in which the seller must seek to produce in the person to whom he wishes to sell ever new and unique needs. The necessity to specialize one's product in order to find a source of income which is not yet exhausted and also to specialize a function which cannot be easily supplanted is conducive to differentiation, refinement and enrichment of the needs of the public which obviously must lead to increasing personal variation within this public.

All this leads to the narrower type of intellectual individuation of mental qualities to which the city gives rise in proportion to its size. There is a whole series of causes for this. First of all there is the difficulty of giving one's own personality a certain status within the framework of metropolitan life.

Where quantitative increase of value and energy has reached its limits, one seizes on qualitative distinctions, so that, through taking advantage of the existing sensitivity to differences, the attention of the social world can, in some way, be won for oneself. This leads ultimately to the strangest eccentricities, to specifically metropolitan extravagances of self-distanciation, of caprice, of fastidiousness, the meaning of which is no longer to be found in the content of such activity itself but rather in its being a form of "being different"—of making oneself noticeable. For many types of persons these are still the only means of saving for oneself, through the attention gained from others, some sort of self-esteem and the sense of filling a position. In the same sense there operates an apparently insignificant factor which in its effects however is perceptibly cumulative, namely, the brevity and rarity of meetings which are allotted to each individual as compared with social intercourse in a small city. For here we find the attempt to appear to-the-point, clear-cut and individual with extraordinarily greater frequency than where frequent and long association assures to each person an unambiguous conception of the other's personality.

This appears to me to be the most profound cause of the fact that the metropolis places emphasis on striving for the most individual forms of personal existence—regardless of whether it is always correct or always successful. The development of modern culture is characterized by the predominance of what one can call the objective spirit over the subjective; that is, in language as well as in law, in the technique of production as well as in art, in science as well as in the objects of domestic environment, there is embodied a sort of spirit [*Geist*], the daily growth of which is followed only imperfectly and with an even greater lag by the intellectual development of the individual. If we survey for instance the vast culture which during the last century has been embodied in things and in knowledge, in institutions and comforts, and if we compare them with the cultural progress of the individual during the same period—at least in the upper classes—we would see a frightful difference in rate of growth between the two which represents, in many points, rather a regression of the culture of the individual with reference to spirituality, delicacy and idealism. This discrepancy is in essence the result of the success of the growing division of labor. For it is this which requires from the individual an ever more one-sided type of achievement which, at its highest point, often permits his personality as a whole to fall into neglect. In any case this overgrowth of objective culture has been less and less satisfactory for the individual. Perhaps less conscious than in practical activity and in the obscure complex of feelings which flow from him, he is reduced to a negligible quantity. He becomes a single cog as over against the vast overwhelming organization of things and forces which gradually take out of his hands everything connected with progress, spirituality and value. The operation of these forces results in the transformation of the latter from a subjective form into one of purely objective existence. It need only be pointed out that the metropolis is the proper arena for this type of culture which has outgrown every personal element. Here in buildings and in educational institutions, in the wonders and comforts of space-conquering technique, in the formations of social life and in the concrete institutions of the State is to be found such a tremendous richness of crystallizing, depersonalized cultural accomplishments that the personality can, so to speak, scarcely maintain itself in the face of it. From one angle life is made infinitely more easy in the sense that stimulations, interests, and the taking up of time and attention, present themselves from all sides and carry it in a stream which scarcely requires any individual efforts for its ongoing. But from another angle, life is composed more and more of these impersonal cultural elements and existing goods and values which seek to suppress peculiar personal interests and incomparabilities. As a result, in order that this most personal element be saved, extremities and peculiarities and individualizations must be produced and they must be over-exaggerated merely to be brought into the awareness even of the individual himself. The atrophy of individual culture through the hypertrophy of objective culture lies at the root of the bitter hatred which the preachers of the most extreme individualism, in the footsteps of Nietzsche, directed against the metropolis. But it is also the explanation of why indeed they are so passionately loved in the metropolis and indeed appear to its residents as the saviors of their unsatisfied yearnings.

When both of these forms of individualism which are nourished by the quantitative relationships of the metropolis, i.e., individual independence and the elaboration of personal peculiarities, are examined with reference to their historical position, the metropolis attains an entirely new value and meaning in the world history of the spirit. The eighteenth century found the individual in the grip of powerful bonds which had become meaningless—bonds of a political, agrarian, guild and religious nature—delimitations which imposed upon the human being at the same time an unnatural form and for a long time an unjust inequality. In this situation arose the cry for freedom and equality—the belief in the full freedom of movement of the individual in all his social and intellectual relationships which would then permit the same noble essence to emerge equally from all individuals as Nature had placed it in them and as it had been distorted by social life and historical development. Alongside of this liberalistic ideal there grew up in the nineteenth century from Goethe and the Romantics, on the one hand, and from the economic division of labor on the other, the further tendency, namely, that individuals who had been liberated from their historical bonds sought now to distinguish themselves from one another. No longer was it the "general human quality" in every individual but rather his qualitative uniqueness and irreplaceability that now became the criteria of his value. In the conflict and shifting interpretations of these two ways of defining the position of the individual within the totality is to be found the external as well as the internal history of our time. It is the function of the metropolis to make a place for the conflict and for the attempts at unification of both of these in the sense that its own peculiar conditions have been revealed to us as the occasion and the stimulus for the development of both. Thereby they attain a quite unique place, fruitful with an inexhaustible richness of meaning in the development of the mental life. They reveal themselves as one of those great historical structures in which conflicting life-embracing currents find themselves with equal legitimacy. Because of this, however, regardless of whether we are sympathetic or antipathetic with their individual expressions, they transcend the sphere in which a judge-like attitude on our part is appropriate. To the extent that such forces have been integrated, with the fleeting existence of a single cell, into the root as well as the crown of the totality of historical life to which we belong—it is our task not to complain or to condone but only to understand.

COMPANION WEBSITE

1. Go online to Write Out Loud about how living in a city today might lead to a "blasé attitude" toward metropolitan life.
2. Check out the Supplementary Sources for *Rise of the Avatar* for more from Simmel, including *The Philosophy of Money*. You may never look at a dollar bill the same way again.
3. Browse the *Rise of the Avatar* Supplementary Sources for great films about contemporary identity, including the BBC's provocative *Century of the Self*.

36

The Stranger

Georg Simmel

IF WANDERING, CONSIDERED AS a state of detachment from every given point in space, is the conceptual opposite of attachment to any point, then the sociological form of "the stranger" presents the synthesis, as it were, of both of these properties. (This is another indication that spatial relations not only are determining conditions of relationships among men, but are also symbolic of those relationships.) The stranger will thus not be considered here in the usual sense of the term, as the wanderer who comes today and goes tomorrow, but rather as the man who comes today and stays tomorrow—the potential wanderer, so to speak, who, although he has gone no further, has not quite got over the freedom of coming and going. He is fixed within a certain spatial circle—or within a group whose boundaries are analogous to spatial boundaries—but his position within it is fundamentally affected by the fact that he does not belong in it initially and that he brings qualities into it that are not, and cannot be, indigenous to it.

In the case of the stranger, the union of closeness and remoteness involved in every human relationship is patterned in a way that may be succinctly formulated as follows: the distance within this relation indicates that one who is close by is remote, but his strangeness indicates that one who is remote is near. The state of being a stranger is of course a completely positive relation; it is a specific form of interaction. The inhabitants of Sirius are not exactly strangers to us, at least not in the sociological sense of the word as we are considering it. In that sense they do not exist for us at all; they are beyond being far and near. The stranger is an element of the group itself, not unlike the poor and sundry "inner enemies"—an element whose membership within the group involves both being outside it and confronting it.

The following statements about the stranger are intended to suggest how factors of repulsion and distance work to create a form of being together, a form of union based on interaction.

In the whole history of economic activity the stranger makes his appearance everywhere as a trader, and the trader makes his as a stranger. As long as production for one's own needs is the general rule, or products are exchanged within a relatively small circle, there is no need for a middle-man within the group. A trader is required only for goods produced outside the group. Unless there are people who wander out into foreign lands to buy these necessities, in which case they are themselves "strange" merchants in this other region, the trader *must* be a stranger; there is no opportunity for anyone else to make a living at it.

This position of the stranger stands out more sharply if, instead of leaving the place of his activity, he settles down there. In innumerable cases even this is possible only if he can live by trade as a middleman. Any closed economic group where land and handicrafts have been apportioned in a way that satisfies local demands will still support a livelihood for the trader. For trade alone makes possible unlimited combinations, and through it intelligence is constantly extended and applied in new areas, something that is much harder for the primary producer with his more limited mobility and his dependence on a circle of customers that can be expanded only very slowly. Trade can always absorb more men than can primary production. It is therefore the most suitable activity for the stranger, who intrudes as a supernumerary, so to speak, into a group in which all the economic positions are already occupied. The classic example of this is the history of European Jews. The stranger is by his very nature no owner of land—land not only in the physical sense but also metaphorically as a vital substance which is fixed, if not in space, then at least in an ideal position within the social environment.

Although in the sphere of intimate personal relations the stranger may be attractive and meaningful in many ways, so long as he is regarded as a stranger he is no "landowner" in the eyes of the other. Restriction to intermediary trade and often (as though sublimated from it) to pure finance gives the stranger the specific character of *mobility*. The appearance of this mobility within a bounded group occasions that synthesis of nearness and remoteness which constitutes the formal position of the stranger. The purely mobile person comes incidentally into contact with *every* single element but is not bound up organically, through established ties of kinship, locality, or occupation, with any single one.

Another expression of this constellation is to be found in the objectivity of the stranger. Because he is not bound by roots to the particular constituents and partisan dispositions of the group, he confronts all of these with a distinctly "objective" attitude, an attitude that does not signify mere detachment and nonparticipation, but is a distinct structure composed of remoteness and nearness, indifference and involvement. I refer to my analysis of the dominating positions gained by aliens, in the discussion of superordination and subordination,[1] typified by the practice in certain Italian cities of recruiting their judges from outside, because no native was free from entanglement in family interests and factionalism.

Connected with the characteristic of objectivity is a phenomenon that is found chiefly, though not exclusively, in the stranger who moves on. This is that he often receives the most surprising revelations and confidences, at times reminiscent of a confessional, about matters which are kept carefully hidden from everybody with whom one is close. Objectivity is by no means nonparticipation, a condition that is altogether outside the distinction between subjective and objective orientations. It is rather a positive and definite kind of participation, in the same way that the objectivity of a theoretical observation clearly does not mean that the mind is a passive tabula rasa on which things inscribe their qualities, but rather signifies the full activity of a mind working according to its own laws, under conditions that exclude accidental distortions and emphases whose individual and subjective differences would produce quite different pictures of the same object.

Objectivity can also be defined as freedom. The objective man is not bound by ties which could prejudice his perception, his understanding, and his assessment of data. This freedom, which permits the stranger to experience and treat even his close relationships as though from a bird's-eye view, contains many dangerous possibilities. From earliest times, in uprisings of all sorts the attacked party has claimed that there has been incitement from the outside, by foreign emissaries and agitators. Insofar as this has happened, it represents an exaggeration of the specific role of the stranger: he is the freer man, practically and theoretically; he examines conditions with less prejudice; he assesses them against standards that are more general and more objective; and his actions are not confined by custom, piety, or precedent.[2]

Finally, the proportion of nearness and remoteness which gives the stranger the character of objectivity also finds practical expression in the more *abstract* nature of the relation to him. That is, with the stranger one has only certain *more general* qualities in common, whereas the relation with organically connected persons is based on the similarity of just those specific traits which differentiate them from the merely universal. In fact, all personal relations whatsoever can be analyzed in terms of this scheme. They are not determined only by the existence of certain common characteristics which the individuals share in addition to their individual differences, which either influence the relationship or remain outside of it. Rather, the kind of effect which that commonality has on the relation essentially depends on whether it exists only among the participants themselves, and thus, although general within the relation, is specific and incomparable with respect to all those on the outside, or whether the participants feel that what they have in common is so only because it is common to a group, a type, or mankind in general. In the latter case, the effect of the common features becomes attenuated in proportion to the size of the group bearing the same characteristics. The commonality provides a basis for unifying the members, to be sure; but it does not specifically direct *these* particular persons to one another. A similarity so widely shared could just as easily unite each person with every possible other. This, too, is evidently a way in which a relationship includes both nearness and remoteness simultaneously. To the extent to which the similarities assume a universal nature, the warmth of the connection based on them will acquire an element of coolness, a sense of the contingent nature of precisely *this* relation—the connecting forces have lost their specific, centripetal character.

In relation to the stranger, it seems to me, this constellation assumes an extraordinary preponderance in principle over the individual elements peculiar to the relation in question. The stranger is close to us insofar as we feel between him and ourselves similarities of nationality or social position, of occupation or of general human nature. He is far from us insofar as these similarities extend beyond him and us, and connect us only because they connect a great many people.

A trace of strangeness in this sense easily enters even the most intimate relationships. In the stage of first passion, erotic relations strongly reject any thought of generalization. A love such as this has never existed before; there is nothing to compare either with the person one loves or with our feelings for that person. An estrangement is wont to set in (whether as cause or effect is hard to decide) at the moment when this feeling of uniqueness disappears from the relationship. A skepticism regarding the intrinsic value of the relationship and its value for us adheres to the very thought that in this relation, after all, one is only fulfilling a general human destiny, that one has had an experience that has occurred a thousand times before, and that, if one had not accidentally met this precise person, someone else would have acquired the same meaning for us.

Something of this feeling is probably not absent in any relation, be it ever so close, because that which is common to two is perhaps never common *only* to them but belongs to a general conception which includes much else besides, many *possibilities* of similarities. No matter how few of these possibilities are realized and how often we may forget about them, here and there, nevertheless, they crowd in like shadows between men, like a mist eluding every designation, which must congeal into solid corporeality for it to be called jealousy. Perhaps this is in many cases a more general, at least more insurmountable, strangeness than that due to differences and obscurities. It is strangeness caused by the fact that similarity, harmony, and closeness are accompanied by the feeling that they are actually not the exclusive property of this particular relation, but stem from a more general one—a relation that potentially includes us and an indeterminate number of others, and therefore prevents that relation which alone was experienced from having an inner and exclusive necessity.

On the other hand, there is a sort of "strangeness" in which this very connection on the basis of a general quality embracing the parties is precluded. The relation of the Greeks to the barbarians is a typical example; so are all the cases in which the general characteristics one takes as peculiarly and merely human are disallowed to the other. But here the expression "the stranger" no longer has any positive meaning. The relation with him is a non-relation; he is not what we have been discussing here: the stranger as a member of the group itself.

As such, the stranger is near and far *at the same time*, as in any relationship based on merely universal human similarities. Between these two factors of nearness and distance, however, a peculiar tension arises, since the consciousness of having only the absolutely general in common has exactly the effect of putting a special emphasis on that which is not common. For a stranger to the country, the city, the race, and so on, what is stressed is again nothing individual, but alien origin, a quality which he has, or could have, in common with many other strangers. For this reason strangers are not really perceived as individuals, but as strangers of a certain type. Their remoteness is no less general than their nearness.

This form appears, for example, in so special a case as the tax levied on Jews in Frankfurt and elsewhere during the Middle Ages. Whereas the tax paid by Christian citizens varied according to their wealth at any given time, for every single Jew the tax was fixed once and for all. This amount was fixed because the Jew had his social position as a *Jew*, not as the bearer of certain objective contents. With respect to taxes every other citizen was regarded as possessor of a certain amount of wealth, and his tax could follow the fluctuations of his fortune. But the Jew as taxpayer was first of all a Jew, and thus his fiscal position contained an invariable element. This appears most forcefully, of course, once the differing circumstances of individual Jews are no longer considered, limited though this consideration is by fixed assessments, and all strangers pay exactly the same head tax.

Despite his being inorganically appended to it, the stranger is still an organic member of the group. Its unified life includes the specific conditioning of this element. Only we do not know how to designate the characteristic unity of this position otherwise than by saying that it is put together of certain amounts of nearness and of remoteness. Although both these qualities are found to some extent in all relationships, a special proportion and reciprocal tension between them produce the specific form of the relation to the "stranger."

NOTES

1. Simmel refers here to a passage which may be found in *The Sociology of Georg Simmel*, pp. 216–21.—ED.
2. Where the attacked parties make such an assertion falsely, they do so because those in higher positions tend to exculpate inferiors who previously have been in a close, solidary relationship with them. By introducing the fiction that the rebels were not really guilty, but only instigated, so they did not actually start the rebellion, they exonerate themselves by denying that there were any real grounds for the uprising.

COMPANION WEBSITE

1. Go online to Write Out Loud about a contemporary example of a stranger "that comes today and stays tomorrow."
2. Log on to Simmel's Profile Page to learn more about Simmel's life and the breadth of his ideas.

The Presentation of Self in Everyday Life

Erving Goffman

BELIEF IN THE PART ONE IS PLAYING

When an individual plays a part he implicitly requests his observers to take seriously the impression that is fostered before them. They are asked to believe that the character they see actually possesses the attributes he appears to possess, that the task he performs will have the consequences that are implicitly claimed for it, and that, in general, matters are what they appear to be. In line with this, there is the popular view that the individual offers his performance and puts on his show "for the benefit of other people." It will be convenient to begin a consideration of performances by turning the question around and looking at the individual's own belief in the impression of reality that he attempts to engender in those among whom he finds himself.

At one extreme, one finds that the performer can be fully taken in by his own act; he can be sincerely convinced that the impression of reality which he stages is the real reality. When his audience is also convinced in this way about the show he puts on—and this seems to be the typical case—then for the moment at least, only the sociologist or the socially disgruntled will have any doubts about the "realness" of what is presented.

At the other extreme, we find that the performer may not be taken in at all by his own routine. This possibility is understandable, since no one is in quite as good an observational position to see through the act as the person who puts it on. Coupled with this,

the performer may be moved to guide the conviction of his audience only as a means to other ends, having no ultimate concern in the conception that they have of him or of the situation. When the individual has no belief in his own act and no ultimate concern with the beliefs of his audience, we may call him cynical, reserving the term "sincere" for individuals who believe in the impression fostered by their own performance. It should be understood that the cynic, with all his professional disinvolvement, may obtain unprofessional pleasures from his masquerade, experiencing a kind of gleeful spiritual aggression from the fact that he can toy at will with something his audience must take seriously.[1]

It is not assumed, of course, that all cynical performers are interested in deluding their audiences for purposes of what is called "self-interest" or private gain. A cynical individual may delude his audience for what he considers to be their own good, or for the good of the community, etc. For illustrations of this we need not appeal to sadly enlightened showmen such as Marcus Aurelius or Hsun Tzû. We know that in service occupations practitioners who may otherwise be sincere are sometimes forced to delude their customers because their customers show such a heartfelt demand for it. Doctors who are led into giving placebos, filling station attendants who resignedly check and recheck tire pressures for anxious women motorists, shoe clerks who sell a shoe that fits but tell the customer it is the size she wants to hear—these are cynical performers whose audiences will not allow them to be sincere. Similarly, it seems that sympathetic patients in mental wards will sometimes feign bizarre symptoms so that student nurses will not be subjected to a disappointingly sane performance.[2] So also, when inferiors extend their most lavish reception for visiting superiors, the selfish desire to win favor may not be the chief motive; the inferior may be tactfully attempting to put the superior at ease by simulating the kind of world the superior is thought to take for granted.

I have suggested two extremes: an individual may be taken in by his own act or be cynical about it. These extremes are something a little more than just the ends of a continuum. Each provides the individual with a position which has its own particular securities and defenses, so there will be a tendency for those who have traveled close to one of these poles to complete the voyage. Starting with lack of inward belief in one's role, the individual may follow the natural movement described by Park:

> It is probably no mere historical accident that the word person, in its first meaning, is a mask. It is rather a recognition of the fact that everyone is always and everywhere, more or less consciously, playing a role … It is in these roles that we know each other; it is in these roles that we know ourselves.[3]
>
> In a sense, and in so far as this mask represents the conception we have formed of ourselves—the role we are striving to live up to—this mask is our truer self, the self we would like to be. In the end, our conception of our role becomes second nature and an integral part of our personality. We come into the world as individuals, achieve character, and become persons.[4]

This may be illustrated from the community life of Shetland.[5] For the last four or five years the island's tourist hotel has been owned and operated by a married couple of crofter origins. From the beginning, the owners were forced to set aside their own conceptions as to how life ought to be led, displaying in the hotel a full round of middle-class

services and amenities. Lately, however, it appears that the managers have become less cynical about the performance that they stage; they themselves are becoming middle class and more and more enamored of the selves their clients impute to them.

Another illustration may be found in the raw recruit who initially follows army etiquette in order to avoid physical punishment and eventually comes to follow the rules so that his organization will not be shamed and his officers and fellow soldiers will respect him.

As suggested, the cycle of disbelief-to-belief can be followed in the other direction, starting with conviction or insecure aspiration and ending in cynicism. Professions which the public holds in religious awe often allow their recruits to follow the cycle in this direction, and often recruits follow it in this direction not because of a slow realization that they are deluding their audience—for by ordinary social standards the claims they make may be quite valid—but because they can use this cynicism as a means of insulating their inner selves from contact with the audience. And we may even expect to find typical careers of faith, with the individual starting out with one kind of involvement in the performance he is required to give, then moving back and forth several times between sincerity and cynicism before completing all the phases and turning-points of self-belief for a person of his station. Thus, students of medical schools suggest that idealistically oriented beginners in medical school typically lay aside their holy aspirations for a period of time. During the first two years the students find that their interest in medicine must be dropped that they may give all their time to the task of learning how to get through examinations. During the next two years they are too busy learning about diseases to show much concern for the persons who are diseased. It is only after their medical schooling has ended that their original ideals about medical service may be reasserted.[6]

While we can expect to find natural movement back and forth between cynicism and sincerity, still we must not rule out the kind of transitional point that can be sustained on the strength of a little self-illusion. We find that the individual may attempt to induce the audience to judge him and the situation in a particular way, and he may seek this judgment as an ultimate end in itself, and yet he may not completely believe that he deserves the valuation of self which he asks for or that the impression of reality which he fosters is valid. Another mixture of cynicism and belief is suggested in Kroeber's discussion of shamanism:

> Next, there is the old question of deception. Probably most shamans or medicine men, the world over, help along with sleight-of-hand in curing and especially in exhibitions of power. This sleight-of-hand is sometimes deliberate; in many cases awareness is perhaps not deeper than the foreconscious. The attitude, whether there has been repression or not, seems to be as toward a pious fraud. Field ethnographers seem quite generally convinced that even shamans who know that they add fraud nevertheless also believe in their powers, and especially in those of other shamans: they consult them when they themselves or their children are ill.[7]

FRONT

I have been using the term "performance" to refer to all the activity of an individual which occurs during a period marked by his continuous presence before a particular set of observers and which has some influence on the observers. It will be convenient to label as "front" that part of the individual's performance which regularly functions in a general and fixed fashion to define the situation for those who observe the performance. Front, then, is the expressive equipment of a standard kind intentionally or unwittingly employed by the individual during his performance. For preliminary purposes, it will be convenient to distinguish and label what seem to be the standard parts of front.

First, there is the "setting," involving furniture, décor, physical layout, and other background items which supply the scenery and stage props for the spate of human action played out before, within, or upon it. A setting tends to stay put, geographically speaking, so that those who would use a particular setting as part of their performance cannot begin their act until they have brought themselves to the appropriate place and must terminate their performance when they leave it. It is only in exceptional circumstances that the setting follows along with the performers; we see this in the funeral cortège, the civic parade, and the dream-like processions that kings and queens are made of. In the main, these exceptions seem to offer some kind of extra protection for performers who are, or who have momentarily become, highly sacred. These worthies are to be distinguished, of course, from quite profane performers of the peddler class who move their place of work between performances, often being forced to do so. In the matter of having one fixed place for one's setting, a ruler may be too sacred, a peddler too profane.

In thinking about the scenic aspects of front, we tend to think of the living room in a particular house and the small number of performers who can thoroughly identify themselves with it. We have given insufficient attention to assemblages of sign-equipment which large numbers of performers can call their own for short periods of time. It is characteristic of Western European countries, and no doubt a source of stability for them, that a large number of luxurious settings are available for hire to anyone of the right kind who can afford them. One illustration of this may be cited from a study of the higher civil servant in Britain:

> The question how far the men who rise to the top in the Civil Service take on the "tone" or "color" of a class other than that to which they belong by birth is delicate and difficult. The only definite information bearing on the question is the figures relating to the membership of the great London clubs. More than three-quarters of our high administrative

officials belong to one or more clubs of high status and considerable luxury, where the entrance fee might be twenty guineas or more, and the annual subscription from twelve to twenty guineas. These institutions are of the upper class (not even of the upper-middle) in their premises, their equipment, the style of living practiced there, their whole atmosphere. Though many of the members would not be described as wealthy, only a wealthy man would unaided provide for himself and his family space, food and drink, service, and other amenities of life to the same standard as he will find at the Union, the Travellers', or the Reform.[8]

Another example can be found in the recent development of the medical profession where we find that it is increasingly important for a doctor to have access to the elaborate scientific stage provided by large hospitals, so that fewer and fewer doctors are able to feel that their setting is a place that they can lock up at night.[9]

If we take the term "setting" to refer to the scenic parts of expressive equipment, one may take the term "personal front" to refer to the other items of expressive equipment, the items that we most intimately identify with the performer himself and that we naturally expect will follow the performer wherever he goes. As part of personal front we may include: insignia of office or rank; clothing; sex, age, and racial characteristics; size and looks; posture; speech patterns; facial expressions; bodily gestures; and the like. Some of these vehicles for conveying signs, such as racial characteristics, are relatively fixed and over a span of time do not vary for the individual from one situation to another. On the other hand, some of these sign vehicles are relatively mobile or transitory, such as facial expression, and can vary during a performance from one moment to the next.

It is sometimes convenient to divide the stimuli which make up personal front into "appearance" and "manner," according to the function performed by the information that these stimuli convey. "Appearance" may be taken to refer to those stimuli which function at the time to tell us of the performer's social statuses. These stimuli also tell us of the individual's temporary ritual state, that is, whether he is engaging in formal social activity, work, or informal recreation, whether or not he is celebrating a new phase in the season cycle or in his life-cycle. "Manner" may be taken to refer to those stimuli which function at the time to warn us of the interaction role the performer will expect to play in the oncoming situation. Thus a haughty, aggressive manner may give the impression that the performer expects to be the one who will initiate the verbal interaction and direct its course. A meek, apologetic manner may give the impression that the performer expects to follow the lead of others, or at least that he can be led to do so.

We often expect, of course, a confirming consistency between appearance and manner; we expect that the differences in social statuses among the interactants will be expressed in some way by congruent differences in the indications that are made of an expected interaction role. This type of coherence of front may be illustrated by the following description of the procession of a mandarin through a Chinese city:

> Coming closely behind ... the luxurious chair of the mandarin, carried by eight bearers, fills the vacant space in the street. He is mayor of the town, and for all practical purposes the supreme power in it. He is an ideal-looking official, for he is large and massive in appearance, whilst he has that stern and uncompromising look that is supposed to be necessary in any magistrate who would hope to keep his subjects in order. He has a stern and forbidding aspect, as though he were on his way to the execution ground to have some criminal decapitated. This is the kind of air that the mandarins put on when they appear in public. In the course of many years' experience, I have never once seen any of them, from the highest to the lowest, with a smile on his face or a look of sympathy for the people whilst he was being carried officially through the streets.[10]

But, of course, appearance and manner may tend to contradict each other, as when a performer who appears to be of higher estate than his audience acts in a manner that is unexpectedly equalitarian, or intimate, or apologetic, or when a performer dressed in the garments of a high position presents himself to an individual of even higher status.

In addition to the expected consistency between appearance and manner, we expect, of course, some coherence among setting, appearance, and manner.[11] Such coherence represents an ideal type that provides us with a means of stimulating our attention to and interest in exceptions. In this the student is assisted by the journalist, for exceptions to expected consistency among setting, appearance, and manner provide the piquancy and glamor of many careers and the salable appeal of many magazine articles. For example, a *New Yorker* profile on Roger Stevens (the real estate agent who engineered the sale of the Empire State Building) comments on the startling fact that Stevens has a small house, a meager office, and no letterhead stationery.[12]

In order to explore more fully the relations among the several parts of social front, it will be convenient to consider here a significant characteristic of the information conveyed by front, namely, its abstractness and generality.

However specialized and unique a routine is, its social front, with certain exceptions, will tend to claim facts that can be equally claimed and asserted of other, somewhat different routines. For example, many service occupations offer their clients a performance that is illuminated with dramatic expressions of cleanliness, modernity, competence, and integrity. While in fact these abstract standards have a different significance in different occupational performances, the observer is encouraged to stress the abstract similarities. For the observer this is a wonderful, though sometimes disastrous, convenience. Instead of having to maintain a different pattern of expectation and responsive treatment for each slightly different performer and performance, he can place the situation in a broad category

around which it is easy for him to mobilize his past experience and stereotypical thinking. Observers then need only be familiar with a small and hence manageable vocabulary of fronts, and know how to respond to them, in order to orient themselves in a wide variety of situations. Thus in London the current tendency for chimney sweeps[13] and perfume clerks to wear white lab coats tends to provide the client with an understanding that the delicate tasks performed by these persons will be performed in what has become a standardized, clinical, confidential manner.

There are grounds for believing that the tendency for a large number of different acts to be presented from behind a small number of fronts is a natural development in social organization. Radcliffe-Brown has suggested this in his claim that a "descriptive" kinship system which gives each person a unique place may work for very small communities, but, as the number of persons becomes large, clan segmentation becomes necessary as a means of providing a less complicated system of identifications and treatments.[14] We see this tendency illustrated in factories, barracks, and other large social establishments. Those who organize these establishments find it impossible to provide a special cafeteria, special modes of payment, special vacation rights, and special sanitary facilities for every line and staff status category in the organization, and at the same time they feel that persons of dissimilar status ought not to be indiscriminately thrown together or classified together. As a compromise, the full range of diversity is cut at a few crucial points, and all those within a given bracket are allowed or obliged to maintain the same social front in certain situations.

In addition to the fact that different routines may employ the same front, it is to be noted that a given social front tends to become institutionalized in terms of the abstract stereotyped expectations to which it gives rise, and tends to take on a meaning and stability apart from the specific tasks which happen at the time to be performed in its name. The front becomes a "collective representation" and a fact in its own right.

When an actor takes on an established social role, usually he finds that a particular front has already been established for it. Whether his acquisition of the role was primarily motivated by a desire to perform the given task or by a desire to maintain the corresponding front, the actor will find that he must do both.

Further, if the individual takes on a task that is not only new to him but also unestablished in the society, or if he attempts to change the light in which his task is viewed, he is likely to find that there are already several well-established fronts among which he must choose. Thus, when a task is given a new front we seldom find that the front it is given is itself new.

[...]

DRAMATIC REALIZATION

While in the presence of others, the individual typically infuses his activity with signs which dramatically highlight and portray confirmatory facts that might otherwise remain unapparent or obscure. For if the individual's activity is to become significant to others, he must mobilize his activity so that it will express *during the interaction* what he wishes to convey. In fact, the performer may be required not only to express his claimed capacities during the interaction but also to do so during a split second in the interaction. Thus, if a baseball umpire is to give the impression that he is sure of his judgment, he must forgo the moment of thought which might make him sure of his judgment; he must give an instantaneous decision so that the audience will be sure that he is sure of his judgment.[15]

It may be noted that in the case of some statuses dramatization presents no problem, since some of the acts which are instrumentally essential for the completion of the core task of the status are at the same time wonderfully adapted, from the point of view of communication, as means of vividly conveying the qualities and attributes claimed by the performer. The roles of prizefighters, surgeons, violinists, and policemen are cases in point. These activities allow for so much dramatic self-expression that exemplary practitioners—whether real or fictional—become famous and are given a special place in the commercially organized fantasies of the nation.

In many cases, however, dramatization of one's work does constitute a problem. An illustration of this may be cited from a hospital study where the medical nursing staff is shown to have a problem that the surgical nursing staff does not have:

> The things which a nurse does for post-operative patients on the surgical floor are frequently of recognizable importance, even to patients who are strangers to hospital activities. For example, the patient sees his nurse changing bandages, swinging orthopedic frames into place, and can realize that these are purposeful activities. Even if she cannot be at his side, he can respect her purposeful activities.
>
> Medical nursing is also highly skilled work... . The physician's diagnosis must rest upon careful observation of symptoms over time where the surgeon's are in larger part dependent on visible things. The lack of visibility creates problems on the medical. A patient will see his nurse stop at the next bed and chat for a moment or two with the patient there. He doesn't know that she is observing the shallowness of the breathing and color and tone of the skin. He thinks she is just visiting. So, alas, does his family who may thereupon decide that these nurses aren't very impressive. If the nurse spends more time at the next bed than at his own, the patient may feel slighted... . The nurses are "wasting time" unless they are darting about doing some visible thing such as administering hypodermics.[16]

Similarly, the proprietor of a service establishment may find it difficult to dramatize what is actually being done for clients because the clients cannot "see" the overhead costs of the service rendered them. Undertakers must therefore charge a great deal for their highly visible product—a coffin that has been transformed into a casket—because many of the other costs of conducting a funeral are ones that cannot be readily dramatized.[17] Merchants, too, find that they must charge high prices for things that look intrinsically expensive in order to compensate the establishment for expensive things like insurance, slack periods, etc., that never appear before the customers' eyes.

The problem of dramatizing one's work involves more than merely making invisible costs visible. The work that must be done by those who fill certain statuses is often so poorly designed as an expression of a desired meaning, that if the incumbent would dramatize the character of his role, he must divert an appreciable amount of his energy to do so. And this activity diverted to communication will often require different attributes from the ones which are being dramatized. Thus to furnish a house so that it will express simple, quiet dignity, the householder may have to race to auction sales, haggle with antique dealers, and doggedly canvass all the local shops for proper wallpaper and curtain materials. To give a radio talk that will sound genuinely informal, spontaneous, and relaxed, the speaker may have to design his script with painstaking care, testing one phrase after another, in order to follow the content, language, rhythm, and pace of everyday talk.[18] Similarly, a *Vogue* model, by her clothing, stance, and facial expression, is able expressively to portray a cultivated understanding of the book she poses in her hand; but those who trouble to express themselves so appropriately will have very little time left over for reading. As Sartre suggested: "The attentive pupil who wishes to *be* attentive, his eyes riveted on the teacher, his ears open wide, so exhausts himself in playing the attentive role that he ends up by no longer hearing anything."[19] And so individuals often find themselves with the dilemma of expression *versus* action. Those who have the time and

talent to perform a task well may not, because of this, have the time or talent to make it apparent that they are performing well. It may be said that some organizations resolve this dilemma by officially delegating the dramatic function to a specialist who will spend his time expressing the meaning of the task and spend no time actually doing it.

If we alter our frame of reference for a moment and turn from a particular performance to the individuals who present it, we can consider an interesting fact about the round of different routines which any group or class of individuals helps to perform. When a group or class is examined, one finds that the members of it tend to invest their egos primarily in certain routines, giving less stress to the other ones which they perform. Thus a professional man may be willing to take a very modest role in the street, in a shop, or in his home, but, in the social sphere which encompasses his display of professional competency, he will be much concerned to make an effective showing. In mobilizing his behavior to make a showing, he will be concerned not so much with the full round of the different routines he performs but only with the one from which his occupational reputation derives. It is upon this issue that some writers have chosen to distinguish groups with aristocratic habits (whatever their social status) from those of middle-class character. The aristocratic habit, it has been said, is one that mobilizes all the minor activities of life which fall outside the serious specialities of other classes and injects into these activities an expression of character, power, and high rank.

> By what important accomplishments is the young nobleman instructed to support the dignity of his rank, and to render himself worthy of that superiority over his fellow-citizens, to which the virtue of his ancestors had raised them: Is it by knowledge, by industry, by patience, by self-denial, or by virtue of any kind? As all his words, as all his motions are attended to, he learns a habitual regard to every circumstance of ordinary behavior, and studies to perform all those small duties with

the most exact propriety. As he is conscious of how much he is observed, and how much mankind are disposed to favor all his inclinations, he acts, upon the most indifferent occasions, with that freedom and elevation which the thought of this naturally inspires. His air, his manner, his deportment, all mark that elegant, and graceful sense of his own superiority, which those who are born to inferior stations can hardly ever arrive at. These are the arts by which he proposes to make mankind more easily submit to his authority, and to govern their inclinations according to his own pleasure: and in this he is seldom disappointed. These arts, supported by rank and pre-eminence, are, upon ordinary occasions, sufficient to govern the world.[20]

If such virtuosi actually exist, they would provide a suitable group in which to study the techniques by which activity is transformed into a show.

IDEALIZATION

It was suggested earlier that a performance of a routine presents through its front some rather abstract claims upon the audience, claims that are likely to be presented to them during the performance of other routines. This constitutes one way in which a performance is "socialized," molded, and modified to fit into the understanding and expectations of the society in which it is presented. I want to consider here another important aspect of this socialization process—the tendency for performers to offer their observers an impression that is idealized in several different ways.

The notion that a performance presents an idealized view of the situation is, of course, quite common. Cooley's view may be taken as an illustration:

If we never tried to seem a little better than we are, how could we improve or "train ourselves from the outside inward?" And the same impulse to show the world a better or idealized aspect of ourselves finds an organized expression in the various professions and classes, each of which has to some extent a cant

or pose, which its members assume unconsciously, for the most part, but which has the effect of a conspiracy to work upon the credulity of the rest of the world. There is a cant not only of theology and of philanthropy, but also of law, medicine, teaching, even of science—perhaps especially of science, just now, since the more a particular kind of merit is recognized and admired, the more it is likely to be assumed by the unworthy.[21]

Thus, when the individual presents himself before others, his performance will tend to incorporate and exemplify the officially accredited values of the society, more so, in fact, than does his behavior as a whole.

To the degree that a performance highlights the common official values of the society in which it occurs, we may look upon it, in the manner of Durkheim and Radcliffe-Brown, as a ceremony— as an expressive rejuvenation and reaffirmation of the moral values of the community. Furthermore, in so far as the expressive bias of performances comes to be accepted as reality, then that which is accepted at the moment as reality will have some of the characteristics of a celebration. To stay in one's room away from the place where the party is given, or away from where the practitioner attends his client, is to stay away from where reality is being performed. The world, in truth, is a wedding.

[...]

The expressive coherence that is required in performances points out a crucial discrepancy between our all-too-human selves and our socialized selves. As human beings we are presumably creatures of variable impulse with moods and energies that change from one moment to the next. As characters put on for an audience, however, we must not be subject to ups and downs. As Durkheim suggested, we do not allow our higher social activity "to follow in the trail of our bodily states, as our sensations and our general bodily consciousness do."[22] A certain bureaucratization of the spirit is expected so that we can be relied upon to give a perfectly homogeneous performance at every appointed time. As Santayana suggests, the socialization process not only transfigures, it fixes:

> But whether the visage we assume be a joyful or a sad one, in adopting and emphasizing it we define our sovereign temper. Henceforth, so long as we continue under the spell of this self-knowledge, we do not merely live but act; we compose and play our chosen character, we wear the buskin of deliberation, we defend and idealize our passions, we encourage ourselves eloquently to be what we are, devoted or scornful or careless or austere; we soliloquize (before an imaginary audience) and we wrap ourselves gracefully in the mantle of our inalienable part. So draped, we solicit applause and expect to die amid a universal hush. We profess to live up to the fine sentiments we have uttered, as we try to believe in the religion we profess. The greater our difficulties the greater our zeal. Under our published principles and plighted language we must assiduously hide all the inequalities of our moods and conduct, and this without hypocrisy, since our deliberate character is more truly ourself than is the flux of our involuntary dreams. The portrait we paint in this way and exhibit as our true person may well be in the grand manner, with column and curtain and distant landscape and finger pointing to the terrestrial globe or to the Yorick-skull of philosophy; but if this style is native to us and our art is vital, the more it transmutes its model the deeper and truer art it will be. The severe bust of an archaic sculpture, scarcely humanizing the block, will express a spirit far more justly than the man's dull morning looks or casual grimaces. Everyone who is sure of his mind, or proud of his office, or anxious about his duty assumes a tragic mask. He deputes it to be himself and transfers to it almost all his vanity. While still alive and subject, like all existing things, to the undermining flux of his own substance, he has crystallized his soul into an idea, and more in pride than in sorrow he has offered up his life on the altar of the Muses. Self-knowledge, like any art or science, renders its subject-matter in a new medium, the medium of ideas, in which it loses its old dimensions and its old place. Our animal habits are transmuted by conscience into loyalties and duties, and we become "persons" or masks.[23]

Through social discipline, then, a mask of manner can be held in place from within. But, as Simone de Beauvoir suggests, we are helped in keeping this pose by clamps that are tightened directly on the body, some hidden, some showing:

> Even if each woman dresses in conformity with her status, a game is still being played: artifice, like art, belongs to the realm of the imaginary. It is not only that girdle, brassiere, hair-dye, make-up disguise body and face; but that the least sophisticated of women, once she is "dressed," does not present *herself* to observation; she is, like the picture or the statue, or the actor on the stage, an agent through whom is suggested someone not there—that is, the character she represents, but is not. It is this identification with something unreal, fixed, perfect as the hero of a novel, as a portrait or a bust, that gratifies her; she strives to identify herself with this figure and thus to seem to herself to be stabilized, justified in her splendor.[24]

MISREPRESENTATION

It was suggested earlier that an audience is able to orient itself in a situation by accepting performed cues on faith, treating these signs as evidence of something greater than or different from the sign-vehicles themselves. If this tendency of the audience to accept signs places the performer in a position to be misunderstood and makes it necessary for him to exercise expressive care regarding everything he does when before the audience, so also this sign-accepting tendency puts the audience in a position to be duped and misled, for there are few signs that cannot be used to attest to the presence of something that is not really there. And it is plain that many performers have ample capacity and motive to misrepresent the facts; only shame, guilt, or fear prevent them from doing so.

As members of an audience it is natural for us to feel that the impression the performer seeks to give may be true or false, genuine or spurious, valid or "phony." So common is this doubt that, as suggested, we often give special attention to features of the performance that cannot be readily manipulated, thus enabling ourselves to judge the reliability of the more misrepresentable cues in the performance. (Scientific police work and projective testing are extreme examples of the application of this tendency.) And if we grudgingly allow certain symbols of status to establish a performer's right to a given treatment, we are always ready to pounce on chinks in his symbolic armor in order to discredit his pretensions.

When we think of those who present a false front or "only" a front, of those who dissemble, deceive, and defraud, we think of a discrepancy between fostered appearances and reality. We also think of the precarious position in which these performers place themselves, for at any moment in their performance an event may occur to catch them out and baldly contradict what they have openly avowed, bringing them immediate humiliation and sometimes permanent loss of reputation. We often feel that it is just these terrible eventualities, which arise from being caught out *flagrante delicto* in a patent act of misrepresentation, that an honest performer is able to avoid. This common-sense view has limited analytical utility.

Sometimes when we ask whether a fostered impression is true or false we really mean to ask whether or not the performer is authorized to give the performance in question, and are not primarily concerned with the actual performance itself. When we discover that someone with whom we have dealings is an impostor and out-and-out fraud, we are discovering that he did not have the right to play the part he played, that he was not an accredited incumbent of the relevant status. We assume that the impostor's performance, in addition to the fact

that it misrepresents him, will be at fault in other ways, but often his masquerade is discovered before we can detect any other difference between the false performance and the legitimate one which it simulates. Paradoxically, the more closely the impostor's performance approximates to the real thing, the more intensely we may be threatened, for a competent performance by someone who proves to be an impostor may weaken in our minds the moral connection between legitimate authorization to play a part and the capacity to play it. (Skilled mimics, who admit all along that their intentions are unserious, seem to provide one way in which we can "work through" some of these anxieties.)

The social definition of impersonation, however, is not itself a very consistent thing. For example, while it is felt to be an inexcusable crime against communication to impersonate someone of sacred status, such as a doctor or a priest, we are often less concerned when someone impersonates a member of a disesteemed, non-crucial, profane status, such as that of a hobo or unskilled worker. When a disclosure shows that we have been participating with a performer who has a higher status than he led us to believe, there is good Christian precedent for our reacting with wonderment and chagrin rather than with hostility. Mythology and our popular magazines, in fact, are full of romantic stories in which the villain and the hero both make fraudulent claims that are discredited in the last chapter, the villain proving not to have a high status, the hero proving not to have a low one.

Further, while we may take a harsh view of performers such as confidence men who knowingly misrepresent every fact about their lives, we may have some sympathy for those who have but one fatal flaw and who attempt to conceal the fact that they are, for example, ex-convicts, deflowered, epileptic, or racially impure, instead of admitting their fault and making an honorable attempt to live it down. Also, we distinguish between impersonation of a specific, concrete individual, which we usually feel is quite inexcusable, and impersonation of category membership, which we may feel less strongly about. So, too, we often feel differently about those who misrepresent themselves to forward what they feel are the just claims of a collectivity, or those who misrepresent themselves accidentally or for a lark, than about those who misrepresent themselves for private psychological or material gain.

Finally, since there are senses in which the concept of "a status" is not clear-cut, so there are senses in which the concept of impersonation is not clear either. For example, there are many statuses in which membership obviously is not subject to formal ratification. Claims to be a law graduate can be established as valid or invalid, but claims to be a friend, a true believer, or a music-lover can be confirmed or disconfirmed only more or less. Where standards of competence are not objective, and where *bona fide* practitioners are not collectively organized to protect their mandate, an individual may style himself an expert and be penalized by nothing stronger than sniggers.

NOTES

1. Perhaps the real crime of the confidence man is not that he takes money from his victims but that he robs all of us of the belief that middle-class manners and appearance can be sustained only by middle-class people. A disabused professional can be cynically hostile to the service relation his clients expect him to extend to them; the confidence man is in a position to hold the whole "legit" world in this contempt.
2. See Taxel, *op. cit.*, p. 4. Harry Stack Sullivan has suggested that the tact of institutionalized performers can operate in the other direction, resulting in a kind of *noblesse-oblige* sanity. See his "Socio-Psychiatric Research," *American Journal of Psychiatry*, X, pp. 987–88.

   "A study of 'social recoveries' in one of our large mental hospitals some years ago taught me that patients were often released from care because they had learned not to manifest symptoms to the environing persons; in other words, had integrated

enough of the personal environment to realize the prejudice opposed to their delusions. It seemed almost as if they grew wise enough to be tolerant of the imbecility surrounding them, having finally discovered that it was stupidity and not malice. They could then secure satisfaction from contact with others, while discharging a part of their cravings by psychotic means."

3. Robert Ezra Park, *Race and Culture* (Glencoe, Ill.: The Free Press, 1950), p. 249.
4. *Ibid.*, p. 250.
5. Shetland Isle study.
6. H. S. Becker and Blanche Greer, "The Fate of Idealism in Medical School," *American Sociological Review*, 23, pp. 50–56.
7. A. L. Kroeber, *The Nature of Culture* (Chicago: University of Chicago Press, 1952), p. 311.
8. H. E. Dale, *The Higher Civil Service of Great Britain* (Oxford: Oxford University Press, 1941), p. 50.
9. David Solomon, "Career Contingencies of Chicago Physicians" (unpublished Ph.D. dissertation, Department of Sociology, University of Chicago, 1952), p. 74.
10. J. Macgowan, *Sidelights on Chinese Life* (Philadelphia: Lippincott, 1908), p. 187.
11. Cf. Kenneth Burke's comments on the "scene-act-agent ratio," A *Grammar of Motives* (New York: Prentice-Hall, 1945), pp. 6–9.
12. E. J. Kahn, Jr., "Closings and Openings," *The New Yorker*, February 13 and 20, 1954.
13. See Mervyn Jones, "White as a Sweep," *The New Statesman and Nation*, December 6, 1952.
14. A. R. Radcliffe-Brown, "The Social Organization of Australian Tribes," *Oceania*, I, 440.
15. See Babe Pinelli, as told to Joe King, *Mr. Ump* (Philadelphia: Westminster Press, 1953), p. 75.
16. Edith Lentz, "A Comparison of Medical and Surgical Floors" (Mimeo: New York State School of Industrial and Labor Relations, Cornell University, 1954), pp. 2–3.
17. Material on the burial business used throughout this report is taken from Robert W. Habenstein, "The American Funeral Director" (unpublished Ph.D. dissertation, Department of Sociology, University of Chicago, 1954). I owe much to Mr. Habenstein's analysis of a funeral as a performance.
18. John Hilton, "Calculated Spontaneity," *Oxford Book of English Talk* (Oxford: Clarendon Press, 1953), pp. 399–404.
19. Sartre, *op. cit.*, p. 60.

20. Adam Smith, *The Theory of Moral Sentiments* (London Henry Bohn, 1853), p. 75.

21. Charles H. Cooley, *Human Nature and the Social Order* (New York: Scribner's, 1922), pp. 352–53.

22. Emile Durkheim, *The Elementary Forms of the Religious Life*, trans. J. W. Swain (London: Allen & Unwin, 1926), p. 272.

23. Santayana, *op. cit.*, pp. 133–34.

24. Simone de Beauvoir, *The Second Sex*, trans. H. M. Parshley (New York: Knopf, 1953), p. 533.

COMPANION WEBSITE

1. Go online to Write Out Loud about how almost all performances require a little bit of duping on the part of the performer.

2. Log on to the Mid-Twentieth-Century American Theory Profile Page to learn more about Goffman's ideas and influences.

3. Browse the Supplementary Sources for *Rise of the Avatar* for a great *New Yorker* article on the presentation of self in the social world of online dating.

38

The History of Sexuality

Michel Foucault

HISTORICALLY, THERE HAVE BEEN TWO great procedures for producing the truth of sex.

On the one hand, the societies—and they are numerous: China, Japan, India, Rome, the Arabo-Moslem societies—which endowed themselves with an *ars erotica*. In the erotic art, truth is drawn from pleasure itself, understood as a practice and accumulated as experience; pleasure is not considered in relation to an absolute law of the permitted and the forbidden, nor by reference to a criterion of utility, but first and foremost in relation to itself; it is experienced as pleasure, evaluated in terms of its intensity, its specific quality, its duration, its reverberations in the body and the soul. Moreover, this knowledge must be deflected back into the sexual practice itself, in order to shape it as though from within and amplify its effects. In this way, there is formed a knowledge that must remain secret, not because of an element of infamy that might attach to its object, but because of the need to hold it in the greatest reserve, since, according to tradition, it would lose its effectiveness and its virtue by being divulged. Consequently, the relationship to the master who holds the secrets is of paramount importance; only he, working alone, can transmit this art in an esoteric manner and as the culmination of an initiation in which he guides the disciple's progress with unfailing skill and severity. The effects of this masterful art, which are considerably more generous than the spareness of its prescriptions would lead one to imagine, are said to transfigure the one fortunate enough to receive its privileges: an absolute mastery of the body, a singular bliss, obliviousness to time and limits, the elixir of life, the exile of death and its threats.

On the face of it at least, our civilization possesses no *ars erotica*. In return, it is undoubtedly the only civilization to practice a *scientia sexualis*; or rather, the only civilization to have developed over the centuries procedures for telling the truth of sex which are geared to a form of knowledge-power strictly opposed to the art of initiations and the masterful secret: I have in mind the confession.

Since the Middle Ages at least, Western societies have established the confession as one of the main rituals we rely on for the production of truth: the codification of the sacrament of penance by the Lateran Council in 1215, with the resulting development of confessional techniques, the declining importance of accusatory procedures in criminal justice, the abandonment of tests of guilt (sworn statements, duels, judgments of God) and the development of methods of interrogation and inquest, the increased participation of the royal administration in the prosecution of infractions, at the expense of proceedings leading to private settlements, the setting up of tribunals of Inquisition: all this helped to give the confession a central role in the order of civil and religious powers. The evolution of the word *avowal* and of the legal function it designated is itself emblematic of this development: from being a guarantee of the status, identity, and value granted to one person by another, it came to signify someone's acknowledgment of his own actions and thoughts. For a long time, the individual was vouched for by the reference of others and the demonstration of his ties to the commonweal (family, allegiance, protection); then he was authenticated by the discourse of truth he was able or obliged to pronounce concerning himself. The truthful confession was inscribed at the heart of the procedures of individualization by power.

In any case, next to the testing rituals, next to the testimony of witnesses, and the learned methods of observation and demonstration, the confession became one of the West's most highly valued techniques for producing truth. We have since become a singularly confessing society. The confession has spread its effects far and wide. It plays a part in justice, medicine, education, family relationships, and love relations, in the most ordinary affairs of everyday life, and in the most solemn rites; one confesses one's crimes, one's sins, one's thoughts and desires, one's illnesses and troubles; one goes about telling, with the greatest precision, whatever is most difficult to tell. One confesses in public and in private, to one's parents, one's educators, one's doctor, to those one loves; one admits to oneself, in pleasure and in pain, things it would be impossible to tell to anyone else, the things people write books about. One confesses—or is forced to confess. When it is not spontaneous or dictated by some internal imperative, the confession is wrung from a person by violence or threat; it is driven from its hiding place in the soul, or extracted from the body. Since the Middle Ages, torture has accompanied it like a shadow, and supported it when it could go no further: the dark twins.[1] The most defenseless tenderness and the bloodiest of powers have a similar need of confession. Western man has become a confessing animal.

Whence a metamorphosis in literature: we have passed from a pleasure to be recounted and heard, centering on the heroic or marvelous narration of "trials" of bravery or sainthood, to a literature ordered according to the infinite task of extracting from the depths of oneself, in between the words, a truth which the very form of the confession holds out like a shimmering mirage. Whence too this new way of philosophizing: seeking the fundamental relation to the true, not simply in oneself—in some forgotten knowledge, or in a certain primal trace—but in the self-examination that yields, through a multitude of fleeting impressions, the basic certainties of consciousness. The obligation to confess is now relayed through so many different points, is so deeply ingrained in us, that we no longer perceive it as the effect of a power that constrains us; on the contrary, it seems to us that truth, lodged in our most secret nature, "demands" only to surface; that if it fails to do so, this is because a constraint holds it in place, the violence of a power weighs it down, and it can finally be articulated only at the price of a kind of liberation. Confession frees, but power reduces one to silence; truth does not belong to the order of power, but shares an original affinity with freedom: traditional themes in philosophy, which a "political history of truth" would have to overturn by showing that truth is not by nature free—nor error servile—but that its production is thoroughly imbued with relations of power. The confession is an example of this.

One has to be completely taken in by this internal ruse of confession in order to attribute a fundamental role to censorship, to taboos regarding speaking and thinking; one has to have an inverted image of power in order to believe that all these voices which have spoken so long in our civilization—repeating the formidable injunction to tell what one is and what one does, what one recollects and what one has forgotten, what one is thinking and what one thinks he is not thinking—are speaking to us of freedom. An immense labor to which the West has submitted generations in order to produce—while other forms of work ensured the accumulation of capital—men's subjection: their constitution as subjects in both senses of the word. Imagine how exorbitant must have seemed the order given to all Christians at the beginning of the thirteenth century, to kneel at least once a year and confess to all their transgressions, without omitting a single one. And think of that obscure partisan, seven centuries later, who had come to rejoin the Serbian resistance deep in the mountains; his superiors asked him to write his life story; and when he brought them a few miserable pages, scribbled in the night, they did not look at them but only said to him, "Start over, and tell the truth." Should those much-discussed language taboos make us forget this millennial yoke of confession?

From the Christian penance to the present day, sex was a privileged theme of confession. A thing that was hidden, we are told. But what if, on the contrary, it was what, in a quite particular way, one confessed? Suppose the obligation to conceal it was but another aspect of the duty to admit to it (concealing it all the more and with greater care as the confession of it was more important, requiring a stricter ritual and promising more decisive effects)? What if sex in our society, on a scale of several centuries, was something that was placed within an unrelenting system of confession? The transformation of sex into discourse, which I spoke of earlier, the dissemination and reinforcement of heterogeneous sexualities, are perhaps two elements of the same deployment: they are linked together with the help of the central element of a confession that compels individuals to articulate their sexual peculiarity—no matter how extreme. In Greece, truth and sex were linked, in the form of pedagogy, by the transmission of a precious knowledge from one body to another; sex served as a medium for initiations into learning. For us, it is in the confession that truth and sex are joined, through the obligatory and exhaustive expression of an individual secret. But this time it is truth that serves as a medium for sex and its manifestations.

The confession is a ritual of discourse in which the speaking subject is also the subject of the statement; it is also a ritual that unfolds within a power relationship, for one does not confess without the presence (or virtual presence) of a partner who is not simply the interlocutor but the authority who requires the confession, prescribes and appreciates it, and intervenes in order to judge, punish, forgive, console, and reconcile; a ritual in which the truth is corroborated by the obstacles and resistances it has had to surmount in order to be formulated; and finally, a ritual in which the expression alone, independently of its external consequences, produces intrinsic modifications in the person who articulates it: it exonerates, redeems, and purifies him; it unburdens him of his wrongs, liberates him, and promises him salvation. For centuries, the truth of sex was, at least for the most part, caught up in this discursive form. Moreover, this form was not the same as that of education (sexual education confined itself to general principles and rules of prudence); nor was it that of initiation (which remained essentially a silent practice, which the act of sexual enlightenment or deflowering merely rendered laughable or violent). As we have seen, it is a form that is far removed from the one governing the "erotic art." By virtue of the power structure immanent in it, the confessional discourse cannot come from above, as in the *ars erotica*, through the sovereign will of a master, but rather from below, as an obligatory act of speech which, under some imperious compulsion, breaks the bonds of discretion or forgetfulness. What secrecy it presupposes is not owing to the high price of what it has to say and the small number of those who are worthy of its benefits, but to its obscure familiarity and its general baseness. Its veracity is not guaranteed by the lofty authority of the magistery, nor by the tradition it transmits, but by the bond, the basic intimacy in discourse, between the one who speaks and what he is speaking about. On the other hand, the agency of domination does not reside in the one who speaks (for it is he who is constrained), but in the one who listens and says nothing; not in the one who knows and answers, but in the one who questions and is not supposed to know. And this discourse of truth finally takes effect, not in the one who receives it, but in the one from whom it is wrested. With these confessed truths, we are a long way from the learned initiations into pleasure, with their technique and their mystery. On the other hand, we belong to a society which has ordered sex's difficult knowledge, not according to the transmission of secrets, but around the slow surfacing of confidential statements.

The confession was, and still remains, the general standard governing the production of the true discourse on sex. It has undergone a considerable transformation, however. For a long time, it remained firmly entrenched in the practice of penance. But with the rise of Protestantism, the Counter Reformation, eighteenth-century pedagogy, and nineteenth-century medicine, it gradually lost its ritualistic and exclusive localization; it spread; it has been employed in a whole series of relationships: children and parents, students and educators, patients and psychiatrists, delinquents and experts. The motivations and effects it is expected to produce have varied, as have the forms it has taken: interrogations, consultations, autobiographical narratives, letters; they have been recorded, transcribed, assembled into dossiers, published, and commented on. But more important, the confession lends itself, if not to other domains, at least to new ways of exploring the existing ones. It is no longer a question simply of saying what was done— the sexual act—and how it was done; but of reconstructing, in and around the act, the thoughts that recapitulated it, the obsessions that accompanied it, the images, desires, modulations, and quality of the pleasure that animated it. For the first time no doubt, a society has taken upon itself to solicit and hear the imparting of individual pleasures.

A dissemination, then, of procedures of confession, a multiple localization of their constraint, a widening of their domain: a great archive of the pleasures of sex was gradually constituted. For a long time this archive dematerialized as it was formed. It regularly disappeared without a trace (thus suiting the purposes of the Christian pastoral) until medicine, psychiatry, and pedagogy began to solidify it:

Campe, Salzmann, and especially Kaan, Krafft-Ebing, Tardieu, Molle, and Havelock Ellis carefully assembled this whole pitiful, lyrical outpouring from the sexual mosaic. Western societies thus began to keep an indefinite record of these people's pleasures. They made up a herbal of them and established a system of classification. They described their everyday deficiencies as well as their oddities or exasperations. This was an important time. It is easy to make light of these nineteenth-century psychiatrists, who made a point of apologizing for the horrors they were about to let speak, evoking "immoral behavior" or "aberrations of the genetic senses," but I am more inclined to applaud their seriousness: they had a feeling for momentous events. It was a time when the most singular pleasures were called upon to pronounce a discourse of truth concerning themselves, a discourse which had to model itself after that which spoke, not of sin and salvation, but of bodies and life processes—the discourse of science. It was enough to make one's voice tremble, for an improbable thing was then taking shape: a confessional science, a science which relied on a many-sided extortion, and took for its object what was unmentionable but admitted to nonetheless. The scientific discourse was scandalized, or in any case repelled, when it had to take charge of this whole discourse from below. It was also faced with a theoretical and methodological paradox: the long discussions concerning the possibility of constituting a science of the subject, the validity of introspection, lived experience as evidence, or the presence of consciousness to itself were responses to this problem that is inherent in the functioning of truth in our society: can one articulate the production of truth according to the old juridico-religious model of confession, and the extortion of confidential evidence according to the rules of scientific discourse? Those who believe that sex was more rigorously elided in the nineteenth century than ever before, through a formidable mechanism of blockage and a deficiency of discourse, can say what they please. There was no deficiency, but rather an excess, a redoubling, too much rather than not enough discourse, in any case an interference between two modes of production of truth: procedures of confession, and scientific discursivity.

And instead of adding up the errors, naïvetés, and moralisms that plagued the nineteenth-century discourse of truth concerning sex, we would do better to locate the procedures by which that will to knowledge regarding sex, which characterizes the modern Occident, caused the rituals of confession to function within the norms of scientific regularity, how did this immense and traditional extortion of the sexual confession come to be constituted in scientific terms?

1. *Through a clinical codification of the inducement to speak.* Combining confession with examination, the personal history with the deployment of a set of decipherable signs and symptoms; the interrogation, the exacting questionnaire, and hypnosis, with the recollection of memories and free association: all were ways of reinscribing the procedure of confession in a field of scientifically acceptable observations.

2. *Through the postulate of a general and diffuse causality.* Having to tell everything, being able to pose questions about everything, found their justification in the principle that endowed sex with an inexhaustible and polymorphous causal power. The most discrete event in one's sexual behavior—whether an accident or a deviation, a deficit or an excess—was deemed capable of entailing the most varied consequences throughout one's existence; there was scarcely a malady or physical disturbance to which the nineteenth century did not impute at least some degree of sexual etiology. From the bad habits of children to the phthises of adults, the apoplexies of old people, nervous maladies, and the degenerations of the race, the medicine of that era wove an entire network of sexual causality to explain them. This may well appear fantastic to us, but the principle of sex as a "cause of any and everything" was the theoretical underside of a confession that had to

be thorough, meticulous, and constant, and at the same time operate within a scientific type of practice. The limitless dangers that sex carried with it justified the exhaustive character of the inquisition to which it was subjected.

3. *Through the principle of a latency intrinsic to sexuality.* If it was necessary to extract the truth of sex through the technique of confession, this was not simply because it was difficult to tell, or stricken by the taboos of decency, but because the ways of sex were obscure; it was elusive by nature; its energy and its mechanisms escaped observation, and its causal power was partly clandestine. By integrating it into the beginnings of a scientific discourse, the nineteenth century altered the scope of the confession; it tended no longer to be concerned solely with what the subject wished to hide, but with what was hidden from himself, being incapable of coming to light except gradually and through the labor of a confession in which the questioner and the questioned each had a part to play. The principle of a latency essential to sexuality made it possible to link the forcing of a difficult confession to a scientific practice. It had to be exacted, by force, since it involved something that tried to stay hidden.

4. *Through the method of interpretation.* If one had to confess, this was not merely because the person to whom one confessed had the power to forgive, console, and direct, but because the work of producing the truth was obliged to pass through this relationship if it was to be scientifically validated. The truth did not reside solely in the subject who, by confessing, would reveal it wholly formed. It was constituted in two stages: present but incomplete, blind to itself, in the one who spoke, it could only reach completion in the one who assimilated and recorded it. It was the latter's function to verify this obscure truth: the revelation of confession had to be coupled with the decipherment of what it said. The one who listened was not simply the forgiving master, the judge who condemned or

acquitted; he was the master of truth. His was a hermaneutic function. With regard to the confession, his power was not only to demand it before it was made, or decide what was to follow after it, but also to constitute a discourse of truth on the basis of its decipherment. By no longer making the confession a test, but rather a sign, and by making sexuality something to be interpreted, the nineteenth century gave itself the possibility of causing the procedures of confession to operate within the regular formation of a scientific discourse.

5. *Through the medicalization of the effects of confession*. The obtaining of the confession and its effects were recodified as therapeutic operations. Which meant first of all that the sexual domain was no longer accounted for simply by the notions of error or sin, excess or transgression, but was placed under the rule of the normal and the pathological (which, for that matter, were the transposition of the former categories); a characteristic sexual morbidity was defined for the first time; sex appeared as an extremely unstable pathological field: a surface of repercussion for other ailments, but also the focus of a specific nosography, that of instincts, tendencies, images, pleasure, and conduct. This implied furthermore that sex would derive its meaning and its necessity from medical interventions: it would be required by the doctor, necessary for diagnosis, and effective by nature in the cure. Spoken in time, to the proper party, and by the person who was both the bearer of it and the one responsible for it, the truth healed.

Let us consider things in broad historical perspective: breaking with the traditions of the *ars erotica*, our society has equipped itself with a *scientia sexualis*. To be more precise, it has pursued the task of producing true discourses concerning sex, and this by adapting—not without difficulty—the ancient procedure of confession to the rules of scientific discourse. Paradoxically, the *scientia sexualis* that emerged in the nineteenth century kept as its nucleus the singular ritual of obligatory and exhaustive confession, which in the Christian West was the first technique for producing the truth of sex. Beginning in the sixteenth century, this rite gradually detached itself from the sacrament of penance, and via the guidance of souls and the direction of conscience—the *ars artium*—emigrated toward pedagogy, relationships between adults and children, family relations, medicine, and psychiatry. In any case, nearly one hundred and fifty years have gone into the making of a complex machinery for producing true discourses on sex: a deployment that spans a wide segment of history in that it connects the ancient injunction of confession to clinical listening methods. It is this deployment that enables something called "sexuality" to embody the truth of sex and its pleasures.

"Sexuality": the correlative of that slowly developed discursive practice which constitutes the *scientia sexualis*. The essential features of this sexuality are not the expression of a representation that is more or less distorted by ideology, or of a misunderstanding caused by taboos; they correspond to the functional requirements of a discourse that must produce its truth. Situated at the point of intersection of a technique of confession and a scientific discursivity, where certain major mechanisms had to be found for adapting them to one another (the listening technique, the postulate of causality, the principle of latency, the rule of interpretation, the imperative of medicalization), sexuality was defined as being "by nature": a domain susceptible to pathological processes, and hence one calling for therapeutic or normalizing interventions; a field of meanings to decipher; the site of processes concealed by specific mechanisms; a focus of indefinite causal relations; and an obscure speech (*parole*) that had to be ferreted out and listened to. The "economy" of discourses—their intrinsic technology, the necessities of their operation, the tactics they employ, the effects of power which underlie them and which they transmit—this, and not a system of representations, is what determines the essential features of what they have to say. The history of sexuality—that is, the history of what functioned in the nineteenth century as a specific field of truth—must first be written from the viewpoint of a history of discourses.

Let us put forward a general working hypothesis. The society that emerged in the nineteenth century—bourgeois, capitalist, or industrial society, call it what you will—did not confront sex with a fundamental refusal of recognition. On the contrary, it put into operation an entire machinery for producing true discourses concerning it. Not only did it speak of sex and compel everyone to do so; it also set out to formulate the uniform truth of sex. As if it suspected sex of harboring a fundamental secret. As if it needed this production of truth. As if it was essential that sex be inscribed not only in an economy of pleasure but in an ordered system of knowledge. Thus sex gradually became an object of great suspicion; the general and disquieting meaning that pervades our conduct and our existence, in spite of ourselves; the point of weakness where evil portents reach through to us; the fragment of darkness that we each carry within us: a general signification, a universal secret, an omnipresent cause, a fear that never ends. And so, in this "question" of sex (in both senses: as interrogation and problematization, and as the need for confession and integration into a field of rationality), two processes emerge, the one always conditioning the other: we demand that sex speak the truth (but, since it is the secret and is oblivious to its own nature, we reserve for ourselves the function of telling the truth of its truth, revealed and deciphered at last), and we demand that it tell us our truth, or rather, the deeply buried truth of that truth about ourselves which we think we possess in our immediate consciousness. We tell it its truth by deciphering what it tells us about that truth; it tells us our own by delivering up that part of it that escaped us. From this interplay there has evolved, over several centuries, a knowledge of the subject; a knowledge not so much of his form, but of that which divides him, determines him perhaps, but above all causes him to be ignorant of himself. As unlikely as this may seem, it should not surprise us when we think of the long history of the Christian and juridical confession, of the shifts and transformations this form of knowledge-power, so important in the West, has undergone: the project of a science of the subject has gravitated, in ever narrowing circles, around the question of sex. Causality in the subject, the unconscious of the subject, the truth of the subject in the other who knows, the knowledge he holds unbeknown to him, all this found an opportunity to deploy itself in the discourse of sex. Not, however, by reason of some natural property inherent in sex itself, but by virtue of the tactics of power immanent in this discourse.

NOTE

1. Greek law had already coupled torture and confession, at least where slaves were concerned, and Imperial Roman law had widened the practice.

COMPANION WEBSITE

1. Go online to Write Out Loud about how online communication, such as Twitter and Facebook, open up new outlets for confession and, possibly, discipline.
2. Take a look at the *Rise of the Avatar* Supplementary Sources for additional readings from contemporary theorist Nikolas Rose who extends Foucault's ideas on the self to the areas of psychology and biomedicine.
3. Check out the Interactive Reading for contemporary examples of "biopower" and interview footage of Foucault himself.

39

Gender Trouble

Judith Butler

"WOMEN" AS THE SUBJECT OF FEMINISM

For the most part, feminist theory has assumed that there is some existing identity, understood through the category of women, who not only initiates feminist interests and goals within discourse, but constitutes the subject for whom political representation is pursued. But *politics* and *representation* are controversial terms. On the one hand, *representation* serves as the operative term within a political process that seeks to extend visibility and legitimacy to women as political subjects; on the other hand, representation is the normative function of a language which is said either to reveal or to distort what is assumed to be true about the category of women. For feminist theory, the development of a language that fully or adequately represents women has seemed necessary to foster the political visibility of women. This has seemed obviously important considering the pervasive cultural condition in which women's lives were either misrepresented or not represented at all.

Recently, this prevailing conception of the relation between feminist theory and politics has come under challenge from within feminist discourse. The very subject of women is no longer understood in stable or abiding terms. There is a great deal of material that not only questions the viability of "the subject" as the ultimate candidate for representation or, indeed, liberation, but there is very little agreement after all on what it is that constitutes, or ought to constitute, the category of women. The domains of political and linguistic "representation" set out in advance the criterion by which subjects themselves are formed, with the result that representation is extended only to what can be acknowledged as a subject. In other words, the qualifications for being a subject must first be met before representation can be extended.

Foucault points out that juridical systems of power *produce* the subjects they subsequently come to represent.[1] Juridical notions of power appear to regulate political life in purely negative terms—that is, through the limitation, prohibition, regulation, control, and even "protection" of individuals related to that political structure through the contingent and retractable operation of choice. But the subjects regulated by such structures are, by virtue of being subjected to them, formed, defined, and reproduced in accordance with the requirements of those structures. If this analysis is right, then the juridical formation of language and politics that represents women as "the subject" of feminism is itself a discursive formation and effect of a given version of representational politics. And the feminist subject turns out to be discursively constituted by the very political system that is supposed to facilitate its emancipation. This becomes politically problematic if that system can be shown to produce gendered subjects along a differential axis of domination or to produce subjects who are presumed to be masculine. In such cases, an uncritical appeal to such a system for the emancipation of "women" will be clearly self-defeating.

The question of "the subject" is crucial for politics, and for feminist politics in particular, because juridical subjects are invariably produced through certain exclusionary practices that do not "show" once the juridical structure of politics has been established. In other words, the political construction of the subject proceeds with certain legitimating and exclusionary aims, and these political operations are effectively concealed and naturalized by a political analysis that takes juridical structures as their foundation. Juridical power inevitably "produces" what it claims merely to represent; hence, politics must be concerned with this dual function of power: the juridical and the productive. In effect, the law produces and then conceals the notion of "a subject before the law"[2] in order to invoke that discursive formation as a naturalized foundational premise that subsequently legitimates that law's own regulatory hegemony. It is not enough to inquire into how women might become more fully represented in language and politics. Feminist critique ought also to understand how the category of "women," the subject of feminism, is produced and restrained by the very structures of power through which emancipation is sought.

Indeed, the question of women as the subject of feminism raises the possibility that there may not be a subject who stands "before" the law, awaiting representation in or by the law. Perhaps the subject, as well as the invocation of a temporal "before," is constituted by the law as the fictive foundation of its own claim to legitimacy. The prevailing assumption of the ontological integrity of the subject before the law might be understood as the contemporary trace of the state of nature hypothesis, that foundationalist fable constitutive of the juridical structures of classical liberalism. The performative invocation of a nonhistorical "before" becomes the foundational premise that guarantees a presocial ontology of persons who freely consent to be governed and, thereby, constitute the legitimacy of the social contract.

Apart from the foundationalist fictions that support the notion of the subject, however, there is the political problem that feminism encounters in the assumption that the term *women* denotes a common identity. Rather than a stable signifier that commands the assent of those whom it purports to describe and represent, *women*, even in the plural, has become a troublesome term, a site of contest, a cause for anxiety. As Denise Riley's title suggests, *Am I That Name?* is a question produced by the very possibility of the name's multiple significations.[3] If one "is" a woman, that is surely not all one is; the term fails to be exhaustive, not because a pregendered "person" transcends the specific paraphernalia of its gender, but because gender is not always constituted coherently or consistently in different historical contexts, and because gender intersects with racial, class, ethnic, sexual, and regional modalities of discursively constituted identities. As a result, it becomes impossible to separate out "gender" from the political and cultural intersections in which it is invariably produced and maintained.

The political assumption that there must be a universal basis for feminism, one which must be found in an identity assumed to exist cross-culturally, often accompanies the notion that the oppression of women has some singular form discernible in the universal or hegemonic structure of patriarchy or masculine domination. The notion of a universal patriarchy has been widely criticized in recent years for its failure to account for the workings of gender oppression in the concrete cultural contexts in which it exists. Where those various contexts have been consulted within such theories, it has been to find "examples" or "illustrations" of a universal principle that is assumed from the start. That form of feminist theorizing has come under criticism for its efforts to colonize and appropriate non-Western cultures to support highly Western notions of oppression, but because they tend as well to construct a "Third World" or even an "Orient" in which gender oppression is subtly explained as symptomatic of an essential, non-Western barbarism. The urgency of feminism to establish a universal status for patriarchy in order to strengthen the appearance of feminism's own claims to be representative has occasionally motivated the shortcut to a categorial or fictive universality of the structure of domination, held to produce women's common subjugated experience.

Although the claim of universal patriarchy no longer enjoys the kind of credibility it once did, the notion of a generally shared conception of "women," the corollary to that framework, has been much more difficult to displace. Certainly, there have been plenty of debates: Is there some commonality among "women" that preexists their oppression, or do "women" have a bond by virtue of their oppression alone? Is there a specificity to women's cultures that is independent of their subordination by hegemonic, masculinist cultures? Are the specificity and integrity of women's cultural or linguistic practices always specified against and, hence, within the terms of some more dominant cultural formation? If there is a region of the "specifically feminine," one that is both differentiated from the masculine as such and recognizable in its difference by an unmarked and, hence, presumed universality of "women"? The masculine/feminine binary constitutes not only the exclusive framework in which that specificity can be recognized, but in every other way the "specificity" of the feminine is once again fully decontextualized and separated off analytically and politically from the constitution of class, race, ethnicity, and other axes of power relations that both constitute "identity" and make the singular notion of identity a misnomer.[4]

My suggestion is that the presumed universality and unity of the subject of feminism is effectively undermined by the constraints of the representational discourse in which it functions. Indeed, the premature insistence on a stable subject of feminism,

understood as a seamless category of women, inevitably generates multiple refusals to accept the category. These domains of exclusion reveal the coercive and regulatory consequences of that construction, even when the construction has been elaborated for emancipatory purposes. Indeed, the fragmentation within feminism and the paradoxical opposition to feminism from "women" whom feminism claims to represent suggest the necessary limits of identity politics. The suggestion that feminism can seek wider representation for a subject that it itself constructs has the ironic consequence that feminist goals risk failure by refusing to take account of the constitutive powers of their own representational claims. This problem is not ameliorated through an appeal to the category of women for merely "strategic" purposes, for strategies always have meanings that exceed the purposes for which they are intended. In this case, exclusion itself might qualify as such an unintended yet consequential meaning. By conforming to a requirement of representational politics that feminism articulate a stable subject, feminism thus opens itself to charges of gross misrepresentation.

Obviously, the political task is not to refuse representational politics—as if we could. The juridical structures of language and politics constitute the contemporary field of power; hence, there is no position outside this field, but only a critical genealogy of its own legitimating practices. As such, the critical point of departure is *the historical present*, as Marx put it. And the task is to formulate within this constituted frame a critique of the categories of identity that contemporary juridical structures engender, naturalize, and immobilize.

Perhaps there is an opportunity at this juncture of cultural politics, a period that some would call "postfeminist," to reflect from within a feminist perspective on the injunction to construct a subject of feminism. Within feminist political practice, a radical rethinking of the ontological constructions of identity appears to be necessary in order to formulate a representational politics that might revive feminism on other grounds. On the other hand, it may be time to entertain a radical critique that seeks to free feminist theory from the necessity of having to construct a single or abiding ground which is invariably contested by those identity positions or anti-identity positions that it invariably excludes. Do the exclusionary practices that ground feminist theory in a notion of "women" as subject paradoxically undercut feminist goals to extend its claims to "representation"?[5]

Perhaps the problem is even more serious. Is the construction of the category of women as a coherent and stable subject an unwitting regulation and reification of gender relations? And is not such a reification precisely contrary to feminist aims? To what extent does the category of women achieve stability and coherence only in the context of the heterosexual matrix?[6] If a stable notion of gender no longer proves to be the foundational premise of feminist politics, perhaps a new sort of feminist politics is now desirable to contest the very reifications of gender and identity, one that will take the variable construction of identity as both a methodological and normative prerequisite, if not a political goal.

To trace the political operations that produce and conceal what qualifies as the juridical subject of feminism is precisely the task of *a feminist genealogy* of the category of women. In the course of this effort to question "women" as the subject of feminism, the unproblematic invocation of that category may prove to *preclude* the possibility of feminism as a representational politics. What sense does it make to extend representation to subjects who are constructed through the exclusion of those who fail to conform to unspoken normative requirements of the subject? What relations of domination and exclusion are inadvertently sustained when representation becomes the sole focus of politics? The identity of the feminist subject ought not to be the foundation of feminist politics, if the formation of the subject takes place within a field of power regularly buried through the assertion of that foundation. Perhaps, paradoxically, "representation" will be shown to make sense for feminism only when the subject of "women" is nowhere presumed.

THE COMPULSORY ORDER OF SEX/GENDER/DESIRE

Although the unproblematic unity of "women" is often invoked to construct a solidarity of identity, a split is introduced in the feminist subject by the distinction between sex and gender. Originally intended to dispute the biology-is-destiny formulation, the distinction between sex and gender serves the argument that whatever biological intractability sex appears to have, gender is culturally constructed: hence, gender is neither the causal result of sex nor as seemingly fixed as sex. The unity of the subject is thus already potentially contested by the distinction that permits of gender as a multiple interpretation of sex.[7]

If gender is the cultural meanings that the sexed body assumes, then a gender cannot be said to follow from a sex in any one way. Taken to its logical limit, the sex/gender distinction suggests a radical discontinuity between sexed bodies and culturally constructed genders. Assuming for the moment the stability of binary sex, it does not follow that the construction of "men" will accrue exclusively to the bodies of males or that "women" will interpret only female bodies. Further, even if the sexes appear to be unproblematically binary in their morphology and constitution (which will become a question), there is no reason to assume that genders ought also to remain as two.[8] The presumption of a binary gender system implicitly retains the belief in a mimetic relation of gender to sex whereby gender mirrors sex or is otherwise restricted by it. When the constructed status of gender is theorized as radically independent of sex, gender itself becomes a free-floating artifice, with the consequence that *man* and *masculine* might just as easily signify a female body as a male one, and *woman* and *feminine* a male body as easily as a female one.

This radical splitting of the gendered subject poses yet another set of problems. Can we refer to a "given" sex or a "given" gender without first inquiring into how sex and/or gender is given, through what means? And what is "sex" anyway? Is it natural, anatomical, chromosomal, or hormonal, and how is a feminist critic to assess the scientific discourses which purport to establish such "facts" for us?[9] Does sex have a history?[10] Does each sex have a different history, or histories? Is there a history of how the duality of sex was established, a genealogy that might expose the binary options as a variable construction? Are the ostensibly natural facts of sex discursively produced by various scientific discourses in the service of other political and social interests? If the immutable character of sex is contested, perhaps this construct called "sex" is as culturally constructed as gender; indeed, perhaps it was always already gender, with the consequence that the distinction between sex and gender turns out to be no distinction at all.[11]

It would make no sense, then, to define gender as the cultural interpretation of sex, if sex itself is a gendered category. Gender ought not to be conceived merely as the cultural inscription of meaning on a pregiven sex (a juridical conception); gender must also designate the very apparatus of production whereby the sexes themselves are established. As a result, gender is not to culture as sex is to nature; gender is also the discursive/cultural means by which "sexed nature" or "a natural sex" is produced and established as "prediscursive," prior to culture, a politically neutral surface *on which* culture acts. This construction of "sex" as the radically unconstructed will concern us again in the discussion of Lévi-Strauss and structuralism in chapter 2. At this juncture it is already clear that

one way the internal stability and binary frame for sex is effectively secured is by casting the duality of sex in a prediscursive domain. This production of sex as the prediscursive ought to be understood as the effect of the apparatus of cultural construction designated by *gender*. How, then, does gender need to be reformulated to encompass the power relations that produce the effect of a prediscursive sex and so conceal that very operation of discursive production?

GENDER: THE CIRCULAR RUINS OF CONTEMPORARY DEBATE

Is there "a" gender which persons are said to *have*, or is it an essential attribute that a person is said to *be*, as implied in the question "What gender are you?" When feminist theorists claim that gender is the cultural interpretation of sex or that gender is culturally constructed, what is the manner or mechanism of this construction? If gender is constructed, could it be constructed differently, or does its constructedness imply some form of social determinism, foreclosing the possibility of agency and transformation? Does "construction" suggest that certain laws generate gender differences along universal axes of sexual difference? How and where does the construction of gender take place? What sense can we make of a construction that cannot assume a human constructor prior to that construction? On some accounts, the notion that gender is constructed suggests a certain determinism of gender meanings inscribed on anatomically differentiated bodies, where those bodies are understood as passive recipients of an inexorable cultural law. When the relevant "culture" that "constructs" gender is understood in terms of such a law or set of laws, then it seems that gender is as determined and fixed as it was under the biology-is-destiny formulation. In such a case, not biology, but culture, becomes destiny.

On the other hand, Simone de Beauvoir suggests in *The Second Sex* that "one is not born a woman, but, rather, becomes one."[12] For Beauvoir, gender is "constructed," but implied in her formulation is an agent, a *cogito*, who somehow takes on or appropriates that gender and could, in principle, take on some other gender. Is gender as variable and volitional as Beauvoir's account seems to suggest? Can "construction" in such a case be reduced to a form of choice? Beauvoir is clear that one "becomes" a woman, but always under a cultural compulsion to become one. And clearly, the compulsion does not come from "sex." There is nothing in her account that guarantees that the "one" who becomes a woman is necessarily female. If "the body is a situation,"[13] as she claims, there is no recourse to a body that has not always already been interpreted by cultural meanings; hence, sex could not qualify as a prediscursive anatomical facticity. Indeed, sex, by definition, will be shown to have been gender all along.[14]

The controversy over the meaning of *construction* appears to founder on the conventional philosophical polarity between free will and determinism. As a consequence, one might reasonably suspect that some common linguistic restriction on thought both forms and limits the terms of the debate. Within those terms, "the body" appears as a passive medium on which cultural meanings are inscribed or as the instrument through which an appropriative and interpretive will determines a cultural meaning for itself. In either case, the body is figured as a mere *instrument* or *medium* for which a set of cultural meanings are only externally related. But "the body" is itself a construction, as are the myriad "bodies" that constitute the domain of gendered subjects. Bodies cannot be said to have a signifiable existence prior to the mark of their gender; the question then emerges: To what extent does the body *come into being* in and through the mark(s) of gender? How do we reconceive the body no longer as a passive medium or instrument awaiting the enlivening capacity of a distinctly immaterial will?[15]

Whether gender or sex is fixed or free is a function of a discourse which, it will be suggested, seeks to set certain limits to analysis or to safeguard certain tenets of humanism as pre-suppositional to any analysis of gender. The locus of intractability, whether in "sex" or "gender" or in the very meaning of "construction," provides a clue to what cultural possibilities can and cannot become mobilized through any further analysis. The limits of the discursive analysis of gender presuppose and preempt the possibilities of imaginable and realizable gender configurations within culture. This is not to say that any and all gendered possibilities are open, but that the boundaries of analysis suggest the limits of a discursively conditioned experience. These limits are always set within the terms of a hegemonic cultural discourse predicated on binary structures that appear as the language of universal rationality. Constraint is thus built into what that language constitutes as the imaginable domain of gender.

Although social scientists refer to gender as a "factor" or a "dimension" of an analysis, it is also applied to embodied persons as "a mark" of biological, linguistic, and/or cultural difference. In these latter cases, gender can be understood as a signification that an (already) sexually differentiated body assumes, but even then that signification exists only *in relation* to another, opposing signification. Some feminist theorists claim that gender is "a relation," indeed, a set of relations, and not an individual attribute. Others, following Beauvoir, would argue that only the feminine gender is marked, that the universal person and the masculine gender are conflated, thereby defining women in terms of their sex and extolling men as the bearers of a body-transcendent universal personhood.

In a move that complicates the discussion further, Luce Irigaray argues that women constitute a paradox, if not a contradiction, within the discourse of identity itself. Women are the "sex" which is not "one." Within a language pervasively masculinist, a phallogocentric language, women constitute the *unrepresentable.* In other words, women represent the sex that cannot be thought, a linguistic absence and opacity. Within a language that rests on univocal signification, the female sex constitutes the unconstrainable and undesignatable. In this sense, women are the sex which is not "one," but multiple.[16] In opposition to Beauvoir, for whom women are designated as the Other, Irigaray argues that both the subject and the Other are masculine mainstays of a closed phallogocentric signifying economy that achieves its totalizing goal through the exclusion of the feminine altogether. For Beauvoir, women are the negative of men, the lack against which masculine identity differentiates itself; for Irigaray, that particular dialectic constitutes a system that excludes an entirely different economy of signification. Women are not only represented falsely within the Sartrian frame of signifying-subject and signified-Other, but the falsity of the signification points out the entire structure of representation as inadequate. The sex which is not one, then, provides a point of departure for a criticism of hegemonic Western representation and of the metaphysics of substance that structures the very notion of the subject.

What is the metaphysics of substance, and how does it inform thinking about the categories of sex? In the first instance, humanist conceptions of the subject tend to assume a substantive person who is the bearer of various essential and nonessential attributes. A humanist feminist position might understand gender as an *attribute* of a person who is characterized essentially as a pregendered substance or "core," called the person, denoting a universal capacity for reason, moral deliberation, or language. The universal conception of the person, however, is displaced as a point of departure for a social theory of gender by those historical and anthropological positions that understand gender as a relation among socially constituted subjects in specifiable contexts. This relational or contextual point of view suggests that what the person "is," and, indeed, what gender "is," is always relative to the constructed relations in which it is determined.[17] As a shifting and contextual phenomenon, gender does not denote a substantive being, but a relative point of convergence among culturally and historically specific sets of relations.

Irigaray would maintain, however, that the feminine "sex" is a point of linguistic *absence*, the impossibility of a grammatically denoted substance, and, hence, the point of view that exposes that substance as an abiding and foundational illusion of a masculinist discourse. This absence is not marked as such within the masculine signifying economy—a contention that reverses Beauvoir's argument (and Wittig's) that the female sex is marked, while the male sex is not. For Irigaray, the female sex is not a "lack" or an "Other" that immanently and negatively defines the subject in its masculinity. On the contrary, the female sex eludes the very requirements of representation, for she is neither "Other" nor the "lack," those categories remaining relative to the Sartrian subject, immanent to that phallogocentric scheme. Hence, for Irigaray, the feminine could never be the *mark of a subject*, as Beauvoir would suggest. Further, the feminine could not be theorized in terms of a determinate *relation* between the masculine and the feminine within any given discourse, for discourse is not a relevant notion here. Even in their variety, discourses constitute so many modalities of phallogocentric language. The female sex is thus also *the subject* that is not one. The relation between masculine and feminine cannot be represented in a signifying economy in which the masculine constitutes the closed circle of signifier and signified. Paradoxically enough, Beauvoir prefigured this impossibility in *The Second Sex* when she argued that men could not settle the question of women because they would then be acting as both judge and party to the case.[18]

The distinctions among the above positions are far from discrete; each of them can be understood to problematize the locality and meaning of both the "subject" and "gender" within the context of socially instituted gender asymmetry. The interpretive possibilities of gender are in no sense exhausted by the alternatives suggested above. The problematic circularity of a feminist inquiry into gender is underscored by the presence of positions which, on the one hand, presume that gender is a secondary characteristic of persons and those which, on the other hand, argue that the very notion of the person, positioned within language as a "subject," is a masculinist construction and prerogative which effectively excludes the structural and semantic possibility of a feminine gender. The consequence of such sharp disagreements about the meaning of gender (indeed, whether *gender* is the term to be argued about at all, or whether the discursive construction of *sex* is, indeed, more fundamental, or perhaps *women* or *woman* and/or *men* and *man*) establishes the need for a radical rethinking of the categories of identity within the context of relations of radical gender asymmetry.

For Beauvoir, the "subject" within the existential analytic of misogyny is always already masculine, conflated with the universal, differentiating itself from a feminine "Other" outside the universalizing norms of personhood, hopelessly "particular," embodied, condemned to immanence. Although Beauvoir is often understood to be calling for the right of women, in effect, to become existential subjects and, hence, for inclusion within the terms of an abstract universality, her position also implies a fundamental critique of the very disembodiment of the abstract masculine epistemological subject.[19] That subject is abstract to the extent that it disavows its socially marked embodiment and, further, projects that disavowed and disparaged embodiment on to the feminine sphere, effectively renaming the body as female. This association of the body with the female works along magical relations of reciprocity whereby the female sex becomes restricted to its body, and the male body, fully disavowed, becomes, paradoxically, the incorporeal instrument of an ostensibly radical freedom. Beauvoir's analysis implicitly poses the question:

Through what act of negation and disavowal does the masculine pose as a disembodied universality and the feminine get constructed as a disavowed corporeality? The dialectic of master–slave, here fully reformulated within the non-reciprocal terms of gender asymmetry, prefigures what Irigaray will later describe as the masculine signifying economy that includes both the existential subject and its Other.

Beauvoir proposes that the female body ought to be the situation and instrumentality of women's freedom, not a defining and limiting essence.[20] The theory of embodiment informing Beauvoir's analysis is clearly limited by the uncritical reproduction of the Cartesian distinction between freedom and the body. Despite my own previous efforts to argue the contrary, it appears that Beauvoir maintains the mind/body dualism, even as she proposes a synthesis of those terms.[21] The preservation of that very distinction can be read as symptomatic of the very phallogocentrism that Beauvoir underestimates. In the philosophical tradition that begins with Plato and continues through Descartes, Husserl, and Sartre, the ontological distinction between soul (consciousness, mind) and body invariably supports relations of political and psychic subordination and hierarchy. The mind not only subjugates the body, but occasionally entertains the fantasy of fleeing its embodiment altogether. The cultural associations of mind with masculinity and body with femininity are well documented within the field of philosophy and feminism.[22] As a result, any uncritical reproduction of the mind/body distinction ought to be rethought for the implicit gender hierarchy that the distinction has conventionally produced, maintained, and rationalized.

The discursive construction of "the body" and its separation from "freedom" in Beauvoir fails to mark along the axis of gender the very mind-body distinction that is supposed to illuminate the persistence of gender asymmetry. Officially, Beauvoir contends that the female body is marked within masculinist discourse, whereby the masculine body, in its conflation with the universal, remains unmarked. Irigaray clearly suggests that both marker and marked are maintained within a masculinist mode of signification in which the female body is "marked off," as it were, from the domain of the signifiable. In post-Hegelian terms, she is "cancelled," but not preserved. On Irigaray's reading, Beauvoir's claim that woman "is sex" is reversed to mean that she is not the sex she is designated to be, but, rather, the masculine sex *encore* (and *en corps*) parading in the mode of otherness. For Irigaray, that phallogocentric mode of signifying the female sex perpetually reproduces phantasms of its own self-amplifying desire. Instead of a self-limiting linguistic gesture that grants alterity or difference to women, phallogocentrism offers a name to eclipse the feminine and take its place.

NOTES

1. See Michel Foucault, "Right of Death and Power over Life," in *The History of Sexuality, Volume I, An Introduction,* trans. Robert Hurley (New York: Vintage, 1980), originally published as *Histoire de la sexualité 1: La volonté de savoir* (Paris: Gallimard, 1978). In that final chapter, Foucault discusses the relation between the juridical and productive law. His notion of the productivity of the law is clearly derived from Nietzsche, although not identical with Nietzsche's will-to-power. The use of Foucault's notion of productive power is not meant as a simple-minded "application" of Foucault to gender issues. As I show in chapter 3, section ii, "Foucault, Herculine, and the Politics of Sexual Discontinuity," the consideration of sexual difference within the terms of Foucault's own work reveals central contradictions in his theory. His view of the body also comes under criticism in the final chapter.

2. References throughout this work to a subject before the law are extrapolations of Derrida's reading of Kafka's parable "Before the Law," in *Kafka and the Contemporary Critical Performance: Centenary Readings,* ed. Alan Udoff (Bloomington: Indiana University Press, 1987).

3. See Denise Riley, *Am I That Name?: Feminism and the Category of 'Women' in History* (New York: Macmillan, 1988).

4. See Sandra Harding, "The Instability of the Analytical Categories of Feminist Theory," in *Sex and Scientific Inquiry,* eds. Sandra Harding and Jean F. O'Barr (Chicago: University of Chicago Press, 1987), pp. 283–302.

5. I am reminded of the ambiguity inherent in Nancy Cott's title, *The Grounding of Modern Feminism* (New Haven: Yale University Press, 1987). She argues that the early twentieth-century U.S. feminist movement sought to "ground" itself in a program that eventually "grounded" that movement. Her historical thesis implicitly raises the question of whether uncritically accepted foundations operate like the "return of the repressed"; based on exclusionary practices, the stable political identities that found political movements may invariably become threatened by the very instability that the foundationalist move creates.

6. I use the term *heterosexual matrix* throughout the text to designate that grid of cultural intelligibility through which bodies, genders, and desires are naturalized. I am drawing from Monique Wittig's notion of the "heterosexual contract" and, to a lesser extent, on Adrienne Rich's notion of "compulsory heterosexuality" to characterize a hegemonic discursive/epistemic model of gender intelligibility that assumes that for bodies to cohere and make sense there must be a stable sex expressed through a stable gender (masculine expresses male, feminine expresses female) that is oppositionally and hierarchically defined through the compulsory practice of heterosexuality.

7. For a discussion of the sex/gender distinction in structuralist anthropology and feminist appropriations and criticisms of that formulation, see chapter 2, section i, "Structuralism's Critical Exchange."

8. For an interesting study of the *berdache* and multiple-gender arrangements in Native American cultures, see Walter L. Williams, *The Spirit and the Flesh: Sexual Diversity in American Indian Culture* (Boston: Beacon Press, 1988). See also, Sherry B. Ortner and Harriet Whitehead, eds., *Sexual Meanings: The Cultural Construction of Sexuality* (New York: Cambridge University Press, 1981). For a politically sensitive and provocative analysis of the *berdache*, transsexuals, and the contingency of gender dichotomies, see

Suzanne J. Kessler and Wendy McKenna, *Gender: An Ethnomethodological Approach* (Chicago: University of Chicago Press, 1978).

9.   A great deal of feminist research has been conducted within the fields of biology and the history of science that assess the political interests inherent in the various discriminatory procedures that establish the scientific basis for sex. See Ruth Hubbard and Marian Lowe, eds., *Genes and Gender*, vols. 1 and 2 (New York: Gordian Press, 1978, 1979); the two issues on feminism and science of *Hypatia: A Journal of Feminist Philosophy,* Vol. 2, No. 3, Fall 1987, and Vol. 3, No. 1, Spring 1988, and especially The Biology and Gender Study Group, "The Importance of Feminist Critique for Contemporary Cell Biology" in this last issue (Spring 1988); Sandra Harding, *The Science Question in Feminism* (Ithaca: Cornell University Press, 1986); Evelyn Fox Keller, *Reflections on Gender and Science* (New Haven: Yale University Press, 1984); Donna Haraway, "In the Beginning was the Word: The Genesis of Biological Theory," *Signs: Journal of Women in Culture and Society*, Vol. 6, No. 3, 1981; Donna Haraway, *Primate Visions* (New York: Routledge, 1989); Sandra Harding and Jean F. O'Barr, *Sex and Scientific Inquiry* (Chicago: University of Chicago Press, 1987); Anne Fausto-Sterling, *Myths of Gender: Biological Theories About Women and Men* (New York: Norton, 1979).

10.   Clearly Foucault's *History of Sexuality* offers one way to rethink the history of "sex" within a given modern Eurocentric context. For a more detailed consideration, see Thomas Laqueur and Catherine Gallagher, eds., *The Making of the Modern Body: Sexuality and Society in the 19th Century* (Berkeley: University of California Press, 1987), originally published as an issue of *Representations*, No. 14, Spring 1986.

11.   See my "Variations on Sex and Gender: Beauvoir, Wittig, Foucault," in *Feminism as Critique,* eds. Seyla Benhabib and Drucilla Cornell (Basil Blackwell, dist. by University of Minnesota Press, 1987).

12.   Simone de Beauvoir, *The Second Sex*, trans. E. M. Parshley (New York: Vintage, 1973), p. 301.

13.   Ibid., p. 38.

14.   See my "Sex and Gender in Beauvoir's *Second Sex*," *Yale French Studies, Simone de Beauvoir: Witness to a Century*, No. 72, Winter 1986.

15.   Note the extent to which phenomenological theories such as Sartre's, Merleau-Ponty's, and Beauvoir's tend to use the term *embodiment*. Drawn as it is from theological contexts, the term tends to figure "the" body as a mode of incarnation and, hence, to preserve the external and dualistic relationship between a signifying immateriality and the materiality of the body itself.

16.   See Luce Irigaray, *This Sex Which Is Not One*, trans. Catherine Porter with Carolyn Burke (Ithaca: Cornell University Press, 1985), originally published as *Ce sexe qui n'en est pas un* (Paris: Éditions de Minuit, 1977).

17.   See Joan Scott, "Gender as a Useful Category of Historical Analysis," in *Gender and the Politics of History* (New York: Columbia University Press, 1988), pp. 28–52, repr. from *American Historical Review*, Vol. 91, No. 5, 1986.

18.   Beauvoir, *The Second Sex,* p. xxvi.

19.   See my "Sex and Gender in Beauvoir's *Second Sex*."

20.   The normative ideal of the body as both a "situation" and an "instrumentality" is embraced by both Beauvoir with respect to gender and Frantz Fanon with respect to race. Fanon concludes his analysis of colonization through recourse to the body as an instrument of freedom, where freedom is, in Cartesian fashion, equated with a consciousness capable of doubt: "O my body, make of me always a man who questions!" (Frantz Fanon, *Black Skin, White Masks* [New York: Grove Press, 1967] p. 323, originally published as *Peau noire, masques blancs* [Paris: Éditions de Seuil, 1952]).

21.   The radical ontological disjunction in Sartre between consciousness and the body is part of the Cartesian inheritance of his philosophy. Significantly, it is Descartes' distinction that Hegel implicitly interrogates at the outset of the "Master–Slave" section of *The Phenomenology of Spirit*. Beauvoir's analysis of the masculine Subject and the feminine Other is clearly situated in Hegel's dialectic and in the Sartrian reformulation of that dialectic in the section on sadism and masochism in *Being and Nothingness*. Critical of the very possibility of a "synthesis" of consciousness and the body, Sartre effectively returns to the Cartesian problematic that Hegel sought to overcome. Beauvoir insists that the body can be the instrument and situation of freedom and that sex can be the occasion for a gender that is not a reification, but a modality of freedom. At first this appears to be a synthesis of body and consciousness, where consciousness is understood as the condition of freedom. The question that remains, however, is whether

this synthesis requires and maintains the ontological distinction between body and mind of which it is composed and, by association, the hierarchy of mind over body and of masculine over feminine.

22. See Elizabeth V. Spelman, "Woman as Body: Ancient and Contemporary Views," *Feminist Studies*, Vol. 8, No. 1, Spring 1982.

COMPANION WEBSITE

1. Go online to Write Out Loud about why identifying women as "the subject" of feminism is problematic for Butler.
2. Log on to the Feminist Theory Profile Page to learn more about Butler's impact on feminist thought and politics.
3. And check out the *Rise of the Avatar* Supplementary Sources for films and readings that question whether sex or gender can be neatly divided into male and female, masculine and feminine, including the documentary *Paris is Burning* and biologist Anne Fausto-Sterling's short article, "The Five Sexes."

40

Modernity and Self-Identity

Anthony Giddens

A PERSON WITH A REASONABLY stable sense of self-identity has a feeling of biographical continuity which she is able to grasp reflexively and, to a greater or lesser degree, communicate to other people. That person also, through early trust relations, has established a protective cocoon which 'filters out', in the practical conduct of day-to-day life, many of the dangers which in principle threaten the integrity of the self. Finally, the individual is able to accept that integrity as worthwhile. There is sufficient self-regard to sustain a sense of the self as 'alive' – within the scope of reflexive control, rather than having the inert quality of things in the object-world.

The existential question of self-identity is bound up with the fragile nature of the biography which the individual 'supplies' about herself. A person's identity is not to be found in behaviour, nor – important though this is – in the reactions of others, but in the capacity *to keep a particular narrative going.* The individual's biography, if she is to maintain regular interaction with others in the day-to-day world, cannot be wholly fictive. It must continually integrate events which occur in the external world, and sort them into the ongoing 'story' about the self. As Charles Taylor puts it, 'In order to have a sense of who we are, we have to have a notion of how we have become, and of where we are going.'[1]

[...]

'LIVING IN THE WORLD': DILEMMAS OF THE SELF

In conditions of late modernity, we live 'in the world' in a different sense from previous eras of history. Everyone still continues to live a local life, and the constraints of the body ensure that all individuals, at every moment, are contextually situated in time and space. Yet the transformations of place, and the intrusion of distance into local activities, combined with the centrality of mediated experience, radically change what 'the world' actually is. This is so both on the level of the 'phenomenal world' of the individual and the general universe of social activity within which collective social life is enacted. Although everyone lives a local life, phenomenal worlds for the most part are truly global.

Characterising individuals' phenomenal worlds is difficult, certainly in the abstract. Every person reacts selectively to the diverse sources of direct and mediated experience which compose the *Umwelt*. One thing we can say with some certainty is that in very few instances does the phenomenal world any longer correspond to the habitual settings through which an individual physically moves. Localities are thoroughly penetrated by distanciated influences, whether this be regarded as a cause for concern or simply accepted as a routine part of social life. All individuals actively, although by no means always in a conscious way, selectively incorporate many elements of mediated experience into their day-to-day conduct. This is never a random or a passive process, contrary to what the image of the *collage* effect might suggest. A newspaper, for example, presents a collage of information, as does, on a wider scale, the whole bevy of newspapers which may be on sale in a particular area or country. Yet each reader imposes his own order on this diversity, by selecting which newspaper to read – if any – and by making an active selection of its contents.

In some part the appropriation of mediated information follows pre-established habits and obeys the principle of the avoidance of cognitive dissonance. That is to say, the plethora of available information is reduced via routinised attitudes which exclude, or reinterpret, potentially disturbing knowledge. From a negative point of view, such closure might be regarded as prejudice, the refusal seriously to entertain views and ideas divergent from those an individual already holds; yet, from another angle, avoidance of dissonance forms part of the protective cocoon which helps maintain ontological security. For even the most prejudiced or narrow-minded person, the regularised contact with mediated information inherent in day-to-day life today is a positive appropriation: a mode of interpreting information within the routines of daily life. Obviously there are wide variations in terms of how open a given individual is to new forms of knowledge, and how far that person is able to tolerate certain levels of dissonance. But all phenomenal worlds are active accomplishments, and all follow the same basic psychodynamics, from the most local of ways of life to the most cosmopolitan.

'Living in the world', where the world is that of late modernity, involves various distinctive tensions and difficulties on the level of the self. We can analyse these most easily by understanding them as dilemmas which, on one level or another, have to be resolved in order to preserve a coherent narrative of self-identity.

UNIFICATION VERSUS FRAGMENTATION

The first dilemma is that of *unification* versus *fragmentation*. Modernity fragments; it also unites. On the level of the individual right up to that of planetary systems as a whole, tendencies towards dispersal vie with those promoting integration. So far as the self is concerned, the problem of unification concerns protecting and reconstructing the narrative of self-identity in the face of the massive intensional and extensional changes which modernity sets into being. In most pre-modern contexts, the fragmentation of experience was not a prime source of anxiety. Trust relations were localised and focused through personal ties, even if intimacy in the modern sense was generally lacking. In a post-traditional order, however, an indefinite range of possibilities present themselves, not just in respect of options for behaviour, but in respect also of the 'openness of the world' to the individual. 'The world', as indicated above, is not a seamless order of time and space stretching away from the individual; it intrudes into presence via an array of varying channels and sources.

Yet it is wrong to see the world 'out there' as intrinsically alienating and oppressive to the degree to which social systems are either large in scale or spatially distant from the individual. Such phenomena may often be drawn on to supply unifying influences; they are not just fragmenting in their impact on the self. Distant events may become as familiar, or more so, than proximate influences, and integrated into the frameworks of personal experience. Situations 'at hand' may in fact be more opaque than large-scale happenings affecting many millions of people. Consider some examples. A person may be on the telephone to someone twelve thousand miles away and for the duration of the conversation be more closely bound up with the responses of that distant individual than with others sitting in the same room. The appearance, personality and policies of a world political leader may be better known to a given individual than those of his next-door neighbour. A person may be more familiar with the debate over global warming than with why the tap in the kitchen leaks. Nor are remote or large-scale phenomena necessarily factors only vaguely 'in the background' of an individual's psychological make-up and identity. A concern with global warming, for example, might form part of a distinctive lifestyle adopted by a person, even if she is not an ecological activist. Thus she might keep in close contact with scientific debates and adjust various aspects of her lifestyle in relation to the practical measures they suggest.

Fragmentation clearly tends to be promoted by the influences emphasised by Berger and others: the diversifying of contexts of interaction. In many modern settings, individuals are caught up in a variety of differing encounters and milieux, each of which may call for different forms of 'appropriate' behaviour. Goffman is normally taken to be the theorist *par excellence* of this phenomenon. As the individual leaves one encounter and enters another, he sensitively adjusts the 'presentation of self' in relation to whatever is demanded of a particular situation. Such a view is often thought to imply that an individual has as many selves as there are divergent contexts of interaction, an idea which somewhat resembles poststructuralist interpretations of the self, albeit from a differing theoretical perspective. Yet again it would not be correct to see contextual diversity as simply and inevitably promoting the fragmentation of the self, let alone its disintegration into multiple 'selves'. It can just as well, at least in many circumstances, promote an integration of self. The situation is rather like the contrast between rural and urban life discussed previously. A person may make use of diversity in order to create a distinctive self-identity which positively incorporates elements from different settings into an integrated narrative. Thus a cosmopolitan person is one precisely who draws strength from being at home in a variety of contexts.[2]

The dilemma of unification versus fragmentation, like the others to be mentioned below, has its pathologies. On the one hand we find the type of person who constructs his identity around a set of fixed commitments, which act as a filter through which numerous different social environments are reacted to or interpreted. Such a person is a rigid traditionalist, in a compulsive sense, and refuses any relativism of context. On the other hand, in the case of a self which evaporates into the variegated contexts of action, we find the adaptive response which Erich Fromm has characterised as 'authoritarian conformity'. Fromm expresses this in the following way:

> The individual ceases to be himself; he adopts entirely the kind of personality offered to him by cultural patterns; and he therefore becomes exactly as all others are and as they expect him to be ... this mechanism can be compared with the protective colouring some animals assume. They look so similar to their surroundings that they are hardly distinguishable from them.[3]

In such circumstances, we might argue, the false self overrides and blankets out the original acts of thinking, feeling and willing which represent the true motivations of the individual. What remains of the true self is experienced as empty and inauthentic; yet this vacuum cannot be filled by the 'pseudo-selves' brought into play by the individual in different contexts, because these are as much stimulated by the responses of others as drawn from the person's inner convictions. Ontological security in this situation is as weakly founded as in the case of the rigid traditionalist. The individual only feels psychologically secure in his self-identity in so far as others recognise his behaviour as appropriate or reasonable.

POWERLESSNESS VERSUS APPROPRIATION

A second dilemma is that of *powerlessness* versus *appropriation*. If there is one theme which unites nearly all authors who have written on the self in modern society, it is the assertion that the individual experiences feelings of powerlessness in relation to a diverse and large-scale social universe. In contrast to the traditional world, it is supposed, where the individual was substantially in control of many of the influences shaping his life, in modem societies that control has passed to external agencies. As specified by Marx, the concept of alienation has served as the centre-point for analyses of this issue. As the forces of production develop, particularly under the aegis of capitalistic production, the individual cedes control of his life circumstances to the dominating influences of machines and markets. What is originally human becomes alien; human powers are experienced as forces emanating from an objectified social environment. Not only the followers of Marx have expressed such a view; it is also found, in somewhat different guise, in the works of the theorists of 'mass society'. The more extensive modern social systems become, according to this position, the more each particular individual feels shorn of all autonomy. Each, as it were, is merely an atom in a vast agglomeration of other individuals.

The ideas I have sought to develop in this book are distinctively different from such a standpoint. In many pre-modern contexts, individuals (and humanity as a whole) were more powerless than they are in modern settings. People typically lived in smaller groups and communities; but smallness is not the same as power. In many small-group settings individuals were relatively powerless to alter or escape from their surrounding social circumstances. The hold of tradition, for example, was often more or less unchallengeable. There are many other illustrations. Pre-modern kinship systems, for example, were often quite rigid, and offered the individual little scope for independent action. We would be hard pressed to substantiate an overall generalisation that, with the coming of modern institutions, most individuals either are (or feel) more powerless than in preceding times.

Modernity expropriates – that is undeniable. Time-space distanciation and the deskilling effects of abstract systems are the two most important influences. Even if distance and powerlessness do not inevitably go together, the emergence of globalised connections, together with high consequence risks, represent parameters of social life over which the situated individual has relatively little control. Similarly, expropriation processes are part and parcel of the maturation of modern institutions and reach not only spheres of day-to-day life but the heart of the self.

If we understand such processes in dialectical fashion, however, and if we see that globalisation produces not just extensional but intensional change, a complex picture emerges. We cannot say that all forms of expropriation necessarily provide the possibility of reappropriation, certainly on the level of individual conduct. Many of the processes transformed by disembedding, or reorganised in the light of the intrusion of abstract systems, move beyond the purview of the situated actor. On the other hand, others make possible forms of mastery over life circumstances unavailable in pre-modern situations.

Powerlessness and reappropriation intertwine variously in different contexts and at varying times: given the dynamism of modernity, there is little stability in the relations between them. An individual who vests trust in others, or in a given abstract system, normally thereby recognises that she lacks the power to influence them significantly. Yet the vesting of trust can also generate new capacities. Consider the example of money. In order to utilise money, an individual must participate in systems of economic exchange, banking and investment and so forth, over which she has little direct control. On the other hand, this process allows the individual – given sufficient resources – a diversity of opportunities which would otherwise be absent.

The experience of powerlessness, considered as a psychic phenomenon, naturally always relates to aims, projects or aspirations held by the individual, as well as to the composition of the phenomenal world. Powerlessness experienced in a personal relationship may be psychologically more damaging and consequential than powerlessness felt in relation to more encompassing social systems. Of course, these may feed into one another in various ways. Diffuse anxieties about high-consequence risks, for instance, might contribute in a general fashion to feelings of powerlessness experienced by an individual in more local contexts. Conversely, feelings of personal impotence may become diffused 'upwards' towards more global concerns. It seems reasonable to posit that connections of this kind are likely to underlie a 'survival' mentality. A 'survivor' is someone who feels deprived of adequate social mastery in a threatening series of personal and social environments. Yet a survivalist outlook carries connotations of appropriation as well as of powerlessness. Someone who concentrates on surviving in personal relations, as in other spheres of life, cannot be said to have abandoned all autonomy over his or her life's circumstances. Even if only in a somewhat negative sense, the individual clearly seeks active mastery: to survive is to be able in a determined way to ride out the trials life presents and overcome them.

Once again, the dilemma of powerlessness versus appropriation has its pathologies. Where an individual feels overwhelmed by a sense of powerlessness in the major domains of his phenomenal world, we may speak of a process of *engulfment*. The individual feels dominated by encroaching forces from the outside, which he is unable to resist or transcend. He feels either haunted by implacable forces robbing him of all autonomy of action, or caught up in a maelstrom of events in which he swirls around in a helpless fashion. At the other pole of the powerlessness/appropriation divide is *omnipotence*. Like all personality pathologies, it is a fantasy state. The individual's sense of ontological security is achieved through a fantasy of dominance: the phenomenal world feels as if it is orchestrated by

that person as a puppeteer. Since omnipotence is a defence it is brittle, and often links psychologically to the other pole of the powerlessness/appropriation composition: in other words, under pressure it can dissolve into its contrary, engulfment.

AUTHORITY VERSUS UNCERTAINTY

A *third* dilemma is that of *authority* versus *uncertainty*. In conditions of high modernity, in many areas of social life – including the domain of the self – there are no determinant authorities. There exist plenty of claimants to authority – far more than was true of pre-modern cultures. Tradition was itself a prime source of authority, not located within any particular institution, but pervading many aspects of social life. Diffuse though it may have been, tradition was in an important sense a single authority. Although in the larger pre-modern cultures there may quite often have been clashes between rival traditions, for the most part traditional outlooks and ways of doing things precluded other alternatives. Even where there were vying traditions, involvement in a traditional framework was normally quite exclusive: the others were thereby rejected.

When we speak of specific institutions of authority, religion obviously has a leading place. In virtually all smaller pre-modern cultures there was only one main religious order – although such cultures have had their share of sceptics, and magicians and sorcerers were available to those diverging from religious orthodoxy. Yet these alternatives were scarcely substitutes for the overarching authoritative reach of the dominant religious system. In larger traditional societies, where religious orders sometimes were more diversified, there was little pluralism in the modern sense: orthodoxy confronted various heresies. The local community and the kinship system were two further sources of stabilising authority, directly relevant to the sustaining of trust relations in traditional contexts. Both were the source of 'binding doctrines' as well as of forms of behaviour endowed with strong normative compulsion.

Submission to traditional authorities, no matter how deep, did not remove uncertainty from day-to-day life in traditional cultures. The strength of pre-modern forms of authority could almost be understood as a response to the very unpredictability of daily life and to the number of influences felt to be outside human control. Religious authorities in particular quite often cultivated the feeling that individuals were surrounded by threats and dangers – since only the religious official was in a position to be able either to understand or to seek successfully to control these. Religious authority created mysteries while simultaneously claiming to have privileged access to them.[4]

In modern times some forms of traditional authority continue to exist, including, of course, religion. Indeed, for reasons that are to do precisely with the connections between modernity and doubt, religion not only refuses to disappear but undergoes a resurgence. Yet there is now a basic contrast with the past. Forms of traditional authority become only 'authorities' among others, part of an indefinite pluralism of expertise. The expert, or the specialist, is quite different from the 'authority', where this term is understood in the traditional sense. Except where authority is sanctioned by the use of force (the 'authorities' of the state and legal authority), it becomes essentially equivalent to specialist advice. There are no authorities which span the diverse fields within which expertise is claimed – another way of repeating the point that everyone in modern systems is a lay person in virtually all aspects of social activity. Authority in this situation is no longer an alternative to doubt. On the contrary, modes of expertise are fuelled by the very principle of doubt; in assessing the claims of rival authorities, the lay individual tends to utilise that principle in the sceptical outlook which pluralistic circumstances almost inevitably presuppose.

Of course, day-to-day life is not ordinarily experienced as perennially 'in doubt'. The reorganisation of daily life through abstract systems creates many routine forms of activity having a higher level of predictability than most contexts in pre-modern cultures. Through the protective cocoon, most people are buffered most of the time from the experience of radical doubt as a serious challenge either to the routines of daily activity or to more far-reaching ambitions. The dilemma of authority versus doubt is ordinarily resolved through a mixture of routine and commitment to a certain form of lifestyle, plus the vesting of trust in a given series of abstract systems. Yet this 'compromise package', under pressure, can begin to disintegrate.

Some individuals find it psychologically difficult or impossible to accept the existence of diverse, mutually conflicting authorities. They find that the freedom to choose is a burden and they seek solace in more overarching systems of authority. A predilection for *dogmatic authoritarianism* is the pathological tendency at this pole. A person in this situation is not necessarily a traditionalist, but essentially gives up faculties of critical judgement in exchange for the convictions supplied by an authority whose rules and provisions cover most aspects of his life. We should distinguish this attitude from faith, even faith in fundamentalist religious codes. For faith almost by definition rests on trust. Taking refuge in a dominant authority, however, is essentially an act of submission. The individual, as it were, no longer needs to engage in the problematic gamble which all trust relations presume. Instead, he or she identifies with a dominant authority on the basis of projection. The psychology of leadership plays an important role here. Submission to authority normally takes the form of a slavish adherence to an authority figure, taken to be all-knowing.

At the other pole, we find pathological states in which individuals are virtually immobilised through a tendency towards universal doubt. In its most marked versions, this outlook takes the form of paranoia or a paralysis of the will so complete that the individual effectively withdraws altogether from ordinary social intercourse.

PERSONALISED VERSUS COMMODIFIED EXPERIENCE

A fourth dilemma is that between *personalised* versus *commodified* experience. Modernity opens up the project of the self, but under conditions strongly influenced by standardising effects of commodity capitalism. In this book I have not sought to trace out in a detailed fashion the impact of capitalistic production on modern social life. Suffice to affirm that capitalism is one of the main institutional dimensions of modernity, and that the capitalist accumulation process represents one of the prime driving forces behind modern institutions as a whole. Capitalism commodifies in various senses. The creation of the abstract commodity, as Marx pointed out, is perhaps the most basic element in the expansion of capitalism as an overall production system. Exchange-value is only created when use-values become irrelevant to the mechanisms whereby the production, sale and distribution of goods and services are carried on. Exchange-value thus allows for the disembedding of economic relations across indeterminate spans of time-space.

Commodification further, crucially, affects labour power: in fact labour power as such only comes into existence when separated as a commodity from 'labour' as a whole. Finally, commodification directly affects consumption processes, particularly with the maturation of the capitalistic order. The establishing of standardised consumption patterns, promoted through advertising and other methods, becomes central to economic growth. In all of these senses, commodification influences the project of the self and the establishing of lifestyles.

We can detail the impact of commodification in the following ways. The capitalistic market, with its 'imperatives' of continuous expansion, attacks tradition. The spread of capitalism places large sectors (although by no means all) of social reproduction in the hands of markets for products and labour. Markets operate without regard to pre-established forms of behaviour, which for the most part represent obstacles to the creation of unfettered exchange. In the period of high modernity, capitalistic enterprise increasingly seeks to shape consumption as well as monopolise the conditions of production. From the beginning, markets promote individualism in the sense that they stress individual rights and responsibilities, but at first this phenomenon mainly concerns the freedom of contract and mobility intrinsic to capitalistic employment. Later, however, individualism becomes extended to the sphere of consumption, the designation of individual wants becoming basic to the continuity of the system. Market-governed freedom of individual choice becomes an enveloping framework of individual self-expression.

The very corruption of the notion of 'lifestyle', reflexively drawn into the sphere of advertising, epitomises these processes. Advertisers orient themselves to sociological classifications of consumer categories and at the same time foster specific consumption 'packages'. To a greater or lesser degree, the project of the self becomes translated into one of the possession of desired goods and the pursuit of artificially framed styles of life. The consequences of this situation have often been noted. The consumption of ever-novel goods becomes in some part a substitute for the genuine development of self; appearance replaces essence as the visible signs of successful consumption come actually to outweigh the use-values of the goods and services in question themselves. Bauman expresses this well:

> Individual needs of personal autonomy, self-definition, authentic life or personal perfection are all translated into the need to possess, and consume, market-offered goods. This translation, however, pertains to the appearance of use value of such goods, rather than to the use value itself; as such, it is intrinsically inadequate and ultimately

self-defeating, leading to momentary assuagement of desires and lasting frustration of needs. ... The gap between human needs and individual desires is produced by market domination; this gap is, at the same time, a condition of its reproduction. The market feeds on the unhappiness it generates: the fears, anxieties and the sufferings of personal inadequacy it induces release the consumer behaviour indispensable to its continuation.[5]

Commodification is in some ways even more insidious than this characterisation suggests. For the project of the self as such may become heavily commodified. Not just lifestyles, but self-actualisation is packaged and distributed according to market criteria. Self-help books, like *Self Therapy*, stand in a precarious position with regard to the commodified production of self-actualisation. In some ways such works break away from standardised, packaged consumption. Yet in so far as they become marketed as prepackaged theorems about how to 'get on' in life, they become caught up in the very processes they nominally oppose.

The commodifying of consumption, it should be made clear, like other phenomena discussed earlier, is not just a matter of the reordering of existing behaviour patterns or spheres of life. Rather, consumption under the domination of mass markets is essentially a novel phenomenon, which participates directly in processes of the continuous reshaping of the conditions of day-to-day life. Mediated experience is centrally involved here. The mass media routinely present modes of life to which, it is implied, everyone should aspire; the lifestyles of the affluent are, in one form or another, made open to view and portrayed as worthy of emulation. More important, however, and more subtle, is the impact of the narratives the media convey. Here there is not necessarily the suggestion of a lifestyle to be aspired to; instead, stories are developed in such a way as to create narrative coherence with which the reader or viewer can identify.

No doubt soap operas, and other forms of media entertainment too, are escapes – substitutes for real satisfactions unobtainable in normal social conditions. Yet perhaps more important is the very narrative form they offer, suggesting models for the construction of narratives of the self. Soap operas mix predictability and contingency by means of formulae which, because they are well known to the audience, are slightly disturbing but at the same time reassuring. They offer mixtures of contingency, reflexivity and fate. The form is what matters rather than the content; in these stories one gains a sense of reflexive control over life circumstances, a feeling of a coherent narrative which is a reassuring balance to difficulties in sustaining the narrative of the self in actual social situations.

Yet commodification does not carry the day unopposed on either an individual or collective level. Even the most oppressed of individuals – perhaps in some ways particularly the most oppressed – react creatively and interpretatively to processes of commodification which impinge on their lives. This is true both within the realm of mediated experience and of direct consumption. Response to mediated experience cannot be assessed purely in terms of the content of what is disseminated: individuals actively discriminate among types of available information as well as interpreting it in their own terms. Even young children evaluate television programmes in terms of their degree of realism, recognising that some are wholly fictional, and treat programmes as objects of scepticism, derision or humour.[6] The fact that commodification is not all-triumphant at a collective level is also important for realms of individual experience. Space, for example, becomes commodified as a fundamental part of disembedding processes. However, space does not thereby become fully commercialised or subject to the standardising impact of commodity production. Many aspects of the built environment, and other spatial forms too, reassert themselves (through the active engagements of agents) in decommodified modes. Commodification is a driving force towards the emergence of internally referential systems; but, as will be discussed in the following section, external anchorings in aesthetic and moral experience refuse to disappear completely.

It is against this complicated backdrop that we should understand processes of individuation. The reflexive project of the self is in some part necessarily a struggle against commodified influences, although not all aspects of commodification are inimical to it. A market system, almost by definition, generates a variety of available choices in the consumption of goods and services. Plurality of choice is in some substantial part the very outcome of commodified processes. Nor is commodification merely the same as standardisation. Where mass markets are at issue, it is clearly in the interests of producers to ensure the large-scale consumption of relatively standardised products. Yet standardisation can often be turned into a mode of creating individual qualities – as in the previously quoted example of clothing. Mass produced clothing still allows individuals to decide selectively on styles of dress, however much the standardising influence of fashion and other forces affect those individual decisions.

A prime type of behaviour pathology associated with commodifying influences is narcissism – in this respect Lasch's thesis is valid, if over-generalised. Of course, narcissism springs from other sources too, especially as a deepseated phenomenon of personality development. But in so far as commodification, in the context of consumerism, promotes appearance as the prime arbiter of value, and sees self-development above all in terms of display, narcissistic traits are likely to become prominent. Individuation, however, also has its pathological aspects. All self-development depends on the mastering of appropriate responses to others; an individual who has to be 'different' from all others has no chance of reflexively developing a coherent self-identity. Excessive individuation has connections to conceptions of grandiosity. The individual is unable to discover a self-identity 'sober' enough to conform to the expectations of others in his social milieux.

Unification versus fragmentation: the reflexive project of the self incorporates numerous contextual happenings and forms of mediated experience, through which a course must be charted.

Powerlessness versus appropriation: the lifestyle options made available by modernity offer many opportunities for appropriation, but also generate feelings of powerlessness.

Authority versus uncertainty: in circumstances in which there are no final authorities, the reflexive project of the self must steer a way between commitment and uncertainty.

Personalised versus commodified experience: the narrative of the self must be constructed in circumstances in which personal appropriation is influenced by standardised influences on consumption.

Figure 40.1 Dilemmas of the self

NOTES

1. Charles Taylor, *Sources of the Self* (Cambridge: Cambridge University Press, 1989). On narratives of self-identity see also Alasdair MacIntyre, *After Virtue* (London: Duckworth, 1981).
2. Cf. Claude S. Fischer, *The Urban Experience* (New York: Harcourt Brace Jovanovich, 1984).
3. Eric Fromm, *The Fear of Freedom* (London: Routledge, 1960), p. 160.
4. W. Warren Wagar, *Terminal Visions* (Bloomington: University of Indiana Press, 1982).
5. Zygmunt Bauman, *Legislators and Interpreters* (Cambridge: Polity, 1989), p. 189.
6. Robert Hodge and David Tripp, *Children and Television* (Cambridge: Polity, 1989), p. 189. Cf. also John Fiske, *Understanding Popular Culture* (London: Unwin Hyman, 1989).

COMPANION WEBSITE

1. Go online to Write Out Loud about your own personal experiences of unification vs. fragmentation.
2. Log on to Giddens' Profile Page to learn more about one of the foremost theorists of modernity living today.
3. Log on to the Supplementary Sources for *Pathway to Meltdown* to learn more about some of Giddens' other work, including his book, *The Consequences of Modernity*.

Credits

Glossary Index

academia, and Orientalism 437–8

academic capital 189–90

academic positions, and Black women 434–5

academic qualifications: and cultural capital 189–90, 194, 200; as currency 197n.22

accounting practices 85, 86

accumulation of capital 128, 129, 152, 217–18, 219, 220, 240, 316, 327

acquisition of capital: duty of 241; as end in itself 233; and ethics/morality 236, 252n.47; Protestant asceticism 239–40

action(s): class 295; conditioned by crowds 264; meaningful 257, 259; rational 258–9; science of human 259; social *see* social action; subjective meaning of 260; of women 370

activism: and oppression 440, 441; of women 431

actor-network theory 6

administration, cost of 291

administrative democratization 291

administrative law 26

Aeschylus 410

aestheticism 198–200

aesthetics, and art 198–200

affectual social action 265

agency, bureaucratic 287

agricultural capitalism 161–2

agricultural industry, and division of labour 16

agricultural periods, and density of society 30

Akrich, Madeleine 99, 101

Alienation (or, estrangement): According to Marx, a structural condition of capitalism wherein relationships between the worker and his product, labor process, species being, and/or other people are broken or destroyed: advanced industrial society 308, 515; of labor 154, 157; of women 420; of workers 153, 154

altruistic suicide 50

alveolar system, and moral vacuums 29

America: 29 *see* United States

"An Apology to Graft" 77

Anglicanism 242

animism, and religion 52

Anomic suicide: Suicide committed when moral regulation is too low, such as suicide committed by widows 50

Anomie: Feeling of disconnection from rest of society brought about through a pathological division of labor and lack of moral regulation; a state of normlessness 4–5, 34, 39n.43, 45, 47–50

anthropomorphism 101

anticolonialism movement 386

antifeminists 372

antisemitism 337

apartheid, global gendered 431, 432

appearance, and manner 485–6

appointment of officials 290

appropriation versus powerlessness 514–16, 520

apriorism 57–8, 66n.19

Aristotle 17, 37, 368

ars erotica 499

art, and aesthetics 198–200

Arunta, the 62

ascetism: as bourgeois value 253n.65; and modern economic order 243; and pursuit of wealth 240; religious 239, 240–1

assets, structure of 201

attitude of daily life 88

attraction 17

authoritarian conformity 514

authoritarian domination 271

authoritarianism, dogmatic 517

authority, types of 224, 272–3

authority versus uncertainty 516–18, 520

aversion, concealed 473

avowal 494–5

Bacchae, The 410–11

Bachelard, Gaston 409

Bachofen, Jacob, J. 54, 65n.4

background expectancies, as scheme of interpretation 87–8

background understandings, and bewilderment 92–4

Bain, A. 17